Crystal Reports® 8.5:
The Complete Reference

About the Author

George Peck is a software trainer, consultant, and developer with more than 20 years of experience in the computer industry.

After more than 10 years as an internal consultant and trainer in a large corporation, George founded his own consulting and training firm, The Ablaze Group, in 1994 (www.AblazeGroup.com). He has trained, consulted, and developed custom software for large and small clients throughout the United States, Canada, and the United Kingdom.

George is certified by Crystal Decisions as both a trainer and consultant for Crystal Reports 8.5, Crystal Enterprise, and Seagate Info. He is a recipient of the Crystal Decisions *Training Partner of the Year* award.

Prior to his computer career, George was a broadcaster, and his voice may still be heard in various national radio and TV commercial and promotional campaigns.

Crystal Reports® 8.5: The Complete Reference

George Peck

Osborne/**McGraw-Hill**

New York Chicago San Francisco
Lisbon London Madrid Mexico City
Milan New Delhi San Juan
Seoul Singapore Sydney Toronto

Osborne/**McGraw-Hill**
2600 Tenth Street
Berkeley, California 94710
U.S.A.

To arrange bulk purchase discounts for sales promotions, premiums, or fund-raisers, please contact Osborne/**McGraw-Hill** at the above address. For information on translations or book distributors outside the U.S.A., please see the International Contact Information page immediately following the index of this book.

Crystal Reports® 8.5: The Complete Reference

34567890 DOC DOC 0198765432

ISBN 0-07-219327-1

Publisher	**Copy Editor**
Brandon A. Nordin	Dennis Weaver
Vice President & Associate Publisher	**Proofreader**
Scott Rogers	Linda Medoff
Acquisitions Editor	**Indexer**
Ann Sellers	Claire Splan
Senior Project Editor	**Series Design**
Carolyn Welch	Peter F. Hancik
Acquisitions Coordinator	**Computer Designer**
Tim Madrid	Lucie Ericksen, Roberta Steele
Contributing Writer	**Illustrator**
Lauren O'Malley	Michael Mueller, Lyssa Wald
Technical Editors	**Series Design**
Blair Harvey	Peter F. Hancik
Herb Hess	

This book was composed with Corel VENTURA™ Publisher.

For Denise
You endured so much more than these
words can express appreciation for.
Thank You, my Love.

Contents at a Glance

Part II **Web Reporting with Crystal Reports and Crystal Enterprise**

Part III **Developing Custom Window Applications**

Part IV **Appendixes**

Contents

Part I

Crystal Reports 8.5 Introduced

Part IV

Appendixes

Acknowledgments

By the time the third edition of a book comes around, it gets harder and harder to "get creative" when acknowledging those who have been so helpful in its development. But acknowledge them I must, as this tough project would have been infinitely tougher without their help.

The crew at Osborne/McGraw–Hill deserves the first and foremost thanks. For Ann Sellers, I offer a special acknowledgment. You put up with a lot of static during this project, and I thank you so much for your steadfast support. Thanks also to Tim Madrid for keeping all the submissions together. For Dennis Weaver: accept my appreciation for your wonderful editing and for putting up with the *Gentle Ben* and *Dual* jokes. Carolyn Welch also deserves high praise for keeping these sentences structured in proper English. And, I must save a special acknowledgment for Editorial Director Wendy Rinaldi, who came to the rescue when we all needed her.

For technical editors Herb Hess and Blair Harvey, I owe you both a debt of gratitude and a sincere apology. I'm very grateful for your insightful assistance in catching those missing toolbar buttons, forgotten references to version 7, and for generally keeping me on track technically. Please accept my regret for underestimating the time it took you to accomplish this. You are consummate professionals and true friends.

It appears to be a given that panic descends upon these projects in the final days, no matter how many books I write. To Lauren O'Malley: thanks so much for picking up the ball and running with it under what must have certainly been serious pressure. Keep your schedule open—there's another one waiting in the wings!

Thanks, too, to Ryan Marples at Crystal Decisions. Not only did you provide some great insights into the details of the new topics, but I would have completely missed that space between "Visual Studio" and ".Net".

In what has become a *Crystal Reports: The Complete Reference* tradition, I must offer kudos to the Internet radio stations that kept me company during the odd hours I kept while putting this title together. KPIG, 107-oink-5 (www.kpig.com) deserves recognition. I jumped through some serious hoops to keep you coming in at 8,200 feet in the mountains. And KEOM-FM in Mesquite, Texas (www.keom.fm) is the only station around anymore that plays all those 70's hits I grew up with. Thanks, not bad for a high school station!

Dad, the more I write, the more I appreciate your profession. Thanks for your support, kindness, and warmth. I love you.

And, I must admit how oddly unimportant this project suddenly seemed on the morning of September 11, 2001, which came as I was wrapping up development of this book. May I simply offer condolences and my sorrow to those who lost friends and family in what is probably this country's most devastating tragedy of the first half of my life. This event, which will certainly affect our country for the second half of my life and beyond, needs to be acknowledged.

George Peck, September 2001
author@CrsytalBook.com
www.CrystalBook.com

Introduction

With two successful editions of *Crystal Reports: The Complete Reference* sitting on my bookshelf, decision time came as to how to proceed with the latest version of Crystal Reports. As the version number might indicate, Crystal Reports version 8.5 is not as extensive an upgrade to the popular report as previous "full number" versions. So, I began to ask myself all the typical nagging questions: "Is there enough new material in version 8.5 to warrant a new edition of the book?" "Will enough people upgrade to version 8.5 to justify the effort?" "What should I concentrate on in an 8.5 book?"

Welcome to the result of all those questions. Although Crystal Reports 8.5 doesn't contain as many new report design features as past upgrades, there are some notable new features, like Report Alerts, that deserve coverage. And, there have been fairly significant enhancements to developer features. As a Visual Basic programmer myself, I thought the new features needed to be delved into. And then there's *Crystal Enterprise*. This entirely new approach to Web reporting is a monumental change for existing Crystal Reports Web users. This new feature, probably more than any other, cried out for coverage in a new edition of this book.

If you've already purchased Crystal Reports 8.5, you'll certainly benefit from not only the new features introduced in this version, but from all the terrific reporting capabilities built up over this product's previous major releases. If you're considering an upgrade from Crystal Reports version 8, but haven't yet made your final decision, this book will be a great resource for you. Read the following "What's New In Crystal Reports 8.5" section for an overview of the new features. Then, look through individual chapters for more detailed coverage of the new features. If you're planning to integrate Crystal Reports with your Visual Basic applications or post your reports on the Web, make sure you spend time with Parts II and III of the book as well. Once you've visited the new material, you should have no trouble deciding whether the latest version is right for you.

Whether you've faithfully upgraded to each new version of Crystal Reports as it has come out, or if you've finally made the jump to 8.5 from an older version, you're sure to find plenty of good material here to help you find what you're looking for. Look for "real-world" examples and techniques that will help you design great reports to solve countless business and personal requirements. If you're a Visual Basic programmer or Web designer who wants to integrate your finished report into a custom Windows program or Web site, you'll find lots of examples and samples here, too. The accompanying CD-ROM contains sample reports, examples of Visual Basic integration, and a sample custom Web site you can try with Microsoft IIS and Active Server Pages.

The book is organized into three major sections. Part I covers report design techniques, from your very first simple report to complex report formatting, formulas, and advanced approaches to nagging reporting problems. Here you'll find out how to use Crystal Reports 8.5 features to produce reports that rival the quality of page publishing programs. Once you've created an appealing report, you'll see how it can be exported to a number of other file formats, including Adobe Acrobat PDF format, as well as the up-and-coming Extensible Markup Language (XML). Look for chapters that cover Charting, Geographic Mapping, and how to make the most efficient use of your SQL database, such as SQL Server or Oracle.

Part II is an exciting new section that not only discusses how to integrate Crystal Reports with Microsoft Active Server Pages, but covers Web reporting with Crystal Enterprise. You'll learn how to get the most from this brand new tool, whether you choose to use the ePortfolio right out of the box, or decide to create your own completely customized Crystal Enterprise system using new *Crystal Server Pages*. Not only can you learn all about Crystal Enterprise Standard edition, which is included with Crystal Reports 8.5, but you can find out about the separately available Crystal Enterprise Professional if you are planning a large, enterprise-wide Web-based reporting system.

Part III is for the Visual Basic programmer. Here you'll see how to use the updated and streamlined *Report Designer Component* to integrate virtually every Crystal Reports feature right from within your Visual Basic program. Not only can you integrate reports you've already created with the Crystal Reports designer, but you can actually design reports interactively right inside the Visual Basic Integrated Development Environment. And, you'll see how you can now even add report design capability to your application, so your end users can design their own reports right from within your application. If you are using Microsoft's revolutionary Visual Studio.NET (in beta release at time of this printing), you'll see how Crystal Reports fits in with this exciting new development tool by reading Appendix A.

What's New In Crystal Reports 8.5

As the version number indicates, Crystal Reports 8.5 can't really be considered a "full" upgrade. After close examination, it's tempting to say that Crystal Decisions (the new name for the former Seagate Software) used Crystal Reports 8.5 largely as a vehicle to launch Crystal Enterprise. Although there are certainly some interesting new features in the core Crystal Reports program, you'll find the more significant changes if you are a Windows programmer who wants to integrate Crystal Reports with your custom programs. And, if you're a Web designer, get ready for Crystal Enterprise, which is by far the most significant change for version 8.5.

A summary of new features follows. If the new feature warrants more detailed coverage, you'll find a reference to the book chapter where the new feature is detailed.

Report Alerts

You can now set up special conditions that will cause a message box to appear when the report is run. The conditions and messages are completely customizable by you when you design the report. You can also make use of Report Alerts in formulas. Report Alerts are covered in Chapters 5 and 7.

New Data Sources, Including XML Support

Crystal Reports 8.5 supports several new database types and data sources. For example, you can now report directly from ACT 2000 or Exchange 2000 data sources. Probably of most significance is support for Extensible Markup Language, or XML. Crystal Reports will read data stored in XML via the new version of ODBC that is included with version 8.5. Database types supported by Crystal Reports are discussed in Chapter 19.

Note   *Most advanced data source options, such as native connections to SQL databases, XML support, and updated ODBC drivers are included only with Crystal Reports Professional and Developer editions. These features are not available with Crystal Reports Standard edition.*

New Exporting Options, Including PDF and XML

Version 8.5 has added additional formats to its File Export capability. In addition to standard formats, such as ASCII text, Word, Excel, and HTML, you can now export finished reports to Adobe's popular Portable Document Format, or PDF. You can now also export Crystal Reports data to XML to allow data interchange with new-breed applications that take advantage of the emerging XML data format. Exporting is covered in Chapter 13.

Miscellaneous Minor Report Design Enhancements

Additional miscellaneous features fall into the "nice-to-have" category, not warranting special recognition. You may copy Crystal Reports objects, including charts and maps, to the Windows clipboard and then paste them into other Windows applications. If you're creating Hierarchical Groups, you can now include subtotals and summaries within them (discussed in Chapter 3). Chapter 10 covers some minor changes to Charting, including the ability to automatically set most chart options with common defaults. And, you may now save a preview thumbnail of your first report page when you save the report (this is helpful for reports published with Crystal Enterprise).

Crystal Enterprise Web Reporting

No doubt the biggest change in Crystal Reports 8.5 is its approach to Web-based reporting. Responding to a heightened demand in the corporate community for Web-based alternatives, Crystal Decisions announced Crystal Enterprise at the same time it announced Crystal Reports 8.5. In fact, Crystal Enterprise Standard is included right in the box with Crystal Reports 8.5 Professional and Developer Editions. Crystal Enterprise replaces the previous Web Access Server and Web Component Server options for Web reporting with a much higher capacity and more flexible approach to Web reporting. Section II of this book is largely devoted to Crystal Enterprise: both the Standard edition included with Crystal Reports and the Professional edition, available for purchase separately.

New Windows Developer Features

If you are a Windows developer using a developer tool such as Visual Basic to embed Crystal Reports in your custom Windows applications, your options have changed with the release of version 8.5. While most of the original developer interfaces remain in version 8.5 (the ActiveX Control and Report Engine Automation Server being two prime examples), they have not been updated with new features for several Crystal Reports versions. Not only does Crystal Decisions actively encourage developers to migrate their applications to the Report Designer Component or RDC, but the RDC is the only integration method that exposes all the latest Crystal Reports 8.5 features. In addition, version 8.5 of the RDC now includes an Embedded Report Designer ActiveX control that allows your end users to design their own reports within your custom application.

Because of the obvious benefits and future direction of the Report Designer Component, Part III of this book concentrates on its implementation in custom Visual Basic applications. And, if you're using Microsoft's new Visual Studio.NET development environment (in public beta release at time of this printing), you'll find examples of VS.NET's Crystal Reports implementation in Appendix A.

Developer features described in Part III are only available with Crystal Reports Developer edition. Crystal Reports Standard and Professional editions do not contain the Windows developer interfaces.

Crystal Decisions

Although not significant to the use of Crystal Reports, it's helpful to know that the name of the company that produces it has changed. *Crystal Decisions, Inc.* was born the day that Crystal Reports 8.5 was released. Formerly known as Seagate Software, Crystal Decisions changed its company name and corporate brand to more closely align itself with the wide name recognition of its flagship product, Crystal Reports. Along with a name change comes a change in the Internet address for the company. You may learn more about Crystal Decisions products at http://www.crystaldecisions.com.

The Complete Reference

Part I

Crystal Reports 8.5 Introduced

Chapter 1

Common Ground: Creating a Simple Report

Businesses, large and small, continue to find new innovations for personal computer–based information systems. Many of these systems are conversions of older "mainframe"-type computer systems. The world was largely spared major computer problems when passing into the year 2000 partially because so many corporations have moved to these new computer systems.

Some of the buzzwords that have entered or invaded (depending on your point of view) the industry during this trend are *customer relationship management* (CRM), *enterprise resource planning* (ERP), and *business intelligence* (BI). ERP systems from such vendors as PeopleSoft, Oracle, Baan, SAP, and others are organizing and managing human resources, accounting, inventory, and billing functions for businesses of all sizes. Other more specialized PC-based applications used in manufacturing, medicine, service businesses, and countless other areas are also in wide use. And, despite the recent dot-com meltdown, there are still a large number of Internet-based "e-commerce" sites that are becoming part of our everyday lives.

Most of these new PC-based systems all have one core thing in common: an industry-standard database program to manage the data. But after thousands, or often millions, of pieces of data have been put into these databases, how can you extract the right data in a meaningful form? That's where the BI tools come into play. A tool must exist to extract and summarize all of this data in a meaningful fashion—in a way that allows key decision makers to know what's really happening with their business and how to move forward in the best possible direction.

While these varied information systems may have certain BI capabilities "out of the box," many users of database-based systems need more capabilities to create their own specialized views of their centralized data. There is a plethora of query, graphic, spreadsheet, and analysis tools. Still, probably the most often used method of garnering information from corporate information systems is the tried-and-true report. Enter the *database report writer*.

Introducing Crystal Reports 8.5

With the latest release, Crystal Reports remains the market leader and de facto standard for business and corporate report writing. In 1984, a Canadian shipping company wanted to produce custom reports from its accounting system. When the vendor said "We can't help you," the company created Quick Reports, the precursor to Crystal Reports. Crystal Reports' first "bundle" was with that vendor's next version of its accounting software.

Crystal Reports is now bundled with over 150 leading software packages, including many of the aforementioned ERP and accounting packages from vendors including ACCPAC International, Great Plains Software, and PeopleSoft. Versions of Crystal Reports are also included with Microsoft's BackOffice, Visual Studio 6, and the upcoming Visual Studio.NET packages.

Crystal Reports is aimed at three general types of users:

- Casual business users, such as data analysts, executive assistants, and marketing directors, who will design reports around their corporate data to make intelligent business decisions.

- Information technology professionals, who will use Crystal Reports to integrate sophisticated reporting right inside their own Microsoft Windows programs.

- Webmasters, who will use Crystal Reports to provide print-quality reports and graphics over their intranets or the Internet.

Figure 1-1 shows the Crystal Reports 8.5 screen when the program is first started. Note the standard Windows user interface, including different toolbars, pull-down menus, and the Welcome dialog box.

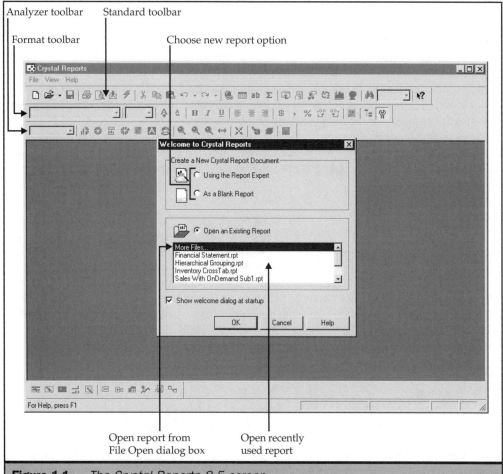

Figure 1-1.   *The Crystal Reports 8.5 screen*

When you first start the program, the only two main functions that you'll usually want to perform are creating a new report and opening an existing report. Like most functions in Crystal Reports, these functions can be accomplished in several ways. If the Welcome dialog box appears, you can choose either function from it by using its various radio buttons. If you've closed the Welcome dialog box, you may redisplay it from the Help menu and choose options from there. You may also open an existing report or create a new report with pull-down menu options, keyboard shortcuts, or toolbar buttons, as described later in the chapter.

Crystal Reports Screen Elements

The Crystal Reports screen consists of four main parts you'll want to familiarize yourself with: the pull-down menus, the toolbars, the report design/preview area, and the status bar.

Pull-Down Menus

The pull-down menus are standard Windows-type menus that you can pull down with your mouse. In some cases, you can also use shortcut key combinations (such as CTRL-N to start a new report) to choose pull-down menu options. You'll notice these shortcut key combinations next to their menu options when you pull down the menus. You can also use the standard Windows convention of holding down the ALT key and typing the underlined letter in the menu, and then choosing a menu option by typing another underlined letter from within the menu. For example, you can display the Field Explorer to add a database field or other object to the report (Insert menu, Field Object option) by typing ALT-I-F.

Toolbars

When you first start Crystal Reports, three toolbars are displayed across the top of the screen by default. One additional toolbar is available for display by choosing View | Toolbars from the pull-down menus. The toolbars contain buttons for almost all of Crystal Reports' available functions (some options still require the use of pull-down menu options, but not many). Many of the icons on the toolbars are self-explanatory. In addition, tool tips are available for each toolbar button—just point to a toolbar button with your mouse and wait a few seconds. A small yellow box containing a short description of the toolbar button's function will appear.

> **Tip**   *You may "undock" the toolbars from their default positions and place them anywhere you want. Just click a blank part of the toolbar and drag it to the desired location. It will become its own "window." If you place it near the edge of the Crystal Reports screen (or back near its original position), it will snap into place along the edge of the screen.*

The Standard Toolbar   This toolbar is the first toolbar just below the pull-down menus. It contains the most-often-used Crystal Reports functions, such as opening and saving report files, printing and exporting the report, selecting records, adding a chart, and so on.

The Format Toolbar   This toolbar is the toolbar just below the Standard toolbar. You should be familiar with this toolbar if you've used most any office suite type of tool, such as word processors or spreadsheets. This toolbar allows you to change the format (font, size, and alignment) of one or more objects that you have selected on your report.

The Analyzer Toolbar   The third toolbar contains options that are available only when you are viewing a chart or map. Some of the buttons are available when you have selected a map or a chart in the main Preview tab (described later in the chapter). Other Analyzer toolbar buttons are available only when you're viewing the chart or map in a separate Analyzer tab in the report design/preview section.

The Supplementary Toolbar   This fourth toolbar is not displayed by default. To display it, choose View | Toolbar from the pull-down menus and check the Supplementary Tools option. Or, you can click the last button in the Formatting toolbar to display the Supplementary toolbar. The Supplementary toolbar, displayed on the bottom of the Crystal Reports screen, contains lesser-used options in Crystal Reports, such as inserting a group, adding a cross-tab object, displaying the Visual Linking Expert, and so on.

Depending on how often you use charts and maps in your reports, you may find that you use the Supplementary toolbar much more often than the Analyzer toolbar. You may prefer to hide the Analyzer toolbar and display the Supplementary toolbar. You may choose this combination by checking and unchecking the appropriate toolbar options after choosing View | Toolbars from the pull-down menus.

Report Design/Preview Area

The large gray area in the middle of the Crystal Reports screen is the report design/preview area. Here, you actually manipulate fields and objects that make up your report. When you want to have a look at the way the report will eventually appear when printed on paper or displayed on a Web page, you can preview the actual report in this area, as well.

   You'll soon see that you can choose different views of a report by clicking a number of tabs that will appear at the top of the report design/preview area. When you initially create a report, you see a Design tab, which shows a design view, or "template," of your report, simply indicating the location of objects in different report sections. When you preview the report, a Preview tab appears, which shows actual data from the database as it will appear in the final report. In addition, as you progress with your report work, you'll see additional tabs for subreports, drill-down views, and Analyzer views. Simply click the tab you wish to see.

Status Bar

The status bar appears at the very bottom of the Crystal Reports screen. Although you can hide the status bar by unchecking the Status Bar option on the View menu, you'll probably want to leave it displayed, because it contains very helpful information for you as you design and preview reports. In particular, the status bar will show more-detailed descriptions of menu options and toolbar buttons. While the short tool tip that appears when you point to a button is handy, it may not offer a good enough description of what the toolbar button does. Just look in the status bar for more information.

Also, the status bar contains more helpful information on its right side, such as how many database records are being used in your report, what percentage of the report processing is finished, and at what location (X-Y coordinates) on the report page a currently selected object is located.

Starting Out: Opening or Creating a Report

To open an existing report, you may use either one of the options from the Welcome dialog box, choosing a recently used report from the list, or choosing the More Files... option. If you've closed the Welcome dialog box, select File | Open, use the shortcut key combination CTRL-O, or click the Open button in the Standard toolbar. A standard file-open dialog box will appear, showing any files with an .RPT extension in the drive and folder. Navigate to any alternate drives or folders to find the existing Crystal Report .RPT file that you wish to open.

To create a new report, choose either the Using the Report Expert or the As a Blank Report radio button on the Welcome dialog box. Or, if you've closed it, start a new report by choosing File | New, pressing the keyboard shortcut CTRL-N, or clicking the New button in the Standard toolbar.

If you use the As a Blank Report option from the Welcome dialog box, you skip the report experts and proceed directly to custom report design (see "Using the Blank Report Option," later in the chapter). Any other new report step (the Using the Report Expert radio button on the Welcome dialog box, or any of the new report options available after closing the Welcome dialog box) will display the *Report Gallery.*

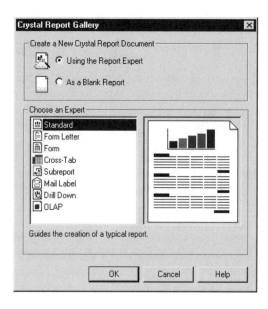

There are two general options you can choose from the Report Gallery:

- Create a report using one of eight report experts
- Use the As a Blank Report option for precise control when designing a new report

Using the Report Experts

The eight standard *report experts* allow you to create "quick and dirty" reports with minimal effort. They're helpful when you want to create a simple report or put together the beginning elements of a more complex report. Choose the expert that most closely matches the type of report that you want to create. When you make the choice, you'll see a thumbnail view of that type of report appear in the Report Gallery.

To create a simple, general-purpose report (for example, an employee phone list or your last year's sales totals), click Standard to use the Standard Report Expert (see Figure 1-2). The Standard Report Expert presents a type of dialog box that's probably familiar to you if you've used other office suites or productivity products. You build your report by choosing options from the different tabbed pages in the dialog box. You advance to the next tab by clicking the tab itself or by clicking the Next button at the bottom of the dialog box.

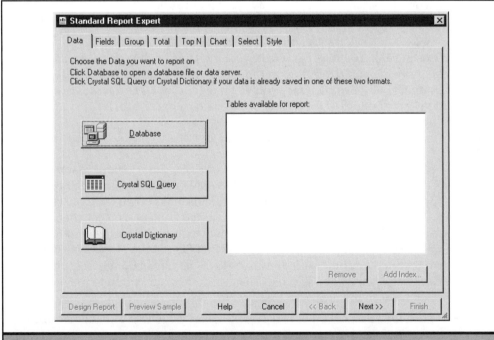

Figure 1-2.   *The Standard Report Expert*

To create a report with the Standard Report Expert, follow these steps:

1. In the Data tab, choose one of the three data types available: Database, Crystal SQL Query, and Crystal Dictionary. The Database button launches the Data Explorer (discussed later in the chapter) that allows you to choose any database Crystal Reports supports, including PC-style "local" databases, as well as client/server databases, such as Oracle or Informix. Clicking either the Crystal SQL Query button or the Crystal Dictionary button displays the Data Explorer with the Metadata/Query category expanded. From here, you may click the plus signs next to Crystal Dictionary / Infoview (discussed in Chapter 18) or Crystal SQL Query (discussed in Chapter 17). Either action displays a File Open dialog box allowing you to open the type of file selected. Note that the SQL Query and Dictionary buttons are redundant—you can also use the Metadata/Query category from within the Data Explorer using the Expert's Database button.

2. As you add tables, you'll see them appear in the Tables Available for Report box in the Data tab. Once you're finished adding tables, you'll be taken to the Links tab automatically. (Note that you won't see the Links tab unless more than one table is chosen.) This tab shows you the tables you've chosen in a visual format, allowing you to *link* the tables together, based on common fields. Crystal Reports will *Smart Link* the tables automatically, showing you lines indicating the fields and tables that are linked. If these links are correct (in the real world they rarely are), you may leave them as is.

3. If you need to delete a link that Crystal Reports added, click the line that connects the tables, and click the Delete Link button or press the DELETE key to remove the existing link. You may then create your own link by dragging from the "from" field and table and dropping on the "to" field and table. A line will appear, indicating your new link. Once you've linked the tables correctly, click the Next button at the bottom of the Expert or the Fields tab.

Note *Linking tables has quite a few fine points. Look for more information in Chapter 14.*

4. Choose the database fields you actually want to appear on your report. You may choose single fields simply by clicking the field name under the Available Fields list. If you want to choose multiple fields, hold down the CTRL key and click. You'll notice that fields are "multi-selected" when you click them. To deselect an already selected field, hold down CTRL and click the field name again. To select a range of fields, click the first field in the range. Then, hold down the SHIFT key and select the last field in the range. Both fields, plus all fields in between, will be selected. Then, click the Add button to move your selected fields to the Fields To Display box.

To search for a particular field (in case the tables you chose contain many fields), click the Find Field button under the Available Fields list. You can enter a full or partial field name to search for. If that field is in any tables in the Available

Fields list, the field will be highlighted. You may also create a formula field (discussed in detail in Chapter 5) by clicking the Formula button. If you select a field in the field list and then click the Browse Data button, you'll see a sample of actual data from that database field. This may be helpful in determining whether or not this is the correct field to add to your report.

5. If you'd like to change the order in which the fields appear on the report, or the column headings that appear above them, you can make those changes in the Fields To Display box. Select a field and click the up or down arrow buttons above the Fields To Display box to reorder the field. You may also type a new column heading for the chosen field in the Column Heading text box. When you're finished, click Next or the Group tab to move on.

Tip   *This is all the information the Standard Report Expert needs to display the report. From this point forward, if you don't want to specify any other report features, such as grouping, totaling, charting, or record selection, you may click the Design Report, Preview Sample, or Finish button after specifying information on the Data, Links, and Fields tab.*

6. If you wish to have your report displayed in order of one or more particular fields, choose one or more fields from the Available Fields list on the Group tab and click the Add button. *Grouping* puts all report records together on the report whose chosen grouping fields are the same. Grouping is similar to just sorting records, but groups can have subtotals, counts, averages, or other summaries at the end. Grouping is covered in more detail in Chapter 3.

7. On the Total tab, you'll find a subtab for every group you created on the Group tab. Click the tab for the group you want to create subtotal or summary fields for. Then, choose fields you want subtotaled or summarized at the end of the group, or grand-totaled at the end of the report. Notice that Crystal Reports has already added any numeric or currency fields to the Summarized Fields box and has chosen to sum them, and also has added grand totals. If you don't want to include one or more of these already chosen fields, select the field or fields you don't want summarized and click the Remove button.

Choose any additional fields that you do want summarized in the Available Fields list. Then, click the Add button. Numeric and currency fields will be summed (added together) by default, while other field types will be assigned the Maximum summary type by default. To change the summary type, choose a different summary from the Summary Type drop-down list. Note that you'll see more limited summary types for nonnumeric or noncurrency fields. Instead of creating an actual subtotal of a number, you may also choose to create a percentage summary field (discussed in more detail in Chapter 3). To do this, check the Percentage Of check box, and choose the field you want to calculate the percentage of.

8. Usually, any groups on your report are presented in alphabetical order (for example, Arizona precedes California, followed by Oregon, Texas, and Wyoming). However, if you want to see the "top five states in order of sales," use the Top N tab to reorder the report groups by one of the subtotal or summary amounts rather than by the name of the group.

   The Top N tab in the Standard Report Expert will show subtabs for each group on the report. Click the tab for the group you want to set up Top N reporting for. To have all the groups still appear on the report, but in order of a summary or subtotal field, leave the default All option chosen in the For This Group Sort drop-down list. Then, choose the summary or subtotal field you want the groups sorted by in the Based On drop-down list. If you only want to see a limited number of groups (say the Top 5 or the Bottom 10), change the All option to Top N or Bottom N. Choose what you want *N* to be—how many groups you want to appear on the report. Finally, click the Include Other Groups check box if you want to include the rest of the report items that aren't in the Top N or Bottom N. They will be placed in one last group with the name you specify in the text box.

9. The Chart tab lets you show your report data graphically in a bar, pie, or other form of chart. Several subtabs show up below the Chart tab that take you through creating a chart step by step. Chapter 10 explains how to create graphs and charts in detail.

10. To limit your report to meaningful database records, use the Select tab. You likely won't ever want to include every record in the database tables in your report. Many tables contain large numbers of records, and your reports will be much more meaningful if they only contain the relevant set of records. Choose one or more fields to select upon, and move them to the Select Fields box by clicking the Add button. When you select a field in the Select Fields box, an additional drop-down list appears below. You can choose the comparison operator you need in the pull-down list (such as equal to, less than, one of, between, and so on). Then, choose the value you want to compare against in the additional drop-down lists that appear. You may type a comparison value directly in the drop-down list box, or you can click the down arrow in the box to choose from a sample of data that will be read from the database field.

Note   *More detailed information on selecting records is contained in Chapter 6.*

11. The Style tab lets you determine the general appearance of your report and add a report title and bitmap graphic (such as a logo) to your report. When you choose one of the available styles, a thumbnail image shows the general appearance of that style.

The Standard Report Expert dialog box has three choices that you can use when you are ready to complete the report:

- Click the Design Report button to create the report and proceed immediately to the Design tab, where you can see or change the database fields and other objects the Expert has laid out.

- Click Preview Sample to see a preview of the entire report, or just a subset of the report's records, based on a number you supply.

- Click Finish to apply the selection criteria you supplied in the Select tab and show the entire report in the Preview tab.

Once you have created the report using the Standard Report Expert, you can print it on a printer, export it to another file format, save it to the Crystal Reports .RPT file format, or use any other function that Crystal Reports provides. You can click the Design tab to make any manual adjustments to the report that you wish. You can also rerun the Standard Report Expert to make changes to the report.

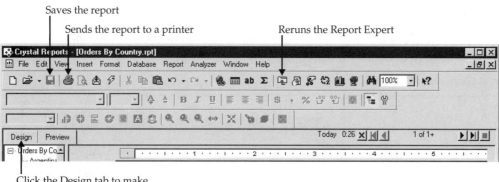

Saves the report

Sends the report to a printer   Reruns the Report Expert

Click the Design tab to make
manual adjustments to the report

Using the Blank Report Option

While the report experts simplify the report design process by presenting a step-by-step approach, they limit your flexibility to create a report exactly as you'd like it to look. You are required to accept the fonts, colors, and layout that the expert chooses. Group total and summary fields are not labeled, and group fields are repeated over and over again in every report line within the group.

Although it's initially more labor-intensive, using the Blank Report option to create a report gives you absolute control over what you put on your report, where you put it, and how it looks. Even if you use the report experts, it's important to understand the concepts involved in the Blank Report option, because you'll want to use those concepts to refine most reports that the report experts create. To use the Blank Report option, click the As a Blank Report radio button on the Report Gallery dialog box when first creating a new report. Then click OK. The Data Explorer will appear.

The Data Explorer

The *Data Explorer,* shown in Figure 1-3, is where you choose the database tables you wish to include in your report. Here, you can select from any database type that Crystal Reports supports, including PC-type "local" databases, such as Microsoft Access, dBASE, Paradox, Btrieve, and others. You can also choose from virtually all popular client/server or SQL databases, such as Microsoft SQL Server, Oracle, Informix, and Sybase. Crystal Reports even supports proprietary data types, such as Web server activity logs, the Windows NT/2000 event log, and Microsoft Exchange systems. And, Crystal Reports 8.5 now allows you to choose an XML file to report on. These data types are all chosen here.

The Data Explorer categorizes types of databases, shown as small folder icons with plus signs next to them. Depending on the type of database you want to report on, click the plus sign next to one of the following database categories:

- **Current Connections** Displays a list of any databases you may already have connected to when working with previous reports.

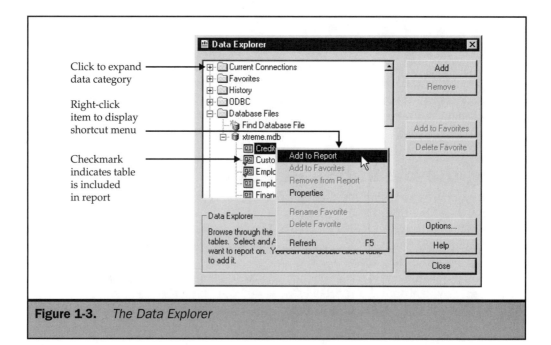

Figure 1-3.   *The Data Explorer*

- **Favorites**   Contains data sources that you've previously added—if you use a data source on a regular basis, you may want to add it to the Favorites category to make it easy to find.

- **History**   Shows data sources that you've recently connected to.

- **ODBC**   Displays any existing ODBC data sources configured on your computer; often contains connections to larger corporate client/server databases, such as Oracle and Microsoft SQL Server. Use this category to connect to XML data with Crystal Reports 8.5.

- **Database Files**   Enables you to report on a local PC-style database, such as Microsoft Access, Xbase .DBF files, Paradox .DB files, or Btrieve .DDF files.

- **More Data Sources**   Provides extra data sources (often proprietary data types) not included in the other categories, such as Web server logs, Microsoft Exchange Server folders, and the local file system. Reporting on these kinds of data types is discussed in Chapter 19.

- **Metadata/Query**   Enables you to create a report based on a Crystal Dictionary .DC5 file or a Crystal SQL Designer .QRY file. Crystal Dictionaries are discussed in Chapter 18 and the Crystal SQL Designer is discussed in Chapter 17.

Note

There may be several different ways of connecting to the same database. If, for example, you wish to report on a corporate Oracle database, you may connect via ODBC or by using a Crystal Reports "native" driver in the More Data Sources category. If you're unsure of how to connect to your database, check with your database administrator.

After you click the plus sign next to the category you wish to use, you see a list of available databases under that category. If you're already logged on to a database in that category, you'll see the database name and all the available tables underneath the database name. Choose the desired database or subcategory. Depending on the category or database you choose, additional dialog boxes will appear, asking you to choose a particular database filename, log in to the database, or choose a database server. Eventually, you'll be able to choose one or more *database tables* that you wish to include in your report.

To add a table to the report, select the table and click the Add button. You can also just double-click the table name. When the table has been added to the report, you'll see a small checkmark on top of the small table icon next to the table name. If you add a table by mistake, just select it and click the Remove button. The checkmark will go away. Once you've selected all the tables you want to include in your report, close the Data Explorer with the Close button.

Tip

If you choose more than one table for your report, you'll automatically be presented with the Visual Linking Expert. Use this dialog box to join or link your tables together. Table linking is discussed in detail in Chapter 14.

The Field Explorer

Once you've chosen and linked tables, Crystal Reports will display the Design tab, along with the Field Explorer, as shown in Figure 1-4. Begin designing your report simply by dragging fields from the Field Explorer and dropping them on the report where you want them to appear.

The Field Explorer contains categories of fields that are available to place on your report. When you first create a new report, you'll see that the Database Fields category is highlighted. Clicking the plus sign next to it will expand the category, showing all the tables you added from the Data Explorer. Plus signs next to the table names, as well as next to the Special Fields category, indicate that fields are available below those

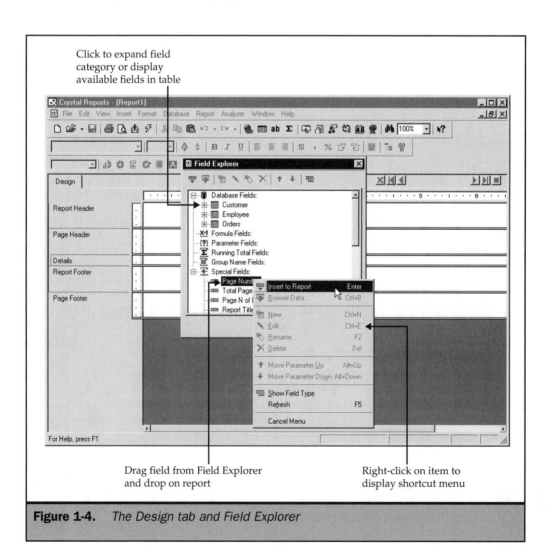

Click to expand field category or display available fields in table

Drag field from Field Explorer and drop on report

Right-click on item to display shortcut menu

Figure 1-4. *The Design tab and Field Explorer*

levels—click the plus sign to see available fields. The other categories of the Field Explorer will not have any plus signs next to them, unless you've opened an existing report that already contains fields of these types. Once you begin creating new formulas, parameter fields, and so on, you'll see plus signs next to these categories as well. Click the plus signs to see available fields in these other categories.

The simplest way to add a field to the report is to drag and drop the field from the Field Explorer to the report's Design tab. When you drag, you'll see an outline of the field object appear on the report as you drag. When you have positioned the field where you want it to appear, simply release the mouse button to drop the field on the report. As an alternative, you may right-click a field and choose Insert To Report from the pop-up menu, select the desired field, and click the Insert To Report button (the first toolbar button) from the Field Explorer toolbar, or just press ENTER. The field will be attached to the mouse cursor, which you can then position to drop the field.

You're not limited to dragging and dropping one field at a time to the report. If you see several fields you'd like to drag and drop at once, use CTRL-click to select or deselect multiple fields. If you wish to select a range of fields, click the first field in the range and then hold down the SHIFT key and click the last field in the range. Both fields, as well as all of those in between, will be selected. After you CTRL- or SHIFT-click the desired fields, drag and drop them as a group. After you add a field to the report, you see a small green checkmark next to the field in the Field Explorer. This indicates that the field is in use somewhere on the report.

 The Field Explorer is not just available in the Design Tab. If you wish to add a field to the report while in the Preview tab, choose Insert | Field Object from the pull-down menus or click the Insert Fields button on the Standard toolbar. Just be careful—you need to be very precise where you drag and drop fields in the Preview tab.

Report Sections

When you first create a new report, Crystal Reports shows five default sections in the Design tab. Table 1-1 outlines where and how many times each section appears in a report, and the types of objects you may want to place in them.

Section	Where It Appears	What to Place in the Section
Report header	Once only, at the beginning of the report	Title page, company logo, introductory information that you want to appear once only at the beginning of the report, charts or cross-tabs that apply to the whole report

Table 1-1.   *Crystal Reports Default Report Sections*

Section	Where It Appears	What to Place in the Section
Page header	At the top of every page	Field titles, print date/time, report title
Details	Every time a new record is read from the database	Database fields and formulas that you want to appear for every record
Report footer	Once only, at the end of the report	Grand totals, closing disclaimers, charts, or cross-tabs that apply to the whole report
Page footer	At the bottom of every page	Page numbers, report name, explanations for figures in the report

Table 1-1.   *Crystal Reports Default Report Sections* (continued)

If you drag a database field into the details section, Crystal Reports places a field title in the page header automatically and aligns it with the database field. If you drag a database field into any other section, no field title will be inserted, even if you drag the field into the details section later—automatic field titles are only created if you drag a field directly into the details section.

Previewing the Report

When you see objects depicted in the Design tab, Crystal Reports is only displaying "placeholders." You'll see the names of fields and objects surrounded by outline symbols, indicating how wide and tall they are. You won't ever see actual data in the Design tab. To see the report containing real data as it might appear when printed on a printer or exported to a Web page, you need to preview the report.

There are several ways of previewing a report. Choose File | Print Preview or click the Print Preview button on the Standard toolbar to preview the entire report. To preview a limited number of records, choose File | Print | Preview Sample and specify the number of records you wish to see.

When you preview a report, the Preview tab appears next to the Design tab, as shown in Figure 1-5. You can scroll up and down through the report, use the Zoom control to change the Zoom level of the report, and use the page navigation buttons to move through various pages of the report. You can easily move back and forth between the Design and Preview tabs by clicking them.

Moving and Sizing Objects

Once you've placed objects on your report, you will probably want to move them around the report as your design progresses. Crystal Reports uses the maximum length of string database fields to determine how wide to make them. Quite often, this results

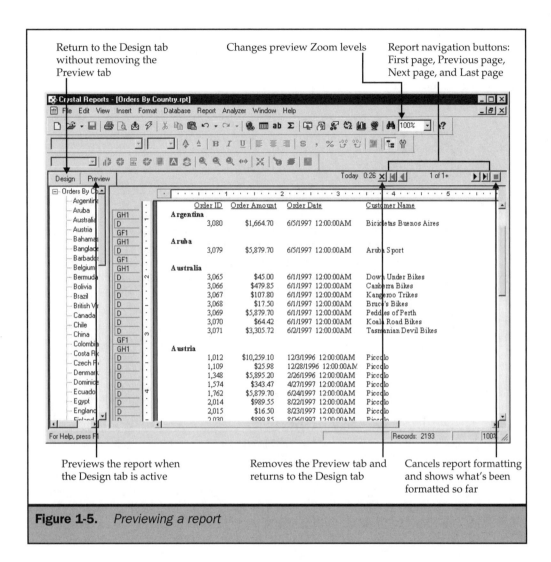

Return to the Design tab without removing the Preview tab

Changes preview Zoom levels

Report navigation buttons: First page, Previous page, Next page, and Last page

Previews the report when the Design tab is active

Removes the Preview tab and returns to the Design tab

Cancels report formatting and shows what's been formatted so far

Figure 1-5. *Previewing a report*

in very wide string fields on the report. Based on the size of the data that these display, you'll probably want to shrink the size of these fields. Also, if you change the font size of an object, you'll usually have to adjust the object size accordingly.

The first step in moving or sizing an object is to select the object. Simply click it. A shaded outline and four blocks appear around the object, indicating that it is selected. Now you can move or size it.

Pointing inside the selected object causes your mouse pointer to turn into a four-way pointer. You can then click and drag the object to a new location with the mouse. If you point at one of the little blue blocks—the *sizing handles* at the top, bottom, left, and right of the object—your mouse pointer turns into a two-way size pointer. Clicking and dragging these handles stretches or shrinks the object. Sizing objects requires very precise accuracy with your mouse! Laptop users with trackpads will probably opt for an external mouse after trying this a few times.

Point inside a selected object to move it   Point at the desired sizing handle to resize an object

You're not limited to moving or sizing one object at a time. You can select multiple objects before moving or sizing them. CTRL-click or SHIFT-click to select more than one field or field title. You can also surround multiple objects with an elastic box. Before you start to draw the elastic box, make sure you deselect any already selected objects by clicking an area of the report where there are no objects.

When the Design tab is displayed, you don't have to use the mouse to move or resize objects. For very fine control of object placement and sizing, use your keyboard's cursor keys. Using the cursor keys by themselves will move selected objects in the direction of the key. If you hold down SHIFT and use the cursor keys, objects will be widened, narrowed, made taller, or made shorter in the direction of the keys.

Using Guidelines to Move Objects

When you insert a database field into the details section, Crystal Reports inserts two other things automatically. The first, the field title, appears directly above the field in the page header. What might not be so obvious is the *vertical guideline*. You'll notice a little "upside-down tent" (officially known as a *guideline* handle) in the ruler above the report. The guideline is actually a vertical line extending from the guideline handle all the way down the report. Crystal Reports automatically placed this in the ruler, and it attached the field in the details section and the field title in the page header to the guideline.

By default, only the guideline handles are visible when you first install Crystal Reports. If you'd like to see the dashed guidelines themselves in the Design tab, choose View | Guidelines in Design from the pull-down menus. To see guidelines in the Preview tab, choose View | Guidelines in Preview from the pull-down menus. Note that even if you make the latter choice, you'll only see the dashed guidelines in the Preview tab if you click any object to select it in the preview window.

You may move objects as a group by dragging the guideline handle left or right inside the ruler. All objects attached to that guideline will move at the same time. If you've placed a database field in the details section and an associated field title in the page header, and have inserted several group subtotals in groups and grand totals in the report footer, they will typically all be attached to the same guideline. Just move the guideline left or right to move all the objects together.

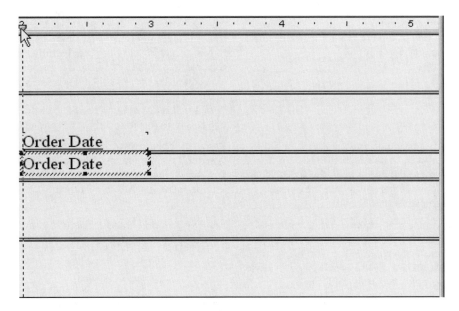

With a little experience, you'll probably quickly develop a love-hate relationship with guidelines. If you have lots of smaller objects positioned closely together on a report, you'll probably give up on the guidelines and just move them by CTRL-clicking or using an elastic box. If you have fewer objects spaced a little farther apart on your report, or lots of aligned objects in several report sections, you'll probably like using the guidelines to rearrange objects. Table 1-2 shows some of the guideline issues that may crop up in your report-design process, along with ways of solving the problems.

What Happened	How Is It Fixed?
You mistakenly dragged a guideline off the ruler when you just wanted to move it left or right. The objects attached to it haven't moved, and the guideline is now gone.	Click the Undo button on the Standard toolbar, or choose Edit | Undo. This will bring the guideline back. If you notice the missing guideline after you've completed other tasks, and you don't want to Undo, just add a guideline back into the ruler by clicking in the ruler; reattach the objects by dragging them to the new guideline.

Table 1-2.   *Guideline Issues*

What Happened	How Is It Fixed?
You selected and moved an individual object or objects with your mouse, but the guideline didn't move with them. Now, when you move the guideline in the ruler, the objects don't move.	You detach an object from a guideline when you move the object in the Design tab. You cannot reattach guidelines to objects by moving the guideline in the ruler. You have to reattach *objects to guidelines* by moving the objects until they snap to the guidelines. You can tell when an object has been reattached to a guideline by looking at the very small red marks on the edge of the object where it's attached to the guideline.
You've resized or moved objects and they now appear to be attached to two guidelines: one on the left and one on the right. When you move either guideline, the objects stretch rather than move.	Resize the objects away from the guideline you don't want them attached to. By resizing, you detach them from one guideline while leaving them attached to the other.
You notice that when you delete objects from the report, the guidelines stay and clutter up the ruler. When you move other objects around on the report, they're always snapping to the stray guidelines.	Remove any unwanted guidelines simply by dragging them off the ruler.

Table 1-2. *Guideline Issues* (continued)

Note   *If you created the report with a report expert, you'll see that Crystal Reports inserted horizontal guidelines on the left side of the Design tab. You can add these yourself if you use the Blank Report option. Just click in the side ruler to add a horizontal guideline. Then, attach objects to them on the top, bottom, or middle. Move the guideline to move whole lines of objects up or down at the same time.*

Formatting Objects

When you place objects on your report, Crystal Reports applies default font faces, sizes, colors, and formatting to the objects. You'll usually want to change some of this formatting to suit your particular report style or standards. There are several ways of formatting objects. As you use Crystal Reports, you may find that one way suits you better than another. Also, all formatting options aren't available with every method, so you may need to use a certain one to perform a specific kind of formatting.

Using the Format toolbar is the quickest way to apply standard formatting. The Format toolbar is similar to other toolbars you may have used in word processors or spreadsheet programs. To format using the Format toolbar, first select the object or objects you want to format, and then change their formatting by clicking Format toolbar buttons or choosing items in scroll boxes.

Some formatting options, such as changing font color or formatting a date field to print in a long date format, aren't available on the Format toolbar. These formatting options, along with all the options available on the Format toolbar, can be chosen in the Format Editor, shown in Figure 1-6. To use the Format Editor, first choose the object or objects that you wish to format, and then do one of the following:

- Click the Format button on the Supplementary toolbar.

- Choose Format Field, Borders and Colors, or Font from the Format menu.

- Right-click the object and choose Format Field, Border and Colors, or Font from the pop-up menu.

All of these options display the Format Editor. The only difference is the tab that will be chosen on the Format Editor when it appears.

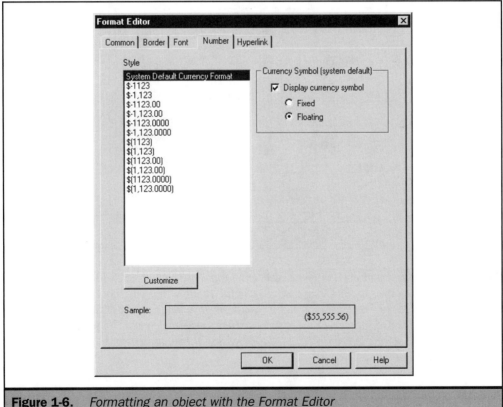

Figure 1-6.   *Formatting an object with the Format Editor*

Choose the desired tab on the Format Editor, and make formatting selections by choosing one of the built-in styles, by using a custom style, or by choosing other specific formatting options on the desired tab. Click OK on the Format Editor to apply all the formatting you chose and close the Format Editor.

There are two general ways you can choose formats in the Format Editor—with a default style, or by customizing the style. In particular, you'll notice a selection of predefined formats for most nonstring data types in the Style list. You can just choose one of these default formats from the list. If, however, the exact format you want isn't in the Style list, click the Customize button at the bottom of the Style list. A Custom Style dialog box will appear where you can make more detailed choices about how to format the field. You'll need to use the Customize button to conditionally format some aspects of the field as well (conditional formatting is discussed in Chapter 7).

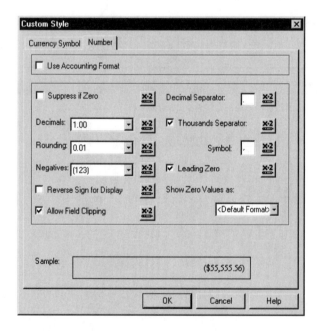

Caution *You can add new objects, or move, size, and format existing objects, just as easily in the Preview tab as in the Design tab. Be careful, though, that you move or size objects accurately in the Preview tab. You may inadvertently move an object from the details section to the page header, or make some similar undesirable move, without realizing it. Formatting objects in the Preview tab is great, but it may be better to size or move them in the Design tab.*

Customizing Crystal Reports' Behavior

When you first install Crystal Reports, it behaves in a certain way that should serve most users well. However, you will probably want to customize the behavior of some Crystal Report options. Other software typically has a Preferences or Options menu item to accomplish this. Crystal Reports has two options that work together to control how the program behaves: Options and Report Options, both chosen from the File menu.

Most often, you will use the Options dialog box, shown in Figure 1-7, to change the default behavior of Crystal Reports. For example, to change the default font face and size from Times Roman 10 point to something else, you would click the Fonts tab in the Options dialog box, click the button for the type of object you want to change, and choose a different font or size. To change the default format of date fields from mm/dd/yy to mm/dd/yyyy, you would click the Fields tab in the Options dialog box and then click the Date button.

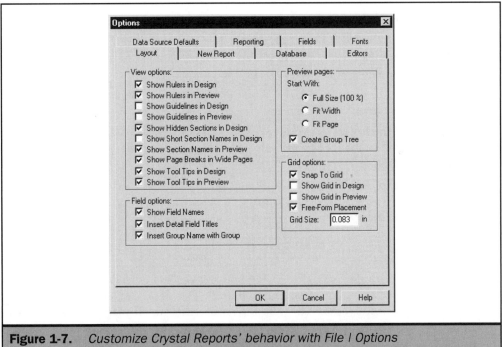

Figure 1-7.   *Customize Crystal Reports' behavior with File | Options*

Note   *Many options you choose here don't change items already placed on the current report, or any existing reports—they will only affect new items added to the report. For example, if you change the default font to 8-point Arial, only new objects that you add to the report from that point forward will take on that new formatting.*

There are a number of options that benefit the new user and make report creation a bit easier. You may want to choose File | Options and set each of the following options to your own personal preference.

Layout Tab

- **Show Guidelines in Design**   Almost always on; the majority of report designing should occur in the Design tab, and guidelines can be useful.

- **Show Guidelines in Preview**   Almost always off; guidelines detract from the "What-You-See-Is-What-You-Get" (or WYSIWYG) view most people are used to.

- **Show Short Section Names in Design**   Once you're more familiar with the Design tab, you may turn this option on to give you more design area.

- **Show Section Names in Preview**   Usually on, to help you troubleshoot sectional problems when you're in preview mode.

- **Snap To Grid**   Great to turn off when you want to be able to truly use freeform placement of objects.

- **Show Grid in Design**   If you leave Snap To Grid turned on, this will actually show the grid in the Design tab, so you can see exactly where objects you are moving will snap.

- **Show Grid in Preview**   Almost always off, to improve clarity, but can be turned on if you are moving and resizing objects in the Preview tab and want to see where they will snap.

Reporting Tab

- **Save Data With Report**   Checks the File | Save Data with Report option automatically when you create a new report. This saves data in the Preview tab along with the report design in the report .RPT file. If you don't want this option turned on when you create a new report, uncheck it here in File | Options.

- **Show All Headers on Drill Down**   Shows all headers above the group being drilled into inside the drill-down tab. See Chapter 8 for information on drill-down reporting.

- **Autosave Reports After *x* Minutes**   This will automatically save your report files every few minutes, preventing a loss of data if you suffer a power failure or your computer hangs. You may choose how often to automatically save reports. Reports are saved in the drive/folder specified as your Windows "Temp" folder with the file extension .AUTOSAVE.RPT.

- **Formula Language**   This feature allows you to choose the default formula language for Crystal Reports formulas. You may change the language used for formulas within each formula, but this allows you to choose the default. Chapter 5 discusses the different formula language options in more detail.

A subset of items from the Options dialog box appears on the File | Report Options dialog box.

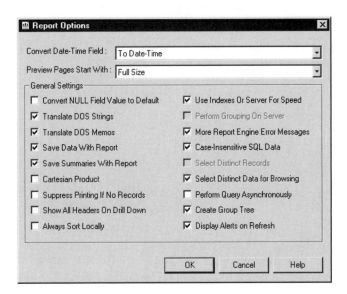

When you create a new report, these options are based on what's chosen in the File | Options dialog box. Later, though, these options can be set to be different than the corresponding File | Options dialog box items. When the report is saved, these options are saved along with the report. The next time the report is retrieved, they will *supersede* the corresponding File | Option items.

The Complete Reference

Crystal Reports

Chapter 2

Enhancing Appearance with Text Objects

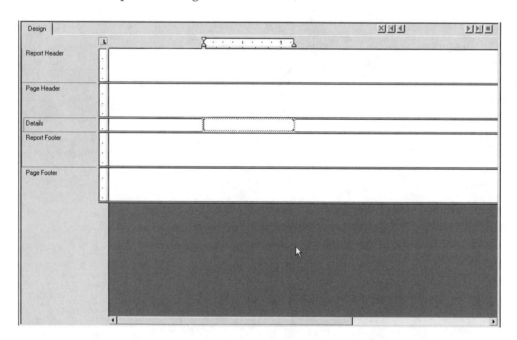

here are many times during the report designing process that you need to just drop some *literal text* into your report. This could be a report title that you place in the report header, a label next to a subtotal in the group footer, or a whole paragraph that you place in the report footer (perhaps explaining the methodology of the report). You can accomplish this with *text objects*.

To insert a text object, choose Insert | Text Object or click the Text Object button on the Standard toolbar. You'll see the text object attached to your mouse pointer. Position the mouse where you want the text object to go, and click. The text object will be dropped at that location, and you'll be immediately placed in *edit mode*. You'll always know when you're in edit mode because you'll see a flashing cursor inside the text object and a small ruler at the top of the Design or Preview tab, as shown here:

Now, just start typing. The material you type will appear inside the text object. When you're finished, just click outside the text object to save your changes.

There are several ways to edit the contents of an existing text object. To use the "long way," select the text object and then choose Edit | Edit Text Object from the pull-down menus, or right-click on the text object and choose Edit Text Object from the pop-up menu. The "short way" is simply to double-click a text object, which places you in edit mode. Once in edit mode, use the cursor keys, BACKSPACE key, and DEL key to move around and edit the text.

Caution *It's commonplace to attempt to exit edit mode by pressing the ENTER key. Not only will this not end editing, it will start a new line in the text object. This can often cause the contents of the text object to partially or completely disappear. If you want to put line breaks in your text object, go ahead and press ENTER, but make sure you resize the text object when you're finished so that you can see all of your text.*

Combining Database Fields

Simply typing literal text into text objects is a waste of their capabilities! Text objects are powerful elements that can help you create very attractive reports. Consider Figure 2-1, the beginning of a form letter that uses the Customers table from XTREME.MDB (included with Crystal Reports 8.5). Note the spacing problems with

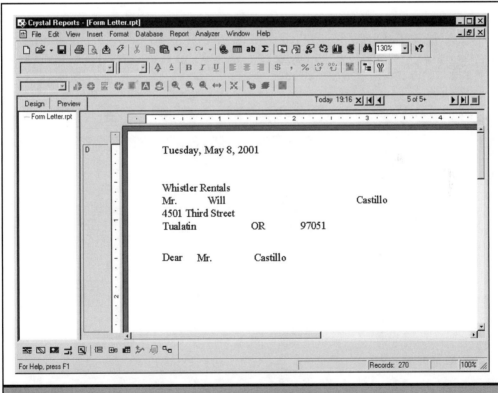

Figure 2-1. *Spacing problems using database fields*

the contact name, city, state, and ZIP code. These lines are composed of separate fields from the Customers table. No matter how much you try or how creative you get sizing and moving these fields, they will not line up properly for every customer. They appear in the same horizontal location in every details section, no matter how wide or narrow the fields are sized.

This type of problem is a dead giveaway that this is a computer-generated letter. Although most consumers are savvy enough to assume that a computer had something to do with the form letters they receive, you don't want to make it obvious. Crystal Reports gives you a better way with text objects.

In addition to containing literal text, text objects allow you to combine database fields with literal text. When the text object appears, it automatically sizes the contents of the database fields so that there is no extra space. Figure 2-2 shows the same form letter as Figure 2-1, but a text object is used to combine the database fields with literal text and spaces.

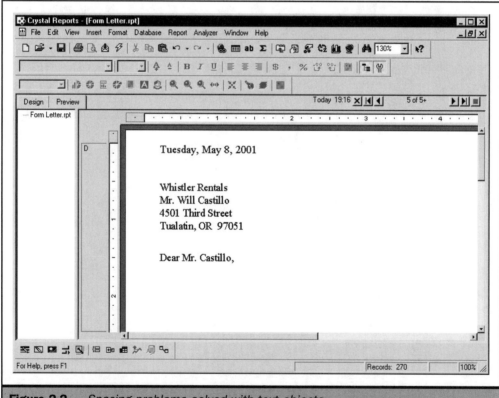

Figure 2-2.   *Spacing problems solved with text objects*

To combine database fields inside a text object, follow these steps:

1. Insert a text object, as described previously. If you need to include any literal text, you may type it either now or after you've inserted the database fields. It doesn't matter whether you leave the text object in edit mode or end editing.

2. From the Field Explorer, choose the field or fields you want to combine in the text object. Drag them from the Field Explorer into the text object. Note that your mouse cursor will change when you move over the text object, and a blinking cursor will appear in the text object at the same time:

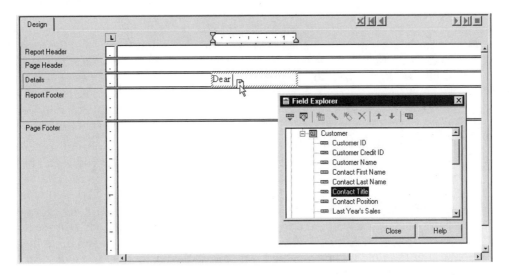

3. Before dropping the database field or fields in the text object, look very carefully at the location of the blinking text object cursor. Wherever the cursor is located is where the database field or fields will go when you release the mouse button. Release the button when the cursor is in the proper position.

4. The text object will go into edit mode, if it wasn't already. You may now type more literal text or add another database field, if you need to.

5. When you're finished combining database fields and literal text, end editing by clicking outside the text object.

Combining Special Fields

You're not limited to combining database fields inside text objects. You can use *special fields* as well. Special fields are system-generated fields, such as the print date, print time, page number, and total page count. You may place them directly on the report, just like database fields. And, like database fields, you'll encounter spacing problems if you try to place them near literal text.

To combine special fields with literal text inside text objects, perform the same steps as for database fields. Just drag the fields from the Special Fields category of the Field Explorer, instead of from the Database Field category. In fact, you can embed any type of field from the Field Explorer in a text object just by dragging and dropping from the desired category.

Figure 2-3 shows the benefits of combining special fields with literal text in text objects.

The following pointers will help you as you combine fields and literal text inside text objects:

- If you place a database or special field in the wrong location inside the text object (suppose you place the Last Name field in between the letters *a* and *r* in the word "Dear"), you can simply use your cursor keys and the BACKSPACE or DEL key to make the correction. In this case, it is easier to just delete the text following the special field, and reenter it before the special field. You may also use CTRL-C to cut text and CTRL-V to paste text inside the text object.

- If you inadvertently drop a subtotal, summary, database field, or some other item inside a text object by mistake (it's pretty easy to do, even if you're careful), you have two choices. If you catch the problem immediately, you can choose Edit | Undo, or click the Undo button on the Standard toolbar. The field will move back where it was. However, if you notice that you accidentally dropped a field inside the text object after it's too late to reasonably undo it, edit the text object, click the field that was mistakenly added to highlight it, and press the DEL key. The field will be removed from inside the text object. You will then need to re-create it and place it in its correct position on the report.

The Can Grow Formatting Option

When you combine database fields or special fields inside text objects, Crystal Reports turns on the Can Grow formatting option automatically. You can turn it back off or change the Maximum Number of Lines option from the Format Editor. To display the Format Editor, use one of these options:

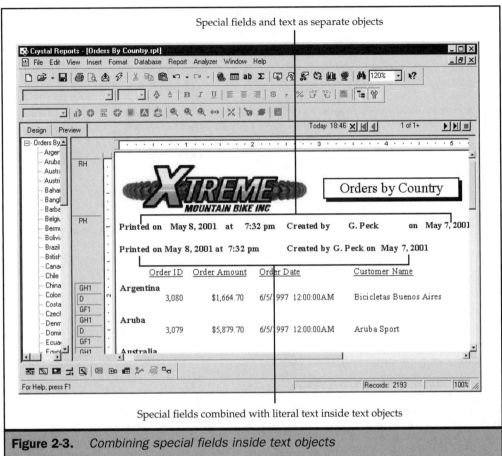

Figure 2-3.   *Combining special fields inside text objects*

- Select the text object and then select Format | Format Text from the pull-down menus.

- Right-click the text object and choose Format Text from the pop-up menu.

- Click the Format button on the Supplementary toolbar.

The Can Grow option is found on the Common tab of the Format Editor.

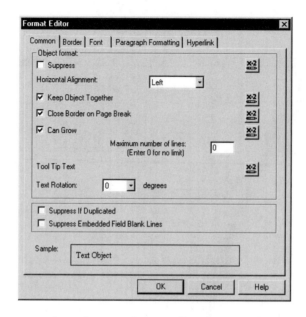

With Can Grow turned on, the text object will automatically grow taller to show all the text inside it. You can specify the maximum number of lines that the text object will grow, or leave the number set to zero for unlimited size. When Can Grow is turned on, the text object will only display as wide as it appears on the report. However, it will word-wrap at spaces in the text, creating additional vertical space up to the maximum number of lines.

This automatic behavior lets you size a text object so that it's only one line high. If the contents of the text object can be displayed in one line, the text object will remain one line tall. If it needs more lines, it will expand only by the amount of vertical space necessary to show the material inside the text object (limited by the maximum number of lines).

Tip   *Can Grow is helpful for other types of objects as well, not just text objects. You can set the Can Grow formatting option for string fields and memo fields. This is particularly helpful for "description" or "narrative" types of fields that could contain as little as a few characters and as much as several paragraphs of text. Can Grow isn't available for any type of object other than a text object, string field, or memo field.*

Formatting Individual Parts of Text Objects

You can format a text object as you would any other object, using the Format toolbar or Format Editor. When you select a text object and change the formatting, such as setting a color or font size, the entire text object takes on that format. This may be the behavior you want.

However, at other times you may want certain characters or words in a text object to take on different formatting than the rest of the text object. Even more prevalent is a situation in which you need to format individual database fields or special fields that reside *inside* a text object.

For example, when you insert the Print Date special field inside a text object, it takes on the default formatting from File | Options, perhaps an mm/dd/yy format. If you select the text object and display the Format Editor, there is no Date tab in which to choose an alternate date format—this is a text object you're formatting! Similarly, if you've placed a number field inside a text object, you may want to change the formatting to show no decimal places or to add a currency symbol.

To accomplish these types of formatting tasks, you must format individual parts of the text object. This is actually quite simple. Start editing the text object by double-clicking it. You are then free to select individual characters or words by dragging over them with your mouse or by holding down the SHIFT key while using the cursor keys. You can then use the Format toolbar or Format Editor to change the formatting for just those selected characters.

To change the formatting of a database or special field inside a text object, edit the text object and then click the field you wish to format. You'll know you've selected the field when it becomes highlighted inside the text object. You can then use the Format Editor (either from the Format menu or by right-clicking—the number-formatting buttons on the Format toolbar won't work here) to change the formatting of the object.

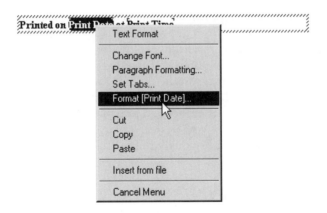

Note   *In Crystal Reports 7 and earlier, text objects were not WYSIWYG (what you see is what you get). That is, they didn't appear the same when printed on paper as they did when previewed on the screen. Screen-to-printer accuracy has been much improved since version 7. However, if you have reports developed in earlier versions that you don't want to look different when opened in Version 8.5, check the setting of Version 7 Text Compatibility on the Reporting tab of the File | Options dialog box. If this option is turned on, Crystal Reports 8.5 will maintain close (if not identical) formatting for text objects on Version 7 reports that are opened with Crystal Reports 8.5.*

Importing Text from a File

If you have large amounts of text that you want to use in Crystal Reports text objects, you may either type it into a text object directly or copy and paste from the Windows Clipboard. However, data for text objects can also be imported directly from plain text, Rich Text Format (RTF), or Hypertext Markup Language (HTML) files.

To import text into a text object, add a text object as described previously in the chapter (using the Insert menu or toolbar button). If the text object isn't already in edit mode, double-click it to place it in edit mode. Then, right-click and choose Insert From File from the pop-up menu.

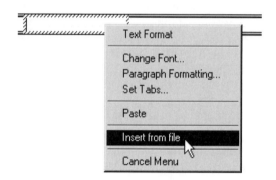

A File Open dialog box will appear. Navigate to the drive and folder where the text, RTF, or HTML file is that you wish to import into the text object. Choose the desired file and click OK. The file will be imported into the text object, alongside any existing text that may already be in the text object. If the text file contains plain text, it will simply be displayed in the text object in the default font style for text objects (set on the Fonts tab of File | Options). If the imported text is in HTML or RTF format, Crystal Reports automatically interprets the embedded font and formatting specifications and includes them in the text object. If you wish to reformat portions of the text object, simply use techniques described previously in the chapter for formatting individual parts of text objects.

The Complete Reference

Crystal
Reports

Chapter 3

Sorting and Grouping

W hen you first create and preview a report, the report shows details sections in *natural order*. That is, the records appear in whatever order the database sends them to Crystal Reports. This order can vary widely, depending on what database you are using, how you link tables, and other variables.

You'll probably want to control the order in which information appears on your report. An employee listing, for example, isn't very useful if it isn't in alphabetical order. A sales breakdown is probably more helpful if you see your sales figures in a particular order. You're probably interested in a highest-to-lowest sequence of order quantities if you're about to send gifts to your best customers at the holidays. On the other hand, lowest-to-highest sequence is probably more appropriate if you're about to send your marketing department out to talk to lower-performing customers.

Sorting Your Report

If you simply want to reorder your report's details sections into a particular order, you need to *sort* the report. Sorting is useful for simple reports that need to present information in a certain order. To sort a report, choose Report | Sort Records from the pull-down menus, or click the Sort Order button on the Standard toolbar. This displays the Record Sort Order dialog box.

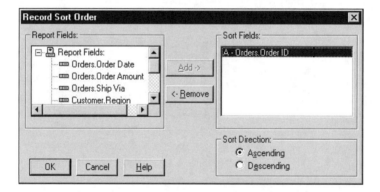

The left Report Fields box shows all the report fields that you've placed in the details section of the report. If you wish to sort on a field you haven't placed on the report, scroll down through the Report Fields list until you find the list of tables and fields you added to your report. Choose one or more fields to control how you want your report sorted. Simply double-click the field you wish to sort on, or select the field and then click the Add button. Either method moves the field to the Sort Fields box on the right. You may then choose between the Ascending and Descending radio buttons to choose the sort order.

An *ascending* sort orders the records alphabetically, A to Z; if the records start with numbers, they will appear before any letters, sorted 0 through 9. In a *descending* sort, the order is reversed. Records appear in Z to A order, followed by any numbers in 9 to 0 order.

You may sort by as many fields as you like—you're not limited to one. This is handy, for example, if you want to sort your customers by state, and within state by customer name. Simply add the additional sort fields to the Sort Fields box and choose the sort order. When you click OK, Crystal Reports will sort by the higher fields first, and then the lower fields.

Here are a few points that will help you sort your reports more effectively:

- You can't reorder the sort fields in the Sort Fields part of the Record Sort Order dialog box. If you want to change the order of the sort, you need to use the Remove button to remove fields, and use the Add button to add them again in correct sort order.

- You can sort just as easily on formula fields (covered in Chapter 5) as you can on database fields. This is often required if you want to customize some aspect of the way records are sorted. Just remember that if you're using a SQL database, such as SQL Server or Oracle, sorting on a formula field makes Crystal Reports sort the records instead of having the database server do the work, which may affect the performance of your report (albeit slightly). This is covered in more detail in Chapter 14.

Grouping Records

Sorting records is handy for lists or other simple reports that just need records to appear in a certain order. It's more common, however, to want not only to have your report sorted by certain fields, but also to have subtotals, counts, averages, or other summary information appear when the sort field changes. To accomplish this, you must use Crystal Reports *groups*.

When you create a report group, you both sort the records on the report and create two additional report sections every time the group field changes. You may place subtotals, averages, counts, and many other types of summary information in these sections. In addition, grouping your report enables the *group tree,* an Explorer-like window on the left side of the Preview tab. The group tree gives you a quick overview of the organization of your report, and enables you to navigate directly to a particular group that you want to see.

To create a report group, you may either choose Insert | Group from the pull-down menus or click the Insert Group button from the Supplementary toolbar. The Insert Group dialog box appears.

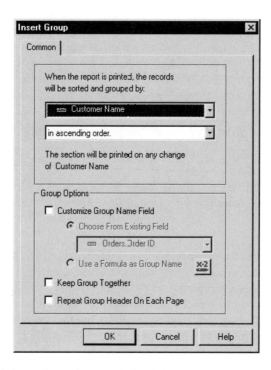

There are several drop-down lists and check boxes that you use to insert a group. Follow these steps to complete the dialog box:

1. Click the top drop-down list to select the field you want to group on. The list will display fields on your report, as well as other fields in the tables that the report is using. You can group based on a field already on the report or based on a database field that you didn't put on the report. You can also group based on a formula field.

2. Click the second drop-down list to select the order in which your groups will appear on the report. There are four options: *ascending order* shows the groups in A to Z order alphabetically; *descending order* shows the groups in Z to A order; *specified order* lets you create your own groups (described later in this chapter); and *original order* groups records in the order in which they appear in the database. (The latter is an interesting feature, but probably not useful in most reports.)

3. If you simply want to have the database field itself appear in the groups on the report and the group tree, leave the Customize Group Name Field check box empty. However, if you'd like to customize the way the groups appear (perhaps you'd like a month fully spelled out along with a four-digit year for a date field), click the Customize Group Name Field check box. You can then make additional choices to determine what appears for the group. "Customizing Group Name Fields" appears later in the chapter.

4. Click the Keep Group Together option if you want Crystal Reports to try to keep your groups from breaking at the end of a page. If you leave this option unchecked, the beginning of a group and just a few detail records in the group may print at the bottom of a page, while the rest of the group's detail records and its subtotals may appear at the top of the next page.

5. Click the Repeat Group Header On Each Page option if you think you will have large groups that will span more than a single page. This option will print the group header section (described later) at the top of each page where a group continues. This allows you to look at details sections on subsequent pages and know which group they belong to.

Caution   *Clicking Keep Group Together can cause odd behavior if the first group in your report won't fit on a page by itself. In this case, Crystal Reports will detect that it can't fit the group on the first page of the report and will start a new page before it starts printing the group. The result will be a blank first page. If this happens, you may resolve the problem by suppressing the report header section. If you do this, but still want material to print at the top of the first page only, create separate Page Header A and B sections, and conditionally format page header A to suppress if the page number is greater than 1. Formatting report sections is described in Chapter 8.*

Figure 3-1 shows the two new sections that are added to the Design tab, the group header and group footer. These sections appear at the beginning and end of every group. Note that Crystal Reports places an object in the group header section automatically. This *group name* object will automatically print the contents of the field on which the group is based in each group header. The group footer section is empty.

Tip   *You may turn off the Insert Group Name with Group option in File | Options if you don't want Crystal Reports to automatically insert a group name object in the group header when a group is created. If this is turned off, or if you inadvertently delete a group name object, you can insert a group name by displaying the Field Explorer and dragging and dropping a group name object after opening the Group Name Fields category.*

Figure 3-2 shows the Preview tab with the now-active group tree. You can see your groups in an outline form and navigate directly to the beginning of one of the groups by clicking the group in the group tree. You can also turn the display of the group tree on and off by clicking the Toggle Group Tree button on the Format toolbar.

Manipulating Existing Groups

After you create a group, you may wish to delete it so that only detail records print again without grouping. Or, you may wish to change the field that the group is based on, change the order of the groups from ascending to descending, customize the group name field, or choose one of the formatting options to control the way Crystal Reports deals with page breaks inside groups.

Group header will print at the start of each group

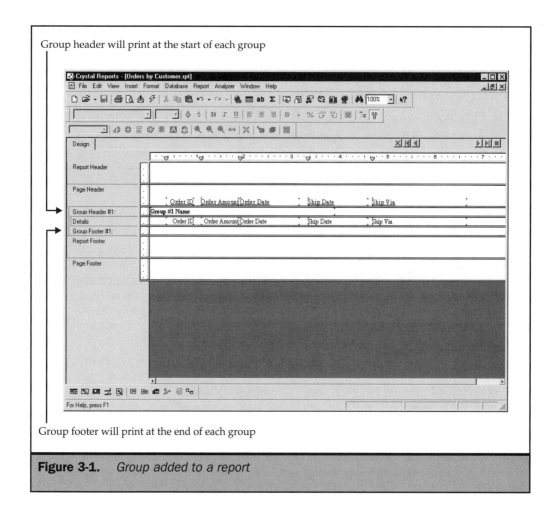

Group footer will print at the end of each group

Figure 3-1. *Group added to a report*

Two different ways exist to delete an existing group. The first is to choose Edit | Delete Group from the pull-down menus. You are presented with a list of groups (or only one, if that's all the report contains). Choose the group you wish to delete and click OK.

The second way is to return to the Design tab and point your mouse to the gray section names on the left side of the screen. You must point to the group header or group footer for the group you wish to delete, and then right-click and choose Delete Group from the pop-up menu.

> **Tip** *You can also delete a group with the right-click method in the Preview tab. Point to the abbreviated section names (GH or GF) in the Preview tab and right-click. You can then choose Delete Group from the pop-up menu.*

Click a group to navigate directly to it   Toggle the group tree on and off

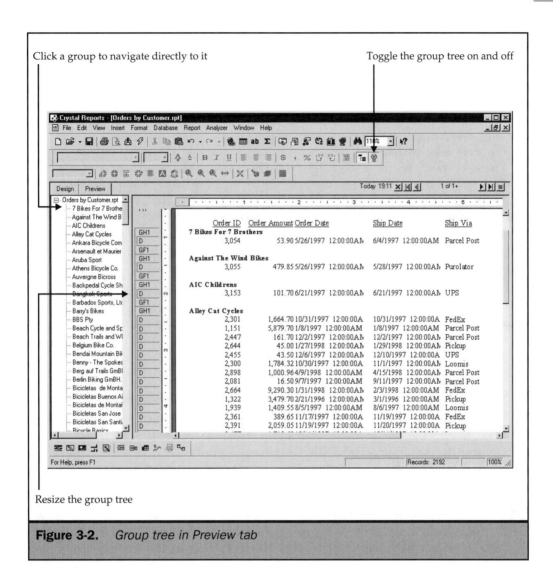

Figure 3-2.   *Group tree in Preview tab*

Resize the group tree

Deleting a group is a permanent operation, and you will be so warned. The group header and group footer sections will be removed from the report, along with any objects in them. You can't undo this: the Undo button on the Standard toolbar and the Undo option in the Edit menu are grayed out. It's not a bad idea to save the report before you delete a group. If it turns out to be a mistake, you can close the changed report (*without* saving changes) and go back to the saved version.

There are also two ways to change existing groups by redisplaying the dialog box that appeared when you created the group. You may change the field that the group is based on, change the order of groups (ascending, descending, specified, original), customize the group name field, or select the Keep Group Together or Repeat Group Header on Each New Page option. The first way is to choose Report | Change Group Expert from the pull-down menus. Though not really an "expert," this option presents you with a list of groups that are defined on the report. Choose the group you want to change and click Options.

The second way to change a group is to right-click on the group header or group footer section of the group you want to change in the Design or Preview tab. Then, right-click and choose Change Group from the pop-up menu. The Change Group Options dialog box will reappear, in which you change group settings and then click OK when you're finished.

Adding Subtotals and Summaries

So, what's the difference between just sorting the report and creating a group? Not only is the group tree useful with grouped reports, but you now have a section available for subtotals, averages, counts, and other summary functions at the end of each group. Although the group footer is empty when first created, you can insert subtotals and summary functions into it with ease.

Inserting subtotals or summaries in your report requires several steps:

1. Select in the details section the field that you wish to subtotal or summarize.

2. Choose Insert | Subtotal or Insert | Summary from the pull-down menus, or right-click the field you've chosen and choose Insert Subtotal or Insert Summary from the pop-up menu. To insert a summary, you can also click the Summary button on the Standard toolbar. The Insert Subtotal or Insert Summary dialog box will appear.

In Crystal Reports 8.5, you don't have to first select the details section field you want to summarize. If you have no fields selected, the first drop-down list in the Insert Subtotal or Insert Summary dialog box lets you choose the field you want to summarize.

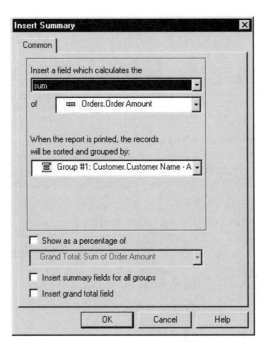

3. Subtotals can be inserted only for numeric or currency fields, whereas summaries can be inserted for any type of field (although not all summary functions are available for non-number fields).

4. If you are inserting a summary, choose the summary function (sum, average, and so on) that you wish to use. Then, choose the group in which you want to place the subtotal or summary. The first (or only) group you've created is displayed in the drop-down list by default.

5. If you want to create a percentage summary field, click the Show As a Percentage Of check box and choose from the drop-down list the field that you want to show the percentage of (percentage summary fields are discussed in detail later in the chapter).

6. If you have more than one group on the report and you want the summary or subtotal created for all groups, click the Insert Summary Fields for All Groups check box. If you want a grand total (*grand summary* is actually a more appropriate term) created as well, click the Insert Grand Total Field check box.

7. Click OK to place the subtotal or summary in the group footer directly below the detail field that you're summarizing.

8. Since Crystal Reports doesn't label group summaries for you, you should add text objects next to the summaries to indicate what they display. For example, a subtotal won't be confused with an average if you place a text object containing "Subtotal:" next to the subtotal object.

Here are a few pointers to keep in mind when inserting subtotals and summaries:

■ Although Crystal Reports places subtotals and summaries in the group footer by default, you don't have to leave them there. If you move them to the group header, they'll print the same information, but at the beginning of groups.

■ Once a summary or subtotal has been created, you don't have to delete it and insert a new summary if you want to change its function (for example, to change a subtotal to an average). Simply click the subtotal or summary and choose Edit | Summary from the pull-down menus, or right-click the summary and choose Change Summary from the pop-up menu.

■ You can actually create a group and a subtotal or summary in the group footer in one step. Simply insert a subtotal or summary as outlined previously. If there are no groups yet on the report, the Insert Subtotal or Insert Summary dialog box will, in essence, turn into a dialog box for inserting a group. If there are already existing groups and you want to create a new one, choose the field that you want to create the group on instead of an existing group. Again, the dialog box turns into an Insert Group dialog box. After you choose the appropriate options and click OK, a group will be created and the subtotal or summary will be placed in the group footer all at the same time.

If you want a grand total or summary to appear but forgot to click the Insert Grand Total Field option when you created the group, or if there are no groups and you just want a grand total, you may add it in a separate step. Select the field in the details section that you wish to summarize, and select Insert | Grand Total from the pull-down menus. You can also right-click the field you wish to summarize and choose Insert | Grand Total from the pop-up menu. In either case, the Insert Grand Total dialog box (very similar to the Insert Summary dialog box) appears. As with inserting group summaries, you don't have to actually select the details section field you want to grand total first. The grand total will be placed in the report footer, where it will summarize for all records on the report.

Tip   *If you pull down the Insert menu and the Subtotal, Summary, and Grand Total options are dimmed, it indicates that you have selected an object on your report (perhaps a text object, group name field, and so forth) that can't be summarized. Either select the object that you actually want to summarize, or deselect everything on the report. Then, the menu options will be enabled.*

Table 3-1 shows the different summary functions that are available in the Insert Summary and Insert Grand Total dialog boxes and what each does.

 If the details field that you summarize contains null values (a special database value where the field actually contains nothing, as opposed to a zero or empty string), the summary function won't "count" that record. For example, a Count or Average won't figure the null record into its calculation. If you wish to avoid this problem with the current report, you can convert database null values to zero or empty string values by choosing File | Report Options and clicking Convert NULL Field Value to Default. If you want this to be the default option for all new reports, you can choose the same option on the Reporting tab from File | Options.

Percentage Summary Fields

Although the default summary functions satisfy most needs for analytical reporting, sometimes you may prefer to calculate percentages rather than whole numbers. For example, if your report groups sales by sales rep within each month, you may want to know both the actual dollars and the *percentage* of revenues each sales rep is responsible for in that month. And, you may also want to calculate the percentage of total sales for the entire year that each month is responsible for. Such an example is

Function	Results
Sum	Returns the subtotal of the chosen field; available only for number or currency fields. Choosing a summary with the Sum function is exactly the same as inserting a subtotal.
Average	Returns the average of the chosen field; available only for number or currency fields.
Maximum	For number or currency fields, returns the highest number in the group. For string fields, returns the last member of the group alphabetically. For date fields, returns the latest date in the group.
Minimum	For number or currency fields, returns the lowest number in the group. For string fields, returns the first member of the group alphabetically. For date fields, returns the earliest date in the group.

Table 3-1. *Summary Functions*

Function	Results
Count	Simply counts the records in the details section and returns the number of records in the group. Although you are required to choose a database field before selecting this option, the Count function will return the same number no matter which field you choose (with the exception of fields that contain null values).
Sample Variance Sample Standard Deviation Population Variance Population Standard Deviation	For number or currency fields only, these functions return the chosen statistical function for all the detail fields in the group. For details of how these values are calculated, refer to a statistics text.
Distinct Count	Similar to the Count function, but returns only the distinct number of occurrences of the field. As opposed to Count, the field you choose in the details section before choosing Distinct Count is very significant. For example, if five records contain the strings Los Angeles, Chicago, Vancouver, Chicago, and Miami, the Count function would return 5, whereas Distinct Count would return 4.
Correlation Covariance Weighted Average	For number and currency fields only. When you choose these functions, an additional drop-down list appears, letting you choose another numeric or currency field to use in the function. These functions vary in use and are explained in standard statistics texts. Crystal Reports online Help has good descriptions of some of these functions.
Median	For number and currency fields only. Returns the median, or middle, number in the group. If there is one number in the group, it is returned. If there are two numbers, their average is returned.
Pth Percentile	For number and currency fields only. When you choose this function, an additional box appears in which you can enter a number between 0 and 100 for P. This function returns the number that indicates what the percentile is for P, based on all the numbers in the group.

Table 3-1.   *Summary Functions* (continued)

Function	Results
Nth Largest	Returns the third, fifth, or tenth (and so forth) largest value in the group, depending on the value you enter for *N*. For example, *N*th largest, with *N* equaling 1, returns the largest value in the group. When you choose this function, an additional box appears in which you can enter the value for *N*. For numeric fields, this function returns the *N*th-highest numeric value. With string fields, it returns the *N*th value alphabetically (for example, if there are three records containing FedEx and two records containing UPS, *N*th largest when *N* equals 2 will be UPS, and *N*th largest when *N* equals 3 will be FedEx).
Nth Smallest	Returns the third, fifth, tenth (and so forth) smallest value in the group. For example, *N*th smallest with *N* equaling 1 returns the smallest value in the group. When you choose this function, an additional box appears in which you can enter the value for *N*. This function behaves similarly to *N*th highest with both numeric and string fields.
Mode	Returns the most frequently occurring value from all the detail records in the group. For numeric fields, Mode returns the most frequently occurring number. For string fields, Mode returns the most frequently occurring string (for example, with detail records containing five occurrences of FedEx, three occurrences of UPS, and eight occurrences of Parcel Post, Mode would return Parcel Post).
Nth Most Frequent	Returns the third, fifth, tenth (and so forth) most frequent occurrence in the group. This is similar to Mode, except that you're not limited to just the *most* frequent occurrence.

Table 3-1. *Summary Functions* (continued)

shown in Figure 3-3. Crystal Reports 8.5 features the *percentage summary field*, which creates this type of calculation without the need for a formula.

To create a percentage summary field, follow the steps previously outlined to insert a summary field (percentage summary fields aren't available when using Insert | Subtotal).

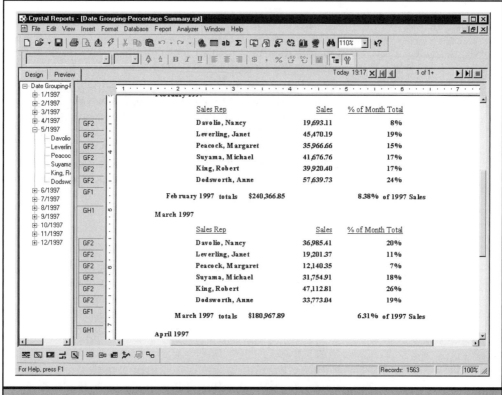

Figure 3-3. *Percentages created with percentage summary fields*

Choose the field you want to use to calculate the percentage (the "numerator") and the group in which you want the percentage placed, as though you are creating a regular summary. Then, click the Show As a Percentage Of check box and use the drop-down list to choose the higher-level group or grand total you want used as the "denominator." If you are placing the percentage in the highest-level (or only) group on the report, you'll only be able to choose a grand total for the denominator. Click OK.

Crystal Reports will place a summary field in the group footer of the group you specified. When you preview the report, however, you'll see a percentage number rather than a count, subtotal, or other number. The percentage summary field will already be formatted to display a percent sign.

Multiple Groups

Crystal Reports does not limit your report to just one level of grouping. In fact, many powerful reporting features can be provided to your report viewer by creative use of multiple groups. The key to many sophisticated reporting requirements lies in creative use of formulas (covered in Chapter 5) in conjunction with multiple levels of grouping.

Multiple groups form a report hierarchy, with increasing levels of detailed information being presented by inner groups. For example, a report might be grouped by country first. Within the country group would be a geographic region group (Northwest, Southwest, and so forth), and then a group by state, a group by county or township, a group by city, and finally detail records showing individual customers or orders within that city. Each group has its own group header and group footer sections, and subtotals and summaries can exist for each group.

The group tree handles multiple levels of grouping very elegantly, following the general style of Windows Explorer. Plus signs (expand buttons) are displayed next to groups that can be expanded to display other groups; minus signs (collapse buttons) are shown beside expanded groups that can be collapsed. Figure 3-4 shows a report with multiple groups. Notice that you can navigate through the group tree by clicking

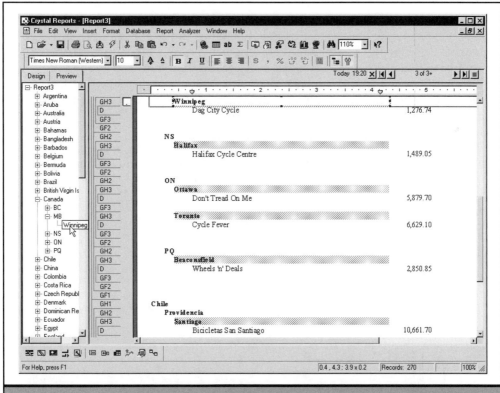

Figure 3-4. *Multiple levels of grouping*

the plus and minus signs to open and close group levels. When you find the group you want to see, click the group name in the group tree to go directly to the beginning of that group in the report, no matter how deep the group is in the hierarchy.

To create additional levels of grouping, simply repeat the process described previously for inserting a group. The groups will appear in the order that you create them. You can use the Insert Subtotal/Summary options to add subtotals and summaries to the group footer and group header sections.

> **Tip** *If you are using multiple groups and forgot to include a summary or subtotal field in all groups or as a grand total when you first created it, you needn't create additional summaries or grand totals using menu options. You can simply copy the subtotal or summary object from a group footer to another group footer, or to the report footer, and get the same result—Crystal Reports uses the location of the object to determine the scope of records it applies to. Use Edit | Copy and Edit | Paste from the pull-down menus to copy and paste the summaries, or select the summary and CTRL-drag to copy the object to another section.*

You may inadvertently create groups in the wrong order. For example, if you wish to have your report grouped by state and then by city, make sure to create the groups in that order. If you create the city group first, followed by the state group, you'll have one group for each city, with whatever state that city is in as a lower-level group. You'd have, for example, a group for Los Angeles containing a California group. Below that, you'd have a group for San Diego containing another California group.

This isn't as much of a problem as it might seem. You don't have to delete groups and reinsert them in the desired order—moving them around is surprisingly easy. Simply return to the Design tab and point to the gray Group Header or Group Footer area on the left side of the screen. Point to the group that needs to be moved, and hold down the left mouse button—the mouse cursor turns into a hand symbol.

```
Design | Preview |

                                     · · · I · ⇩ · 1 · · · I · · ·

Report Header                   ·
                                ·

Page Header                     ·
                                ·
                                ·                    Customer Name

Group Header #1:        🖑  ·  Group #1 Name
Group Header #2:            ·  Group #2 Name
Details                        ·                    Customer Name
Group Footer #2:               ·
Group Footer #1:               ·
Report Footer                   ·
                                ·

Page Footer                     ·
                                ·
                                ·

                                ◄|
```

You can now simply drag and drop the group header or group footer on top of the group that you wish to swap it with. When you release the mouse button, the groups swap locations. Don't be confused by the fact that the groups stay numbered in sequential order—the groups have been moved. In the preceding example, simply dropping the state group header (Group Header #2) on the city group header (Group Header #1) will swap the groups. The state group header becomes Group Header #1 and the city group header becomes Group Header #2.

Specified Order Grouping

Sometimes, you may need data grouped on your report in a special order that the database doesn't offer. For example, the database may contain a state field, but not a field indicating what geographic location the record belongs to (Northwest, Southwest, and so on). One option that may be appropriate for more sophisticated customized grouping is basing a group on a sophisticated formula. However, if your customized grouping is not particularly complicated, *specified order grouping* may be more straightforward. This allows you to create customized groups without having to know the Crystal Reports formula language.

Specified order grouping lets you use a dialog box similar to the Select Expert (discussed in Chapter 1) to create your own groups, based on an existing database field. In the geographic location example used previously, you could create a Northwest group consisting of Washington, Oregon, Idaho, and Montana. The Southwest group could include Nevada, California, Texas, and Arizona. The Northeast group could consist of New York, Maine, Vermont, and New Hampshire. Southeast could include Florida, Alabama, Louisiana, and Mississippi. All the other states not in these four groups could either be ignored, placed in their own individual groups, or lumped together in one final group given a name of your choice, such as Midwest.

To specify your own groups, choose Specified Order in the Insert Group dialog box instead of Ascending or Descending order when you create a new group or change an existing group. (Don't forget that the quickest way to change an existing group is to point to the desired group header or group footer gray section name in the Design tab, right-click, and choose Change Group from the pop-up menu.) When you choose Specified Order, a Specified Order tab is added to the Change Group Options dialog box.

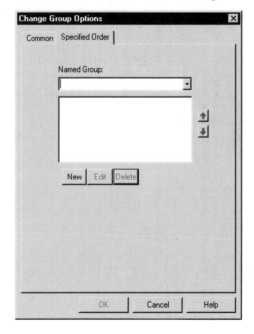

The title of this dialog box changes depending on whether you are inserting a new group or changing an existing group. The dialog boxes are identical (including Specified Grouping) except for the dialog box title.

Click the New button to create a new named group. This will display the Define Named Group dialog box, shown next. Type the name the group should have on the report, such as Northwest. Then, using options in the tabs, indicate which records will be included in the group. For example, you may want the Northwest group to include records in which Customer.Region is one of BC, OR, and ID.

```
┌──────────────────────────────────────────────────────────┐
│ 🖫 Define Named Group                                  [×] │
│                                                            │
│  Group Name:  │Northwest                              │   │
│                                                            │
│  Customer.Region │ <New> │                                │
│  ┌────────────────────────────────────────────────────┐  │
│  │ │is one of        ▼│  │                        ▼│   │  │
│  │                                                     │  │
│  │              ┌──────┐   ┌──────────────────────┐   │  │
│  │              │ Add  │   │BC                    │   │  │
│  │              └──────┘   │OR                    │   │  │
│  │              ┌──────┐   │ID                    │   │  │
│  │              │Remove│   │                      │   │  │
│  │              └──────┘   └──────────────────────┘   │  │
│  └────────────────────────────────────────────────────┘  │
│                                                            │
│  ┌────┐   ┌──────┐   ┌──────┐        ┌────────────┐      │
│  │ OK │   │Cancel│   │ Help │        │Browse Data...│    │
│  └────┘   └──────┘   └──────┘        └────────────┘      │
└──────────────────────────────────────────────────────────┘
```

If you need to use several different criteria for the named group, you can click the <New> tab and add additional criteria for the group. When you're finished, click OK on the Define Named Group dialog box. The named group will be created and will appear in the list of named groups in the Change Group Options dialog box. You can now click the New button again to add additional named groups (for example, Southwest, including AZ, CA, and TX).

Remember that clicking the <New> tab to create more than one selection tab still only allows you to select based on one field—the field your group is created on. The criteria on the tabs will be joined using a logical Or operation—this is different from the Select Expert.

As you add new named groups, they appear in the Specified Order tab of the Change Group Options dialog box in the order that you created them, *not* in alphabetical order. If you wish to change the order in which the named groups appear on the report, select a named group and use the up or down arrow next to the list of named groups to change its position. The Other group, however, will always be last, no matter what you name it or how you position named groups with the arrow buttons.

After you create at least one named group, the Others tab appears in the Group dialog box. You use this tab to deal with any records that haven't been caught by your specific named groups. You can discard the remaining records, place them in one "catchall" group with the name of your choice, or leave them in their own groups based on the database field. In the geographic example, Northwest, Southwest, Northeast, and Southeast have all been created as named groups. The Others tab is used to lump any regions that weren't otherwise specified into a Midwest group.

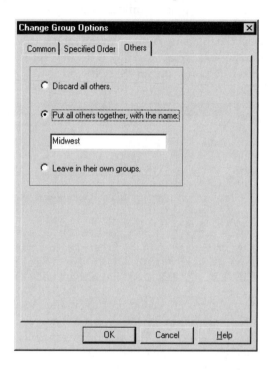

Tip

You might have noticed the Named Group drop-down list on the Specified Order tab. This list will browse the database, showing you samples of the actual field you're grouping on. If you choose one of these samples, Crystal Reports will create a named group with the same name as the actual database field. This is handy if you want to create the same groups as you would by using Ascending or Descending order, but place the groups in the specific order you desire.

After you create your named groups and click OK on the Change Group Options dialog box, the report will reflect your new grouping. Figure 3-5 shows a list of orders grouped by the five geographic areas described previously. If you wish to change any of your specified grouping options, or remove them altogether so that records appear in their own groups, just use the steps mentioned previously to change an existing group. The Change Group Options dialog box will open, and you can edit your specified groups or change grouping to ascending or descending order, which will remove specified grouping.

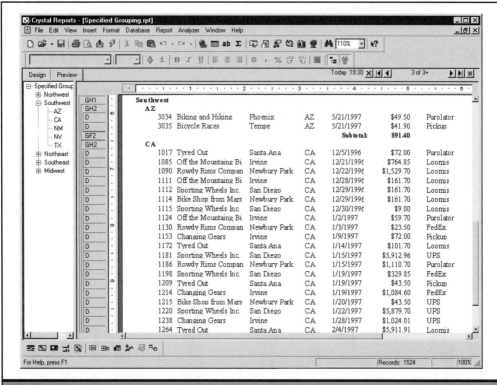

Figure 3-5. *Report with specified order grouping*

Drilling Down on Data

One of the most powerful features of Crystal Reports is its online reporting capability. Although you can print reports on a printer and export them to other file formats, such as Word or Excel, the real power of many reports becomes available only when users can view and interact with them *online*. This means that the user directly views the .RPT file that Crystal Reports creates. This affords two benefits:

- A user can rerun the report whenever they want, seeing an updated view of the database at that moment.

- A user can interact with the report by using the group tree and drill-down capabilities.

Various Crystal Reports 8.5 versions offer online interactive reporting to users in several ways:

- Giving users their own copy of Crystal Reports, letting them open, view, and modify reports at will
- Providing Seagate Analysis, Crystal Decisions' free query, light reporting, and OLAP analysis tool, for report viewing and interaction
- Including a Crystal Report in a custom Windows application (covered in Part III, starting with Chapter 25)
- Reporting with a Web browser and Crystal Enterprise (covered in Part II, starting with Chapter 20)

All of these interactive methods allow a user to *drill down* on data in the report. This technique, a feature that has been carried over from early PC-based decision-support system software, allows a report viewer to initially look at higher-level data. For example, a report might start at the country level. If the viewer sees a subtotal or summary number (or an element in a pie chart or other chart) for a particular country that interests them, they can double-click that number. This will drill down to the next level in the report, possibly the region or state level, where they can see summary numbers for each of those states or regions. If the report is designed with several levels of drill-down ability, the user could then double-click a region that piqued their interest to display all the cities in that region. The drilling down could progress further, allowing users to drill down on cities and finally ZIP codes, where individual detail items at the ZIP-code level would appear.

Crystal Reports automatically sets up a drill-down hierarchy when you create groups. Every group you create can be drilled into, exposing the lower-level group and finally the details section. So, for our drill-down example to work, you would create multiple groups on the report in the following order: country, region (state), city, and finally ZIP code.

After you create groups, you can drill down on the group name (automatically placed in the group header) or any summary or subtotal that you place in a group header or group footer. When you point at these objects, you'll notice that the mouse pointer changes from an arrow to a magnifying glass, called a *drill-down cursor*. This indicates that you can drill down on the group by double-clicking this object. When you double-click, a *drill-down tab* appears next to the main Preview tab, containing the lower-level group or detail data. Every time you drill down, a separate drill-down tab appears.

If you drill down enough times, there won't be enough room to see all the drill-down tabs, along with the main Preview and Design tabs. In this situation, two small arrows appear next to the last drill-down tab. You can click these arrows to move back and forth among the tabs to see tabs that have disappeared off the screen. You can also close any drill-down tab by clicking the red X button next to the page-navigation buttons. This closes the current tab and displays the tab to the left. You can close every tab this way (including the Preview tab), except for the Design tab.

> **Tip** *If you wish to print the report to a printer or export it to another file format, only the material appearing in the current tab will print or export. If you're displaying the Preview tab at the time, the summarized report will print or export. If, however, you have a drill-down tab selected when you print or export, only the material in that drill-down tab will be included.*

Figure 3-6 shows a report with several drill-down tabs visible. Notice that there isn't enough room to show all the tabs, so small arrows appear to the right of the last drill-down tab. Also notice that the mouse cursor has changed to a magnifying glass because it is over a summary/subtotal object.

You can drill down on any report that has at least one group on it, even if all the details sections are showing already. Drill-down ability is really helpful with summary reports that start out showing only high-level data. A viewer will only want to see the lower-level groups and the detail when they drill down. Therefore, you'll want to hide

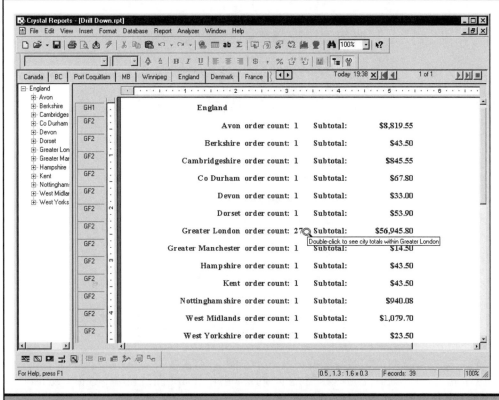

Figure 3-6. *Drill-down report*

the details section, as well as the lower-level group headers and group footers, to create a truly useful drill-down report. You'll see how to hide or suppress sections in Chapter 8.

Caution   *If one or more drill-down tabs appear alongside the Preview tab, there are very few report-design modifications you can make without receiving a message indicating that you won't be able to keep the drill-down tabs. Don't worry about this—just make the modifications and drill down again to redisplay the drill-down tabs.*

Grouping on Date Fields

When you create report groups based on date fields, you probably don't want a new group to appear every time the date changes from one day to another. You may only want a new group for every week, month, or calendar quarter. You could create a complicated formula that breaks down groups in this manner and groups on the formula, but Crystal Reports provides a much easier way.

When you select a field to group on, Crystal Reports automatically adds an additional drop-down list to the Insert Group dialog box.

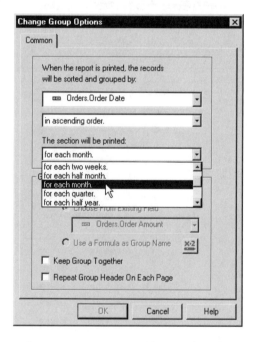

You can choose how often a new group will be created by selecting the appropriate item from the list. Then click OK. The groups will now appear in the group tree for every month, quarter, year, or whatever period was chosen. The group name in the group header will indicate the beginning date for each group (the first month of the quarter, the first day of the week, and so forth).

Customizing Group Name Fields

The group name field takes on the Crystal Reports default format for the data type of the group field. For example, the default format for date fields is the same as your Windows default date format. Thus, a group name for a calendar quarter group may show up as 1/97, 4/97, and so on. What if you prefer the group names to appear as "January, 1997" and "April, 1997"?

You can format a group name field just like any other field or object. Click the group name field and then format it just like any other object (by using the Format menu or right-clicking and using the pop-up menu). For a group name based on a date field, for example, you can choose how the month and year appear, as well as what character should be used as the separator between them.

However, you'll notice that even when you format the group name field as mentioned here, the group tree will not reflect the change. It continues to use the default formatting regardless of how you format the group name field. Also, you may find situations in which you want to show information for the group that is different from what is actually supplied by the field you group on. For example, you may be grouping by a fiscal month number in a database. You'll want to show the spelled-out month name despite the fact that the group tree and group headers will show the number (1 for January, 8 for August, and so on). Or, you may be grouping by employee number rather than employee name, to avoid the possibility of lumping employee data together for employees that share the same name. But, you still want the report to show the employee name instead of the number.

You may create a formula and group on it instead of the database field to accomplish this type of specialized group display. However, you'll often not get exactly the results you want (in the numeric month example mentioned previously, you will need to add the month number in front of the spelled-out month if you want to still show the months in chronological order). However, Crystal Reports 8.5 provides the *customized group name field*, which gives you much more flexibility in controlling what the group tree and group header display.

You may customize the group name field when you initially create a group. Or, if you decide later that you'd like to customize the group name field in an existing group, you can change the group by using Report | Change Group Expert, or by right-clicking the appropriate group header or group footer gray section name and choosing Change Group from the pop-up menu. Once the Change Group Options dialog box appears, perform the following steps to customize the group name field.

1. Click the Customize Group Name Field check box.

2. To choose an alternate database field to display (for example, if you'd like to show an employee name field instead of the employee number field the group

is based on), click the Choose From Existing Field radio button and then pick the desired database field in the associated drop-down list.

3. To create a specialized formula to display instead of the field the group is based on, click the Use a Formula As Group Name radio button. Then, click the Conditional Formula button next to the radio button. The group name Formula Editor appears, in which you can create a string formula to display instead of the field the group is based on. For example, to show an employee's last name, a comma, and then the employee's first name, you could create the following formula:

```
{Employee.Last Name} + ", " + {Employee.First Name}
```

Look at Chapter 5 for details on creating formulas.

Figure 3-3, earlier in the chapter, shows examples of both date grouping and customized group fields. You'll notice that the report shows new groups for every month in 1997, and that employee information is indicated with the employee's last and first names, rather than the employee ID, which the group is actually based on.

Grouping on Formula Fields

As your reports become more sophisticated, you'll find more and more often that you won't be able to create the groups you need just from database fields. You may be able to use specified order grouping, but even it is limited by its simple Select Expert–like approach. For the really tough grouping jobs, you need to create formula fields and group on them. Creating formula fields is covered in Chapter 5.

Grouping on a formula field is very simple (at least the grouping is, after you create the formula). The formula appears at the end of the list of report fields in the Insert Group or Change Group Options dialog box. Simply choose it as the field you wish to group on.

A good example of when you might need to group based on a formula field is the geographic grouping case mentioned earlier in this chapter. Suppose you want to first group by geographic location (Northwest, Southwest, and so on), and then within these groups you want to group on individual states or regions. That way, you'll be able to see group totals for both individual states and the higher-level geographic regions.

The problem is this: After you create the specified-order grouping based on the Customer.Region database field for the geographic groups, Crystal Reports won't let you create a second group on the same database field in ascending order for the state groups. If you try to choose a database field that's already been grouped on, the OK button in the Insert Group or Change Group Options dialog box is disabled.

To solve this problem, here's a formula field called @Region that simply returns the Customer.Region database field.

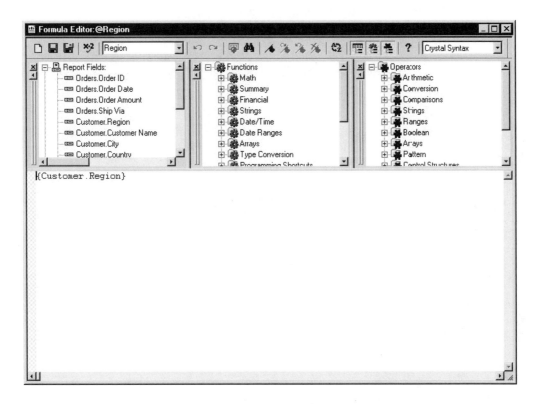

The @Region formula field can now be used instead of the database field to create the second group. Figure 3-5, shown earlier in the chapter, gives an example of two levels of grouping (specified order and regular grouping) using the same field—once directly from the database and once with a formula.

Caution   *Although you gain great flexibility when you group on a formula field, you may lose a little performance along the way. When you group on a database field, Crystal Reports can have the database server (SQL Server, Oracle, and so on) sort records in the proper group order before sending them to Crystal Reports. When you group on a formula field, the server won't be able to sort the records in advance, leaving that for Crystal Reports to do once the records begin to arrive from the server. You may or may not notice any performance degradation, depending on the size of the report and the speed of your computer. If you really want to maximize performance and still have a customized group, you may be able to substitute a SQL expression for a formula as the source for your group. SQL expressions are covered in Chapter 14.*

Top N Reporting

Figure 3-7 shows a typical order summary report by customer name. This is a great drill-down report example—the details section is hidden and only the summary

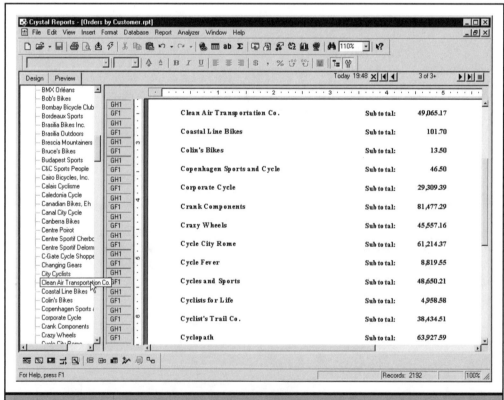

Figure 3-7.   *Order summary report by customer name*

information for each customer is showing (hiding sections is covered in Chapter 8). This is a good report for the sales manager who is asked, "How did Clean Air Transportation Co. do last year?" All the viewer has to do is click Clean Air Transportation Co. in the group tree to go directly to its summaries.

However, what if the sales manager has ten boxes of Godiva chocolates that she wants to send to her ten best customers? Or, consider the new sales associate who's been assigned the task of visiting the 15 worst-performing customers to try to bolster sales. The report shown in Figure 3-7 is not very useful if you want to find the top 10 or bottom 15 customers. The sales manager and sales associate would be much happier with a Top *N* report.

A Top *N* report lets you sort your groups by a subtotal or summary function (subtotal of order amount, for example), instead of by the name of the group. That way, your groups will appear, for example, in order of highest to lowest sales or lowest to highest sales. In addition, Top *N* reporting enables you to see only the top or bottom *N* groups, where you specify the *N*.

Crystal Reports uses the Top N/Sort Group Expert to reorder your groups by a subtotal or summary. Choose this option from the pull-down menus by selecting Report | Top N/Sort Group Expert. You can also click the Top N Expert button in the Supplementary toolbar. Or, finally, if you select a summary or subtotal in a group footer and click the Sort button on the Standard toolbar, the Top N/Sort Group Expert will appear instead of the Record Sort Order dialog box.

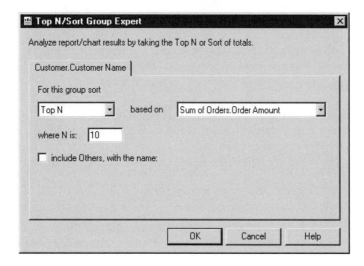

The Top N/Sort Group Expert (again, not really an "expert," just a dialog box) presents a tab for every group you've created on your report. Click the tab for the group that you want to reorder. When you first open the Top N/Sort Group Expert, the default setting for the first drop-down list is All and the default setting for the second drop-down list is empty. This simply indicates that this group initially will not be a Top *N* group and that groups will appear in the order you chose when you created the groups. If none of the groups on your report have subtotal or summary fields in them, the Top N/Sort Group Expert won't be available, as it uses summary fields to sort the groups. And, when you display the Top N/Sort Group Expert, only groups that contain subtotal or summary fields will appear as tabs.

When you click the down arrow of the second drop-down list, you see all the summaries or subtotals you've created for that group (only subtotals and summaries you created with Insert Subtotal or Insert Summary will be there—you won't see any formulas or other fields). Choose the one that you want the Top *N* report to be based on. For example, if you want to see the top ten customers according to last year's sales, choose Sum of Customer.Last Year's Sales. If you leave the first drop-down list set to All, all groups will remain on the report, but will be sorted in ascending or descending order, based on the radio buttons at the bottom of the dialog box. If you want the groups sorted by more than one summary (for example, first by sum of order amount and then by count of order ID), select additional summaries from the drop-down list and choose an ascending or descending sort for each.

> **Tip** *Using the All option to sort groups in a different order can be a very innovative way to solve unique reporting problems. If you need to create a group based on one field but then have the groups appear in a different order, insert a summary field in the group footer based on the field you want to sort the groups by. Then, using the All option, choose the summary field you created.*

If you are only interested in the Top *N* or Bottom *N* groups, change the first drop-down list from All to Top N or Bottom N. Top N sorts the groups from the highest to lowest value, and Bottom N sorts from lowest to highest. The second drop-down list enables you to select one summary or subtotal to use for Top *N* or Bottom *N*. Choose the summary you want to use. Once you've done that, type the value of *N* in the appropriate text box. You also have a check box and text box that let you choose whether to include other groups not in the Top or Bottom *N* in the report. If you do include them, they will be lumped together in one other group with the name you type.

Using the Godiva and worst-performing-customer example earlier:

- The sales manager's Godiva chocolate report would be Top *N* of Sum of Orders.Order Amount, where *N* is 10 and other groups are not included.

- The sales associate's follow-up visit report would be a Bottom *N* of Sum of Orders.Order Amount, where *N* is 15 and other groups are not included.

The following Top *N* report shows who will be getting chocolates this year.

If you wish to change the report from Top *N* to Bottom *N*, change the value of *N*, or remove the Top/Bottom *N* sorting altogether and show all of your groups sorted in the order you originally chose, simply redisplay the Top N/Sort Group Expert and change the values. Remember that a group will be sorted in its original ascending or descending order if you set the first drop-down list to All and the second drop-down list to blank.

 If you create a Top N report and don't include others, any grand totals you place in the report footer will still include all records on the report. If you want to include accurate grand totals in a Top N report, either include others or use a running total instead of grand totals (explained in Chapter 5).

Hierarchical Groups

Crystal Reports 8.5 also features *hierarchical groups,* which can be helpful in certain reporting situations where one table in a database contains fields that relate to other fields in the same table. A specific example would be an employee table that includes a field indicating what other employee *in the same table* this employee reports to. Without hierarchical grouping, creating an organizational chart utilizing this table would be difficult. At the very least, you would need to perform a seldom-used database scenario known as a *self-join,* in which you add the same table to the report twice (using an alias name the second time), linking the second table to the first (in essence, joining a table to itself). Even after this was accomplished, it could be difficult, if not impossible, to show the multiple levels of hierarchy that the table structure contained.

With Crystal Reports, no self-join or complex reporting logic is required. You may simply choose hierarchical grouping options to indicate the relationship between the two fields in the same table, and to specify how much indentation you wish to show between the hierarchies. As an example, you may create a simple report using the Employee table from the XTREME sample database included with Crystal Reports. If you create a group based on Employee ID, you'll simply see one group for each employee in the table. To show the reporting relationship among the employees, choose Report | Hierarchical Grouping Options. This displays the Hierarchical Options dialog box.

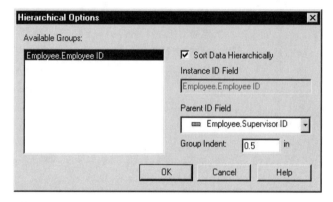

Choose the group (if there is more than one) for which you want to show the hierarchy. Then, click the Sort Data Hierarchically check box and choose the field that relates to the group field in the Parent ID Field drop-down list. Then, type the distance by which you wish to indent the lower-level hierarchies. Click OK.

The report will now create additional occurrences of groups to show the hierarchies created by the relationship of the two chosen fields. Here's an example of hierarchical reporting using the XTREME sample database:

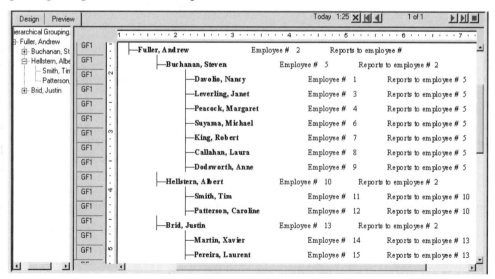

Note *The lines in this illustration are not created automatically. You may use Crystal Reports' line drawing tools to create this kind of effect. This example also uses a customized group name field, to show the employee name instead of the employee number in the group tree and the report.*

Crystal Reports 8.5 now includes the ability to add subtotals or summaries in hierarchical groups. Once you've created your group hierarchy with the features discussed previously, just use the same Insert Subtotal, Insert Summary, and Insert Grand total features covered earlier in the chapter to summarize data in hierarchical groups. The Sum Across Hierarchy check box will appear.

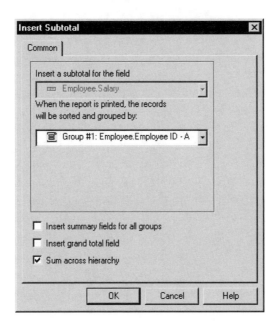

Chapter 4

Creating
Geographic Maps

A
lthough there are few changes from previous Crystal Reports versions, the Geographic Map feature remains a handy tool for those that need to graphically display geographic data. Your report can include not only textual information (for example, states, cities, and sales totals), but also a colorful map that plots sales totals by state. Using maps, you can display information in a way that helps to analyze geographical data more easily. In addition to regular groups and details section fields, Crystal Report allows you to create maps based on online analytical processing (OLAP) grids and groups using specified order grouping.

Once you create a map, you can view it onscreen in the Preview tab or launch the Crystal Reports Analyzer. The Analyzer tab appears next to the Preview tab, giving you access to specific functions for analyzing maps and charts. Another Crystal Reports mapping feature is the Map Navigator, which is available when you use the Analyzer.

Different Map Types

Crystal Reports provides five different types of maps. The type you should choose depends on the data that you'll be depicting in the map and the way you wish to show it. Table 4-1 discusses the different types of maps and their uses.

Caution *Crystal Reports 8.5 contains a limited number of maps. If you use a field that Crystal Reports can't resolve to an existing map, the map may not show any meaningful data, or may show up as a blank area on your report. Crystal Reports mapping modules are provided by a third party, MapInfo. You may also get more information from MapInfo at http://www.mapinfo.com.*

You have several ways of choosing the data that will populate your map:

■ **Group map** Requires you to use existing groups with their subtotals and summaries for the map. A report grouped by country, for example, can be used to show the concentration of customers by country if you include a summary function that counts customers for each group.

■ **Advanced map** Allows you to create a map based on data in the report's details section. You may have a detail report containing a sales figure for each customer. If you include the state each customer is in, you can create an advanced map based on the state and the amount of sales for that state. The map will show how sales compare by state. In effect, the map will group and subtotal your records by state, even if no state group exists on the report. You also would use an advanced map when you need to map multiple values per geographic region (as in the pie chart and bar chart explained in Table 4-1).

Map Type	Description	Uses and Comments
Ranged	Assigns different colors to *ranges* of numbers. For example, a state that contains over $500,000 in sales would be bright red, a state that contains between $250,000 and $500,000 in sales would be orange, and a state that contains less than $250,000 in sales would be a deep magenta.	Useful for comparing different regions or countries to each other by shade or color. There are four ways to choose how the ranges are colored: **Equal count** Evenly divides the number of map ranges so that an equal number (or as close as possible to an equal number) of mapped values appear in each range. This avoids map views containing almost all one color, which may occur if the data you are mapping is heavily concentrated on the low or high end of the overall range of values. **Equal ranges** Divides the map ranges by the summary numbers being shown on the map. This option assigns equal ranges of summary values, regardless of how many groups or regions make up each range. **Natural break** Also uses the summary numbers to determine map ranges, but bases range breakdowns on the average amounts of the ranges. **Standard deviation** Divides the map ranges such that the middle interval breaks at the average of the summary values. The ranges above and below the middle break at one "standard deviation" above or below the middle.
Dot density	Displays a dot on the map for every occurrence of the item being mapped. A higher concentration of dots appears in areas of the map that have the most occurrences.	Used to show a concentration of activity (for example, quantities or subtotals) in certain states or countries.

Table 4-1.   *Crystal Reports Map Types*

Map Type	Description	Uses and Comments
Graduated	A symbol (a circle, by default) represents data, and the size of the symbol is based on the concentration or level of the amount—small amounts are represented by small circles, large amounts by large ones.	Shows just one symbol per country, state, etc., but shows a different size depending on the number the map is based on. The default symbol is a circle, but you can choose from other characters, as well as apply special effects (for example, a drop shadow, halo, etc.) to the symbol.
Pie chart	Displays a pie chart over the related geographic area.	Only useful when comparing multiple related data points for the same geographic area. A pie chart is better for comparing items against each other, where all items total 100 percent. For example, if you are graphing sales by account rep, grouped by state, you would see a pie chart on each state showing how much of the "state pie" each rep has.
Bar chart	Displays a bar chart over the related geographic area.	Only useful when comparing multiple related data points for the same geographic area. A bar chart is better for comparing items over time, or other comparisons that aren't "piece of the pie" oriented. For example, if you are graphing sales for the past five years, grouped by state, you would see a bar chart on each state comparing the sales for the past five years.

Table 4-1. *Crystal Reports Map Types* (continued)

■ **Cross-Tab map or OLAP map** Plots data from a cross-tab object (covered in Chapter 9) or an OLAP grid (covered in Chapter 16). The cross-tab object must have at least one row or column field that's based on a geographic item, such as a country or state. OLAP grids must have a certain type and organization of dimensions (see "OLAP Maps," later in the chapter, for details). Because cross-tabs and OLAP grids can contain multiple summary fields, you can use them to create pie chart or bar chart maps.

Adding a Map

To insert a map on your report, choose Insert | Map from the pull-down menus, or click the Insert Map button on the Standard toolbar. The Map Expert appears, containing three main tabs: Data, Type, and Text.

The Data Tab

The Data tab is where you choose the type of map you want to create, as well as the fields and summaries from the report that you want to base your map on.

Group Maps

To create a group map, click the Group button on the Data tab.

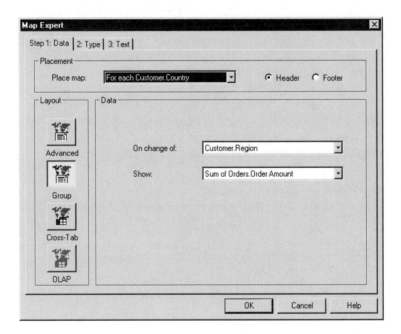

This map will include data based on an existing group on your report. The group needs to be based on some kind of geographic field, such as a country or state. The map will depict your chosen subtotal or summary field for each group.

The Place Map drop-down list lets you choose how often you want the map to appear on the report. The options in this list will vary according to how many groups you have on your report. If you only have one group on your report, the only option available in the drop-down list is Once Per Report. If you have more than one group, you also have For Each *Group Field* options for every group, *except* for the top-level group, because you must always place a map at least one level higher in your report than the group your map is based on.

For example, if you only have a state group on your report, the only option for a group map is Once Per Report, because you must have the map at a level higher than the group. However, if you have a country group, and a region group within the country group, the drop-down list allows you to choose For Each Customer.Region (or whatever field the region group is based on). If you choose this lower level, you'll have a map appearing in every country group, showing the geographic breakdown *by region* for that country.

You can then choose whether to have Crystal Reports initially place the map in the group or report header or footer, by clicking the desired radio button. After the map has been created initially, you can drag the map object from the header to the footer, or vice versa.

Use the On Change Of drop-down list to choose the geographic group that you want the map to be based on. Choose the summary or subtotal field you want the map to depict from the Show drop-down list.

Because Group Maps must be based on a summary or subtotal field in a group, any groups that don't have at least one subtotal or summary field won't show up in the Map Expert. If you only have one group on your report, and it doesn't contain a subtotal or summary field, the Group button in the Map Expert will be dimmed.

Advanced Maps

To create an advanced map, click the Advanced button on the Data tab.

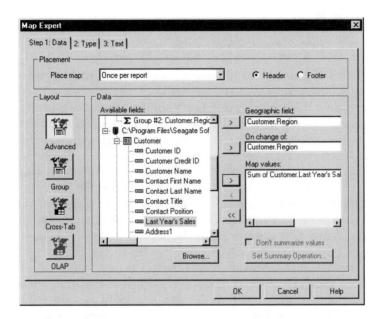

This map will include data based on fields in the details section of your report. One of your detail fields needs to be a geographic field, such as a country or state. The map will summarize one or more other detail fields and depict them on the map for each geographic field.

The Place Map drop-down list lets you choose how often you want the map to appear on the report. The options in this list will vary according to how many groups (if any) you have on your report. If there are no groups, the only option available in the drop-down list is Once Per Report. If you have one or more groups, you also have For Each *Group Field* options for every group.

You can then choose whether to have Crystal Reports initially place the map in the group or report header or footer, by clicking the desired radio button. You are also free to drag the map object from the header to the footer, or vice versa, after the map has been created.

The Available Fields list contains all the report, database, and formula fields available for the map. Choose the geographic field that you want your map to use, and then click the right arrow next to the Geographic Field box to choose the field. The same field will also automatically be placed in the On Change Of box. If you wish to just summarize values for the geographic field (for a range or dot density map, for example), simply leave the same field in the two boxes. If, however, you wish to show a pie or bar chart on the map for another field (for example, to show a pie chart in each country comparing states), then choose the field you want to "compare" in the Available Fields list and click the right arrow next to the On Change Of text box. Finally, click one or more fields (using CTRL-click or SHIFT-click) in the Available Fields list that you want summarized in the map. Use the right arrow next to the Map Values box to add them. If you wish to remove a Map Value field or fields, click it in the Map Values box and click the left arrow. If you wish to remove all the Map Value fields, click the double left arrow.

Even though this is an advanced map (based on individual report records in the detail section), Crystal Reports still summarizes values by default, as though report groups exist for the fields you've placed in the Geographic Field and On Change Of boxes. You can choose the summary function (Sum, Average, Count, and so on) you want the map to use when summarizing the detail fields you've added to the Map Values box. Select a field in the box, click the Set Summary Operation button, and choose the function (Sum, Average, Count, and so on) that you wish to use. In previous Crystal Reports versions, if you checked the Don't Summarize Values box, the map wouldn't summarize the values like a grouped report, but just depicted the *first* value in the details section. In the initial release of Crystal Reports 8.5, the Don't Summarize Values box has been disabled, so your map will always depict a summary of the chosen detail field.

Crystal Reports mapping can sometimes be particular about the geographic field you base your map on. For example, if the field contains USA, the map will recognize it. If it just contains US, the map won't recognize it. The same holds true for state names. Two-letter abbreviations and completely spelled state names are recognized, whereas inconsistently abbreviated state names or standard two-letter state names followed by periods may not. Sometimes you'll need to experiment, and in some cases you may want to create a formula (discussed in Chapter 5) that changes the way the geographic data is presented, and then base the map on the formula field. Also, Crystal Reports 8.5 provides the ability to resolve data mismatches that exist between the geographic names that maps recognize and the actual data in the database (see "Resolving Data Mismatches" later in the chapter).

If you add a nonnumeric field to the Map Values box, it is automatically summarized with a count function. The only other choice in the Change Summary Operation list is DistinctCount.

Cross-Tab Maps

To create a cross-tab map, click the Cross-Tab button on the Data tab.

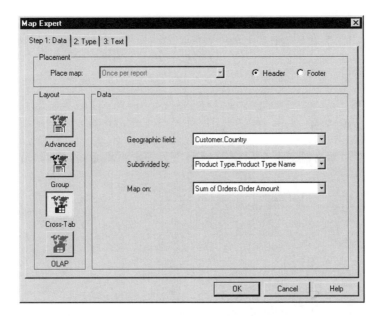

This map depicts data contained in a cross-tab object already on your report. The Cross-Tab button is enabled only if you already have a cross-tab object selected on your report before you start the Map Expert (or, if you have only one cross-tab object on the entire report, the button is enabled and will default to the lone cross-tab). The row or column of the cross-tab must be a geographic field, such as a country or state. Because cross-tabs can have multiple summarized fields, you can create pie chart and bar chart maps from cross-tabs. Creating cross-tab objects is covered in Chapter 9.

The Place Map drop-down list will be dimmed, because you must place the map on the same level as the cross-tab (in the same group, once per report, and so forth). You can choose whether to have Crystal Reports initially place the map in the group or report header or footer, by clicking the desired radio button. You can also drag the map object from the header to the footer, or vice versa, after the map has been created.

In the Geographic Field drop-down list, choose the row or column of the cross-tab that contains the geographic field the map will be based on. If you want the cross-tab to be mapped as a pie or bar chart map, choose the other row or column in the Subdivided By drop-down list. In the Map On drop-down list, choose the summary field from the cross-tab that you want depicted. If you have multiple summary fields, you'll have multiple options here.

OLAP Maps

To create an OLAP map, click the OLAP button on the Data tab.

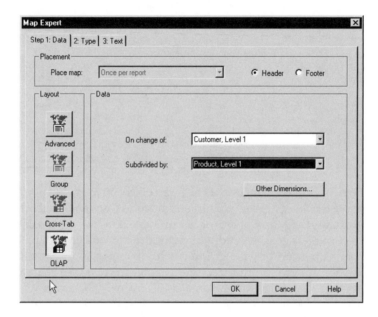

This map depicts data contained in an OLAP grid object already on your report. The OLAP grid button is enabled only if you already have an OLAP grid object selected on your report before you start the Map Expert (or, if you have only one OLAP grid object on the entire report, the button is enabled and will default to the lone OLAP grid). At least one dimension of the OLAP grid must be based on a geographic field, such as a country or state. Because OLAP grids can have multiple dimensions, you can create pie chart and bar chart maps from OLAP grids. Creating OLAP grid objects is covered in Chapter 16.

The Place Map drop-down list will be dimmed, because you must place the map on the same level as the OLAP grid (in the same group, once per report, and so forth). You can choose whether to have Crystal Reports initially place the map in the group or report header or footer, by clicking the desired radio button. You can also drag the map object from the header to the footer, or vice versa, after the map has been created.

In the On Change Of drop-down list, choose the dimension of the OLAP grid that contains the geographic field the map will be based on (this may be a "lower-level" dimension—go back and look at the results of your OLAP grid if you're unsure where the geographic data is). If you want the OLAP grid to be mapped as a pie or bar chart map, choose another dimension in the Subdivided By drop-down list.

The Type Tab

After you've chosen the data elements for your map, click the Type tab to choose the type of map you want to display. Click one of the following buttons to select a map type:

- **Ranged**   Presents options for a ranged map, including how many intervals the map will contain, how the intervals are broken down, the beginning and ending color for the intervals, and whether the map should show empty intervals.

- **Dot Density**   Enables you to choose large or small dots for the map.

- **Graduated**   Presents the symbol used for the graduated map. A circle symbol is chosen by default, but you can click the Customize button to change the symbol and color and add special effects to the symbol, such as a halo or drop shadow.

- **Pie Chart**   Presents options for a pie chart map. You can choose small, medium, or large pies. If you click the Proportional Sizing check box, the pies will be sized according to the quantities contained in the data being mapped: larger quantities create larger pies, and smaller quantities create smaller pies.

- **Bar Chart**   Enables you to choose the size of the bars: large, medium, or small.

Tip   *You are restricted to either the first three or the second two buttons, depending on how many data elements you've chosen for your map. If you chose only one data element to map, you can use only the Ranged, Dot Density, or Graduated option. If your map contains multiple elements from a detail report, or you chose a Subdivided By item with a cross-tab object or OLAP grid, you can use only the Pie Chart or Bar Chart option.*

The Text Tab

The Text tab lets you customize textual elements, such as the title and legend, that appear with the map. Type in the Map Title box the title you wish the map to display. Crystal Reports automatically creates a legend for the map. You can choose whether to display a full legend, a compact legend, or no legend at all by clicking the appropriate radio button. If you choose to include a legend, you can display the map-generated legend or specify your own by using the radio buttons and text boxes in the Legend Title section.

After you choose all the necessary options, click OK. Crystal Reports creates the map and places it in the report or group header or footer that you specified. To modify an existing map, simply click the map to select it in either the Design or Preview tab. Then, choose Format | Map Expert from the pull-down menus, click the Format button in the Supplementary toolbar, or right-click the map and choose Map Expert from the pop-up menu.

If you change the geographic item that a group is based on, you may need to delete and re-create the map. Maps automatically choose their geographic field when first created, but may not rechoose a different field if the group they're based on changes. For example, if you create a ranged map based on a country group, you'll see the world appear with different colors inside the countries. If you then change your group to state and add record selection to only include the USA, your map might still show the world. If this happens, you need to delete and re-create the map to have it show just the USA with different colors for the states.

Drilling Down on Maps

Crystal Reports lets you drill down on Group maps, just like on group names and summaries (discussed in Chapter 3) and on charts and graphs (covered in Chapter 10). When you view a map in the Preview tab, simply point your mouse to the geographic region you wish to look at in more detail. The mouse cursor turns into a magnifying glass. Double-click the desired area of the map to open up a drill-down tab next to the Preview tab. This drill-down tab will contain just the information for the report group represented by that map segment.

To close a drill-down tab, click the red X that appears next to the page navigation buttons on the right side of the preview window. The current tab closes and the next tab to the left is displayed.

 Because an Advanced map is already mapping the lowest level of information on your report, you cannot drill down on this type of map. Nor can you drill down into Cross-Tab or OLAP maps.

The Map Analyzer

Crystal Reports 8.5 includes the chart and map *Analyzer*, an additional viewing tab separate from the Preview tab. The Analyzer tab displays a map (or chart, as discussed in Chapter 10) by itself in a separate tab next to the Preview tab. The Analyzer tab lets you concentrate on the map by itself—no other report data is displayed. Also, the Analyzer tab lets you actually look at two maps simultaneously, one on top of the other. This may be helpful for comparing map breakdowns for different countries or regions, for example.

The Analyzer features its own pull-down menu, as well as its own toolbar that displays below the Formatting toolbar. To display the Analyzer tab, select the map you want to analyze in the Preview tab. Then, right-click and choose Map Analyzer from the pop-up menu, or choose Analyzer | Map Analyzer from the pull-down menus. The map is displayed in the Analyzer tab.

If you have multiple maps on your report (different maps or the same map in different groups), you can show two maps in the Analyzer tab at the same time. Just choose the other map you want to display, and follow the same steps. The Analyzer tab will show both maps, separated by a movable border. If you try to add a third map to the Analyzer tab, you'll receive a message indicating that the Analyzer is limited to two maps. You'll have the choice of replacing the top or bottom pane with the new map you've selected. If you want to remove one of the maps in the Analyzer split screen, just drag the moveable border all the way up or down to "erase" the top or bottom map.

With the Analyzer tab displayed, you can choose options from the Analyzer pull-down menu, right-click the Analyzer tab and choose options from the pop-up menu, or use the Analyzer toolbar. You can zoom in and out on the map; pan the map up, down, left, or right; or center the map on the screen. You can also change the type of map (ranged, dot density, and so forth) and the order in which map "layers" are displayed.

Figure 4-1 shows the Analyzer with two maps displayed on top of each other. Notice the functions available on the Analyzer toolbar.

> **Tip** *You don't have to launch the Analyzer to perform many of the Analyzer functions. You can right-click the map in the Preview tab and choose the Zoom or Pan option from the pop-up menu. You can also use buttons on the Analyzer toolbar. As soon as you select a map in the Preview tab, certain buttons in the toolbar become enabled. From this toolbar, you can select Zoom and Pan functions while displaying the Preview tab. Note that the Change Map Type and Change Map Layers buttons work only when the Analyzer tab is displayed. Drill-down, however, is not available in the Analyzer. Return to the Preview tab to drill down.*

The Map Navigator

Another feature in Crystal Reports 8.5 is the Map Navigator. When you view a map in the Analyzer tab, a smaller "thumbnail" of the map appears in its own window in the lower right of the Analyzer tab. You may drag the Map Navigator by its title bar to move it around the Analyzer tab, as well as resize the window by dragging a border of the window.

A magenta outline in the Map Navigator shows the portion of the map that you see in the Analyzer tab. If you zoom in on the map (using the Analyzer toolbar or the pop-up menu), the magenta outline shrinks, outlining the zoomed-in portion of the map. You can also use the magenta outline to zoom in, zoom out, and pan the Analyzer tab to a particular area of the map. If you point inside the magenta outline, your mouse cursor changes to a four-arrow move cursor—simply drag the magenta outline around to pan to a different area of the map. If you point to a corner of the magenta outline, the mouse cursor changes into a diagonal two-arrow cursor. Drag the corner to expand or contract the magenta outline. This zooms in or out on the map.

Resolving Data Mismatches

One of the serious limitations of geographic maps when they were initially introduced with Crystal Reports 7 was the inability to resolve mismatches of geographic data in

Use the Analyzer toolbar to manipulate the map in either the Preview or Analyzer tab

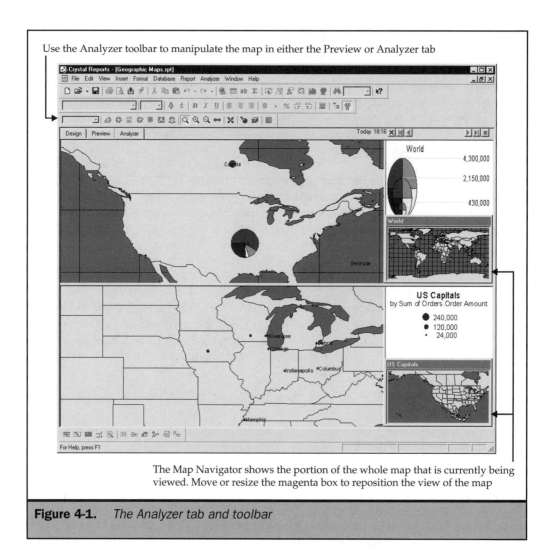

The Map Navigator shows the portion of the whole map that is currently being viewed. Move or resize the magenta box to reposition the view of the map

Figure 4-1. *The Analyzer tab and toolbar*

the database to what the map would understand. If your database contained, for example, spelled-out state names instead of two-letter abbreviations, the map would not be able to resolve the names to actual states. Crystal Reports 8 and later has improved on this limitation somewhat by allowing you to resolve data mismatches that may cause database data to be improperly mapped, or not mapped at all.

If you suspect that the map may not be interpreting database data correctly, first display the map in the Analyzer tab. Crystal Reports attempts to determine whether any data mismatches exist. If it detects a data mismatch, it enables the Resolve Mismatch option, which can be chosen from the Analyzer pull-down menu, by right- clicking the map in the Analyzer tab, or by clicking the Resolve Mismatch button in the Analyzer toolbar.

This will display the Map Region Resolver dialog box (it may take some time to generate the data for this dialog box).

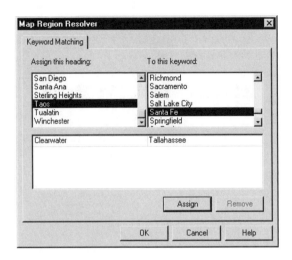

On the left, the Assign This Heading list shows geographic data being supplied to the map by the report. To the right is the To This Keyword list, showing the geographic data that the current map understands. When you select a value in the first list, the next alphabetical name is automatically highlighted in the second list. Scroll up and down in the list until you find the substitute data, which you can then select (such as substituting Santa Fe for Taos). Click the Assign button, which adds the assignment to the box below the two lists. Each assignment you add is added to the bottom box. If you decide that you don't want to use an assignment, select it in the lower list and click the Remove button.

When you're finished assigning values, click the OK button to show the map with the updated mapping assignments.

Map Layers

A map is displayed in the Analyzer tab using *layers*. If you are looking at a USA map, for example, the map may be composed of layers consisting of USA, US Highways, and US Major Cities. You can think of a map layer as a transparency containing just that layer's information that lies on top of the lower layers, which lie on top of the map. By using layers, the map can be displayed showing different levels of detail, usually determined by how far in the map is zoomed. If you are fully zoomed out on the map, you'll only see the states. As you zoom in, you eventually see highways appear across the states. And, as you zoom in even further, you see dots and the names of cities within the states.

Although maps include layers in a default order with default settings, you can choose which layers to display, hide, include, or not include. You can also change the order in which the layers "lie" on the map, and change the zoom level at which layers become visible. To work with map layers, click the Change Map Layers button on the Analyzer toolbar; right-click the Analyzer and choose Format Map | Layers from the pop-up menu; or choose Analyzer | Fomat Map | Layers from the pull-down menus. The Layer Control dialog box is displayed.

You see all the layers included in the map by default. You can change the order in which the layers appear by selecting an individual layer and then clicking the Up or Down button to change the order of the layers. If you want to hide a layer so that it doesn't show in the map, select the layer and clear the Visible check box. If you decide that you no longer want the layer at all, select it and click the Remove button.

If you later decide you want to redisplay a layer you removed earlier, or you want to add a new layer not already on the map, click the Add button. A File Open dialog box appears. Additional layers are located in \PROGRAM FILES\MAPINFO MAPX\ MAPS. Point to that folder and look for the appropriate .TAB file. After you choose it, it appears in the Layer Control dialog box.

To change the zoom level at which a layer appears, select the layer and click the Display button. The Display Properties dialog box for that layer opens.

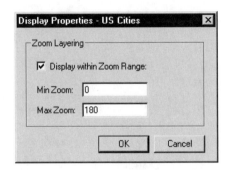

If you uncheck Display Within Zoom Range, the layer appears in the map at all times, regardless of the zoom level. If you leave it checked, you can set the minimum and maximum zoom levels at which the layer will become visible. After you make your choices, you can zoom in or out on the map to see the layer changes.

 If you are displaying two maps in the Analyzer, you must perform a zoom or pan operation inside the appropriate map to select that map. You can then use the Layer Control dialog box to work with map layers.

Figures 4-2 and 4-3 show the same map at the same zoom level with different settings for the US Highways layer.

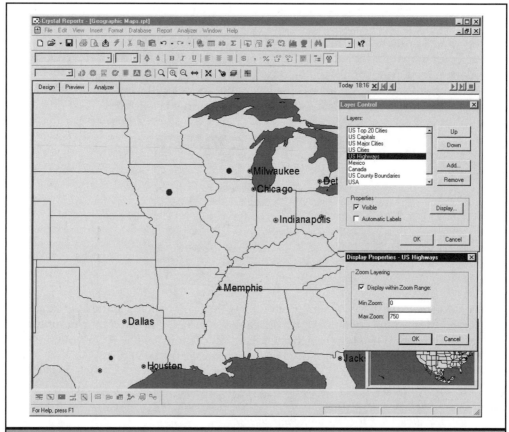

Figure 4-2. *Map with US Highways layer set to show only in certain zoom levels*

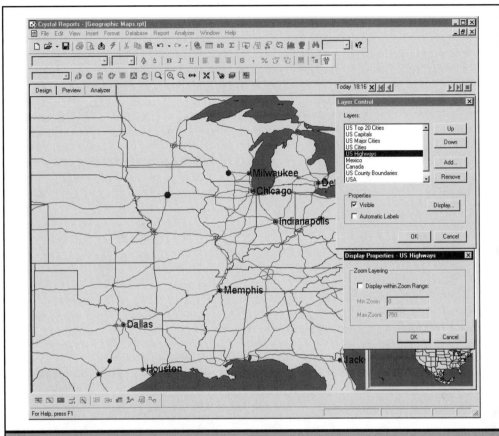

Figure 4-3. *Map with US Highways layer set to show in all zoom levels*

Chapter 5

Using Formulas

When you first start using Crystal Reports, you'll be able to write some simple reports using data that comes entirely from the database. You simply drag fields from the Field Explorer onto the report, and away you go. However, it won't be long until you find that you want some information to appear on your report that isn't contained in the database. Or, you may find that you want to display a field differently on the report than it appears in the database. For these, and many similar situations, use Crystal Reports *formulas.*

A formula can be thought of as a math calculation or a small piece of computer programming code. If you're not used to them at first, creating formulas can appear to be very complicated. Depending on your background, you may like the fact that some formulas are very much like programming. Or, this may be one characteristic of formulas that you would prefer not to deal with. Formulas can be as simple or as complex as you want to make them—you can start with simple math computations and, as you get more comfortable, graduate to full Basic-like formulas using Case statements, variables, and other advanced programming techniques. Formulas bring the ultimate power and flexibility to Crystal Reports.

You can create formulas with either the Design or the Preview tab displayed, although creating them in the Design tab is probably better because you will have a more accurate idea of where the formulas will really end up when you place them on your report. All formula work begins at the Formula Fields category of the Field Explorer. Display the Field Explorer by using the Standard toolbar Insert Fields button or choose Insert | Field Object from the pull-down menus.

To create a new formula, first select the Formula Fields category. Then click the New button in the Field Explorer toolbar, use the CTRL-N shortcut key combination, or right-click the Formula Fields category and choose New from the pop-up menu. You'll be asked to supply a formula name. Remember, you're *not* creating a file on disk when you add a formula, so you don't need to worry about file-naming conventions—the formula is simply stored inside the .RPT file of your report. Your formula names can contain upper- and lowercase letters, spaces, and anything else that makes them descriptive. Use an easy-to-understand formula name—not only does it help you to recognize what the formula is when you look at the list of formulas you've created, but it also is used for the field title when you place a formula in the details section. When you click OK, the Formula Editor is displayed.

The Formula Editor

Figure 5-1 shows the Formula Editor, which you use to create all of your new formulas, as well as to edit any existing formulas. The Formula Editor has been completely redesigned in Crystal Reports 8.5. It may look a little foreboding at first, but don't worry—it will soon become second nature to you as you create and edit more formulas.

If you wish to customize the font face, size, colors, and other appearance options that the Formula Editor uses, select File | Options on the pull-down menus and make your choices on the Editors tab of the dialog box that opens.

Field Tree box contains a hierarchical tree of database fields, other formula fields, group subtotals, etc.

Choose the formula language syntax to use for this formula

Toolbar provides access to the most common Formula Editor functions

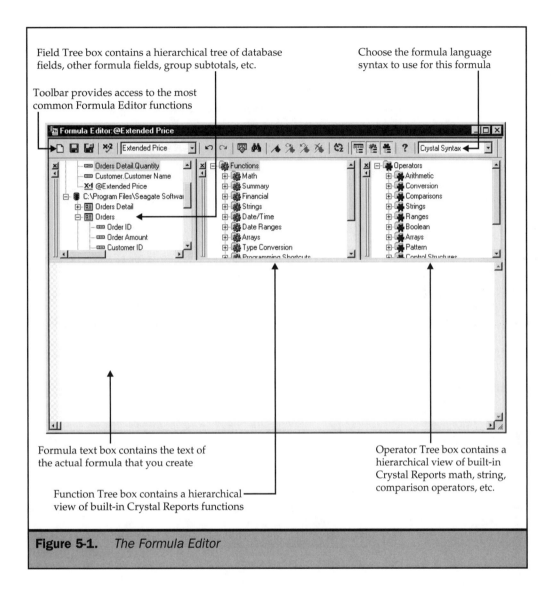

Formula text box contains the text of the actual formula that you create

Function Tree box contains a hierarchical view of built-in Crystal Reports functions

Operator Tree box contains a hierarchical view of built-in Crystal Reports math, string, comparison operators, etc.

Figure 5-1. *The Formula Editor*

Before you actually create a formula, familiarize yourself with the layout of the Formula Editor. Notice that the toolbar, as well as the Field Tree, Function Tree, and Operator Tree boxes, can be closed, resized, moved, and undocked (detached from the main window and put in their own windows). You have a great deal of flexibility in customizing the way the Formula Editor looks.

Figure 5-2 shows the Formula Editor with the toolbar and Operator Tree box undocked.

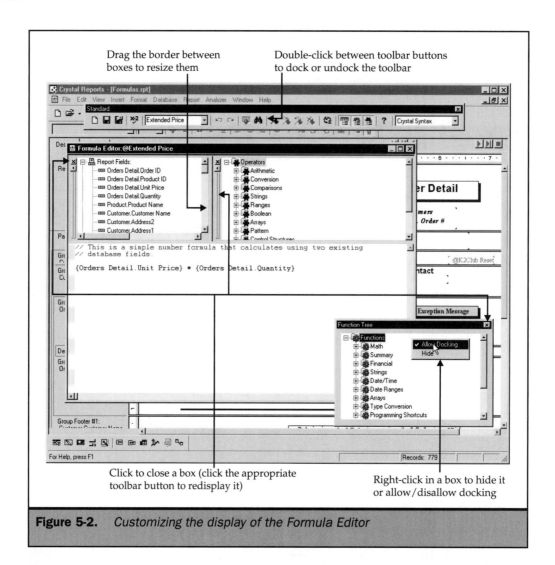

Figure 5-2.   *Customizing the display of the Formula Editor*

Caution   *If you mistakenly undock and then close the toolbar, you can get it back by right-clicking anywhere in the Format Editor and choosing Show Toolbar from the pop-up menu. You may also press ALT-T.*

When you're working with the Formula Editor, you'll want to familiarize yourself with the toolbar, because you'll need to use it on a regular basis. There are buttons to create new formulas, save the formula you're working on, edit another formula, manipulate bookmarks, and on and on. If you're unfamiliar with a toolbar button's function, point to it with your mouse and wait a second or two—a tool tip for that button will appear. Table 5-1 shows the functions of the Formula Editor's toolbar buttons.

Button/Key Combo	Name	Function
or CTRL-N	New	Creates a new formula. You'll be asked to give the formula a name.
	Save	Saves the current formula and leaves the Formula Editor displayed.
or CTRL-S	Save and Close	Saves the current formula and closes the Formula Editor.
or ALT-C	Check	Checks the syntax of the formula and reports any errors.
Customer Address or CTRL-M	Name	Lets you choose another formula to edit, without closing and reopening the Formula Editor.
or CTRL-Z	Undo	Undoes the latest action.
or CTRL-SHIFT-Z	Redo	Redoes the latest action.
or ALT-B	Browse Data	Displays sample data from the database for the selected database field.
or CTRL-F	Find/Replace	Allows searching and replacing for specific characters in the current formula.
or CTRL-F2	Toggle Bookmark	Places a bookmark at the current line of formula text. If a bookmark is already there, removes it.

Table 5-1.   *Formula Editor Toolbar Buttons*

Button/Key Combo	Name	Function
or F2	Next Bookmark	Moves the cursor to the next bookmark in the current formula.
or SHIFT-F2	Previous Bookmark	Moves the cursor to the previous bookmark in the current formula.
or CTRL-SHIFT-F2	Clear All Bookmarks	Removes all bookmarks from the current formula.
or CTRL-O	Sort Trees	Sorts the contents of the three Tree boxes alphabetically, instead of in the default logical order.
or ALT-F	Field Tree	Displays/hides the Field Tree box.
or ALT-U	Function Tree	Displays/hides the Function Tree box.
or ALT-P	Operator Tree	Displays/hides the Operator Tree box.
or ALT-H	Help	Displays Formula Editor Help.
Crystal Syntax ▾ or CTRL-T	Syntax	Chooses syntax (Crystal or Basic) to use for this formula only.

Table 5-1.   *Formula Editor Toolbar Buttons (continued)*

Tip   *There are many other shortcut keys you can use while in the Formula Editor. Search Crystal Reports online Help for "Formula Editor Key Controls."*

There are two general approaches to building a formula: type in the parts of the formula directly or double-click in the tree boxes. Once you become more familiar with the Crystal Reports formula language, you will probably create at least some parts of your formula by typing the formula text right into the Formula text box at the bottom of the Formula Editor. For example, simply typing an asterisk when you want to multiply numbers often is easier than clicking around in the Operator Tree box to find the multiplication operator.

Other parts of your formula, however, are best created automatically by double-clicking elements in one of the three tree boxes. For example, to include a database field as part of your formula, just find the field you want to include in the Field Tree box and double-click it. The field will be placed at the cursor position in the Formula text box, using proper formula language syntax.

Using the trees is easy. Simply find the general area of the tree that you are interested in and click the plus sign next to the category that you want to use. All the functions or operators within that category will appear. Double-click the one you want to use and it will be placed at the cursor position in the Formula text box. If you click a function that requires *arguments* (or parameters), such as an UpperCase function that needs to know what you want to convert to uppercase, the function name and parentheses will be placed in the formula with the cursor positioned at the location of the first argument. You can either type it in or move it to another tree (the Field Tree, for example) and double-click the field you want to add as the argument. After a while, you'll be able to find the functions or operators you're looking for quickly and create fairly large formulas simply by pointing and double-clicking.

Formula Syntax Choices in Seagate Crystal Reports 8.5

Prior to Crystal Reports 8, formulas could only be written in one formula language. Crystal Reports 8.5 continues a feature first introduced in Version 8 that allows the choice of two languages or *syntaxes*.

The syntax you use for individual formulas can be chosen with the syntax drop-down list, located at the far-right end of the Formula Editor toolbar. When you choose the desired syntax, you'll notice that the Function and Operator trees will change, showing all the built-in functions and operators for the chosen syntax. When you check the formula with the Check button, the formula must conform to the syntax chosen in the drop-down list. If, for example, you create a formula that is correct for Crystal syntax, and then choose Basic syntax in the drop-down list, you'll probably get an error message if you check the formula. Crystal Reports will not automatically convert from one syntax to the other when you change the syntax drop-down value in an already existing formula.

The choice of syntax is largely one of personal preference. If you are a Basic programmer who often encounters syntax errors with Crystal syntax because you instinctively use Basic, you'll probably be pleased with Basic syntax. If you've used previous versions of Crystal Reports and aren't a Basic programmer, you'll most likely want to continue to use Crystal syntax because you're familiar with it. You don't have to do this at the expense of flexibility, either—most, if not all, of the Basic-like constructs in Basic syntax are also available in Crystal syntax. You can always choose which syntax to use in each formula that you create (the notable exceptions being record- and group-selection formulas—these can only use Crystal syntax, and you aren't given a choice). You may choose the default syntax for all new formulas by choosing File | Options and clicking the Reporting tab. At the bottom of the dialog box is a Formula Language drop-down list that you use to set the default for all new formulas.

The remainder of this chapter focuses largely on Crystal syntax, showing most examples in the Crystal Reports' "original" formula language. This choice has been made for two reasons:

■ If you are using previous versions of Crystal Reports, most of this chapter will still apply to you.

■ The Basic language is well documented in many other texts. Since this book is specific to Crystal Reports, language syntax that is specific to Crystal Reports is best documented here.

Any examples or issues that are specific to Basic syntax will be so noted.

Notice the syntax that Crystal Reports uses when it places objects in the Formula text box (the small formula illustrated in Figure 5-2 is a good example). If you decide to type material into the formula yourself, you'll need to adhere to proper formula language syntax. Table 5-2 identifies special characters and other syntactical requirements of the formula language.

Crystal Syntax	Basic Syntax	Uses
. (period)	. (period)	Used to separate the table name from the field name when using a database field. You must always include the table name, a period, and the field name—the field name by itself is not sufficient.

Table 5-2.   *Formula Editor Special Characters*

Crystal Syntax	Basic Syntax	Uses
{} ("curly" or French braces)	{} ("curly" or French braces)	Used to surround database fields, other formula names, and parameter fields. The formula won't understand fields if they're not surrounded by curly braces.
// (two slashes)	' (apostrophe) or Rem	Denotes a comment. These can be used at the beginning of a line in a formula, in which case the Formula Editor ignores the whole line. You can also place two slashes or an apostrophe anywhere in a formula line, in which case the rest of the line will be ignored.

" " or ' ' (quotation marks or apostrophes)	" " (quotation marks)	Used to surround string or text *literals* (fixed-string characters) in formulas. With Crystal syntax, you can use either option, as long as they're used in matched pairs. For example:
		`If {Customer.Country} = "USA"`
		`Then ""United States" Else`
		`'International'`
		If you are using Basic syntax, you must use quotation marks only—an apostrophe will be interpreted as a comment.

( ) (parentheses)	( ) (parentheses)	Used to force certain parts of formulas to be evaluated first, as in the following:
		`({Orders.Amount} +`
		`{Orders.Amount}) * {@Tax Rate}.`
		`Also used to denote arguments or`
		`"parameters" of built-in`
		`functions, as in this example:`
		`UpperCase({Customer.Customer`
		`Name}).`

Table 5-2. *Formula Editor Special Characters* (continued)

Crystal Syntax	Basic Syntax	Uses
@ ? # %	@ ? # %	Crystal Reports automatically precedes certain fields with these characters. The @ sign precedes formulas, ? precedes parameter fields, # precedes running total fields, and % precedes SQL expression fields. When including these types of fields in a formula, make sure you surround the field with curly braces.
# (pound sign)	# (pound sign)	If you don't include curly braces around a pound sign, Crystal Reports will expect a value appearing between two pound signs that can be converted to a date/time value, as in this example: `#2/10/2000 1:15 pm#`

,
(comma)
	,
	(comma)
		Used to separate multiple arguments in functions. For example:
		`ToText({Orders.Amount},0," ")`
		`Don't add a comma as a thousands`
		`separator when using a numeric`
		`constant in a formula. For`
		`example:`
		`{Orders.Amount} + 2,500`
		`will cause a syntax error.`

; (semicolon)	: (colon)	If your formula contains multiple statements, you must separate them with a semicolon in Crystal syntax. With Basic syntax, you may separate multiple statements on the same line with a colon.

Table 5-2. *Formula Editor Special Characters* (continued)

Crystal Syntax	Basic Syntax	Uses
ENTER key	_ (space followed by underscore)	In Crystal syntax, you may press ENTER to start a new line in your formula anywhere between a field or function and an operator (don't put new lines or spaces in the middle of field or function names!). Long formulas are more readable on multiple lines. For example:

```
If {Order.Amount} > 5000 Then
     "Qualifies for bonus"
Else
     "Not eligible for bonus"
```

In Basic syntax, you may press ENTER only at the end of a complete statement. If you want a line break in the middle of a statement, you must use a line continuation sequence (a space, followed by the underscore). For example:

```
If {Order.Amount} > 5000 Then
    Formula = _
    "Qualifies for bonus"
Else
    Formula = _
    "Not eligible for bonus"
End If
```

Table 5-2.   *Formula Editor Special Characters* (continued)

Crystal Syntax	Basic Syntax	Uses

:=
(colon followed by
equal sign)
	=
	(equal sign)
		Used for variable assignment, such as:
		`NumberVar Quota := 1`
		In Crystal syntax, don't confuse
		this with the equal sign alone,
		which is used for comparison:
		`If {Customer.Region} = "BC" Then`
		`        "Canadian Customer"`
		In Basic syntax, the equal sign is used for
		both comparison and assignment, as in:
		`If {Customer.Region} _`
		`    = "BC" Then`
		`Formula = "Canadian Customer"`
		`End If`

Table 5-2.   *Formula Editor Special Characters* (continued)

Data Types

As you begin to work with formulas, it's very important to understand the concept of *data types*. Every database field has a certain data type, and every formula you create will result in a single data type. These concepts are important, because if the formula you create doesn't deal with data types properly, you'll get errors when you try to save the formula, or the formula won't give you the result you're looking for. You can't, for example, add the contents of a number field to the contents of a string field with a plus sign—both fields have to be numbers. You can't convert a date field to uppercase characters, because only a string field can be converted to uppercase.

By default, Crystal Reports doesn't display objects in the Design tab by their data types. It shows their names instead. You may prefer to see the data-type representation instead of the field name. To do this, choose File | Options from the pull-down menus and turn off the Show Field Names check box in the Field Options section of the Layout tab. Notice the difference between showing field names and showing data types:

Order ID	Order Amount	Order Date	Ship Via
-5,555,555	($55,555.56)	12/27/00 1:23:45AM	XXXXXXXXXXXX

You may want to turn off Show Field Names when you first start working with formulas. Seeing the data types can help you determine the type of operators and functions that will work with the database fields you're including in your formulas. Also, whenever you *browse* database fields in the Formula Editor, the data type shows up in the Browse dialog box. In the preceding illustration, the fields have the following data types:

- **Order ID**   A *number* data type, which can contain only numbers (along with a period to indicate a decimal point, and a hyphen or minus sign if it's a negative number). You can add, subtract, multiply, divide, and perform other math operations on number data types.

- **Order Amount**   A *currency* data type (only available from certain databases). This is similar to a number data type, but it avoids rounding errors that sometimes occur when performing math operations on number data types.

- **Order Date**   A combined *date/time* data type (again, only supported by certain databases). This can contain a date, time, or a combination of both. Other databases have date-only data types, and some have time-only data types.

- **Ship Via**   A *string* (or *text*) data type. The string data type allows any combination of characters to be placed in the field. However, because letters and punctuation marks can reside in the field, you normally can't perform mathematical calculations with the field.

You may encounter other data types in your databases that aren't shown in this example:

- **Boolean**   Represents data that can only have a true or false value.

- **Memo**   Designed to contain large amounts of text (larger than the 254-character string limit), such as narratives and comments.

- **BLOB**   Designed to contain photos, graphics, or large amounts of plain ASCII text.

 Memo and BLOB (Binary Large Object) fields can be placed on the report only for display. They cannot be used or manipulated inside formulas. They won't even show up in the Formula Editor Field Tree box.

Creating a New Formula

Creating a simple math calculation is easy. Using the Orders Detail table of the sample XTREME.MDB database included with Crystal Reports, you can calculate the extended price of each order-line item with the following formula.

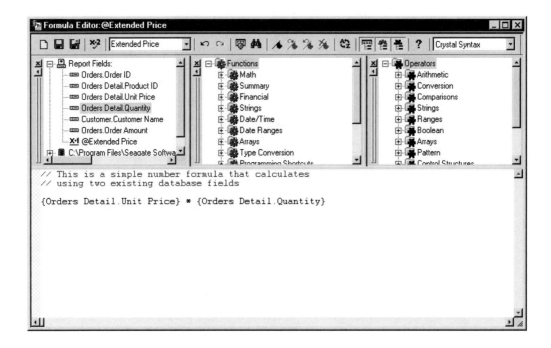

To create this formula, follow these steps:

1. Create a new report using the XTREME.MDB Microsoft Access sample database included with Crystal Reports. Choose the Orders Detail table from this database.

2. Select the Formula Fields category and then click the New button in the Field Explorer toolbar.

3. When asked to name the formula, call it **Extended Price**, and click OK or press ENTER.

4. When the Formula Editor appears, double-click the Orders Detail.Unit Price report field in the Field Tree box to add it to the Formula text box. If the field you want to add has already been placed on the report, you will actually find it in the Field Tree under both the Report Fields section and the Database name—there is absolutely no difference if you choose the field from either area.

5. Click the plus sign next to Arithmetic in the Operator Tree box to see all the arithmetic operators that are available. Double-click the multiply operator. (You can save yourself some mouse clicks by typing an asterisk directly in the Formula text box, if you'd like. Although you don't have to put a space before or after the asterisk, the formula is easier to read if you do.)

6. Double-click the Orders Detail.Quantity field in the Field Tree box to place it after the asterisk.

After you finish the formula, you have several ways to save it and close the Formula Editor. When you first start to use formulas, you'll probably want to check for correct syntax of the formula before you save it. This will ensure that Crystal Reports can at least understand the different parts of the formula and how they are supposed to be calculated or manipulated. Check the formula's syntax by clicking the Check button in the Formula Editor toolbar, or press ALT-C. If Crystal Reports can understand all parts of the formula, a dialog box will appear indicating that no errors were found. (If you've ever written computer programs or used spreadsheet formulas before, though, you know that correct syntax doesn't guarantee that the formula will return the right answer!)

If there is a syntax error in the formula, Crystal Reports will display an error message and place the cursor at the point in the formula where it stopped understanding it. As you can see here, sometimes these messages may be very descriptive:

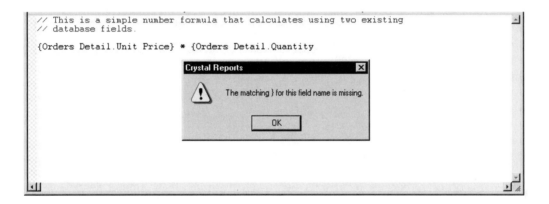

or they can be very cryptic:

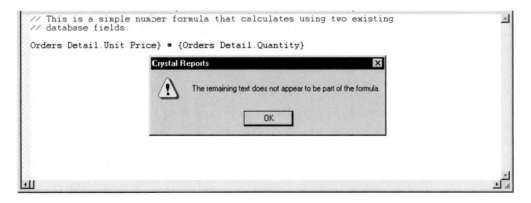

even though both of these examples result from simply forgetting curly braces. You'll learn over time what most error messages indicate and how to resolve them.

Even though you may not get any syntax errors when you first check the formula after you create it, you may still get an error when the report runs, depending on the actual data in the database. This may happen, for example, if you create a formula that divides two fields, but the "divided by" field returns a zero during a certain record. You'll then get a Can't Divide by Zero syntax error in the middle of the report process. If there's a chance that this type of error may occur based on the data, you'll probably want to add some type of "If {field} > 0 Then..." logic to ensure these types of run-time syntax errors won't occur.

After you determine that there are no syntax errors, it's time to save the formula. You may either save the formula and remain in the Formula Editor or save the formula and close the Formula Editor. There are two toolbar buttons for this, or CTRL-S will save the formula and close the Formula Editor.

If you choose to skip the syntax check and immediately save the formula, Crystal Reports will check the syntax anyway. If there is an error, you'll be given the opportunity to save the formula with the error. This makes little sense, because Crystal Reports will stop as soon as you try to run the report and display the error message in the Formula Editor. If you try to save and get a syntax error, correct the error and try to save the formula again. If there are no errors, you'll no longer get a syntax error message and the formula will be saved.

Once the formula has been saved and the Formula Editor has closed, you will see the formula name under the Formula Fields category of the Field Explorer. You can simply drag and drop the formula on the report, just like a database field. In the case of the Extended Price formula, notice that the formula has taken on the currency data type. This occurred because a currency field was multiplied by a number field. The resulting formula will be a currency formula. If you used the ODBC connection to the XTREME database to create this formula, Extended Price will be numeric, as the Microsoft Access ODBC driver converts currency fields to numbers.

Editing, Renaming, or Deleting an Existing Formula

After you create a formula, you may wish to change its calculation or add to its function. You can *edit* the existing formula in the Field Explorer by performing any of these steps:

- Selecting the formula you wish to change and clicking the Edit button in the Field Explorer toolbar
- Selecting the formula you wish to change and typing CTRL-E
- Right-clicking on the formula and choosing Edit from the pop-up menu.

Any of these options will redisplay the Formula Editor with the formula in it.

An even quicker method of editing is available after you've placed the formula on your report. In either the Design or Preview tab, click the formula. Notice in the status bar that the formula name is preceded by the @ sign. Crystal Reports automatically adds this symbol to the beginning of all formulas you create. Now that you've selected the formula, simply right-click and choose Edit Field Object from the pop-up menu. The formula will reappear in the Formula Editor, ready for you to modify.

If you wish to *rename* a formula, you must do so from the Formula Fields category of the Field Explorer. Begin by selecting the formula you want to rename in the Field Explorer. Then, you may either click the Rename button in the Field Explorer toolbar or press the F2 key. You may also right-click the formula and choose Rename from the pop-up menu. Even quicker, just click a second time on the formula field name after a slight pause. The name will become "editable"—type the new name and press ENTER. If you've used this formula inside other formulas or elsewhere on your report, Crystal Reports will change the name there, too.

If you select a formula on the report and click the DEL key, you remove that particular occurrence of the formula from the report. However, the formula remains in the Field Explorer and takes up memory and storage space when you save the report. If you're sure you no longer need the formula, delete it entirely. This must be done from the Formula Fields category of the Field Explorer. Select the formula you want to delete and press the DEL key. You can also choose the Delete button from the Field Explorer toolbar, or right-click the formula name and choose Delete from the pop-up menu. The formula will be removed from the dialog box.

Caution   *If you remove a formula that is in use somewhere else on the report, such as in another formula or in a hidden section, you'll be given a warning, because when you delete this formula, other formulas dependent upon it may stop working. You cannot Undo a formula deletion either, so you may want to save your report first when you get this warning—then go back and delete the formula. That way, you can retrieve the old report from disk if you inadvertently delete an important formula.*

Number Formulas

Probably the most common type of formula is a number formula, such as the Extended Price formula discussed earlier. Number formulas can be as simple as multiplying a database field by 1.1 to increase its amount by 10 percent, or as complex as calculations that include sophisticated statistical math. There is no special procedure required to declare a formula as a "number formula"—the formula simply takes on that data type based on the fields and operators that you use in the formula. As the Extended Price formula, shown here, demonstrates, multiplying a number field by a currency field results in a currency formula:

```
{Orders Detail.Unit Price} * {Orders Detail.Quantity}
```

Many number formulas will use a mathematical *operator*, such as a plus sign, a hyphen or minus sign, an asterisk for multiplication, or a slash for division. You also need to use built-in *functions* that Crystal Reports supplies. You'll find all the built-in functions listed in the Function Tree box. By double-clicking a function, the function name is placed in the Formula text box with the cursor located in between the opening and closing parentheses. You can then either type in the function's *arguments* or parameters, or double-click other fields or formulas in the Field Tree box to add them as arguments to the function.

For example, if you have a group on the report and want to include a group subtotal in a formula, you would use the Sum function. You'll find that three Sum functions actually are available, with one, two, or three arguments. Here are some examples:

```
Sum({Orders.Order Amount})
```

returns a total of all order amounts for the entire report.

```
Sum({Orders.Order Amount},{Customer.Region})
```

returns a total of just the order amounts in the region group where the formula is evaluated. If the formula was evaluated in the Colorado group, the formula returns the order amount subtotal for Colorado only.

```
Sum({Orders.Order Amount},{Orders.Order Date}, "weekly")
```

returns the order amount subtotal for the current order date group, calculating the subtotal based on a week of orders. Note that this third argument corresponds to the time periods that are available when creating a group based on a date field. (Refresh your memory about date-field grouping by looking at Chapter 3.)

So, you could calculate each order amount's percentage of the region subtotal by using the percentage operator and the Sum function as follows:

```
{Orders.Order Amount} % Sum({Orders.Order
Amount},{Customer.Region})
```

There are built-in functions to calculate all the summary-type information discussed in Chapter 3, such as average, subtotal, *P*th percentile, and on and on. By opening the Arithmetic category of functions in the Function Tree box, you'll also find functions to calculate remainders, determine absolute value, and round numbers.

Tip *If you need to calculate a group subtotal as a percentage of a grand total or higher-level group total, there's no need to create a formula. Instead, use percentage summary fields as described in Chapter 3. However, you'll still need to create a formula as described previously if you want to determine what percentage of a group subtotal a particular detail field is responsible for.*

The Basic Syntax Formula Variable

When you use Crystal syntax, the formula simply returns the results of the last statement in the formula. If the formula consists of only one statement, such as the multiplication in the previous example, the formula returns the results of the multiplication. If the formula contains several statements separated by semicolons, the last statement determines what's returned to the report.

But if you are using Basic syntax, you must keep in mind one slight difference from any Basic-like programming languages you've used. In a Basic computer language, you typically assign and manipulate variables throughout your code. When you wish to display the value of a variable, you use a Print or ? statement or set the value of a text box or other form element to the value of the variable. Because Crystal Reports has no Print statement, you need an alternative method of displaying a value on the report. This is accomplished with the *Formula variable*.

The word "Formula" is a reserved word in Basic syntax—you can't use it for any other purpose, such as using it as your own variable name with a Dim statement. By assigning a value to the Formula variable, you determine what the formula returns to the report. You can use the Formula variable over and over within a formula, just like any other variable (as an accumulator, for example). The last occurrence in the formula where a value is assigned to the Formula variable determines what the formula returns to the report. Consider the following Basic syntax formula:

```
' Calculates extended price
Formula = {Orders Detail.Unit Price} * {Orders Detail.Quantity}
If {Customer.Region} = "CO" Then
    ' add 4.25% sales tax to Colorado orders
    Formula = Formula * 1.0425
End If
```

Here, the Formula variable is used like a regular variable (it doesn't even have to be declared with a Dim statement first). It's first used just to calculate the extended price. Then, it's included in an If statement to add sales tax for Colorado orders. If the If statement is true, the existing value of the Formula variable is multiplied by 1.0425 to add 4.25 percent. If the If test fails, the last statement that assigns a value to the Formula variable (the extended price calculation) will be what's returned to the report.

Order of Precedence

You'll sometimes find situations where you're unsure of the order in which Crystal Reports evaluates a formula's operators. For example, if you wish to add sales tax to an extended price, you might use the following formula, which is supposed to add 8 percent sales tax to the extended price of an order (already calculated in the @Extended Price formula):

```
{@Extended Price} + {@Extended Price} * .08
```

The question of how Crystal Reports calculates this is crucial. Does it calculate the addition operator first and then the multiplication operator, or does it calculate the multiplication operator first and then the addition operator? The results will vary dramatically based on the calculation order. Consider an Extended Price of $100 with addition performed first:

```
100 + 100 = 200
200 * .08 = 16.00
```

or with multiplication performed first:

```
100 * .08 = 8.00
100 + 8.00 = 108.00
```

While your customer might be very pleasantly surprised by the first calculation showing up on their invoice, the second calculation is certainly the correct one. But, looking at the formula, you'll notice that the multiplication operator is the second operator. Will it be evaluated second?

The answer is no, based on the *order of precedence.* Although it may sound like a computer concept, order of precedence is actually a concept that you should recall from your ninth grade math class. In this formula, multiplication and division are evaluated first from left to right across the formula; then, addition and subtraction are evaluated from left to right across the formula.

The order of precedence for both Crystal syntax and Basic syntax is as follows:

- Exponentiation (^)
- Negation (-)
- Multiplication, division, left to right (*, /)
- For Crystal syntax only, percent (%) is evaluated at the same time as multiplication and division
- Integer division (\)
- Modulus (Mod)
- Addition and subtraction, left to right (+, -)

Based on this, the formula to add tax to the Extended Price shown earlier will work just fine. But, what if, for some reason, you want the addition performed first, not the multiplication. Again, thinking back to ninth grade math, you surround the part of the formula you want evaluated first with *parentheses*. The following formula will perform the addition before the multiplication:

```
({@Extended Price} + {@Extended Price}) * .08
```

Tip   *If you use one formula inside another formula, as in this example, Crystal Reports calculates the embedded formula first (using the order of precedence), and then calculates the second formula.*

String Formulas

Many times, the database will contain string or text data that is insufficient for your reporting needs. For example, you may want to sort a report by ZIP code, but the database only contains ZIP code as part of a City_State_Zip field. Or, you may want to write a report to print checks, spelling out the dollar amount in words, using a number or currency field in the database. All of these are applications for a formula that either manipulates or creates string data.

Strings can be *concatenated,* or "tacked together," using the plus sign or the & sign (ampersand). Although the plus operator is the same one used to add numbers, the results will be very different depending on the data type. For example, this formula

```
25 + 7 + 100
```

returns a numeric result of 132. Because all the elements of the formula are numbers, the plus sign will add the numbers together and return a numeric answer.

Contrast that with this formula:

```
"25" + "7" + "100"
```

or

```
"25" & "7" & "100"
```

which returns a string result of 257100. By enclosing the numbers in quotation marks, Crystal Reports interprets the values in the formula as strings, not numbers. When you use a plus sign or ampersand with strings, the result is the concatenation of the individual string elements.

This is very useful for many situations you'll encounter when reporting against databases. The following illustration shows the beginning of a form letter that simply uses database fields on the report.

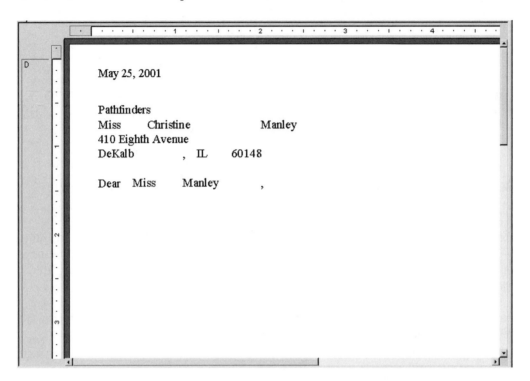

Notice the spacing problems for the contact name, city-state-ZIP line, and salutation. While you may be able to improve the appearance of this report slightly by resizing and moving the individual database fields, you'll never achieve a perfect result. By placing the database fields on the report in fixed locations, the report will never be able to accommodate varying widths of first names, last names, cities, and so on.

The next illustration shows the same report using formulas to concatenate the database fields together.

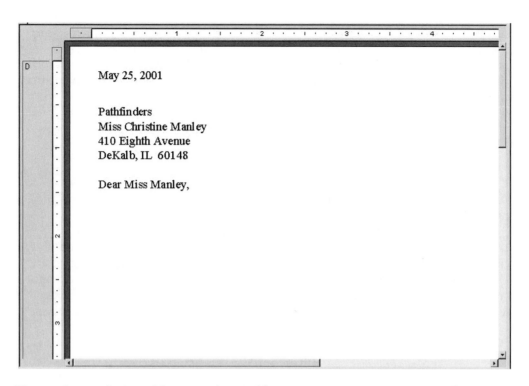

The results are obvious: No matter how wide or narrow names or cities are, they are placed right next to the other items (with a space in between).

But why use formulas to achieve these results instead of just combining the database fields inside text objects? (Refer to Chapter 2 if you forgot about text objects.) Formulas give you a lot more flexibility in how your report looks. For example, you can display only the first initial of a contact name on the report using a formula. You can't do that with a text object.

Concatenating string fields is as simple as using the plus sign operator, as in the following:

```
{Customer.Contact Title} + " " + {Customer.Contact First Name} +
" " +{Customer.Contact Last Name}
```

Notice that a space is hard-coded into the formula using a *string literal,* which is simply a fixed string surrounded by quotation marks. You'll use string literals often in concatenation formulas and If-Then-Else formulas (discussed later in this chapter). So, the literal space in this formula will separate the title from the first name, and the first name from the last name.

You could create a salutation line using several string literals, as follows:

```
"Dear " + {Customer.Contact Title} + " " +
{Customer.Contact Last Name} + ","
```

Notice that the word "Dear" and a space precede the title, a space separates the title from the last name, and a comma follows the last name.

There are many situations in which you may want to use only certain parts of strings in a formula, not the whole string. For example, you may want to use only a first initial as part of the contact name on a form letter. By following a string field with a number or range of numbers enclosed in square brackets (Crystal syntax) or parentheses (Basic syntax), you can extract certain characters from the string field. This function is known as the *subscript* function. For example, look at this formula in Crystal syntax:

```
{Customer.Contact Title} + " " + {Customer.Contact First Name}[1] +
". " + {Customer.Contact Last Name}
```

Notice that only the first character from the first name will be included in the formula, and a period has been added to the space literal between the first and last names.

Many older database systems contain date information in string fields, because earlier versions of mainframe systems or older database systems did not include a date data type. To allow dates to sort correctly, the year needs to precede the month and day in these fields as well. So, it is very common to find January 10, 1999 coded into a string database field as 19990110.

If you want to display the date in an mm/dd/yyyy format to make the date more readable, you could use string subscript operators to pick out the individual parts of the date, add some string literals, and rearrange the date's appearance. Assuming that the hire date in a "legacy" database is an eight-character string field in the form yyyymmdd, this formula will redisplay it as mm/dd/yyyy:

```
{EMP.HIRE_DATE}[5 to 6] + "/" + {EMP.HIRE_DATE}[7 to 8] +
{EMP.HIRE_DATE}[1 to 4]
```

Notice that the subscript operator can also return a *range* of characters, not just one.

In addition to the subscript operator, there are many built-in string functions that you can use in your formulas. There are functions to return characters from the left of a string, the middle of a string, and the right of a string. Using these, the preceding date formula could be rewritten in Crystal syntax as follows:

```
Mid({EMP.HIRE_DATE},5,2) + "/" + Right({EMP.HIRE_DATE},2) +
Left({EMP.HIRE_DATE,4})
```

In this case, the Mid function takes three arguments: the field or string to use, the position in the string from which to start reading, and the number of characters to return (there's also a two-argument version of Mid). The Right and Left functions take two arguments: the field or string to use and the number of characters to return.

Caution *Crystal Reports doesn't deal well with formulas that may include a database field containing a null value (a special database value equating to empty, as opposed to zero for a number field, or an empty string for a string/text field). If any part of the formula that you're using contains a null, the entire formula will return null. Use an If-Then-Else formula, along with the IsNull built-in function (described later in the chapter), to deal with potential null situations. Or, you may check the* Convert NULL Field Value to Default *option by choosing File | Report Options from the pull-down menus to convert any null fields from the database to empty string fields on the report.*

The ToText Function

A crucial built-in function that you will use very often in string formulas is ToText, which is used to convert other data types to a string data type so that you can use them in concatenation or comparison formulas. You can use ToText to convert numbers, dates, times—virtually any other data type—to strings. You need this functionality to avoid the type of problem shown here:

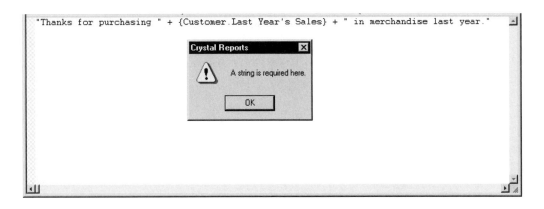

This problem occurs because you can't concatenate a currency field onto a string literal (or any other combination of mismatched data types). To convert a number or currency field to a string, such that you can concatenate it to another string, use ToText. The following will solve this problem:

```
"Thanks for purchasing " + ToText({Customer.Last Year's Sales}) +
" in products last year."
```

That formula will return

```
Thanks for purchasing $32,421.27 in products last year.
```

If you look in the Function Tree box under Strings, you'll see several permutations of ToText, with anywhere from one to five arguments.

The ampersand operator (&) can be used in place of the plus sign to concatenate string values. The advantage of the ampersand is that it performs an implicit conversion if you are mixing data types in your formula. As such, if you use the ampersand for concatenation, rather than the plus sign, you won't need to use ToText. However, if you want to control formatting of the converted values in your formula, you'll still want to use ToText to provide customized formatting.

While the best place to look for all the ToText details is Crystal Reports online Help, here are a few additional ToText examples:

- Determine the number of decimal places:

```
"Thanks for purchasing " + ToText({Customer.Last Year's Sales},0) +
" in products last year."
```

will return

```
Thanks for purchasing $32,421 in products last year.
```

A second number argument to ToText determines how many decimal places Crystal Reports uses when it converts the number or currency field to a text string.

- Determine the thousands separator:

```
"Thanks for purchasing " + ToText({Customer.Last Year's Sales},0,"") +
" in products last year."
```

will return

```
Thanks for purchasing $32421 in products last year.
```

A third string argument to ToText determines what thousands separator
Crystal Reports uses when it converts a number or currency field to a text
string. In this example, the two quotation marks side by side indicate an
empty string, so ToText doesn't use a thousands separator.

■ Format date fields:

```
"Your order was placed on " +
ToText({Orders.Order Date},"dddd, MMMM d, yyyy.")
```

will return

```
Your order was placed on Friday, May 25, 2001.
```

This version of ToText uses a *format string* as the second argument. The
format string (sometimes referred to as a *mask*) uses special characters,
such as pound signs, zeros, decimal points, the letters *d*, *m*, *y*, and so forth,
as placeholders to indicate how data should be formatted when converted
to a string. In this example, the *dddd* characters specify the day of the week
to be spelled out fully. *MMMM* specifies a fully spelled month, *d* specifies
the day of the month without a leading zero, and *yyyy* specifies a four-digit
year. Any characters included in the format string that can't be translated
into placeholders (such as the commas and periods) are simply added to
the string as literals.

Tip   *It's important to remember that the case of the placeholder characters is significant.
When formatting time fields, for example, lowercase h characters indicate hours with a
12-hour clock, whereas uppercase H characters indicate hours with a 24-hour military
clock. Or, if you use placeholder characters of the wrong case, Crystal Reports will just
include the characters in the resulting string as literals.*

Another built-in function, ToWords, comes in handy when writing checks with Crystal Reports. Consider the following formula:

```
ToWords({PAYROLL.NET_CHECK_AMT})
```

When placed on the report, this formula returns the following for an employee record with net pay of $1,231.15:

```
one thousand two hundred thirty-one and 15/100
```

Date/Time Formulas

There are many reporting situations in which you need to manipulate date, time, or date/time data types. Most modern PC and SQL databases support some or all of these data types. Although date and time fields don't appear on the report as pure numbers (they often include other characters and words, depending on how they're formatted), they are actually stored by the database and Crystal Reports as numbers. Therefore, it's possible to do mathematical calculations on date fields. There are also built-in date and time functions that return just parts of date and time fields and that convert other data types to date or time fields.

Number of Days Between Dates

When Crystal Reports performs math on date-only fields, the result of the calculation is in whole days. Crystal Reports returns fractional days if fields in the formula are date/time fields. For example, if you subtract a date-only field containing the value May 1, 2001 from a date-only field containing the value May 5, 2001, the result will be the whole number 4. If the fields are date/time fields and the May 1 field contains a time of 12 noon and the May 5 field contains a time of midnight, the result will be the fractional number 3.5.

So, determining how long it took to ship an order is as simple as creating the following formula:

```
{Orders.Ship Date} - {Orders.Order Date}
```

Even though both the database fields in this formula are dates (or date/time if these fields are coming from the sample XTREME database included with Crystal Reports), the result of the formula will be a number—the number of days between the two dates. This formula will return the number of calendar days between the two dates—it uses all days in the calendar. If you wish to exclude weekends from this calculation, it gets a little trickier. Crystal Reports 8.5 provides the Visual Basic–like function DateDiff in both syntaxes to do more flexible date math. An example of using DateDiff to exclude weekends from this type of calculation can be found in Crystal Reports online Help. Search for "DateDiff function."

 Tip *If you wish to exclude company holidays as well (holidays that might be stored in a database table), this could very well become a candidate for a User Function Library (discussed later in this chapter and in Chapter 27).*

You can calculate a date in the future. If, for example, you want to create an accounts receivable report that shows the actual due date of an invoice, the date itself could be calculated by using the invoice date (a date field) and terms (a number field), as follows:

```
{AR.INV_DATE} + {AR.TERMS}
```

Although you don't explicitly define this formula as a date formula, it returns a date data type showing the date on which the invoice is due, provided the terms field contains the number of days required for payment (30, 45, and so forth).

Another function in both Crystal Reports 8.5 formula syntaxes can be a lifesaver with future and past date calculations. The DateAdd function operates similar to its Visual Basic counterpart. For example, to determine a date exactly one month prior to today's date, you would use this formula:

```
DateAdd("m", -1, CurrentDate)
```

The "m" argument indicates a month time interval. The second argument indicates the number of "time intervals" to add (in this case, a negative one, thereby subtracting a month). And, the third argument is the date or date/time value to add to. What's particularly powerful about DateAdd is the automatic adjustment for various numbers of days in months and years. For example, if you evaluated this formula on March 31, 2000, it would return February 29, 2000 (there is no February 31, but 2000 was a leap year, therefore resulting in February 29).

Number of Hours and Minutes Between Times

You can also perform mathematical functions directly on time fields. When you calculate two time fields together, the result is in seconds. For example, the following formula will return the elapsed time, in seconds, between a starting time and ending time field in a college database's course table:

```
{COURSE.EndTime} - {COURSE.StartTime}
```

You may not want the time returned as seconds, but perhaps as hours and minutes, minutes and seconds, or any combination separated with colons. To accomplish this, you have a bit more work to do, but not as much as you might think. Examine the following:

```
Time(0,0,0) + ({COURSE.EndTime} - {COURSE.StartTime})
```

You'll notice that parentheses force the time calculation to be performed first, resulting in the number of seconds between the two times. The Time built-in function is also being used to return a time data type, using three arguments: hour, minute, and second. The particular time being returned by the Time function is midnight. By adding the seconds between the two times to midnight, you essentially have the number of hours, minutes, and seconds that have elapsed since midnight.

When you place this on your report, you'll see hours, minutes, and seconds, followed by AM or PM (AM if the time difference is less than 12 hours, PM if more, assuming that you're using Crystal Reports' default *hh:mm:ss AM/PM* date format). Now it's simply a matter of using the Format Editor to suppress the AM/PM indicator by choosing 24-hour time display. You can also suppress any combination of hours, minutes, and seconds to show the elapsed time the way you wish.

The new DateDiff function is not limited to just calculating differences between dates. You can also do time calculations similar to the previous example with DateDiff.

Month, Day, Year, Hour, Minute, and Seconds Functions

There are many built-in functions to help you use date and time fields. You can use the Month, Day, and Year functions with a date or date/time field as an argument to return just the month, day, or year of the date as a number. Conversely, with the Hour, Minute, and Seconds functions, you can supply a time or date/time field as a single argument and have just the hour, minute, or second of the field returned as a number.

DateValue Function

Two very important functions are DateValue and CDate, both of which are functionally equivalent. The DateValue function is much easier to use than the Date function, which was the only similar option in versions of Crystal Reports prior to Version 8. While there are several variations on DateValue, probably the most intriguing is the variation that accepts one string argument. This string can contain several variations of date-like strings, such as 10/1/99, March 17, 2000, 21 Feb 2003, and so on. Crystal Reports will evaluate the string to determine where the month, day, and year portions reside, returning a "real" date value as the result.

Note   *If you supply a two-digit year to DateValue, Crystal Reports applies a "sliding scale" approach to determining the century. If the two-digit year is between 0 and 29, Crystal Reports assumes the century is 2000. Otherwise, the two-digit year will be converted to the 1900s.*

This greatly simplifies date conversion in Crystal Reports 8.5. Previously, the Date function required three numeric arguments: year, month, and day. If you needed a date data type to use in comparison formulas or other formulas that worked well with dates, you had to perform fairly involved conversion routines to pick apart a date string. You needed to determine its individual month/day/year parts, convert these to numbers, and supply them to the Date function. For example, if your legacy database contained dates in string fields formatted as "mm/dd/yyyy," you would have used a combination of string subscripts, the ToNumber function, and the Date function to turn them into dates. Examine the following formula:

```
Date(ToNumber({EMP.HIRE_DATE}[7 to 10]),
     ToNumber({EMP.HIRE_DATE}[1 to 2]),
     ToNumber({EMP.HIRE_DATE}[4 to 5]))
```

While this worked, it is now much easier simply to use the following:

```
DateValue({EMP.HIRE_DATE})
```

There may be times when DateValue can't properly evaluate a date string, due to misspellings or other nonconforming string contents in a database field. This is a prime candidate for a run-time formula error. When you check the formula in the Formula Editor with the Check button, you'll get the popular No Errors Found message. However, when the report runs and the formula encounters the nonconforming string value, you'll see the following:

To avoid these run-time errors, use an If-Then-Else statement (described later in the chapter) in conjunction with another function, IsDate, to perform the conversion to a Date value only if the string can be interpreted by Crystal Reports as a date.

A number of related Time and DateTime conversion and detection functions are also available in Crystal Reports 8.5. Look in the Functions Tree or online Help for DateTimeValue, TimeValue, IsDateTime, and IsTime.

If-Then-Else Formulas

If you don't consider yourself a computer programmer, you may want to reevaluate your skills after you read this section. Crystal Reports allows the use of If-Then-Else logic in formulas. The If-Then-Else combination is the cornerstone of much computer programming code, so once you learn If-Then-Else concepts, you'll be on your way to new heights. Even if you're not contemplating a career change, you'll need to use If-Then-Else formulas to perform really sophisticated report customization.

If-Then-Else formulas perform a test on a database field, another formula, or some combination of them. Your test can be as simple or as complex as you need it to be—perhaps just checking to see if a sales figure exceeds the $1,000 bonus threshold. Or, you may want to check the number of days a product took to ship, in conjunction with the carrier who shipped the product and the sales level of the customer, to determine if a shipment met your company's shipping goals. If the test passes (returns *true*), the formula will return a certain result. If the test fails (returns *false*), a different result will be returned.

If-Then-Else formulas are created with the following syntax:

```
If <test> Then <result if true> Else <result if false>
```

The test portion of an If-Then-Else formula must use comparison operators found in the Operator Tree box (or a Boolean formula, discussed later in the chapter). You'll find a Comparisons section of the box that, when opened, shows operators that test for equal, less than, greater than, and other combinations of conditions. These can be used in conjunction with And, Or, and Not Boolean operators to combine multiple conditional tests together. Here's a simple If-Then-Else formula that will return a string based on an order amount:

```
If {Orders.Order Amount} > 5000 Then "Bonus Order" Else "Regular Order"
```

The Order Amount database field is tested to see if its value is greater than 5,000. If the test is true, the formula returns the "Bonus Order" string. Otherwise, the formula returns the "Regular Order" string.

Boolean operators can also be used to combine multiple comparisons together. You can use And, Or, and Not Boolean operators. The preceding formula has been slightly enhanced in the following formula, using a Boolean operator to combine two comparisons:

```
If {Orders.Order Amount} > 5000 And Month({Orders.Order Date}) = 12
Then
    "Holiday Bonus Order"
Else
    "Regular Order"
```

Here, the order amount has to exceed 5,000 *and* the order must have been placed in December for the formula to return Holiday Bonus Order. Orders over 5,000 in other months will still be regular orders. If you change the And to an Or in the preceding formula, then *all* orders in December will be bonus orders, regardless of amount. Orders over 5,000 will also be considered bonus orders the rest of the year.

Data Types in If-Then-Else Formulas

While creating If-Then-Else formulas, you must pay special attention to the data types that you're using in the formula. In the If test of the formula, make sure you use similar data types in each individual comparison operation. For example, if you want to test whether Customer.Country is USA, the test will be

```
If {Customer.Country} = "USA"
```

Since Customer.Country is a string field, you need to compare it to a string literal, enclosed in quotation marks or apostrophes (just quotation marks in Basic syntax). If the field you are testing is numeric, you need to use a number constant, as in the Orders.Order Amount sample shown previously. If you mismatch data types, such as these:

```
If {Orders.Order Amount} > "5000"
```

you'll receive an error.

If you use multiple comparisons separated by Boolean operators, each comparison can have a different data type. For example, if you want to combine the two tests mentioned previously, your formula would start out as follows:

```
If {Customer.Country} = "USA" And {Orders.Order Amount} > 5000
```

In this case, the different data types in the If part of the formula are fine, as long as each "side" of each comparison is of the same data type.

For example, you may have an existing formula on your report, @Ship Days, that calculates the number of days it took to ship an order. But, since @Ship Days is a numeric formula, it will display a zero on your report if the order was placed and shipped on the same day. Therefore, you would write the following If-Then-Else formula to show the words "Same Day" on the report if @Ship Days is zero, or to show just the contents of the @Ship Days formula if it is not zero:

```
If {@Ship Days} = 0 Then
    "Same Day"
Else
    @Ship Days
```

But, if you use the Check button in the Formula Editor to check the syntax of this formula, you'll receive an error:

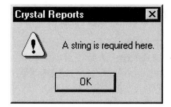

The problem is that Crystal Reports doesn't know what data type to assign to the formula. If the test returns true, the formula will return a string for the words "Same Day". However, if the test returns false, the formula will return @Ship Days, which is a number. Crystal Reports must assign a data type to a formula when it's first created—it can't wait until the report is running. Therefore, even though the If part of a formula can contain various data type tests, the Then and Else parts must contain the same data types.

Remember the function that converts other data types to strings? The following will solve this problem:

```
If {@Ship Days} = 0 Then
    "Same Day"
Else
    ToText(@Ship Days,0)
```

This result is better, because it doesn't show zero as the number of ship days. But, we want to take it a step further to make the report more readable. Look at the enhanced version of this formula:

```
If {@Ship Days} = 0 Then
    "Shipped Same Day"
Else
    "Shipped in " + ToText(@Ship Days,0) + " days"
```

This looks better on the report, particularly if the report isn't a straight columnar report. You might want to put this in a group header for an order, before the individual line items for the order show up in the details section. But, there's just one more problem. What will this formula return if it only took one day to ship the order?

```
Shipped in 1 days
```

While this probably won't mean your dismissal from the report development team, why not go one easy step further to make the report look even better? Try the following:

```
If {@Ship Days} = 0 Then
    "Shipped Same Day"
Else
    If {@Ship Days} = 1 Then
        "Shipped in 1 day"
    Else
        "Shipped in " + ToText({@Ship Days},0) + " days"
```

This is an example of a *compound* or *nested* If-Then-Else statement. Notice that you're not limited to one If, Then, or Else clause in a formula. You can make another If statement the result of the first Then, or the result of the first Else, and on and on. There is no specific limit to how many levels you can nest these, but obviously the formula becomes hard to follow after only one or two levels. Also, don't forget that the Else clause isn't required, so when you nest these, you won't have to always have a matching Else clause for every If.

Multiple Actions with One If-Then-Else Statement

You'll notice in all the preceding examples that only one action occurred as the result of the Then and Else parts of the statement. While this is okay for many types of formulas, sometimes you may want several things to happen, particularly when you need to set the contents of several variables as the results of a single Then or Else clause (variables are discussed later in this chapter). In this situation, you can simply repeat the

If-Then-Else test several times, with a different result for each Then and Else clause. Just be sure to separate each If-Then-Else statement from the next with a semicolon. For example, to set the contents of several variables in one formula, you might use the following:

```
NumberVar GroupBonus;
NumberVar GroupFollowUpCount;
NumberVar ReportBonus;
NumberVar ReportFollowUpcount;
StringVar GoodCustomer;

If {Orders.Order Amount} > 5000 Then
    GroupBonus := GroupBonus + 1
Else
    GroupFollowUpCount := GroupFollowUpCount + 1 ;

If {Orders.Order Amount} > 5000 Then
    ReportBonus := ReportBonus + 1
Else
    ReportFollowUpCount := ReportFollowUpCount + 1 ;

If {Orders.Order Amount} > 5000 Then
    GoodCustomer := {Customer.Customer Name}
```

All of these If statements will be evaluated and the resulting variables will be set. The formula will display the result of the last action in the If statement on the report. In this example, if the Order Amount is over $5,000, all the bonus variables will be incremented by one and the GoodCustomer variable will be assigned the customer name. But, because the GoodCustomer variable assignment is the last action that executes, the customer name is what the formula actually displays on the report. If the Order Amount is less than $5,000, then the two FollowUpCount variables will be incremented by one. But, because the last statement still tries to set the GoodCustomer variable and fails (and there's no Else clause), the GoodCustomer variable won't be assigned a value and the formula will return an empty string.

If you look at the previous example, you see quite a bit of duplicate typing (the If test is repeated three times). This duplication can be eliminated by creating just one If-Then-Else statement, but supplying several actions to the Then and Else clauses, separating the action statements with a semicolon and surrounding them all with parentheses. Here's the same formula created using this shortened approach:

```
NumberVar GroupBonus;
NumberVar GroupFollowUpCount;
```

```
NumberVar ReportBonus;
NumberVar ReportFollowUpcount;
StringVar GoodCustomer;

If {Orders.Order Amount} > 5000 Then
    (GroupBonus := GroupBonus + 1 ;
    ReportBonus := ReportBonus +1 ;
    GoodCustomer := {Customer.Customer Name})
Else
    (GroupFollowUpCount := GroupFollowUpCount + 1 ;
    ReportFollowUpCount := ReportFollowUpCount + 1;
    GoodCustomer := "")
```

Caution   *In the preceding example, you'll need to make sure to include the statement to assign the GoodCustomer variable an empty string in the Else clause. Otherwise, you'll receive the "A String is Required Here" error. This is because the Then and Else clauses must still return the same data type. Without the GoodCustomer assignment in the Else clause, the Then clause will be returning a string value (a string variable is being assigned) and the Else clause will be returning a numeric value (a numeric variable is being assigned).*

Enhanced Crystal Reports If-Then-Else Options

If the If-Then-Else logic described so far isn't enough to propel you toward (or perhaps away from) a programming career, Crystal Reports 8.5 includes a bevy of other If-Then-Else possibilities to help you reconsider!

First, the If-Then-Else statements in Basic syntax differ from those Crystal syntax versions described previously. Basic syntax follows the more typical If-Then-Else-EndIf approach familiar to Basic language programmers. In particular, this makes performing multiple actions as the result of a single If-Then-Else statement more straightforward by introducing the End If clause:

```
If <test> Then
    <statement>
    <statement>
    <more statements...>
Else
    <statement>
    <statement>
    <more statements...>
End If
```

Also, you can use the Basic syntax ElseIf clause (don't forget it's one word—no space) to allow nesting of multiple If conditions in one statement:

```
If <first test> Then
    <statements...>
ElseIf <second test> Then
        <second test statements...>
Else
    <statements if first test fails...>
End If
```

And, another permutation of If-Then-Else logic exists in both Crystal and Basic syntaxes of version 8.5. If you've used Microsoft Office products, such as Microsoft Access, you may be familiar with the IIF *Immediate If* function. This shortened version of protracted If-Then-Else logic is actually a single function, similar to ToText or UpperCase (it appears in the Function tree under Programming Shortcuts) that accepts three arguments. The function syntax is as follows:

```
IIF(<Boolean expression>, <result if true>, <result if false>)
```

This function can simplify If-Then-Else logic for small, simple formulas, or when you want to perform a "mini" If-Then-Else statement as part of a larger formula. For example, consider the following string formula using traditional If-Then-Else logic:

```
If {Customer.Country} = "USA" Then
    {Customer.Customer Name} + " requires domestic shipping charges"
Else
    {Customer.Customer Name} + " requires international shipping charges"
```

By using the Immediate If function, this can be simplified to the following:

```
{Customer.Customer Name} + " requires " +
IIF({Customer.Country} = "USA", "domestic", "international") +
" shipping charges"
```

Helpful Built-In Functions for If-Then-Else Formulas

If you look in the Function Tree box of the Formula Editor, you'll notice a Print State category (labeled *Other* in versions of Crystal Reports prior to 8.0). Opening this category shows a variety of built-in functions that you can use in If-Then-Else (and other) formulas to enhance your reporting flexibility. For example, all the Special Fields discussed in Chapter 2, such as Page Number, Total Page Count, Print Date and Time, Record Number, Group Number, and others, are available. There are other special functions that you can use to test for a null database value in the current, next, or last record; to check whether the current database record is the first or last; or to check whether the formula appears in a repeated group header. By using these special built-in functions, you can create formulas that make your reports more intuitive and easier to read.

Here are some examples:

- IsNull function

```
If IsNull({Customer.Region}) Then
    ""
Else
    ", " + {Customer.Region}
```

The IsNull function is critical if you may encounter null values in database fields that you include in your formulas. By design, a Crystal Reports formula will return a null value if any part of the field contains a null value. If a numeric formula performs addition on a field containing a null value, the formula won't treat the null as a zero and return a numeric result with the rest of the addition—the formula will return a null. If you are performing string concatenation and one of the string fields is null, the whole formula will return null, not the rest of the concatenation.

By using the If-Then-Else test with the IsNull function described previously, you can check whether the region field contains a null value. If so, the formula will return an empty string (denoted by the two sets of quotation marks). Otherwise, the formula will return a comma, a space, and then the region name. This formula can then be concatenated with city and ZIP database fields in another formula to form a city-state-ZIP line. If the region in the database is null, the other formula won't become null.

| Tip |

Several factors determine whether or not the database will contain null values. In many cases, this is determined by the way the database is initially designed. If you prefer to avoid null values appearing on the report, Crystal Reports allows you to convert them to a "default" format (typically a zero for number fields, and an empty string for string fields). To do this for all new reports in the future, check Convert NULL Field Value To Default on the Reporting tab of the File | Options pull-down menu. If you want to set this for just the current report, check the same option after choosing File | Report Options from the pull-down menus.

- Next function

```
If {Customer.Customer Name} = Next({Customer.Customer Name}) Then
    {Customer.Customer Name} + " continues on next page..."
```

The Next function reads a field in the next record of the database. This formula compares the field in the next record to the same field in the current record. If the values are the same, you know that the same customer will appear in the first record on the next page, and you can note this with a text message. This formula would typically be placed in the page footer.

 Notice that there is no Else clause in this formula. Crystal Reports doesn't require an Else clause in an If-Then-Else formula in Crystal syntax. If you leave the Else off and the test returns false, the formula will produce an empty string.

■ InRepeatedGroupHeader function

```
If InRepeatedGroupHeader Then
    GroupName ({Customer.Customer Name}) + "   - continued -"
Else
    GroupName ({Customer.Customer Name})
```

If you place this formula in the group header of a group with the Repeat Group Header on Each New Page option turned on (this can be set when you create or change a group—see Chapter 3), "- continued -" appears only when the group header is repeated. This also uses the GroupName function to return the group name field for a particular group. An InRepeatedGroupHeader test also comes in handy if you are resetting variables in formulas you are placing in the group header (assuming that you'll always be encountering a new group when the group header prints). Because you don't want to reset your variables in a *repeated* group header, you can condition your variable assignment statement on the value of InRepeatedGroupHeader. You might use something similar to the following:

```
If Not InRepeatedGroupHeader Then GroupBonus := 0
```

Crystal Reports 8.5 Logic Constructs

Although Crystal Reports versions prior to 8.0 provided a very robust formula language, many advanced users (particularly those with programming backgrounds) needed some of the procedural capabilities of high-level computer languages. If you fall into this category, not only will the typical procedural constructs in Basic syntax open up new flexibility for you, but similar logic constructs in Crystal syntax will also make your reporting life easier. Even if you're not a programmer, you'll probably soon find that these features come in handy in the more advanced reporting situations you'll encounter.

The term *logic construct* refers to the features of the Crystal Reports formula language that enable you to go beyond basic If-Then-Else logic. In versions of Crystal

Reports prior to 8.0, it was tedious to write long repetitive If-Then-Else formulas to perform tasks such as testing for more than a small number of conditions, picking apart strings, or cycling through multiple-value parameter fields or other arrays. With Crystal Reports 8.5, logic functions such as Select Case, For loops, and Do loops make these tasks much easier. These new functions enable Crystal Reports formulas to move closer and closer to a full procedural language, such as Visual Basic.

Select Case Statement

Select Case is very similar to its Visual Basic counterpart. It provides a much simpler and cleaner approach to testing for multiple conditions and returning appropriate results—those complex If-Then-Else statements can now be replaced with more readable and easy-to-maintain logic.

Look at the following compound If-Then-Else statement:

```
If {@Ship Days} = 0 Then
    "Shipped Same Day"
Else
    If {@Ship Days} = 1 Then
        "Shipped in 1 day"
    Else
        "Shipped in " + ToText({@Ship Days},0) + " days"
```

This is a relatively simple formula that checks whether the @Ship Days formula returns a 0 or a 1, returning a different string value in each case. If neither of these conditions is true, a catchall Else clause displays another string value. While this particular example isn't particularly complicated, it could quickly become much more difficult to interpret and maintain if more than two conditions have to be tested for.

Select Case is much better suited to this type of logic. Consider the following:

```
Select {@Ship Days}
    Case 0:
        "Shipped Same Day"
    Case 1:
        "Shipped in 1 day"
    Default:
        "Shipped in " + ToText({@Ship Days},0) + " days"
```

You may choose Select Case from the Operator Tree or simply by typing the correct syntax. Begin with the word "Select" followed by a database field, formula, or other expression. Then, supply multiple Case clauses, each testing the value of the Select expression (make sure the value you supply to each Case clause is the same data type as the Select expression). If you want to have the formula return the same result for several different values of the Select expression, you may separate the values after the Case clause with commas, and include the To operator to supply a range of values. After the Case clause, supply a colon (don't use a semicolon—this isn't the end of the statement) and then supply the expression you want the formula to return if the Select value equals the Case clause. Remember that all expressions that result from a Case clause must be the same data type—you can't have one Case clause return a string and another Case clause return a number. After the Case clauses have been defined, you may supply an optional Default clause, followed by a colon, and the expression you want the formula to return if none of the Case clauses match the Select value.

For Loop

Basic programmers have always enjoyed the capability to loop through fragments of program code over and over to perform repetitive logic. This was difficult, if not impossible, in versions of Crystal Reports prior to 8.0 and 8.5. In particular, if you needed to cycle through a multiple-value parameter field or other type of array (such as to look at each character of a string value), you couldn't perform a loop for each member of the array or each character of the string.

Crystal Reports 8.5 includes the ubiquitous For loop in both syntaxes (except there's no Next clause in the Crystal syntax version). The For loop uses a counter variable to keep track of how many times a specified piece of logic has been cycled through. The For clause sets both the beginning and ending values of the counter variable. The optional Step clause tells the For statement how to increment the counter variable (the default is 1 if the Step clause is left out). The For statement is closed off by the word "Do", followed by one or more statements enclosed in parentheses (use a semicolon to separate more than one statement within the parentheses). The statements inside the parentheses will be executed once for every increment of the counter variable.

The following formula displays all the entries a user has chosen in the multiple-value Region parameter field:

```
NumberVar Counter;
StringVar Message := "Regions Chosen: ";

// cycle through all members of the multi-value ?Region parameter field
For Counter := 1 to Count({?Region}) Step 1 Do
(
    // build the Message variable, along with comma/space
    Message := Message & {?Region}[Counter] + ", "
);

// strip off last comma/space added by the loop
Left(Message, Length(Message) - 2)
```

First, this formula declares two variables: Counter to increment the For loop, and Message to accumulate the parameter field values (look at the next section of the chapter for information on using variables). The For loop then cycles Counter from 1 to the number of elements in the parameter field (returned by the Count function). For each loop, Counter is used to retrieve the next element of the parameter field and accumulate it, along with a comma and a space, in Message. The final statement of the formula, which is not associated with the loop, strips off the last comma and space that were added inside the last occurrence of the loop.

Note   *Good formula logic dictates adding a test in this formula that uses the Exit For statement to exit the For loop if the Message variable exceeds 254 characters in length (the maximum length of a string variable). If the loop tries to accumulate more than 254 characters in the variable, a run-time error will occur.*

Using the Join and Split Functions to Avoid Loops

While the previous code is a great For loop example, there's actually another built-in formula function that negates the need for the variable declarations, the looping logic, and the removal of the training comma/space when creating a single string containing multi-value parameter field entries. Look at the following code:

```
"Regions chosen: " + Join({?Region}, ", ")
```

This formula uses the *Join function*, similar to its Visual Basic counterpart, which takes all the *elements* of the array supplied in the first parameter (a multi-value parameter field actually is an array), concatenates them together, and optionally separates each with the string supplied in the second parameter. Join performs the same thing as all the looping logic and variable manipulation demonstrated earlier, with one simple function.

Conversely, you may wish to take a string value or variable that contains multiple strings separated by a common delimiter (such as a slash) and create an array of string values. You could create a loop that cycles through the string one character at a time, looking for the delimiter (the slash), and performing complex logic to extract the substring and add it to an array. But the *Split function*, like its equivalent in Visual Basic, will perform all this logic for you automatically. Look at the following code:

```
Var array Regions;
Regions :=
Split("Northwest/Southwest/Northeast/Southeast/Midwest", "/")
```

The second line of code will populate the Regions array variable with five elements by looking through the string and separating the five substrings that are separated by slashes.

While Do Loop

A looping construct similar to the For loop described previously can be used to repeat statements while a certain condition is met. Whereas the For loop uses a counter variable to determine how many times the loop executes, the While Do loop evaluates a condition before each occurrence of the loop and stops if the condition is no longer true. This construct is similar to Do and While loops used in Visual Basic and other procedural languages.

The following listing is a formula that sets a variable to a phone number database field and then uses a While Do loop to look for hyphens in the variable. As long as a hyphen exists in the variable, the Do loop will execute a statement to "pick out" the hyphen, leaving behind only the pure numbers from the phone number. When there are no more hyphens in the variable, the While condition will fail and the statement after the closing parenthesis of the While Do loop (the variable name, which will display the number without the hyphens) will execute.

```
StringVar NewPhone := {Customer.Phone};

While Instr(NewPhone,"-") > 0 Do
(
    NewPhone := Left(NewPhone, Instr(NewPhone,"-") - 1) &
    Right(NewPhone, Length(NewPhone) - Instr(NewPhone, "-"));
);

NewPhone
```

Although this is a good example of how a While Do loop can cycle while a condition is true, it's a fairly complex process for the relatively simple "search and replace" function that it performs. For a more streamlined formula, you can use the Crystal Reports 8.5 Replace function, as in the following example:

```
Replace({Customer.Phone}, "-", "")
```

In this case, the Replace function makes use of three parameters: the first being the string field or value that you want to modify, the second being the character or characters you want to search for, and the third being the character or characters you want to replace the search characters with. Be careful, though, if you're using Crystal Reports 8 instead of Version 8.5. In Version 8, the Replace function doesn't operate as it should if you supply an empty string for the third parameter, as in this example. For this reason, you have to use the While Do loop to remove hyphens from the phone number in Version 8.

The previous logic construct examples are presented in Crystal syntax. Basic syntax logic constructs are very similar, if not identical, to their Visual Basic counterparts.

Boolean Formulas

The one remaining type of formula that you may need to create is the *Boolean formula*, which can return just two values, true and false. You can think of a Boolean formula as just the "test" part of an If-Then-Else formula. When the formula is evaluated, it ultimately returns only one of the two states.

Here's a simple Boolean formula:

```
{@Ship Days} > 3
```

In this formula, the existing @Ship Days formula (a number formula) is tested to be greater than 3 (indicating a shipping exception). It either is or isn't greater than 3! If it is greater than 3, the formula returns a true value—if it's not, the formula returns a false value.

When you then place this formula on your report, it will appear with a Boolean data type. If you have Show Field Names turned off in File | Options (discussed earlier in the chapter), then you'll see the formula show up with the word "True" in the Design tab. If you format the field, you'll notice a Boolean tab in the Format Editor that lets you choose how you want the true/false values to appear on the report.

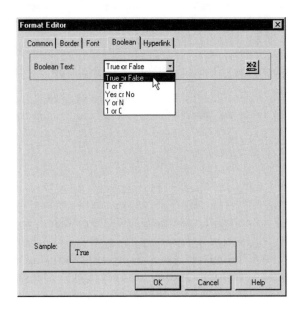

Although you may occasionally find Boolean formulas helpful when they're actually placed on the report, you'll probably use them much more often as a cornerstone for other formulas. For example, the Boolean formula shown previously indicates that Xtreme Mountain Bikes considers orders that took longer than three days to ship as exceptions. But, Xtreme really wants to break down the shipping exception rule based on Last Year's Sales. If the customer purchased more than $50,000 in merchandise last year, the three-day shipping exception will apply. However, if a customer purchased less, a six-day shipping exception applies.

This requires a *compound* Boolean formula, such as

```
({@Ship Days} > 3 And {Customer.Last Year's Sales} > 50000)
Or {@Ship Days} > 6
```

which uses a combination of And and Or operators, along with the comparison operators, to create a more complex Boolean formula. What's important to remember, though, is that the ultimate result will still be either true or false. You can make a Boolean formula as complex as you want, using combinations of comparison operators along with And, Or, and Not operators, but in the end, only true or false will result.

Tip   *Notice the parentheses around the first part of this compound Boolean formula. They ensure that both @Ship Days is less than 3 and Last Year's Sales is greater than $50,000 before "Or'ing" the @Ship Days greater than 6 test. Although this may make the formula more understandable, it is optional. Crystal Reports considers all Boolean operators (And, Or, and Not) equally in the order of precedence (discussed previously in this chapter). That is, it evaluates them equally as it travels through the formula from left to right.*

There are several benefits to creating Boolean formulas in this fashion:

■ After you create a complex Boolean formula, you can include it in other formulas as the test part of an If-Then-Else formula, as in the following:

```
If {@Shipping Exception} Then
    "*** Shipping Exception ***"
Else
    "Shipped Within Goal"
```

This makes the second formula much easier to read and understand.

■ By using the Boolean formula throughout the report, you eliminate the need to retype the complex Boolean test repeatedly, thus reducing the chance of errors. Even more important, you have only one formula to change if the report requirements change down the road. For example, if you use the @Shipping

Exception formula as the cornerstone for 50 other formulas in your report, and you later decide to reduce the Last Year's Sales qualification from $50,000 to $35,000, you have only *one* formula to change on your report, not 50. All the rest will follow the change.

■ You can use the Boolean formula in advanced record selection (covered in Chapter 6) and conditional formatting (covered in Chapter 7) to limit the report to certain records or to have certain objects on the report appear with different formatting.

 Tip *Crystal Reports' online Help is a wealth of wisdom on formula concepts and built-in functions. You'll find samples of every built-in function and many sample formulas that you can use as building blocks for your reports. Use this great resource as often as possible.*

Variables in Formulas and Evaluation Times

As a general rule, formulas contain their value only for the duration of one database record. If you put a formula in the details section, it will evaluate every time a new record is processed and put its result in the details section. If you put a formula in a group footer, it will be evaluated when each group footer prints. In every case, the formula will not "remember" anything from the previous record or previous group footer. Once the next record or footer comes along, the formula evaluates completely "from scratch."

Sometimes, though, you may need a formula to remember material from record to record or from group to group. You may want to accumulate some value as the report progresses so that you can print a total in a group footer or report footer. For example, you may want to check the value of a subtotal in a group footer. If it exceeds a certain threshold, you may want to increment a counter so that you can show how many groups exceeded the threshold at the end of the report.

To accomplish this, you need to somehow store information from record to record or from group to group. This can be accomplished by using *variables*. A variable is simply a "placeholder" that Crystal Reports sets aside in the computer's memory. As the report progresses from record to record or from group to group, your formula can refer back to the variable or change its contents. You can then use the variable in other formulas or display its accumulated contents in a group or report footer.

Note *Crystal syntax and Basic syntax use different statements to maintain variables. Like Visual Basic, Basic syntax requires use of the Dim statement to declare a variable before use. And, like Visual Basic, you can either assign a data type to a variable when you Dim it, or simply assign a value to it after you have used Dim without a data type (and the variable will automatically take on the data type of the value you assign it). Because of this similarity to Visual Basic, Basic syntax variables won't be discussed here, because they are well documented in Visual Basic texts. The rest of the discussion on variables applies to Crystal syntax.*

Declaring a Variable

The first step in any formula that uses a variable is to *declare* the variable. This sets aside a specific amount of memory for the variable, based on its data type. You'll find variable declarations listed in the Operator Tree box of the Formula Editor under Variable Declarations.

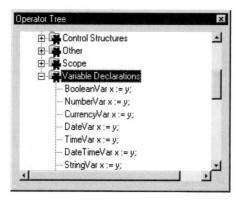

Notice that a different variable declaration statement exists for each Crystal Reports data type. You must consider in advance what kind of data your variable is going to hold, and declare the correct type of variable accordingly. If, for example, you want to keep track of a customer name from record to record, and the customer name field in the database is a string data type, you need to declare a string variable to hold the information.

You must also give each variable a name. You can give it any descriptive name you wish, provided it doesn't contain spaces or conflict with another Crystal Reports formula language *reserved word*. You can't, for example, use variable names such as Date, ToText, or UpperCase—these are reserved by the formula language for its own built-in functions.

To declare a variable, type the variable declaration followed by the variable name, such as this example:

```
NumberVar BonusAmount;
```

This declares a number variable called BonusAmount that can later be assigned a numeric value. The semicolon at the end of the statement separates this statement from the next one in the formula (presumably a statement to assign or test the contents of the variable).

If you wish to use more than one variable in the formula, you may declare them together, again separated by semicolons. For example:

```
NumberVar BonusAmount;
StringVar BonusCustName;
DateVar DateBonusReached;
```

> **Tip** *You may be used to assigning variables in other programming languages. Remember that Crystal Reports treats variables differently. You must declare a variable in each formula where you want to refer to the variable. However, even if you declare a variable and assign it a value in one formula, and then declare it again in a formula that appears later in the report, it will retain the value from the first formula. Unlike many other languages, declaring a variable more than once in Crystal Reports does not reset its value to zero or empty (with the exception of local variables, as described in the following section). These considerations apply to both syntaxes, Crystal and Basic. Even if you're used to using the Dim statement only once in Visual Basic, you must use it with Basic syntax in every formula where you want to refer to a variable. If the variable has been declared with a Dim statement in another formula, declaring it again will not reset its value.*

Variable Scope

The whole idea and benefit of variables is that they retain their values as the report progresses from record to record or from group to group. So, for variables to be of real benefit, they need to keep their values throughout the report process. And, because you may have several formulas that you want to refer to the same variable, you need to be able to refer to a variable in one formula that was already declared and assigned a value in another.

Exactly how long and where a variable keeps its value is determined by the variable's *scope*. If a variable has a narrow scope, it will retain its value only in the formula where it is initially declared—any other formula that refers to a variable with the same name will be referring to a brand new variable. If a variable has a wide scope, its value will be retained for use not only in other formulas, but also in subreports within the main report. (Subreports are covered in Chapter 11.) The following are three additional words you can place in front of your variable declarations (or use in place of the Dim statement in Basic syntax) to determine the variable's scope:

Local	The variable remains in scope only for the formula in which it is defined. If you declare a variable with the same name in another formula, it won't use the value from the first formula.
Global	The variable remains in scope for the duration of the entire main report. You can declare a global variable in one formula, and another formula will be able to use the contents placed in the variable by the first formula. Global variables, however, are not visible in subreports.
Shared	The variable not only remains in scope for the duration of the entire main report, but can also be referred to in formulas in subreports. You can use shared variables to pass data around the main report, back and forth between the main report and subreports, and from subreport to subreport.

Add these keywords in front of variable declarations to determine their scope, as follows:

```
Local NumberVar BonusAmount; //will only be visible in this formula
Global StringVar BonusCustName; //available to the whole main report
Shared DateVar DateBonusReached; //available to main and subreports
```

Caution   *If you leave off the variable scope keyword in Crystal syntax, the default scope for a variable will be global—it will be available to other formulas in the main report, but not to subreports. If you use the Dim statement in Basic syntax, the default scope for the variable will be local—it will be available for use only in the rest of the formula where it's declared. If you don't want to use the default scope, make sure you always add the proper scope keyword. And, make sure you add the keyword to the declaration in every formula that will be using the variable!*

Assigning a Value to a Variable

After you declare a variable, it won't do you much good if you don't assign a value to it. You may want to use it as an accumulator, to "add one" to it each time some condition is met for the database record. You may want to assign a string value to it, concatenating additional string values onto the variable as records progress. You then might display the value of the accumulated variable in the group footer, and assign the variable an empty string in the group header to start the whole process over again for the next group.

Tip   *If you declare a variable but don't assign a value to it, it takes on a default value based on its data type. Numeric and Currency variables default to 0, string variables default to an empty string, Boolean variables default to false, and Date variables default to a "0/0/00" date. Date/Time and Time variables have no default value.*

Crystal syntax provides two instances in which you can assign a variable a value: at the same time the variable is declared, or on a separate line later in the formula. In either event, you must use the assignment operator, consisting of a colon followed by an equal sign, to assign a value to a variable. This is important—it's easy to get confused and just use the equal sign by itself. The equal sign works only for comparison—you must place a colon in front of the equal sign to make assignment work properly unless you are using Basic syntax, in which case the equal sign by itself is used for both assignment and comparison. Here's a Crystal syntax example of assigning a variable a value on a separate line:

```
NumberVar CustomerCount;
CustomerCount := CustomerCount + 1
```

Here, the CustomerCount variable is declared on the first line (terminated with a semicolon) and assigned on the second line. In this particular formula, the CustomerCount variable will keep its value from record to record, so it will be incremented by one every time the formula executes.

If you want to reset the value of the CustomerCount variable in a group header, you need to reset it to 0. Here's a Crystal syntax example of how to declare and assign a variable at the same time:

```
NumberVar CustomerCount := 0;
```

Here, the variable is declared, followed by the assignment operator and the value to assign the variable. In this example, placing this formula in the group header will reset the CustomerCount variable at the beginning of each group.

 Tip *Notice that a semicolon doesn't have to appear in the last line of a formula, because it is used to separate one statement from another. If your formula only declares and assigns a variable, you don't need the semicolon at the end of the declaration/assignment statement.*

You don't have to assign a value to a variable every time the formula executes, nor do you need to assign the same value every time. Creative use of logic constructs, such as If-Then-Else or Select Case, along with variable assignment, provides report flexibility that rivals that of many programming languages. Look at the following formula, which declares and conditionally assigns several variables:

```
CurrencyVar BonusAmount;
StringVar HighestCustName;
DateTimeVar DateBonusReached;

If {Orders.Order Amount} > BonusAmount Then
    (HighestCustName := {Customer.Customer Name};
     DateBonusReached := {Orders.Order Date};
     BonusAmount := {Orders.Order Amount})
```

Look at this formula closely. Assuming it's placed in the details section, it keeps track of the highest order amount as the records progress. When an order exceeds the previous high amount, the customer who placed the order and the date the order was placed are added to variables. Then, the new high order amount is assigned to the bonus amount. The following are some important points to note about the formula:

■ There are multiple variable assignments separated by semicolons inside the parentheses. They will all execute, but only the last statement will determine how the formula appears on the report. In this example, the last statement uses a currency data type, so the formula will appear on the report as currency.

- If you are keeping track of the bonus amounts, dates, and customer names for a certain group, such as a region or country, make sure to reset the variables in the group header. If you fail to reset the variables, and the next group doesn't have an order as high as the top value in the previous group, the previous group's values will appear for the following group as well.

- If you want to keep track of quotas or similar values for both group and report levels (for example, you want to see the bonus customer for each region and for the entire report), you'll need to assign and maintain two sets of variables: one for the group level that is reset in the group header, and one for the report level that's not reset.

Displaying a Variable's Contents

In the preceding example, you saw how to accumulate values in variables in the details section, and how to reset them by assigning them a value of 0 in the group header (or in another area of the report). You also need to have a way to show exactly what's contained in a variable on the report, or to use the variable's value in a formula some other way.

To show the contents of a variable, you simply need to declare it. If the formula contains no other statements, declaring the variable will also return it as the formula value. For example, you might place the following formula in the group footer to show the customer who reached the bonus in the region group:

```
StringVar HighestCustName
```

You neither need to place any other statements in the formula to show the value of the variable nor even need the semicolon at the end of the declaration line—it's the last line in the formula.

You may have situations in which you want to show the contents of a variable, but are using other statements to assign the variable in the formula. In that case, just declaring the variable won't display it, because the declaration statement won't be the last line in the formula. In this situation, just add the name of the variable as the last line of the formula. This will then display the contents of the variable when the formula executes. Here's an example:

```
CurrencyVar BonusAmount;
StringVar HighestCustName;
DateTimeVar DateBonusReached;

If {Orders.Order Amount} > BonusAmount Then
    (HighestCustName := {Customer.Customer Name};
```

```
    DateBonusReached := {Orders.Order Date};
    BonusAmount := {Orders.Order Amount});

HighestCustName
```

This formula performs the test and variable assignments as before, but the last line of the formula simply shows the HighestCustName variable, a string variable. So, this formula shows up with small *x*'s in the Design tab (if Show Field Names is turned off in File | Options), and the contents of the HighestCustName variable will be shown whenever the formula executes.

You can go even one step further by testing and assigning variables and then using them later in other calculations or concatenations. Here's another permutation of this formula:

```
CurrencyVar BonusAmount;
StringVar HighestCustName;
DateTimeVar DateBonusReached;

If {Orders.Order Amount} > BonusAmount Then
    (HighestCustName := {Customer.Customer Name};
     DateBonusReached := {Orders.Order Date};
     BonusAmount := {Orders.Order Amount});

"As of this order, the amount to beat is " + ToText(BonusAmount) +
" set by " + HighestCustName + " on " + ToText(DateBonusReached,"M/d/yy")
```

This formula not only declares variables, it also conditionally assigns them and then concatenates and displays them, converting them to text as necessary.

Evaluation Times and Report Passes

As you may have gathered by this time, formulas that contain variables are affected by where they are placed physically on the report. If you want to check values and assign variables during record-by-record processing, you must put the formula in the details section. If you want to show the accumulated totals for each group, you place a formula in the group footer to show the total variables. And, to reset the variables for the next group, you need to place the formula that resets them in the group header.

However, just placing the formulas in these sections doesn't necessarily guarantee that they will actually evaluate in that section or during the logical "formatting" process of the report (during which a group header prints, then the detail sections for that group print, then the group footer prints, and so on). Consider the following example.

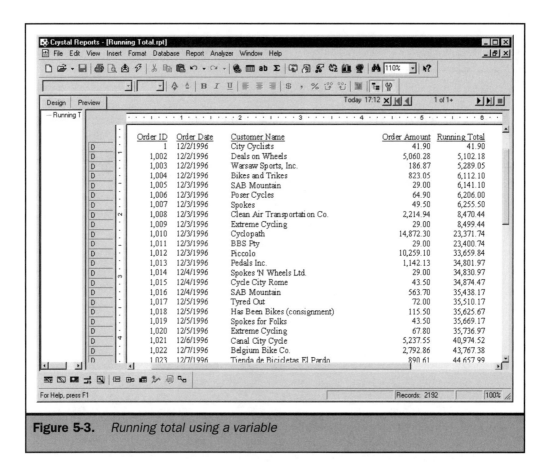

Figure 5-3.   *Running total using a variable*

Figure 5-3 contains a report that calculates a "running total" using a variable. The variable accumulates the order amounts in each detail section as the report progresses.

As you can see, the report is a simple detail report—there are no groups. In Figure 5-4, the report is grouped by Customer Name. Look what happens to the running totals.

Why does adding a group result in the oddity with the running total? This happens because the formula is accumulating the running total at a different time from when it's actually displaying it on the report. The formula is calculating while records are being read from the database, not when records have been grouped and are actually being printed or formatted. The formula is said to be calculating in a different *report pass* than the pass that actually formats the report. So, the running total has already been calculated for every record before Crystal Reports sorts the records to be placed in groups.

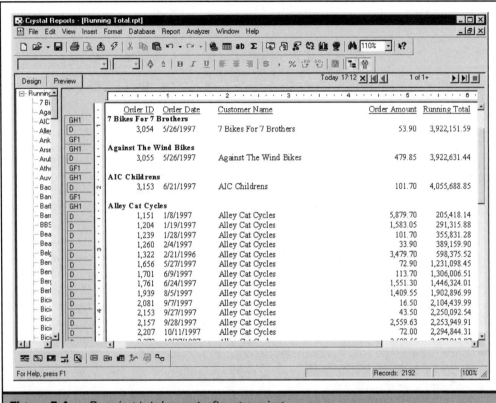

Figure 5-4. *Running total report after grouping*

Tip *This behavior may not be repeatable with a SQL database. When using a PC-style database, such as Microsoft Access, Crystal Reports actually reads and sorts the data itself, creating the two-pass concept. With a SQL database, the data may be selected and sorted by the database server before it is sent to Crystal Reports. In that case, you won't necessarily see this odd behavior.*

Crystal Reports generally breaks down its report processing into the following three passes, during which certain types of formulas automatically evaluate:

Before Reading Records	Occurs before any records are read from the database. If formulas don't include any references to database fields or summary functions, they calculate in this pass.

While Reading Records	Occurs as records are being read from the database, but before any record selection, sorting, or grouping is performed. Formulas that include references to database fields, but don't contain any subtotal or summary functions, are calculated in this pass. These formulas are often called *first pass* formulas.
While Printing Records	Occurs after records have been read and are being formatted for display or printing. Sorting and grouping occurs during this pass. Formulas that include sum, average, or other summary functions are included in this pass. These formulas are often called *second pass* formulas.

In most cases, you can trust Crystal Reports to accurately determine in which pass it needs to evaluate a formula. The glaring exception, however, is when a formula uses variables. If a formula simply declares a variable, or declares the variable and assigns it a literal or constant value, Crystal Reports evaluates that formula in the Before Reading Records pass, because it makes no reference to database fields or summary functions. If you assign a variable a database value, Crystal Reports evaluates that formula in the While Reading Records pass (the formula will become a first pass formula). Only if you have some type of summary or subtotal function in the formula will Crystal Reports automatically evaluate the formula in the While Printing Records pass (the formula then becomes a second pass formula).

This default behavior can cause very strange results, as the previous running total example illustrates. When you use variables in your formulas, you may need to force the formula to evaluate in a different pass than it would by default. You do this by changing the formula's *evaluation time*. To do this, add an evaluation-time statement as the first statement in the formula. Look in the Formula Editor Function Tree box and you'll notice an Evaluation Time section. Open that section to see several evaluation-time statements that should now be mostly self-explanatory.

To force the formula that accumulates the running total to the second pass, where it will calculate the running total correctly after the records have been grouped, add the WhilePrintingRecords evaluation-time statement to the formula, as follows:

```
WhilePrintingRecords;
CurrencyVar RunningTotal := RunningTotal + {Orders.Order Amount}
```

Caution	*Don't get confused if you can't insert a subtotal, summary, or grand total on a second pass formula. When you click this type of formula in the details section, no subtotal, summary, or grand total options will be available on the pull-down or pop-up menus, because subtotals, summaries, and grand totals are calculated in the While Printing Records pass. If the formula is already evaluating in that pass, you can't create a summary or grand total on it.*

The one evaluation-time function that may not be self-explanatory is EvaluateAfter, which takes one argument: the name of another formula. This forces one formula to evaluate after another formula when they evaluate in the same pass and are in the same section of the report. Because Crystal Reports automatically evaluates formulas that contain other formulas in the proper order, you'll use this function very rarely. However, it may be necessary to use it with formulas that contain variables.

When Crystal Reports evaluates two formulas that contain the same variable in the same section of the report, the order in which it will evaluate them is not predictable. One example is if you place two formulas in a group footer. The first formula shows the values of the variables:

```
WhilePrintingRecords;

CurrencyVar BonusAmount;
StringVar HighestCustName;
DateTimeVar DateBonusReached;

"The highest order of " + ToText(BonusAmount) +
" was placed by " + HighestCustName + " on " +
ToText(DateBonusReached,"M/d/yy")
```

The second resets the variables to zero or an empty string to prepare for the next group:

```
WhilePrintingRecords;

CurrencyVar BonusAmount := 0;
StringVar HighestCustName := "";
DateTimeVar DateBonusReached := DateTime(0,0,0);
```

Because there's a chance that the formula that resets the variables will evaluate before the formula that shows them, you have two choices. First, and probably most logical, is simply to move the formula that resets the variables to the group header. That way, the variables will be reset when a new group begins, after they have been displayed in the previous group footer. Or, if there is some logical reason why both formulas must exist in the group footer, you can use EvaluateAfter in the formula that resets the variables, as follows:

```
EvaluateAfter ({@Bonus Show});

CurrencyVar BonusAmount := 0;
StringVar HighestCustName := "";
DateTimeVar DateBonusReached := DateTime(0,0,0);
```

By placing EvaluateAfter as the first statement in the formula, you force the reset formula to evaluate after the display formula. Because you are forcing this formula to evaluate after a formula that's in the second pass, there's no need to include WhilePrintingRecords in this formula.

As you begin to add formulas that calculate and reset variables, you may find quite a few instances of things appearing in details and group header sections that show zeros or other unnecessary information. You can't delete the formulas from these sections, because then they won't evaluate properly. To hide them, just click Suppress on the Common tab of the Format Editor. You'll then see them on the Design tab, but not on the Preview tab or any other report output.

When Not to Use Variables

It's fairly common to learn how to use certain "spiffy" features of a tool, and then to use them to excess! Variables have that potential. Although they are fast and, if used judiciously, don't consume significant extra memory or resources, they can sometimes be "overkill." If you find a use for variables, first look closely at your report to see whether an easier, quicker way exists to accomplish the same task.

Figure 5-5 is an example of a report that counts orders that exceed a $1,000 bonus level. The number of orders needs to be shown both at the group level and at the end of the report.

Using variables to accomplish this requires the creation of several formulas. Two variables are also required: one to accumulate the bonus order count for each group, and one to count for the whole report. Following are the formulas.

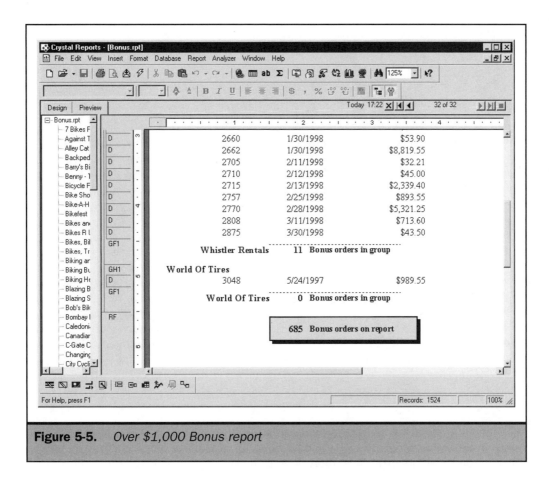

Figure 5-5. *Over $1,000 Bonus report*

@Bonus Calc is placed in the details section and suppressed:

```
WhilePrintingRecords;
NumberVar CountCustomer;
NumberVar CountReport;
If {Orders.Order Amount} > 1000 Then
    (CountCustomer := CountCustomer + 1;
     CountReport := CountReport + 1)
```

@Show Group Bonus is placed in the group footer:

```
WhilePrintingRecords;
NumberVar CountCustomer;
"This customer had " + ToText(CountCustomer,0) + " bonus orders."
```

@Reset Group Bonus is placed in the group header and suppressed:

```
WhilePrintingRecords;
NumberVar CountCustomer := 0;
```

@Show Report Bonus is placed in the report footer:

```
WhilePrintingRecords;
NumberVar CountReport;
"This report had " + ToText(CountReport,0) + " bonus orders."
```

While this will work, there is a much simpler way to accomplish the same task with just one formula using no variables. Create a single formula, place it in the details section, and suppress it. It will simply consist of the following:

```
If {Orders.Order Amount} > 1000 Then 1
```

When you place this in the details section, it will return a number constant of 1 when an order exceeds $1,000. If an order is under $1,000, the number formula will return 0 (because the formula is numeric and there is no Else clause, it will return 0 if the If test fails). You then simply need to insert a group subtotal and a report grand total on the formula to calculate group and report totals.

The result: the same totals with much less effort. This simple technique of assigning a formula a value of 1 if a test is passed can become the cornerstone for a lot of statistics-type reports you may have to write.

You may also be able to save time by using running total fields instead of formulas with variables. The running total report earlier in the chapter that illustrates evaluation times is a perfect example. In this type of report, there's no need to create formulas to calculate the running total. Running total fields are covered later in this chapter.

Tip   *Many of the types of formulas illustrated in this chapter are included in a report on the accompanying CD. Open FORMULAS.RPT to see how these, and similar formulas, are implemented.*

User Function Libraries

Crystal Reports has been designed as an *extensible* reporting tool. With respect to formulas, that means that you can develop your own functions to add to the Function Tree box if Crystal Reports doesn't provide one that you need. Look at the built-in functions that appear under the Additional Functions category.

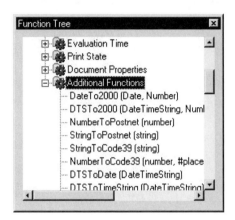

The functions in this category aren't really "built-in." These functions are being supplied to Crystal Reports by *User Function Libraries* (UFLs). The UFL is supplied to Crystal Reports by an external dynamic link library developed in another programming language. You can write your own custom functions using a Windows programming language, such as C++ or Visual Basic, and have them appear in this section of the Function Tree box. For example, you could write a function that calculates the number of business days between two dates you supply, excluding any weekends and company holidays. You might write a function that converts a text string to proper case (that is, uppercase letters at the beginning of the string and after every space, lowercase letters otherwise).

You can learn how to write your own UFLs in Visual Basic in Chapter 27.

Running Total Fields

In certain situations, the use of formulas with variables (discussed earlier in the chapter) is inevitable. But, many of the examples shown previously can actually be accomplished without even creating a formula. If you need to accumulate, display, and reset running totals, you will probably prefer the *running total field*. A running total field can be inserted just like a database field. It gives you great flexibility to accumulate or increment values as the report progresses, without the need for formulas or variables.

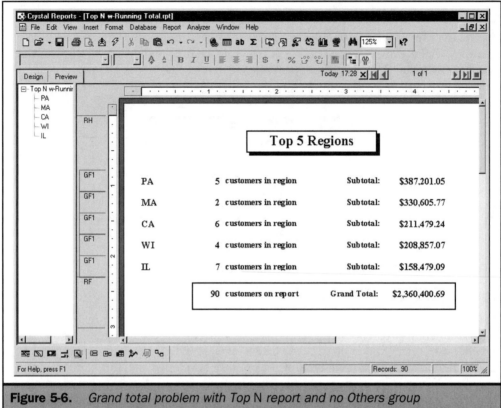

Figure 5-6.   *Grand total problem with Top N report and no Others group*

Figure 5-6 shows a Top *N* report (discussed in Chapter 3) that shows regional subtotals for the top five regions in the U.S. This particular Top *N* report does not include Others. As mentioned in Chapter 3, this causes the report grand totals not to agree with the sum of all the group totals. The grand totals are based on all report records, not just those that fall into the top five groups. Using running total fields is the perfect answer to this problem.

All new running total fields are created from the Field Explorer. Just click the Running Total Fields category to begin. First, select the Running Total Fields category in the Field Explorer. Click the New button in the Field Explorer toolbar to create a new running total field. You may also select an existing field in the Details section, right-click, and choose Insert | Running Total from the pop-up menu. The Create Running Total Field dialog box appears, as shown in Figure 5-7.

Fields available to
use in running total

Field and type of summary
used to calculate running total

When the running total
will be incremented

Running total field name

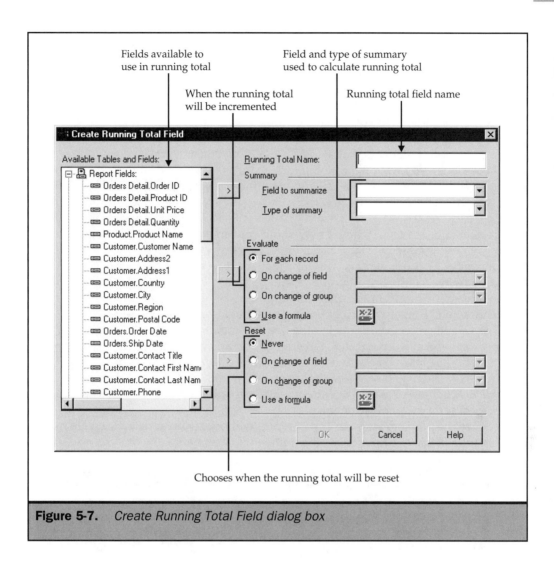

Chooses when the running total will be reset

Figure 5-7. *Create Running Total Field dialog box*

Start by giving the running total field a name (if you don't like the default name given by Crystal Reports). It can contain mixed case characters and spaces and won't conflict with formula or database field names. Crystal Reports will precede the running total field name with a pound sign (#).

If you select a detail field and use the right-click method to insert the running total field, the field you choose will already appear in the Field To Summarize drop-down list, and a default summary function will appear in the Type of Summary drop-down list. If you're creating a new running total field from the Field Explorer, choose the report, database, or formula field that you want to use to calculate the running total by selecting the field in the Available Tables and Fields list and clicking the right arrow next to the Field To Summarize box. Choose the type of calculation you want to use from the Type of Summary pull-down list. If you just want to increment the running total by one for certain records, use the Count or DistinctCount summaries (depending on how "unique" the field you are summarizing is), along with any field from the report that won't contain null values. Nulls don't increment counts.

Choose when you want the running total to increment, by making choices in the Evaluate section. Then, choose when you want the running total to reset, by making choices in the Reset section. If you select a field in the Available Tables and Fields list and then click the arrow next to the On Change of Field radio button, the running total will increment or reset every time a new value appears in that field. If you click the On Change of Group radio button, you can then choose an existing report group in the pull-down list. The running total will increment or reset every time the chosen group changes. If you click the Use a Formula radio button, you can then click the Formula button next to it. The Formula Editor will appear, in which you can enter a Boolean formula that will trigger when the running total field is incremented or reset.

Click OK when you've completed the Create Running Total Field dialog box. The running total will now appear in the Field Explorer and can be dragged and dropped on the report just like a database field. If you'd like to edit, rename, or delete the running total field, you have these choices in the Field Explorer. You can also right-click a running total field in either the Design or Preview tab and choose Edit Field Object from the pop-up menu.

To solve the problem with the Top *N* report without "Others," simply create two running total fields: one to calculate the number of customers:

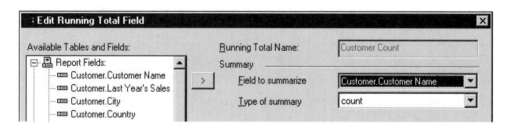

and one to calculate the sale grand total:

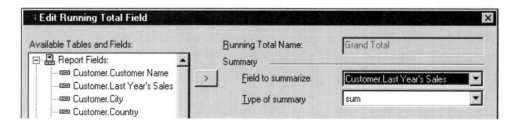

Place these running totals in the report footer instead of grand totaling the fields from the details section. Because running totals evaluate only during the While Printing Records pass, the extra records in the Others group won't be included in the report footer. Figure 5-8 shows the correct totals now displayed on the Top *N* report.

Caution *Because running total fields are calculated in the While Printing Records pass of the report, you cannot create running total fields based on second pass formulas.*

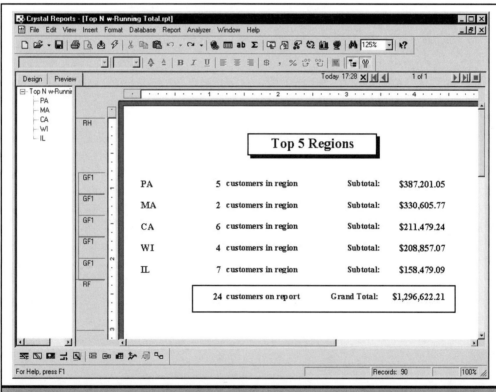

Figure 5-8. *Correct Top N report using running total fields*

The Complete Reference

Crystal Reports

Chapter 6

Analyzing with Advanced Selection Criteria

159

Creating a simple report is as quick as choosing tables, dragging and dropping fields on the report, and clicking the Preview button. However, if you only perform those few steps, you may have a much larger report show up than you bargained for! One important step missing is *record selection*. If you don't enter some sort of record-selection criteria, every record that exists in the tables you choose will appear on the report.

In the case of a small PC-type database with, say, 1,000 records, this won't be terribly time- or resource-intensive. However, if you're connected to a large SQL database with potentially millions of records, the consequences of not including record selection will probably be felt on your network, and will certainly be felt on your desktop PC. Since Crystal Reports needs to store the data that makes up a report somewhere, you may run out of memory or temporary disk space in such a situation. Regardless of these concerns, your report will be terribly slow, and probably not very useful, if you have that many records on the report.

Virtually all reports will need some form of record-selection criteria. You may want to limit the report to only USA customers, only orders placed in 2000, or only invoices that are more than 30 days past due. Record-selection criteria can be used to limit your report to any of these sets of records. In any event, it's very wise to apply your record-selection criteria early on in your report-design process—certainly *before* you preview or print the report!

The Select Expert

Crystal Reports includes the *Select Expert* to help you create useful record-selection criteria. You can use the Select Expert for simple, straightforward record selection, and as a starting point for more sophisticated record selection. The Select Expert can be run from within the Select tab on any of the report experts, or after you have chosen and linked tables using the Blank Report option. In either case, you'll want to make sure to use it before you preview the report.

To use the Select Expert while using one of the report experts, choose at least one table on the Data tab, and, if necessary, link the tables on the Links tab (table linking is covered in more detail in Chapter 14). You can then either progress through the other tabs until you reach the Select tab, or go to it directly. When you click the Select tab, the Select Expert will appear inside the Standard Report Expert, as shown in Figure 6-1.

If you are using the Blank Report option to create a report, you must initially select and link tables. Once the Field Explorer appears, you can either immediately run the Select Expert or add fields to the report before running the Select Expert. Again, you'll want to run the Select Expert before you preview the report.

Run the Select Expert by clicking the Select Expert button in the Standard toolbar. You can also choose Report | Select Expert from the pull-down menus. If you have already added fields to the report and want to use one of them from the Design tab or Preview tab for record selection, select the field on the report before you start the Select

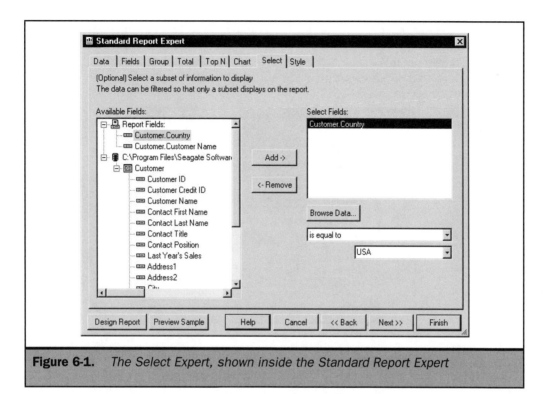

Figure 6-1.   *The Select Expert, shown inside the Standard Report Expert*

 Expert. You can also right-click your selected field and choose Select Expert from the pop-up menu. In each case, the Select Expert will start with a tab already created for the chosen field.

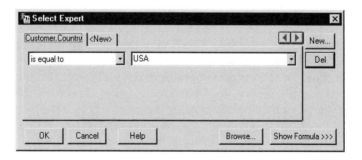

 You may use this feature unintentionally. If you start the Select Expert and see a tab for a field that you don't want to select on, just click the Del button on the right side of the expert to delete the current tab. Then click the <New> tab or the New button to choose the correct field to select.

If this is the first time you've run the Select Expert, and you haven't chosen an existing report field, you'll see a Choose Field dialog box listing all report and database fields. You'll also see this dialog box if you are already displaying the Select Expert and click the <New> tab or New button to add additional criteria.

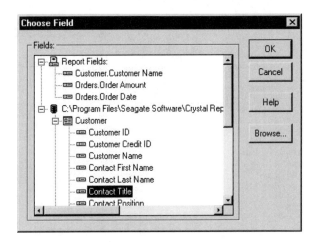

Click the report or database field that you want your record selection to be based on. If you want to see sample data from the database for that field, click Browse. Once you're satisfied with the field you want to use for record selection, select it and click OK. The Select Expert will appear with a tab for that field.

Once you've chosen a field to select on, you'll see an additional pull-down list with the default of Is Any Value. You will use this list to choose the comparison operation you want to use for your record selection. The pull-down list will reveal all the comparisons you can use to select records, and may vary somewhat based on the type of field you've chosen for record selection. Table 6-1 explains the different operators that may appear in the pull-down list. Note that the pull-down list will contain the operators discussed in the table, as well as operators that add the word "Not" in front of the operator. As you might imagine, choosing the "Not" version of the operator will include all records where the condition is *not* true, instead of where the condition is true.

Once you've chosen a comparison operator in the pull-down list, the Select Expert will change based on the selection you've made. If you've chosen an operator that only compares to one item (such as Equal To, Less Than, or Greater Than), one additional pull-down list will appear. If you've chosen an operator that can compare to multiple items (such as One Of, Like, or Starts With), a pull-down list will appear, along with a multiple-item box. You can add and remove items from the multiple-item box by clicking the Add and Delete buttons that appear next to the box.

Operator	Description
Is Any Value	This is the same as having no selection criteria at all. Is Any Value means it doesn't matter what's in the field—all records will be included in the report.
Is Equal To	The field must be exactly equal to what you specify.
Is One Of	You can specify more than one item to compare to by adding multiple comparison items to a list. If the field is exactly equal to any of them, the record will be included.
Is Less Than	The field must be less than the item you're comparing to. If you are comparing numbers, the field must be smaller numerically. If you are comparing dates, the field must be an earlier date. If you're comparing strings, the field must be lower in the alphabet. If you choose the Less Than Or Equal To option, the field can be equal to or less than what you're comparing to.
Is Greater Than	The field must be greater than the item you're comparing to. If you are comparing numbers, the field must be larger numerically. If you're comparing dates, the field must be a later date. If you're comparing strings, the field must be higher in the alphabet. If you choose the Greater Than Or Equal To option, the field can be equal to or greater than what you're comparing to.
Is Between	Allows you to select two items to create a comparison range. The field must be between, or equal to, the two items. Is Between uses the same type of comparison as is used with Is Less Than and Is Greater Than: numbers compare numerically, dates compare chronologically, and strings compare alphabetically.
Starts With	Allows you to specify "leading" characters to compare to. If the first characters in the field equal the specified characters, the record will be returned. If you want to perform several Starts With comparisons, you can add multiple criteria to a list. This operator will only appear when you are using a string field.

Table 6-1. *Select Expert Comparison Operators*

Operator	Description
Is Like	You can look for partial text matches using wildcard characters to search for records that contain particular characters or groups of characters. When you specify your comparisons, you can use a question mark to indicate that one character in the field at that position can contain anything. You can use an asterisk to indicate that the rest of the field from that point on can contain anything. If you want to perform several Like comparisons, you can add multiple criteria to a list. This operator will only appear when you are using a string field.
Is In the Period	Allows you to compare a date field to a group of built-in date ranges, such as the last week, last month, last quarter, current year, etc. These built-in ranges are all based on the system clock of your computer when you run the report. This operator will only appear when you are using a date field.
Is True	Includes records where the field equates to true. This operator will appear only when you are using a Boolean field.
Is False	Includes records where the field equates to false. This operator will appear only when you are using a Boolean field.
Formula	Allows you to enter any Boolean formula using the Crystal Reports formula language. Similar to the Show Formula button in the lower-right corner of the Select Expert.

Table 6-1. *Select Expert Comparison Operators* (continued)

The new pull-down list allows you to choose the item you want to compare the field to in either of two ways: type it directly or choose it from the pull-down list. You can simply type the literal item you want to compare to directly in the pull-down list.

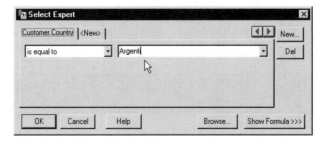

If you click the arrow on the pull-down list, the Select Expert will browse the database and list a few sample items from that database field. You may choose one of the items in the pull-down list for comparison.

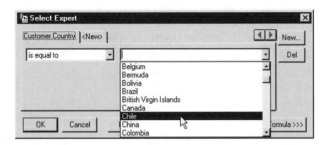

If the comparison operator you've chosen allows multiple entries, you can add an item you've typed to the multiple-item box by clicking the Add button. If you choose a browsed database item from the pull-down list, it will be added to the multiple-item box automatically. In either case, you can remove an item from the multiple-item box by selecting it and then clicking the Remove button.

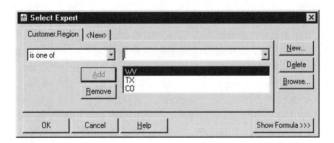

Note that you can choose *Is Not* versions of the comparison operators as well. This will, in essence, *reverse* the selection criteria you've chosen. If, for example, you chose a country field, the Is Not Equal To operator, and specified "USA" as the item to compare to, your report will now include records for every country *except* the USA.

The Select Expert does not limit you to comparing just one field. Once you have added one database field, you can click the <New> tab or the New button. This will redisplay the Choose Field dialog box, from which you can pick another field to compare to. Once you pick this field, a new tab will display in the Select Expert, enabling you to create another comparison. You may create as many tabs and comparisons as you need.

Crystal Reports applies a logical AND to all the tabs in the Select Expert—all the criteria have to be true for a record to be selected. If you would rather have a logical OR applied to some or all of the tabs (so that if any one of them is true, but not all of them, a record is returned), you must manually edit the selection formula created by the Select Expert. This is discussed later in this chapter in "Manipulating the Record-Selection Formula Directly."

Refreshing the Report Versus Using Saved Data

When you preview a report on the screen for the first time, Crystal Reports has to actually read the database and perform record selection, and only thereafter can it format and display the report. To enhance future performance while you work with the report, Crystal Reports creates a set of *saved data*. This saved data consists of the records that were retrieved from the database, which are then kept either in memory or in temporary files on your hard drive. If you perform simple formatting changes, move fields around, or make other minor modifications that won't require the database to be re-queried, Crystal Reports will use the saved data every time you preview the modified report, thus improving performance. If you add new fields to the report, Crystal Reports knows it has to re-query the database, and does so without prompting. You may notice a bit of a wait (or maybe a long wait, depending on your database) while it runs the new query.

But, when you change record-selection criteria, Crystal Reports doesn't know whether or not it needs to re-query the database. You will be given the option to Refresh or Use Saved Data. The choice you make is dependent upon whether you widened or narrowed the selection criteria. If you *narrowed* your selection criteria so that the new selection criteria can be completely satisfied with the existing saved data, you can choose to use the saved data. Since the database doesn't have to be re-queried, the changes will appear very quickly in the Preview tab.

 If, however, you *widened* the selection criteria so that the saved data won't contain all the records you're specifying, you need to refresh the report so that the database can be re-queried. Choosing to use saved data in this situation will result in your report showing too few (if any) records, even though they actually exist in the database. However, the re-query will take time to perform. If you make the wrong choice and end up with too few, or no, records, you can refresh the report manually by clicking the Refresh button in the Standard toolbar, pressing the F5 key, or choosing Report | Refresh Report Data from the pull-down menus.

When you save a report, you have the option to store the saved data in the .RPT file. If you include the saved data, the report will immediately display the Preview tab showing the saved data the next time you open the .RPT file—no database re-query will be required. However, this will also make the .RPT file larger (sometimes significantly so), since it has to keep the saved data along with the report design.

Tip   *Even if you open a report with saved data, the saved data will be discarded and only the Design tab will appear if the Discard Saved Data When Loading Reports option is checked on the Reporting tab of File | Options.*

To choose whether or not to save data, check or uncheck File | Save Data with Report from the pull-down menus, and then re-save the report after making your choice. You can also make the choice with the appropriate check box on File | Report Options. If you wish to set default behavior for this option for all new reports in the future, turn on or off the Save Data with Report option on the Reporting tab of File | Options.

Record Selection with Date Fields

Many reporting requirements can be satisfied by creatively using date fields in record selection. Crystal Reports provides a good selection of built-in date ranges you can use to compare to, or you can use other operators to compare date fields. When you choose a date field in the Choose Field dialog box, the Select Expert makes the In the Period comparison operator available. If you choose this operator, another pull-down list containing Crystal Reports' built-in date ranges appears.

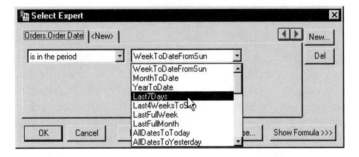

By using these built-in ranges, you can create a report that will return, say, only orders in the previous month by comparing to the LastFullMonth. What's particularly appealing about using built-in date range functions is the "self-maintenance" of the report. When you use the LastFullMonth range, for example, the report will always use the system clock in your computer to include orders from the previous month, no matter when the report is run. You don't have to manually change the date range every month.

There may be times, however, when you have to manually enter a date range for record selection. If, for example, you want to see all orders for 1997, you need to specify those dates manually. There is no built-in *X* Years Ago date range. In this case, you choose the date field you want to select on (for example, Order Date), and use a Between comparison operator to indicate orders between January 1, 1997 and December 31, 1997. You need to enter the dates by using the proper Crystal Reports formula syntax, which is Date(yyyy,mm,dd). Simply entering "1/1/97" and "12/31/97" in the Between pull-down lists will result in an error when you click OK.

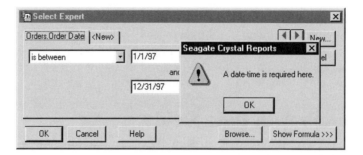

To correct this problem, enter a beginning date of **Date(1997, 1, 1)** and an ending date of **Date(1997, 12, 31)**. Even easier is the Version 8.5 *date literal* character, the pound sign (#). By surrounding the dates you type with pound signs, Crystal Reports will attempt to convert "free-form" dates into Crystal's internal date format. You won't have to use the Date function. In this example, entering dates of **#1/1/1997#** to **#12/31/1997#** would also solve the problem.

 If you're selecting on a Date/Time field, supplying just a date will work, but will automatically assume times on or after midnight of the first date. However, only records that include times of exactly midnight for the second date will be included—any times of even one second after midnight for the second date won't be included. Also, if you only supply a date instead of a Date/Time value, the Select Expert will not be able to interpret the Date function sufficiently to remember the comparison operator. The next time you open the Select Expert, it will have replaced the operator for the date field with a formula including the Date function.

Manipulating the Record-Selection Formula Directly

When you create record-selection criteria with the Select Expert, it actually creates a formula using the Crystal Reports formula language behind the scenes. For most simple record-selection criteria, you won't have to worry about manipulating this formula directly. Also, by using the Select Expert directly and not manipulating the actual formula that it creates, you will often maximize performance, particularly when using SQL databases.

However, there are times when the Select Expert itself won't provide enough flexibility for the record selection you need to accomplish. Consider the following scenario—you have two fields on their own tabs included in the Select Expert: Region Is Equal To CA, and Order Amount Is Greater Than 2500.

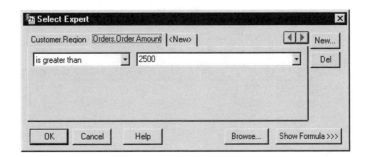

Since the Select Expert performs a logical AND between the tabs, what do you do if you want to see all orders from California, regardless of the order amount, as well as orders from any other state over $2,500?

In this case, the Select Expert doesn't provide sufficient flexibility to create this type of special record selection. Thus, you must use a *record-selection formula*. The Select Expert creates a record-selection formula automatically as you add tabs and selection criteria. You can modify the formula it creates in one of two ways:

- By clicking the Show Formula button on the Select Expert itself
- By choosing Report I Edit Selection Formula I Record from the pull-down menus

If you know you'll need extra features that the Select Expert doesn't provide, you can skip it entirely and create your record-selection formula right in the Formula Editor. Choose Report I Edit Selection Formula I Record from the pull-down menus to create the formula this way.

In the scenario previously mentioned, you need to change the relationship that exists between the two criteria from an And to an Or. This is a simple process that you can apply either right from the Select Expert or by using the Formula Editor. To use the Select Expert, simply click the Show Formula button.

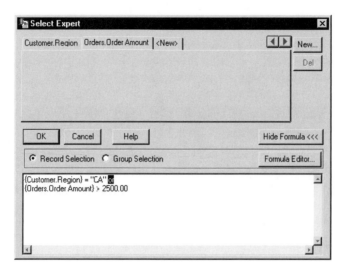

You can now modify the formula created by the Select Expert to show you all California orders, regardless of amount, and other orders over $2,500. Notice that the Select Expert has placed the And operator between the two parts of the selection formula. Simply position the cursor in the formula and change the And to Or, and then click OK.

If you click Show Formula in the Select Expert and then decide you want to use the full-featured Formula Editor, just click the Formula Editor button in the expanded Select Expert dialog box. The formula will be transferred to the Formula Editor, where you can modify or enhance it.

Since you will ultimately be using the Crystal Reports formula language for your record selection, most of the features of the language are available for record selection. In this situation, it may be preferable to edit the selection formula in the Formula Editor so that you can see and use all the built-in functionality. The formula that the Select Expert created will appear when you choose Report | Edit Selection Formula | Record from the pull-down menus.

You can modify this formula to your heart's content, provided that the ultimate finished formula is a Boolean formula—it will ultimately just return true or false (refer to Chapter 5 for more information on Boolean formulas). The formula will be evaluated for each record in the database. If the formula evaluates to true, the record will be included in the report; otherwise, the record will be ignored.

Case Sensitivity with Record Selection

A question that you will probably ask yourself fairly quickly when using record selection is, "Is it case sensitive?" In other words, if you ask to see records where the country is "USA", will a record be returned if the database field contains mixed-case characters, such as "Usa".

Case sensitivity is generally ignored when using SQL databases and PC databases via ODBC, as well as certain PC-style databases using a direct database driver. Although this case insensitivity is the default behavior "out of the box," be sure to check the Case-Insensitive SQL Data option in the File | Report Options dialog box to affect the current report, or check the same option on the Database tab of File | Options to set the default for all new reports you create in the future.

Even if this option is checked, some databases and ODBC drivers may not support case insensitivity with Crystal Reports. It's best to run a test with your own database to make sure you're retrieving all desired records with your record selection.

Tip *If you modify the formula the Select Expert created, or create your own formula, running the Select Expert again is fine. However, if the Select Expert is unable to fully interpret the formula you created, you'll see slightly different behavior for one or more tabs. You may see a tab with a field set to Is Formula and part of the selection formula showing in the third list box. You may also see a message indicating that the formula uses a "composite expression" and prompting you to edit the formula directly.*

Limiting Data with a Group-Selection Formula

When you use the Select Expert or create a record-selection formula with the Formula Editor, you affect the way Crystal Reports initially selects data from the database. Record selection occurs during the *first pass* of the report, before data has been sorted or grouped. Because of this, you can't use record selection to limit your report, say, to groups where the total sales exceeds $100,000—the record selection occurs before these totals are calculated. (See Chapter 5 for a discussion of report passes.)

You may also want to use an existing report formula in record selection. However, if you use the WhilePrintingRecords function or a summary function in the formula, it will evaluate in the report's *second pass* and won't show up in the Field Tree box when you create a record-selection formula. Again, the record selection occurs during the first pass, and second-pass formulas can't be used.

If you want to limit the report based on group subtotals or summaries, or somehow limit the report using second-pass formulas, you must use a *group-selection formula* instead of a record-selection formula. Create a group-selection formula from the Select Expert by clicking the Show Formula button and then clicking the Group Selection radio button. You can also select Report | Edit Selection Formula | Group. You can now create a Boolean formula to limit records using group summaries or second-pass formulas. And, if you choose a group summary or subtotal from the Field List when initially using the Select Expert, you'll be creating a Group Selection formula automatically because of your use of a summary or subtotal.

One word of caution: Group selection occurs *after* the group tree, subtotals, and grand totals have been calculated. This can lead to apparent inaccuracies on your report. For example, look at the report shown in Figure 6-2.

You'll notice that the group tree shows many more regions than actually appear on the report. And, it doesn't take a math degree to see that the grand totals don't quite add up. Don't forget that selection of a summary or subtotal field in the Select Expert will create a group-selection formula instead of a record-selection formula. You may see this kind of odd behavior and not fully understand why. Look back at the Select Expert to see if your selection is based on a subtotal or summary field.

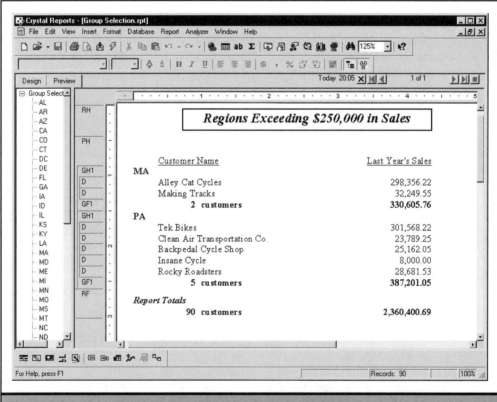

Figure 6-2. *Report with a group-selection formula applied*

This report applies a group-selection formula to limit the report to groups where the sum of Last Year's Sales exceeds $250,000. This group selection is applied after the group tree and grand totals have been created. Although there is no way to change the group tree in this situation, you can correct the totaling problem by using running totals instead of grand totals. Look at Chapter 5 for information on running total fields.

Performance Considerations with Record Selection

In many cases, record selection is the most time-consuming portion of the report process, particularly with larger databases. If you're using a PC-style database located on a local or network hard drive, Crystal Reports performs the record selection itself, reading every record in the database and only keeping those that match.

In this situation, performance considerations dictate using *indexed fields* for your record selection if at all possible. Indexed fields are fields that are specially designated when the database is designed. The field's index stores all the values in the field in a presorted state that makes it much faster to select records based on the field. To determine if a field is indexed, you may wish to consult the database designer.

You can also see which fields are indexed by using the Visual Linking Expert. Click the Visual Linking Expert button on the Supplementary toolbar, or choose Database | Visual Linking Expert from the pull-down menus.

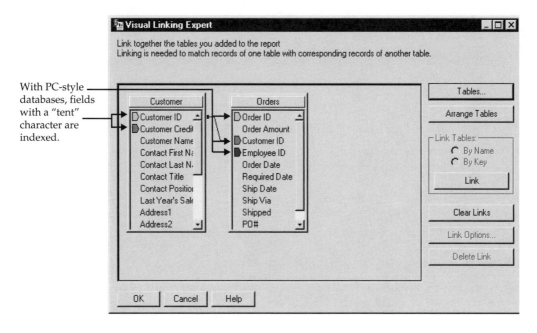

With PC-style databases, fields with a "tent" character are indexed.

You'll notice a small "tent" character appearing next to every indexed field (the different colors you may see are generally insignificant to record selection, as long as you select on a field with the symbol). Make note of the indexed fields and attempt to use them in record selection. If the field you need to select on is not indexed, and record selection appears very sluggish, you may wish to consult the database designer about adding an index for that field.

Finally, double-check the setting of the Use Indexes or Server for Speed option. To check the option for the current report, look in the File | Report Options dialog box. If you wish to check the option for all new reports in the future, look for the option on the Database tab of File | Options. If this is turned off, Crystal Reports won't use field indexes at all.

SQL databases (or PC-style databases accessed via ODBC) present a different set of performance considerations. As a general reporting rule, you want to always have the database server perform the record selection, if at all possible. This can typically be accomplished by only using the Select Expert to create selection criteria—using the Formula Editor makes it entirely too easy to introduce functions that Crystal Reports can't move to the database server. And, making changes to what the Select Expert creates with an Is Formula operator or the Show Formula button may also seriously degrade database server record-selection performance. As with PC-style databases, make sure the Use Indexes or Server for Speed option is turned on in File | Report Options.

Tip   *More in-depth discussion and examples of performance issues, including record selection, are found in Chapter 14.*

The
Complete
Reference

Chapter 7

Making Your Reports Visually Appealing

Crystal Reports, as a Windows-based report writer, has many features that can help you create eye-catching, visually effective reports. You can often use Crystal Reports to create reports right from the database, whereas you formerly had to use a word processor or page publishing program to create such reports. The next time you're tempted to export database records to a text file and merge them in a word processing or page publishing document, use some of the techniques covered in this chapter and save the extra work.

You may consider using geographic maps (discussed in Chapter 4) and charts and graphs (discussed in Chapter 10) as visual elements to make your reports more appealing. But, even using just the textual elements of Crystal Reports can be very creative. Not only can you use a variety of fonts and typefaces in your reports, you also can set object foreground and background colors, choose unique borders on all four sides of objects, add drop shadows, and use other graphical features. You can include bitmap pictures on your report, either directly from the database (if the database you're using supports and includes them) or add bitmaps right into a report section. You can draw lines and boxes around the report to highlight important portions. New to Version 8.5, you can use Report Alerts to trigger a message when a certain condition is met, as well as highlight portions of the report that met that condition.

One of the features of Crystal Reports that you'll want to use first is *conditional reporting*, which lets you change the appearance of objects based on their contents or the contents of other fields, objects, or formulas. Although the possibilities of conditional formatting are only limited by your imagination and creativity, some immediate uses of conditional reporting that may come to mind are

- Showing sales figures in red if they fall below a predefined level
- Using a different font to highlight long-time customers
- Adding a border around an invoice number if it's past due
- Showing a report title that's different on the first page than on the rest of the pages
- Graphically indicating with file-folder icons whether a case file has been opened or closed

The Highlighting Expert

Probably the simplest conditional formatting tool with Crystal Reports is the *Highlighting Expert*, which lets you change the appearance of number and currency fields based on their contents. If a sales figure falls below a preset goal for the department, you can have it stand out with a white font color on a red background. Or, you can change the border on a Days Overdue formula that exceeds, say, 60 days.

To highlight a number or currency field, select the field you want to change. Start the Highlighting Expert by clicking the Highlighting button on the Format bar and choosing Format | Highlighting Expert from the pull-down menus, or right-clicking the object and choosing Highlighting Expert from the pop-up menu. Figure 7-1 shows the Highlighting Expert.

The key to using the Highlighting Expert is knowing which conditions to declare for the field's contents. Begin by choosing a comparison operator in the Value Is drop-down list. You'll find most of the standard comparison operators you've used in formulas or in the Select Expert, such as Less Than, Greater Than, Equal To, Not Equal To, and so forth. After making this choice, enter a constant number to compare to in the text box below (you can also click the drop-down arrow and choose a value from the sample data in the list). Finally, choose any combination of font and background colors and border styles you want the field to have if the comparison is true.

To format the sales figure to show up as white text on a red background if it falls below the preset sales figure of $1,000, choose a comparison of Less Than, type **1000**, and then choose a Font Color of White and a Background of Red. You will see a sample in the Sample box in the lower right of the Highlighting Expert, as well as to the left of

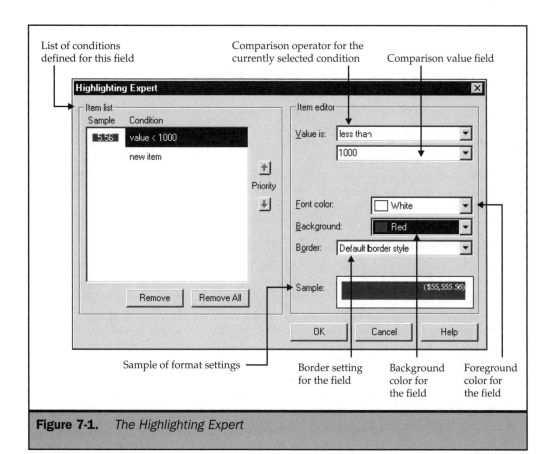

Figure 7-1.   *The Highlighting Expert*

the now-created condition in the Item List box on the left. When you click OK, the field will show white text on a red background for any sales figures less than $1,000.

You may want to set up multiple conditions if you want more than one formatting option displayed. To expand on the previous example, suppose you want to show bonus sales (over $5,000) in blue, in addition to the existing red background for those that fall below $1,000. Just click New Item in the Item List box. You can enter a new condition and another set of formatting options. Both will apply to the field.

You may have two conditions that conflict with each other. For example, you could have a condition that formats field contents over $1,000 in red, and another that applies blue formatting for contents over $5,000. Since both conditions would satisfy the over-1000 condition, will everything over $1,000 (including anything over $5,000) be in red? It depends on the *priority* you assign the conditions. If the over-1000 condition is higher in the Item List box, everything over $1,000 will be in red. However, if the over-5000 condition is set higher, then it has priority—everything over $5,000 will be in blue. Then, the second item in the list (the over-1000 item) will be tested, placing anything over $1,000 in red. To change priority, click the condition you want to move and then click the up or down Priority arrow.

Conditional Formatting Formulas

The Highlighting Expert is a simple and quick way to format fields, because you don't have to know the formula language to use it. However, the trade-off is in flexibility. As your reports become more sophisticated, sometimes the Highlighting Expert won't provide all the flexibility you need. You may need to conditionally format fields other than number or currency fields. You may want to apply formatting other than just color and borders. For these situations, you need to use *conditional formatting formulas*. Conditional formatting formulas use the Formula Editor to create one or more conditions to determine how the object appears.

Absolute Versus Conditional Formatting

Before you learn how to set formatting conditionally, it's important to have a fundamental grasp of *absolute formatting*, which simply refers to applying normal formatting to objects with the Format Editor. If you right-click an object and choose Change Font from the pop-up menu, the Format Editor will appear with the Font tab selected. If you change the color of the font to Red, *all* occurrences of the object on the report will be red. If you click the Border tab and select the Drop Shadow check box, *all* occurrences of the object will have a drop shadow. This is the process of absolute formatting.

As you approach conditional formatting, it's important to distinguish between two types of formatting properties: *multiple-choice* properties and *on-off* properties. On the Font tab, Font and Color are good examples of multiple-choice properties. You can click a drop-down list and choose from any one of several fonts or colors. An example of an on-off property is Drop Shadow on the Border tab, which just has a check box: it can only be turned on or off. Whether a formatting property is multiple choice or on-off determines the type of formula you'll use to set it conditionally. Multiple-choice properties are conditionally formatted with If-Then-Else formulas, while on-off properties are conditionally formatted with Boolean formulas.

 You need to be familiar with the Crystal Reports formula language to use conditional formatting effectively. To refresh your memory, look for information on If-Then-Else and Boolean formulas in Chapter 5.

 To set formatting conditionally, click the Conditional Formula button that appears on the Format Editor next to the property that you want to format.

This will display the *Format Formula Editor* (essentially the same Formula Editor discussed in Chapter 5, but with a new title), shown in Figure 7-2. Notice that you can set conditional formatting with either Crystal or Basic syntax by making your choice from the Syntax drop-down list. If you are formatting a multiple-choice property, all

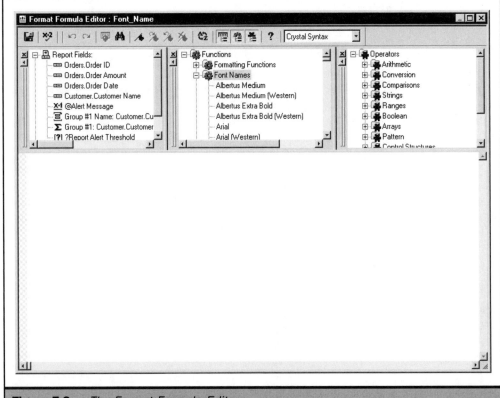

Figure 7-2. *The Format Formula Editor*

the available options for the property appear at the top of the Function Tree box. If, for example, you are conditionally formatting the Color property, you'll see all the available colors listed. If you're formatting a border, you'll see the different available line styles.

Use an If-Then-Else formula to determine the formatting of the object. Your formula can be as simple or as complex as you need. For example, you may have a formula to set font color that is as simple as the following:

```
If {Customer.Last Year's Sales} > 5000 Then Blue Else Black
```

or a formula to set a bottom border as complex as this:

```
If {Orders.Order Amount} > 5000 And {Orders.Ship Via} = "Fedex"
Then
    DoubleLine
Else
    If {Orders.Order Amount} > 1000 And {@Ship Days} < 3 Then
        SingleLine
    Else
        NoLine
```

You can use any type of simple or compound If-Then-Else formula, as long as the results of every Then and Else are one of the available formatting properties in the Function Tree box.

When you have finished with the formula, you can use the Check button to select the syntax of the formula, or save the formula and close the Format Formula Editor with the Save button. The Format Editor will remain on the screen. Notice that the Conditional Formula button changes from blue to maroon, and the pencil character inside the button points at a different angle. This indicates that a conditional formula is set for this property.

To change the existing formula, click the Conditional Formula button again and change the formula that appears in the Format Formula Editor. To delete conditional formatting and return to absolute formatting (or no formatting at all), just highlight and delete the whole conditional formula. Then, click the Save button. You'll notice that the Conditional Formula button has returned to a blue color with the pencil pointed in its original direction.

   While most conditional formulas must use a built-in formatting function for the Then and Else clauses of your formula, the Size property is a little different from other properties. In this case, the result of your conditional formula must be a number.

If you're formatting an on-off property, the general procedure for conditional formatting is the same. But when you click the Conditional Formula button next to the property, you won't see any additional functions in the Function Tree box of the Format

Formula Editor, because you can't use an If-Then-Else formula to format this property. Because the property can have only one of two states, on or off, you must format it with a Boolean formula that can return only one of two results: true or false.

To add a drop shadow to Customer Name fields of customers who have last year's sales greater than $100,000, start by right-clicking the Customer Name field. Choose Change Border from the pop-up menu and click the Conditional Formula button next to the Drop Shadow property. When the Format Formula Editor appears, type in the following Boolean formula:

```
{Customer.Last Year's Sales} > 100000
```

The Boolean formula will evaluate to only one of two states: true or false. If the formula returns true, the formatting property will be turned on and the field will have a drop shadow around it. If the formula returns false, the property will be turned off and the field won't have a drop shadow.

You may be curious about how conditional formatting and absolute formatting interrelate. Consider the following scenario. You choose an absolute color of Red on the Font tab of the Format Editor and click OK. Of course, every occurrence of the field will be red. You then return to the Format Editor and, without changing the absolute formatting, click the Conditional Formula button next to the Color property and add the following formula:

```
If {Customer.Last Year's Sales} > 50000 Then Blue
```

Note the missing Else clause. Remember that Crystal Reports does _not_ require an Else clause in an If-Then-Else formula. In a regular formula, if the If test fails and there's no Else clause, the formula returns an empty string, zero, or other default value, based on the data type of the formula. But, what color will the font take on here if there's no Else clause and absolute formatting is set to Blue?

Contrary to what might seem logical, when the If test fails in this case, the font will show up in black type, despite the absolute formatting of Blue. This is by design—if conditional formatting is applied, absolute formatting is ignored. If the conditional formula fails (and there's no condition to "catch" the failure, like an Else clause), the Windows Control Panel default color or format for that type of object will be used. Be careful with this if you don't use Else clauses, especially if you're formatting background colors. A font color of black isn't necessarily problematic, but a background color of black will often cause your report to look like someone plastered electrical tape all over it!

The exception to this rule, and a way to combine absolute and conditional formatting, is to use the DefaultAttribute function, located in the Formatting Functions category of the Function Tree box in the Format Formula Editor. If you use this function with the

Then or Else clause, the formula will use the setting from the absolute formatting property. Hence,

```
If {Customer.Last Year's Sales} > 50000 Then Blue
Else DefaultAttribute
```

will show sales figures over $50,000 in blue and others in red (provided that the absolute color chosen in the Format Editor is red). If you change the absolute color, then figures over $50,000 will still show up in blue, but the rest will take on whatever color you specified as absolute.

 If you've applied conditional formatting to a field that's also being formatted with the Highlighting Expert, the Highlighting Expert will take precedence. Only if it doesn't change the formatting of a field will conditional formatting be visible.

Creative Use of the Suppress Property

If you search through the Format Editor, you'll notice that virtually all formatting properties can be set conditionally. One of the most flexible is the Suppress property on the Common tab. You may consider that absolutely setting the Suppress property is of limited usefulness. (Why even bother putting the object on the report if you're just going to suppress it?) There are some good reasons for suppressing the object; for example, a formula that sets a variable to zero in a group header has to be physically placed in the header to work properly, but you don't want zeros showing up at the top of every group.

There are many more situations in which *conditionally suppressing* an object can be useful. Here are some examples, and the corresponding Boolean formulas you will apply to the Suppress property:

- **Placing the word "continued" in a repeated group header** In Chapter 3, the repeated group header was introduced. If you select this option in the Group Options dialog box, a group header section will repeat at the top of a page if a group continues from the previous page. Indicating that this group continues from the previous page adds readability to your report. Place a text object that contains the word "continued," or something similar, in the group header close to the Group Name field. You must now suppress it if it is *not* in a repeated group header. Conditionally suppress the text object with the following Boolean formula:

```
Not InRepeatedGroupHeader
```

 When you conditionally suppress an object, you use a Boolean formula; and when your formula returns true, the object will be suppressed, not shown. So, you may have to think "backward" when conditionally suppressing.

■ **Showing a bonus message only for certain records**   You may want a report to indicate that a certain record (for example, a certain order or a certain sales person) has exceeded a predefined goal amount. Simply create a text object that displays something like "Congratulations! You've exceeded the sales goal." Again, you have to think about when you *don't* want the text object to appear, not when you do. Assuming a $10,000 sales goal, conditionally suppress the text object with the following Boolean formula:

```
{AccountRep.Sales} <= 10000
```

■ **Showing a different heading on page 2 and later**   You may want to have a larger report title, perhaps including the company logo and a large font, on page 1 of the report. However, every other page needs to contain a smaller title without the logo, and perhaps include the word "continued." If you put the large title in the report header, you'll only see it at the beginning of the report. But, putting the smaller title in the page header will result in it showing up on every page, including page 1. Create the text object that contains the smaller title and place it in the page header along with any column headings or other objects you want to appear on every page. But, conditionally suppress the text object containing the title with the following Boolean formula (PageNumber is a built-in function from the Print State category of the Formula Editor Function Tree box that returns the current page number):

```
PageNumber = 1
```

 You can also create string formulas that provide roughly the same functionality as these examples and place them in appropriate report sections. However, to minimize potential "formula clutter," it sometimes may be preferable to just create text objects and conditionally suppress them.

Special Fonts, Graphics, and Line Drawing

As mentioned at the beginning of the chapter, Crystal Reports is a true Windows report writer. This means that it can use most of the fonts and graphical capabilities of Windows.

Using Special Fonts

Don't hesitate to use symbol fonts that are installed on your computer. In particular, the Symbol and Wingdings symbol fonts are included as part of Windows and should be available to most "target" systems that will be running your report.

 Don't forget that any fonts you use when designing your reports must also be present on the machine that runs your reports if you expect the report to look identical on both machines. Using Times Roman, Helvetica, Symbol, and Wingdings fonts, at a minimum, is pretty safe, because they are installed by default on all Windows systems.

Both Symbol and Wingdings fonts contain typographical symbols instead of letters and numbers. Although you type letters and numbers into a text object or formula formatted with a text font initially, you'll see them replaced with the symbol characters once you change the font from a text font to one of the symbol fonts. You'll need either a font table (typically available from Windows Control Panel) or a little extra time to experiment and figure out what symbols display when you type certain letters, numbers, or special characters.

Figure 7-3 shows a report using the Wingdings font. In this example, the following formula is being displayed on the report next to the order amount, formatted using the Wingdings font:

```
If {Orders.Order Amount} < 1000 Then
    "L"
Else
    If {Orders.Order Amount} > 1000 And {Orders.Order Amount} < 2500 Then
        "K"
    Else
        "J"
```

Using Bitmap Graphics

If you are planning to create reports that approach the quality of output from page publishing programs, you'll soon have a need to use *bitmap graphics* in your reports. Bitmap graphics are common graphics files most often associated with the Web (such as .JPG files) or Windows paint program files (such as .BMP and .PCX files). You may have a company logo that you want included on the title page of the report. Or, you may want to add a smaller graphical element, such as an icon, to another section of the report.

 To insert a bitmap graphic, first make sure you are displaying the Design tab. Although it's possible to add a graphic while viewing the Preview tab, this is risky, because you won't always be sure which report section the graphic will end up in. Click the Insert Picture button on the Supplementary toolbar, or choose Insert | Picture from the pull-down menus. A familiar File Open dialog box will appear, asking you to choose a bitmap format file. Navigate to the necessary drive and folder, and the dialog box will show any files at that location that can be added to the report. Choose the correct file and click OK.

An outline will appear alongside your mouse cursor. Drag the outline to the section of the report where you want the graphic to be placed, and click the left mouse button to drop it there. If the graphic happens to cover more than one report section, it will be dropped in the section where the upper-left corner of the outline is when the mouse is clicked. Once you drop the graphic, you'll see it appear in the Design tab.

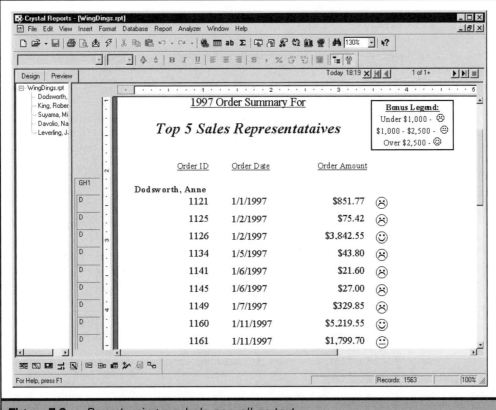

Figure 7-3. *Report using symbols as well as text*

You have complete control over how the graphic is sized and cropped. You can simply drag the graphic to a new location on the report, or resize it using the sizing handles on the sides and corners. You can also position the graphic (or any other object on the report, for that matter) with the Object Size and Position dialog box. Select the object that you want to position, right-click, and choose Object Size and Position from the pop-up menu. You can also choose Format | Object Size and Position from the pull-down menus.

To format the graphic more precisely, you can use the Format Editor. Make sure the graphic is still selected. Then, click the Format button in the Supplementary toolbar, right-click the graphic, and choose Format Graphic from the pop-up menu; or choose

Format | Format Graphic from the pull-down menus. The Picture tab allows you to specify exact cropping and scaling specifications.

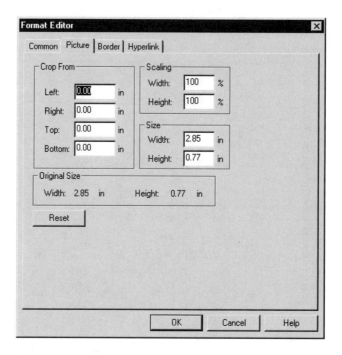

Caution   *Only common bitmap graphic formats are supported in Crystal Reports. It will not recognize specialized formats, such as Adobe Photoshop, or any vector formats, such as those from CorelDRAW or Adobe Illustrator. If you wish to use these graphics in a report, you need to convert them to common bitmap formats with another program before adding them to your report.*

Although using symbol fonts, such as Wingdings, is very powerful, you are limited to what is included in the font itself. Also, the symbols are generally simple two-dimensional images and can only be displayed in a single color. Wouldn't it be nice if you could use smaller bitmap files, such as icon-like graphics that look more three-dimensional and include several colors, on your report?

Because you can suppress bitmap files conditionally, just like other objects, you have real power and flexibility in creating visually appealing and interesting reports using bitmap graphics. Figure 7-4 shows a report with unique icons indicating the status of an order. Orders that have been shipped (or are "closed") have a closed file folder next to them. Open orders (not shipped) have an open file folder next to them.

This report uses a technique that could be called *mutually exclusive suppression*. There are two different bitmap files on the report: an open-file bitmap and a closed-file bitmap. They are placed right on top of each other in the details section. They are conditionally

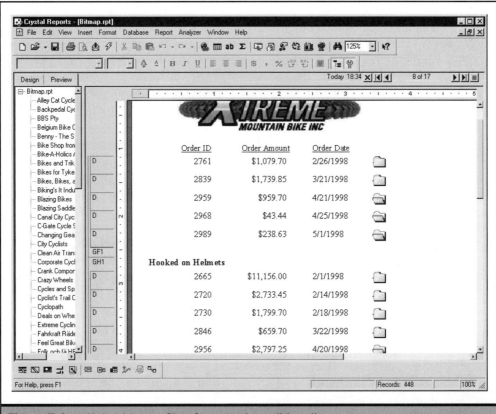

Figure 7-4.   *Using bitmap files formatted conditionally*

suppressed in such a way that only one will ever be displayed at a time. In this case, they are suppressed using the Shipped field (a Boolean field that returns true or false) from the XTREME.MDB Orders table.

The open-file bitmap is conditionally suppressed using this formula:

```
{Orders.Shipped}
```

while the closed-file bitmap is conditionally suppressed using this formula:

```
Not {Orders.Shipped}
```

Because of this, only one will ever be visible at a time.

The success of this technique depends on Crystal Reports allowing multiple objects to be placed right on top of each other. You have the ability to do this with any text or graphic object whenever and wherever you choose. Just make sure you implement some technique similar to this to prevent them from splattering all over each other. You can also use the Move to Back, Move Backward, Move Forward, and Move to Front options from the Format pull-down menu or from the pop-up menu that appears when you right-click an object. These options determine which objects have "priority" when they are placed on top of each other.

Line and Box Drawing

You can use the Border tab on the Format Editor to control lines on all four sides of individual objects. While this lets the individual objects stand out by having lines or boxes appear around them, you may want more flexibility, to have groups of objects highlighted with boxes or to have lines stretch partially or completely across sections.

Crystal Reports lets you use line and box drawing tools to create these boxes and lines. To create a line or box, ensure that you have the Design tab chosen. Inserting lines or boxes in the Preview tab may give you undesirable results if you don't put them in the right section.

To add a line or box to your report, perform these steps:

1. Click the Insert Line or Insert Box button in the Supplementary toolbar. You can also choose Insert | Line or Insert | Box from the pull-down menus.

2. When you make either of these choices, your mouse cursor changes to a pencil. Point the pencil to where you want to begin the line or box, and hold down the left mouse button.

3. Drag the line or box to its ending position and release the button. Notice that you can draw only perfectly vertical or horizontal lines—diagonal lines can't be drawn.

The line or box will appear on the report, complete with sizing handles. You can now drag or resize the line or box just like any other object. You may also format the line or box with the Format Editor (using options from the Format pull-down menu, or by right-clicking the line or box and choosing Format from the pop-up menu). You can choose the color, size, and style of the line or box, along with other options (Crystal Reports 8.5 allows you to create rounded boxes, for example). Figure 7-5 shows a report that uses a horizontal line to delineate group footers, and places a filled, rounded box around report totals.

Tip *You can draw lines and boxes that traverse multiple report sections. This is handy if you want to have a single box enclose a column starting in the page header and ending in the page footer, including all the sections in between. However, this can sometimes result in odd behavior if, for example, you start a line in the page header but end it in the details section or a group footer. If your lines or boxes traverse sections, make sure you preview the report to check that you get the desired results.*

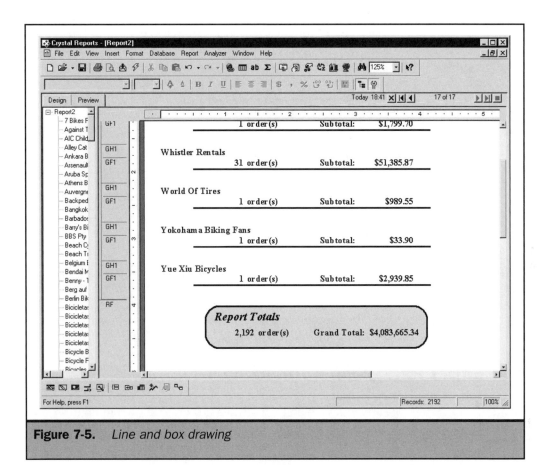

Figure 7-5. *Line and box drawing*

Text and Paragraph Formatting

Crystal Reports 8.5 includes formatting features that enhance reporting capabilities. Some are designed for use with foreign-language versions of the report writer (such as Japanese), while others simply provide enhanced functionality for more reporting situations.

A subtle feature that may not be immediately noticeable is *fractional point sizes* for fonts. If you use the point size drop-down list either in the Format toolbar or from the Font tab of the Format Editor, you'll see that only whole-number point-size values are available. However, if you click inside the drop-down list, you can then type values directly into the drop-down list, rather than choosing predefined numbers. If you want to use a 10.5 point size instead of a whole number, simply type **10.5** and press ENTER. You may type in sizes in ½ point increments (10.5 will work, but 10.25 will round to 10.5).

You'll also notice a *Text Rotation* option on the Format Editor Common tab. This allows you to rotate objects based on TrueType or built-in printer fonts to 90 degrees (sideways from bottom to top) or 270 degrees (sideways from top to bottom). Just choose the desired rotation from the drop-down list. You'll probably need to adjust the height and width of the now-rotated text to properly show all the material in the object.

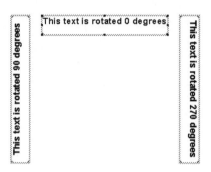

 You can make innovative use of text rotation by using multiple report sections and the Underlay section formatting option, described in Chapter 8. For example, by placing a rotated text object in Page Header b (which is formatted with the Underlay option), you can have vertical text flow down alongside the rest of your report on every page. This technique can be helpful for replicating special forms, for example.

Format Editor Paragraph Formatting Tab

If you format a string or memo database field or a text object, Crystal Reports 8.5 presents an additional *Paragraph Formatting* tab on the Formula Editor, as shown in Figure 7-6. Use these options to determine how multiple lines of text or data will be formatted:

- **Indentation—First Line**   Indicates the amount of space the first line in each paragraph will be indented. The first line of the text or any line after a carriage return is considered the first line of a paragraph.

- **Indentation—Left**   Indicates the amount of space that the entire field will be indented from the left side of the object.

- **Indentation—Right**   Indicates the amount of space that the entire field will be indented from the right side of the object.

- **Spacing—Line Spacing**   Adds vertical blank space between each line in the paragraph. Choose the Multiple option to choose a multiple of the normal spacing (for example, two times normal spacing). Choose the Exact option to choose a specific point size for line spacing (for example, 5 points).

- **Spacing—Of *x* Times Normal**   Specifies the associated number for the Multiple or Exact Line Spacing option.

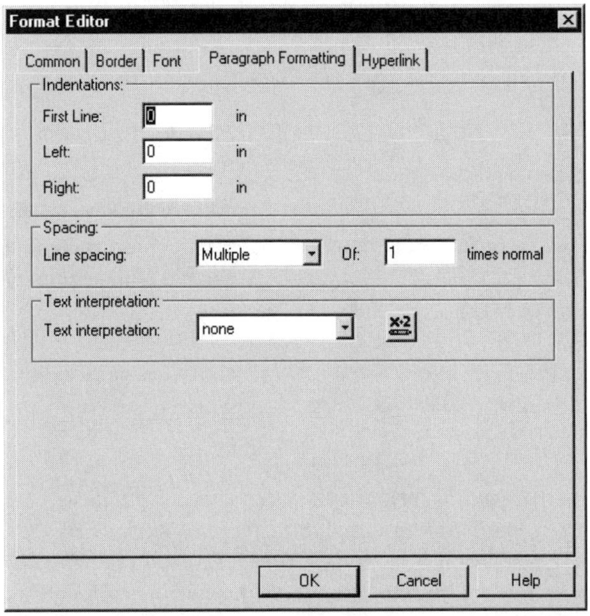

Figure 7-6.   *Paragraph Formatting tab on Format Editor*

Using HTML and RTF Text Interpretation

Figure 7-6 also shows the *Text Interpretation* drop-down list on the Paragraph Formatting tab (you'll see this option only with string or memo database fields—not with text objects). Available options in this drop-down list are None (the default), HTML Text (Hypertext Markup Language), and RTF Text (Rich Text Format). HTML text is often associated with the Web—Web pages are encoded in HTML. RTF is a standard text format that is interchangeable between most popular word processors and page publishing programs.

If you leave the default Text Interpretation option of None chosen, Crystal Reports 8.5 simply displays the value from the database as it actually appears in the database. If the field contains special formatting codes, they'll just appear on the report directly. If your database string or memo fields contain text with special HTML or RTF formatting codes to describe fonts, colors, and special formatting, choose the appropriate HTML or RTF Text Interpretation option. Crystal Reports will convert these formatting codes into actual typeface, point size, color, and formatting options. Notice how a Text Interpretation setting

of None versus a setting of HTML displays a database field that's encoded using the
Hypertext Markup Language.

```
<HTML>
<HEAD>
<META
HTTP-EQUIV="Content-Type"
CONTENT="text/html;
charset=windows-1252">
<META NAME="Generator"
CONTENT="Microsoft Word
97">
</HEAD>
<BODY>

<I><FONT
FACE="Arial"><P>Now</I> is
the time for all
```

Now is the time for all
<u>good</u> men to come to
the aid of their country.

Caution	*Remember that many of the formatting options and techniques discussed in this chapter may not export properly to non-Crystal file formats, such as Word, Excel, or HTML (although Crystal Report 8.5's DHTML and RTF exports are much improved over previous versions). If you wish to use special formatting techniques in a report exported to one of these formats, perform a test export early in your report-design process to avoid unexpected results after a large report-design effort. Information on exporting to alternative file formats is discussed in Chapter 13.*

Report Alerts

A new feature to Crystal Reports 8.5 is *Report Alerts*. Report Alerts allow you to set up a
condition that Crystal Reports checks for every time you refresh the report (by clicking
the Refresh button in the Standard toolbar, by selecting Report | Refresh Report Data
from the pull-down menus, or by pressing the F5 key). Report Alerts can also be used to
highlight desired conditions when reports are scheduled with the new Crystal Enterprise
Web-based reporting system (covered in Part II of this book).

While you've always been able to conditionally format report sections and objects
based on a condition, you might not have always known which customers, sales reps,
months, and so forth, had "triggered" this condition without going through the report
page by page looking for the conditionally formatted sections. Now when a report with
Report Alerts defined runs, a separate dialog box will pop up if any of the conditions
on the report have been met. You can then click a button on the dialog box to display
a separate tab (similar to a drill-down tab) that shows only report records that meet
the alert condition.

To work with Report Alerts, choose Report | Create Alerts from the pull-down menus.
The Report Alerts dialog box will appear, as shown in Figure 7-7. If any existing alerts
have already been created in the report, they'll appear inside this dialog box. If you

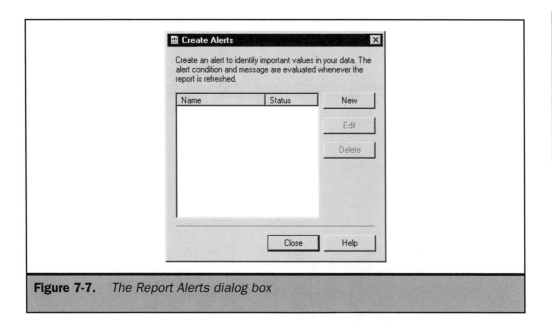

Figure 7-7.   *The Report Alerts dialog box*

wish to modify any existing alert, select it in the dialog box and click the Edit button. To delete an existing alert, select it and click the Delete button. If there are no alerts in the report yet, the dialog box will be empty.

To create a new alert, click the New button. The Create Alert dialog box will appear, as shown in Figure 7-8. At minimum, you must specify the name of the Report Alert in the Name text box, and the condition that will trigger the alert by clicking the Condition button. You may optionally type a message that will appear when the alert is triggered in the Message text box, or customize the message with a string formula you create by clicking the conditional formula button. Clicking the Condition button will display the Formula Editor, where you enter a Boolean formula that determines when the alert will be triggered (see Chapter 5 for information on Boolean formulas). If you wish to temporarily disable the alert without deleting it entirely, deselect the Enabled check box.

For example, you may wish to create a simple report showing orders that were placed. If the order amount exceeds a certain level ($5,000, for example), you wish to trigger a report alert. Create the report as you usually would and then create a new Report Alert. Give the alert a name of your choosing (perhaps "Order Exceeds 5,000"), type any message you want to appear when the alert is triggered, and then click the Condition button. Enter a Boolean formula to indicate what records should trigger the alert, such as

```
{Orders.Order Amount} > 5000
```

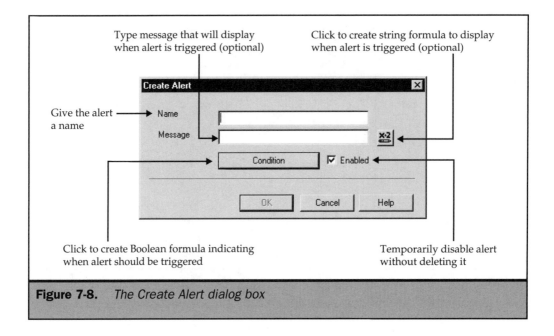

Type message that will display
when alert is triggered (optional)

Click to create string formula to display
when alert is triggered (optional)

Give the alert
a name

Click to create Boolean formula indicating
when alert should be triggered

Temporarily disable alert
without deleting it

Figure 7-8.   *The Create Alert dialog box*

Once you've saved the alert, simply refresh the report. If any order amounts in the report exceed $5,000, you'll receive an alert dialog box indicating that the alert has been triggered.

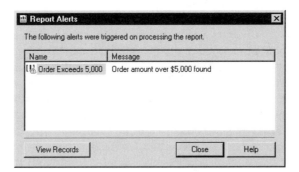

To see a separate tab showing all report records with orders that exceed $5,000, just click the View Records button. A separate tab (similar to a drill-down tab, discussed in Chapters 3 and 8) will appear showing just the relevant records.

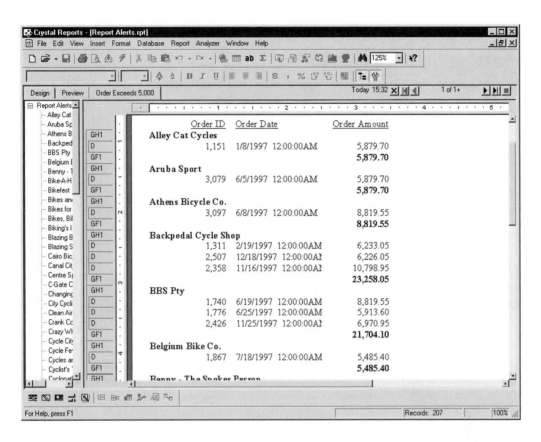

You don't have to just base Report Alerts on database fields, as in the previous example. You can also base report alerts on summary or subtotals in group footers (although you can't base Report Alerts on WhilePrintingRecords or "second pass" formulas). For example, you may prefer to create a parameter field (discussed in Chapter 12) to prompt the user for a customer total threshold. You can then create a Report Alert that will be triggered if an order subtotal in a customer name group footer exceeds the value supplied by the parameter field. In this situation, the Boolean formula used to trigger the alert will look something like this:

```
Sum ({Orders.Order Amount}, {Customer.Customer Name}) >
{?Report Alert Threshold}
```

Basing Report Formulas or Conditional Formatting on Report Alerts

While a dialog box showing that a Report Alert has been triggered, and the ability to view a separate tab of report items that triggered the alert, you may appreciate the additional power afforded to your formulas by Report Alerts as well. Three new functions have been added to the formula language in Crystal Reports 8.5 to support alerts: *IsAlertEnabled*, *IsAlertTriggered*, and *AlertMessage*. Each of these new functions takes one parameter, the name of a previously created report alert:

- **IsAlertEnabled**   Returns a true or false value, depending on the state of the Enabled check box in the Create Alert dialog box (shown in Figure 7-8, earlier in the chapter). If the alert is enabled, then this function will return true. Otherwise, it will return false.

- **IsAlertTriggered**   Returns a true or false value, depending on whether the record the formula is evaluating for triggers the alert or not. For example, if you create a formula containing the IsAlertTriggered("Order Exceeds 5,000") function, the function will return true for records with order amounts greater than $5,000, and false for records with order amounts equal to or less than $5,000.

- **AlertMessage**   Returns the message specified for the Report Alert. This is either the "hard-coded" message that was typed into the Message text box when the alert was created, or the results of the message string formula that was created with the alert.

For the previously discussed customer subtotal example, you may wish to create a formula that displays a message in group footers that trigger the alert. The formula might look similar to this:

```
If IsAlertTriggered ("Beat 1997 Goal") Then
    GroupName ({Customer.Customer Name}) & " beat the 1997 goal"
```

And, you might wish to highlight the entire group footer with a different background color if the group triggered a Report Alert. You can use these new formula functions in conditional formatting formulas, as well as report formulas. For example, you could conditionally set the background color of the Customer Name Group Footer to aqua by using the Section Expert. The conditional formula would be similar to this:

```
If IsAlertTriggered ("Beat 1997 Goal") Then crAqua Else crNoColor
```

Note   *For complete information on formatting sections and the Section Expert, refer to Chapter 8.*

Chapter 8

Using Sections
and Areas

In previous chapters you learned how to change the appearance of individual objects on the report, such as changing the color of a field or adding a drop shadow to a text object. However, you also have the ability to format *entire sections* of your report. Just a few of the section formatting options available to you are

- Add a gray background to every other details section
- Format a group header so every group starts anew on its own page
- Create multiple columns in your details section for labels
- Add a light-colored watermark graphic in its own page header section that appears behind the rest of your report

Formatting Sections with the Section Expert

There are several ways to change the appearance of an entire report section. You'll often just want to change the *size* of a section. Consider this "single-spaced" report:

Customer Name	City	Region	Last Year's Sales
City Cyclists	Sterling Heights	MI	$19,426.76
Pathfinders	Allenspark	CO	$42,601.14
Bike-A-Holics Anonymous	Blacklick	OH	$18,708.52
Psycho-Cycle	Huntsville	AL	$66,791.39
Sporting Wheels Inc.	San Diego	CA	$61,767.84
Rockshocks for Jocks	Austin	TX	$41,443.97
Poser Cycles	Eden Prairie	MN	$21,812.40

Notice the details sections appearing very close to each other. Maybe you'll just want to "double-space" the report. However, there is no double-space, space-and-a-half, or any similar function available in Crystal Reports. Instead, you choose how tall you want a section to be by using one of several techniques.

The simplest technique is simply to drag the bottom border of a section down to make the section taller. Point to the line at the bottom of the section you want to resize—the mouse cursor will turn into two lines with up and down arrows. This section-sizing cursor indicates that you can drag the section border down to make a section taller, or drag the border up to make the section shorter.

By simply making the details section taller, the white space that's exposed becomes the "double-space" when you re-preview the report, as shown here:

Customer Name	City	Region	Last Year's Sales
City Cyclists	Sterling Heights	MI	$19,426.76
Pathfinders	Allenspark	CO	$42,601.14
Bike-A-Holics Anonymous	Blacklick	OH	$18,708.52
Psycho-Cycle	Huntsville	AL	$66,791.39

Although this is the most straightforward way to resize a section, you have other options available. By right-clicking in the gray section name on the left side of the Design tab, you display the section pop-up menu. For example, right-clicking the Details section brings up this menu:

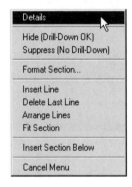

This pop-up menu contains four additional features for resizing sections, as listed here:

Insert Line   Adds an additional horizontal guideline to the section ruler on the left side of the section. If the section isn't tall enough to show the additional guideline, the section grows taller.

Delete Last Line   Removes the bottom guideline in the section and shrinks the size of the section proportionally. If you choose this option and there is no more room to shrink the section because of the objects in the section, you'll receive an error message.

Arrange Lines   Rearranges any horizontal guidelines in an even fashion. If there aren't enough horizontal guidelines to fill the section, additional guidelines will be added.

Fit Section   Automatically shrinks the size of the section to the bottommost object in the section. If there are any horizontal guidelines below the bottom object, they are removed before the section is resized.

Although you may sometimes use the Insert Line, Delete Last Line, or Arrange Lines options from the section pop-up menu, you'll most likely find Fit Section the only useful option. It's particularly useful if the section is very large (perhaps you've deleted a large map, chart, or picture from the section and all the white space it took up is still there), and you want to shrink it without having to scroll down to find the bottom section border.

The Section Expert

Whereas the Format Editor is used to format individual objects, you use the *Section Expert,* shown in Figure 8-1, to format entire sections of your report. The Section Expert has a surprising number of options for formatting individual report sections. Using these options provides a new level of flexibility for your reports.

The Section Expert can be displayed in several ways. You can click the Section Expert button on the Standard toolbar, choose Format | Section from the pull-down menus, or right-click in the gray area of the section you wish to format and choose Format Section

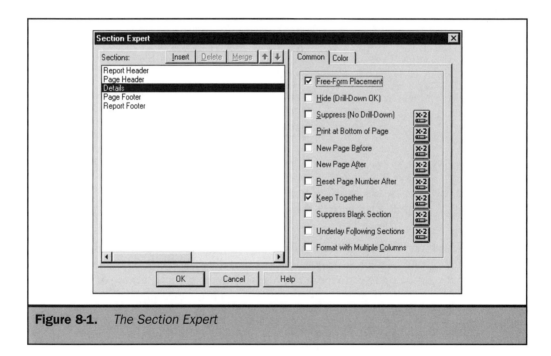

Figure 8-1.   *The Section Expert*

from the pop-up menu. If you choose the toolbar button or menu option, the first section will be highlighted in the Section Expert. If you right-click in the gray area of a section and use the pop-up menu, that particular section will be highlighted.

By selecting different sections of the report in the Section Expert, you can view and set formatting properties for the section. Note that the properties will vary slightly, and some won't be available, depending on which section you select. For example, the New Page Before property doesn't make much sense for a page header section, so it will be grayed out when a page header is selected. Table 8-1 explains the different section formatting properties available in the Section Expert's Common tab.

Caution   *Don't confuse the Keep Together section property and the Keep Group Together group property in the Change Group dialog box. Keep Together in the Section Expert just prevents the particular section from splitting over two pages; whereas Keep Group Together will attempt to keep the group header, all details sections, and the group footer for the same group from printing across multiple pages.*

Property	Function
Free-Form Placement	Allows objects to be moved freely throughout the section without snapping to horizontal guidelines. If turned off, horizontal guidelines are added to the left of the section and objects snap to them when moved.
Hide (Drill-Down OK)	Hides a section and all objects in it. However, if the section is within a higher-level group and that group is drilled into, this section *will* appear in the drill-down tab.
Suppress (No Drill-Down)	Suppresses a section and all objects in it. If the section is within a higher-level group and that group is drilled into, this section *will not* appear in the drill-down tab, even though a drill-down tab will appear.

Table 8-1.   *Section Expert Common Tab Formatting Properties*

Property	Function
Print at Bottom of Page	Prints the section at the bottom of the page. Typically used for invoices, statements, or other similar reports that require a group footer with a total to print at the bottom of the page, regardless of how many details sections print above it.
New Page Before	Starts a new page before printing this section. Useful in a group header if you want each group to start on its own page.
New Page After	Starts a new page after printing this section. Useful in a group footer if you want the next group to start on its own page.
Reset Page Number After	Resets the page number back to 1 after printing this section. Useful in a group footer if you want each group to have its own set of page numbers, regardless of the total number of pages on the report. Also resets the Total Page Count field.
Keep Together	Prevents Crystal Reports from putting a page break in the middle of this section. For example, this would avoid having the first few lines of a multiple-line details section appearing on the bottom of one page and the last few lines appearing on the next page.
Suppress Blank Section	Suppresses the entire section if all the objects inside it are blank. Useful in situations where you want to avoid white gaps appearing in your report if all the objects in a section have been conditionally suppressed or suppressed "if duplicated."
Underlay Following Sections	Prints the section, and then all following sections print right on top of the section. Useful for printing maps, charts, or pictures alongside data or underneath the following sections.
Format with Multiple Columns	Creates multiple newspaper- or phonebook-style columns. The Layout tab will appear when this property is checked. This is only available when the details section is chosen.

Table 8-1.   *Section Expert Common Tab Formatting Properties* (continued)

You'll also notice Conditional Formula buttons for many properties on the Common tab. These properties can be set conditionally with a Boolean formula, if necessary. There are many uses for both absolute and conditional properties on the Common tab. Here are some common examples.

Starting a Group on Its Own Page

Checking New Page Before in a group header or New Page After in a group footer (but not both) will cause each group to start on a new page. There is one problem with setting this property absolutely—you can end up with "stranded" pages. If you set New Page Before on a group header, you'll often encounter a stranded first page, because the report header will print and Crystal Reports will skip to the next page before printing the first group header. Conversely, if you set New Page After on a group footer, you'll often encounter a stranded last page, because the last group footer will be followed by a page break before the report footer prints.

To avoid these pitfalls, you can set the New Page Before or New Page After properties conditionally. To avoid a stranded first page, you can use a conditional formula to set the New Page Before property only on the second and subsequent groups—the first group will stay on the first page with the report header. Since the first group header will print at the same time the first record is printing, you can use the following Boolean conditional formula for New Page Before:

```
Not OnFirstRecord
```

To avoid a stranded last page, you want a new page after every group footer *except the last one*. Since the last group footer will only occur on the last record of the report, you can use this conditional formula for New Page After:

```
Not OnLastRecord
```

Printing an Invoice Total at the Bottom of the Page

You may be creating invoices grouped by invoice number, or statements grouped by customer number. You want the invoice or statement total, located in the group footer, to print at the bottom of the page, regardless of how many details records print. Crystal Reports' normal behavior is to print the group footer immediately following the last details record. If there are only a few invoice items or statement lines, the total will print high up the page, right after the last details line. If you want the total to print at the bottom of the page in this situation, check the Print at Bottom of Page property for the group footer.

Starting Page Numbers Over for Each New Group

You might have a large report grouped by department that you want to "burst" apart and distribute to each individual department. Initially, you'll want to make sure to use

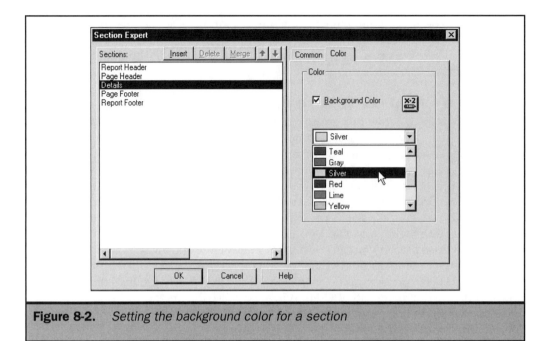

Figure 8-2. *Setting the background color for a section*

the New Page Before property with the group header or the New Page After property with the group footer so that you won't ever have the end of one department appearing on the same page as the beginning of the next.

However, you also don't want to confuse those who may look at page numbers on later groups in the report. Even though a page may be the first one for the IT department, it will probably have a much larger page number than 1. Simply check the Reset Page Number After property for the department group footer. Page numbers will then start over at 1 for each department.

Changing Color for Entire Sections

The Color tab in the Section Expert, shown in Figure 8-2, lets you change the background color for an entire section, separate from any color formatting that individual objects in the section may have.

If you check the Background Color property, you can then choose from various colors in the pull-down list below it. This will set the background color for the entire section. This lets you highlight entire sections with different colors, if you choose—for example, a report with the group footer section showing a different background color:

2805	Rad Bikes	Tualatin	OR	3/9/1998	$1,739.05	UPS
2839	Craze Cycle	Tualatin	OR	3/2?/1998	$1,739.85	Pickup
2866	Whistler Rentals	Tualatin	OR	3/28/1998	$845.55	FedEx
2894	Our Wheels Follow Us Ev	DeKalb	OR	4/6/1998	$32.73	FedEx
2914	Rad Bikes	Tualatin	OR	4/14/1998	$373.35	Pickup
2939	Whistler Rentals	Tualatin	OR	4/18/1998	$2,084.59	Loomis
2940	Our Wheels Follow Us Ev	DeKalb	OR	4/18/1998	$161.70	UPS
2959	Craze Cycle	Tualatin	OR	4/2?/1998	$959.70	Parcel Po
2968	Craze Cycle	Tualatin	OR	4/25/1998	$43.44	FedEx
2989	Craze Cycle	Tualatin	OR	5/1/1998	$238.63	FedEx

Subtotal: $617,204.64

Southwest
 CA
1026	Tyred Out	Santa Ana	CA	12/?/1996	$33.00	Pickup
1059	Off the Mountain Biking	Irvine	CA	12/?2/1996	$364.67	Pickup
1065	Tyred Out	Santa Ana	CA	12/?3/1996	$1,275.70	UPS

Notice the Conditional Formula button on the Color tab. This lets you set the background color conditionally, which can be helpful if you want to base a background color on some particular condition.

The location of the Conditional Formula button on the Color tab may confuse you. Since it's located next to the Background Color check box, you may think it requires a Boolean formula to set the Background Color property. In fact, it conditionally sets the background color itself with an If-Then-Else formula.

Creating a "Banded" Report

Mainframe reports often were printed on "green bar" or "blue bar" paper with alternating shades of color and white. This was designed to make columns of numbers easy to follow across the page. Now that many PC-based reports are printed by laser printers on plain paper, you must create your own "banded" reports if your reports would benefit from this kind of look.

Simply giving the details section a silver background color isn't visually appealing, as shown here:

2712	Alley Cat Cycles	Concord	MA	2/12/1998	$1,619.74	Parcel Post
2735	Alley Cat Cycles	Concord	MA	2/19/1998	$8,819.55	Parcel Post
2753	Alley Cat Cycles	Concord	MA	2/24/1998	$1,619.55	UPS
2788	Alley Cat Cycles	Concord	MA	3/5/1998	$1,085.40	Loomis
2797	Alley Cat Cycles	Concord	MA	3/7/1998	$959.70	UPS
2898	Alley Cat Cycles	Concord	MA	4/9/1998	$1,000.96	Parcel Post

31 orders   Subtotal: $54,565.39

Backpedal Cycle Shop
1222	Backpedal Cycle Shop	Philadelphia	PA	1/23/1997	$6,116.82	UPS
1327	Backpedal Cycle Shop	Philadelphia	PA	2/22/1997	$3,479.70	Pickup
1429	Backpedal Cycle Shop	Philadelphia	PA	3/16/1997	$2,294.55	Parcel Post
1498	Backpedal Cycle Shop	Philadelphia	PA	4/7/1997	$49.50	Pickup
1550	Backpedal Cycle Shop	Philadelphia	PA	4/20/1997	$973.98	Parcel Post

However, setting every other details section to silver provides a good way to help report readers follow columns of material across the page. You can set the background color conditionally to accomplish this. Use the following conditional formula:

```
If Remainder(RecordNumber,2) = 0 Then Silver Else NoColor
```

This uses several built-in Crystal Reports functions. The Remainder function takes two arguments, the numerator and the denominator. It divides the numerator by the denominator, but returns the *remainder* of the division operation, not the result of the division. The RecordNumber built-in function simply counts records consecutively, starting at 1. Therefore, *every other* record number, when divided by 2, will return 0 as the remainder. This will alternate the details section background color for every record.

D	.	2712	Alley Cat Cycles	Concord	MA	2/12/1998	$1,619.74	Parcel Post
D	.	2735	Alley Cat Cycles	Concord	MA	2/19/1998	$8,819.55	Parcel Post
D	_	2753	Alley Cat Cycles	Concord	MA	2/24/1998	$1,619.55	UPS
D	.	2788	Alley Cat Cycles	Concord	MA	3/5/1998	$1,085.40	Loomis
D	.	2797	Alley Cat Cycles	Concord	MA	3/7/1998	$959.70	UPS
D	∞	2898	Alley Cat Cycles	Concord	MA	4/9/1998	$1,000.96	Parcel Post
GF1	.		31 orders			Subtotal:	$54,565.39	
GH1	_							
		Backpedal Cycle Shop						
D	.	1222	Backpedal Cycle Shop	Philadelphia	PA	1/23/1997	$6,116.82	UPS
D	.	1327	Backpedal Cycle Shop	Philadelphia	PA	2/22/1997	$3,479.70	Pickup
D	N	1429	Backpedal Cycle Shop	Philadelphia	PA	3/16/1997	$2,294.55	Parcel Post
D	.	1498	Backpedal Cycle Shop	Philadelphia	PA	4/7/1997	$49.50	Pickup
D	.	1550	Backpedal Cycle Shop	Philadelphia	PA	4/20/1997	$973.98	Parcel Post

You can make modifications to this formula to shade more than just every other line. If you want *every two* lines shaded, you could change the formula slightly:

```
If Remainder(RecordNumber,4) In [1,2] Then Silver Else NoColor
```

This divides the record number by 4 and checks for remainders of 1 or 2. This will be true for every two records. The result is shown here:

D	.	2735	Alley Cat Cycles	Concord	MA	2/19/1998	$8,819.55	Parcel Post
D	_	2753	Alley Cat Cycles	Concord	MA	2/24/1998	$1,619.55	UPS
D	.	2788	Alley Cat Cycles	Concord	MA	3/5/1998	$1,085.40	Loomis
D	.	2797	Alley Cat Cycles	Concord	MA	3/7/1998	$959.70	UPS
D	∞	2898	Alley Cat Cycles	Concord	MA	4/9/1998	$1,000.96	Parcel Post
GF1	.		31 orders			Subtotal:	$54,565.39	
GH1	_							
		Backpedal Cycle Shop						
D	.	1222	Backpedal Cycle Shop	Philadelphia	PA	1/23/1997	$6,116.82	UPS
D	.	1327	Backpedal Cycle Shop	Philadelphia	PA	2/22/1997	$3,479.70	Pickup
D	N	1429	Backpedal Cycle Shop	Philadelphia	PA	3/16/1997	$2,294.55	Parcel Post
D	.	1498	Backpedal Cycle Shop	Philadelphia	PA	4/7/1997	$49.50	Pickup
D	.	1550	Backpedal Cycle Shop	Philadelphia	PA	4/20/1997	$973.98	Parcel Post

You probably get the general idea of how this works. You can now modify the formula in any number of ways to change the way background shading works.

Tip   *When setting the background color of a section, as well as background colors for individual objects, you may want to use NoColor instead of White to indicate a normal color. By using White, you will have solid white colors that can sometimes look unpleasant in combination with other solid colors. If you use NoColor, you often achieve a certain amount of transparency that will look better when mixing colors on the report.*

Creating Summary and Drill-Down Reports

A *details report* shows every individual details record in the database. This may often be preferable for certain listings or smaller transaction-type reports. Often, however, a viewer will only want to see subtotals, counts, averages, or other summary information for certain groups on the report. The details information used to arrive at those summaries isn't as important. This calls for a *summary report*.

In its simplest form, a summary report is a report with one or more groups with the details section hidden or suppressed. Consider Figure 8-3, a details report of orders, grouped by customer.

This shows every order for the customer, with an order count and order amount subtotal appearing in the group footer. While this may be useful for a report viewer

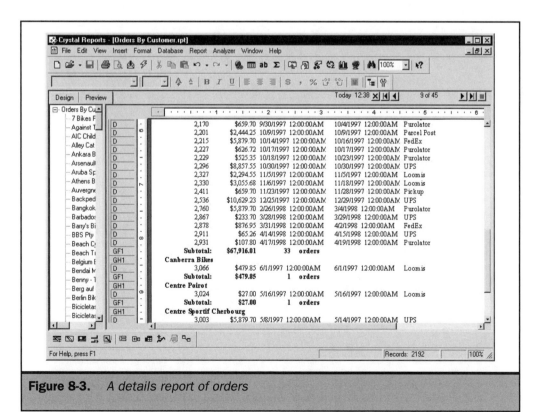

Figure 8-3.   *A details report of orders*

concerned about individual orders, the sales manager or account representative may often just be interested in the summary information for each customer. All the order details just get in the way of their analysis.

In this case, simply hiding or suppressing the details section will create a much more meaningful report for these viewers. You can hide or suppress the details section from the Section Expert. As a shortcut, there are Hide and Suppress options available right in the section pop-up menu, as well. Just right-click the gray details section name at the left of the Design tab and choose Hide (Drill-Down OK) or Suppress (No Drill-Down) from the pop-up menu.

The details section will simply disappear from the Preview tab, while the group header and footer still show up. Figure 8-4 shows the resulting summary report, which is much more succinct and meaningful to a viewer looking at the big picture.

If you later want to change your report back to a details report, you need to have the details section reappear. Just display the Section Expert by using the toolbar button or pull-down menu option. Select the details section and turn off the Hide or Suppress property. You can also display the Design tab and right-click the gray area to the left of the screen where the details section is hidden or suppressed. To redisplay the details section, choose the opposite of the Suppress or Hide option you initially set.

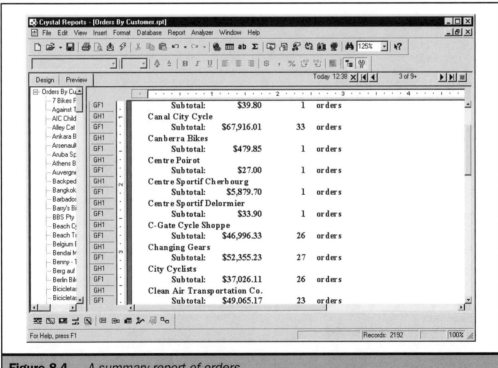

Figure 8-4.   *A summary report of orders*

| Tip |

You can choose how a hidden or suppressed section appears in the Design tab. Choose File | Options from the pull-down menus and look for the Show Hidden Sections in Design option on the Layout tab. If this is checked (the default), hidden or suppressed sections will still appear in the Design tab, but they will have gray shading. If you turn this option off, they will only show the bottom border of the hidden or suppressed section in the Design tab.

Choosing whether to hide or suppress a section determines whether or not you want a report viewer to drill down into the section (discussed next). Also, note that the Suppress property can be conditionally set in the Section Expert, while the Hide property cannot.

Drill-Down Reports

One of the most powerful features of an online reporting tool like Crystal Reports is interactive reporting. You may be creating a report to distribute to a large audience via a Web page in Crystal Enterprise (covered in Part II), or as part of a custom Windows application (covered in Part III). A truly useful report will initially present viewers with higher-level summary or total information. If the viewer sees a number or other characteristic of the report that interests them, you want them to be able to drill down into just that particular area.

| Note |

Drill-down is an interactive feature only applicable to viewers looking at a Crystal Report in its "native" format. Drill-down isn't available in any reports exported to another format, such as Word or Excel. And, obviously, drill-down isn't a feature that applies to reports printed on paper!

In its simplest form, a drill-down report can be created by hiding the details section (hence, the Drill-Down OK notation alongside the Hide property) in a report that has one or more groups. When you point at the group name field, or a subtotal or summary object in a group header or footer, you'll notice your mouse cursor change to a magnifying glass, or *drill-down cursor*. When you double-click, a separate drill-down tab will appear, showing the group header, footer, and details sections for that group. You can then navigate to the main Preview tab to see the summary report, or back to individual drill-down tabs to see the details information. You can double-click in the Preview tab as many times as you want in order to create additional drill-down tabs.

More complicated drill-down reports can be created by using multiple levels of grouping, along with creative use of section hiding. Figure 8-5 shows a drill-down report containing a details section and three groups: country, region, and city. Initially the report just shows countries and their totals. If you drill down on a country, you'll find region subtotals for that country. Drilling down on a region will show city totals. And finally, drilling down on a city total will show individual orders placed from that city.

The Group tree shows the drill-down hierarchy

Click to print the contents of the current tab

Click the Design, Preview, or any drill-down tab to display it

Moves among the tabs, if there are too many to display at once

Closes the current drill-down tab and displays the tab to the left

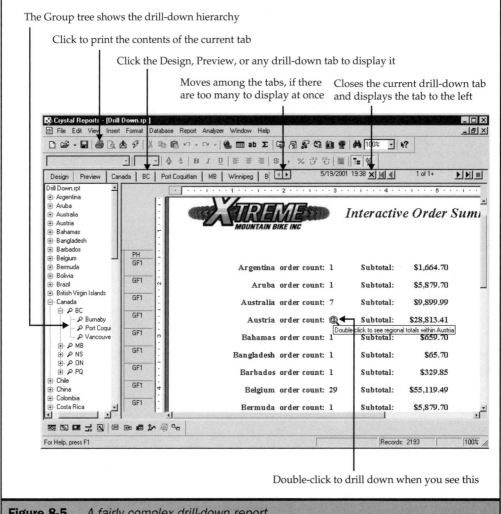

Double-click to drill down when you see this

Figure 8-5. *A fairly complex drill-down report*

Tip *Make note of the Show All Headers on Drill Down option. By turning this option on (it's off by default), your report will display all higher levels of group headers when you drill into a group, instead of showing just the previous level of group headers. Choose this option for the current report only by selecting File | Report Options. To choose the option for all new reports in the future, set the option on the Reporting tab after choosing File | Options.*

If you're interacting with a report, it's important to remember what will print or export if you click the Print button on the Standard toolbar, or choose File | Print from the pull-down menus. Only what's shown in the current drill-down tab (or Preview tab) will print or export. If you want to just print one drill-down tab, choose the drill-down tab and then click the Print button. If you want to print all the summary information in the main Preview tab, make sure it's selected before you print or export. If you want to print or export both summary and details information *in the same report,* you must either display the details section and print from the Preview tab, or create a separate report more appropriate for printing.

Using Tool Tip text can help a viewer determine what will happen when they double-click an object. By creating a string formula with the Tool Tip text Conditional Formula button in the Format Editor, you can give a viewer more information about what the object contains. The tool tip illustrated in Figure 8-5 comes from the following Tool Tip text Conditional Formula added to the summary field in the Country group footer:

```
"Double-click to see regional totals within " +
    GroupName ({Customer.Country})
```

Creative Use of Column Headings and Group Headers in Drill-Down Reports

If you leave Crystal Reports' default column headings in the page header and simply hide or suppress lower-level group headers in your drill-down reports, you may get undesirable results when the viewer sees the initial Preview tab.

Column Heading Problems   The first problem will be the appearance of column headings in the Preview tab above the first group header, but with no matching details records. But, when you eventually drill down to the details level, the page header won't appear, so the viewer won't see the column headings.

There are two ways of resolving this problem, depending on how many levels of grouping exist on the report. If you only have one level of grouping, perform the following steps:

1. Move the column headings from the page header to the group header, either above or below the group name field (or remove the group name field altogether), depending on how you want the drill-down tab to appear.

2. Copy the group name field from the group header into the group footer.

3. Hide the group header along with the details section.

This way, the summary report will just show one line per group until you drill down. Then, the group header (containing the column headings) will appear inside the drill-down tab, along with the details sections.

However, if you have more than one level of grouping, the previous technique won't work properly—you'll see the column headings appear over and over again at the last group level. In this case, use this approach:

1. Create a second details section (Details b) and move the column headings into it.

2. Swap Details b and Details a so that the column headings are on top of the details section that contains database fields.

3. Select the text objects that comprise the column headings. You may multi-select them with CTRL-click or an elastic box. Using the Format Editor, choose the Suppress if Duplicated formatting option.

4. Using the Section Expert, choose the Suppress Blank Section formatting option for Details a.

This technique, while a little more time-consuming, provides perfect results. When the lowest level of grouping appears, there will be no column headings (because they've been moved to the details section). But, when you drill down to the details level, the column headings only show up once at the top of the drill-down tab, because of the Suppress if Duplicated/Suppress Blank Section formatting combinations.

Repeating Group Headers   If you simply choose the Hide (Drill-Down OK) formatting option on group header sections, your report may suffer from extra sets of group headers that appear when you drill down. For example, if you drill down into a country group to see all the regions within the country, the region group header will print before every group footer. To solve this problem, you may try to suppress the region group header so that it will never show up. However, when you then drill into a region group to see cities within the region, the region group header won't print at the top of the list of cities.

In theory, you'd like the region group header to show up when you've drilled into the region group to see cities, but *not* show up when you're looking at the region group at its summary level. But, what conditional formula can you use to suppress the region group header so that it only shows up when there isn't a country group header there as well?

There is an advanced technique available to solve this problem, using one or more formulas that contain variables. By setting the variable in the higher-level group header, and using the value of the variable to conditionally suppress the lower-level group header, you can achieve the results you need. While this is even more work than the earlier techniques that deal with column headings, this process will allow you the ultimate control over your report behavior when the viewer drills down.

Look at the Drill Down.RPT sample report on the book's companion CD to see examples of these drill-down techniques.

Multiple-Column Reports for Labels and Listings

Crystal Reports is designed to replace much of the repetitive printing that you may have used a word processor for in the past. Immediate uses include form letters and mailing labels. You can also use the multicolumn feature of Crystal Reports to create newspaper-style columns in your reports. If you have just a few fields that you'd like to print in columnar form, the Section Expert provides the necessary section formatting.

To create mailing labels in Crystal Reports, click the Mail Label Expert button in the Report Gallery when first creating a new report. This brings up the Mailing Labels Report Expert, shown in Figure 8-6, which takes you step by step through the process of choosing the table and fields that make up your mailing label, and choosing from a predefined list of continuous-feed and laser printer labels.

Since there is no similar expert for creating newspaper-style reports, you have to create such reports using the Custom option and the Section Expert. Recall from Table 8-1 one of the Section Expert's formatting properties, Format with Multiple Columns. This property is only available for the details section—it won't even appear in the Section Expert if you have any other section selected. Once you check this property, the Layout tab appears in the Section Expert, as shown in Figure 8-7.

On the Layout tab, you determine the specifics of the columns you want to create. Although you might expect to see a "number of columns" setting, this is actually determined by page margins (set with File | Page Setup), the width of the details section, and the

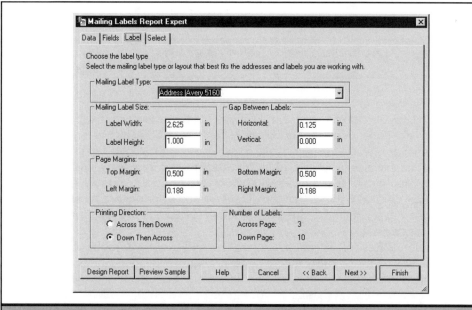

Figure 8-6.   *Creating mailing labels with a report expert*

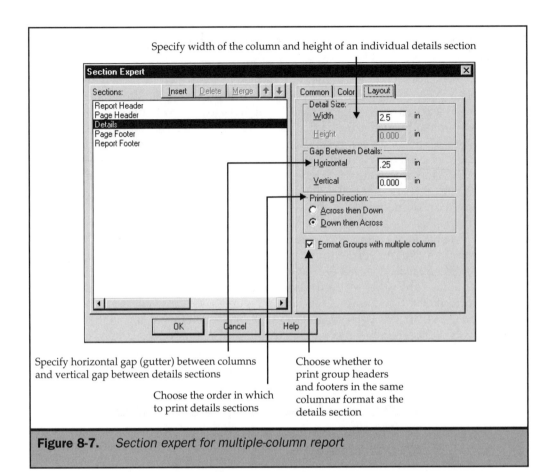

Specify width of the column and height of an individual details section

Specify horizontal gap (gutter) between columns and vertical gap between details sections

Choose the order in which to print details sections

Choose whether to print group headers and footers in the same columnar format as the details section

Figure 8-7.   *Section expert for multiple-column report*

horizontal gap between details. For example, if you have quarter-inch margins with standard letter-size paper in portrait orientation, you'll have 8 full inches of printable space. If you choose a details-size width of 2.5 inches and a horizontal gap of a quarter inch, you'll have three evenly spaced columns with a quarter inch on all sides.

When you choose to format the details section with multiple columns, the Design tab changes slightly. You'll notice that the details section's bottom border shrinks to equal the width you set in the Layout tab. The other sections of the report retain the full width of the page.

The exception to this rule occurs when you check the Format Groups with Multiple Column check box on the Layout tab. In this case, all group headers and footers take on the same width as the details section. This can make a marked difference in the appearance of your report, depending on the size of your groups. As a general rule, not formatting groups with multiple columns will cause smaller groups to print only in one column on the left side of the page. Usually, the only small groups that print across multiple columns are ones that start at the bottom of the page. Figure 8-8 shows the difference.

You'll typically experience more predictable behavior by formatting groups with multiple columns.

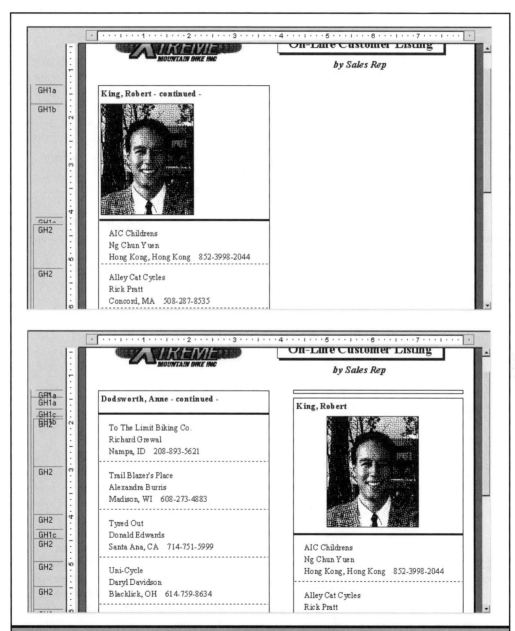

Figure 8-8.   *Report groups formatted without and with multiple columns*

Multicolumn reporting works fine when previewing your report online or when printing to a printer. Also, Crystal Reports 8.5 .PDF and HTML 4 (DHTML) exports support multicolumn reports. However, multiple columns may be lost when you export reports to other file formats. Perform a sample export with a simple multicolumn report to your desired file format before expending a great deal of effort on the report. That way you won't discover later that you don't get the desired results.

Using Multiple Sections

To be precise, the five default sections that first appear in a new report, and any additional group headers and footers that are added later, are referred to as *areas*, because Crystal Reports lets you create multiple occurrences of the same area, and each of these occurrences is called a *section*. Creating multiple sections can be accomplished from the Section Expert by using the pop-up menu that appears when you right-click in the gray area on the left side of the screen.

To insert an additional details section, for example, right-click in the details gray area on the left side of the Design tab and choose Insert Section Below from the pop-up menu. Or, from the Section Expert, select the area that you wish to duplicate and click the Insert button. You'll see the details area split into two sections: Details a and Details b. Once you've created multiple sections in an area, the pop-up menu, shown next, and Section Expert, shown in Figure 8-9, take on a great deal of additional capability.

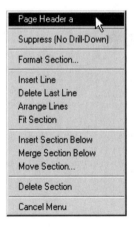

You can also rearrange the order in which sections appear right in the Design tab. Simply point to the gray section name on the left of the screen, hold down the mouse button, and drag the section you wish to move—the mouse cursor will change to a "hand." Drop the section in its new location in the same area. Although the section contents will swap, the consecutive lettering will not change—the first section will still be lettered a; the second, b; and so on.

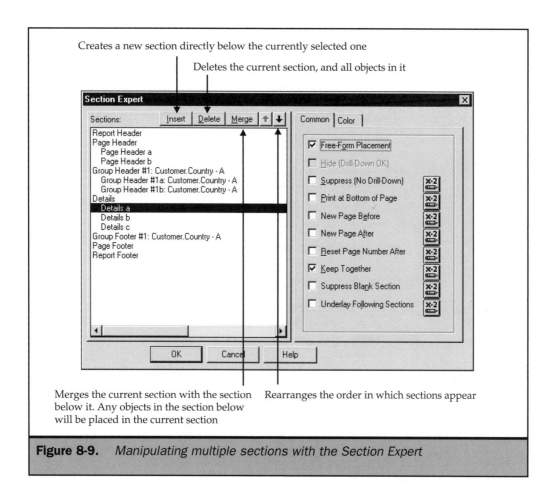

Creates a new section directly below the currently selected one

Deletes the current section, and all objects in it

Merges the current section with the section below it. Any objects in the section below will be placed in the current section

Rearranges the order in which sections appear

Figure 8-9.   *Manipulating multiple sections with the Section Expert*

You can insert as many sections in an area as you wish—there can be Details a, b, c, d, and on and on (when Crystal Reports runs out of letters, it starts doubling them up, as in "Details ab"). Any area can be comprised of multiple sections. Nothing prevents you from having three report headers, five details sections, two group footer #1s, or any other combination.

Once you've created the multiple sections, you can add objects to any of the sections. You can even add the same object to some, or all, of them. When the report prints, the sections will simply print one right after the other, with the objects showing up one below the other. Probably the biggest question you have right now is "What's the benefit of multiple sections anyway? Everything just prints as though it were in one bigger section!"

Figure 8-10 is a great example of the benefit of multiple sections. This shows a form letter based on the Customer table from the sample XTREME.MDB database included

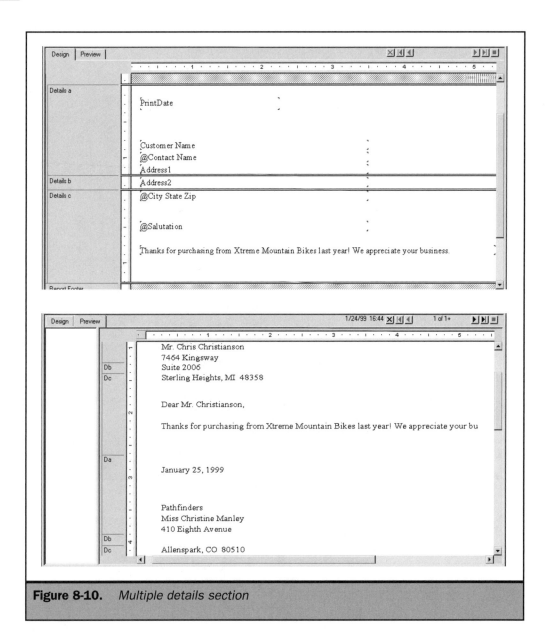

Figure 8-10. *Multiple details section*

with Crystal Reports. Notice that the letter consists of three different details sections. Details a contains the Print Date, Customer Name, and Address 1; Details b contains Address 2; and Details c contains the rest of the letter. When you preview the report, it just shows the details sections one on top of the other, as though everything is in one big details section.

But look at the letter for Pathfinders. Notice the empty line that appears when there is no Address 2 database field. This behavior, again, is identical to what you'd expect if you had put all the objects in one tall details section.

Here's the benefit: you may *conditionally suppress* individual sections—in this case, Details b—so that they appear or disappear according to your specifications. To eliminate the blank line that appears when there's nothing in Address 2, format Details b with Suppress Blank Section. If the objects contained in it all contain empty values (as is the case with Pathfinders), the section will not appear at all. You can also use the Conditional Formula button next to the Suppress property to suppress based on any condition you need.

> **Tip** *The more you work with areas and sections, the more you may notice the large amount of space the area and section names take up on the left side of the Design tab. If you wish to have more space for actual report objects, you can change the way Crystal Reports shows section names. Choose File | Options and check Show Short Section Names in Design on the Layout tab. "Report Header" will now be abbreviated "RH," "Page Header a" will become "PHa," and so on. You'll now have more room to work with actual report objects.*

Conditionally Suppressing Sections

You may think that conditional suppression is only useful when you have multiple sections. Actually, there may be times when you want to control the appearance of just a single section. Using the Conditional Formula button next to the Suppress property lets you supply a Boolean formula to determine when the section appears or doesn't appear. Consider the following examples.

Printing a Bonus Message for Certain Records

You are designing a list of orders by salesperson. You want a bonus message and a "lots o' money" graphic to appear below the order if it exceeds $2,500. However, if the order doesn't exceed the bonus level, you *don't* want the large blank space to appear where the graphic and message are located. If you just use the Format Editor to conditionally suppress the graphic and text object containing the message, they won't appear, but the empty space still will.

Simply create a Details b section and place the graphic and text object in it. Then, suppress Details b when the bonus isn't met, using the following conditional formula for the Suppress property:

```
{Orders.Order Amount} < 2500
```

Figure 8-11 shows the result.

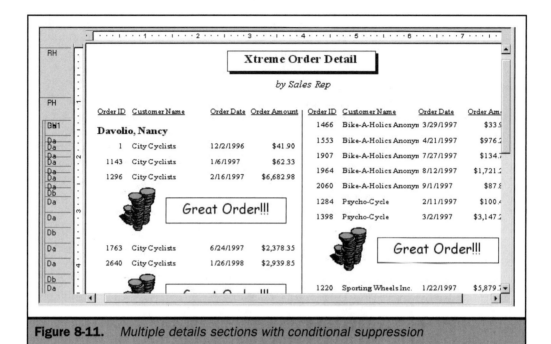

Figure 8-11.   *Multiple details sections with conditional suppression*

Printing a Different Page Header on Page 2 and Later

You may wish to print a title page or other large page header on page 1 of the report, perhaps containing a logo and large formatted title. However, on subsequent pages of the report, you want a less flashy header with smaller type and no graphic. You want column headings and the print date and time to show up on all pages of the report, including the first.

This presents a special reporting problem. The flashy page header can simply be put in the report header section. It will then appear only on the first page. However, if you put the smaller report title in the page header along with the column headings and other information, it will appear on page 1 along with the report header. You can use the Format Editor to suppress the object containing the smaller header, but then extra white space will appear on page 1.

The solution is to create a second page header section. Put the smaller report title in Page Header a and put the column headings and print date/time in Page Header b. Then, conditionally suppress Page Header b so that it won't show up on page 1. Here's the conditional formula, which uses the PageNumber built-in function:

```
PageNumber = 1
```

Printing Odd and Even Page Headers or Footers

You may be printing your report on a "duplex" laser printer that can print on both sides of the paper. Or, you may want to photocopy your report from one to two sides and place it in a three-ring binder or other bound format. Crystal Reports lets you create separate odd and even page headers and footers to add a real page-published look to your report.

Simply create separate Page Headers a and b (and, perhaps, Page Footers a and b). Place the appropriate material in each section and position it properly for odd/even appearance. Now, conditionally suppress the sections. The sections containing the material for odd page numbers will be suppressed for even page numbers with the following conditional formula:

```
Remainder(PageNumber,2) = 0
```

And, the sections containing the material for even page numbers will be suppressed for odd page numbers with the following conditional formula:

```
Remainder(PageNumber,2) = 1
```

These formulas use the PageNumber built-in function illustrated previously. In addition, they use the Remainder function, which will indicate whether a page number is even or odd (even page numbers divided by 2 return a remainder of 0, and odd page numbers return a remainder of 1, as explained earlier in the chapter).

Underlaying Sections

The Section Expert includes the Underlay Following Sections property. As described in Table 8-1, this property prints the underlaying section in its usual position, but prints the following sections right over the top. Initially, this may seem of limited usefulness. How readable will a report be if sections are printing right over the top of earlier sections?

Look at Figure 8-12 to get an idea. This report includes a large, light "Draft" graphic that has been placed in the page header. When Underlay Following Sections is checked for the page header in the Section Expert, all the other sections will print right over the top of the page header, creating the watermark effect.

If you want to include column headings in the page header, along with the watermark, you experience a problem. The watermark will be underlaid as you desire, but so will the column headings! The solution, as you might expect, is to add a Page Header b. Place the watermark graphic in one page header section and format it to Underlay Following Sections. Place the column headings in the other page header section and don't underlay it. Which page header you place the objects in will determine whether or not the column headings are underlaid. If you put the watermark in Page

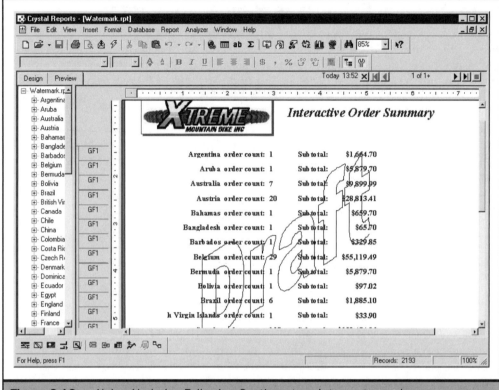

Figure 8-12. *Using Underlay Following Sections to print a watermark*

Header a (which is formatted to Underlay Following Sections) and the column headings in Page Header b (not underlaid), the watermark will underlay the column headings. If you choose the other way around, the column headings won't be underlaid.

Tip *When you underlay a section, all sections will print over the top of it, until Crystal Reports comes to its "companion" section, which will not underlay it. For example, if you underlay a page header, all sections will print on top until Crystal Reports gets to the matching page footer. If you underlay Group Header b, all other sections will print on top until the report hits Group Footer b, which will not be underlaid.*

You can also use the Underlay Following Sections feature to place maps or charts beside the data they refer to, rather than on top or bottom of the related data. Figure 8-13 shows a

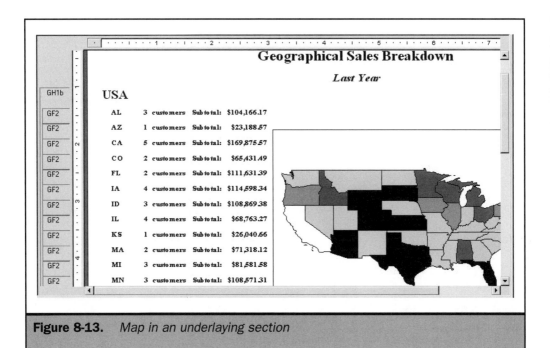

Figure 8-13.   *Map in an underlaying section*

report containing a map. Notice that the map appears alongside the data that the map refers to, rather than above. The map is still contained in the group header, but the map object has been moved to the right of the section, and the group header section is formatted to Underlay Following Sections.

Again, so that the USA Group Name field isn't also underlaid along with the map, it has been placed in a second group header, which is not underlaid.

Chapter 9

Analyzing with Cross-Tabs

D atabase report writers and spreadsheet programs are typically considered to be two completely separate products. The database report writer sorts and selects data very well, while the spreadsheet is great for analyzing, totaling, and trending in a compact row-and-column format. Crystal Reports provides a tool that, to a limited extent, brings the two features together: the *cross-tab object*. A cross-tab is a row-and-column object that looks similar to a spreadsheet. It summarizes data by using at least three fields in the database: a row field, a column field, and a summarized field. For each intersection of the row and column fields, the summarized field is aggregated (summed, counted, or subjected to some other type of calculation).

Consider two common summary reports. The first summary report shows total sales in dollars for each state in the United States. The second report shows total units sold by product type. If a marketing analyst wanted to combine these two reports together to more closely analyze both sales in dollars by state and units sold by product type, you would be limited in what you could offer with the standard grouped summary report.

You can create a report, similar to that shown in Figure 9-1 (initially grouped by state, and within state grouped by product type), that provides the information the analyst desires. But, if the analyst wanted to compare total mountain bikes sold in the country with total kid's bikes sold in the country, this report would make the process very difficult. Product type is the inner group, so there are no overall totals by it. Also,

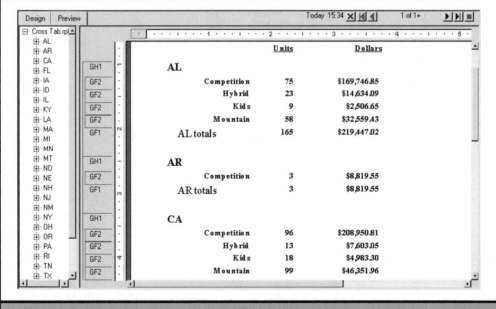

Figure 9-1. *Standard summary report with two groups*

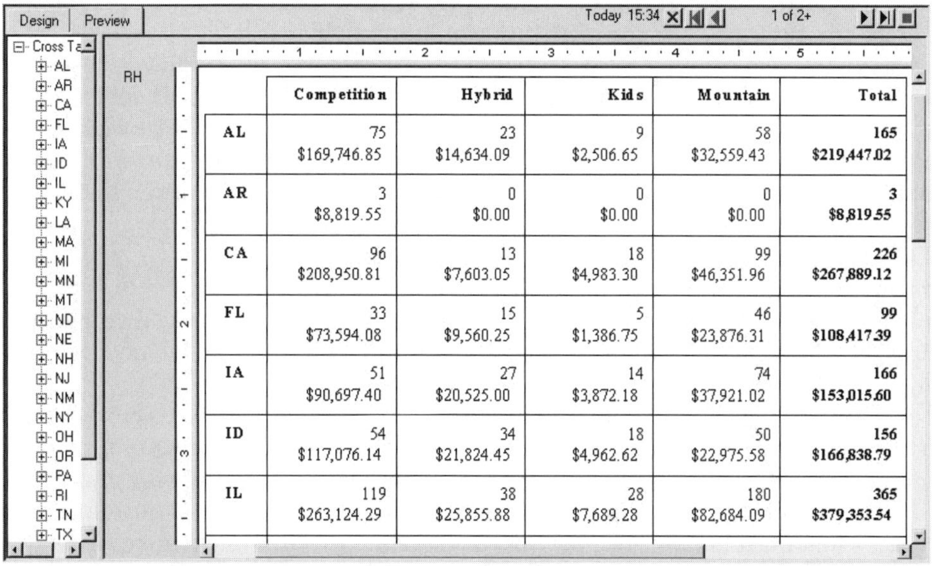

	Competition	Hybrid	Kids	Mountain	Total
AL	75 $169,746.85	23 $14,634.09	9 $2,506.65	58 $32,559.43	165 $219,447.02
AR	3 $8,819.55	0 $0.00	0 $0.00	0 $0.00	3 $8,819.55
CA	96 $208,950.81	13 $7,603.05	18 $4,983.30	99 $46,351.96	226 $267,889.12
FL	33 $73,594.08	15 $9,560.25	5 $1,386.75	46 $23,876.31	99 $108,417.39
IA	51 $90,697.40	27 $20,525.00	14 $3,872.18	74 $37,921.02	166 $153,015.60
ID	54 $117,076.14	34 $21,824.45	18 $4,962.62	50 $22,975.58	156 $166,838.79
IL	119 $263,124.29	38 $25,855.88	28 $7,689.28	180 $82,684.09	365 $379,353.54

Figure 9-2.   *Cross-tab showing units/dollars by region and by product type*

comparing Alabama totals with Vermont totals would be difficult, because they would be several pages apart on the report.

This scenario is a perfect example of where a cross-tab object would be useful. A cross-tab is a compact, row-and-column report that can compare subtotals and summaries by two or more different database fields. Whenever someone requests data to be shown by one thing and by another, it's a cross-tab candidate. Just listen for the "by this and by that" request. Figure 9-2 will probably be much more useful to the analyst.

Creating a Cross-Tab Object

When you look at a cross-tab, it's tempting to think of it as an entire report unto itself, much like an Excel spreadsheet is entirely independent. In fact, a cross-tab is just an object that resides in an existing report section. Even when you choose the Cross-Tab Expert from the Report Gallery, Crystal Reports just creates a cross-tab object and puts it in the report header. You can create more than one cross-tab per report, if you wish. In fact, you can even copy an existing cross-tab and put it in several different sections of the same report. It's just an object, like a text object, map, or database field.

A cross-tab can exist by itself on a report (as evidenced by the Cross-Tab Expert), or can be placed on a report that already contains fields in the details section, as well as one or more groups. The report can be completely functional in every respect before the cross-tab is added—the cross-tab just gets dropped in.

The first step in creating a cross-tab is to ensure that the tables you've chosen and linked for your report contain enough data to populate the cross-tab. If, for example, you want to look at order totals for the years 1995, 1996, 1997, and 1998 by state, make sure you choose tables that include the order amount, the year the order was placed, and the state of the customer who placed the order. While this may seem rather obvious, you may not have enough data to adequately populate your cross-tab if you don't think ahead carefully.

You may or may not want to use actual report fields as cross-tab fields. If the fields are already on the report, you can add them to the cross-tab object. Or, if you've added completely different fields to the report, you can still base the cross-tab on other fields that exist in the tables you chose when creating the report.

You can use the Cross-Tab Expert from the Report Gallery, or add a cross-tab to an existing report you've already created. To use the Cross-Tab Expert, simply choose it from the Report Gallery when creating a new report. Once you've chosen and linked the tables you want to make up your cross-tab report, click the Cross-Tab tab. The same three tabs that make up the Format Cross-Tab dialog box (discussed in more detail later in this chapter) will appear inside the Cross-Tab Expert.

If you've already created another report using another Expert or the Blank Report option, you may insert a cross-tab object whenever you want. To create a cross-tab object, it's best to select the Design tab first. Although you can place a cross-tab on the report in the Preview tab, you may not be able to accurately tell where it's being placed. In the Design tab, there's no question. Click the Insert Cross-Tab button on the Supplementary toolbar, or choose Insert | Cross-Tab from the pull-down menus. The Format Cross-Tab dialog box will appear, as shown in Figure 9-3.

The Format Cross-Tab dialog box has three tabs: Cross-Tab, Style, and Customize Style. The Cross-Tab tab is used to define the database fields or formulas that make up the cross-tab. The Style tab lets you choose a predefined formatting style for the cross-tab. And, the Customize Style tab displays a large number of custom formatting options to precisely control the appearance of the cross-tab.

The first step to creating a cross-tab is to define the fields that will make up the row, column, and summarized fields in the cross-tab. This is done with the Cross-Tab tab. Look through the Available Fields box to find the fields you want to use for the cross-tab's row and column fields. Just drag your chosen field from the Available Fields box and drop it on the Rows or Columns box. You can also select the field in the Available Fields box and click the Add Row or Add Column button.

Then, choose the field you want summarized in each *cell* (the intersection of each row and column). This will typically be a number or currency field, such as Quantity Sold or Order Amount, but it doesn't have to be. If you choose a number field, Crystal

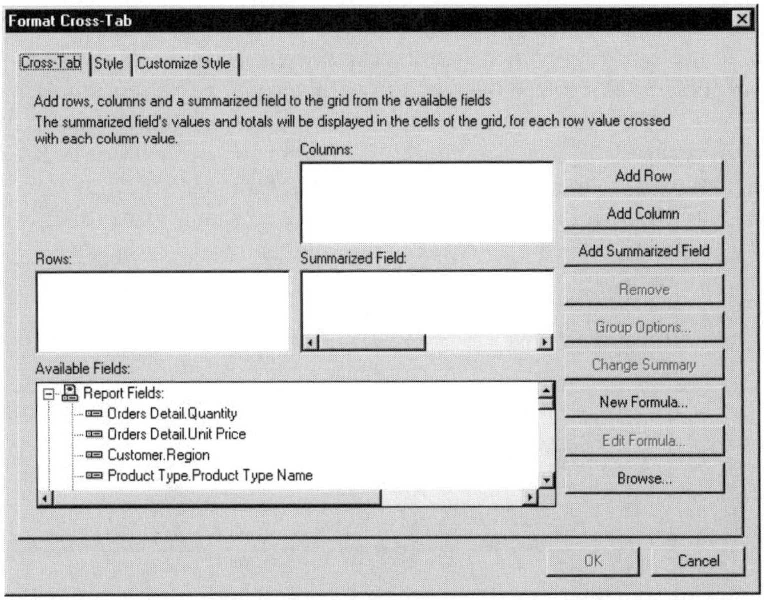

Figure 9-3.   *The Format Cross Tab dialog box*

Reports will subtotal the field for each cell. If you choose a field with another data type, a count of the number of occurrences of the field for each row/column combination will be shown. Drag the field to be summarized from the Available Fields box to the Summarized Field box, or select the field and click the Add Summarized Field button.

If you'd like to use an existing formula for a row, column, or summarized field, just select the formula in the Available Fields box. If you'd like to create a new formula or edit an existing formula before using it in the cross-tab, click the New Formula button or Edit Formula button, either of which launches the Formula Editor, where you can create or edit the formula. The formula will then appear in the Available Fields box, from which you can drag it to the Rows, Columns, or Summarized Field box.

If you're not concerned initially about doing any customized formatting for your cross-tab object, you're ready to place it on the report (formatting options on the other two tabs of the Format Cross-Tab dialog box are discussed later in the chapter). When you click OK on the Format Cross-Tab dialog box, you are returned to the report, with a small object attached to your mouse cursor. You can drop the cross-tab object in the report header or footer, or in a group header or footer. Cross-tabs can't be placed in the details section or in a page header or footer—you'll get a "no-drop" cursor (a circle with a line through it) if you try to position the cross-tab in these sections.

Drop the cross-tab below any other objects in the section, such as summaries, group names, or text objects. Although the cross-tab will appear relatively small in the Design tab, when you actually preview or print the report, the cross-tab will grow both horizontally and vertically to accommodate all of its rows and columns. If there are other objects below or to the right of the cross-tab, it will print right over the top of them. When you drop the cross-tab, the small object on the mouse cursor turns into a larger cross-tab object, showing a layout of the row, column, summarized field, and row and column totals.

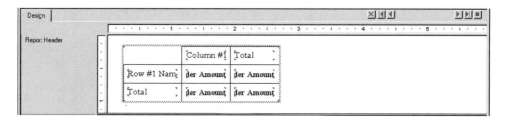

When you preview the report, Crystal Reports will cycle through the database several times to properly calculate the totals for all row and column combinations—you may note some extra time required to do this. The cross-tab will then appear in the section where you placed it.

	Argentina	Austria	Canada	France	Italy	Mexico
Competition	$57,616.33	$55,339.27	$233,640.81	$60,971.15	$79,756.29	$34,992.6
Gloves	$12,744.29	$5,425.03	$29,347.18	$7,019.81	$9,972.65	$5,999.6
Helmets	$27,136.42	$14,536.93	$55,633.80	$16,160.25	$28,640.44	$2,707.5

The section in which you place a cross-tab is critical in determining the data that the cross-tab will encompass. If you place a cross-tab in the report header or footer, only one occurrence of the cross-tab will appear on the report (remember, the report header and footer appear only once, at the beginning and end of the report, respectively). This cross-tab will encompass all the data on the report. If you place a cross-tab in a group header or footer, you get as many cross-tabs on your report as there are groups, each encompassing only data for that group.

Figure 9-4 shows a cross-tab using the XTREME.MDB sample database included with Crystal Reports. This cross-tab includes product names as the rows, and cities as the columns. Notice that all cities in all states show up in the cross-tab.

Contrast this with Figure 9-5, which is the exact same cross-tab object that's just been moved to a state group footer. Now there will be a cross-tab on the report for every state group, but each cross-tab will contain data only for that particular group. If you choose to, you can copy the cross-tab object between a group header or footer to the report header or footer and actually see cross-tabs for individual groups, as well as an all-encompassing cross-tab for the whole report.

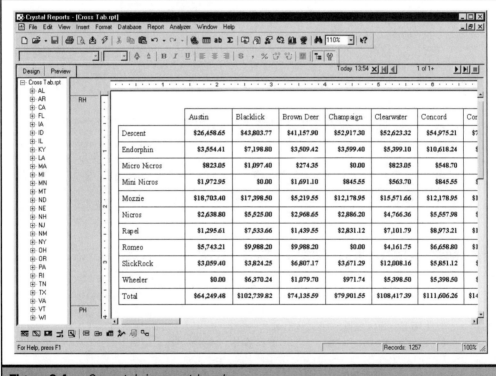

Figure 9-4. *Cross-tab in report header*

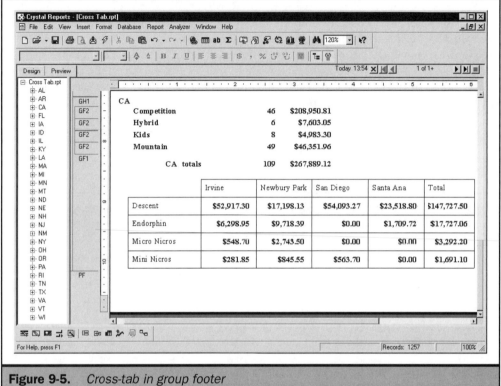

Figure 9-5.   *Cross-tab in group footer*

Editing an Existing Cross-Tab

After you create a cross-tab and drop it on your report, making changes to it is easy. You must first select the entire cross-tab object, not just one of its individual objects, by clicking either the small white space in the upper-left corner of the cross-tab (above the first row and to the left of the first column) or the grid lines between cells. You'll know you've selected the entire cross-tab if the status bar displays Cross-Tab: you can select the cross-tab in either the Design tab or the Preview tab.

After you select the cross-tab that you want to modify, choose Format | Cross-Tab from the pull-down menus, or right-click and choose Format Cross-Tab from the pop-up menu. This simply redisplays the Format Cross-Tab dialog box, allowing you to change row, column, or summarized fields on the Cross-Tab tab, or format the cross-tab with the Style tab or the Customize Style tab.

You can also *pivot* the cross-tab, which simply refers to swapping the rows and columns around so that what used to be the row will now be the column, and vice versa. Choose Format | Pivot Cross-Tab from the pull-down menus, or right-click the selected cross-tab object and choose Pivot Cross-Tab from the pop-up menu.

Creative Use of Grouping and Formulas

As discussed previously, Crystal Reports chooses a default calculation for the summarized field when it creates the cross-tab. If you choose a number or currency field for a summarized field, Crystal Reports will use the Sum function to subtotal the numbers in each cell. This typically is what you want for this type of field (for example, the total sales figure for Green Bikes in the USA). If you use any other type of field (string, date, Boolean, and so forth), Crystal Reports will automatically use the Count function to count the occurrences of the particular summarized field for each row/ column combination.

You are, however, completely free to change the function that Crystal Reports assigns to the summarized field. If you want to see the average sales figure in each cell instead of the total figure, it's easy to change. In either the Design or Preview tab, click the object in the cell (the intersection of the row and column). The status bar will indicate that you've selected Sum of <summarized field>. Change the summary operation from Sum to Average (or any other available summary) by choosing Edit | Summary Field from the pull-down menus or by right-clicking and choosing Edit Summary Operation from the pop-up menu. This brings up the Change Summary Operation dialog box:

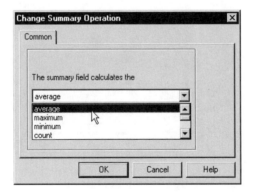

If you've used a nonnumeric field for the cross-tab summarized field, you can change the summary operation from Count to Minimum, Maximum, Distinct Count, or any other summary function that is available for nonnumeric fields. This is similar to how you can change the summary operation with existing group summaries and subtotals, as discussed in Chapter 3. In fact, the cross-tab in essence groups database records for every row/column combination, creating the summary or subtotal field for each cross-tab "group." Chapter 3 has more information on available summary functions and what they calculate.

No matter how hard you try or how creative you might be, cross-tab cells cannot contain anything but numbers created from summary functions. Reports such as calendars, schedules, or other row/column reports may look like potential cross-tabs. However, to have some textual information at the intersection of the rows and columns, you need to design the report using other techniques. Cross-tabs are strictly for numeric analyses.

Changing Cross-Tab Grouping

Because Crystal Reports uses a procedure to create cross-tabs that's similar to its procedure for creating groups, you have some of the same flexibility to change the way the cross-tab is organized. You can change a cross-tab "group" when first creating the cross-tab or formatting an existing cross-tab. In the Cross-Tab tab, select the row or column field you want to change, and then click the Group Options button. The Cross-Tab Group Options dialog box appears.

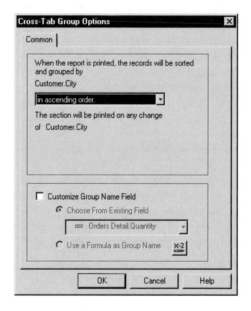

For a nondate field, there are three available options:

- **Ascending Order**   Shows the cross-tab row or column in A to Z order.
- **Descending Order**   Shows the cross-tab row or column in Z to A order.
- **Specified Order**   Lets you create custom rows or columns, based on the contents of the database field you chose for the row or column. This works identically to Specified Order Grouping, discussed in Chapter 3.

The Customize Group Name Field check box, radio buttons, and formula button work identically to the same options in the Change Group dialog box discussed in Chapter 3. You may customize the appearance of the text that displays in the row or column of the cross-tab with these options.

If the row or column field is a date field, time field, or date/time field, the Cross-Tab Group Options dialog box offers additional options that give you even greater flexibility, similar to creating report groups with similar fields.

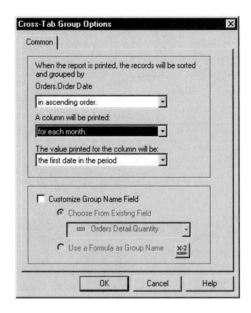

The A Column Will Be Printed pull-down list gives you a choice of how often you want a new row or column to appear in the cross-tab. Choices include every day, every week, every two weeks, every hour, every minute, and so on. Again, these are identical to the date/time grouping choices discussed in Chapter 3.

The next pull-down list, The Value Printed for the Column Will Be, gives you two choices: the first date in the period and the last date in the period. If you choose the first-date option with, say, a quarterly date period for 1997, the cross-tab will show 1/97, 4/97, 7/97, and 10/97. If you choose the last-date option, the cross-tab will show the exact same data in the cells, but the dates will be 3/97, 6/97, 9/97, and 12/97.

To give you a better idea of the flexibility that date group options provide, look at Figures 9-6 and 9-7, both showing cross-tabs based on the same date field. Figure 9-6 shows weekly date grouping with the first-date option, and Figure 9-7 shows quarterly grouping with the last-date option.

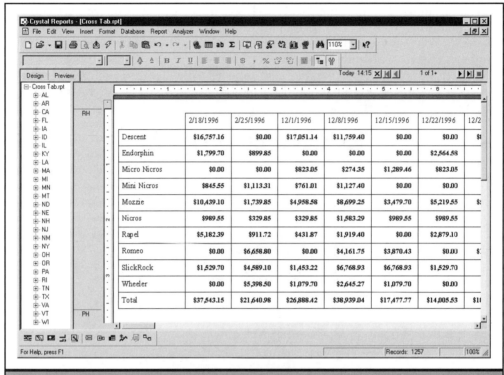

Figure 9-6. *Cross-tab date field with weekly first-date group options*

Using Formulas in Cross-Tabs

Even with the powerful grouping options and the ability to change the summary function used to calculate cell values, you may not always be able to display material in a cross-tab exactly the way you want using just the database fields in the Available Fields box. You are completely free to use formulas in your cross-tabs as a row, column, or summarized field. You can create the formulas in advance with the Formula Editor, or click the New Formula button right in the Format Cross-Tab dialog box to display the Formula Editor. After you create the formula, it will appear in the Available Fields box under the Report Fields category. Simply drag it to the Rows, Columns, or Summarized Field box.

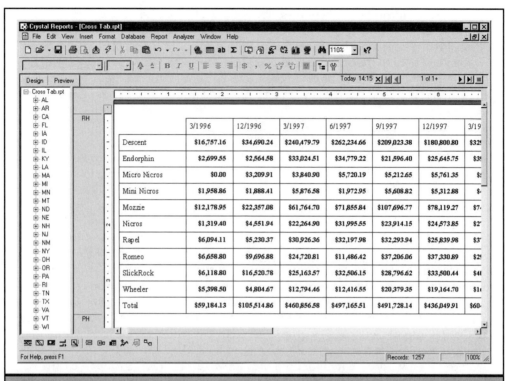

Figure 9-7. *Cross-tab date field with quarterly last-date group options*

Caution Because cross-tabs are calculated during the first report pass (WhileReadingRecords), you cannot use second-pass formulas in cross-tabs. You can only use formulas that calculate during the first pass. However, you can base a chart or a map on a cross-tab, because cross-tabs are processed before charts and maps. See Chapter 5 for a discussion on report passes.

Multiple Rows, Columns, and Summarized Fields

The Rows, Columns, and Summarized Field boxes in the Format Cross-Tab dialog box obviously are more than one field tall. Yes, that means that you can add more than one database field or formula to any of these cross-tab sections. It's important to understand, though, how this will affect cross-tab behavior and appearance.

Probably the simplest place to start is with multiple summarized fields. If you add more than one field to the Summarized Field box, the cross-tab will simply calculate the additional summary or subtotal in each cell. You could, for example, use Product Name as the row, Region as the column, and *both* Quantity and Price as summarized fields. The cross-tab would simply include two numbers in each cell—the total quantity and total price for that particular product and region.

You can even add the same field to the Summarized Field box more than once and choose a different summary function for each occurrence. You could, for example, add both the Quantity and Price fields to the Summarized Field box again. However, you might choose an Average summary function instead of a Sum for the second occurrence of the fields. The cross-tab would then show four numbers in every cell: total quantity, total price, average quantity, and average price.

Adding multiple fields to the Rows or Columns boxes causes a little different behavior that you need to understand. Whereas multiple summarized fields simply calculate and print in the same cell, multiple row or column fields don't just print over and over, side by side. When you add multiple fields to these boxes, you create a *grouping relationship* between the fields. Consider a cross-tab in which you add the Product Type field as the first row field, and the Product Name field as the second row field. Crystal Reports will create a group hierarchy by Product Type, and within that, by Product Name. The resulting cross-tab would look like Figure 9-8.

Notice that rows are created for both the "inner" and "outer" groups—each product name has its own row within its product type, and each product type has its own subtotal row. And, at the end of the cross-tab is a grand total row for everything.

You can set up this multiple-field group hierarchy for either rows or columns. And, you can include as many fields as you want in the Rows box or the Columns box (although it won't make much sense if you go beyond two or three levels).

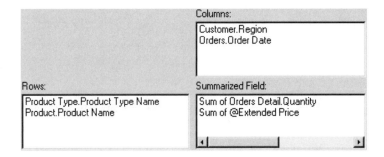

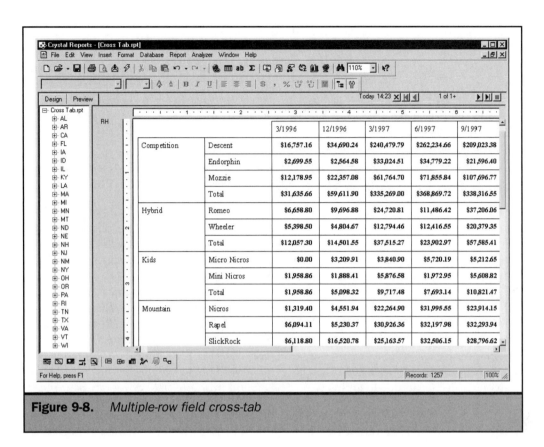

Figure 9-8. *Multiple-row field cross-tab*

Here's a portion of the resulting cross-tab:

Note   *What section of the report you place the cross-tab in is particularly important when you are using multiple row or column fields. If you create a cross-tab that's based on Country, and then Region, you'll see different behavior depending on where you put the cross-tab. If you put it in the report header or footer, you'll have rows or columns for each country, and all the regions within those countries. However, if you have already grouped your report by country, and you place the cross-tab in a country group header or group footer, you'll then have one cross-tab for every country. However, that cross-tab will have only one country row or column in it, followed by any regions within that country. If you find cross-tabs at group levels with only one high-level row or column, there's not a great deal of benefit to using multiple row or column fields in that cross-tab.*

If you plan to use multiple row or column fields, choosing fields that have a logical, groupable relationship with each other is crucial. You may think of this relationship as being *one-to-many*. The Product Type/Product Name relationship is a good example— every one product type has many product names. Country/Region is another good example—every one country has many regions.

Placing two fields in the Rows or Columns boxes that don't have this relationship will cause an odd-looking cross-tab. For example, if you add Customer Name and Address fields to the same row or column box, you'll simply see the customer name row or column, immediately followed by a single address row or column. The summaries in each will be exactly the same, because there's no logical one-to-many relationship between the fields. (The exception would be if a single customer had more than one office location—then this would be a valid multiple-field cross-tab example.)

Note   *You may yearn for a cross-tab that allows multiple row or column fields that don't act as groups. You might, for example, want to see Actual $, Budget $, Variance $, and Variance % all as separate column fields that just calculate and print side by side. Sorry, but any time you add multiple fields to the Rows box or Columns box, Crystal Reports displays the fields in a grouping hierarchy from top to bottom.*

Reordering Fields in the Rows, Columns, or Summarized Field Boxes

The multiple fields you add to the Rows box or Columns box not only have to have a logical relationship, they also need to appear in the box in the right order. Using the previous Country/Region example, Country must be the first field in the box, followed by Region. If they're added the other way around, then each region will appear first, followed by a single row or column containing numbers from the country the region is in.

If you happen to add fields to the Rows, Columns, or Summarized Field boxes in the wrong order, you can use the long way or the short way to fix the problem. The long way: delete the fields from the boxes and add them again in the proper order. The short way: simply drag and drop the fields in the right order directly inside the box. You can click and drag a field in any of the boxes and drop it in a different location in the box.

Customizing Cross-Tab Appearance

So far, this chapter has concentrated on the basic steps required to create cross-tabs, on grouping options, and on some of the finer points of multiple row, column, and summarized fields. In all of these examples, the resulting cross-tab object looks fairly plain. In keeping with the ability of Crystal Reports to create publication-quality reports, you have numerous options available to help you improve the appearance of your cross-tab reports.

The most basic type of formatting options for cross-tabs lies in the individual cross-tab objects themselves. A cross-tab actually consists of a series of individual objects. The best way to see this is to look at a cross-tab in the Design tab.

	Column #1 N	Total
Row #1 Name	ail.Quantity	ail.Quantity
Total	ail.Quantity	ail.Quantity

Notice the row and column name fields, which are similar to group name fields in a regular report—they display the database fields that make up the row and column headings. The Total text objects indicate the subtotal and total rows and columns. These are standard text objects—simply double-click them to change their contents, if you wish. And, in the actual cells, notice the subtotal or summary functions that calculate the cross-tab totals.

Each of these individual objects can be resized or formatted to change the appearance of the cross-tab. For example, if a column in the cross-tab isn't wide enough to show its contents, the contents will just be cut off, or *truncated*. Examine the following cross-tab:

	1/96	10/96	1/97	4/97	7/97	10/97	1/98
Descent	#########	#########	#########	#########	#########	#########	######
Endorph	$3,651.08	#########	#########	#########	#########	#########	######
Micro N	$0.00	#########	$5,651.36	#########	#########	#########	######
Mini Nic	$7,300.90	#########	#########	#########	#########	#########	$9,983
Mozzie	#########	#########	#########	#########	#########	#########	######

Notice that the row labels are being truncated. Also, note that many of the cells contain pound signs, indicating that the cells aren't wide enough to show all the data in them.

Although you may be tempted to look on one of the tabs of the Format Cross-Tab dialog box for some sort of column width setting, you simply need to select the individual object that makes up the column and resize it. This can be done in either the Design or Preview tab. Simply select the object, noting that all other similar cells are selected as well. Then, point to the desired *sizing handle* (one of the small blue blocks on all sides of a selected object) until the mouse cursor changes to the two-way sizing cursor. Then, simply resize the object to its desired width.

	1/96	10/96	1/97
Descent	############	############	############
Endorphin	$3,651.08	############	############
Micro Nicro	$0.00	############	$5,651.36
Mini Nicros	$7,300.90	############	############

You can format the individual pieces of the cross-tab just like any other text object or number field, using either the Formatting toolbar or the Format Editor. You can change the object's color, font face and size, horizontal alignment, or any other standard formatting option. If you choose one of the summary or subtotal objects in the middle, you can choose one of the default formatting styles, or choose a custom style to specify the number of decimal places, whether to include a thousands separator or currency symbol, or any other formatting option available to numeric or currency fields. If you base a row or column on a date or time field, you can choose how the field is displayed— month/year, month/day/year, hour:minute, hour:minute:second, or any other variation provided by the Format Editor.

You can select multiple objects in a cross-tab by using CTRL-*click. You can then format them all at the same time with the Formatting toolbar or the Format Editor.*

The Style Tab

When you select a cross-tab object and format it with Format | Cross-Tab or right-click and choose Format Cross-Tab from the pop-up menu, the Format Cross-Tab dialog box will appear. Two tabs in this dialog box control formatting: Style and Customize

Style. The Style tab lets you choose from several predefined formatting styles for the cross-tab object.

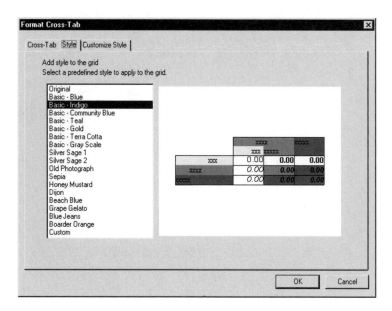

The Original option simply displays the cross-tab object with no special formatting—this is the original formatting option when a cross-tab is first created. You may choose from any of the predefined styles in the list. When you click a style, a sample of the style appears in the right side of the Style tab. Then, just click OK. The cross-tab will be formatted according to the built-in style that you chose.

Crystal Reports behaves somewhat oddly when using the Style tab on the Format Cross-Tab dialog box. Even if you haven't chosen any customized settings, you'll always receive a warning that you'll lose customized settings when you choose one of the built-in styles. And, if you return to the Style tab later after choosing one of the built-in styles, the Custom setting will be highlighted, not the built-in style you chose before.

The Customize Style Tab

For very specific formatting of a cross-tab object, you need to use the Customize Style tab on the Format Cross-Tab dialog box. This tab contains advanced cross-tab options that more precisely control cross-tab behavior. The Customize Style tab is shown in Figure 9-9.

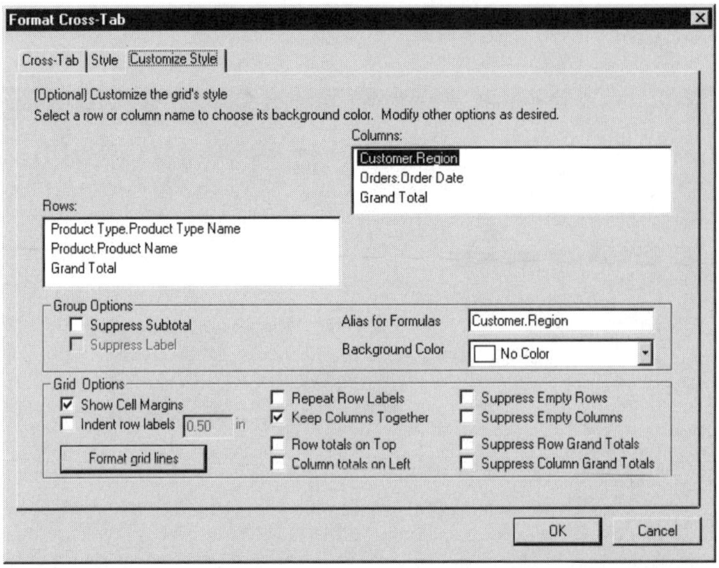

Figure 9-9.   The Format Cross-Tab dialog box's Customize Style tab

If you've already chosen one of the built-in styles on the Style tab, you'll see the settings for that built-in style when you choose the Customize Style tab. For example, you'll see background colors for each row or column item that the built-in style selected. If the built-in style shows totals before rows and columns instead of after, you'll see those options chosen. If you haven't chosen one of the built-in styles, or you want to change some of the settings that the built-in style selected, you may choose the various options in the Custom Style tab. The various options are explained in Table 9-1.

Several of the options on the Customize Style tab, particularly the Repeat Row Labels and Keep Columns Together options, dictate how a cross-tab appears when printed on paper. This is significant, because Crystal Reports displays cross-tabs differently in the Preview tab than it will print them on a printer. Even if the cross-tab width exceeds the width of the page, the Preview tab will show the entire cross-tab across the screen. You can continue to scroll farther right to see the rest of the cross-tab.

Option	Description
Rows list	Select the row that you want to format. If you've added multiple row fields, you'll see each row field listed. You can also choose separate formatting options for the row grand total.
Columns list	Select the column that you want to format. If you've added multiple column fields, you'll see each column field listed. You can also choose separate formatting options for the column grand total.
Group Options	
Suppress Subtotal	If you select this option, the subtotal row or column (depending on what's selected in the Rows or Columns list) won't appear. In this case, the cross-tab still shows the hierarchical grouping relationship among the multiple row or column fields, but the subtotals for the selected field won't appear. This option is only available for higher-level fields when you've chosen multiple row or column fields—the option is disabled if you select the lowest-level (or if you added only one) row or column field.
Suppress Label	If you choose the Suppress Subtotal option, this option becomes enabled. Checking this option will completely eliminate the field you chose from the row or column. The grouping hierarchy will remain, but the higher-level group won't appear at all in the cross-tab.

Table 9-1.   *Customize Style Tab Options*

Option	Description
Alias for Formulas	Used to refer to an entire row or column when performing conditional formatting on the cross-tab. See "Conditionally Formatting Cross-Tabs" later in the chapter.
Background Color	Sets the background color for the entire row or column that's chosen in the Rows or Columns list. This color is independent of any individual cell colors you may choose by selecting an object in the cross-tab and using the Format Editor.

Grid Options

Option	Description
Show Cell Margins	Pads cells with white space on all sides. Turning this option off will place cells right next to each other.
Indent Row Labels	Checking this option will indent the label for the chosen row from the left of the cross-tab. You may specify how much to indent the row in the text box after the Indent Row Labels check box. This is typically used to highlight a hierarchical grouping relationship when you've added multiple row fields to the cross-tab.
Format Grid Lines button	Displays the Format Grid Lines dialog box (described later in the chapter) to customize where and how grid lines appear in the cross-tab.

Table 9-1.   *Customize Style Tab Options* (continued)

Option	Description
Repeat Row Labels	If Keep Columns Together is checked, this option will repeat the row labels when a cross-tab exceeding the width of the page is printed on two or more pages.
Keep Columns Together	Prevents columns from being cut in half when a cross-tab exceeding the width of the page is printed.
Row Totals on Top	Displays row totals on top of the actual rows containing the data being totaled, rather than at the bottom of the rows.
Column Totals on Left	Displays column totals to the left of the actual columns containing the data being totaled, rather than on the right of the columns.
Suppress Empty Rows	Rows with no data will not appear in the cross-tab.
Suppress Empty Columns	Columns with no data will not appear in the cross-tab.
Suppress Row Grand Totals	Prevents row grand totals from appearing in the cross-tab.
Suppress Column Grand Totals	Prevents column grand totals from appearing in the cross-tab.

Table 9-1.   *Customize Style Tab Options* (continued)

When Crystal Reports prints the cross-tab on paper, however, it must add page breaks if the cross-tab exceeds the width of the printed page. You can control how Crystal Reports formats the cross-tab across multiple pages with the options in the Customize Style tab. When you display the cross-tab in the Preview tab, you can see where Crystal Reports will insert page breaks when the cross-tab is printed on paper. In the following example, notice that the page break occurs between columns (it's not running right through the numbers of a column) and that the row labels are repeating after the page break. This is the result of turning on both Keep Columns Together and Repeat Row Labels.

Dashed line indicates where page break will appear when printed on paper

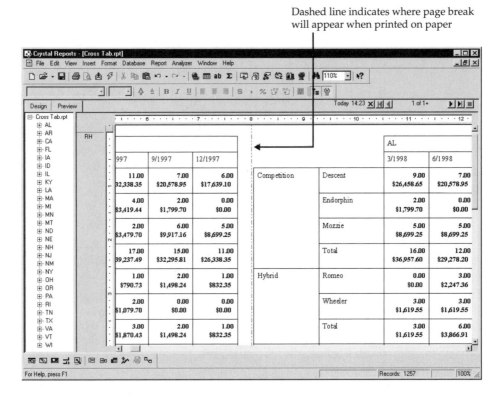

Formatting Grid Lines

Crystal Reports provides the ability to customize grid line appearance, including which grid lines appear and how they look. Customize the grid lines by clicking the Format Grid Lines button in the Grid Options area of the Customize Style tab. The Format Grid Lines dialog box will appear, as shown in Figure 9-10.

You may simply choose to not show any grid lines at all by unchecking the Show Grid Lines option. Or, to control individual grid lines, you may either select the grid line you want to customize in the grid line list or actually click a particular line in the grid lines diagram at the top of the dialog box. Then, choose individual options for the grid line in the Line Options portion of the Format Grid Lines dialog box.

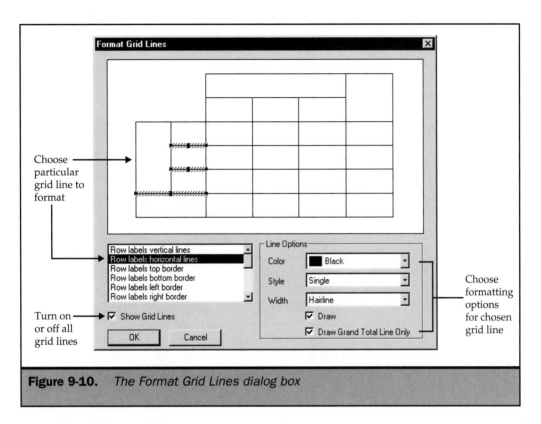

Figure 9-10. *The Format Grid Lines dialog box*

Adding Legends to Cross-Tabs

If you add multiple summarized fields to a cross-tab, it may not be clear to your viewer what the numbers mean. Consider the following cross-tab that contains multiple summary fields:

		Canada		USA			
		BC	Total	AL	AZ	CA	CO
Competition	Descent	38.00 $55,269.19	38.00 $55,269.19	30.00 $38,071.06	12.00 $20,137.98	39.00 $51,741.38	$14_
	Endorphin	13.00 $4,499.25	13.00 $4,499.25	5.00 $2,699.55	0.00 $0.00	23.00 $7,918.69	$4_
	Mozzie	31.00 $27,750.61	31.00 $27,750.61	12.00 $8,699.25	0.00 $0.00	26.00 $18,964.37	$6_
	Total	82.00 $87,519.05	82.00 $87,519.05	47.00 $49,469.86	12.00 $20,137.98	88.00 $78,624.44	$26_

There are several summarized fields in each cell. However, it's not apparent to the viewer what these numbers are—they may be totals, averages, or counts. Although Crystal Reports does not have a legend capability for cross-tabs, you can create your own legends using text objects and, optionally, with filled-box drawing. Here is the multiple-summary cross-tab with a legend:

		Canada		USA			
Quantity ■ Price ■		BC	Total	AL	AZ	CA	C(
Competition	Descent	38.00 $55,269.19	38.00 $55,269.19	30.00 $38,071.06	12.00 $20,137.98	39.00 $51,741.38	$
	Endorphin	13.00 $4,499.25	13.00 $4,499.25	5.00 $2,699.55	0.00 $0.00	23.00 $7,918.69	
	Mozzie	31.00 $27,750.61	31.00 $27,750.61	12.00 $3,699.25	0.00 $0.00	26.00 $18,964.37	
	Total	82.00 $87,519.05	82.00 $87,519.05	47.00 $49,469.86	12.00 $20,137.98	88.00 $78,624.44	$

Text objects have simply been placed in the same report section as the cross-tab, so that they appear in the upper-left corner of the cross-tab. The small white area in the cross-tab above the first row and to the left of the first column can be placed right over the top of the text objects. The summary fields have been formatted to show in a different color, and small filled boxes of the same color have been drawn with the box-drawing tool (discussed in Chapter 7).

Conditionally Formatting Cross-Tabs

You may wish to conditionally format cross-tab cells, depending on their contents. *Conditional formatting* (discussed in more detail in Chapter 7) is the process of changing the appearance of a cross-tab cell based on its contents. You may wish to highlight certain cells that exceed a certain sales goal or shipping level; you can change the color, shading, or border of just those cells.

Select the summary or subtotal object that you want to conditionally format. Then, choose Format | Highlighting Expert from the pull-down menus, or right-click the cell and choose Highlighting Expert from the pop-up menu. You can choose Highlighting Expert conditions and formats to highlight certain cells.

You can also use conditional formulas. After selecting a summary or subtotal object in the cross-tab, display the Format Editor by choosing options from the Format pull-down menu or by right-clicking and choosing options from the pop-up menu. You can click a Conditional Formula button anywhere on the Format Editor to set that formatting property conditionally.

What Is CurrentFieldValue?

When you choose to use conditional formulas instead of the Highlighting Expert, you must be careful about the tests you use to conditionally format cross-tab summaries. Since the summaries are calculations based on database fields, but are not actually the database fields themselves, you can't just test a database field to conditionally format the cross-tab. And, contrary to what you see if you've placed subtotals or summaries in a group footer, you won't see the summaries or subtotals that make up the cells in the field list of the Formula Editor.

You must test the built-in CurrentFieldValue function when conditionally formatting cross-tabs. CurrentFieldValue, as its name suggests, returns whatever the cell or "field" being tested contains. You can, therefore, use a conditional formula similar to the following to apply a silver background color to cross-tab subtotals that exceed $10,000:

```
If CurrentFieldValue > 10000 Then Silver Else NoColor
```

Figure 9-11 shows a cross-tab with this formatting.

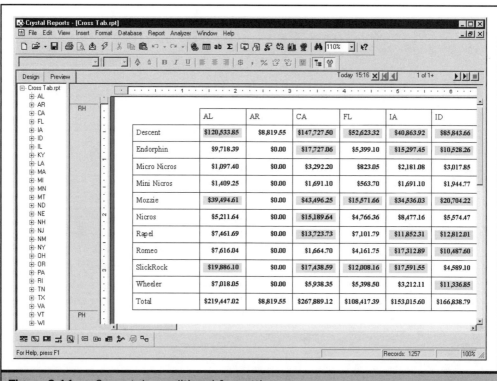

Figure 9-11.   *Cross-tab conditional formatting*

What Are GridRowColumnValue and the Alias for Formulas?

Using the CurrentFieldValue function described in the preceding section, you can only set conditional formatting in the cross-tab based on the value of the current cell. However, you may also want to set conditional formatting based on the row or column that the cell is in, not just the value in the cell. Crystal Reports provides this capability using two functions, GridRowColumnValue and Alias for Formulas.

When you conditionally format a cell, notice the GridRowColumnValue function in the Functions box of the Format Formula Editor. By using this function with an If-Then-Else formula (when setting a multiple-choice formatting property) or a Boolean formula (when setting an on/off formatting property), you can determine which row or column the cell is in and format accordingly. Consider the following Boolean formula that conditionally sets the Drop Shadow property on the Format Editor Border tab:

```
GridRowColumnValue("Customer.Region") = "CA"
```

The result is shown in Figure 9-12. Notice that only cells under the CA column have drop shadows applied to them. By supplying an *alias name* as the parameter for the

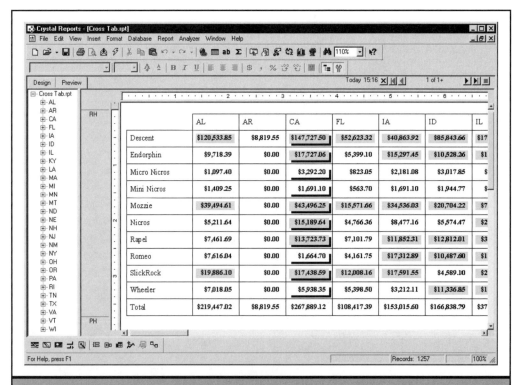

Figure 9-12.   *Cross-tab conditional formatting with GridRowColumnValue*

GridRowColumnValue function, you can determine which row or column the formula will refer to. In this scenario, Customer.Region is supplied as the alias name. So the GridRowColumnValue for the Region column is tested. If the value of the column is CA, the drop shadow is applied.

By default, each row or column's alias is the field or formula name of the row or column (without the curly braces). If you want to change the alias name to something more meaningful (perhaps just the field name instead of the entire table/field name combination), you may change it on the Customize Style tab of the Format Cross-Tab dialog box (refer to Figure 9-9). Select a row or column field in the Rows or Columns list. Then, type a new value in the Alias for Formulas text box. You may then use the new text you typed as the parameter for the GridRowColumnValue function to refer to the row or column.

 As much as you might like to, you cannot drill down on a cross-tab object. If you include a cross-tab in a summary report, you can drill down on the summary report groups, but not on the cross-tab.

The Complete Reference

Chapter 10

Creating Charts

Early database report writers were notoriously "textual" in nature. Crystal Reports, however, features a very flexible charting package to complement its complete formatting capabilities for textual information. Not only can you create attractive, meaningful, text-based reports, you can present the information graphically as well. Using Crystal Reports charting and graphing capabilities, you can see your database data presented in colorful bar charts, pie charts, three-dimensional area charts, and in many other ways. These charts can be seen in the Preview tab right inside Crystal Reports, on Web reports, included in reports exported to other external file formats, or printed on a black and white or color printer.

Minimal charting changes have occurred between Crystal Reports 8 and 8.5. However, if you're making an 8.5 upgrade from Version 7 or earlier, charting has undergone fairly major changes. Not only has the Chart Expert (the tool used to create charts, discussed later in the chapter) changed significantly, the advanced charting tool from previous versions, alternatively known as Seagate Charts and the PG Editor, is gone. Virtually all the advanced functions from this previous tool are now built in to the Chart Expert or the chart formatting options that are available in Version 8.5.

You should ask yourself (or your reporting audience) a couple of questions before you start to create a chart:

- Will my viewers really benefit from a graphical representation of the data?
- What kind of chart best matches the information to be shown?

While it's tempting to create lots of pretty, colorful charts, they aren't always an appropriate way to get across the "message" of the report. But for the many instances when a chart will add value to a report, you have a great number of charting options available to you.

Types and Layouts of Charts

Once you've decided to use a chart, you have two general choices to make about how you'll create your chart: what type of chart to use, and how the chart will be laid out. The *chart type* refers to what the chart will look like—whether it will show the data in bars, lines, a pie, or some other graphical representation. The *chart layout* refers to the data that will be used to make up the chart, whether it comes from the details section, group summaries, or a cross-tab or OLAP grid (OLAP reporting is discussed in Chapter 16).

Chart Type

The first choice to make is which type of chart best represents the data to be charted. Although some types may be prettier than others, you again need to consider what type of chart will add real meaning to the data, allowing the viewer to get the most benefit from the report. Table 10-1 discusses the main types of charts available in the Crystal Reports Chart Expert and where they are best used. When you begin to use the Chart Expert, you'll notice that each of these main chart types actually has several variations.

Chart Type	Usage
Bar	Shows a series of bars side by side on the page, which is effective for showing how items compare to each other in terms of volume, size, dollars, etc., and may also be effective in plotting growth over time.
Line	Shows trends over time, particularly for multiple groups of data.
Area	Similar to a line chart, except that the area below the line is filled in with a color. Like the line chart, it is helpful for showing trends over time, but for just one or a few groups of data.
Pie	A circle with colored slices for each item, which is good for showing which item is the biggest "piece of the pie." The pie chart represents percentages for each item, and is effective for small to moderate numbers of items.
Doughnut	Similar to a pie chart, showing who has the biggest bite of the donut. The only difference from a pie chart is that the doughnut has a hole in the middle, where the grand total for the chart is displayed.
3-D riser	A three-dimensional version of the bar chart. You can choose what shape you want for the bars—a cone, pyramid, etc. Because this chart is three-dimensional, it can show multiple groups of data side by side.
3-D surface	A three-dimensional version of the area chart; it shows multiple groups of data in a three-dimensional view.

Table 10-1.   *Crystal Reports Chart Types*

Chart Type	Usage
XY scatter 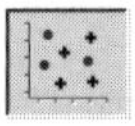	Plots data as points on two axes, allowing you to see if a correlation exists between the individual items.
Radar 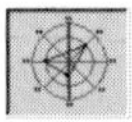	Looks a little like a radar screen, with concentric circles expanding from the center. Each group of data is drawn as a line from the center to the outside of the chart, with the subtotal of that group displayed on the line in its relative location.
Bubble 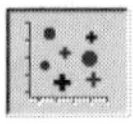	Very similar to an XY scatter chart, plotting individual points within two axes, but provides more quantitative information by varying the size of the plotted points as well.
Stock 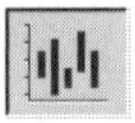	Similar to a bar chart in that it displays side-by-side bars. However, all the bars don't start at the bottom of the chart. Both the top and bottom of the bars are based on data supplied. This chart is helpful for viewing minimum and maximum financial data, such as stock prices.

Table 10-1. *Crystal Reports Chart Types* (continued)

Chart Layout

In addition to the type of chart, you have a choice as to what data the chart will represent. *Cross-tab charts* and *OLAP charts* are fairly easy to understand—they graph data in existing cross-tab objects or OLAP grids on your report. A *Group chart* graphs data contained in subtotal or summary fields in existing group headers or footers. An *Advanced chart* graphs data in the details section. Your choice of which to use will be based on your individual report design and the way you want to graphically display the data.

It's particularly important to understand the difference between a Group chart and an Advanced chart, and to know where they can be placed on a report. Consider the following illustration:

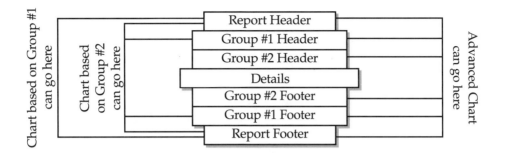

In essence, a chart must always be placed *at least one level higher* than the data it's graphing. An Advanced chart must be placed in a group header or footer or the report header or footer. A Group chart must be placed in a group header or footer of a higher-level group (if there is one), or the report header or footer. Because of the one-level-higher requirement, you can *never* place an Advanced chart or Group chart in the details section—cross-tab and OLAP charts can't go there either.

Cross-tab and OLAP charts don't fit the one-level-higher scenario. Because they depict data in a specific cross-tab or OLAP grid, they make sense only if they're in the same section as the cross-tab or OLAP grid they're based on. If you base a chart on a cross-tab or OLAP grid, you'll be able to drop it only in the same section. If you later move the cross-tab or OLAP grid to another report section, the chart will automatically move along with it.

Where you place a chart determines the data that it depicts. If you create an Advanced chart and place it in a group header, it will depict just the details sections for that group—a different chart will appear for each group. If you place the same Advanced chart in the report header or footer, it will depict data for the entire report. You'll see the same behavior for a Group chart. If you place it in a higher-level group, it will graph data only for subgroups within the group where it is located. If you place the Group chart in a report header or footer, it will include data for all groups on the report.

Creating Charts with the Chart Expert

You can create a chart by using the Standard, Cross-Tab, Subreport, Drill Down, or OLAP Report Experts from the Report Gallery, or the Chart Expert after you've created a report with the Blank Report option. If you're using one of the report experts, clicking the Chart tab will display the Chart Expert right inside the report expert. If you've already created a report with an expert and simply want to add a chart to it without re-running the expert, or if your report is designed with the Blank Report option, you can display the Chart Expert in one of two ways. Either click the Insert Chart button on the Standard toolbar or choose Insert | Chart from the pull-down menus. The Chart Expert will appear.

The Chart Expert is a tabbed dialog box that gives you tremendous flexibility for designing your charts. You specify chart options by progressing through the Chart Expert's five tabs: Type, Data, Axes, Options, and Text (of which only three are visible if Automatically Set Chart Options is checked).

The Type Tab

When the Chart Expert first appears, the Type tab will be displayed. Figure 10-1 shows the Type tab.

First, choose the general type of chart (such as pie, bar, area, and so forth) that you want to use from the list. When you make a general choice, you typically see a more specific set of choices shown as thumbnails on the right. To use the specific type of chart, click the thumbnail that best represents what you want to use. You'll see a description of the layout and uses of the chart in the scroll box below.

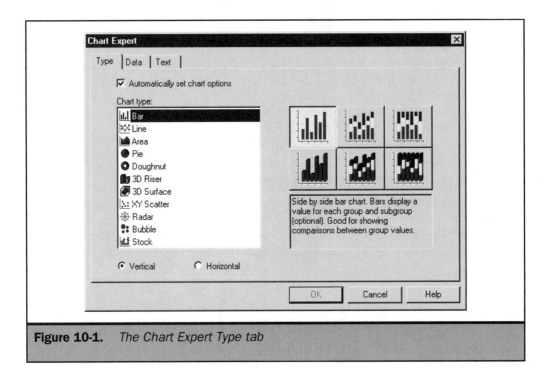

Figure 10-1.   *The Chart Expert Type tab*

Certain chart types give you a choice of horizontal or vertical direction. If you choose vertical with a bar chart, for example, the bars will grow out of the bottom of the chart. If you choose horizontal, they will spread from the left of the chart toward the right.

A new option in Crystal Reports 8.5 is the Automatically Set Chart Options check box on the Type tab. By checking this box, the Axes and Options tabs (discussed later in the chapter) will disappear from the Chart Expert and default settings for items on those tabs will be chosen. If you don't like the default settings or need to customize some settings on the Axes or Options tabs, uncheck this option. The tabs will return to the Chart Expert where you may choose your custom settings.

The Data Tab

The Data tab is where you choose the layout for the chart—whether it will be an Advanced, Group, Cross-tab, or OLAP chart. You also use the Data tab to select the actual database or formula fields you want Crystal Reports to use when creating your chart, to choose where you want the chart placed, and to specify when you want the chart to "change" graphically (when you want a new bar or pie slice to be created, when you want a new point plotted on the line, and so on).

Begin by choosing the chart layout you want to use. The following four buttons on the left side of the Data tab may or may not be enabled, based on other elements in your report:

- **Group** Available only if at least one group has been created on your report.

- **Advanced** Always available, although it is the default button only if nothing else is available.

- **Cross-Tab** Available only if one or more cross-tab objects already are on the report. If you have more than one cross-tab, but haven't selected the cross-tab you want to chart first, this button will be disabled.

- **OLAP** Available only if one or more OLAP grids already are on the report. If you have more than one OLAP grid, but haven't selected the grid you want to chart first, this button will be disabled.

The only parts of the Data tab that remain constant regardless of the button you choose are the Place Chart drop-down list and the Header and Footer radio buttons. The Place Chart drop-down list lets you choose where on the report you want Crystal Reports to initially place your chart. Again, depending on the chart type you use, the choices here will be different. Group charts can be placed in a higher-level group or in the report header and footer. Advanced, Cross-tab, and OLAP charts can be placed in a group or report header or footer. Choose Once per Report or For Each *group* from the drop-down list. Then click the radio button that corresponds to where in the report you want the chart placed—the header or footer.

The rest of the Data tab will change based on the chart layout button you click.

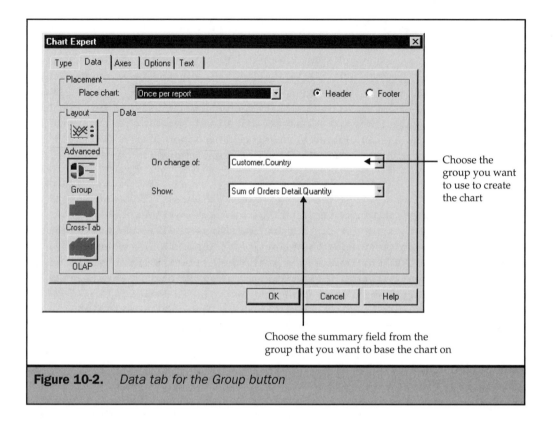

Figure 10-2. *Data tab for the Group button*

Group

A Group chart will graph data based on fields in an existing report group. You have to have at least one group defined, with at least one subtotal or summary field, before you can use this button.

Figure 10-2 shows the Data tab when the Group button is clicked.

The On Change Of drop-down list lets you choose when you want the graph to start a new element. If, for example, you choose Customer.Country, a new bar will show up in a bar chart for every country. On Change Of Employee.Last Name, for example, will create a new slice in a pie chart for every employee.

The On Change Of drop-down list's contents change in correlation with what you choose in the Place Chart drop-down list. In essence, the On Change Of drop-down list shows you one or two levels lower than where you're placing your chart. For example, if you choose to place the chart Once per Report, the On Change Of drop-down list will show the highest-level group on the report. If there is more than one group, it will also show an additional option of showing the highest-level group and the next-highest-level group. If you choose to place the report in a group, On Change Of will show the next two lower-level groups, and so on.

Here's an example of what shows up in the On Change Of drop-down list when the chart is placed Once per Report and there are country and region groups on the report:

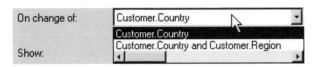

If you choose a single group, your chart will just summarize the values in that group, as shown here:

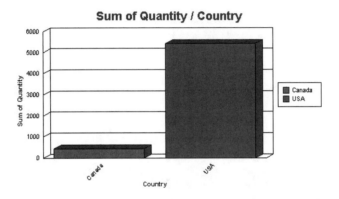

If you choose the two-group option, Crystal Reports actually creates multiple sections of the chart—the first section based on the first group, each containing individual chart elements based on the second group, like this:

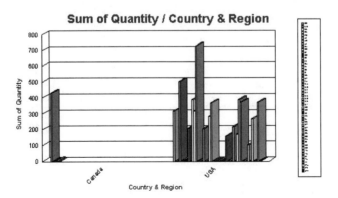

The Show drop-down list lets you choose what makes up the chart element. If, for example, you create a bar chart with On Change Of set to Customer.Country, and Show set to Sum of Orders Detail.Quantity, you'll see a new bar for every country. The bar's height or width (based on whether you chose a horizontal or vertical bar chart) will be based on the subtotal of Order Quantity for the group.

The Show drop-down list is populated based on what subtotal and summary fields you place in the group header or footer of the group chosen in On Change Of. For a group graph to work, you must have at least one summary or subtotal for the group—if you don't, the Group layout button won't even be available.

Advanced

An Advanced chart (known as a Detail chart in Crystal Reports 7 and earlier) graphs data from the details section of your report. Although you can create an Advanced chart even if you have groups defined, it won't be affected by the groups at all. Figure 10-3 shows the Data tab when the Advanced button is clicked.

This rather busy dialog box lets you choose data from your details section to create a chart. Because there can be several different fields in the details section that can affect the chart's appearance, a little more forethought is required when using this dialog box.

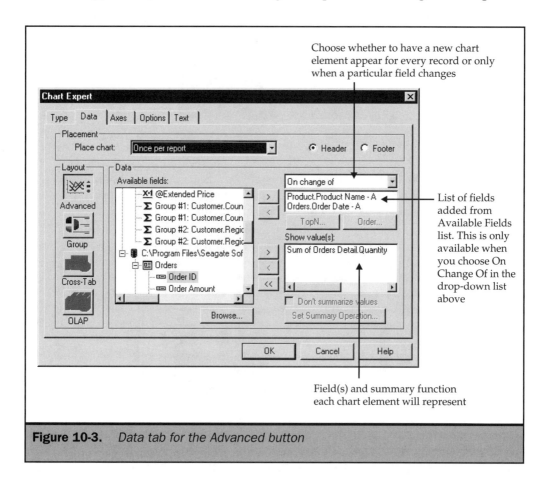

Figure 10-3. *Data tab for the Advanced button*

The Available Fields list shows report, formula, subtotal/summary, running total, and database fields in the report. You can select any of these fields that you need for creating your chart (except summary/subtotal fields, which can only be used in the Show Value(s) list). If you're unsure what kind of data is in a field, select it and click the Browse button to see a sample of database data. Once you're ready to use a field as either an On Change Of or Show Value(s) field, select the field and click the right arrow next to the box where you want the field placed. It will be copied to the box on the right.

The drop-down list in the upper right gives you three choices: On Change Of, For Each Record, and For All Records. The choice you make here determines how often a new chart element (bar, pie slice, and so on) will appear in the chart.

If you choose For Each Record, a new element appears in the chart for every record in your details section. This may be useful for very small tables that have only a few records in them. However, if your database has more than a few records, making this choice will probably render a chart that's too crowded to be of any real value. If you choose For All Records, you essentially create a *grand total* chart, showing just one element that displays a total of all records on the report. If you make either of these choices, the box below the drop-down list remains empty—you won't be able to add any fields to it from the Available Fields list.

By choosing On Change Of in the drop-down list and choosing one or more fields from the Available Fields list (except group summary or subtotal fields), you can create a chart that summarizes values in your details section. This option basically creates an invisible group on your report and creates a new chart element every time the chosen field changes. For example, if your report contains no groups, but you choose On Change Of Customer.Country, your chart will have a new element appear for each unique country that appears in your details section. Whatever field you add to the Show Value(s) list will be summarized or subtotaled by country, and the result will be used as the value for the chart.

Tip   *You can choose one or two fields to add to the On Change Of list. This works like the Group chart option, described previously, in which you can choose to show the highest-level group and the next-highest-level group. If you choose one field, the chart will contain only one section with all the elements located in it. If you choose two fields, the chart will be broken into side-by-side sections, with the first-chosen field making up the first section. Then, individual elements for the second field will appear within each of the sections based on the first field.*

Although there isn't an actual group on the report, Crystal Reports is creating an "invisible" group to base your chart on. You have control over the way the Chart Expert uses these groups. The TopN and Order buttons control this. If you click the TopN button, you'll see the Top N/Sort Group Expert dialog box, in which you can choose to include only the top N or bottom N groups in your chart, and choose which number to use for N.

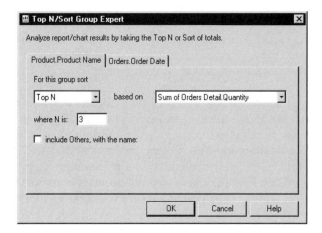

If you click the Order button, you'll see the Chart Sort Order dialog box with a drop-down list containing Ascending, Descending, Specified Order, and Original Order options. You may choose to show the chart elements in A to Z order, Z to A order, or using specified grouping (and, if you recall from Chapter 3, although Original Order is an option, it's probably of little use). If the chosen field is a date, time, or date/time field, you can choose how often you want a new chart element to appear (monthly, weekly, every minute, hourly, and so on). Refer to Chapter 3 for information on Top N, Specified Order grouping, and grouping on date/time fields.

Once you've chosen a field in the On Change Of box to determine when a new chart element will appear, you can add a field or fields to the Show Value(s) list to indicate which values Crystal Reports will use to size the chart element. If you add multiple fields to this list, the chart will contain multiple bars, lines, and so forth—one for each field you add to the list.

If you add a number or currency field to this list (and you haven't chosen For Each Record in the top drop-down list), Crystal Reports automatically uses the Sum function to subtotal the field for each invisible group. If you choose another type of field, Crystal Reports automatically uses the Count function. If you wish to change the summary function (for example, to graph the average sales amount instead of the total), you can select the field you want to change in the Show Value(s) list and click the Set Summary Operation button. A dialog box will appear with a drop-down list containing the available summary functions for that type of field. Choose the summary function you want used to size the chart element. The Percentage Summary Field option for group summaries, discussed in Chapter 3, is also available here. By checking the Show As a Percentage Of check box, you can choose a higher-level group total or grand total, and chart elements will display the percentage of the higher totals that each of the invisible group totals represents.

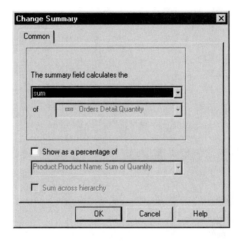

If you choose For Each Record in the top drop-down list, Crystal Reports will display a new chart element for every record on the report—no invisible group will be created. In this case, any fields you add to the Show Value(s) list won't be summarized. If you choose On Change Of in the top drop-down list and the invisible groups are created, you can specify that one or more values in the Show Value(s) list *not* be summarized, by selecting the field and checking Don't Summarize Values. Be careful if you do this— only the first occurrence of the field in the invisible group will be included in the chart. The rest will simply be ignored.

The following illustration shows the resulting chart for the Data tab shown in Figure 10-3, including limiting the chart to the top three product names with the TopN button, and with date grouping set to "for each year" with the Order button.

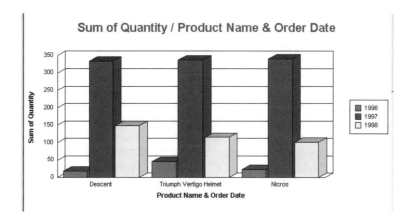

Cross-Tab

The Cross-Tab button is available only if you have one or more cross-tab objects on your report. If you have only one cross-tab object, this button will be enabled even if you haven't selected the cross-tab first. However, if you have more than one cross-tab, you must select the cross-tab that you want to chart *before* you start the Chart Expert. Chapter 9 discusses cross-tab objects.

Figure 10-4 shows the Data tab when the Cross-Tab button is clicked.

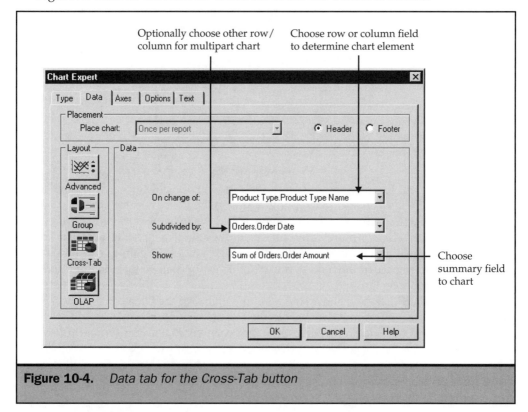

Figure 10-4. *Data tab for the Cross-Tab button*

The On Change Of drop-down list includes the two outer fields you chose for your cross-tab row and column; if you used multiple row and column fields, only the first row or field can be used. Crystal Reports will create one chart element (bar, pie slice, and so on) for each occurrence of this field in the cross-tab.

The Subdivided By drop-down list is initially set to None. If you leave it this way, the chart will create only one series of chart elements, based on the field in the On Change Of drop-down list. If, however, you want to create two series of elements for side-by-side comparison, or if you're using a 3-D riser or 3-D area chart and want to see multiple elements three-dimensionally, choose the other row/column field in the Subdivided By drop-down list.

The Show drop-down list shows the summary field or fields you placed in your cross-tab. Choose the field that you want to use in your chart. This field determines the size of the chart elements (height of a bar, size of a pie slice, and so forth).

The following illustration shows the resulting 3-D riser chart for the Data tab shown in Figure 10-4:

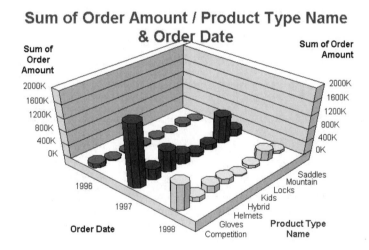

OLAP

The OLAP button is available only if you have one or more OLAP grid objects on your report. If you have only one OLAP grid, this button will be enabled even if you haven't selected the OLAP grid first. However, if you have more than one OLAP grid, you must select the grid that you want to chart *before* you start the Chart Expert. Chapter 16 discusses OLAP reporting.

Figure 10-5 shows the Data tab when the OLAP button is clicked.

Creating a chart based on an OLAP grid is very similar to creating a chart based on a cross-tab. There are just a couple of differences between the two. There is no summary field to choose (OLAP grids display only one value, so there is no choice to make). Also, the dimension hierarchy of your OLAP grid may be a little different than the multiple row/column fields you added to a cross-tab object.

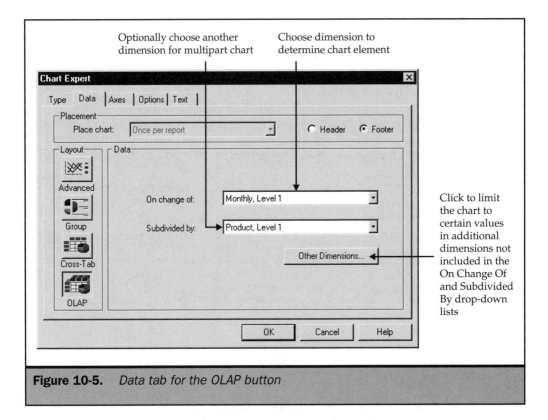

Figure 10-5. *Data tab for the OLAP button*

Choose a dimension on which to base the chart from the On Change Of drop-down list. A new chart element will be created for every occurrence of this dimension. If you leave the Subdivided By drop-down list set to None, the chart creates only one series of chart elements, based on the dimension in the On Change Of drop-down list. If, however, you want to create two series of elements for side-by-side comparison, or if you're using a 3-D riser or 3-D area chart and want to see multiple elements three-dimensionally, choose another dimension in the Subdivided By drop-down list. You can choose a next "deeper" level dimension here if you've created multiple levels of dimensions in your OLAP grid.

Depending on how many dimensions your OLAP grid contains, and how the fields that make up the dimension relate to each other (their *hierarchy*), you may need to filter the chart to just certain field values in a dimension. To do this, click the Other Dimensions button in the lower right of the Data tab. This displays the Other Dimensions dialog box, where you can choose the particular subdimension of the OLAP grid that you want charted.

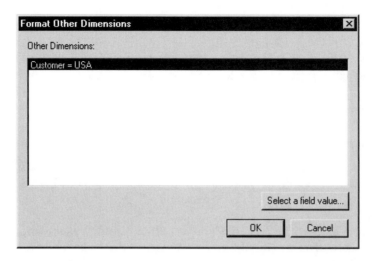

Click one of the available Other Dimensions and click the Select a Field Value button. The Select a Field for Dimension dialog box appears, with the dimension hierarchy displayed in an Explorer-like fashion.

Navigate through the dimension hierarchy and choose a level that you want to limit the chart to. For example, if you navigate down from USA and choose FL, your OLAP chart will just contain totals for the Florida region in the OLAP grid.

You can experiment with OLAP grids and charts by using a sample OLAP cube file installed with Crystal Reports. Create an OLAP grid (using the steps described in Chapter 16) based on the Holos HDC cube file Crystal Reports program directory\ Samples\en\Databases\Olap Data\Xtreme.HDC. Note that you must have included the OLAP Data data access type when you installed Crystal Reports in order to create an OLAP grid. You can then create a chart based on this OLAP grid.

The Axes Tab

The Axes tab will appear if you leave the Automatically set chart options check box unchecked on the Data tab. The Axes tab gives you complete control over how Crystal Reports displays the X, Y, and Z (if you're using a 3-D chart) axes of the chart. Figure 10-6 shows the Axes tab.

By making choices in the Axes tab, you can control how Crystal Reports displays axes on your charts. The *axes* are the areas of the chart that describe or depict the data values in the chart. If, for example, you have a bar chart in which each bar represents sales volume for a salesperson, the bottom of the chart where each salesperson is listed

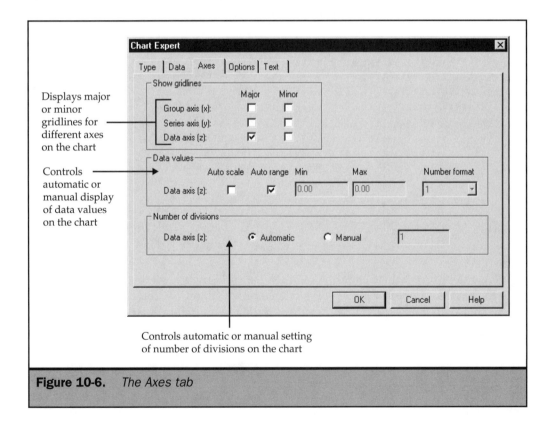

Figure 10-6. *The Axes tab*

is called the *group axis* (also sometimes called the *X axis*). The left side of the chart where the numbers representing the volume appear is called the *data axis* (sometimes called the *Y axis*), as shown here:

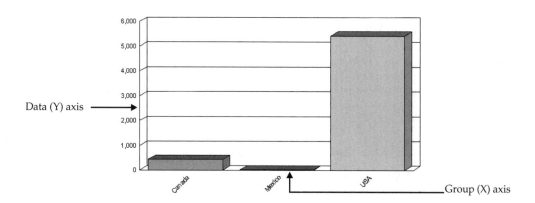

If you are using a 3-D chart, the data axis is the Z axis, and a new axis called the *series axis* is the Y axis, like this:

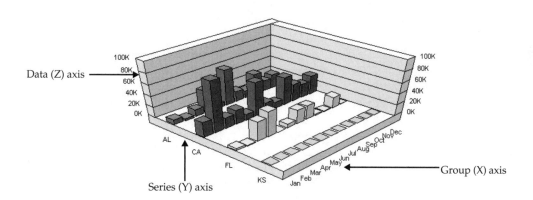

Click the Major or Minor check boxes to add gridlines to the chosen axes. *Major gridlines* fall directly in line with the axis labels that Crystal Reports assigns to the axis. *Minor gridlines* appear in between the axis labels, and work only for numeric labels. Depending on the type of chart you're using, you may not notice any difference between major and minor gridlines. Also, some charts will always have a group axis gridline, regardless of what you choose on the Axes tab.

If you leave the Auto Range check box for the Data Values option on, Crystal Reports automatically formats the chart based on the number of elements it includes.

If you wish to customize this, you can turn off the Auto Range option and add starting and ending values for the axes, as well as choose the number format (decimals, currency symbols, and so on) to use for the labels. If you choose a certain number format, such as a currency symbol, and then recheck Auto Range, the axes will be automatically renumbered, but the number format you chose will stay in place. The Auto Scale option affects the beginning numeric value that the data axis starts with. If you choose Auto Scale, Crystal Reports uses the values of the chart elements to choose an appropriate starting number for the data axis.

If you leave the Number of Divisions set to Automatic, Crystal Reports will create a predefined number of labels and gridlines for the data axes. Clicking the Manual radio button and specifying a number in the text box will create your specified number of divisions, along with labels and gridlines, for the data axes.

 Not all of the options on the Axes tab will necessarily apply to the style of chart you are using. For example, a pie chart doesn't use any axes options. If the chart you've chosen doesn't use axes, the tab won't appear in the Chart Expert.

The Options Tab

The Options tab will appear if you leave the Automatically set chart options checkbox unchecked on the Data tab. The Options tab allows you to customize general options for your chart, such as whether to display it in color or black and white, whether to show a legend and where to place it, and other options. The Options tab will change based on the type of chart you've chosen. Figure 10-7 shows the Options tab for a bar chart.

 If you're printing your reports on a black and white printer, it may be preferable to leave the chart in color and let the printer assign gray tones to the chart elements. These may actually look better than the ones Crystal Reports assigns. Experiment to determine what works best with your particular printer.

The Data Points section lets you choose whether you want labels or numbers to appear on your chart elements. If, for example, you choose Show Label with a pie chart, each of the slices of the pie will be labeled with the item that the slice refers to. If you choose Show Value with a bar chart and choose a number format of $1, you'll see the actual dollar amounts (with no decimal places) appear above each bar.

The Marker Size and Marker Shape drop-down lists let you choose how markers look on a line chart. *Markers* are the points on the line chart that are connected by the lines.

The Show Legend check box determines whether or not a legend appears on your chart. The *legend* is the color-coded key that indicates what the elements of your chart refer to. You can also choose where to place the legend with options in the Placement drop-down list. You might want legends for a pie chart with no labels, for example.

CRYSTAL REPORTS 8.5
INTRODUCED

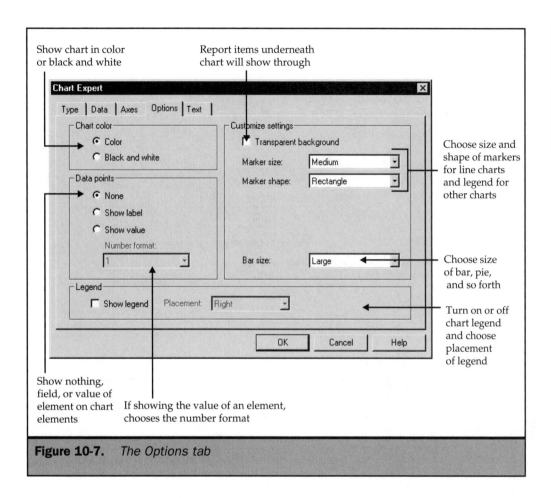

Figure 10-7.   *The Options tab*

However, if you are using a bar chart with labels already appearing along the bottom of the chart, a legend is redundant and should be turned off.

The Text Tab

The Text tab, shown in Figure 10-8, allows you to assign text to different parts of your chart, and change the appearance of these text items. You can add a chart title, subtitle, and footnote. And, you can place titles on the group, data, and series (or data2) axes of your chart.

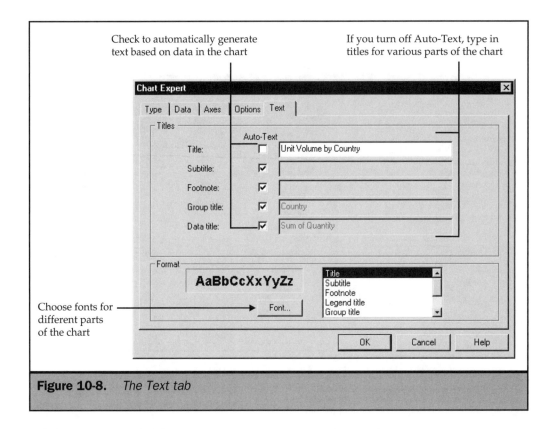

Figure 10-8. *The Text tab*

By default, the Auto-Text check boxes are all selected and the text boxes next to them are dimmed. You'll notice that Crystal Reports has added titles into certain items automatically, based on the data that the chart is based on. If you don't wish to use Crystal Reports' default titles on the chart, uncheck the Auto-Text check box for the desired title and then type the material you want to appear on the chart in the associated text boxes on the Text tab. If you leave a text box blank, that title won't appear on the chart.

To change the appearance of the different items, select the item you want to change in the list on the lower right of the Text tab. Then, click the Font button to choose the font face, size, and appearance for that item. A sample of the font you choose appears in the shaded box above the Font button.

Figure 10-9 shows a chart with all the labels set. You can see where each of the labels appears on a typical chart.

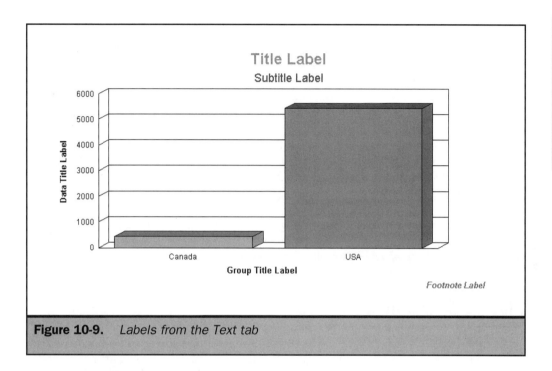

Figure 10-9. *Labels from the Text tab*

Placing and Sizing Charts

Once you complete all the information on the Chart Expert and click OK, Crystal Reports places the chart in the upper-left corner of the header or footer section you chose. Unlike other objects you add, it won't be attached to a mouse cursor allowing you to drop it where you wish. If other objects are already in the section, the chart is placed on top of them (the Transparent Background option on the Chart Expert's Options tab allows objects underneath the chart to show through).

When the chart is placed, it remains selected, however. You'll notice the shaded outline and sizing handles around the chart. You can now drag it to another location in the same section, or move it to another section on the report. You can also resize the chart by using the sizing handles, or move and resize the chart by choosing Format | Object Size and Position from the pull-down menus, or by right-clicking the chart and choosing Object Size and Position from the pop-up menu.

Remember that where you place a chart determines the data that it displays. If you place an Advanced or Group chart in the report header or footer, it will display data for the whole report. If you place the chart in a group header or footer, the chart will appear for every group, only showing data for that particular group. Cross-tab and

OLAP charts display the data from the particular objects they're based on. If you place a cross-tab object and matching chart in a group header or footer, the cross-tab and chart will display data only for the group they're in. Since OLAP grids don't change based on their location on the report, a matching OLAP chart won't change based on where you place it.

In Crystal Reports 8.5, Cross-tab and OLAP charts are always in the same section as their matching cross-tab object or OLAP grid object. You may have an OLAP grid in the report footer and its matching chart in the report header, but if you try to move the chart into a group header or footer, it won't work. And, if you then move the OLAP grid from the report footer to a group footer, the chart will automatically move to the matching group header.

If you create a chart based on, say, a Region field, but years appear in the Design tab, don't be surprised. The charts that appear in the design tab are "dummy" charts that don't depict actual data in the database. When you preview the report, however, you will see live data depicted in the chart.

Placing Charts Alongside Text

When you first create a chart in a section, it's placed in the upper-left corner of the section by default. If the chart is in a report or group header, the chart will print before the rest of the report or the group, because the section containing the chart prints first. Sometimes, you may want a chart to appear *alongside* the data it's referring to. Typically, this might be an Advanced chart that you've placed in a group header. Instead of having the chart print by itself, followed by the details that belong to the group, you may want the chart to print alongside the details sections.

By using the Underlay option in the Section Expert, you can format the group header section to underlay the following details sections, thereby printing the chart alongside the other items. For this to work effectively, you need to size and move the details section objects so that they won't be overprinted by the chart. Then, move and size the chart so that it will appear to the side of the details section objects. Using the Section Expert, choose the Underlay Following Sections option for the section containing the chart. If there is a group name, column headings, or other information in the group header that you *don't* want to be underlain, you need to create a second group header section for the chart that you underlay. Format it to use the Underlay feature and format the first group header containing the textual information with Underlay turned off. See Chapter 8 for more information on multiple sections and the Underlay feature.

Figure 10-10 shows an Advanced chart placed in Group Header b with Underlay Following Sections turned on.

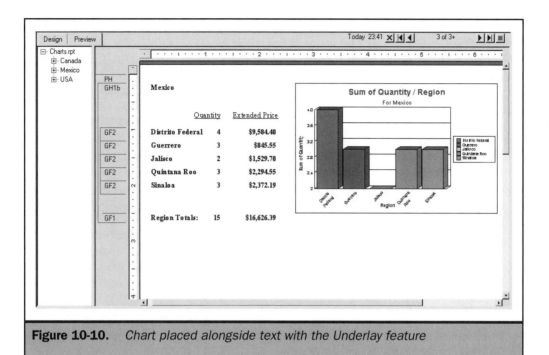

Figure 10-10. *Chart placed alongside text with the Underlay feature*

Modifying Existing Charts

Once you've created a chart, you may wish to change it. Perhaps you prefer to see a pie chart instead of a bar chart. Or, you may want to change the titles that appear on the chart. You may even want to change the chart from an Advanced chart to a Group chart, or vice versa.

First, select the chart you want to change in either the Design or Preview tab. Then, choose Format | Chart Expert from the pull-down menus, or right-click the selected chart and choose Chart Expert from the pop-up menu. The Chart Expert will reappear and you can make any desired changes before clicking OK.

Zooming In and Out on Charts

A feature of Crystal Reports 8.5 is the ability to zoom in and out on a limited number of chart types. If you have created a Bar or Line chart, you'll notice additional options available on the pop-up menu when you right-click the Chart: Select Mode (selected by default) and Zoom In. You may also select a chart and use the Zoom options from the Analyzer pull-down menu. And, if you display the Analyzer toolbar by using the View | Toolbars pull-down menu, you may choose toolbar buttons to control zoom in and zoom out on the chart.

If you choose the Zoom In option from the chart pop-up menu or associated Analyzer toolbar button, your mouse cursor will change to a magnifying glass with a plus sign. While you may be tempted to just click somewhere inside the chart expecting to zoom in, you must actually hold down your mouse button and draw an elastic box with the mouse. When you release the mouse button, the chart will zoom in to the area you surrounded. You may continue to highlight additional areas to zoom in further on the chart.

To zoom back out, right-click the chart and choose Zoom Out from the pop-up menu, or click the associated button on the Analyzer toolbar. The mouse cursor will change to a magnifying glass with a minus sign. Just click anywhere on the chart to zoom back out.

When you're finished zooming in or out on a chart, choose Select Mode from the chart pop-up menu, or click the associated button on the Analyzer toolbar. Your mouse cursor will return to its default "four-arrow" state so that you can select the chart to move or resize it on the report.

Drilling Down on Charts

If you create a Group chart, you'll notice the mouse cursor change to a magnifying glass when you point to a chart element. This drill-down cursor indicates that you can double-click a chart element that you're interested in to drill down on the chart. When you drill down on a chart element, another tab appears next to the Preview tab for the particular group you drilled down on. Drill-down allows your report viewer to interact with charts, much as they interact with group footer and group header subtotal and summary fields.

By creative use of Group charts and hiding of details and group header/footer sections, you can create a very visually appealing interactive report for use in online reporting environments. You could, for example, create a large Group pie chart and place it in the report header, along with grand totals and text objects. You might add a text object that directs the viewer to double-click a pie slice for more information. You may also set Tool Tip text for the chart, prompting the viewer to double-click the slice they're interested in. Select the chart and right-click, choosing Change Border from the pop-up menu. Click the Common tab and use the Conditional Formula button to add Tool Tip text.

To add even more interactivity, you could add lower-level Group or Advanced charts in the report's group headers or footers, hiding them with the Section Expert. When the user drills down on the higher-level chart in the report header, a drill-down tab showing a more detailed chart will open. You can create drill-down levels until the user eventually reaches details sections to see low-level transaction data.

Get more information about creating multiple groups, drill-down, and hidden sections in Chapter 3 and Chapter 8.

Note

Drill-down is only available and useful when viewing a report in its native format. Viewers can drill down on reports displayed right on the Preview tab of Crystal Reports, by using a report integrated with a custom Windows application, by opening the report in Seagate Analysis, or by using a Crystal Enterprise and a Web browser. Drill-down doesn't work with reports exported to other file formats, such as Word and Excel. Obviously, drill-down won't be effective with printed reports.

Using the Analyzer with Charts

You'll be able to view charts in the Preview tab alongside other report elements around them. However, although you can change the zoom level of the report, as well as choose a chart and zoom in and out on it, you are limited in your ability to interact with just the chart itself. To work "intimately" with only one particular chart that you're interested in, use the *Analyzer*. The Analyzer actually displays an additional tab on the screen next to the Preview tab that shows only the chart—no other report elements appear. Not only does this give you a better overall view of information in the chart, but the Analyzer also allows you to interact more fully with, and do more specific formatting on, the specific chart.

Pick in the Preview tab the specific chart instance that you want to analyze, and choose Analyzer | Chart Analyzer from the pull-down menus, or right-click the chart and choose Chart Analyzer from the pop-up menu. The chart you chose will be displayed in a new Analyzer tab next to the Preview tab.

Tip

If you return to the Preview tab and analyze another chart, the Analyzer tab will be split in half, showing one chart on top of the other. If you try to analyze a third chart, you will be prompted to discard one of the existing charts, because the Analyzer can view a maximum of two charts.

While you can use the Zoom In/Zoom Out feature described earlier in the chapter with the Analyzer (don't forget—Zoom is only available for bar and line charts), the Analyzer's true power is the custom formatting it enables you to perform on the chart.

Customizing Charts with the Format Chart Option

If you've created charts of any sophistication in Crystal Reports 7 or earlier, you're probably familiar with the separate charting package known alternately as the PG Editor or Seagate Charts. This tool, which was based on a separate charting package from Three D Graphics, Inc., was required for any moderate-to-advanced chart customization. In Crystal Reports 8 and later, this tool is now gone and all chart formatting options are built entirely into just two available charting options: the Chart Expert (discussed in the previous part of this chapter) and the Format Chart option. These options are now based on a Three D Graphics product called Amigo 2000. When you find situations where you want to have even more control than the Chart Expert provides, it's time to look at the Format Chart option.

There are several ways to perform custom formatting on a chart. With the Analyzer tab as the active tab, either select Analyzer | Format Chart from the pull-down menus or right-click the chart and choose Format Chart from the pop-up menu. A submenu will appear with various chart-formatting options.

You may also choose these formatting options by using the *Analyzer toolbar*. If you don't already see the Analyzer toolbar, turn it on with the View | Toolbars pull-down menu option.

Use these buttons to display
chart formatting dialog boxes

 You don't necessarily have to display a chart in the Analyzer tab to format it with the Format Chart option. If you select the chart in either the Design or Preview tab, these options are still available. However, not all formatting options, such as customizing individual chart elements like bars and pie wedges, are available when you format from the Design or Preview tab.

Depending on the type of chart you're using and the formatting option you choose, different dialog boxes will appear with different options. Some dialog boxes can be quite complex, with both vertical and horizontal sets of tabs to provide a wide array of options.

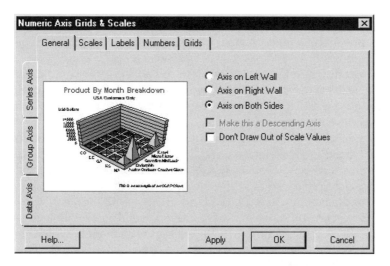

Notice the thumbnail miniature picture of the chart in the dialog box. As you make changes to the dialog box, you'll see the changes immediately reflected in the thumbnail. When you click OK, the changes will appear in the Analyzer tab.

Tip   *Any changes you make to a chart in the Analyzer tab will appear only in that one instance of the chart back on the Preview tab. If, for example, you choose a chart in the Canada group header and customize it in the Analyzer tab, the other charts in the USA and Mexico group headers won't be affected when you return to the Preview tab. If you want to have the changes you make in the Analyzer propagate to all other chart instances, right-click the chart in the Analyzer tab and choose Apply Changes to All Charts from the pop-up menu, or choose Analyzer | Apply Changes to All Charts from the pull-down menus.*

Virtually all of the customization capabilities that existed previously with the PG Editor/Seagate Charts have been transferred to these formatting options. Some of the more useful capabilities are discussed in the following sections.

Changing Colors and Shades of Chart Elements

When you create a chart in the Chart Expert, your only choices on the Options tab for affecting chart colors are the Color and the Black and White radio buttons. You have no control at all over what individual colors or shades the chart elements will have. The ability to completely customize element colors and shades is a feature available with the Format Chart options.

Begin by selecting the element you wish to color. This can be an individual bar, pie slice, or line. Note that it may look as though you've selected only a part of an element—for example, just one side or just the top of the bar. Whenever you change the color, however, it will apply to the entire element.

To change the color of the element, simply choose a different color from the color drop-down list in the Analyzer toolbar. You'll notice that the chart element changes color, along with any associated value in the chart legend (if the legend is being displayed).

You change not only the color of the chosen chart element, but also the pattern displayed in the element. By default, all charts created with the Chart Expert contain solid colors. However, you may want to replace the solid color with a graduated color, a pattern, or maybe even a picture. After selecting the element to which you want to apply the pattern, gradient, or bitmap, right-click and choose Format Chart | Selected Item from the pop-up menu, choose Analyzer | Format Chart | Selected item from the pull-down menus, or click the Formatting button on the Analyzer toolbar. The Formatting dialog box will appear with the Fill tab selected, as shown in Figure 10-11.

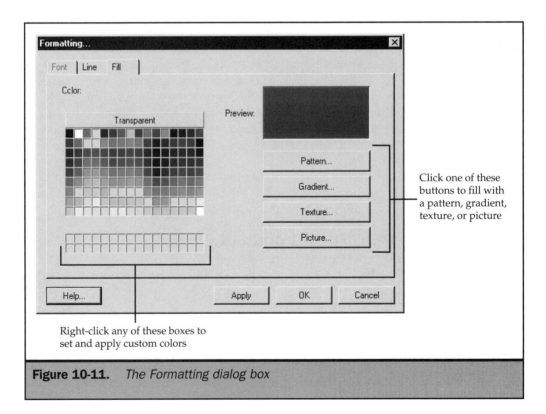

Figure 10-11. *The Formatting dialog box*

You may change the solid color to use for the element by choosing a predefined color from the palette. If you want to use a color that's not in the standard palette, right-click one of the gray boxes below the standard palette. A Custom Color dialog box appears, in which you can choose a custom color. Then, click the button you just modified to apply the custom color to the chart element.

To apply a pattern, gradient, or texture, or to fill the chart element with a picture, choose one of the corresponding buttons on the right side of the Formatting dialog box. For example, clicking the gradient button displays a dialog box showing preset color gradients. If you click the Advanced Options button, the gradient dialog box displays an extra section that lets you design your own gradients.

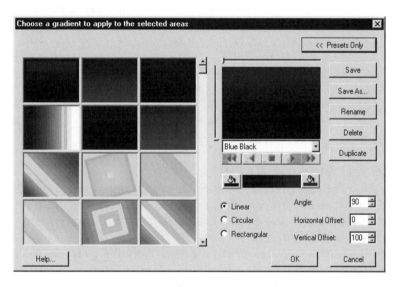

Either choose one of the preset gradients, or use the dialog box options to customize your own gradient. When you click OK, the solid color previously appearing in the Formatting dialog box will be replaced by the selected gradient.

Click Apply or OK on the Formatting dialog box to apply your selected color, pattern, gradient, or picture to the chart element.

Often, gradients and patterns, or even certain solid background colors, can add visual appeal if applied to the whole background of the chart. To do this, click a blank area of the chart where there are no other chart elements. Then, choose menu options or the toolbar button to display the Formatting dialog box. You'll notice a black line surrounding the entire chart after you've selected the background area. Color and gradient/pattern options you choose will then apply to the chart background.

Customizing and Moving Chart Titles, Labels, and the Legend

When you add a title, labels, and legend to your chart with the Options and Text tabs of the Chart Expert, Crystal Reports places them in specific locations, using specific colors and alignment. If you choose to display a legend on your chart, you have only a few predefined locations on the Options tab where you can place it. The Analyzer gives you much more flexibility to move, change, and format these objects as you see fit.

Chart titles and labels are all objects that you can select by pointing and clicking in the Analyzer tab. Once you've selected an object (as denoted by the "sizing handle" blocks on all sides), you can reposition the text simply by pointing inside the text frame and dragging it to a new location. To resize the object, position the cursor on one of the sizing handles and narrow or stretch the object. Use the Analyzer toolbar Format button, or the pull-down or pop-up menu options described in the previous section, to display the Formatting dialog box. You may choose alternate colors, fonts, alignment, and other text-related options on the Font tab of the Formatting dialog box.

If you want to move the legend to a specific place on the chart, just drag it (you can't resize it) to its new location. You can actually select and format three different parts of the legend: the frame, the textual items, and the symbols. Select each piece and use the Formatting dialog box to change them. Note that if you change the symbol, the associated chart element (bar, pie slice, and so forth) changes along with it.

Changing 3-D Viewing Angles

Some of the more impressive chart types that Crystal Reports can create are 3-D charts. There are several types of 3-D charts, some of which actually chart only one data item, such as the 3-D bar, pie, and doughnut charts, and others that chart two data items, such as 3-D riser and 3-D surface charts.

Once you create these types of charts, the Analyzer gives you a great deal of control over the three-dimensional appearance of the chart. For example, if you choose a single doughnut chart, Crystal Reports gives it a certain 3-D appearance by default. Using the Analyzer, you can completely change the viewing aspects of the chart. To make these selections, display the chart in the Analyzer. Then, click the General button in the Analyzer toolbar, or choose the General option from either the Analyzer pull-down or pop-up menu Format Chart option. The Chart Options dialog box will appear.

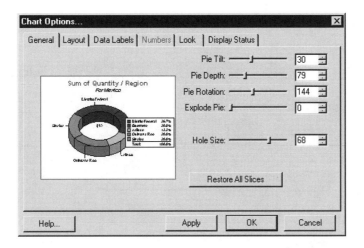

The General tab contains various sliders and spin boxes that allow you to change all visual aspects of the 3-D doughnut chart.

Dual-data-item 3-D charts, such as the 3-D riser and 3-D surface charts, have even more "whiz-bang" 3-D capabilities. Not only can you choose from a variety of viewing angles right on the Chart Expert's Options tab when you create the chart, but you also can perform almost unlimited 3-D customizations within the Analyzer.

After creating one of these charts, display the chart in the Analyzer. Then, either click the Viewing Angle button from the Analyzer toolbar or choose the Viewing Angle option from either the Analyzer pull-down or pop-up menu Format Chart option. The Choose a Viewing Angle dialog box appears. If you click the Advanced Options button, the dialog box displays an extra section that lets you completely customize the viewing angle, rather than just choosing presets, as shown in Figure 10-12.

This dialog box offers numerous options for changing the 3-D appearance of the chart. You can simply choose from any of the 12 built-in angles by clicking one of the 12 boxes on the left side of the dialog box, or choose from a large number of saved angle definitions by clicking the drop-down list or forward/backward buttons below the main thumbnail. You can also manually change all kinds of 3-D viewing aspects of the chart by making manual adjustments on the Rotate, Pan, Walls, and Move tabs.

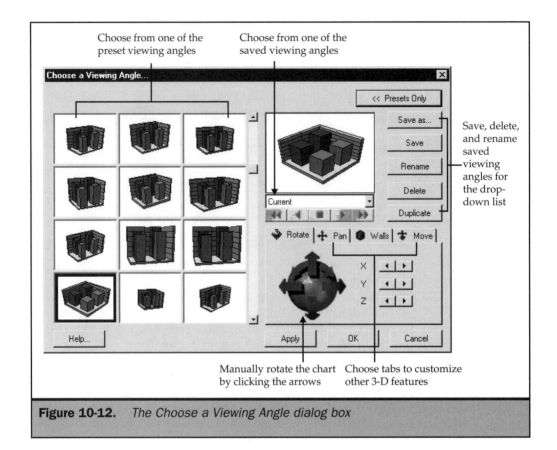

Figure 10-12. *The Choose a Viewing Angle dialog box*

You'll see the main thumbnail in the middle of the dialog box change as you choose alternative viewing options.

You may be confused by the prompt to name and save a viewing angle that you've customized when you click Apply or OK. If you make manual changes to the viewing angle with options on the tab, rather than choosing one of the built-in presets or named angles, you'll be prompted to save the settings before you apply them. While you can replace an existing named angle, or create a new one, before you actually apply the viewing angle to the chart, you don't have to. Just click the Cancel button on the Enter 3D Viewing Angle Preset name dialog box. The changes will still be applied to the chart.

Choosing Additional Chart Types

Although the Chart Expert contains many different types and variations of charts (bubble, scatter, and so forth), the Format Chart option contains even more (provided you selected the Custom Charting option when you installed Crystal Reports). To look at the available additional chart types, click the Template button in the Analyzer toolbar, or choose the Template option from either the pull-down or pop-up menu Format Chart option. The Choose a Chart Type dialog box will appear.

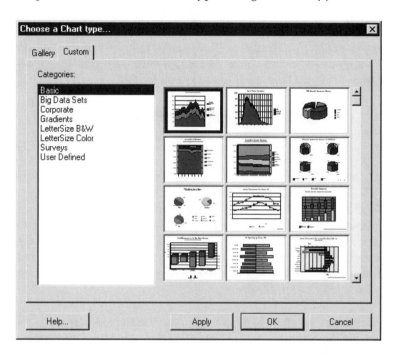

This dialog box contains two tabs: the Gallery tab and the Custom tab. The Gallery tab mostly contains the standard chart types that you find in the Chart Expert. You can choose some variations of these with the various options that appear, and then view the results of your choices in the thumbnail at the top of the Gallery tab.

If you click the Custom tab, you'll see a list of chart categories on the left. When you click each category, a large assortment of chart thumbnails from within that category appears on the right. Scroll down through the different thumbnails until you find a custom chart type that appeals to you. Select it and click Apply or OK. The new chart type will be applied to what appears in the Analyzer tab. If you want to customize the look of the chart further, use any of the techniques discussed earlier in the chapter.

Note *You must have chosen the Custom Charting option when you installed Crystal Reports for these additional chart types to be available. If they're not available, re-run Crystal Reports setup and choose the Custom Charting option.*

Saving and Reusing Chart Settings

If you have a particular set of Analyzer settings you'd like to use on more than one chart, you can save the settings in a chart *template.* You can then apply the template to another chart that you create or edit.

To save a template, make any desired changes to your chart, such as changing label positions, element colors, perhaps the legend position, and any other settings you want to make. Then, either choose Analyzer | Save as Template from the pull-down menus or right-click the chart and choose Save As Template from the pop-up menu. A message box appears, indicating that the template has been saved.

 Be judicious about how many times you save chart templates. The list of user-defined templates will grow quickly if you're not careful. The only way to remove a user-defined template once you've saved it with these steps is to use Windows Explorer to remove the file directly. Template files are located in the \Program Files\Seagate Software \SSChart \Templates\User Defined folder.

To apply the saved template to a new chart, use the steps described in the preceding section, "Choosing Additional Chart Types." Notice that the last category on the Custom tab is *User Defined.* When you choose that category, the collection of thumbnails consists of all the templates you've saved. Choose the thumbnail that you wish to apply to your current chart. When you click Apply or OK, the template settings will be applied to the existing chart.

Chapter 11

Using Subreports

A s you become more sophisticated in your report designing abilities, you will find at times that it's difficult, if not impossible, to create certain kinds of reports. For example, you might want to create one of the following:

■ A single-page Company Condition report that contains an accounts receivable summary in the upper left, an accounts payable summary in the upper right, a payroll expense summary in the lower left, and a sales summary in the lower right. At the bottom of the report, you'd like some grand totals for each of the summary reports.

■ A listing of orders by customer for the month that also has a summary of the top five products sold during the month, regardless of customer.

■ A sales report grouped by state, with a list of all credit granted in the same state in the group footer.

■ A report based on a PC-style database that you can't properly link because of the lack of indexed fields.

■ A report that contains a report title, logo, and company information from a separate Company Information table in the database that doesn't contain any field that can be linked to other fields in other tables.

In each of these cases, you can't create the report using traditional Crystal Reports methods. The first three instances are prohibitive because a report, by nature, can only use a single result set, or a single group of fields returned all at once, from the database. The fourth instance exhibits Crystal Reports' requirement that PC-style databases be linked using indexed fields. And the fifth instance (a fairly common situation), exhibits the problem encountered when there are no common fields that can be linked between the two tables.

Crystal Reports provides an innovative way to deal with these types of reporting challenges. *Subreports* allow you to solve these problems by, in essence, placing one report inside another report. A subreport is simply another report that appears inside the original *main report* as an object. Even though both reports have separate layouts and separate Design tabs, they appear together in the same place. The main report is created initially, after which one or more subreports are added to the main report.

Each subreport is designed separately, based on its own database tables and fields. You can preview each subreport in its own Preview tab, format individual objects in each subreport, and create unique selection criteria for the subreport. However, when you return to the main report's Preview tab or print the main report, the subreports will be processed and printed at the same time, appearing inside the main report.

The following are the two main types of subreports:

■ **Unlinked subreports**   Have no tie-in to the main report at all—they exist completely on their own and don't typically communicate with the main report. The Company Condition report mentioned previously falls into this category.

Each of the unlinked subreports stands on its own and won't change based on any controlling field in the main report.

- **Linked subreports**   Are controlled by the main report. The subreport will "follow" the main report, only returning a certain set of records based on the main report's controlling field or fields. The subreport containing sales by state followed by matching credit, mentioned previously, is an example of a linked subreport. When the state group changes in the main report, the subreport will only return records for that particular state.

You can also choose when subreports are processed by the main report. *In-place* subreports process at the same time as the main report and return their results at the same time. *On-demand* subreports only appear in the Preview tab with a placeholder and don't process until a viewer double-clicks them. This improves the performance of the main report, because all the subreports don't have to be processed at the same time as the main report.

Unlinked Subreports

The most straightforward subreport is an unlinked subreport. An unlinked subreport can be thought of as a completely separate report that just shows up on the main report—there's no connection at all. The subreport has its own layout, its own database connection, and its own selection criteria. It is not affected at all by what appears on the main report.

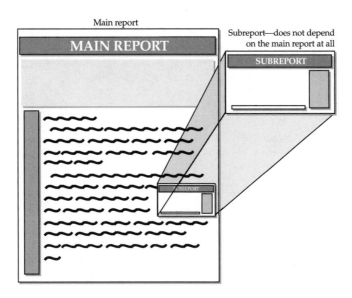

It's important to understand that Crystal Reports will not create another .RPT file when you create a subreport. Even though you will see another Design tab with separate tables and record selection, the subreport definitions are all contained in the main .RPT file.

To create an unlinked subreport, you must first create at least the skeleton for the main report, and then create the subreport. You can use the Subreport Expert from the Report Gallery, or create the main report using the Blank Report option and then add the subreport later.

To use the Subreport Expert, choose it from the Report Gallery when you create a new report. Create at least the basic components of your main report by choosing options in the Data and Fields tabs, at a minimum. When you click the Subreport tab, the Insert Subreport dialog box will appear inside the Report Expert.

 If you use the Blank Report option to create a report, or you wish to add a subreport to an existing report, it's best to add a subreport in the Design tab. That way, you'll know exactly what section you will be placing the subreport in when you drop it on the main report. Start to create the subreport by clicking the Insert Subreport button on the Supplementary toolbar or by choosing Insert | Subreport. The Insert Subreport dialog box will appear.

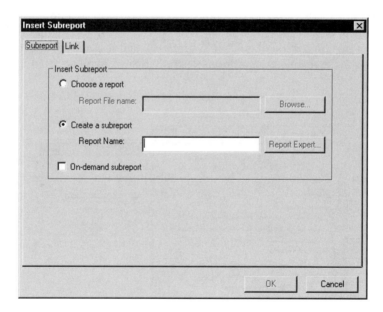

The Insert Subreport dialog box contains two tabs: Subreport and Link. The Link tab, discussed later in the chapter in "Linked Subreports," is used to create a linked subreport. The Subreport tab contains two radio buttons, Choose a Report and Create a Subreport, and one check box, On-Demand Subreport (on-demand subreports are discussed later in this chapter). If you've already created another report that you would like to import as a subreport now, you can click the Choose a Report radio button and type in the path and filename of the existing report, or use the Browse button to navigate to the existing report. When you click OK, a subreport object outline will be attached to your mouse cursor. Place the subreport object in the desired location on the main report. As soon as you place the subreport, you'll notice that another Design tab will appear. If you click it, you'll find the report layout for the report you just imported.

When you import an existing report as the subreport, Crystal Reports will not create a real-time link to it. The report design characteristics of the existing report will just be added to the main report and then "forgotten." If you later make changes to the original report that you imported, the changes won't be reflected here. However, Crystal Reports 8.5 provides the ability to update the subreport to reflect any changes to the original .RPT file. You may update the subreport manually or automatically.

To update a subreport with any changes made to the original .RPT file manually, right-click the subreport object on the main report Design tab (the placement of the subreport object is discussed later in the chapter). Choose Re-import Subreport on the pop-up menu. The .RPT file that was used to originally import the subreport will be read again and any changes will now be reflected in this report. To have Crystal Reports automatically update imported subreports every time the main report is opened, format the subreport by selecting the subreport object in the main report Design tab or Preview tab. Then either use the Format menu or right-click on the subreport object and choose Format Subreport, which will display the Format Editor. On the Subreport tab, check the Re-import when Opening check box. You may also set this option globally by choosing File | Options and then checking the Re-import Subreports when Opening Reports option on the New Report tab.

Caution   *If you re-import a subreport using these methods, any changes you made to the subreport design will be overwritten by the updated subreport. You won't be warned that your changes are going to be overwritten, and you cannot undo the import. If you realize that you've overwritten subreport changes that you wanted to keep, close the report without saving it. Then, re-open the report.*

If you wish to create a new subreport from scratch, click the Create a Subreport radio button and give the subreport a descriptive name in the Report Name text box. Remember that you are not creating a new .RPT file when you create a subreport, so the subreport name doesn't have to conform to file-naming conventions. It should be descriptive of the subreport, because the name will appear on the main report Design tab wherever the subreport object is placed. Notice that once you enter a name, the only button that becomes enabled is the Report Expert button. The OK button at the bottom of the dialog box is still dimmed. This indicates that you must use a Report Expert to create at least a minimal portion of your subreport. Once you close the Report Expert and return to the Insert Subreport dialog box, the OK button will be enabled. When you click the Report Expert button, the Subreport Expert appears.

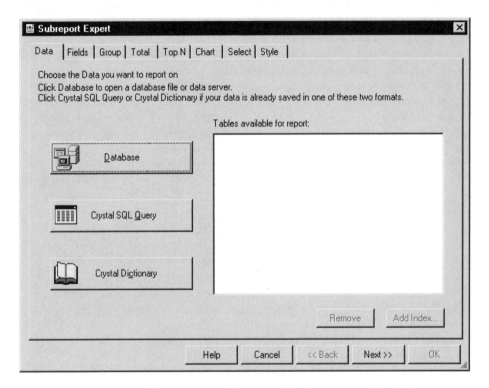

Don't forget that one of the powerful features of subreports is the ability to create reports based on entirely different databases and tables. You can select completely different databases, tables, and fields than are used on the main report. You must choose options on at least the Data and Fields tabs before you can click the OK button on the Subreport Expert. You can use the other tabs to refine your subreport before you click OK, or wait and work in the subreport Design tab directly.

When you've selected your desired options in the Subreport Expert and clicked OK, you'll be returned to the Insert Subreport dialog box. Notice that the OK button is now enabled, because you have specified the necessary information with the Subreport Expert. When you click OK, you will be returned to the main report Design tab, and a box-like subreport object will be attached to your mouse cursor. Drop the object by clicking in the report section of the main report where you want the subreport to appear. Choose this section carefully; it typically makes no sense for an unlinked subreport to appear more than once in the main report. For example, if you place the subreport in the details section, the same unlinked subreport will appear over and over again, once for each details record. You'll typically place an unlinked subreport in a report header or footer, unless you want it to repeat on more than one page.

Don't forget the Underlay formatting option on the Section Expert (discussed in detail in Chapter 8). You can, for example, easily create a second page header section for your subreport object and format the second page header to Underlay Following Sections. That way, your subreport will print alongside—not on top of—any data on the main report.

When you place your subreport in the main report Design tab, it simply shows up as a box with the subreport name centered inside it. Notice, however, that another Design tab labeled with the subreport name now appears alongside the main report Design tab. If you click the new tab, the subreport Design tab will appear.

Design	1997 Top 10 Products	
	· · · · 1 · · · · 2 · · · · 3 · · · ·	
Report Header		1998 Top 10 Products
Group Header #1: Product.Product Name - A	Group #1 Name	
Details	Product Name	Order Amount
Group Footer #1: Product.Product Name - A	Group #1 Name	rs.Order Amount
Report Footer		

You can now move, resize, reformat, and otherwise modify objects in the subreport just as you would in the main report. The subreport will present its own Data and Field Explorers, allow a separate set of formulas to be created, and allow you all the flexibility you have on the main report. However, the subreport Design tab has one limitation: You cannot add another subreport to it—subreports can only be created one level deep.

Caution   *Since subreports can only be one level deep, an existing report that already contains subreports will not include the subreports when it is imported from the Insert Subreport dialog box. The main report will be imported into the subreport Design tab, but the lower-level subreports won't show up. You may need to modify the imported report to make up for the empty space that appears where the subreport used to be.*

You can even preview a subreport in its own Preview tab. With the subreport Design tab displayed, preview the report using the Preview toolbar button, the F5 key, or the pull-down menu options. A separate Preview tab for the subreport will appear next to the subreport Design tab.

When you now preview the main report, you'll see the subreport where you placed it in the Design tab. By default, subreports are surrounded by a border, so you'll see a box around the subreport. If the subreport is not entirely visible (it may be partly off the right side of the page, or it may be overwriting main report data if you set it to Underlay Following Sections), return to the main report Design tab and reposition or resize the subreport object. If you don't have sufficient room in the subreport Design tab to properly place objects, return to the main report Design tab and resize the subreport object. The subreport Design tab's width is determined by the subreport object's width in the main report.

  You may save a subreport in its own .RPT file to use elsewhere or on its own. Select the subreport object in the main report Design or Preview tab and choose File | Save Subreport As, or right-click the subreport object and choose Save Subreport As from the pop-up menu.

Drilling Down on Subreports

You have the same flexibility for drill-down reporting in subreports as you do in the main report. If you design a subreport with grouping, hidden sections, or charts, you can drill down in the subreport, too.

When you first preview the main report, the subreport will appear inside it. If you point to the subreport, you'll notice the mouse cursor change to a magnifying glass, indicating drill-down capability. When you double-click the subreport, it will be displayed in its own Preview tab (but no actual subreport drill-down will occur). If you've designed the subreport to allow drill-down, you'll notice the mouse cursor displaying a drill-down cursor again in the subreport Preview tab. If you then double-click again, additional drill-down tabs will appear for groups you've created in the subreport.

If Crystal Reports runs out of room to display all the tabs, two small left-right arrows will appear to the right of the group of tabs. You can use the arrows to cycle through the tabs from the left or right. If you wish to close some of your drill-down tabs, click the red X next to the page navigation controls. This will close the tab you are currently viewing and display the tab to the left. Figure 11-1 shows an unlinked subreport with more tabs than can be displayed at once.

When you add a subreport to the main report, a Design tab for the subreport is created automatically. You can close the subreport Design tab by clicking the red X button. To redisplay a subreport Design tab, display the Design tab for the main report and then either double-click the subreport object, select the subreport and choose Edit | Subreport from the pull-down menus, or right-click the subreport object and choose Edit Subreport from the pop-up menu.

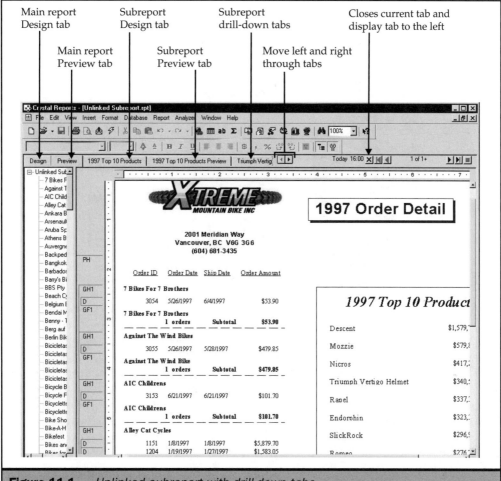

Figure 11-1. *Unlinked subreport with drill-down tabs*

Linked Subreports

A linked subreport is handy when you want to have multiple records from one database appear after multiple related records from another database. The previous example of a report that shows all sales in a region, followed by all credits in a region, fits this category. The subreports follow along with the main report.

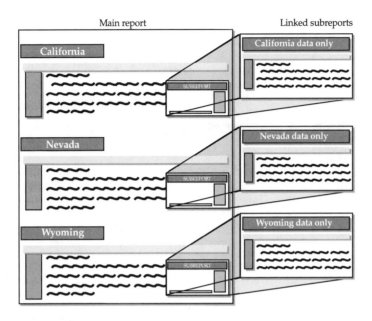

A linked subreport is also required if you have a report based on a PC-style database that requires linking to a field that's not indexed. Since a linked subreport can show matching records based on a non-indexed field, you can create reports using a linked subreport that you would normally be unable to create.

The initial steps for creating a linked subreport are the same as creating an unlinked subreport. Use the Insert Subreport toolbar button or menu options to create a subreport. Then, import an existing report or create a new subreport with the Subreport Expert. However, before you click OK in the Insert Subreport dialog box, click the Link tab. This will display the Subreport Links dialog box, shown in Figure 11-2, in which you can choose how to link the subreport with the main report.

Tip   *If you inadvertently click OK in the Insert Subreport dialog box before linking, you can still link the subreport after you place it in the main report. You can also choose to change links for an existing linked subreport or link a previously unlinked subreport. Choose Edit | Subreport Links from the pull-down menus, or right-click the subreport object and choose Change Subreport Links from the pop-up menu.*

If you are linking right from the Link tab on the Insert Subreport dialog box, the For Subreport drop-down list will be dimmed—you will be setting links for the subreport you are currently creating. If you are linking a subreport already on the main report, you can choose the subreport you want to set links for (don't forget—there can be more than one subreport on a main report).

The Available Fields list shows fields and formulas available in the main report. Select the field from the list you want to link from, and add it to the Field(s) To Link To

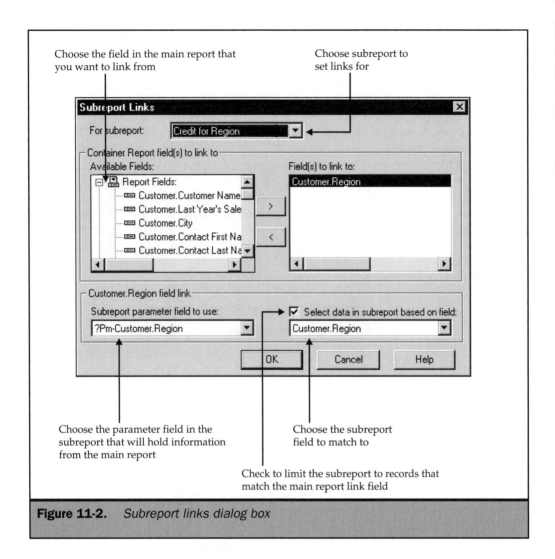

Choose the field in the main report that you want to link from

Choose subreport to set links for

Choose the parameter field in the subreport that will hold information from the main report

Choose the subreport field to match to

Check to limit the subreport to records that match the main report link field

Figure 11-2. *Subreport links dialog box*

list by clicking the right arrow button. If you later decide you don't want to link on that field, select it in the Field(s) To Link To list and remove it with the left arrow button.

Once you've added a main report field to link on, three additional options appear at the bottom of the Subreport Links dialog box. The Subreport Parameter Field To Use drop-down list contains any parameter fields you have created in the subreport (see Chapter 12 for information on parameter fields). In addition to any that you have created, Crystal Reports will create a parameter field consisting of the main report field prefixed with Pm-. If you want to link the subreport so that it only shows matching records for the main report field, just leave this automatically created parameter field selected.

The general approach of linked subreports is to limit the subreport to records that match the linking field from the main report. If this is the behavior you want, make sure Select Data in Subreport Based on Field is checked. Then, use the drop-down list below the check box to choose the field in the subreport that you want to use to limit records (Crystal Reports will automatically show a subreport field that has the same field name as the main report linking field). If you want to use more than one field to link the main report to the subreport, just add additional fields to the Field(s) To Link To list and match them up to the corresponding subreport fields.

Clicking OK closes the Subreport Links or Insert Subreport dialog box and creates the links between the main report and the subreport. A subreport link is based on two concepts: passing data from the main report into a subreport parameter field, and creating a record-selection formula in the subreport based on the parameter field. This way, every time the main report runs the subreport, it places the value of the main report linking field in the parameter field, which is used to select records for the subreport.

Because of this method of subreport linking, whenever you try to preview a linked subreport on its own, you'll see a prompt similar to this:

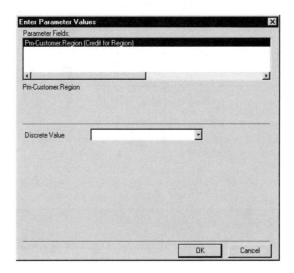

This indicates that the value for the parameter field is not being passed from the main report and you need to provide it. Type a valid value for the linked field (such as a state abbreviation, customer number, department code—whatever value is appropriate for the linked field) and click OK. The subreport Preview tab will appear showing just the records that you specified.

When you preview the main report, it will pass data to the subreport via the parameter field every time the subreport is processed; the subreport will use the parameter field in its record-selection formula and will return the limited set of resulting records to the main report. Figure 11-3 shows the customer/credit report mentioned previously, with the credit subreport appearing in the state group footer.

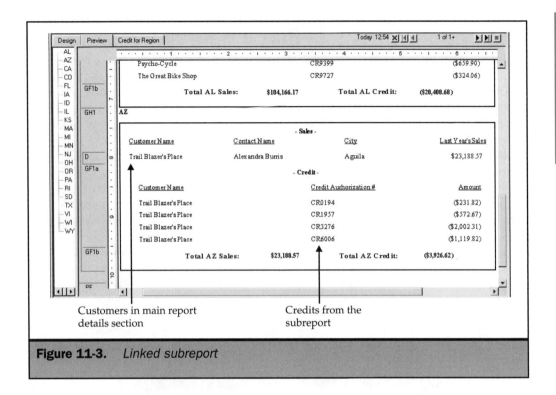

Customers in main report
details section

Credits from the
subreport

Figure 11-3.   *Linked subreport*

Linking Based on Formula Fields

If you use the Visual Linking Expert (discussed in Chapter 14) to link tables together in the
main report, you can only link based on database fields. This may be a problem if a field in
one table doesn't exactly match the data type or organization in another table. For example,
you may want to link two tables together based on a First/Last Name field because there
is no other common number field or other linkable field. The problem, however, might be
that the fields are separated into individual First and Last Name fields in one table, and
contained in a single Name field in the other table. The link will never work in the Visual
Linking Expert because of the differences in the data layout.

One of the benefits of using subreports is their ability to link based on a formula
field, instead of just using database fields. By creating a subreport, you can link the two
tables together. The key is to use a formula to concatenate the individual First and Last
Name fields together into one combined formula field. You can then use the formula
field to link to the subreport that contains the single Name field. Once you've created
the formula in the main report or subreport, it will appear in the Subreport Links
dialog box and you can choose it as a From or To linking field.

Chapter 5 discusses concatenating string fields and other formula-creation techniques.

On-Demand Versus In-Place Subreports

By default, a subreport will process *in-place* as soon as Crystal Reports encounters it during main-report processing. Therefore, if you place a subreport in a group footer and preview the report, the subreport will process every time Crystal Reports comes to a group footer. If the report contains 75 groups and you click the last page-navigation button (or you have a Total Page Count special field on your report), 75 subreports will have to be processed before you see the page.

Depending on subreport size, database speed, or any of a number of other factors, this subreport processing may present a prohibitive performance problem. That's why Crystal Reports provides the *on-demand* subreport. An on-demand subreport simply exists as a placeholder on the main report, but it doesn't process as the main report progresses. Only when you drill down on the subreport placeholder by clicking on it does the subreport actually process and appear in its own Preview tab.

There are two ways to denote a subreport as on-demand versus in-place. When you first create the subreport, check the On-Demand Subreport check box in the Insert Subreport dialog box. Or, you may format the subreport using the Format Editor. On the main report Design or Preview tab, select the subreport object that you wish to denote as on-demand. Then, display the Format Editor by clicking the Format button in the Supplementary toolbar, by choosing Format | Format Subreport, or by right-clicking the subreport object and choosing Format Subreport from the pop-up menu. The Format Editor will appear with a Subreport tab.

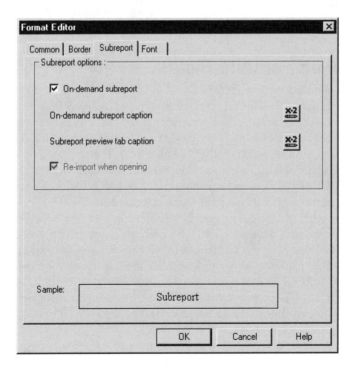

Check On-Demand Subreport to make the currently selected subreport on-demand. Now, when you preview the main report, only a placeholder outline will appear where the subreport would be. When the viewer double-clicks the placeholder, the on-demand subreport will process and appear in its own Preview tab.

Since data is not saved in on-demand subreports, you may wish to avoid them if you distribute a report to a viewer who doesn't have access to the database. Even if a viewer opens a report with File | Save Data with Report checked, on-demand subreports will have to connect to the database to be shown.

There are two helpful text options that make on-demand subreports more intuitive and interactive. The On-Demand Subreport Caption and Subreport Preview Tab Caption properties also exist on the Format Editor's Subreport tab. Both of these properties are set via Conditional Formula buttons, which allow you to create a conditional string formula that determines what appears inside the subreport placeholder in the main report and in the subreport Preview tab, respectively.

Since both are conditional formulas, you can use the complete Crystal Reports formula language to create a string formula to display. This gives you the flexibility to include actual database data in the formulas. For example, to prompt the user to double-click a subreport placeholder to see credit information for a particular state, you could enter the following formula for the On-Demand Subreport Caption:

```
"Click to see Credit records for " + GroupName ({Customer.Region})
```

To show the state name in the Preview tab for the particular on-demand subreport that a viewer chooses, you could use the following conditional formula for the Subreport Preview Tab Caption:

```
GroupName ({Customer.Region}) + " credits"
```

The Subreport Preview Tab Caption works with either on-demand or in-place subreports (if in-place subreports are drilled down on). The On-Demand Subreport Caption will only be available if you check On-Demand Subreport.

You can use other options on the Format Editor to choose the font face, size, and color, the border style, and the background color that appear on the placeholder. By using these formatting options creatively, you can make an on-demand subreport placeholder look clickable.

Figure 11-4 shows the resulting main report Preview tab. Notice that several subreports have been double-clicked and their Preview tabs have been customized.

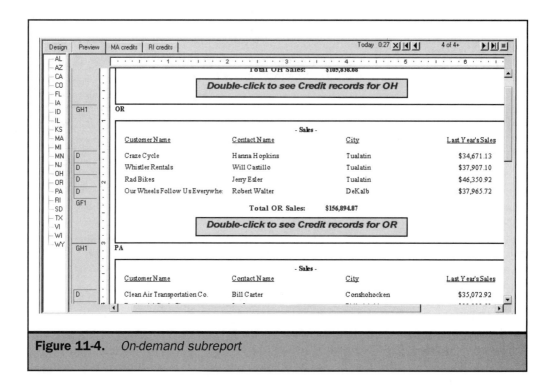

Figure 11-4. *On-demand subreport*

Caution *If you are passing data back to the main report from a subreport (discussed later in the chapter), making the subreport on-demand will prevent the data from being passed back when the main report runs. Since the subreports aren't processing as the main report runs, there's nothing for them to pass back!*

Passing Data Between Main Reports and Subreports

In addition to passing a linking field to a subreport from a main report to limit the subreport's record selection, you may want to pass data from a main report to a subreport for other purposes. Or, you may want to pass data from a subreport back to the main report to use in summary calculations or similar functions. You can pass data to a subreport from the main report by using a parameter field. Crystal Reports also provides the *shared variable,* which allows you to pass data back and forth between main reports and subreports.

Passing data to a subreport from the main report but not having the subreport use it in record selection is fairly straightforward. Display the Subreport Links dialog box, as explained earlier in this chapter. Choose a linking field from the main report and add it to the Field(s) To Link To list. This will automatically add a parameter field prefixed with Pm- (all parameter fields automatically begin with a question mark) to the Subreport Parameter Field To Use drop-down list. Now, simply uncheck Select Data in Subreport Based on Field.

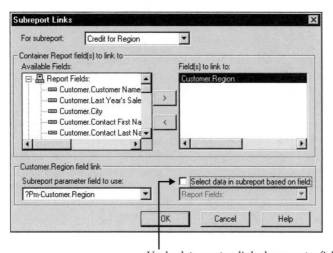

Uncheck to create a linked parameter field
that doesn't change subreport record selection

These steps will create the Pm- parameter field in the subreport and pass data to it, but the parameter field won't be used for subreport record selection. Then, just use the parameter field in subreport formulas or place it on the subreport for display, as desired.

Note *Chapter 12 discusses how to use parameter fields in your report.*

Using shared variables is a consistent way to pass data back and forth between the main report and one or more subreports, or even from subreport to subreport. You'll need to create formulas that declare the same shared variable in both the main report and subreport. You can assign the variable a value in the subreport and then read the contents of the variable in the main report. Or, you can assign a value in the main report and read it in the subreport.

Here's an example of a formula in a subreport that places the sum of a currency field into a shared variable:

```
WhilePrintingRecords;
Shared CurrencyVar CreditTotal := Sum ({Credit.Amount})
```

And, here's the corresponding formula in the main report that retrieves the value of the shared variable:

```
WhilePrintingRecords;
Shared CurrencyVar CreditTotal
```

For more information on assigning and using variables, and other formula topics, refer to Chapter 5.

Note	*Because subreports process after formulas in the main report processing cycle, you must take special steps to retrieve the contents of a shared variable set in a subreport. For example, if you place both the subreport and a formula to retrieve the contents of a shared variable set in that subreport in a group footer, you'll notice odd behavior. Typically, you'll find that the formula returns the value of the shared variable from the* previous *group, instead of the current group. This is because the subreport is setting the value of the shared variable after the formula to retrieve the variable has already processed. To resolve this problem, insert an additional section (for example, a Group Footer #1 b) as described in Chapter 8. Then, place the formula that retrieves the value of the shared variable in the second section (Group Footer #1 b), while leaving the subreport in the first section (Group Footer #1 a). The formula that retrieves the contents of the shared variable will not retrieve the value from the correct corresponding subreport.*

Showing an Informational Message Instead of the Empty Subreport

When you link subreports, there may be situations in which the subreport won't retrieve any records that match the linking field from the main report. Typically, this will just result in a subreport showing up without any details sections. If there are column headings or other information in other sections, they will appear with zeros for subtotals. You may prefer to display an informational message instead, similar to what's shown in Figure 11-5.

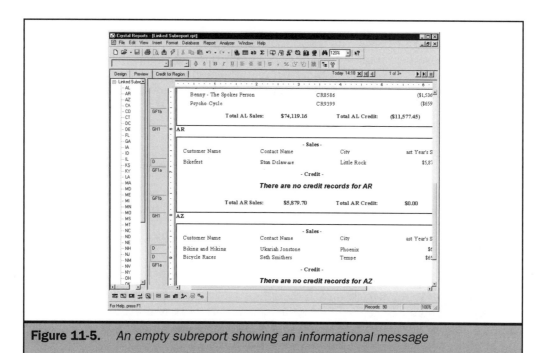

Figure 11-5.   *An empty subreport showing an informational message*

This is accomplished by conditionally suppressing different sections of the subreport, based on a condition indicating the presence or absence of details records. Look at the Design tab for the subreport.

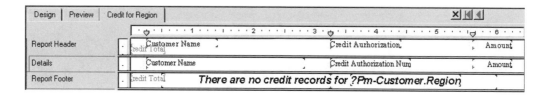

The report header and details sections contain objects that you want to appear if the subreport will return records. The report footer contains the object (the text message) that you want to appear if the subreport doesn't return records. This can be controlled by conditionally suppressing all sections using the Section Expert.

Conditionally suppress the section containing the informational message by adding the following formula with the Conditional Formula button next to the Section Expert's Suppress property:

```
Not IsNull({Credit.Credit Authorization Number})
```

Then, conditionally suppress the sections that contain the actual subreport data with the following conditional formula applied to the Suppress property:

```
IsNull({Credit.Credit Authorization Number})
```

Don't forget—you are conditionally *suppressing* these sections, not displaying them, so you may need to think backward. If the subreport is empty because no records were returned based on the linked field from the main report, the Credit Authorization Number will be null. In this case, you'll want to suppress the actual subreport data but not the informational message. If data is returned, then the Credit Authorization Number will contain data and will not be null. In this case, you want to suppress the informational message but not the actual subreport data.

Tip   *You can use this technique for all of your Crystal Reports, not just subreports. If you might potentially have main reports that return no records, you can display an informational message in them. See Chapter 8 for more information on conditionally formatting sections.*

Performance Considerations

Subreports create potential performance problems for your reporting projects. Here are some tips to help maximize performance for your report viewer. Obviously, these considerations are more important if a viewer will be viewing a report online using Crystal Reports or as an on-demand report on the Web with Crystal Enterprise. If a report is being printed or exported, subreports affect performance as well, but the user won't be staring at the screen waiting for them.

■ Use on-demand subreports if you can. That way, a viewer won't have to wait for many subreports to process. Viewers can double-click the individual subreports they want to see when they want to see them.

■ If you are creating a linked subreport, try to base the link on an indexed field in the subreport. This will cause record selection in the subreport to occur substantially faster. If the subreport is based on an ODBC or SQL database, make sure you are keeping as much of the SQL query on the server as possible (see Chapter 14 for SQL database performance considerations).

■ If you are linking subreports with formula fields, try to keep the formula field in the main report and use a database field in the subreport. Using formula fields in the subreport, particularly with subreports based on SQL databases, will move part or all of the subreport query off the server, impeding performance.

Chapter 12

Viewer Interaction
with Parameter Fields

If you are designing reports to distribute to a viewer audience that may not be familiar with Crystal Reports or the Select Expert, you will soon have the need to prompt the viewer for values that affect record selection, conditional formatting, or some other ad hoc information. This becomes even more crucial when the viewer doesn't actually have a copy of Crystal Reports, but wants to view a report presented in some "turnkey" fashion, such as an on-demand report run on the Web with Crystal Enterprise (discussed in section II of this book). In these situations, the viewer won't have the ability to make changes with the Select Expert anyway.

The ideal solution for these types of ad hoc reporting requirements would be to present the viewer with a dialog box prompt, preferably including a choice of default values or a range of values, to help the user enter the correct values for the prompt. The response the viewer provides could then be passed to the Select Expert to customize record selection, and the values the viewer supplied could also be included on the report to indicate what data makes up the report.

This ideal solution is made possible by *parameter fields*, prompts that are presented to the viewer when he or she refreshes the report. The value the viewer provides is then passed on to the Select Expert, report formulas, or conditional-formatting formulas to customize the way the report appears, based on the viewer's response. The viewer doesn't have to know how to enter selection criteria or conditional formulas to customize the way the report behaves.

Consider the following report:

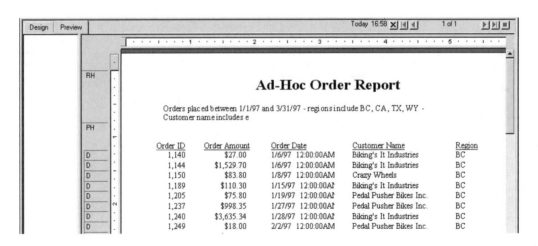

This report uses three fields in record selection:

- **Order Date** Filtered with a Between selection criterion to include orders that were placed in the first quarter of 1997 (between January 1 and March 31).

- **Region** Filtered with a One Of selection criterion to include orders placed from BC, CA, TX, and WY.

■ **Customer Name**   Filtered with a Like selection criterion to include customer names that contain a lowercase *e*.

These criteria are hard-coded into the Select Expert, and a text object appears in the report header to indicate the restrictions.

The difficulty comes when you want the person reviewing the report to be able to easily change these criteria whenever the report is refreshed. The way this report is currently designed, the viewer must have the ability to alter record selection (and know enough about its intricacies to be able to change it). That person also must be able to edit the text object that displays what records are included. Even in this case, it's time-consuming to change this information every time the viewer wants to change these options. Parameter fields are the answer.

Using parameter fields is, at minimum, a two-step process. The third step is optional:

1. Create the parameter field.

2. Use the parameter field in record selection.

3. Place the parameter field on the report, perhaps embedded in a text object, to indicate what is included on the report.

Creating a Parameter Field

Parameter fields are created from the Field Explorer, which can be displayed when either the Design or Preview tab is selected. You can click the Field Explorer button in the Standard toolbar, or choose Insert | Field Object from the pull-down menus. If the Field Explorer is already displayed, just click on the plus sign next to the Parameter Fields category to show existing parameter fields.

If there are parameter fields in the report already, you can edit them by selecting the desired parameter field and clicking the Edit button on the Field Explorer toolbar. You can also rename or delete existing parameter fields with the Rename and Delete buttons on the toolbar. If there are no existing parameter fields, or if you wish to create a new parameter field, ensure that the Parameter Fields category of the Field Explorer is selected (click on it), then click the New button. You can also right-click on the Parameter Fields category of the Field Explorer and choose New from the pop-up menu. The Create Parameter Field dialog box appears, as shown in Figure 12-1; the various fields and options are described in Table 12-1.

Choose a name for your parameter field. It can be the same name as other database or formula fields, because Crystal Reports distinguishes parameter fields by preceding the parameter field name with a question mark. Choose a descriptive yet reasonably short name for your parameter field.

Although not absolutely required for parameter fields, you'll want to enter the message that will appear in the Supply Parameter Field dialog box when a viewer is prompted to provide the value. The message is entered in the Prompting Text field and

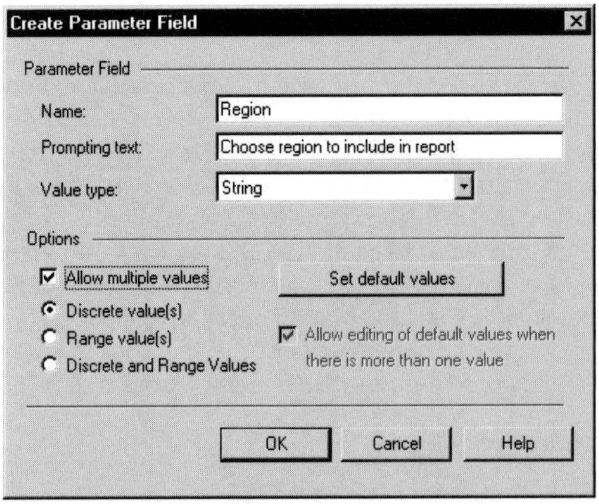

Figure 12-1.   *The Create Parameter Field dialog box*

Field or Option	Description
Name	Name of the parameter field being created.
Prompting Text	Descriptive text that appears when the viewer is prompted for the parameter value.
Value Type	Data type to assign to the parameter field.
Allow Multiple Values	Check this box to allow more than one value to be assigned to the parameter field.
Discrete Value(s) Range Value(s) Discrete and Range Values	Choose between a single parameter field value, a beginning and ending value range, or a combination of both. You may choose Discrete and Range Values only if you check Allow Multiple Values. If you then choose Discrete and Range Values, you'll be able to enter a combination of one or more discrete (single) values and range (from/to) values.

Table 12-1.   *Create Parameter Field Dialog Box Options*

Field or Option	Description
Set Default Values	Displays the Set Default Values dialog box (described later in the chapter).
Allow Editing of Default Values When There Is More Than One Value	Check this box to allow the viewer to type values into the parameter field, even if the values are not in the drop-down pick list.

Table 12-1. *Create Parameter Field Dialog Box Options* (continued)

should be easy to understand and helpful to the user, such as "Enter the state code (2 characters only) for this report." The prompting text can be up to 254 characters long, although prompting text that long will probably look unsightly when the parameter value is prompted for. Crystal Reports will word-wrap the prompting text when the viewer is prompted, if the prompting text won't all fit on one line.

Choose a value or data type for the parameter field from the Value Type drop-down list. This is a crucial step, as it determines how your parameter field can be used in record selection, formulas, and conditional formatting. For example, if you are planning on using the parameter field to compare to a string database field in the Select Expert, choose a String value type. If you are going to limit the report to a certain date range, based on a date/time field in the database, choose a DateTime value type.

These are the only items that are actually required for using a parameter field. However, there are many features in Crystal Reports 8.5 that enhance the flexibility of parameter fields. You can set up a *pick list* that provides one or more default values for a viewer to select. You can allow the viewer to select a from/to *range of values,* which is helpful for selecting beginning and ending date ranges. And, if you are using a string parameter field, you can set minimum and maximum lengths for the parameter field, or use an *edit mask* to force the viewer to enter the string in a certain way. These features are selected in the Set Default Values dialog box. To display this dialog box, shown in Figure 12-2, click the Set Default Values button. The various options for this dialog box are described in Table 12-2.

Note *The Set Default Values dialog box will change, depending on the value type you choose for the parameter field, and whether you choose discrete or range values. You'll find options on this dialog box that are appropriate for the settings you choose on the Create Parameter Field dialog box.*

Setting Up a Pick List

If you don't add any default values when you first create a parameter field, the viewer will have to type in the value for the parameter field. While this sometimes may be

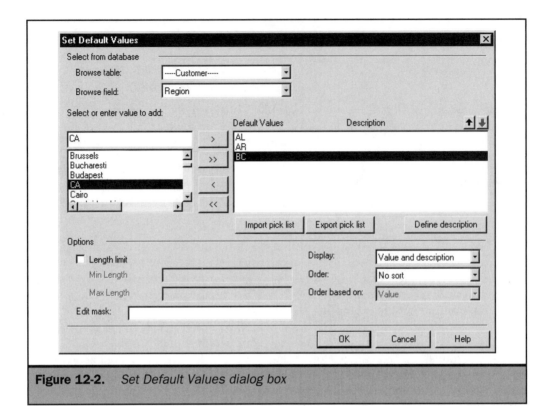

Figure 12-2. *Set Default Values dialog box*

Field or Option	Description
Browse Table	Choose a database table to help provide default values.
Browse Field	Choose a database field to help provide default values.
Select or Enter Value To Add	Type a value to be added to the Default Values list or select a value from the database with the scrolling list.
Default Values	List of values that will appear in the parameter field's pick list. Use the up and down arrow keys to the right of this list to change the order the default values will appear in the pick list.

Table 12-2. *Set Default Values Dialog Box Options*

Field or Option	Description
Up/Down arrows	Use the up and down arrows above the upper-right corner of the Default Values list to change the order that the default values will appear in when the viewer displays the pick list.
Import Pick List Export Pick List	Imports an ASCII text file into the default values list or exports the values you've already added to an ASCII text file that can be used with other reports.
Define Description	Displays a dialog box allowing you to type a description for the parameter field value that's currently selected. This is helpful when you are using coded fields for the parameter field and want the report viewer to see a description of the coded value.
Length Limit	Check this box to limit the length of data that can be added to the parameter field (will only appear with string parameter fields).
Min Length Max Length	If Length Limit is selected, enter the minimum and maximum lengths for the value to be entered into the parameter field (will only appear with string parameter fields).
Range-Limited Field	By checking this box, will allow the values a user enters into the parameter field to be forced to be within a certain range of values (will only appear with numeric or date/time parameter fields)
Min Value/Max Value or Start Date-time/End Date-time	Enter the minimum and maximum values or beginning and ending dates/times that a user will be allowed to enter for the parameter field (will only appear with numeric or date/time parameter fields)

Table 12-2. *Set Default Values Dialog Box Options* (continued)

Field or Option	Description
Edit Mask	Control how information can be entered into the parameter field (will only appear with string parameter fields).
Display	If you enter descriptions for parameter fields, determines whether both the value and description, just the value, or just the description appears when prompting for the parameter field.
Order	Choose whether to not sort the default values at all (leaving them in the same order you entered them here) or to sort them in ascending or descending order when prompting for the parameter field.
Order Based On	If you choose a sort order, determines whether the order is based on the parameter field value or description.

Table 12-2. *Set Default Values Dialog Box Options* (continued)

desirable, it requires that the viewer know enough about the parameter field and the way the report and database are designed that they can type the value correctly. They may make a mistake by misspelling a name or entering an incorrect code for the field. By creating a pick list, you can let the viewer choose from a predefined list of default values.

The pick list presented to the viewer will be the set of values contained in the Default Values list (refer to Figure 12-2). You can add items to this list by typing them in the text box under the Select or Enter Value To Add label and clicking the right arrow next to the text box.

Or, you can choose a database table and field to choose values from. To do this, choose a table and field in the Browse Table and Browse Field drop-down lists. This will fill the list under the Select or Enter Value To Add label with sample data from the database. You can then select an item in the list to place in the text box. Then, by clicking the right arrow, you can add the selected item to the Default Values list. If you want to add all the sample database values, click the double right arrow. If you decide you don't want some existing values to be included in the pick list, you can remove specific items by selecting them in the Default Values list with the left arrow, or you can remove all the values by clicking the double left arrow.

 While it might be a nice feature for a future Crystal Reports release, choosing a Browse Table and Browse Field in the Set Default Values dialog box will not automatically populate the parameter field's pick list with live database data whenever the viewer is prompted for the value. This table and field combination is only used to provide a list of sample values for you to manually add to the Default Values list. If the database later changes, the pick list won't reflect the changes unless you manually edit the parameter field and add new values to the Default Values list.

You can force the viewer to only choose values from the pick list by unchecking the Allow Editing of Default Values check box back in the Create Parameter Field dialog box. If you leave this option checked, the viewer will be able to select an entry from the pick list or type in their own entry.

Crystal Reports 8.5 includes some additional features to improve flexibility with pick lists. You can add descriptive values to hard-to-remember codes, as well as import or export ASCII text files that contain the values that appear in the Default Values list. You'll soon find situations in which you're using a parameter field to limit record selection based on a coded field. Perhaps you have one-letter codes to indicate colors of products, such as B equates to black, L to blue, R to red, and G to green. If you'd prefer that the report viewer not have to remember these codes, but be able to choose the actual colors, define a description for the single-letter default values. Then, even though the user chooses Blue, the parameter field will supply the letter *L* to the Select Expert. Do this by selecting the default value you want to add the description to and then clicking the Define Description button.

If you have a large number of default values (and potentially descriptions) that you'd like to add to your pick list, you may want to import a pick list file. When you click the Import Pick List button, you are presented with a standard File Open dialog box that asks you to select the ASCII text file containing your pick list data. When you choose the appropriate pick list text file and click OK, the Default Values list will be populated with the data from the text file. If you wish to create a pick list file from the existing values that you've already added to the Default Values list (to use in another report, for example), click the Export Pick List button. A standard File Save dialog box will appear in which you can specify the filename for the pick list file.

Pick List File Format

If you wish to create pick list files on your own, using Notepad or some other programmatic option, such as a custom Visual Basic program, you need to know the particular file format that Crystal Reports requires for pick lists. The sample Region Pick List.TXT file that appears on the CD accompanying this book looks like this:

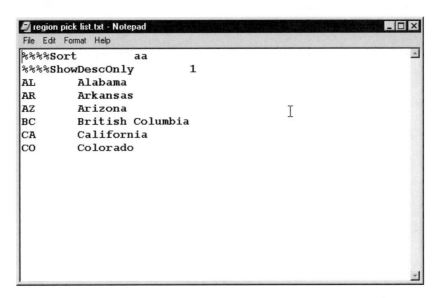

At a minimum, you simply need to type in the parameter field default values you want to appear in the pick list and press ENTER after each (or have your program follow each value with a carriage return/line feed combination). If you wish to add descriptions for the values, press the TAB key between the parameter field value and the description (if you're programmatically creating the pick list, a tab character can be added by inserting an ASCII value of 9).

You may optionally add one or two *directives* at the top of the file. Directives are words that control how Crystal Reports will display the pick list—either showing values and descriptions, or just descriptions only, and how to sort the pick list. Begin a directive with four percent signs, followed by the name of the directive. Directive names are **Sort** and **ShowDescOnly**. Then, press the TAB key and type in a value for the directive.

The Sort directive accepts four values:

aa	Sort the pick list in ascending order using an alphabetical sort.
ad	Sort the pick list in descending order using an alphabetical sort.
na	Sort the pick list in ascending order using a numeric sort.
nd	Sort the pick list in descending order using a numeric sort.

The **ShowDescOnly** directive accepts two values:

1   Show Descriptions only. However, the actual code matching up to the chosen description (the value) will be provided to the report.

0   Show Values and Descriptions. Will show both the code and descriptions for the code.

Responding to Parameter Field Prompts

Once you've created a parameter field, you will be prompted for it the first time you preview the report after the parameter field has been created. The Enter Parameter Values dialog box will be displayed.

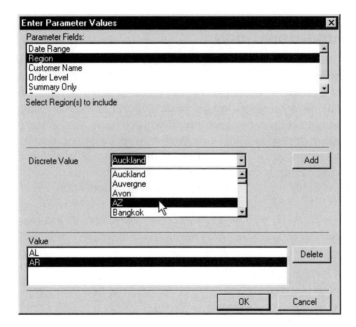

If you haven't entered any default values or created a pick list, the viewer will need to type their response to the prompt. If you've created a pick list, the prompt will be a drop-down list from which one of the predefined values can be selected. If you have created more than one parameter field for the report, only one Enter Parameter Values dialog box will appear, but each parameter field will appear in the list. Click the parameter field you want to select.

Typically, parameter fields will appear in the Enter Parameter Values dialog box in the order you created them. If you'd like to change the order in which they appear, return to the Parameter category of the Field Explorer and reorder the parameter fields with the small up and down arrow buttons in the upper right of the box.

When you refresh the report, the Refresh Report Data dialog box will ask whether to use the currently set parameter field values or to prompt for new values. If you use the current values, the database will be reread with the current values in the parameter fields. If you choose to prompt for new values, the Enter Parameter Values dialog box will appear again, and you'll need to specify new values for all parameter fields. When you refresh the report and select Prompt for New Parameter Values, you'll need to resupply all parameter values. The information you had placed in them previously won't be retained.

Value Type Considerations

The value type you choose for your parameter field determines how the parameter field can be used in the rest of the report. If, for example, you need to compare a parameter field to a date database field, you'll need to use a date parameter field. The value type will also determine how the report viewer must respond to the parameter field prompt.

String and number/currency parameter fields are fairly straightforward. In the case of strings, a viewer can respond with any combination of letters, numbers, or special characters. For numbers, only the numbers 0 through 9 and a minus sign can be used—other characters will result in an error message. Using date, time, date/time, or Boolean parameter fields will introduce some new features and limitations.

 Ranges and edit masks may limit what a viewer can enter into a parameter field. These special features are discussed later in this chapter.

Dates and Times

You'll often want to use date or time parameter fields to limit your report to certain date or time ranges. You can choose value types of Date, Time, or DateTime. You can build a pick list for these value types just like you can for number or string fields. And, if you leave Allow Editing of Default Values checked in the Create Parameter Field dialog box, you'll be able to choose dates or times other than those in the pick list.

When you are prompted for a date or time parameter field, a few special features are available to you:

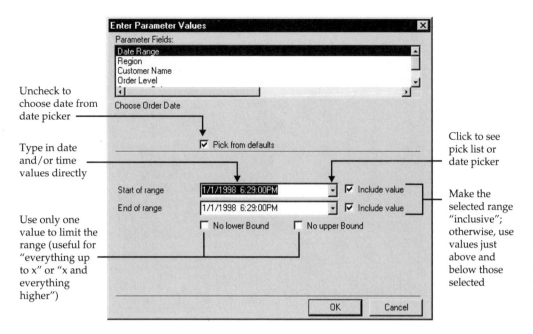

Uncheck to choose date from date picker

Type in date and/or time values directly

Use only one value to limit the range (useful for "everything up to x" or "x and everything higher")

Click to see pick list or date picker

Make the selected range "inclusive"; otherwise, use values just above and below those selected

If you didn't check Allow Editing of Default Values… when you created the parameter field, you'll only be able to click the drop-down list and choose from the pick list. If you did check Allow Editing of Default Values… when you created the parameter field, you can just type a date and/or time value into the prompt.

Preformatted dates and times will appear in the dialog box—just type the correct date and time over any existing default value. If no pick list or default has been specified, the current date and time will appear in the prompt. These can be left as they are or you can use them as a guide for typing in the correct values.

If a pick list is available, click the down arrow to see the available values in a drop-down list. There may also be a Pick from Defaults check box available if Allow Editing of Default Values was checked when the parameter field was created. If you uncheck this option, the pick list will no longer be available.

If you are working with a time value, there will be increment and decrement arrows to the right of the time value. Use these to increment the selected hour, minute, or second up or down. If you are working with a date value, the down arrow will show the *date picker*, which is a small calendar from which you can choose the desired date.

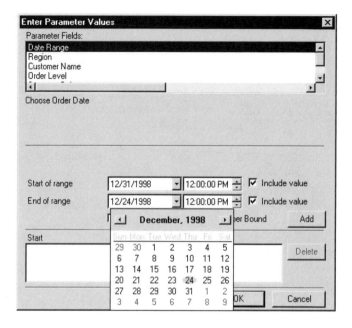

Boolean Parameter Fields

You may find a Boolean parameter field helpful when using record selection based on a Boolean database field or when conditionally formatting based on a parameter field value. A Boolean parameter field, like a Boolean formula (discussed in Chapter 5), can contain one of only two values: true or false.

When you choose a value type of Boolean in the Create Parameter Field dialog box, the dialog box changes to accommodate the special features of a Boolean parameter field, as shown in Figure 12-3. Specify the Name of the field and the Prompting Text for the parameter field just as you would for other parameter fields. You can also choose a True or False default value, as well as specify descriptions for the values, by clicking the Set Default Values button.

The Options section is different for a Boolean parameter field. If you check the Place in Parameter Group check box, you will add this parameter field to a grouping of one or more other Boolean parameter fields. Boolean parameter field groups allow you to simulate the "radio button" behavior you see in Crystal Reports and other Windows applications. Since you can have more than one group of parameter fields, use the Parameter Group Number text box to specify a group number for this parameter field.

If you check Group Is Exclusive, only one parameter field in a group can be chosen at a time in the drop-down list. The chosen field will return true, and all others will

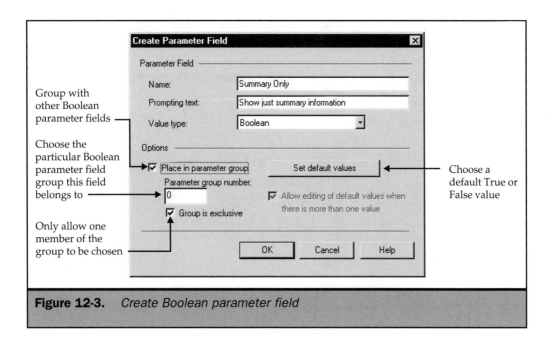

Group with
other Boolean
parameter fields

Choose the
particular Boolean
parameter field
group this field
belongs to

Only allow one
member of the
group to be chosen

Choose a
default True or
False value

Figure 12-3. *Create Boolean parameter field*

return false. If you don't check Group Is Exclusive, you will be able to click the Add button to choose more than one member of the group. Each chosen parameter field will return true, while others not chosen will return false.

For example, you might create six Boolean parameter fields. The first won't be placed in a group, three of them will be assigned to group number 0 and the group will be exclusive, and the remaining two will be assigned to group number 1, which will not be exclusive.

The first parameter field will appear on its own when the prompting dialog box appears. There will be two other Boolean parameters in the dialog box:

- **Group #0**   Contains a drop-down list containing the prompting text for the three parameter fields placed in the first group—you can only choose one of these three parameters because the group is exclusive.

- **Group #1**   Includes the prompting text for the last two parameter fields. You may choose one *or more* of these parameter fields by choosing it and clicking the Add button. Any parameter fields added this way will be set to True.

The following illustration shows a prompt for a Boolean parameter field group.

Choose available parameters from all those in group →

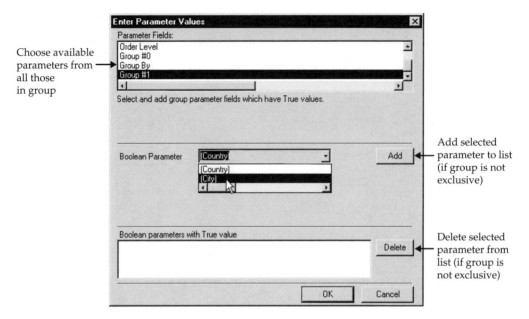

Add selected ← parameter to list (if group is not exclusive)

Delete selected ← parameter from list (if group is not exclusive)

This group is not exclusive, so you can choose more than one of the Boolean parameter fields and add them to a list. Any parameters added to the list will return true when the report runs. If you create an exclusive group, the Add and Delete buttons, as well as the list box below the drop-down list, won't appear. You'll only be able to choose one of the parameter fields in the drop-down list. It will return true, while all others in the group will return false.

Using Parameter Fields in Record Selection

Probably the most common use for a parameter field is in report record selection. By creating a parameter field and using it with the Select Expert or a record-selection formula, you can prompt the viewer to provide variable information when the report runs, and have the report record selection reflect the viewer's choices.

After creating the desired parameter fields, use the toolbar button or pull-down menu option to start the Select Expert. Add a selection tab for the database field you want to compare to the value the viewer enters into the parameter field. When you choose the drop-down list to see sample database values, you'll see parameter fields of the same data type in the list. Choose the correct parameter field.

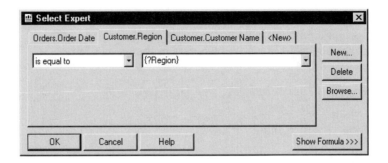

 Only parameter fields of the same data type as the database field will show up in the Select Expert. If you don't see the parameter field you expect in the Select Expert, it wasn't created with the same data type as the database field you are using. Change the value type of the parameter field and rerun the Select Expert.

If you use the Formula Editor to edit the record-selection formula, you'll see all parameter fields (regardless of data type) in the Field Tree box. Choose the parameter field you want to use in the record-selection formula. The formula may look something like this:

```
{Customer.Region} = {?Region}
```

Make sure you choose a parameter field of the same data type, or use functions to convert the parameter field to the correct data type. If you try, for example, to compare a numeric parameter field to a string database field, you'll receive an error in the Formula Editor.

Displaying Parameter Fields on the Report

One of the other major benefits of using parameter fields is that you can place them on your report just like database or formula fields. Whatever value the viewer placed in them before the report ran will appear on the report. By creatively using parameter fields, you can have a customized report that changes record selection and shows the values used in record selection on the report.

To place a parameter field on the report, drag and drop it from the Field Explorer just like you would a database or formula field. Depending on the value type of the parameter field, you can format it using all the usual Format toolbar or Format Editor features discussed earlier in this book. You can also combine parameter fields with other fields and literal text inside text objects (as discussed in Chapter 2). A text object combining a parameter field that looks like this in the Design tab:

Orders over ?Order Level are highlighted

will use the value supplied by the viewer when the report runs.

Orders over $2,500.00 are highlighted

Special Parameter Field Features

Parameter fields have become increasingly sophisticated as new versions of Crystal Reports have been released, particularly Versions 7 and 8. For example, a viewer can choose multiple values for a single parameter field to allow One-Of types of record selection. Parameter fields can be specified to include entire ranges of values, so a viewer can, for example, include all orders placed between January 1, 1998 and December 31, 1998. And, string parameter fields can be limited to certain lengths (for example, no less than three nor more than six characters) or limited to certain formats with edit masks.

Multiple Values

Often, you may want to be able to choose more than one value for a parameter field and have the report recognize the multiple values in record selection. You may, for example, want to initially specify only one region for a report, and later run the same report including ten different regions. If you're not using parameter fields, you'll need to change the Select Expert operator from Equal To to One Of and select the multiple regions.

By clicking the Allow Multiple Values check box in the Options section of the Create Parameter Field dialog box, you allow multiple entries to be added to a parameter list—you, in essence, turn the parameter field into a single object called an *array* that contains more than one value. Even if you choose an Equal To operator in the Select Expert with a multiple-value parameter field, all the values in the array will be included in record selection. When you are prompted for a multiple-value parameter field, you can use the Add and Delete buttons to add or remove multiple values. The values that are added to the list can be either chosen from a pick list or typed in the text box and then added with the Add button (typing values is dependent upon the setting of the Allow Editing of Default Values… check box in the Create Parameter Field dialog box).

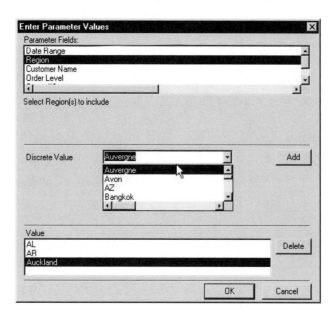

<table>
<tr><td>**Caution**</td><td>*If you add a multiple-value parameter field to your report to display selected values, only the first value will actually appear on the report, even though all values will be used by the Select Expert. Use array functions in a formula, such as the Join function, to retrieve all the values in the parameter field. The Join function is described in detail in Chapter 5.*</td></tr>
</table>

Range Values

Crystal Reports provides *range-value* parameter fields, which allow you to create just one parameter field that can contain both low and high values. When this parameter field is supplied to the Select Expert with the Equals operator, it effectively supplies both the low and high values and changes the operator to Between.

To create a range-value parameter field, click the Range Value(s) radio button in the Create Parameter Field dialog box (this is the opposite of a discrete-value parameter field, which doesn't contain high/low values). This will change the way the parameter field prompt appears when the report is refreshed.

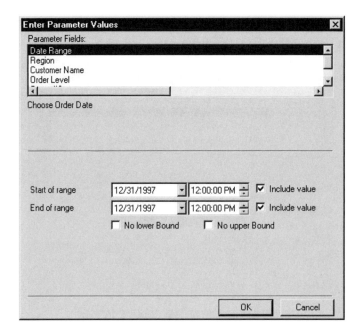

There are now two prompts to choose or enter values: the Start of Range prompt and the End of Range prompt. These two prompts behave the same way a single prompt would behave, being based on pick list creation, allowing editing of default values, and so forth. However, when the viewer clicks OK, both prompts will be supplied to the Select Expert or record-selection formula, and all records between and including the selected values will be returned.

Normally, range-value parameter fields are "inclusive"—that is, the values returned to the report *include* the two values that are specified in the Enter Parameter Values dialog box. If you uncheck Include Value, however, the chosen value *will not* be included in the range. For example, if you choose the number 300 as the Start of Range and leave Include Value checked, any records including the number 300 will be included in the report. If you uncheck Include Value, anything over 300 will be included, but not 300 itself.

There are also No Lower Bound and No Upper Bound check boxes to allow you to make the range an open-ended range. If you leave both boxes unchecked (the default), the range will be limited to the finite values you enter as Start of Range and End of Range. If you check No Lower Bound or No Upper Bound (you can't select both), the corresponding range value will be discarded and the range will only include the other value. For example, if you specify a range of 100 to 1000, checking No Lower Bound will discard 100 and return records where the value is simply less than 1000 (or less than and including 1000 if you leave Include Value checked). Checking No Upper Bound will return records exceeding 100 (or equal to or greater than 100 if you leave Include Value checked).

CRYSTAL REPORTS 8.5
INTRODUCED

If you add a range-value parameter field directly to your report to display selected values, the parameter field will not show anything, because the parameter field is actually a range value. A *range* value is a single object (in this case, the parameter field) that actually contains the entire range of values specified by the parameter field. If you just put the object on the report by itself, Crystal Reports won't return a value, because it's not sure which value in the range you want to return. You can use range functions in the Formula Editor to return the first or last entries in the range. For example, the following formula will display the starting and ending dates of a date-range parameter field:

```
"Orders between " + ToText(Minimum({?Date Range}),"M/d/yyyy") + " and " +
ToText(Maximum({?Date Range}),"M/d/yyyy")
```

The Minimum and Maximum functions return the first and last entries in the range, respectively. The ToText function turns the date values from the array into strings.

If, in addition to checking the Range Value(s) check box, you click the Allow Multiple Values check box in the Create Parameter Field dialog box, the parameter field will allow entry of multiple range values, or an *array of ranges*. For example, you could choose to see orders placed between January 1, 1998 and January 31, 1998; March 1, 1998 and March 31, 1998; and December 1, 1998 and December 31, 1998. When you are prompted for a range-value parameter field that allows multiple values, a list will appear in which you can add multiple ranges.

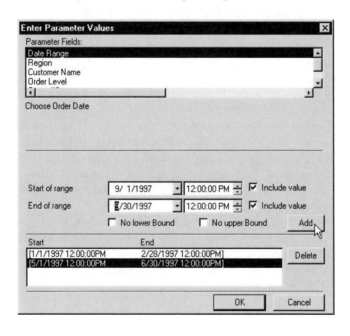

Different values can be specified in the Start of Range and End of Range areas and added to the list with the Add button. If you want to delete an existing range, select it in the list and click the Delete button.

This single parameter field, when supplied to the Select Expert or record-selection formula, will effectively change the selection operator to Between *and* One Of at the same time.

The Minimum and Maximum array functions demonstrated earlier behave a little differently with combination range/multiple-value parameter fields. In this case, the array will only have two values: the first entry in the first range, and the last value in the last range.

Controlling Parameter Field Data Entry

One of the issues Crystal Reports users face is how to best customize the user interface for "turnkey" report users—those that aren't familiar with the intricacies of Crystal Reports. In an ideal world, the user interface will contain business rules, limits, and customized formatting to guide an end user through proper choices of parameters. While this ideal world is best provided with a customized "front end" program developed, perhaps, in Visual Basic, Crystal Reports 8.5 still gives the report developer a fair amount of control over how end users can enter data into parameter fields.

Limiting Entry to Certain Ranges of Values

For parameter field types, except string and Boolean, you can limit the range of entries that a viewer can supply. By checking Range Limited Field in the Set Default Values dialog box, you can specify a beginning and ending value for the range in the controls that become enabled below the check box. When the viewer is prompted for the parameter field, they will be unable to enter values that are below the beginning range or above the ending range.

An extra-added feature of range limiting is the group of default values that can be added to the parameter field. When you range-limit a parameter field and choose a database table and field to help populate the Default Values list, only database items that fall within the specified range can be added to the Default Values list. If you use the double right arrow to add all browsed database values to the list, only those that fall within the beginning and ending ranges will be added.

When a viewer is prompted to supply a range-limited number or currency parameter field, they will receive an error message if they type in a value outside the range. If the range-limited parameter field is a date, time, or date/time field, the viewer will not be able to even type dates or times outside the range. The date picker will only display dates that fall within the range.

Minimum and Maximum Lengths

If you create a string parameter field, the Length Limit check box appears in the Set Default Values dialog box. By checking this option, a Min Length and a Max Length text box are enabled below the check box. You can specify the minimum and maximum number of characters that must be supplied when responding to the parameter field's prompt. If you enter too few or too many characters, an error message will appear.

If you supply a length limit, you are also restricted from adding any default values to the pick list that fall outside the minimum and maximum lengths.

Edit Masks

The most flexibility for controlling string parameter field entry comes from *edit masks*. An edit mask is a string of characters that controls many different aspects of data entry. One example might be an edit mask that allows only two uppercase characters to be entered (perhaps for a state abbreviation). Another example would be an edit mask that sets up the parameter field to accept data in a social security number format, only accepting number characters, and automatically adding hyphens between the third and fourth characters and between the fifth and sixth characters.

The key to using edit masks is learning the correct use of masking characters. These are listed in Table 12-3. Note that not only is the character you use significant, but so is the *case* of the character—uppercase and lowercase versions of the same character perform different masking functions.

Character	Usage
A	Requires entry of an alphanumeric character.
a	Allows an alphanumeric character to be entered, but doesn't require it.
0 (zero)	Requires a digit between 0 and 9 to be entered.
9	Allows a digit between 0 and 9 or a space to be entered, but doesn't require it.
#	Allows a digit, space, or plus or minus sign to be entered, but doesn't require it.
L	Requires entry of a letter between A and Z to be entered.
?	Allows a letter between A and Z to be entered, but doesn't require it.
&	Requires entry of any character or space.
C	Allows entry of any character or space, but doesn't require it.
>	Automatically converts any subsequent characters to uppercase.
<	Automatically converts any subsequent characters to lowercase.
\	Causes the next character to be included in the parameter field as a literal—helpful if you want to actually include masking characters in the parameter field.
. , : ; - / or any character not listed in this table	These characters will be included in the parameter field as literals—they will appear in the parameter field exactly as typed.
Password	Causes characters typed in the parameter field to be displayed with asterisks instead of their actual characters; the actual characters are passed to the report.

Table 12-3.   *Parameter Field Masking Characters*

So, an edit mask of (000) 000-0000 when used with a phone number parameter field will require entry of the area code and phone number portions, and will include the parentheses and hyphen in the parameter field as literals. An edit mask of Password will replace characters typed in the parameter field with asterisks. This is commonly used for entry of passwords or other sensitive information to prevent the information from being learned by someone looking at the screen. When the viewer clicks OK, the actual characters typed will be passed to the report.

Conditional Formatting with Parameter Fields

Parameter fields can be used to customize other parts of the report, not just record selection. If a viewer wishes to highlight orders over a certain amount, they can specify the amount in a parameter field and use the parameter field to set conditional formatting. If they wish to see summary data instead of details data, they can respond to a Boolean parameter field that is used to suppress the details section. Basically, any place you can do conditional formatting, you can base it on parameter fields just as easily as you can on database or formula fields.

Highlighting Data Based on Parameter Fields

Once a parameter field has been created, it can be used for conditional formatting just as easily as any database or formula field. As with any parameter field, you need to consider the value type used to create the parameter field. For example, you might wish to prompt the viewer for an order amount threshold, so that you can highlight orders over that amount in red. If the Order Amount field in the database is contained in a currency data type, you'll need to either create the parameter field with the currency data type or do some data-type conversion in the conditional formula.

A currency parameter field will prompt the viewer to enter an order amount threshold. Then, you can use two conditional formulas: one for the background color of the details section and one for the font color of the order amount and customer name fields. The details section background color can be formatted to show in silver if the order exceeds the parameter field, as follows:

```
If {Orders.Order Amount} > {?Order Level} Then Silver Else NoColor
```

The following conditional formula, when applied to the font color of both the order amount and customer name, will display the fields in red if the order amount exceeds the threshold:

```
If {Orders.Order Amount} > {?Order Level} Then Red Else Black
```

Figure 12-4 shows the result when a threshold of $2,500 is supplied to the parameter field prompt.

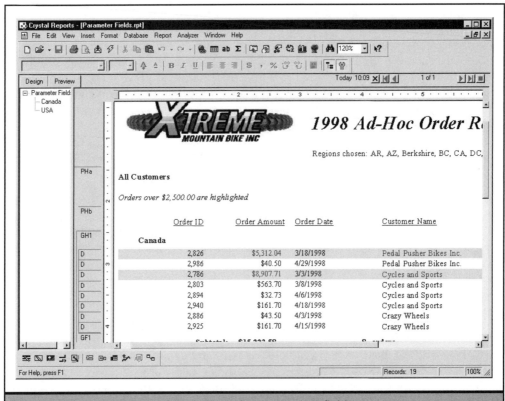

Figure 12-4. *Conditional formatting using parameter fields*

  Since the Highlighting Expert only allows you to compare to actual database values to set formatting conditionally, the Highlighting Expert will not work with parameter fields. You must use the Conditional Formula buttons that appear in the Format Editor if you wish to conditionally format with parameter fields.

Conditionally Suppressing Based on Parameter Fields

Use a parameter field just like a database or formula field to conditionally suppress individual objects or sections. Since the Suppress property requires a Boolean formula when being set conditionally, you can create a Boolean parameter field and supply it as the sole part of the Boolean formula, or you can create a Boolean formula by using a comparison operator with another type of parameter field.

You could, for example, create a Boolean parameter field called Summary Only that returns a true or false value based on the viewer's choice. By simply supplying the Boolean parameter field as the only item in a section or object's Suppress conditional formula, you could control whether the details section or a page header section containing column headings for the details section appears or doesn't appear.

When prompted for this parameter field, the viewer could select a True or False option for the Summary Only parameter field. You could then place this parameter field directly in the Suppress conditional formula for the details section. If the Summary Only parameter were true (indicating that the viewer wants a summary-only report), the details section would be suppressed. You could also suppress the page header section that contains column headings for the details fields.

Using Parameter Fields with Formulas

There will be many situations in which you need to prompt for a parameter field in a certain way or choose a particular value type for a parameter field so it will work properly with record selection. However, you might want to display the parameter field on the report in a different way, perform some calculation based on the parameter field, or otherwise manipulate the parameter field in a formula. Or, you may want to provide some variable information to a formula, such as a sales tax rate. By setting up a parameter field to prompt for the tax rate, it's very easy to run the report for different states or cities that have varying sales tax rates.

When you create a parameter field, it will appear in the Formula Editor's Field Tree box under Report Fields. It can be added to a formula just like a database field or another formula. Just remember the value type you choose when creating the parameter field—you must use it correctly inside the formula to avoid type-mismatch errors. You may need to use ToText, ToNumber, or other conversion functions.

Using a Parameter Field for Partial Text Matches

A handy capability of the Select Expert is the Like operator that can be used when selecting records based on string database fields. Like allows you to supply *wildcard characters,* such as the question mark (?) and asterisk (*) to indicate single-character and whole-field matches, respectively. For example, supplying a Select Expert operator of Like with the literal *?eor?e* would return George, Jeorge, Jeorje, or Georje. Using the Like operator with an asterisk in the literal *Je** would return Jean, Jenny, Jennifer, and Jerry.

 A more complete discussion of record selection is contained in Chapter 6.

By allowing question marks and asterisks to be included in parameter fields, and by using the Like operator in the Select Expert, you give your report viewer great flexibility in choosing only the records they want to see. However, if you want a meaningful message to appear on the report indicating what the user has chosen, you'll need to use a formula to display different information than the parameter field actually supplies to the Select Expert.

Consider a parameter field called Customer Name that will prompt the viewer to add question marks or asterisks for partial-match searches:

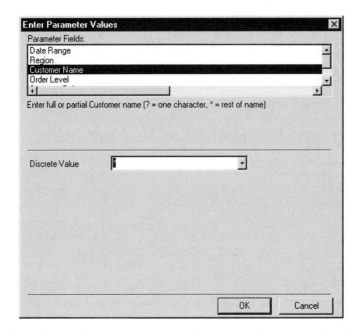

If you wish to place a descriptive message in the page header indicating which customers have been chosen, you can create the following formula:

```
If {?Customer Name} = "*" Then
    "All Customers"
Else
    If Instr({?Customer Name},"?") > 0 or
        Instr({?Customer Name},"*") > 0 Then
        "Customers matching the pattern " + {?Customer Name}
    Else
        "Customer: " + {?Customer Name}
```

This formula simply uses the Customer Name parameter field as you would another database or formula field in an If-Then-Else statement. If the parameter field only contains an asterisk, it will return all records, so the formula returns "All Customers." Otherwise, if the parameter field contains at least one asterisk or question mark (the Instr function will return the location of the first occurrence of the character, or zero if there isn't any occurrence), the formula indicates that the report is based on a partial pattern. Finally, if there are no asterisks or question marks at all, the report will be returning an exact text match to the parameter field, and this formula indicates that.

Using a Parameter Field to Change Sorting or Grouping

You may often wish to have a report viewer choose the report sorting or grouping on the fly. Since a parameter field can't actually return a database or formula-field name itself, you need to create a formula based on the parameter field, and use that formula as the sort or group field in the report.

You could, for example, create a parameter field called Group By that prompts for grouping by Customer or Region. These would be the only two options, as the viewer will not be allowed to edit the default values. The prompt for this parameter field would look like this:

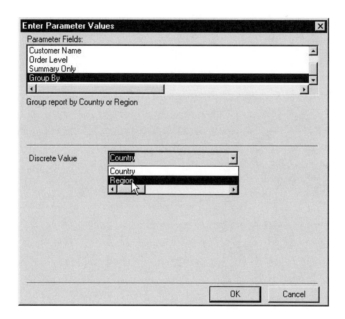

Because the parameter field will only contain the string Region or Country, you can't use the parameter field directly as a sort or group field. You need to create a formula based on the parameter field and supply it as the sort or group field. Look at this formula:

```
If {?Group By} = "Country" Then {Customer.Country}
Else {Customer.Region}
```

This will actually return a different database field based on the parameter field's value. Then, this formula can be supplied as the grouping or sorting field, and the group or sort will change based on the viewer's response to the parameter field.

You may pay a slight performance penalty when you use this method with SQL or ODBC databases. Since the sorting or grouping will be done with a formula field and not directly with a database field, the ORDER BY clause won't use this formula, requiring Crystal Reports to actually sort the data once it arrives from the database server.

Chapter 13

Exporting Reports

When you save a Crystal Report, your report file is saved on disk with an .RPT extension. This Crystal Reports native format can only be used with another copy of Crystal Reports, with Seagate Analysis (Crystal Decisions' query, light reporting, and OLAP analysis tool), with Crystal Enterprise (discussed in Part II of the book), or with a customized Windows application (discussed in Part III of the book). Since everyone who might ever need to view a report probably won't have their own copy of Crystal Reports, there are many ways to *export* a report to a different file format for use with such products as Microsoft Word, Microsoft Excel, Lotus 1-2-3, Acrobat Reader, and others. You can also export your reports to HTML format for viewing in a Web browser. Furthermore, you can attach these differently formatted files to e-mail messages or place them in a Lotus Notes database or a Microsoft Exchange public folder.

Although exporting is a handy way of distributing reports to non-Crystal Reports viewers, your exported reports are *static*, meaning they contain a picture of the database as it existed when the report was exported. As soon as the database changes (perhaps the second after the report was exported), the report becomes outdated. If your viewers have their own copies of Crystal Reports, they can solve this problem by opening and refreshing the report, but this also means that they can *change* the report. This solution also assumes that your viewers know enough about Crystal Reports to be able to open and refresh a report.

If your viewers do not have their own copies of Crystal Reports, and do need real-time data reporting, you may want to consider implementing Crystal Enterprise to allow real-time running of reports in a Web browser. See Part II for more information. Or, you may be able to provide your report viewers with a copy of Seagate Analysis, which will allow them to open reports and run them directly against the database in real time.

| Note | *Previous versions of Crystal Reports allowed creation of compiled reports—stand-alone programs that allowed reports to be run in real time without a copy of Crystal Reports. Although compiled reporting has been eliminated from the shipping version of Crystal Reports as of Version 8, you may still download an add-in that restores this functionality. This is discussed later in this chapter.* |

The examples in this chapter are based on a report, shown in Figure 13-1, containing both text and a chart placed beside the text with the Underlay feature. In addition, some of the text contains special formatting, such as drop shadows. The report also contains additional graphical elements, such as line and box drawing.

Exporting Reports to Office Applications

You'll often wish to convert or export a report you've designed to a popular office file format, such as Excel, Word, WordPerfect, Lotus 1-2-3, or Acrobat Reader. With Crystal Reports, this is as simple as choosing an option from the File menu. You can also

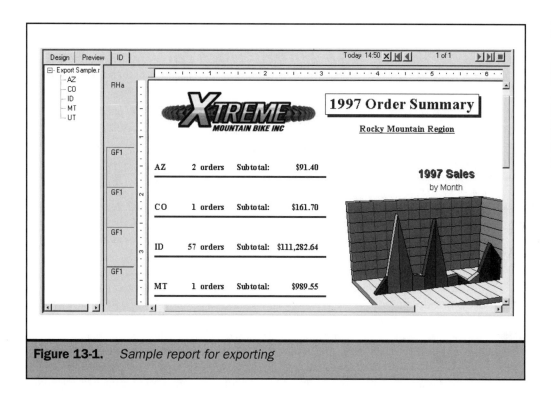

Figure 13-1. *Sample report for exporting*

export the file to a temporary location and immediately launch the application you want to view the file in, provided it's installed on your PC.

Exporting to Different File Formats

To export a file, first open the report you wish to export. Refresh and preview the report, if necessary, to ensure that it contains the most up-to-date data from the database. Then, click the Export button on the Standard toolbar or choose File | Print | Export. The Export dialog box will appear.

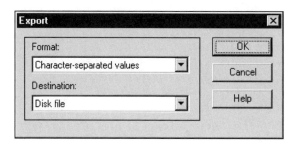

You have two simple choices to make for your export: the file format of the export, and the destination of the export. The Format drop-down list lets you choose from the large number of file formats that Crystal Reports will export to. You can choose from several different ASCII or "straight-text" formats, several versions of Microsoft Excel, Microsoft Word, Lotus 1-2-3, and others.

The Destination drop-down list lets you choose how you want the report exported: to a disk file, attached to an e-mail message, placed in a Microsoft Exchange public folder, or launched in an application on your workstation. If you choose Disk File, the Choose Export File dialog box will prompt you for the folder and filename to export to. Choose a folder and type a filename, if the default folder and filename aren't sufficient.

If your report contains several drill-down tabs or subreport Preview tabs, ensure that the tab you want exported is selected before you begin exporting. Whatever appears in the current tab (and all pages generated by that tab) is what will be exported by Crystal Reports.

Figure 13-2 shows the sample report from Figure 13-1 after it has been exported to a Microsoft Word document.

Notice in the Word document example that the drop shadows around the report title and the title of the chart weren't converted, and the chart is not underlain as the original was. You'll find that some of the Crystal Reports formatting doesn't translate to other file formats. You should export to your ultimate destination format throughout your report design process to make sure everything you want to include will be exported correctly.

If you drill down on a report, a different report "view" will appear inside the drill-down tab. Only the material inside this drill-down tab will be exported. The main Preview tab won't be included. Exporting the Idaho (ID) drill-down tab will result in a Microsoft Excel file, shown in Figure 13-3.

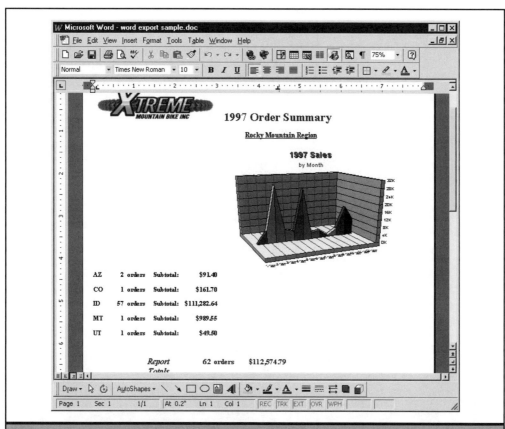

Figure 13-2. *Exporting to a Word document*

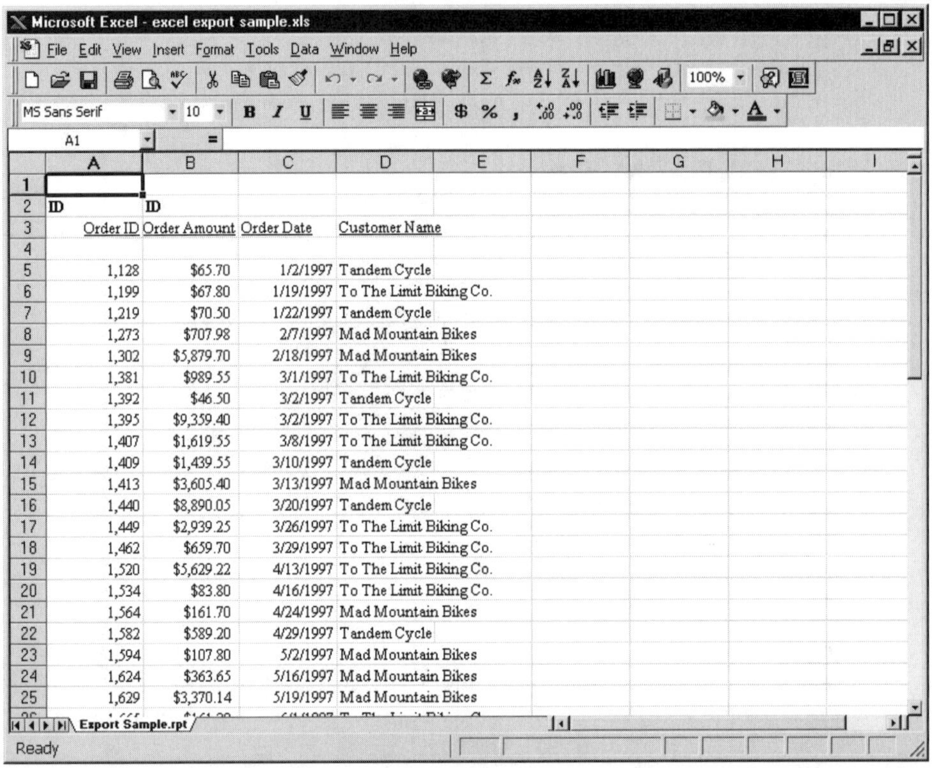

Figure 13-3. Drill-down tab exported to Excel

Depending on the file format you choose, you may receive an additional dialog box prompting you for extended information about the export. If, for example, you choose one of the Excel extended formats, a dialog box will allow you to choose more customized information when exporting to Excel.

Format Options   ☒

☐ Column Headings
☑ Use worksheet functions to represent subtotal fields in report

Set column width
○ Constant column width |10. |
● Column width based on objects in area |Details   ▼|

Format
● Non-Tabular format
○ Tabular format (Arrange all objects in one area into one row)

            OK   Cancel

Exporting to various text file formats, such as Character Separated Values, will present additional dialog boxes prompting you for, among other things, the characters to surround and separate fields.

Exporting to an Adobe Portable Document Format, or *PDF* format, may be the most effective way to export a report that contains complex formatting and graphics, including underlain sections, as shown in Figure 13-4. This is a new feature of Crystal Reports 8.5.

Exporting and Launching an Application

If you choose Application in the Destination drop-down list, Crystal Reports will export the file to a temporary folder and immediately open the file in the corresponding application. If you choose a file format for an application that isn't installed on your computer, you may be presented with a dialog box asking you to choose an application to open the file with. If there is an alternative application that will open that file type, choose it from the list.

The temporary files that Crystal Reports creates will be located in the Windows temporary folder (typically, \WINDOWS\TEMP) and may not automatically be deleted when you close the application. If you wish to periodically "clean out" your Windows temporary folder, use Disk Cleanup or another appropriate utility or measure to remove temporary files.

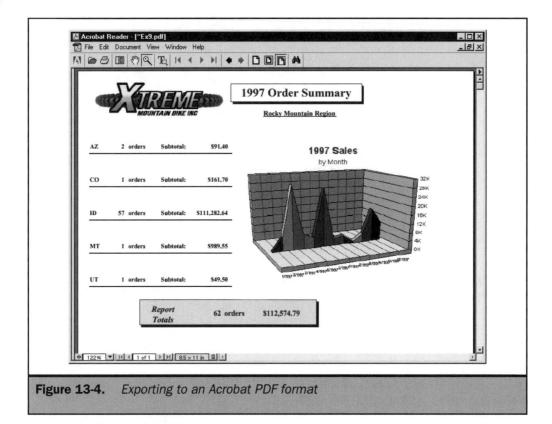

Figure 13-4.   *Exporting to an Acrobat PDF format*

Exporting to an ODBC Data Source

You can export a Crystal Report to an ODBC data source, such as a Microsoft SQL Server or Oracle database. Typically, you'll want to do this with a simple columnar details report that you might be using to transport data from a PC database to a client/server database.

You cannot create a new ODBC data source inside Crystal Reports. Use the ODBC icon in the Windows Control Panel to modify or create ODBC data sources.

To export to an ODBC data source, choose the data source you want to export to in the Format drop-down list. You'll then be asked to supply a table name, which Crystal Reports will create in the database referred to by the data source. If the data source refers to a secure database, you will be asked to supply a database logon user ID and password before the export starts. And, if the data source does not contain a specific database reference, you may be asked to choose a database in addition to the table name.

Crystal Reports will create a new table in the ODBC database and define fields to hold data from the exported report. If you want to change field names or the layout of the table, you need to use a utility specific to the ODBC database that you exported to.

ODBC is "picky" about the organization of data you export. You may need to modify the report (perhaps removing groups or changing the formatting of parts of the report) to get the report to export without ODBC errors.

Creating a Report Definition File

When you create reports, you may want to keep documentation that details the report design, such as the tables that are included, what formulas you've created, and what objects are contained in the report sections.

The Export dialog box in Crystal Reports provides a Report Definition format in the Format drop-down list. When you choose this format, Crystal Reports will save a text file containing a great deal of helpful information about the makeup of the report. You may wish to create and keep these text files in a central location to document the design of your reports. You may also open the text files in a word processor and reformat them to look more appealing.

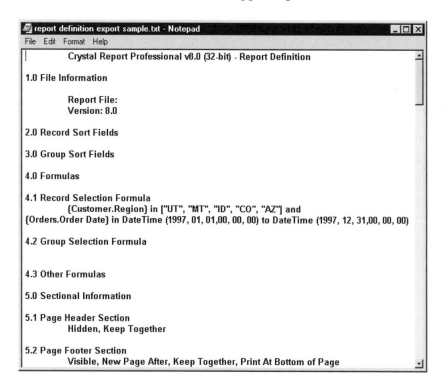

Exporting to XML

One of the more notable new features of Crystal Reports 8.5 is the ability to export your reports to Extensible Markup Language, or *XML*. XML, which is an extension of Hypertext Markup Language (HTML—the original "language" of the World Wide Web), is gaining more acceptance as a method of data exchange among disparate organizations and companies. XML describes the data that it encompasses with a set of descriptors, or *tags*, similar to HTML. These tags format the report content according to standardized language rules established (and still under development) by a consortium of technology and business organizations. XML files can vary in content from very simplified data output to formatted definitions of hierarchically organized data. Each element in an XML file is identified by tags, which define the name of the element, the type of element, and additional optional attributes.

Crystal provides two basic XML output format options: the Crystal ML Schema, which provides a standard set of tags and structure that includes extensive formatting content, or the Custom Format, which allows the user to suppress elements, change the names of elements, and add attributes to elements.

The Crystal ML Schema is the default XML output when you select the Export to XML format. The resulting XML file can be viewed by a Web browser, but will not be interpreted/formatted by the browser the way an HTML file would be. Figure 13-5 shows the XML file output from a simple columnar Orders report (similar to the one in Figure 13-3), using Crystal ML Schema. This schema is published at http://www.crystaldecisions.com/xml/schema.xsd.

Note that this XML file includes format-oriented tags for each section of the report as well as the data elements.

If you wish to customize the XML output format, or request an external schema validation file to accompany the XML file to document the tag conventions used in the XML file, you'll want do it before exporting your report. To customize the format, choose Format | XML Format from the Crystal Reports pull-down menus. When the XML Format dialog box is displayed, click the Options tab.

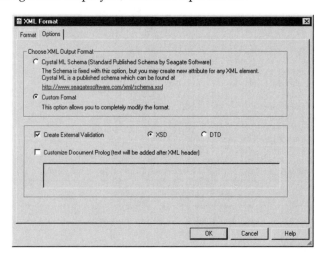

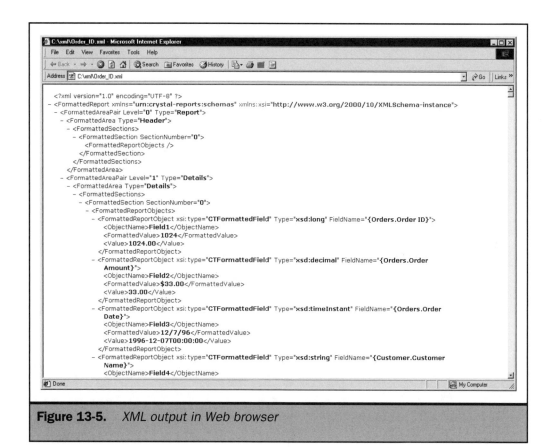

Figure 13-5. *XML output in Web browser*

On the Options tab, you can select XSD if you want an external schema document to accompany your Crystal ML Schema file, and also enter any custom text you want to insert after the header in the XML file to further define the output. Or, if you want to customize the XML output (perhaps to limit the file to data fields rather than formatted section tags), click the Custom Format radio button.

Tip   *Selecting Custom Format also allows the creation of a Document Type Definition external document, or DTD; this option creates a short DTD file, but also changes the XML output itself, eliminating most of the formatting elements and leaving data field elements.*

On the Options tab, after selecting the Custom Format radio button, click the Format tab to display your customization options, shown in Figure 13-6.

To limit the XML file to just data elements, rather than report/formatting elements, you'll want to suppress some or all of the report section parent elements, such as ReportArea:Report Area and Detail:Detail. To do this, select the desired parent element

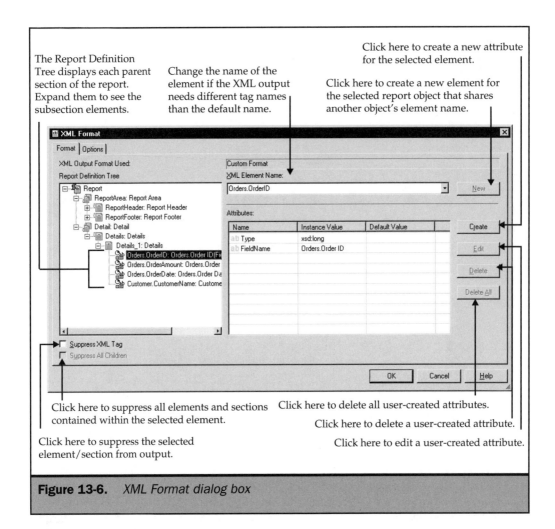

The Report Definition Tree displays each parent section of the report. Expand them to see the subsection elements.

Change the name of the element if the XML output needs different tag names than the default name.

Click here to create a new attribute for the selected element.

Click here to create a new element for the selected report object that shares another object's element name.

Click here to suppress all elements and sections contained within the selected element.

Click here to delete all user-created attributes.

Click here to delete a user-created attribute.

Click here to suppress the selected element/section from output.

Click here to edit a user-created attribute.

Figure 13-6.   *XML Format dialog box*

or section and click the Suppress XML Tag check box beneath the tree. You can use the Suppress All Children check box when you don't want to produce XML tags for *any* subsets of a section/element. However, you would not use the Suppress All Children check box for any of the Details area elements, as it would also suppress tags for the data layer of the Details section. When an element is suppressed, the element can no longer be customized.

To customize attributes or element names, select the element you wish to customize. The element name and the attributes of the element are displayed on the right side of the dialog box. In the example illustrated in Figure 13-6, the selected element is the data field containing the order ID. If desired, the name of the element (Orders.OrderID) can be changed for output purposes by simply entering the modified name in the XML Element Name field. By default, Crystal has assigned two attributes to each data field element: Type and FieldName. The gray "ab" designation beside the attribute name indicates that these cannot be changed or deleted. However, additional attributes can be created, changed, and deleted as needed according to the XML output required. For example, if you need to add a "use" attribute to this field, you can click the Create button to produce the XML Attribute Dialog box seen in Figure 13-7.

For this example, supplying an attribute name of "use" and text of "required" will result in the standard XML field use attribute being inserted into the OrderID data element tag:

```
<Orders.OrderID FieldName="{Orders.Order ID}"
use="required">1128.00</Orders.OrderID>
```

Figure 13-8 shows the XML file exported from the Orders report with all report section areas suppressed, all data element names changed to eliminate the table name, and a use=required attribute added to the OrderID element.

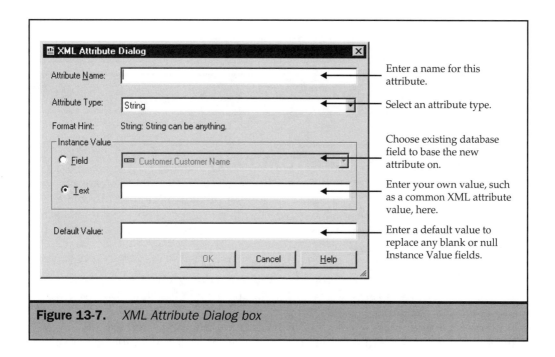

Figure 13-7.   *XML Attribute Dialog box*

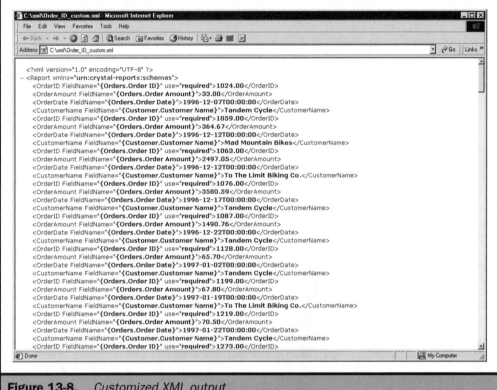

Figure 13-8. *Customized XML output*

Sending Reports Electronically

In addition to exporting reports to office applications, you may want to create an exported report and attach it to an e-mail message or put it in a Microsoft Exchange public folder. You might expect to have to do this in two steps: export to your chosen file format and then run a separate e-mail package to send the file. However, Crystal Reports lets you do it all in one step.

Display the Export dialog box, and in the Format drop-down list, choose the format you want the report exported to. From the Destination drop-down list, choose the e-mail system you wish to send the report with. Choosing Lotus Notes Database will place a report on the Lotus Notes Desktop; choosing Exchange Folder will add the report to a Microsoft Exchange or Outlook Folder; and choosing Microsoft Mail (MAPI) will use a Microsoft-compatible e-mail program, such as Microsoft Outlook, to attach the report to an e-mail message. Note that you need to have the appropriate "client" software installed on your PC for this to work.

Although you can choose File | Print | Mail, the same dialog box will be displayed as with the Export toolbar button or menu command. Just choose the correct e-mail type from the Destination drop-down list to electronically send your exported report.

If Microsoft Outlook is installed on your PC and you choose Microsoft Mail (MAPI) as the destination, the following dialog box will appear:

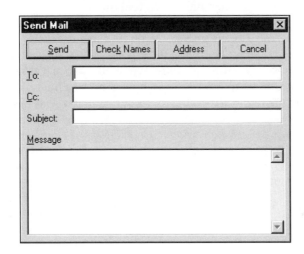

Specify the e-mail address or addresses you want the message to go to, along with the message you want to appear in the e-mail body. The message will be sent with the report file attached (in the format you specified).

You'll probably notice that several HTML file formats for the Web are available from the Export dialog box. Exporting Crystal Reports as HTML, as well as other alternatives for viewing Crystal Reports on the Web, is covered in Part II, starting with Chapter 20.

Compiling and Distributing Real-Time Reports

All the export and distribution methods mentioned previously in the chapter export the report with the data that was current when you went through the exporting process. If the report is based on a constantly changing database, such as a real-time transaction database, the reports you export or distribute may be out-of-date by the time your recipient receives them. While you can just give viewers a copy of the .RPT file and require them to open and refresh it in their own copy of Crystal Reports or Seagate Analysis, or you may post the report to the Web with Crystal Enterprise, you may still want a more cost-effective or efficient way of letting viewers run reports themselves—directly against the database, in real time.

Compiled reporting is a feature of Crystal Reports Version 7 and earlier that lets you create a royalty-free, stand-alone version of a report that a user can run without having Crystal Reports. Once you have compiled the report, you can use the Report Distribution Expert to create a Windows setup program on diskettes or on a shared network drive. Any viewer who runs the setup program will have a copy of the report installed on their own PC and can run the report in real time without having a copy of Crystal Reports.

Note
Compiled reporting is not provided with Crystal Reports after Version 7, but is referenced here for users of earlier versions. With Crystal Reports 8 and 8.5, you may use Crystal Enterprise (discussed in Part II) or Seagate Analysis, to provide real-time reporting capability to viewers lacking their own copies of Crystal Reports. Also, you can download a Crystal Reports add-in to allow compiled reporting with Versions 8 and 8.5. Visit http://support.crystaldecisions.com/updates and search for the file SCR8_Distr_Expert.exe.

Compiling the Report

A compiled report will run on a viewer's PC without Crystal Reports being installed. This is accomplished by creating an *executable* version of the report file, with an .EXE extension. Windows can run this file from the desktop or a Windows program group—Crystal Reports doesn't need to be running to use the report.

To compile a report, open the report that you wish to use. If the report is already open and you are ready to compile it, make sure you save it first—a report must be saved on disk before it can be compiled. Then, click the Compile button on the Supplementary toolbar, or choose Report | Compile Report. The Compile Report dialog box will appear, as shown in Figure 13-9.

By default, Crystal Reports will use the same name as the .RPT file for the compiled report .EXE file. If you wish to use a different name, choose it in the Compiled File Name text box. If you want to run the compiled report on your own computer, choose Create a Program Item for the Report and choose the Start button submenu where you want the icon for the report placed. This will place the icon on your own computer so that you can run the compiled report yourself without having to open Crystal Reports.

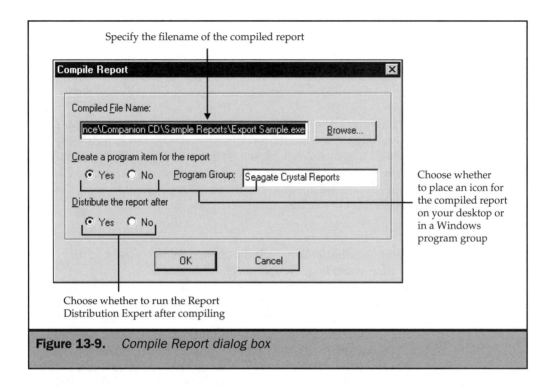

Specify the filename of the compiled report

Compile Report

Compiled File Name:

nce\Companion CD\Sample Reports\Export Sample.exe   Browse...

Create a program item for the report

⦿ Yes   ○ No   Program Group: Seagate Crystal Reports

Distribute the report after

⦿ Yes   ○ No

OK   Cancel

Choose whether to place an icon for the compiled report on your desktop or in a Windows program group

Choose whether to run the Report Distribution Expert after compiling

Figure 13-9.   *Compile Report dialog box*

If you also want to distribute the report immediately after it has been compiled, choose Yes under Distribute the Report After.

Once you click OK, Crystal Reports will create the .EXE file you specified and, if you so choose, put an icon that points to the compiled report in a Start button submenu. Double-click the icon to run the compiled report.

It's tempting for Windows developers to create compiled reports and then call them from within their custom Visual Basic programs. While this may work, it's much more efficient and flexible to use one of the Visual Basic programming interfaces to call a report directly. If you just want to give a stand-alone report to a viewer, use compiled reports. However, if you want to include one or more Crystal Reports as part of a custom Windows application, refer to Part III of this book for integration methods.

Using the Report Distribution Expert

It's important to remember that compiling a report won't create one large .EXE file that can stand completely on its own. In fact, the .EXE file is very small and simply points to many other files that are required to run a compiled report, such as the .RPT file itself, the CRRUN.EXE run-time file, and a .CRF file that contains initialization information about the report. In addition to these files, the compiled report will need to use any database access dynamic link library (.DLL) files that Crystal Reports uses. And, if your viewer wants to be able to export or e-mail reports in other file formats, another set of .DLL files will need to be available as well. The Report Distribution Expert is designed to easily "collect" all the necessary files and create an automatic setup package to install them on a viewer's PC.

The Report Distribution Expert will run immediately after you compile a report, if you choose the option in the Compile Report dialog box. Or, you can run the Report Distribution Expert directly by clicking the Distribution Expert button on the Supplementary toolbar or by choosing Report | Report Distribution Expert. The Report Distribution Expert dialog box will appear, consisting of four different tabs: Options, File List, Third Party DLLs, and Distribution.

Options Tab

The first tab in the Report Distribution Expert is Options, shown in Figure 13-10. Specify general information about your compiled report on this tab.

By default, the report you are compiling will be included in the setup package. If you need to include other reports, you can click the Add button to select additional report files. If you need to distribute the database, as well as the report itself, check the Database File(s) Used by Report check box to set that option. If the compiled reports will be using a common database, perhaps located on a central database server, there will be no reason to distribute the database with the report. However, you may want the viewer to be able to export the compiled report to Microsoft Word or Excel, or to attach the report to an e-mail message. If so, you need to check the DLLs for Exporting check box so that the proper .DLL files for export are included in the setup package. And, if any formulas you've included in the report use User Function Libraries, make sure you include the .DLL files for these as well (Chapter 27 discusses how to create these libraries in Visual Basic).

You can choose to have the setup package created on multiple diskettes or in a single directory of files. Choose the diskette option if you need to distribute the report to an audience that may not have access to a central installation directory (on a LAN server, perhaps). If your viewers do have access to a shared directory, or if you will be placing the setup package on a recordable CD, it is preferable to create an installation directory for the setup package on the common directory. In either case, the Report Distribution Expert will compress all the associated files to save disk space, and create a SETUP.EXE file to uncompress and properly install the files on the target computer.

Remove the selected .RPT file

Add additional .RPT files to the list of distributed files

Include the database file or files with the setup package

Include necessary dynamic link libraries for exporting reports

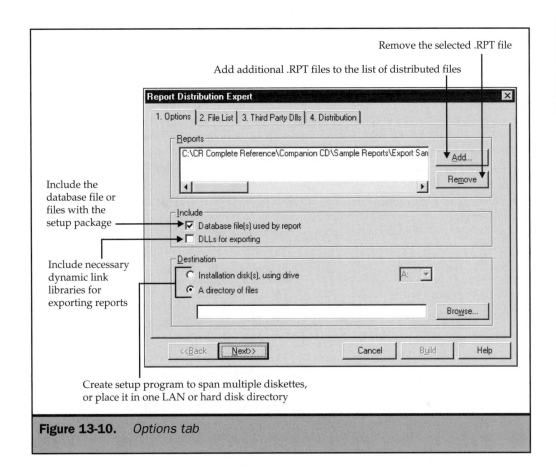

Create setup program to span multiple diskettes, or place it in one LAN or hard disk directory

Figure 13-10. *Options tab*

Caution *If your report is based on a PC-style database (such as Microsoft Access), the Report Distribution Expert may present an error message indicating that you must set the report's database location to be "same as report." Use the Database | Set Location command to set this option. You also need to ensure that the database and the report share the same drive and directory. If the report is based on an ODBC data source, you need to ensure that the same data source is set up on each target machine. The Crystal Reports Setup program will not do this, so you need to ensure this with other means.*

File List Tab

When you click the File List tab, the Report Distribution Expert may give you extra prompts to include database drivers, such as the Microsoft DAO driver. If you are unsure whether the target machine has these necessary drivers, you should choose to include them in the setup package. Then, the Report Distribution Expert will evaluate the report and create a list of support files that it believes may be required by the compiled report, as shown in Figure 13-11. Be patient—this analysis may take a little while.

When the list appears, you can scroll through the filenames to make sure all the support files that your report needs are included. If you want to see different information about the files, click the Description, Path, and Size radio buttons at the top of the screen. You can also add additional files or remove unnecessary files by using the Add and Remove buttons.

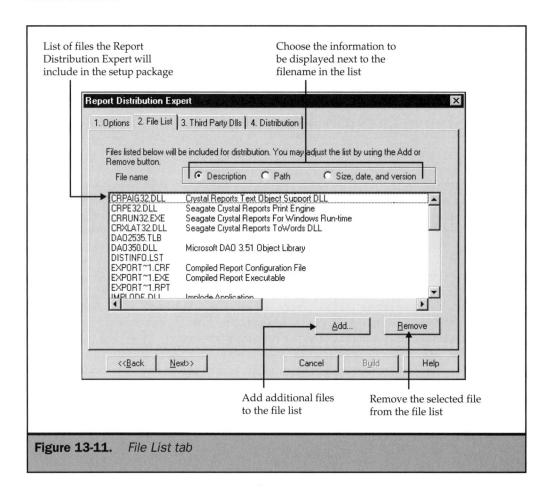

Figure 13-11. File List tab

For more information on which files you may need to include, look at the *RUNTIME.HLP file in Crystal Reports program directory\Developer Files\Help.*

Third Party DLLs Tab

If your report is using a particular DLL that was not included on the Crystal Reports CD-ROM (perhaps a third-party DLL required to connect to a proprietary database), you'll see a list of those DLLs on the Third Party DLLs tab, shown in Figure 13-12.

If you want to include any or all of these third-party files in your setup package, select the files that you want to include and click the Add To The Distribution List button to add them. If this tab is empty and the Add To The Distribution List button is disabled, no third-party DLLs are required for this report.

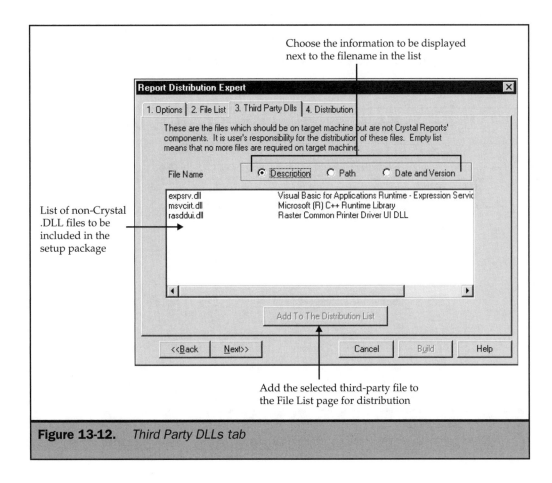

Figure 13-12.   *Third Party DLLs tab*

Distribution Tab

The final step in the Report Distribution Expert is the Distribution tab, shown in Figure 13-13. This tab simply displays a message indicating that the Report Distribution Expert is ready to prepare the setup package. Click the Build button when you're ready to proceed. If you chose to distribute on diskettes, you'll be prompted to insert formatted, blank diskettes into the chosen diskette drive. If you chose to place the setup package in a single directory, the directory will be created. Then, the Report Distribution Expert will compress all the included files to make them as compact as possible. It will also create a standard Windows SETUP.EXE program that can be run on the report viewer's PC to install the compiled report.

Using a Compiled Report

If the compiled report setup package was placed on diskettes or in a common directory, the viewer will need to run the SETUP.EXE program to install the compiled report. This is a standard Windows setup program that copies files to their correct locations and creates a new program group to contain the compiled report's icon.

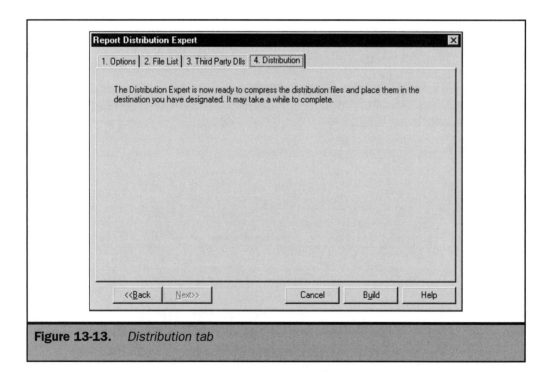

Figure 13-13.   *Distribution tab*

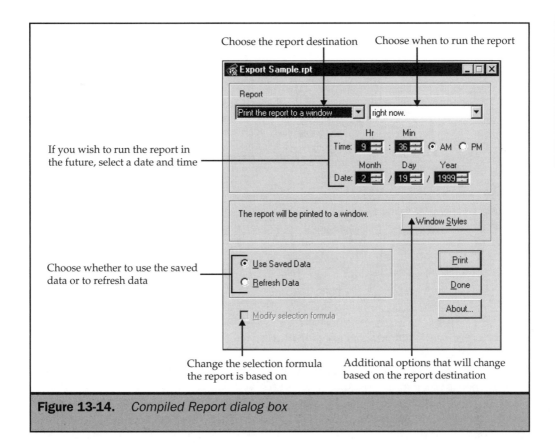

Figure 13-14. Compiled Report dialog box

Once the setup program has been run (or if you just compiled a report on the same machine that Crystal Reports is installed on), you can start your compiled report by choosing the icon from the Start button submenu. The Compiled Report dialog box will appear, as shown in Figure 13-14.

The first Report drop-down list lets you choose where you want the report output to go. The report can be previewed in an onscreen window, printed on a printer, or exported or e-mailed in another file format (provided you included the export DLLs when you created the report setup package). You can also choose whether you want the report to run immediately or at a later time by choosing options in the second Report drop-down list and using the Time and Date options.

A button will appear in the middle of the dialog box that changes based on the report destination. If you choose to print to a printer, clicking the button will let you choose different print options, such as which printer to use and what pages to print. If you choose to export the report, clicking the button will display the Export dialog box that lets you choose the report format and destination. If you choose to preview the report in a window, clicking the button will let you change window styles, by presenting this dialog box:

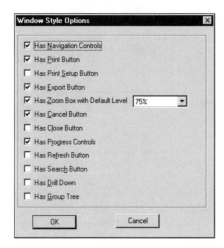

Here, you can choose many options for the preview window, such as whether to display a group tree, whether to allow drill-down, what the initial zoom level should be, and much more.

If the compiled report has the Save Data with Report option chosen from the File menu, you can choose whether to view the report with saved data or to refresh the report data. Using saved data is faster and doesn't require you to connect to the database the report is based on. However, the saved data is "static" and the report may not represent the most current data in the database. Because this is little better than having received the report in a Word or Excel document, the viewer will most probably want to select Refresh Data. If the report was not saved with the Save Data with Report option chosen, the only option will be Refresh Data and the viewer will have to connect to the database to run the report.

If the viewer chooses to Refresh Data, they can also check the Modify Selection Formula check box. If this is checked, the viewer will be able to change record selection before the report processes. A series of dialog boxes will prompt the viewer to enter new selection options.

 A viewer can change the selection criteria only if you limit your Select Expert or record-selection formula operators to those that take one value, such as Equal To or Less Than. Those that can take more than one value, such as One Of, will prevent the viewer from being prompted when they run the compiled report, even if they check Modify Selection Formula.

Once you are satisfied with these options, click the Print button to view, print, or export the report. If the report contains parameter fields, the viewer will be prompted to supply them before the report runs. If you choose to preview the report in a window, the preview window with the compiled report will appear, as shown in Figure 13-15.

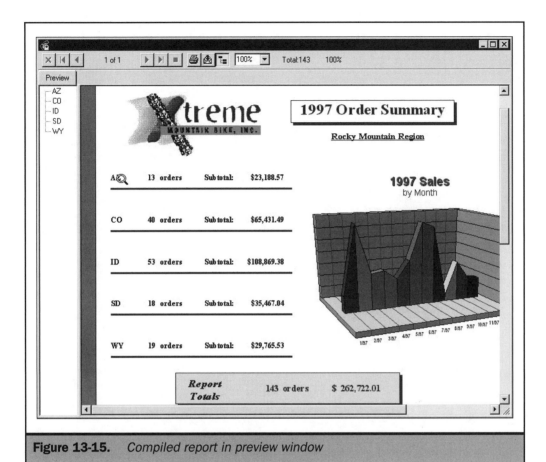

Figure 13-15.   *Compiled report in preview window*

Based on what was chosen with the Windows Styles button, you'll be able to print and export the report from the preview window, as well as drill down and navigate with the group tree. When you have finished viewing the report, simply close the preview window.

Note   *Because compiled reports can only be run by the viewer and not modified, make creative use of parameter fields (discussed in Chapter 12) to allow the viewer as much flexibility as possible in customizing the report to their needs.*

Chapter 14

Reporting from SQL Databases

Although many companies and smaller software packages still rely on PC-style databases for their day-to-day functions, most "downsized" mainframe programs and many newer, department or enterprise applications rely on *client/server* database systems. A client/server system includes two parts: a *client*, typically a PC running software such as Crystal Reports or a data-entry application, and a *server*, typically a larger, high-end PC running Windows NT/2000, or a midrange or even a mainframe Unix computer. The server maintains the database, and the client makes requests of the server for database access. Many different client/server databases exist, with Microsoft SQL Server, Oracle, Sybase, Informix, and IBM DB2 being among the more popular ones.

Caution	*Many SQL databases can be used only with the Professional or Developer Editions of Crystal Reports 8.5. The Standard Edition reports only on PC-style databases, Microsoft SQL Server, and limited databases via ODBC and OLE DB. If you plan to use Crystal Reports 8.5 with Oracle, Informix, or any other common SQL databases, you should purchase the Professional or Developer Edition.*

It's important to understand and contrast the differences between a client/server database system and a PC-style database system that is installed on a shared local area network (LAN). For reporting purposes, in particular, a LAN-based database system presents a much more serious performance hurdle than a client/server database. Figure 14-1 shows a PC reporting on two database environments. The first depicts a Microsoft Access database on a LAN server. The second depicts the same database on a SQL Server system.

The LAN-based scenario places heavy burdens on both the network and the PC making the reporting request. In this scenario, the PC must read the entire 100,000-record Access database across the network, picking and choosing the records that meet the report-selection criteria. This requires large amounts of data to be passed across the network, and the PC has to perform all the selection logic itself.

The client/server environment is much more efficient. The client PC simply makes a request to the database server via a Structured Query Language (SQL) request. The database server, presumably a larger, high-powered PC, Unix computer, or mainframe, runs database software designed to process such queries very efficiently. It directly queries the 100,000-record database and sends only the required 1,000 records back across the network. This places less demand on the client and the network, and the whole process typically takes less time.

Logging On to SQL Databases

The first step to creating a Crystal Report is to select the SQL database that you want to base your report on. There are three general communication methods you can use to connect to a client/server database with Crystal Reports: direct database drivers, ODBC, and OLE DB (pronounced oh-LAY-dee-bee).

CRYSTAL REPORTS 8.5
INTRODUCED

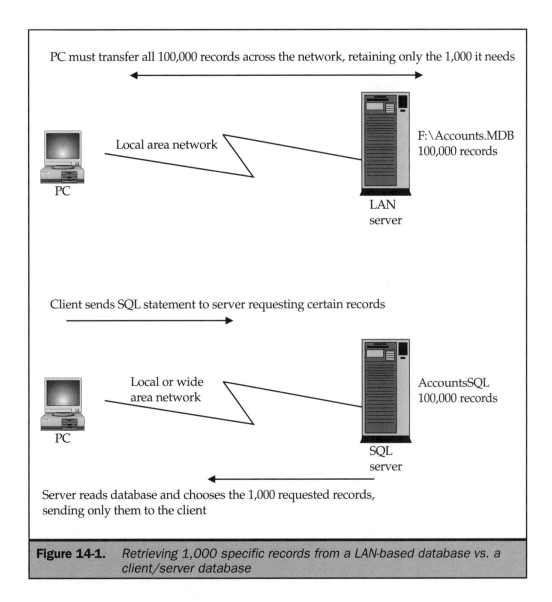

PC must transfer all 100,000 records across the network, retaining only the 1,000 it needs

Local area network

PC

LAN
server

F:\Accounts.MDB
100,000 records

Client sends SQL statement to server requesting certain records

Local or wide
area network

PC

SQL
server

AccountsSQL
100,000 records

Server reads database and chooses the 1,000 requested records,
sending only them to the client

Figure 14-1. *Retrieving 1,000 specific records from a LAN-based database vs. a client/server database*

Direct Database Drivers

Crystal Reports provides direct database drivers that work with many industry-standard client/server databases, including, among others, Microsoft SQL Server, Oracle, and IBM DB2. A direct database driver uses the native communication methods provided by the server vendor to communicate with the database server. This typically requires installing the specific client software provided by the database vendor on the PC. Examples of these packages include Query Analyzer and Enterprise Manager for Microsoft SQL Server 7, and SQL + for Oracle.

Crystal Reports will recognize the existence of these packages and provide a direct database driver to connect to the database. In addition, Crystal Reports provides other direct drivers to allow you to report from Microsoft Outlook folders, Microsoft Exchange folders, Lotus Notes databases, Internet Web server activity logs, and the Windows NT event log. You can even write reports based on the *local file system,* which consists of the file and directory structure of your C drive or a network drive. More details on these specialized types of reports can be found in Chapter 19.

Using direct database drivers to connect to the database server has two general advantages:

- Because fewer layers of communications protocols are being used, there may be a slight performance improvement when reporting.

- The direct database driver may allow more flexibility for creating server-specific SQL statements or other query features for reporting.

ODBC

Although many companies standardize on database servers that Crystal Reports provides direct database drivers for, many other database systems and specialized data systems exist that you may want to report on. Some standard method of communication is needed to connect standard PC clients with the myriad specialized servers and systems that exist. Microsoft designed open database connectivity (ODBC) to accomplish this communication.

Without too many exceptions, any server or proprietary data platform that is ODBC-compliant can be used with Crystal Reports. If the database or system vendor provides a Windows ODBC driver for its system, Crystal Reports should be able to report against that server or system. Because it has been accepted as an industry standard, ODBC is in widespread use.

Tip *Crystal Reports installs ODBC automatically. In addition, it installs some generic ODBC data sources for common database files and formats, including an ODBC data source for using the sample XTREME.MDB database. Before you can use Crystal Reports to report against other ODBC data systems, you must set up an ODBC data source. Use the ODBC Administrator from the Crystal Reports Program Group or Control Panel to set up the data source.*

OLE DB

Microsoft has introduced OLE DB to extend its previous universal data connectivity method, ODBC. OLE DB provides data access in much the same manner as ODBC.

A *data provider* acts as an interface between disparate client and server systems. Data providers are available not only for typical relational database systems, but also for more nontraditional data sources, such as spreadsheets, Web servers, and multidimensional OLAP data sources.

Crystal Reports supports OLE DB data sources that are installed on your client PC. Various client applications, such as OLAP client software, will automatically install OLE DB data providers. More information on OLE DB is available on Microsoft's Web site or in documentation accompanying client applications.

Choosing the Database

When you first start Crystal Reports, you can immediately choose and log on to a client/server database before you open an existing report or create a new report. If you don't log on, but open a report based on a client/server database, you will be prompted to log on as soon as you try to refresh the report or choose any other function that requires the database to be read.

If you want to create a new report based on a client/server database, you can use a report expert or the Blank Report option. If you use a report expert, just click the Database button to connect to a database. The Data Explorer will appear.

Click the Database button to launch the Data Explorer

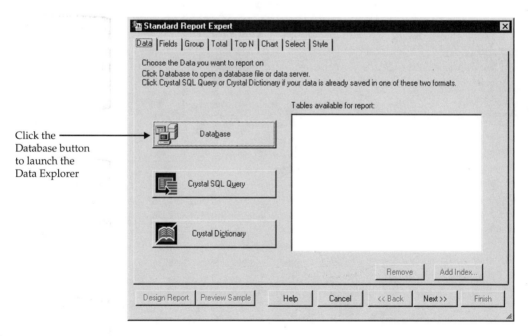

If you chose the Blank Report option to create a new report, the Data Explorer will appear immediately.

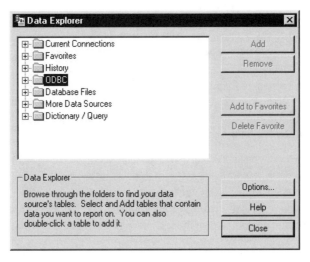

The Data Explorer combines in one place all data sources, including direct database drivers, ODBC, and OLE DB. ODBC data sources appear in the ODBC category, and direct database drivers, as well as OLE DB, are available from the More Data Sources category. Click the plus sign next to the category you wish to choose from, and select the data source or driver that you want to use in your report. Based on the source you choose, another dialog box will appear and prompt for other information, such as a logon ID and password, the database you want to use, or other information that varies based on the driver or data source you choose. After you successfully log on, the Data Explorer shows a list of available tables, stored procedures, and views within the chosen database.

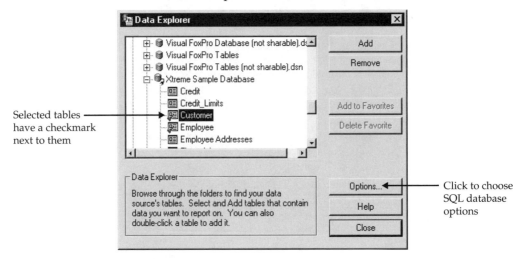

Select the table, stored procedure, or view that you want to include in your report, either by double-clicking it or by selecting it and clicking the Add button. You'll see a green checkmark next to each table that you've chosen. If you don't see all the tables you expect, or you wish to limit the set of available tables to a certain database owner or certain table name pattern, click the Options button to display the Database Options dialog box (discussed later in the chapter under "Changing SQL Options"). After you select all the tables that you want to include, click the Close button to close the Data Explorer and proceed to selecting database fields.

Keep in mind that once you log on to a SQL database from the Data Explorer, you remain connected to that database even if you close any reports that are based on that database connection. If you then begin a new report and attempt to either choose a PC-style database or log on to another SQL database, the database you chose will appear in the Current Connections category of the Data Explorer. If you don't want to use these tables in your report, you need to log off the original server first, either by closing and restarting Crystal Reports or by using the Log On/Off Server option. If you have a report open, choose Database | Log On/Off Server. If you don't have a report open, choose File | Log On/Off Server.

Changing SQL Options

Depending on the data source you choose, you may not see all the database elements you're looking for. In particular, if your database supports *SQL stored procedures* (precompiled SQL statements that may contain parameters) or *views* (virtual tables that may combine several actual database tables together into one group), you will want to make sure you can see these in the Data Explorer. Or, you may want to limit the tables that you see in the Data Explorer to only the table names that match a certain pattern or that are owned by a certain database user.

Clicking the Options button on the Data Explorer, which displays the Database Options dialog box (shown in Figure 14-2), can customize these options.

The Show area of this dialog box lets you limit the tables that appear in the Data Explorer when you log on to a database. Check the table types (Tables, Views, Synonyms, Stored Procedures, and System Tables) to determine the types of tables you want to appear. You can also add a table or table owner *pattern* to limit the list of tables to those that are named like the pattern, or owned by a database user who matches a pattern.

The List Tables and Fields By section lets you determine how tables and fields appear in the Data and Field Explorers. You have several choices for how you want table and field names sorted.

Advanced options determine various database behavior, depending on the type of database you're using and how you want it to behave. Some more notable Advanced options are the following:

■ **Use Indexes or Server for Speed** Choose this option to use index files for PC-style databases (such as Microsoft Access and Paradox), and use a SQL WHERE clause with SQL databases. In most cases, choosing this option dramatically improves reporting performance.

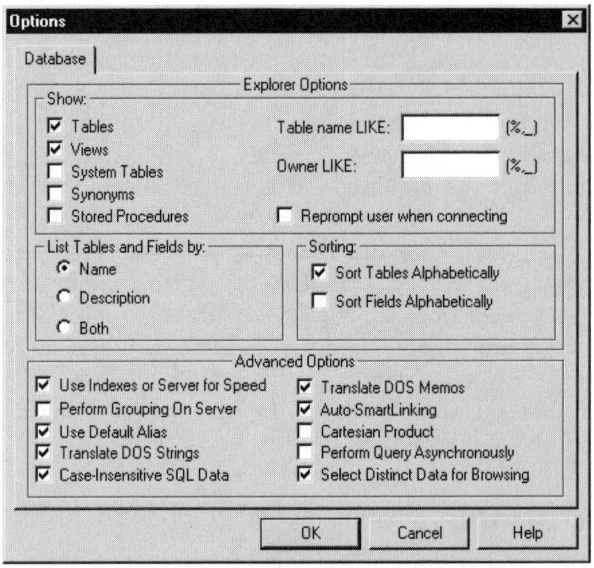

Figure 14-2. *Database Options dialog box*

■ **Perform Grouping On Server** Choose this option to have Crystal Reports "push" as much of the subtotaling and aggregation as possible to the database server, to improve reporting performance. Certain conditions required to take full advantage of this feature are discussed later in the chapter under "Enabling Server-Based Grouping."

■ **Case-Insensitive SQL Data** Choose this option to ignore case when doing record selection with a SQL database. Case insensitivity is discussed in more detail later in the chapter under "Case Sensitivity".

■ **Auto-SmartLinking** Choose this option to have Crystal Reports automatically link database tables when they're added to the report. In many cases, this actually causes more trouble than it's worth, as discussed later in the chapter under "Linking Tables".

■ **Perform Query Asynchronously** This option allows you to stop a query from processing on the database server before report records are returned to Crystal Reports. In some cases, queries submitted to the SQL database can take minutes (sometimes hours) to run. By selecting this option, you can click the Stop button (the black square) at the right of the Preview tab to cancel the query on the database server. Note that this option only applies to certain databases and database drivers—not all databases and drivers support this option.

■ **Select Distinct Data for Browsing**   This option will continuously read the database until it has retrieved the first 500 *unique* values of a field when you browse the field in the Field Explorer or Formula Editors. If you leave this option turned off, Crystal Reports reads only the first 500 records in the table, even if there are a few (or no) unique values. Although you'll have bigger browse lists with this option turned on, you may also suffer from slower performance.

If you want to customize certain options on this dialog box on a permanent basis, instead of doing it each time you display the Data Explorer, choose File | Options and click the Database tab to set options in the dialog box for all new reports you create in the future.

   Another Crystal Reports 8.5 feature is Select Distinct Records. By turning on this option, you can instruct the SQL database server to send only unique records back to Crystal Reports—any duplicate records will be ignored by the server. Choose this option by choosing Database | Select Distinct Records from the pull-down menus, or by checking the Select Distinct Records option on File | Report Options.

Converting a PC-Style Database Report to a Client/Server Database

You may initially create a report based on a PC-style database, such as Microsoft Access, and then decide later to convert the report to use a similarly organized SQL database. Perhaps the Access database has been upsized to SQL Server. Or, you may initially be developing reports against a test database in Btrieve, but the reports will eventually have to run against an identical Oracle database.

In each of these situations, you need to choose a different database driver after you initially create the report, because you'll actually be changing the type of database you are using. Choose Database | Convert Database Driver from the pull-down menus. The Convert Database Driver dialog box will appear.

Check Convert Database Driver on Next Refresh. This enables the To drop-down list. Next to the From label, you'll also see the driver that the report is currently based on. The drop-down list shows the dynamic link library names of all installed Crystal

Reports database drivers, followed by a description of the database that the driver connects to. Choose a new database driver for the report from the list and click OK. If you chose a secure database, you'll be prompted to log on to the database.

If table or field names have changed in the new database (for example, spaces will probably have been replaced with underscores if an Access database was upsized to SQL Server), you'll have to remap old fields to their new names. This is explained in detail in Chapter 15.

If you simply need to choose a different database of the same type, use Database | Set Location instead of Convert Database Driver. Also, Crystal Reports 8.5 automatically converts the database driver if you choose a different database type in the Set Location dialog box.

Changing from One SQL Database to Another

You may have other situations in which you initially develop a report against a particular database, perhaps a test ODBC database. You then need to point the report to another ODBC production database. Since both databases use ODBC connections, you can't use the Convert Database Driver dialog box to change to the production database. Instead, choose Database | Set Location from the pull-down menus. The Set Location dialog box will appear.

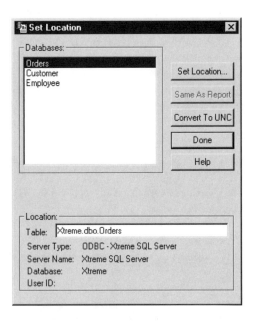

Select the first table you want to point to the production database, and click the Set Location button. The Data Explorer appears, showing all databases that you are currently logged on to in the Current Connections category. If you are already logged on to the production database, simply click the plus sign next to it and then select the new table.

If you aren't logged on to the production database, choose the category and data source that will connect to the production database. Once you've logged on, tables in the production database appear underneath the data source name. Double-click the corresponding table in the production database, or choose it and click Set. You may be asked if you wish to propagate server and database changes across tables with the same original information. If you choose Yes, any other table in the report that belonged to the original database will be pointed to the new database.

If table or field names have changed in the new database, you'll be prompted to remap old fields to their new names. This is covered in more detail in Chapter 15.

Linking Tables

Although you may have rare instances in which you design a report based on just one database table, you usually need to use at least two, and often more, tables in your report, because most modern relational databases are *normalized*. Database normalization refers to breaking out repetitive database information into separate tables in the database for efficiency and maintenance reasons. Consider the following Employee table:

Employee Name	Department Name	Salary
Bill	Information Technology	50,000
Karen	Human Resources	32,500
Renee	Information Technology	37,500
John	Executive	85,000
Carl	Mail Room	24,000
Jim	Information Technology	48,000
Julie	Executive	87,000
Sally	Mail Room	23,500

Although this makes for a simple reporting environment, because you don't need to choose more than one table to print an employee roster or paycheck, it becomes more difficult to maintain. Notice that department names repeat several times throughout this small table. (Think about this same scenario for a 50,000-employee company!) This not only takes up a large amount of storage space, but if a department name changes, much work has to be done to make the change in this table. For example, if the Information Technology department changes its name to Information Systems, a search-and-replace function must be performed through the entire Employee table, replacing every occurrence of the old name with the new name.

Contrast this single-table layout with the following database environment:

Employee Table:

Employee Name	Department Number	Salary
Bill	25	50,000
Karen	17	32,500
Renee	25	37,500
John	8	85,000
Carl	13	24,000
Jim	25	48,000
Julie	8	87,000
Sally	13	23,500

Department Table:

Department Number	Department Name
s8	Executive
13	Mail Room
17	Human Resources
25	Information Technology

Here, you can see that the database has been normalized by placing the department information in its own lookup table. In this environment, much less storage is used by the Employee table, because only a department number is stored for each employee, not the entire department name. And, if the Information Technology department's name changes, only one record in the Department table has to be changed in the entire database.

Visual Linking Expert

Using multiple tables complicates the reporting environment, because you need more than just the Employee table to print an employee roster or paycheck. In the preceding example, you not only have to include the two tables in your report, but must also link them together with a common field. *Linking* tables (often also known as *joining* tables) consists of choosing the common field that will allow the second table to follow the main table as the main table is read record by record. You link tables in Crystal Reports with the Visual Linking Expert, illustrated in Figure 14-3.

The Visual Linking Expert appears automatically if you initially choose two or more tables when you first create a report, or whenever you choose additional tables

Tables chosen from the Data Explorer

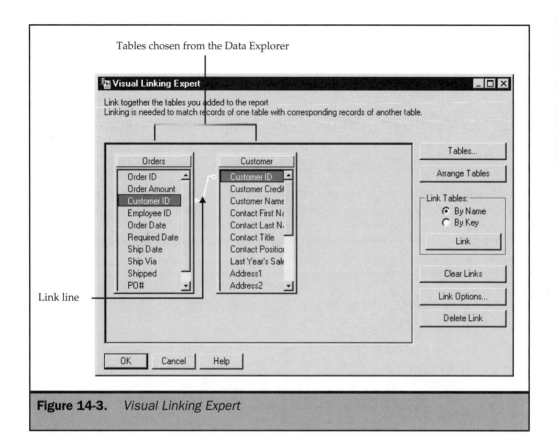

Figure 14-3.   *Visual Linking Expert*

with Database | Add Database To Report from the pull-down menus. You can also display the Visual Linking Expert by clicking the Link Expert button in the Supplementary toolbar or by choosing Database | Visual Linking Expert from the pull-down menus.

The Visual Linking Expert shows all tables that have been included in your report, and it may have already chosen links between the tables. If you see lines with arrows connecting fields in the tables, the Visual Linking Expert has already applied Smart Linking to the tables (discussed later in the chapter). You may need to delete these existing links if they are incorrect, or add new links yourself.

To delete a link, click the line connecting the two tables. If you're not successful in selecting a link at first, keep trying—Crystal Reports 8.5 displays a tool tip for links, and you can't select it when the tool tip is displayed. The link line, along with the fields it connects, will be highlighted. Click the Delete Link button or press the DEL key. If you want to change link options, such as the join type (discussed later in the chapter under "Join Types"), the index used by the link, or multiple-table link behavior, click the Link Options button or double-click the selected link.

To draw a link, click a field in the table you want to link from, drag your mouse to the other table you want to link, and then drop onto the field you want to link to. A link line will be drawn between the two tables. Note that the "from" side of the link line will display a small block, and the "to" side of the link line will display an arrow.

 A persistent bug in Crystal Reports involves dropping on the first field in the "to" table. If you drop much above the middle of the field, the link line won't be drawn. Drop on the lower part of the "to" field to ensure that the link line will be drawn. This problem only occurs if you're dropping on the very first field in the "to" table.

If Crystal Reports detects no potential problems with the link you've drawn, the link line simply appears and you see no messages. If, however, Crystal Reports detects a potential problem with the link, such as mismatched field types, you'll receive a warning message before the link line appears, or the link may not be created at all.

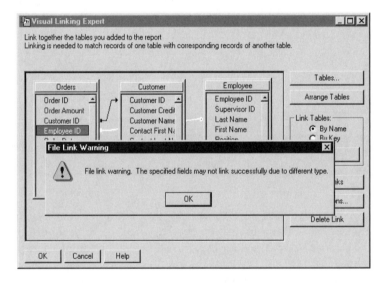

Adding New Tables to the Visual Linking Expert

You will often find that you need to add additional tables to your report as your report design progresses. To do so, choose Database | Add Database To Report from the pull-down menus to open the Data Explorer, in which you can choose additional tables. You may also add tables directly from the Visual Linking Expert by clicking the Tables button. The Choose Tables To Use In Visual Linking dialog box will appear, as shown in Figure 14-4.

Any tables that you've previously added to your report will already appear in the Linked Tables list. If you attempt to add one of these existing tables again, you'll be prompted to give the second occurrence of the table an *alias*, because each table used in

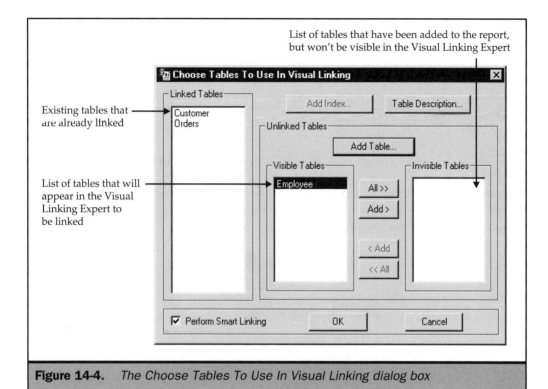

List of tables that have been added to the report,
but won't be visible in the Visual Linking Expert

Existing tables that
are already linked

List of tables that will
appear in the Visual
Linking Expert to
be linked

Figure 14-4.   *The Choose Tables To Use In Visual Linking dialog box*

the Visual Linking Expert must have a unique name. You can add additional tables by
clicking the Add Table button to display the Data Explorer (the Add Index and Table
Description buttons don't apply to SQL databases). After you choose the table or tables,
they appear in the Visible Tables list. These tables will be added to the Visual Linking
Expert when you close this dialog box. Use the Add and All arrow buttons to move
tables between the Visible Tables and Invisible Tables lists, depending on whether you
want to add the tables to the Visual Linking Expert. If you want the Visual Linking
Expert to link the tables automatically, check the Perform Smart Linking check box
(Smart Linking is discussed in more detail later in the chapter). Once you click OK, the
Choose Tables To Use In Visual Linking dialog box closes and the additional tables
appear in the Visual Linking Expert. You can now add or delete links as necessary.

Tip   *You may want to intentionally add the same table to a report more than once.
If, for instance, you have a common lookup table that is used with several master
or transaction tables, you won't be able to retrieve lookup information by linking all
the transaction or master tables to the same lookup table. You'll need to add the lookup
table to the report multiple times, using a different alias each time. You can then link
each transaction or master table to the different aliased versions of the lookup table.*

Removing Unused Tables from the Report

You may inadvertently add too many tables to your report, or you may no longer need tables that you used earlier in the report design process. While this might be a good future enhancement for Crystal Reports, you cannot currently remove any unused tables from the Visual Linking Expert. Close the Visual Linking Expert to return to the report Design tab or Report Expert.

To remove tables using the Report Expert, just remove any fields from the report that come from the table you want to remove. Then, return to the Data tab, select the table you no longer want, and click the Remove button. If you used the Blank Report option and are working directly in the report Design tab, choose Database | Remove from Report from the pull-down menus. Choose the table you no longer want and click Remove. If any fields remain on the report or are used in existing formulas, you'll receive a warning before the table is removed.

 Make sure you really want to remove the table before you click Remove. You can't undo a table removal. Also, if you remove a table that is referenced in any formulas, the formulas will no longer work after the table is gone. If you remove a table by mistake, the best approach is to use the Visual Linking Expert or choose Database | Add Database To Report from the pull-down menus to add the table back in.

Linking Differences Between PC-Style and SQL Databases

While most concepts surrounding table linking apply equally to both PC-style and SQL databases, there are a few specific issues that you should keep in mind when dealing with PC-style databases.

So, Which Tables and Fields Should I Link?

You'll quickly figure out that you have to be very familiar with the database you are reporting against to accurately link tables and fields. You have to know the layout of the tables and the data that the common fields contain to successfully link them. This task is complicated even further by database designers who insist on protecting their jobs by creating confusing and cryptic table and field names.

Probably the most expeditious approach is to consult with someone who either designed the database or is familiar with its layout and contents. Barring that, you may be able to discern the proper tables and fields to link if they are named logically. If nothing else, you can browse individual fields in the Visual Linking Expert by right-clicking a field name and choosing Browse Field from the pop-up menu. By looking for similar data types and sample data that seems to match up in both tables, you can find good candidates for links.

Always make sure you test your report and verify that correct data is being returned once you've linked tables. It's *very easy* to create an incorrect link that displays no error message but doesn't return the correctly matched data to the report.

If you have a large group of report designers who are not familiar with the intricacies of the database, you may want to create a Crystal Dictionary for them to use in reporting. This feature is discussed in Chapter 18.

First, notice the visual differences in the Visual Linking Expert when using a PC-style database.

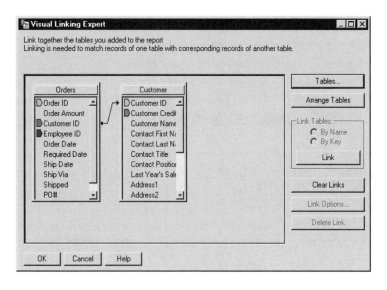

Notice next to various fields the small "tent" arrows that you don't see when using a SQL database. These arrows indicate that the field is indexed. An *index* is a special setting that the database designer creates to speed up access to a table. Searching for specific records from that table will be much faster when the search is based on an indexed field. Based on your video settings, you may also notice different colors for the index arrows. The different colors indicate Crystal Reports' best guess as to which fields may be the table's unique indexes for the fields. As a general rule, you needn't worry about the colors on the index arrows—just make sure that the field you're trying to link to has one.

In some cases, a single field in a table might be indexed more than once—perhaps once individually and also as part of another multiple-field index. In these situations, you may prefer to use one index instead of the other, based on the type of link you are trying to create. For example, if you are linking on only one field that's included in a multifield index, using the individual index for the field instead of the multifield index will probably be preferable (and sometimes mandatory). You can choose an alternate index for a field by clicking the Add Index button in the Choose Tables for Visual Linking dialog box when you add a new table, or in the Link Options dialog box (illustrated later in the chapter in Figure 14-5).

Regardless of the visual differences you may see in the index arrows, PC-style databases impose one unavoidable requirement: The "to" field on which you drop a link *must* be an indexed field. The "from" field doesn't have this requirement, but you have no choice with the "to" field. If you try linking to a nonindexed field, the link won't stick and you'll see an error message.

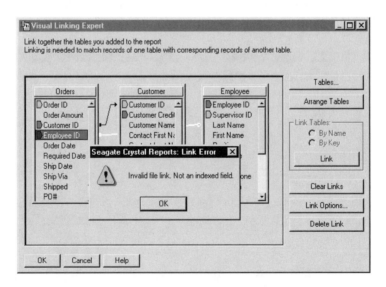

Choosing which fields to index when designing a database is a balancing act. The more indexed fields, the more choices you as a report developer have for linking.

However, creating too many indexes results in larger databases with potential performance problems. If you can't link to a table properly because the target field is not indexed, you may be able to contact the database designer or administrator and request that an index be added. If this isn't practical, you still may be able to create the same, or a very similar, report with the use of subreports. See Chapter 11 for more information.

Is Smart Linking Really That "Smart"?

When you first install Crystal Reports, Smart Linking is turned on by default. Smart Linking is a feature with good intentions, but it is often more trouble than it's worth. Smart Linking automatically links fields in two adjacent tables if the fields meet these criteria:

- The field names are exactly the same.
- The data types are identical.
- In the case of string fields, the field lengths are the same.
- In the case of PC-style databases, the "to" field is indexed.

In an ideal setting (such as the XTREME.MDB sample database provided with Crystal Reports), Smart Linking works perfectly. In the real world, however, things are usually quite different.

Consider, for example, a report that includes a Vendor table and a Customer table. Both tables contain fields named Address, City, State, and Zip_Code. It's perfectly conceivable that these fields have identical data types and field lengths. Smart Linking will dutifully link the two tables together on all four fields. But, these aren't the proper fields with which to link these two tables together.

In Version 8.5, you can use *Linking by Key*, available in the Visual Linking Expert. If Smart Linking is turned on, Crystal Reports automatically uses the field-naming scenario described previously to link fields. If this creates incorrect links, you may want to delete the bad links and re-create them using database key information instead of field name information. After deleting bad links, select the By Key radio button in the Visual Linking Expert and then click the Link button to re-link based on database key information. Crystal Reports can detect "foreign" and "primary" key information in a limited set of databases, such as Oracle and SQL Server, Informix via ODBC and OLE DB, and Microsoft Access using the Microsoft OLE DB Provider for Access.

Because Smart Linking can often result in you taking more time to delete incorrect links and then manually create the correct links, it can be turned off. Select File | Options from the pull-down menus and uncheck Auto-Smart Linking on the Database tab. When the Visual Linking Expert appears, you can then manually link by dragging and dropping or by using Linking by Key.

Tip *When using SQL databases, you won't see the colored "tent" arrows in the Visual Linking Expert, and the indexed "to" field requirement does not exist. However, you'll probably still want to link to indexed fields whenever and wherever possible. All too often, a viewer chastises Crystal Reports for poor performance when the problem actually lies within the speed of the query (or lack thereof) on the server. In many cases, this can be attributed to linking on nonindexed fields. Because there's no visual cue as to which fields are indexed, you should contact the database administrator or designer if you suspect performance problems are related to linking on nonindexed fields.*

Using Multiple Database Types in the Same Report

Crystal Reports doesn't limit you to using just one type of database per report. You may, for example, wish to get the main transaction table for your report from a client/server database using a direct access database driver, one smaller lookup table from a Microsoft Access database on a shared LAN drive, and another lookup table from a Microsoft Excel spreadsheet on your C drive via ODBC or OLE DB.

To accomplish this, simply choose all the different tables from different categories of the Data Explorer when you first create the report. Or, to add additional tables (even from different database types) after you've already started designing a report, choose Database | Add Database To Report from the pull-down menus. After choosing the additional table or tables, close the Data Explorer to add the new tables to the Visual Linking Expert and link them appropriately.

In general, this type of mixed reporting is perfectly acceptable, with one caveat: If you are joining two tables from different data sources, such as a table from an Oracle database and another table from a SQL server database, you can link on only *one field*. If you try to link on more than one field, you receive a message stating "Invalid file link. Not all fields in same index expression." This is a Crystal Reports limitation.

Join Types

When you link two tables, you must consider carefully what records will be returned from both tables. Consider a slight modification to the normalized table structures illustrated earlier in this chapter.

Employee Table:

Employee Name	Department Number	Salary
Karen	17	32,500
Renee	25	37,500

Employee Name	Department Number	Salary
John	8	85,000
Carl	13	24,000
Denise	32	125,000

Department Table:

Department Number	Department Name
8	Executive
13	Mail Room
17	Human Resources
4	Finance
25	Information Technology

A quick glance at these two tables reveals two inconsistencies: Denise has no matching record in the Department table, and the Finance department has no employees in the Employee table. These two tables are said to lack *referential integrity*—a fancy computer term that simply means the two tables don't completely match up. Fancy term or not, this will be *very* important to you as a report designer. You have to decide how you want to deal with a lack of referential integrity.

Many databases can enforce referential integrity, so the situation described previously will never happen. If the database designer chooses to enforce referential integrity between these two tables, an employee cannot be given a department number that doesn't exist in the Department table, and a department record can't be deleted from the Department table if any Employee table records still contain that department. However, enforcing referential integrity often introduces other complexities in the database, and there are many times when the basic function of the database will not allow referential integrity to be enforced. The database designer or administrator should be consulted if you have questions about the way your database is designed.

A situation in which you would be very concerned about referential integrity is if you were designing a report to print paychecks for employees. Consider the tables previously shown as the basis for your paychecks. If you wish to have the employee's department printed on the check stub to help in check distribution, you would need to link the Employee and Department tables together on the Department Number field. It's a fair assumption that your paycheck run would get at least this far:

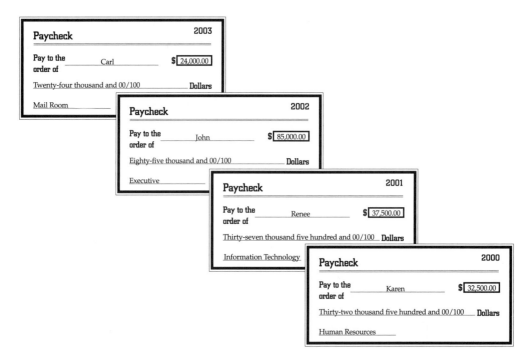

The big question for you, the report designer, is "What happens to Denise?" (the last employee in the Employee table). Considering that she's a highly paid employee, at least from most viewpoints, she will probably be very interested in being paid, regardless of referential integrity. Another interesting question is "Will any checks print for the Finance department?" The answers to your questions are dependent upon which *join type* you use when linking these two tables together.

The following are the two join types that you will be concerned with most of the time:

- **Equal join (often referred to as an *inner join*)**   Includes records from both tables *only when the joining fields are equal.*
- **Left outer join (sometimes simply referred to as *outer join*)**   Includes *all* records from the left table, and records from the right table only when the joining fields are equal.

Even though Denise probably doesn't know what a left outer join is, she probably will be much happier if you choose it. This will result in her receiving a paycheck that simply doesn't have a department name printed on it. This is particularly important in Crystal Reports, because the default join type for SQL databases is an equal join.

A third type of join that you may use less frequently is the following:

■ **Right outer join**   Includes *all* records from the right table, and records from the left table only when the joining fields are equal.

Denise would be as displeased with this choice as she would with an equal join. You would also get a wasted paycheck with the Finance department on the pay stub, but no employee or salary printed on it.

Choosing the Join Type in the Visual Linking Expert

Choose the join type in the Visual Linking Expert by double-clicking the link line between the two tables you are interested in, or by selecting the link and clicking the Link Options button. The Link Options dialog box, shown in Figure 14-5, will appear.

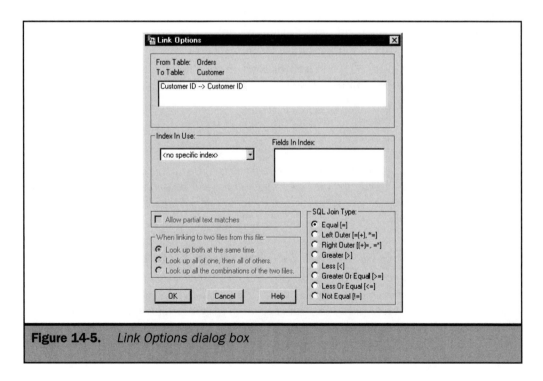

Figure 14-5.   *Link Options dialog box*

Select the desired join type by clicking a radio button in the lower-right corner of the dialog box.

Note *If tables are linked by more than one field, choosing a join type for any of the links will set the same join type for all the links. You cannot have different join types for multiple links between the same tables.*

Although most typical business reporting can be accomplished with equal joins and left outer joins, you may have occasion in specialized reporting situations to use these other join types:

- **Greater join** Repeats records from the left table, matching records from the right table every time the joining field in the left table *is greater than* the joining field in the right table.

- **Less join** Repeats records from the left table, matching records from the right table every time the joining field in the left table *is less than* the joining field in the right table.

- **Greater or equal join** Repeats records from the left table, matching records from the right table every time the joining field in the left table *is greater than or equal to* the joining field in the right table.

- **Less or equal join** Repeats records from the left table, matching records from the right table every time the joining field in the left table *is less than or equal to* the joining field in the right table.

- **Not equal join** Returns all combinations of records from the two tables where the joining fields *are not equal*.

Tip *You can change the join type only for SQL databases. If you display link options for a PC-style database, the SQL Join Type radio buttons will be dimmed. The fixed join type for PC-style databases is a left outer join, even though the dimmed radio buttons indicate an equal join.*

Linking One PC-Style Table to Multiple Tables

When you're using a PC-style database, you have some choices when you create certain types of links between multiple tables. These issues arise when you link a primary or "driving" table to two or more secondary lookup tables. The number and combination of records returned can vary, depending on how many matching records there are in the lookup table for each record in the primary table. These types of links

Which Should Be the Left "From" Table and Which Should Be the Right "To" Table?

When you use the Visual Linking Expert, you begin to draw a link by clicking a "from" table. You then drop the link onto the desired field in the "to" table. You can tell which table is the "from" and which is the "to" by looking at the direction of the link line, as well as the block and arrow. The link line will move *from* one table *to* the other, and the "from" side of the line will display a small block, while the "to" side will display an arrow.

This begs the question, "Does it make any difference which is the "from" and which is the "to" table?" The answer, again, relates to the join type you choose. Generally speaking, if you select an equal join, it doesn't make a great deal of difference. However, if you use any other join type, it makes a great deal of difference, because the "from" or left table and the "to" or right table determine how records are returned.

A relationship between tables is often referred to as a *one-to-one relationship* or a *one-to-many relationship*. If there is always only one matching record in both tables, it doesn't matter which table is the "from" and which is the "to"—it's a one-to-one relationship. However, if there are many matching records in one table for each record in another table, the direction of the link is significant. For example, if a table containing many orders placed by the same customer is linked to a table containing only one matching customer record, you will want to link *from* the Orders table (the "many" table) *to* the Customer table (the "one" table).

If you're concerned that the link may be in "reverse" order, and you'd like to switch the "from" and "to" tables, you can simply delete and redraw the link, or right-click the link and choose Reverse Link from the pop-up menu.

are sometimes called "A to B, A to C" links. Because you can't change join types for PC-style databases, you may occasionally need to change the way Crystal Reports reads records in these situations.

Consider the example shown in Figure 14-6 of a Microsoft Access database that contains three tables: Cust, containing a few customers; Orders, containing several orders for each customer; and Credits, containing credit memos for two customers.

If you are designing a report that lists customers, along with orders and credits for each customer, you will see that there are several ways the report could conceivably

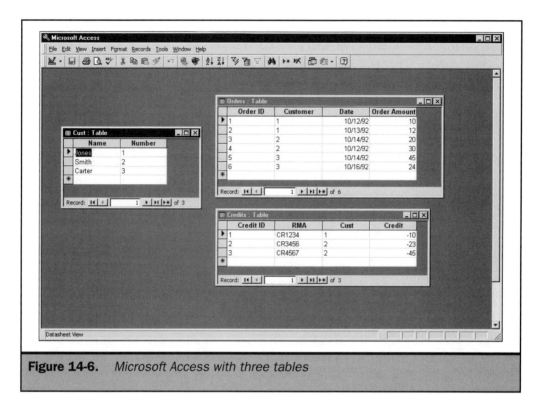

Figure 14-6. *Microsoft Access with three tables*

show these combinations of records. For this example, the tables have been linked as follows in the Visual Linking Expert:

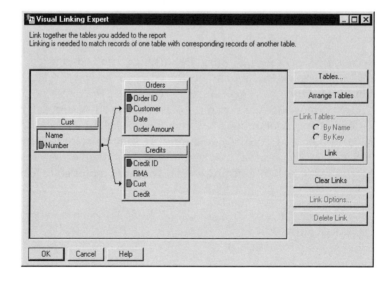

Notice that the Cust table is linked to both secondary tables on the Number field. Whenever you link multiple tables to a single table in this fashion, Crystal Reports gives you an extra choice—When Linking To Two Files from This File—on the Link Options dialog box, which appears when you double-click any link line. With these options, you can choose the lookup method for a multiple-table link:

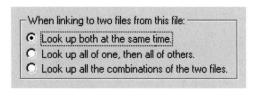

The When Linking To Two Files from This File radio buttons apply only to PC-style databases. They are dimmed whenever you use a SQL database. If you are concerned about the way your SQL database returns records in similar situations, try different join types or check with your database administrator.

The following three examples were created with the previous Access database, showing the Customer Name from the Cust table (referred to here as Table A), the Order ID and Order Amount from the Orders table (Table B), and the Credit ID and Credit Amount from the Credits table (Table C). Each example shows the results of one of the three choices under the When Linking To Two Files from This File area of the Link Options dialog box.

Look Up Both at the Same Time   This method begins by reading a record from Table A, along with the first matching record in Table B and the first matching record in Table C. The *same* record from Table A will then repeat (if there are additional matching records in Table B or C), and the next matching Table B and Table C records will be included. If Crystal Reports runs out of matching records in Table B or C while there are still some left in the other secondary table, null values will appear for that table. Here's the sample report with this option chosen:

Name	Order ID	Order Amount	Credit ID	Credit
Jones	1	10.00	1	-10.00
Jones	2	12.00	1	-10.00
Smith	3	20.00	2	-23.00
Smith	4	30.00	3	-45.00
Carter	5	45.00		
Carter	6	24.00		

Look Up All of One, Then All of Others   This option, in essence, completely separates the secondary tables from each other. Crystal Reports will read a record from Table A, and then read all matching records from Table B first, leaving fields for Table C blank. It then continues repeating the same record from Table A and includes all matching records from Table C, leaving Table B fields blank. Here's the sample report with this option chosen:

Name	Order ID	Order Amount	Credit ID	Credit
Jones	1	10.00		
Jones	2	12.00		
Jones			1	-10.00
Smith	3	20.00		
Smith	4	30.00		
Smith			2	-23.00
Smith			3	-45.00
Carter	5	45.00		
Carter	6	24.00		

Generally, this is the only one of the three options that will not repeat the same record from the secondary tables (although primary table records will repeat). For this reason, this method may be the most straightforward if you're calculating group subtotal or summary fields.

If the method you use does result in repeating records that skew group or report totals or summaries, you need to use running total fields or formulas containing variables to calculate totals without including duplicated records. Both of these features are discussed in Chapter 5.

Look Up All the Combinations of the Two Files

This option can quickly turn records for a relatively small database into a monstrous report. It begins by reading the first Table A record and matching it to a Table B record. It then repeats both the Table A and Table B records for every matching Table C record. It then goes to the next matching Table B record (while *still* on the first Table A record) and repeats the A and B records for the next matching C record. When Crystal Reports runs out of Table B records, it proceeds to the next Table A record and starts the whole process over again. Here's the sample report with this option chosen:

Name	Order ID	Order Amount	Credit ID	Credit
Jones	1	10.00	1	-10.00
Jones	2	12.00	1	-10.00
Smith	3	20.00	2	-23.00
Smith	3	20.00	3	-45.00
Smith	4	30.00	2	-23.00
Smith	4	30.00	3	-45.00
Carter	5	45.00		
Carter	6	24.00		

Working with the SQL Statement

Recall from earlier in the chapter that SQL (the letters can be pronounced individually, or many people pronounce it as *sequel*) is an acronym for *Structured Query Language*. This database query language has been established as a pseudostandard method of querying databases. The term "pseudo" is used because although the American National Standard Institute (ANSI) settled on a standard SQL, virtually every database vendor adds its own personal touches, although they all claim to adhere to the ANSI standard.

Viewing the SQL Query

Because Crystal Reports works with SQL databases, it must eventually translate the tables, fields, links, sorting, and grouping that you've used to design your report into SQL. You can view the SQL statements Crystal Reports creates by choosing Database | Show SQL Query from the pull-down menus.

Consider the following report Design tab that uses data from the XTREME sample database, converted from Microsoft Access to Microsoft SQL Server, accessed via ODBC. This report uses the Orders and Customer tables, linked with a left outer join on Customer ID. The Select Expert is limiting the report to U.S.A customers only. Notice the fields that have been placed in the details section. Also, notice that a group based on Customer.Region has been created.

To view the SQL statement that Crystal Reports creates to query the database, select Database | Show SQL Query. You will see the dialog box illustrated in Figure 14-7. Notice the different parts, or *clauses*, of the SQL statement:

- **SELECT** Matches the database fields that your report needs (for the details section, formulas, grouping, and so on).

- **FROM** Chooses the tables to use and specifies the join type for table linking.

- **WHERE** Supplies record selection to the server.

- **ORDER BY** Requests that the SQL server sort records in Customer.Region order (for the Region group) before sending them back to the client.

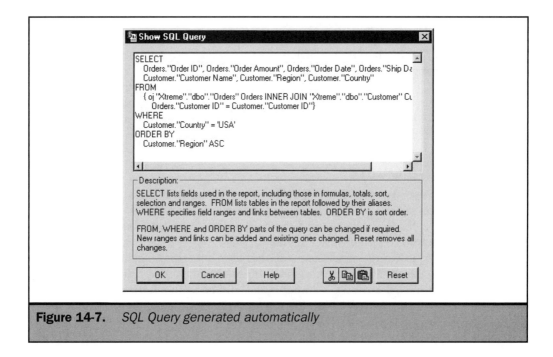

Figure 14-7. SQL Query generated automatically

The SQL syntax may change, based on the type of database you are reporting against and whether you're using ODBC or direct database drivers to communicate with it. You'll also see different syntax for joining tables. And, you may see the actual table join appear in either the FROM or WHERE clause.

Here is the exact same Show SQL Query dialog box using the direct database driver to Microsoft SQL Server:

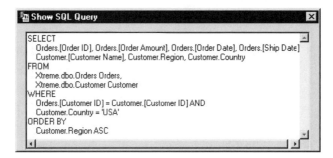

and, for the Microsoft Access version of the XTREME.MDB sample database via ODBC:

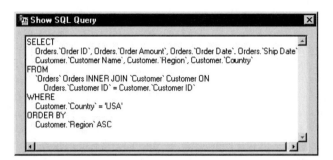

Although you may not consider yourself a database expert and might not make a habit of writing huge SQL statements off the top of your head, there are two big advantages to being able to see and manipulate the SQL query:

■ You can see what Crystal Reports is submitting to the database server, which can be useful if you are experiencing performance problems or other peculiarities.

■ You can actually change most of the SQL query manually if you do have a basic understanding of SQL.

Modifying the SQL Query

Sometimes Crystal Reports may not take full advantage of your server's SQL language extensions, and you may want to modify the SQL to include them. You may also want to paste SQL copied from another query tool into the Show SQL Query dialog box. You are completely free to modify the FROM, WHERE, and ORDER BY clauses of the SQL statement to your heart's content. The SELECT clause is off-limits, though. You can type over it, but any changes you make won't be saved. (Don't even bother to try changing the SELECT to a DELETE or UPDATE—your changes will never make it to the server!)

Make sure the modifications comply with the particular syntax of SQL that your report is based on. The three SQL statement examples shown previously give you an idea of the small syntax differences between different connection methods to the same data. If you enter SQL using incorrect syntax, you'll receive an error message when you refresh the report. If you change the SQL query manually and later think better of it, you can always click the Reset button in the bottom-right corner of the Show SQL

Query dialog box. This erases any changes you've made to the query and returns it to the Crystal Reports default.

It's very important to understand how using the Show SQL Query dialog box and selecting report records interact with each other. The two methods used to be, in effect, mutually exclusive: You could use either the Select Expert or record-selection formula to specify record selection that Crystal Reports performs locally, or the WHERE clause to specify a query limit for the server, but not both.

When you first create a report using a SQL database and use record selection, either with the Select Expert or by entering a record-selection formula, Crystal Reports attempts to convert the record selection into a SQL WHERE clause. As with previous Crystal Reports versions, if you then change the WHERE clause manually in the Show SQL Query dialog box, the record selection you chose with a formula or the Select Expert disappears. Crystal Reports then depends on your "custom" SQL to limit report records.

You can then return to the Select Expert or Record Selection Formula Editor and see that nothing is there. If you then reenter Select Expert choices or a record-selection formula, you are presented with a message:

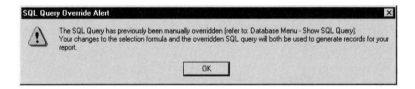

In Crystal Reports 7 and earlier, the selection change would replace the changes you made to the WHERE clause. Now, Crystal Reports actually uses *both* sets of criteria: the Select Expert/record-selection formula *and* the custom WHERE clause to limit records. The WHERE clause is executed first, and then the database result set is run through the local record selection that you chose with the Select Expert or record-selection formula. Be careful when you see this message: it's very possible that the two selection options directly conflict with each other and your report won't display any records. At the very least, it may not make the most efficient use of the database server, as the additional record selection criteria you selected after manually modifying the SQL query won't be moved to the server for processing.

Case Sensitivity

You may recall from Chapter 6 that some PC-style databases are case sensitive when using record selection. An example of case sensitivity is that when comparing a country database field to the literal "USA," any data in the database stored as "usa" or "Usa" won't be retrieved for the report.

You may also recall that you have a choice of case-sensitivity behavior when dealing with SQL databases. To change the option for the current report only, select File | Report Options and check Case-Insensitive SQL Data. If you want SQL queries to be case insensitive for any new report you create from this point forward, select File | Options and check Case-Insensitive SQL Data on the Database.

Remember that this option still may not work if the particular database server, ODBC driver, or direct database driver that you're using doesn't support case insensitivity. In such situations, you may be able to manually modify the SQL statement to ignore case. For example, the following Microsoft Access (via ODBC) WHERE clause is case sensitive:

```
WHERE
    Customer.'Country' = 'USA'
```

By using the specific "flavor" of Microsoft Access SQL, you can make the query case-insensitive by changing it to the following:

```
WHERE
    UCASE(Customer.'Country') = 'USA'
```

This uses the built-in SQL UCASE function to force database records to all uppercase letters before the server compares them to the uppercase "USA" literal.

Using SQL Stored Procedures

Most SQL database systems include the capability to use stored procedures. A *stored procedure* is a SQL query that has been evaluated, or "compiled," by the database server in advance, and is stored on the server along with regular database tables. Because the stored procedure is compiled in advance, it often performs faster than a SQL query submitted on-the-fly. Stored procedures can be created by the database designer or administrator for specific queries that will be run on a frequent basis.

To enhance flexibility, stored procedures can contain one or more stored procedure *parameters* that prompt the user to enter a value. The stored procedure then uses the value to run the query. For example, if you have a stored procedure that returns several fields from linked tables, based on Country and Order Date parameters, you'll be prompted to enter a particular country and order date when the stored procedure runs. The procedure will then return a result set containing only records matching the two-parameter values you supplied.

Choosing Stored Procedures

Crystal Reports treats stored procedures almost identically to regular database tables. Stored procedures appear in the Data Explorer and are used in a report just like regular database tables. The only difference is that a stored procedure may have parameters associated with it. However, you do have a choice of whether or not stored procedures will appear in the Data Explorer in the first place. The quickest way to ensure that they show up is to click the Options button on the Data Explorer and then check the Stored Procedure check box in the Database Options dialog box (shown earlier in Figure 14-2). You may also make the change permanent for all new reports in the future by checking the same option on the Database tab after choosing File | Options from the pull-down menus.

Now, when you open a SQL database, you'll see stored procedures appear along with regular database tables.

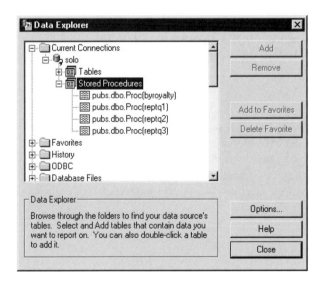

Your report can be based on a stored procedure or a combination of one or more database tables, but not both. You cannot link a stored procedure in the Visual Linking Expert, so you won't be able to fully use a stored procedure in the same way you use a table. If the stored procedure does not include all the data you need, ask your database administrator to add additional fields to the stored procedure, or use a linked subreport (described in Chapter 11) to retrieve the necessary data.

Working with Stored Procedure Parameters

After you choose a stored procedure to report on, you are prompted to supply any values for any stored procedure parameters in the Enter Parameter Values dialog box. This dialog box is identical to the one that prompts for report parameter fields, discussed in Chapter 12.

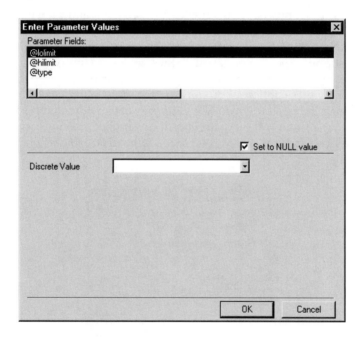

Type your desired parameter values, and click OK. You can then simply continue your report design process normally. The stored procedure will supply a list of fields you can use in your report, just like a normal database table.

Stored procedure parameters behave almost identically to Crystal Reports parameter fields. The stored procedure parameters will appear in the Parameter Fields category of the Field Explorer.

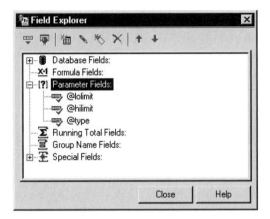

You can edit a stored procedure parameter by selecting it and clicking the Edit button, typing CTRL-E, or right-clicking the parameter and choosing Edit from the pop-up menu. Although you can't change the value type or select multiple or range values, you can supply a pick list of default values, set length limits or an edit mask for string parameters, or range limits for number or date parameters. See Chapter 12 for more information on these options. You can even rename a stored procedure parameter in the Field Explorer the same way you would rename a regular parameter field (although this won't change the name of the stored procedure parameter on the server).

When you refresh the report, you receive the same prompt as when using parameter fields.

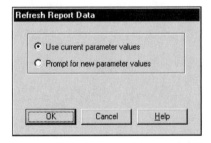

You can choose whether to use the existing values for the stored procedure parameters or to prompt for new values. When you prompt for new values, the server will run the stored procedure with the new values and return a new result set to Crystal Reports.

Using SQL Expression Fields

Sometimes you'll want to have the database server actually perform some calculations for you, sending the already calculated field back with the database result set. This is accomplished with SQL expression fields, which can be created right from the Field Explorer. A *SQL expression* is like a formula, except that it's made up entirely of database fields and SQL functions that are supported by the language of the particular SQL server that you're working with. Sometimes there are advantages to using a SQL expression instead of a Crystal Reports formula. The expression is evaluated on the server, not by the client, which can improve performance.

A particular advantage involves calculations or other specialized functions that are used in record selection. If you use a Crystal Reports formula in record selection, the database server typically won't be able to perform the selection, because it doesn't understand the Crystal Reports formula language. However, by creating a SQL expression and using that in record selection, the SQL server will fully understand the expression, and the record selection will be performed by the database server.

Creating SQL Expressions

The first prerequisite for using SQL expressions is that you must be using a SQL or ODBC database. If you're using a PC-style database, SQL expressions don't apply and you won't even see the SQL Expression category in the Field Explorer. However, when you are using a SQL database, the Field Explorer includes an additional category labeled SQL Expression Fields. Click the Insert Field button in the Standard toolbar, or use Insert | Field Object from the pull-down menus to display the Field Explorer. Then, click the SQL Expression Fields category and click the New button in the Field Explorer toolbar, type CTRL-N, or right-click on the SQL Expression Fields category and choose New from the pop-up menu.

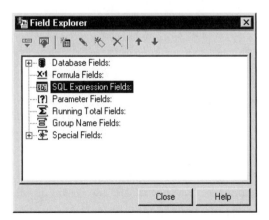

 You can't use SQL expression fields with stored procedures. If your report is based on a stored procedure, the SQL Expression Fields category won't even appear in the Field Explorer.

Creating a SQL expression is very similar to creating a Crystal Reports formula (discussed in detail in Chapter 5). You first are asked to give the SQL expression a name. As with formula names, you should make the SQL expression name reasonably short and easy to understand. You may include spaces as well as upper- and lowercase letters in the name. The name you give the SQL expression will also be the column heading if you place the SQL expression in the report's details section.

After you give the SQL expression a name and click OK, the SQL Expression Editor appears, as shown in Figure 14-8.

Note the similarities between the SQL Expression Editor and the other Crystal Reports formula editors. Creating SQL expressions is essentially the same as creating other formulas: you can type the expression directly into the Formula text box, or double-click in the top three boxes to help build the expression. Notice that, like formulas, parameter fields, and running total fields, Crystal Reports appends a special

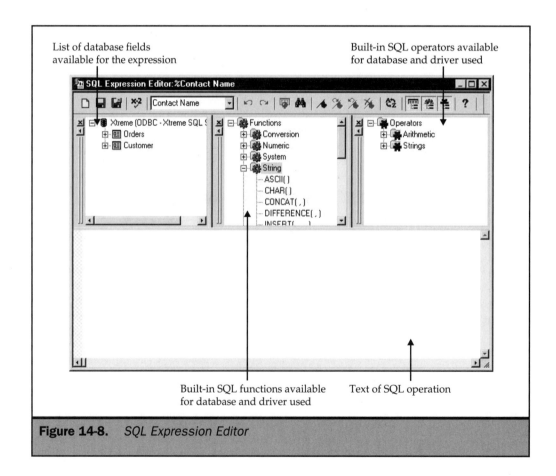

List of database fields available for the expression

Built-in SQL operators available for database and driver used

Built-in SQL functions available for database and driver used

Text of SQL operation

Figure 14-8. *SQL Expression Editor*

character to the beginning of the SQL expression's name. The percent symbol (%) is used to denote SQL expression fields.

The functions and operators available in the SQL Expression Editor change, depending on the database and database driver in use. If you look at the Function Tree box in Figure 14-8, you'll notice a certain set of available SQL functions. This example is for a report using Microsoft SQL Server via ODBC. If you use the direct database driver to connect to the same database, however, the SQL Expression Editor will show a completely different set of SQL functions. For this reason, you will probably have to edit or modify some SQL expressions if you change your report from one database to another using Set Location or Convert Database Driver, both available from the Database pull-down menu. To get detailed descriptions of the different built-in SQL functions for your particular database or driver, consult documentation for that database or driver.

For example, you may want a report viewer to be able to specify with just one parameter field a full or partial contact name to search for. If a customer exists whose contact matches what's entered, the customer will be included on the report. In the Customer table of the XTREME sample database that's included with Crystal Reports,the contact information is actually split into separate first and last name database fields. Without using a SQL expression, you have two choices for setting up this search:

- Create two parameter fields—one for first name and one for last name—and try to compare those to database fields.

- Create a Crystal Reports formula that combines the contact's first and last names, and compare the formula to the parameter field.

There are problems with both approaches, however. If you choose the first option, it's much harder for the viewer to simply type a full or partial contact name, such as "Chris" (to find both Christopher and Christine, for example), because some additional logic will be necessary to ignore the last name parameter field if the viewer just wants to search for full or partial first names. Or, if the viewer wants to see everyone whose last name is "Jones," regardless of first name, then similar logic will have to apply for the first name parameter field. It would be much simpler for the viewer to be able to type **Chris*** or ***Jones** to search for their desired customers.

If you choose the second option, the full or partial searches mentioned in the previous paragraph will work; but because the first and last names are combined in a formula, the record selection will not take place on the database server (remember that most Crystal formulas can't be converted to SQL, so the client will perform record selection).

By using a SQL expression, you can have the best of both worlds. The first and last names can be concatenated into one object and compared to the parameter field. But because the concatenation takes place on the database server, it will still perform the record selection, sending only the resulting customers back to the client, not all customers.

The SQL expression to accomplish this is surprisingly similar to a Crystal Reports formula:

```
Customer."Contact First Name" + ' ' + Customer."Contact Last Name"
```

Notice that a couple of differences exist, however:

- There are no French or "curly" braces around the field names.
- The literal string that separates the first and last name fields must use apostrophes—quotation marks won't work.

Once this SQL expression has been created, it can be dropped onto the report just like a database field, formula field, or other object. It can also be used inside regular report formulas or in conditional formatting formulas. Notice the change to the SQL query (viewed with Database | Show SQL Query) after placing this SQL expression in the details section:

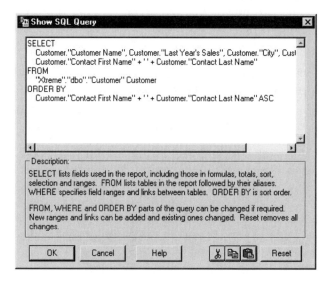

Even though the SQL expression field was given a name in the report, Crystal Reports just adds the SQL expression formula itself right into the SQL statement. The name is simply used by Crystal Reports in the Select Expert or elsewhere on the report.

To now use this SQL expression in record selection, you use the Select Expert's Like operator to allow a wildcard search on the combined first and last names of the contact. If you have already created a string parameter field called {?Contact Prompt}, the Select Expert will look like this:

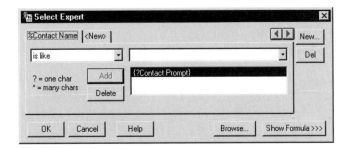

When you refresh the report and are prompted for the Contact Prompt parameter field, entering the Chris* wildcard will return the following records:

Customer Name	Contact Name	Last Year's Sales	City	Region
City Cyclists	Chris Christianson	$20,045.27	Sterling Heights	MI
Pathfinders	Christine Manley	$26,369.63	DeKalb	IL
Orléans VTT	Christophe Jolicoeur	$6,655.90	Troyes	Champagne-Ardenne
The Bike Cellar	Christopher Carmine	$30,938.67	Winchester	VA

Now, look at the SQL query being sent to the database server:

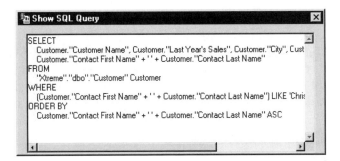

Notice that the WHERE clause includes the SQL expression formula text and a SQL comparison operator that allows wildcard searches. The end result: the flexibility of Crystal Reports formulas with the speed of server-based record selection.

Grouping on the Database Server

Another powerful feature of SQL database servers is server-side processing, or server-based grouping. *Server-based grouping* refers to the ability of the SQL server to perform aggregate calculations on groups of records, returning only subtotals, summaries, and other aggregates to the client. If you are creating a summary report (very often the case), this server capability can significantly decrease the amount of data being passed over the network. Also, the summary calculations can be performed on the server rather than on the client.

Consider the following simple Sales by Region report:

Customer Name	Last Year's Sales	City
AL		
Psycho-Cycle	$52,809.11	Huntsville
Benny - The Spokes Person	$6,091.96	Huntsville
The Great Bike Shop	$15,218.09	Huntsville
3 customers	Subtotal: $ 74,119.16	
AR		
Bikefest	$5,879.70	Little Rock
1 customers	Subtotal: $ 5,879.70	
AZ		
Bicycle Races	$659.70	Tempe
Biking and Hiking	$65.70	Phoenix
2 customers	Subtotal: $ 725.40	

This is the beginning of a report that simply shows all U.S.A. customers, grouped by region, with a customer count and sales subtotal for each group. Because the details section is shown, the database server will need to send all customers in the U.S.A. to Crystal Reports. Crystal Reports is actually calculating the subtotal and count for each group on the client machine as the report processes. This is confirmed by looking at the SQL query for this report:

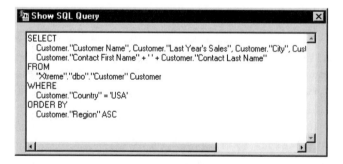

Notice that this fairly simple SQL statement just selects database fields and limits records to the U.S.A. The only server feature used here that helps with grouping is the ORDER BY clause, which presorts the result set into Region order before sending it to the client.

To create a summary report, simply hide the details section by right-clicking in the gray details area in the left of the Design tab, and choose Hide (Drill-Down OK) from the pop-up menu. The report will now show just the summary data, with no individual customers appearing on the report.

Customer Name		Last Year's Sales	City
AL			
	3 customers	Subtotal: $ 74,119.16	
AR			
	1 customers	Subtotal: $ 5,879.70	
AZ			
	2 customers	Subtotal: $ 725.40	
CA			
	6 customers	Subtotal: $ 211,479.24	
CO			

However, if you look at the SQL query, even after refreshing the report, you'll notice that it hasn't changed, because server-based grouping is turned off by default. The server is still sending all customers in the U.S.A to Crystal Reports, and Crystal Reports still has to cycle through the individual customer records to calculate the customer count and sales subtotals. Database fields in the details section are hidden, but the database returns them anyway.

Enabling Server-Based Grouping

There are several different ways to turn on server-based grouping:

- To turn it on for the current report only, choose Database | Perform Grouping on Server from the pull-down menus. You can also choose File | Report Options from the pull-down menus and check Perform Grouping on Server. And, you can choose the same option when you click the Options button on the Data Explorer.

- To turn it on for all new reports you create from this point forward, choose File | Options from the pull-down menus and check Perform Grouping on Server on the Database tab.

Once this option is enabled, the report should look the same. There will be some significant changes to the SQL query, however.

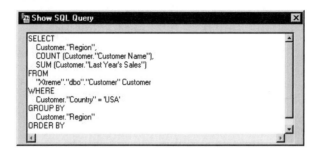

You will see that the SELECT clause now only includes the group field (in this case, Region) and two *aggregate functions* that perform the sum and count functions right on the database server before data is sent to the client. You will also see a new GROUP BY clause that you have not seen before. This new SQL function tells the server to group database records and perform the summary calculations all on the server. Only the summary totals will be sent to the client.

What's Required to Use Server-Based Grouping

Your report must meet certain criteria and be designed in a certain way to use server-based grouping. When you think about the way the server groups and summarizes records, you'll begin to realize why your report must meet these requirements, shown in Table 14-1.

Effects of Drill-Down

When Crystal Reports is performing its own grouping, the concept of report drill-down is fairly straightforward. Even though the details section or lower-level group headers and footers aren't being shown, Crystal Reports is still processing them and storing the data they create. When a viewer double-clicks to drill down on a group, Crystal Reports simply opens a new drill-down tab and displays the data it had previously not displayed.

However, when you enable server-side grouping, there is no detail data to display when a viewer drills down—only the summary data has been sent to the client! Crystal Reports still enables drill-down, however; it just sends another query to the SQL server whenever a viewer drills down. This second query requests just the detail data for the group that was drilled into by adding additional criteria to the WHERE clause. This method provides the benefits of server-based grouping, while still allowing the powerful interactivity of drill-down. The price a viewer pays is the additional time the SQL server may take to process the drill-down query.

Requirement	Reasoning
There must be at least one group on the report.	For the GROUP BY clause to be added to the SQL query, there needs to be at least one group defined on the report.
The details section must be hidden.	If the details section is visible, no grouping will occur on the server, because the server must send down individual database records to show in the details section.
Only include the group fields or summary fields in group headers and footers.	If you include any other database fields (or formula fields that contain anything other than group fields or summary fields), the server will have to send detail data to the client to properly display the report.
Don't group on Crystal Reports formulas.	Because most Crystal Reports formulas can't be converted to SQL, they must be calculated on the client before the report can group on them. Because of this requirement, the server has to send detail records to the client. This is another reason you may want to use SQL expressions as an alternative to formulas, as SQL expressions can still be used for server-based grouping.
Running totals must be based on summary fields.	If running totals (described in Chapter 5) are based on detail fields, Crystal Reports needs the detail data to calculate them as the report processes. This prevents grouping from being done on the server.
The report cannot contain Average or Distinct Count summaries or Top *N* values.	Crystal Reports can't convert these particular functions to SQL. Therefore, the grouping will be performed by the client if these functions are used.
Report groups can only be sorted in ascending or descending order. Specified-order grouping won't work.	Since Crystal Reports bases specified-order grouping on its own internal logic, it needs detail records to properly evaluate what specified groups to place them in. This requires detail records to be sent by the server.

Table 14-1. *Server-Based Grouping Requirements*

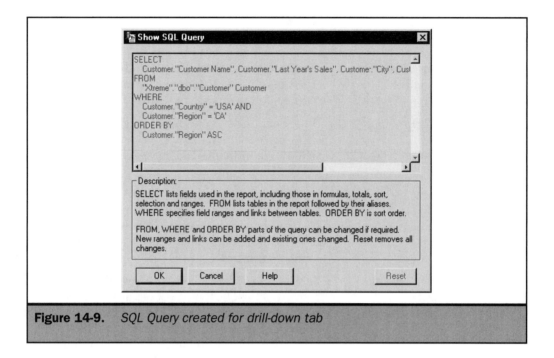

Figure 14-9. *SQL Query created for drill-down tab*

Look at the example shown in Figure 14-9. Notice that a viewer has drilled down on a particular region. A new drill-down tab appears, showing detail data for that region. Notice the new SQL query that was created on-the-fly.

You can view drill-down SQL queries by choosing Database | Show SQL Query when viewing the drill-down tab. If you return to the main Preview tab and show the query, you'll once again notice the GROUP BY clause.

Performance Considerations

SQL databases (or PC-style databases accessed via ODBC) present a very different set of performance considerations than do PC-style databases. As has been discussed throughout the chapter, one of the main benefits of SQL databases over PC databases is the ability of the database server to perform record selection and grouping locally as soon as a SQL query is received from Crystal Reports. Only when the database server has performed record selection or grouping itself will it return the result set back to Crystal Reports.

Let the Server Do the Work

As a general reporting rule, you want to always have the database server perform as much of the processing as possible. Database server software is designed and tuned to perform just such operations, and server software is often placed on very high-end hardware platforms to enhance this performance even further. Any glitch that might cause the database server to send back every record in its database (million-plus-record SQL databases are not at all uncommon) to be selected or summarized locally by Crystal Reports will often result in unsatisfactory performance.

To see how much (or if any) of the query is being evaluated on the database server, view the query by choosing Database | Show SQL Query from the pull-down menus. Look at the SQL statement for the WHERE clause. If you don't see one, no selection at all will be done on the server—every record in the database will come down to the PC, to be left to Crystal Reports to sort through. This can be *very* time-consuming!

Look for an ORDER BY clause if you are sorting or grouping your report. If you see this clause, the database server will presort your data before sending it to Crystal Reports. This can speed the formatting of your report. If you don't see an ORDER BY clause, but you specified grouping or sorting in your report, the server will send records to Crystal Reports unsorted, and the client will have to sort the records.

If you wish to use server-based grouping, make sure you see a GROUP BY clause in the query. This ensures that the server is grouping and aggregating data before sending it to Crystal Reports. If you don't see this clause, check back to the server-based grouping requirements earlier in this chapter.

To ensure record selection occurs on the server, Crystal Reports must convert your record-selection formula to a SQL WHERE clause. Several rules of thumb help to ensure that as much record selection as possible is converted to SQL and that it is done on the server:

- Don't base record selection on formula fields. Crystal Reports usually can't convert formulas to SQL, so most record selection based on formula fields will be passed on to Crystal Reports.

- Don't use Crystal Reports formula language's built-in functions, such as ToText, in your selection criteria. Again, Crystal Reports usually can't convert these to SQL, so these parts of record selection won't be carried out on the server. You may be able to find a similar function in a SQL Expression field and use the expression in record selection.

- Avoid using string subscript functions in record selection. For example, {Customer.Contact First Name}[1 to 5] = "Chris" cannot be converted to SQL, so record selection will be left to Crystal Reports. Create a SQL expression instead, perhaps using a SQL LEFT statement, such as LEFT(Customer.Contact_First_Name, 5). Then use it in record selection.

Use Indexed Fields

You may be lulled into a false sense of performance security because SQL databases don't have the indexed-field linking requirement (remember, PC-style databases only allow you to link to an indexed field). Because you can't even see what fields are indexed in the Visual Linking Expert when using a SQL database, you may think that it really doesn't matter what fields you link to or select on.

Depending on the database system that you're using, linking to nonindexed fields or performing record selection on nonindexed fields can prove disastrous to the performance of your report. Most SQL database systems have indexing capabilities that the database designer probably considers when designing the database.

If at all possible, work with the database designer to ensure that indexes are created to solve not only your database application needs, but your reporting needs as well. Since you won't be able to tell what indexes exist, ask the database designer or administrator what database fields are indexed. Then, try to use those fields as much as possible as "to" fields in linking, and for record selection.

Also, it may improve performance to select records based on as many fields as possible from the main or driving table. For example, you may have a main transaction table that is linked to five lookup tables, and you may want to use the descriptions from the lookup tables in record selection. Instead, consider using the fields in the *main* table for record selection (even if you have to use the codes in the main table, and not the descriptions from the lookup table). Again, if these fields in the main table are indexed, you'll probably see a performance improvement.

The
Complete
Reference

Crystal
Reports

Chapter 15

Accommodating Database Changes and Field Mapping

There are many situations in which the database you initially developed a report against will change. Perhaps the database is in a state of flux and will be changing dynamically as your report design proceeds. Or, you may develop a report against a test database and then change the report to point to a production database later. For true flexibility, you need to be able to accommodate these changes easily, so that you don't have to re-create any features or functions of your report just because the database has changed.

As part of these database changes, the database designer or administrator may rename fields. When Crystal Reports detects these changes, it gives you the opportunity to change the field references inside your report, so the new field names can be automatically associated with the previous field names. This field mapping prevents you from having to add fields to the report again or modify formulas that refer to changed fields.

There are several ways to accommodate changes that have been made to the database:

- Verify a database
- Change database drivers
- Set a location

These are all explained in this chapter.

Verifying or Changing the Database Location

If the database layout changes (field names change, data types are altered, and so forth), if the database is moved to a new location, or if you want to point your report to a different database than it was originally designed with, you need to use Crystal Reports' functions to recognize these changes.

Verifying a Database

If the database your report is based on changes (perhaps the database designer adds new fields, deletes old fields, or gives existing fields new names or data types), your report won't automatically recognize these changes when the report is opened. Even if you refresh the report, Crystal Reports won't detect the changes. To detect changes to the database the report is based on, you must verify the database.

Choose Database | Verify Database from the pull-down menus. If the database has not changed, you'll see a dialog box indicating so:

However, if the database has changed, you'll receive a message like this:

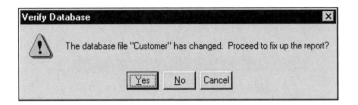

If you click Yes at this prompt, Crystal Reports will read the database structure and make any changes to table names, field names, and data types. When you display the Field Explorer, you'll notice the changes. And, if you have previously linked tables together and table structures have changed significantly, you may need to re-link tables in the Visual Linking Expert. If field names have changed, you will see the Map Fields dialog box (discussed later in the chapter).

Verify on Every Print

If the database changes and you don't verify the database thereafter, your report may show incorrect data if fields have been moved or renamed, or it may display an error message if tables have been removed or renamed. Be very careful when working with a database that may be changing. You'll want to verify the database often to catch any changes.

One way to accomplish this is to select Database | Verify on Every Print from the pull-down menus. When you check this menu option, Crystal Reports will verify the database every time a report is refreshed. The on/off state of Verify on Every Print will be saved with the report—if it was turned on when a particular report was saved, it will be turned on when that report is opened.

Changing the Database Driver

Sometimes, you may want to change the *type,* rather than the name, of the database your report is based on. A fairly common situation occurs when a report is initially developed on a PC-style database and is later upsized to some form of client/server or SQL Server database. In this situation, you must change the database driver the report is based on. A database driver is an underlying dynamic link library (a special Windows data file with a .DLL extension) that Crystal Reports uses to communicate with the different layers of database communication on your PC. A unique driver exists for every type of database that Crystal Reports recognizes.

For example, if you create a report based on a Microsoft Access test database using the Data Explorer Database Files category, you use the PDBDAO.DLL database driver to communicate with the Access database directly. If this Access database is upsized to a production Microsoft SQL Server, you need to change the report to use the PDSSQL.DLL database driver (if you want to use a direct driver to get to SQL Server; see Chapter 14 for more information about direct database drivers). If you want to get to SQL Server (or any other ODBC-compliant database for that matter) using ODBC, you need to change the report to use the PDSODBC.DLL database driver.

Choose Database | Convert Database Driver from the pull-down menus. This displays the Convert Database Driver dialog box:

After you check the Convert Database Driver on Next Refresh check box, you see the From name of the driver that your report is currently based on, followed by a To drop-down list showing all the available drivers that you can convert your report to. Choose the new driver you want to use, based on the type of database you want to convert to. When you click OK, you will be prompted to log on to a new database or choose a new ODBC data source (depending on the driver you are converting to).

As soon as you log on to the new database, your report will be connected to the new database, and the database will be verified (as discussed previously in this chapter). When you display the Field Explorer, you'll notice the changes. If you have previously linked tables together and the table structures have changed significantly, you may need to re-link tables in the Visual Linking Expert. If field names have changed, you will see the Map Fields dialog box (discussed in the "Mapping Old Fields to New Names" section later in this chapter).

Crystal Reports 8.5 provides automatic driver conversion if you use the Set Location command. If you choose Set Location (discussed in the following paragraphs) and choose a database from a different category in the Data Explorer, Crystal Reports 8.5 will perform an automatic driver conversion.

Using Set Location

There will be other situations in which the database your report is based on is physically moved to a new location on the network. Or, you may be developing a report against a test database using ODBC and then need to move the report to a production ODBC database. In these situations, the database type won't change (therefore, you won't need to change to a different database driver), but you will need a method to point the report to the new database location. The Set Location option will accomplish this.

Choose Database | Set Location from the pull-down menus. The Set Location dialog box will appear, displaying a list of all the tables in your report.

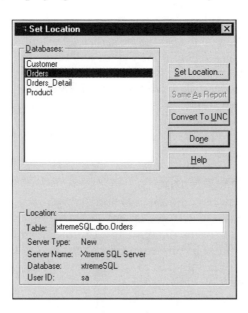

Select the table that you wish to set the new location for. Then, click the Set Location button. The Data Explorer will appear, showing any databases you're already connected to, as well as allowing you to choose or connect to other databases. Choose the table that you wish to replace the previously selected table in the Set Location dialog box with.

After you specify the new database location, you may be asked whether you wish to propagate those changes to other tables with the same original information.

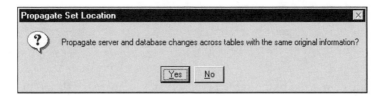

If you click Yes, any other tables in the report that originally were pointed to the same database as the one you just changed will be pointed to the new location automatically. If you click No, all other tables will point to their original locations.

Once you change the location of the database, Crystal Reports will verify the database. When you display the Field Explorer, you'll notice the changes. If you had previously linked tables together and table structures have changed significantly, you may need to re-link tables in the Visual Linking Expert. If field names have changed, you will see the Map Fields dialog box (discussed in the "Mapping Old Fields to New Names" section later in the chapter).

Same As Report Option

The Same As Report button on the Set Location dialog box only applies to reports based on PC-style databases. Clicking Same As Report will remove any drive letter and path name from the database location. From that point forward, Crystal Reports will look for the database on the same disk drive and in the same folder as the report.

This allows you to create and save a report for distribution to other report viewers. The other viewers can place the report on any drive and in any folder that they choose. As long as the database the report is based on is in the same folder as the report, the report will be able to find it.

Converting to a UNC Name

The Convert To UNC button on the Set Location dialog box only applies to reports based on PC-style databases. Clicking Convert To UNC will change the hard-coded drive letter and path name for the database to a Uniform Naming Convention (UNC) name that can easily be found by any computer on the network, regardless of its drive mapping. UNC is a way of pointing to a file on a network disk drive without using a drive letter. Consider the following scenario:

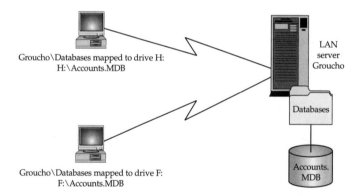

The two PCs are connected to the same LAN server, but are using different drive letters to reach the server. If the first PC creates a report based on Accounts.MDB, the report will have the drive letter and filename H:\Accounts.MDB hard-coded into it. When the second PC opens the report, the report will fail—the database won't be found on drive H.

To avoid this kind of problem, you can use a UNC name to replace the drive letter. A UNC name appears in the following format:

\\<Server Name>\<Share Name>\<Path and Filename>

- *Server Name* is the actual name of the computer or server where the file is located (in this case, Groucho). Two backslash characters precede the server name.

■ *Share Name* is a name that the LAN administrator has given to a particular group of shared files and folders on the server. When a PC maps a drive letter to a LAN server, the drive letter is mapped to a particular share name (in this case, Databases). A single backslash character separates the *Server Name* from the *Share Name*.

■ *Path and Filename* are similar to path names and filenames used on a local PC hard drive, except they are located on the LAN server. In this case, the Accounts.MDB file is in the root of the Databases share name. A single backslash character separates the *Share Name* from the *Path and Filename* (and this path may contain additional backslash characters).

Based on these rules, the corresponding UNC name for the Accounts.MDB file will be as follows:

```
\\Groucho\Databases\Accounts.MDB
```

Notice that the drive letter has been removed. Now, any PC on the network can find the file based on the UNC name—the PC doesn't have to have a drive letter mapped to the LAN server.

Using Set Alias

When you first create a new report based on certain database tables, you'll notice that the actual name of the table you originally chose shows up in the Field Explorer, the Visual Linking Expert, and other places in the report. Although it may appear that Crystal Reports must refer to a database table by its physical name, you have the flexibility to change the name Crystal Reports uses to refer to this table.

Crystal Reports can use an *alias* to refer to a table with a different name of your choice, regardless of what the physical file or table name for the table is. By default, Crystal Reports just assigns the physical name as the alias when the report is first created. To change the alias, choose Database | Set Alias from the pull-down menus. The Set Alias dialog box will appear.

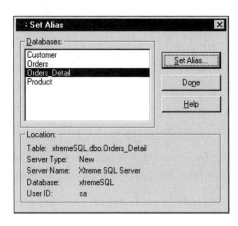

Here, you see a list of all the tables in your report. Select the table that you want to change the alias for, and click the Set Alias button. You'll be prompted to set a new alias for the table. Choose an alias name that's not already in use by another table (you'll be warned if you select an existing alias name) and click OK. Set aliases for as many tables as you'd like, and then click Done to close the Set Alias dialog box. You'll now see the new name applied to the table in all dialog boxes, formulas, and the Visual Linking Expert.

Sometimes, you may need to add the same physical table to a report more than once. Perhaps you're using a lookup table with more than one primary table, or you need to use a self-join, in which a table needs to be added twice and joined to itself for a particular report. You may also need to add two tables with the same name from different databases. When this occurs, you are prompted to set the alias for the second occurrence of the table. Just give it a new alias name. You'll then see the two tables with different names throughout the report.

Mapping Old Fields to New Names

Database changes can cause a mismatch of field names in your report. For example, your original report may be developed against a Microsoft Access database that includes a field named "Account Number" (note that the space between the words is significant to Crystal Reports). You may need to eventually have the same report work

What to Do if Table Names Change

If a database designer or administrator changes the name of a table in the database, the next time you try to refresh your report, you will receive an error indicating that the table can't be found. Unfortunately, refreshing the report or verifying the database will not solve this problem—the message will persist and the report will not print properly.

To solve this problem, perform the following simple steps:

1. Use the Set Location command. When the Set Location dialog box appears, choose the table whose name has changed. Then, just type the new table name directly in the text box at the bottom of the dialog box. (Make sure to leave the exclamation point that separates the table name from the database name if this is a PC-style database.) This will point the table to the new name in the database.

2. If you want the new name to appear throughout the report, use the Set Alias command to change the alias of the old table to the new table name. Using Set Location will correctly point the report to the new table name, but won't change the name in the report—it will still be referred to by the old name. Set Alias will change the name of the table as well, avoiding confusion as to which physical table is actually being used.

with a SQL Server database where the field is known as "Account_Number" (notice that the space has been replaced with an underscore).

Whenever Crystal Reports detects these kinds of database changes, it can't be sure which new database field the old report object should be associated with. By using Field Mapping, you can point the old object to the new database field. Field mapping simply allows you to change the field name that a report refers to, so that, for example, all objects that used to be associated with "Account Number" will now be associated with "Account_Number." No formulas have to be changed, no old objects have to be removed, and no new objects need to be added.

The Field Mapping function cannot be chosen from a menu. It is triggered when Crystal Reports detects any field name changes in the source database. Crystal Reports will check for these changes whenever you verify the database, change the database driver, or use the Set Location command. When Crystal Reports detects that fields in the report are no longer in the database, it displays the Map Fields dialog box, as shown in Figure 15-1.

The Map Fields dialog box is divided into four boxes or lists. The upper-left Unmapped Fields list shows report fields that don't match up to any field names in the new database. The upper-right list shows a choice of fields in the new database that you can map the report fields to. To map the report field to the new database field, select the report field you want to map in the upper-left box, select a matching database field in the upper-right box, and then click the Map button. The fields will be moved from the upper boxes to the lower boxes.

The list of database fields will change based on whether or not you click the Match Type check box on the right side of the dialog box. If the box is checked, only fields of the same data type (string, number, date, and so forth) as that of the selected report field will show up. This helps to ensure that you're making the correct match of fields, by not inadvertently mapping a string field on the report to a number or date field in the new database (although you may want to do this sometimes). There may be times that you won't see the field you want to map to in the right list, however, because of data type mismatches. For example, if you're remapping fields originally from a Microsoft Access database to a SQL Server database, you may not find any SQL Server field that matches a currency field in the Access database. In this situation, uncheck Match Type and look for the field to map to.

When the Map Fields dialog box first appears, some fields probably will already be present in the lower two Mapped Fields boxes. The lower-left list shows report fields that already have a matching field in the new database. And, once you've mapped fields from the upper lists, they will be moved to the lower lists as well. If existing mapping was assumed by Crystal Reports (because of identical field names), or you mistakenly mapped fields that don't belong together, you can select a field in the lower-left or lower-right list. The mapped field will appear highlighted in the other box. You can then click the Unmap button to unmap the fields and move them back to the top lists.

Once you have finished mapping fields, click the OK button to close the Map Fields dialog box. Crystal Reports will now associate the mapped fields with the new database.

List of report fields that have no matching field names in new database

List of fields in the new database that can be mapped to

Limit the mapped-to list of fields to those of the same data type as the selected field in the Unmapped Fields list

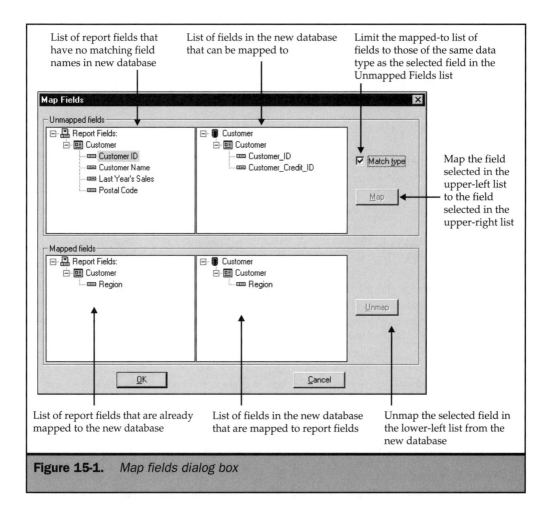

Map the field selected in the upper-left list to the field selected in the upper-right list

List of report fields that are already mapped to the new database

List of fields in the new database that are mapped to report fields

Unmap the selected field in the lower-left list from the new database

Figure 15-1.   *Map fields dialog box*

The Design tab, as well as any formulas, will reflect the new field names. If additional tables have mismatched fields, you'll be presented with the Map Fields dialog box for each subsequent table.

Caution   *Any fields that no longer exist in the source database must be remapped to new fields. If you don't map old field names to new fields, the old fields and objects they're based on will be deleted from your report!*

The
Complete
Reference

Chapter 16

Reporting from OLAP Cubes

Relational database systems provide the vast majority of the data analysis and reporting capabilities that most organizations need. However, there is a smaller segment of many organizations that can benefit from more flexible and sophisticated analysis tools. In many cases, an organization's higher-level analysts are still using spreadsheet tools in combination with relational databases to make strategic company decisions.

Online analytical processing (OLAP) is a newer analysis technique that provides much more flexibility in analyzing company data. Crystal Reports supports most standard OLAP tools and enables you to create reports based on these database systems.

What Is OLAP?

Most typical company data is viewed in two dimensions, whether it is viewed by a reporting tool such as Crystal Reports, or a spreadsheet program such as Microsoft Excel. In the case of a spreadsheet, the rows and columns constitute the two-dimensional analysis. You may be viewing product sales by state, salesperson volume by product category, or customer totals by demographics. In each of these cases, you typically can see only two dimensions at any one time, even though you actually may prefer to analyze a combination of three or more of these factors.

	USA	CAN	UK
PROD 1	534	212	231
PROD 2	45	21	12
PROD 3	321	324	112
PROD 4	204	120	40
PROD 5	78	43	31
PROD 6	32	12	2
PROD 7	786	512	49
PROD 8	123	23	17

Online analytical processing is a leading-edge analysis approach that allows data to be analyzed and viewed in multiple dimensions in real time. With a typical OLAP tool, you may initially be presented with a spreadsheet-like view that shows information using two dimensions, such as product sales dollars by state (or perhaps by country or region, allowing drill-down to the state level).

Even though only two dimensions are visible, additional dimensions are available "behind the scenes" to control the two dimensions you are viewing; you can limit dollars by state by using other dimensions. Perhaps you want to see dollars by state limited to just certain sales reps, certain customer demographics, or certain product categories—you still see the original Dollars and State dimensions, but the numbers are *filtered* by the other dimensions. You may also want to quickly see a sales by product category, demographics by state, or some other combinations of dimensions. Using an OLAP analysis tool, "slicing and dicing" through the different dimensions is typically as easy as dragging and dropping one dimension on top of another. Figure 16-1 shows Seagate Analysis viewing a multidimensional "FoodMart" database included with Microsoft SQL Server 7.0 OLAP Services or Microsoft SQL Server 2000 Analysis Services.

Whereas relational databases represent data in a two-dimensional, row-and-column (or field-and-record) structure, OLAP databases utilize a multidimensional structure known as a *cube* (which, despite its name, is capable of storing more than three dimensions of data). Often, cubes are built based on regular relational database systems—the relational database is populated using typical data-entry or data-import

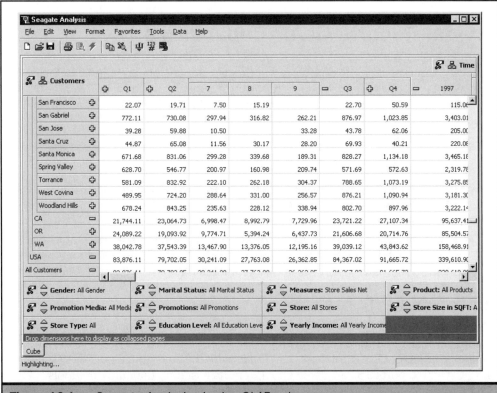

Figure 16-1. *Seagate Analysis viewing OLAP cube*

techniques, and a cube is built based on the relational database. Cubes can be refreshed or repopulated on a regular basis to allow multidimensional, real-time analysis of the data in the relational database.

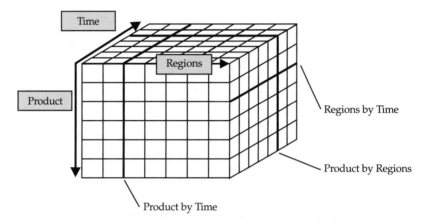

Crystal Reports OLAP Capabilities

You might ask, "Where does Crystal Reports fit into all of this?" Crystal Reports, obviously, can report on the data stored in the two-dimensional relational database. However, Crystal Reports also allows reporting against many industry-leading OLAP cubes. In fact, Crystal Reports can combine reports that are based on both relational databases and OLAP cubes, all in the same report. You have several choices:

- Create a standard report against the relational database the cube is based on.
- Create an OLAP-only report based solely on the cube.
- Create a standard report against a relational database (either the same database the cube is based on or an entirely different database) *and* include an OLAP report based on a cube inside the standard report.
- Create several *different* OLAP reports based on the same, or different, cubes. These OLAP-based reports can exist individually, or be included together inside a standard report based on a relational database.

Supported OLAP Systems

While OLAP technology has been somewhat fragmented and proprietary until recently, industry standards are starting to emerge. Crystal Reports will work with leading proprietary OLAP databases, as well as with the emerging *Open OLAP* standard. Thus, Crystal Reports 8.5 can create OLAP reports based on the following tools:

- Hyperion Essbase
- Seagate Holos and Seagate Info/Crystal Info

- IBM DB2 OLAP Server
- Informix MetaCube
- Microsoft SQL Server 7.0 OLAP Services or SQL Server 2000 Analysis Services via OLE DB
- OLE DB for OLAP sources (or other "Open OLAP" sources)

Types of OLAP Reports

Crystal Reports can create several different types of OLAP reports, depending on the OLAP cube that the report is based on. The common type of report is based on an OLAP grid object. An *OLAP grid* is very similar in appearance and functionality to a cross-tab object (discussed in detail in Chapter 9). An OLAP grid displays one or more cube dimensions in rows and columns on the report. As with a cross-tab, you may format individual rows and columns to appear as you wish. You may also easily swap, or *pivot*, the rows and columns to change the appearance of the OLAP grid.

In addition to the standard OLAP grid, Crystal Reports 8.5 allows an additional type of OLAP report to be created with Informix MetaCube. Reporting with the Informix MetaCube SQL method is very similar to using a standard relational database for reporting on OLAP data. For more information, display Crystal Reports online Help, click the Contents tab, and navigate to "Using the Informix MetaCube SQL Method for Reporting" in the "Creating and Updating OLAP Reports" category.

Note	*Because the OLAP grid object is common to all supported OLAP tools, this book will concentrate on it as the OLAP reporting method. For specific information on the other methods, refer to Crystal Reports documentation or online Help.*

Creating reports with OLAP cubes is straightforward and very similar to creating reports with regular relational databases. You may either use the OLAP Report Expert right from the Report Gallery or choose the Blank Report option. The OLAP Report Expert leads you step by step through choosing the cube and dimensions you want to use in the row and column of your report. The expert will then create a report containing an OLAP grid. If you choose the Blank Report option, you can create one or more OLAP grid objects in your report manually. Creating an OLAP grid object is very similar to creating a cross-tab object.

Using the OLAP Report Expert

The OLAP Report Expert is available from the Report Gallery that appears whenever you create a new report. Just click the OLAP button to use the expert. A tabbed dialog box, similar to Crystal Reports' other report experts, will appear.

The first step is to use the Data tab to choose the OLAP database you wish to base your OLAP report on. Click the Server Type button to choose from Crystal Reports–supported OLAP databases. A list of database types will appear.

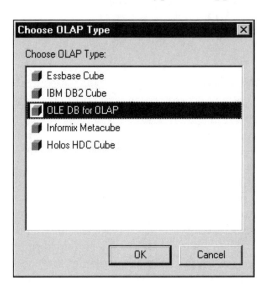

If your OLAP database type doesn't appear on the list, you may need to install client software specific to your particular OLAP system, such as a cube-viewing application, on your PC. After you install this software, restart Crystal Reports and try creating the report again.

Choose the type of OLAP database you wish to use. Depending on your choice, you'll need to log on to your OLAP server, or navigate to the proper folder and filename for the OLAP database you want to report on. Once you've made these choices, the fields on the Data tab of the Expert will be filled. If the database you chose contains more than one cube, choose the cube you want to report on from the Cube drop-down list.

After you make these choices, click the Rows/Columns tab, shown in Figure 16-2, to choose the dimension or dimensions you want to include in the rows and columns of your report.

Crystal Reports 8.5 includes a sample Holos OLAP cube for Xtreme Mountain Bike, Inc., that you can use to experiment with OLAP reporting. The file, XTREME.HDC, can be found in Crystal Reports program directory\Samples\en\Databases\Olap Data. However, the examples in this chapter are based on a sample OLAP cube provided with Microsoft SQL Server.

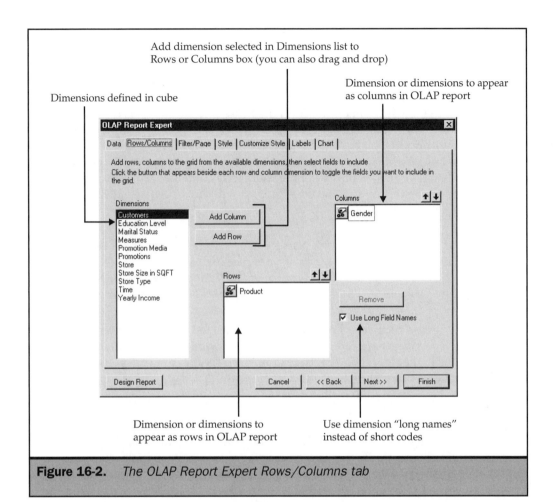

Add dimension selected in Dimensions list to
Rows or Columns box (you can also drag and drop)

Dimensions defined in cube

Dimension or dimensions to appear
as columns in OLAP report

Dimension or dimensions to
appear as rows in OLAP report

Use dimension "long names"
instead of short codes

Figure 16-2. *The OLAP Report Expert Rows/Columns tab*

Choose from the Dimensions list the dimension that you want to appear as the row in your OLAP report. Then, simply drag and drop it into the Rows box or click the Add Row button. Use the same drag-and-drop method to add to the Columns box the dimension you want to appear as the column in your OLAP report. Or, select a dimension and click Add Column.

You aren't limited to placing just one dimension in the Rows and Columns boxes. If you add multiple dimensions, Crystal Reports will "group" the dimensions in the OLAP report. For example, if you add a State dimension, followed by a Customer dimension, Crystal Reports will print states and show customers broken down within each state. If you place the dimensions in the Rows or Columns box in the wrong order, you can simply drag and drop the dimensions into the correct order within the Rows or Columns box. Or, you can select the dimension you want to move, and use the up and down arrows next to the Rows and Columns boxes.

If you wish to remove a dimension from the Rows or Columns box, drag the dimension back to the Dimensions list. Or, you can select the desired dimension and click the Remove button.

Check Use Long Field Names if you want Crystal Reports to use the "long name" or "alias" in the OLAP report, instead of the short code contained in some cubes. For example, by checking this option, the OLAP report will show spelled-out state names instead of two-letter state codes.

Note *The behavior of the Use Long Field Names option is dependent on the OLAP database and cube you are using. If you see abbreviated code-like material in your OLAP report, ensure that this option is checked. However, if the OLAP database or cube isn't designed with long field names or aliases, selecting this option will have no effect.*

Depending on the cube you choose for your report, you may find dimensions that contain many levels or generations. A *generation* is a lower level of information that breaks down the higher level above it. For example, a Products dimension could contain several generations: product type, product name within product type, and size within product name. Each generation further breaks down the information shown by the generation above it, creating a hierarchy for data in the dimension.

By default, if the dimension you choose for your OLAP report contains generations, Crystal Reports will show only the highest generation in a group hierarchy when it displays the dimension. While this may be the way you want the report to appear, it may actually display a data level that is too high. Often, you'll add dimensions to a report's Rows and Columns boxes, only to have the OLAP report show just one number at the intersection of one row and column. If you need to increase the generations inside a dimension that appears on the report, you can use the Field Picker to select the additional generations that you want to see.

To display the Field Picker, click the button next to the dimension you want to work with. The Select Fields dialog box will appear, allowing you to pick the generations you want to use in this particular OLAP report.

The Select Fields dialog box shows the dimension generations in a hierarchy, with pluses and minuses to the left, much like the display of folders and files in Windows Explorer. You can expand the hierarchy to see lower generations by clicking the plus signs next to the generations. If you want to see just the higher-level generations, click the minus sign to collapse them.

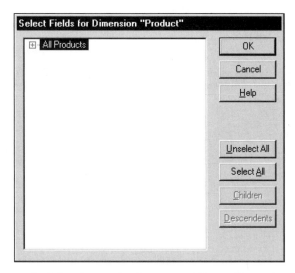

Once you've expanded the dimension's generations sufficiently, you can simply click individual generations to select or deselect them. Those that are highlighted will be included in the report—those that aren't won't. You can select or deselect all the generations by using either the Select All or Unselect All button. These buttons give you a good "starting point" if you want to include just a few, or almost all, of the generations in your report.

If you select a higher-level generation (a generation that has at least one level below it), you can use the Children or Descendents button to select specific levels of generations below the selected generation. Consider the following generations for a Product dimension:

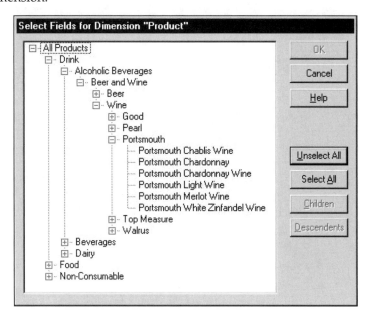

By selecting a higher-level generation and then clicking the Children button, only the *next-lower* generation will be selected:

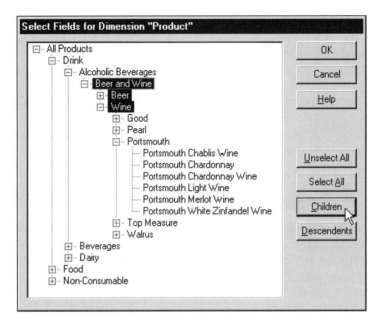

If you select a higher-level generation and then click the Descendents button, *all lower-level* generations will be selected, not just the next level:

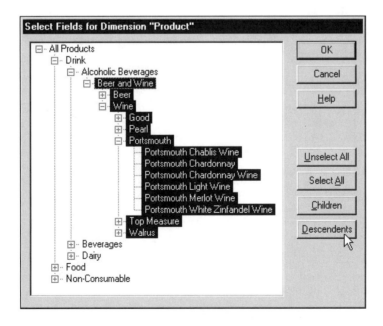

After you choose the generations you want included in the report, click OK. You won't notice any difference in the Rows/Columns tab—you'll need to click the Field Picker again to see what generations you've chosen.

Click the Filter/Page tab, shown in Figure 16-3, to determine how the remaining dimensions included in the cube will affect your OLAP report.

In the Filter/Page tab, you'll see all the other dimensions in the cube that you didn't include in the Rows or Columns boxes. You can use these dimensions to either filter or group your OLAP report. *Filtering* the OLAP report limits the report to certain occurrences of data in these dimensions. *Paging* the OLAP report is very similar to setting up report grouping. Like the grouping of other reports, discussed in Chapter 3, this creates a new section of the OLAP report showing a different OLAP grid every time the value of the chosen dimension changes. Each resulting OLAP report section will contain data just for that one generation.

To *filter* the report based on a dimension, look at the Filter part of the dialog box. You'll notice that each dimension displays a filter criterion, such as Time = 1997. Typically, this default value will be either All or a particular general value that was set as the default when the OLAP cube was defined. Click the Field Picker next to the dimension in the Filter part of the dialog box. The Select Fields dialog box, described earlier, will appear, in which you can choose a particular value to limit the OLAP

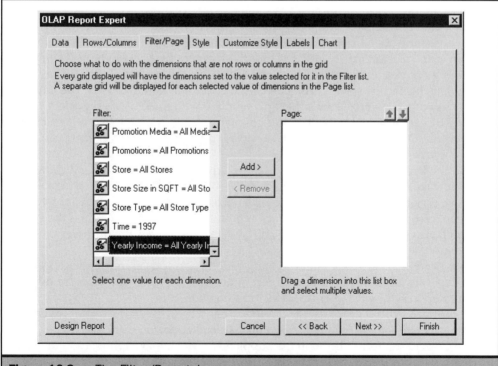

Figure 16-3.   *The Filter/Page tab*

report. After you make your choice and click OK, the criterion in the Filter list will change to indicate the value you picked. The OLAP report will now be limited to only values that are included in the field you chose.

 Unlike the previous example with the Select Fields dialog box, you can choose only one value in the box here. Selecting a new value deselects the previous value.

To *page* the OLAP report based on a dimension, select the desired dimension in the Filter list and click the Add button. Once again, the Select Fields dialog box appears, in which you can again select any combination of generations (using the Children and Descendents buttons, if you'd like). After you make your choices, click OK to close the Select Fields dialog box. The dimension you chose for paging will appear in the Page list at the right of the Filter/Page tab. If you wish to later change the generations you chose to page the report, return to the Filter/Page tab and click the Field Picker next to the dimension in the Page list.

You can add more than one dimension to the Page list. If you do so, you can change the order in which Crystal Reports will group the OLAP report, by selecting one of the dimensions and clicking the up or down arrow. If you want to remove one of the Page dimensions, select it in the Page list and click the Remove button. Once you've made any filtering and grouping choices, you're ready to display the OLAP report if you're satisfied with the default formatting Crystal Reports will apply.

If you want to customize the formatting of the *OLAP Grid objects* the Expert will create (very similar to the cross-tab object discussed in Chapter 9), you can make choices on the Style and Customize Style tabs of the OLAP Report Expert before proceeding. These tabs work exactly the same as they do with cross-tab objects. Refer to Chapter 9 for complete details on how to format an OLAP grid with these two tabs. The Labels tab allows you to customize labels that appear along with the OLAP grid object. OLAP labels are discussed in detail later in this chapter. And, if you want to create a chart based on your OLAP grid, you may make choices on the Chart tab. Charting on OLAP grids is discussed in Chapter 10.

Click the Finish button in the OLAP Report Expert to run the report and show it in the Preview tab. If you want to go immediately to the Design tab to further customize the report, click the Design Report button. Depending on any page dimensions you chose, you'll see a few simple objects on the report, such as the print date and the report title. You'll also see one or more OLAP grid objects, plus any groups that were created to accommodate the page dimensions.

 If you need to make any changes to the OLAP report, you can rerun the OLAP Report Expert by clicking the Report Expert button in the Standard toolbar, or by choosing Report | Report Expert from the pull-down menus.

 Alternatively, you can simply click in the upper-left corner of the OLAP grid object to select it (if there is more than one, select the particular one you want to change). Then, click the Object Properties button in the Supplementary toolbar, right-click, and choose Format OLAP Grid from the pop-up menu, or choose Format | OLAP Grid from the pull-down menus. The Format OLAP Grid Object tabbed dialog box will appear, in which you can make changes to the dimensions and layout of the OLAP grid object.

Using the Blank Report Option

You probably will encounter situations in which you want to create a standard database report that includes one or more OLAP grids. By choosing the Blank Report option from the Report Gallery, you have more flexibility in creating this type of report. Simply create the base report using the techniques discussed elsewhere in the book.

You may even find it useful to base the main report on some fields from your OLAP database. To use the OLAP database for the main report, look for your OLAP database type in the Data Explorer. For example, you may see an ODBC data source set up specifically for your OLAP database, or you may use OLE DB in the Other Data Sources category to connect to an Open OLAP data source. After you choose, and log on to, your OLAP database, you'll see either a list of the OLAP cube or cubes, or associated tables that are used to build the cubes in the Data Explorer. You can add as many of these cubes or tables as necessary for the report. Depending on the type of OLAP database you've chosen, the Field Explorer will show the dimensions and generations for your chosen cubes, or the fields in the chosen tables. You can add these fields to your main report as you would a regular database field. You may need to try some experimentation to determine which dimensions or fields can be used—OLAP data often doesn't behave the same as relational database data. Once the main part of your report is finished, you can add the necessary OLAP grid objects.

Caution   *Even though you can access the OLAP cube by using the Blank Report option, you won't be able to actually include any cube values in any report sections. You'll only be able to include and manipulate dimension names. The only way to actually include the numeric values from the cube is to create an OLAP grid object.*

Adding an OLAP Grid Object

To create an OLAP grid on an existing report, choose Insert | OLAP Grid from the pull-down menus. The Insert OLAP Grid Object dialog box appears.

The tabs in this dialog box behave almost identically to the same tabs on the OLAP Report Expert, described earlier in the chapter. Follow the same steps for the Data and Rows/Columns tabs to choose the cube and dimensions for your OLAP grid. You may also use the Style and Customize Style tabs to format the OLAP grid, similar to formatting a cross-tab object (covered in detail in Chapter 9). Two of the tabs deserve more discussion, however: the Filter/Page tab and the Labels tab.

Filter/Page Tab

As discussed earlier in the chapter, you can set up a dimension filter by clicking the Field Picker next to a dimension in the Filter list. This technique works the same way here. However, the technique for selecting Page dimensions differs slightly here, as opposed to using the OLAP Report Expert described earlier in the chapter.

When using the OLAP Report Expert, any dimensions you choose as Page dimensions will automatically create one or more report groups on the resulting report (see Chapter 3 for a detailed discussion of grouping). However, the Blank Report option allows you to create a report structure on your own, potentially with your own grouping. If you want an OLAP grid to appear within your groups (perhaps you've grouped your report by region and want an OLAP grid to appear in each group header showing data only for that region), you need to think about how you want to add a Page dimension. The Page dimension you choose determines the proper "alignment" of your OLAP grid with your existing report grouping.

Choosing a dimension to use as a Page dimension is the same: select the dimension in the Filter list and click the right arrow. But now, a different dialog box appears.

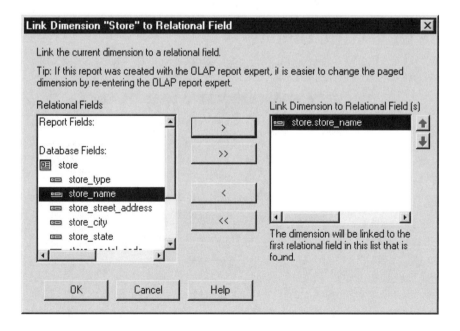

As the title of the dialog box suggests, you need to link the dimension you chose as a Page dimension to the relational database field that the associated report group is based on. In this illustration, the Store dimension from the OLAP grid is being linked to a Store Name field that is used to group the existing report. By making the correct choice here, you'll ensure that the OLAP grid shows data only for the particular group that it is contained in.

OLAP Labels

Many OLAP cubes of even moderate complexity often contain many dimensions. However, unlike a "slice and dice" OLAP analysis tool (like Seagate Analysis), an OLAP grid object doesn't offer a high level of interactivity. As such, you'll probably use only a few (if not just one) dimensions for a row and column. The remainder of the dimensions not actually appearing as a row or column (often called *qualified dimensions*) can simply be ignored, used as Filter dimensions, or used as Page dimensions. Of particular interest is how the report viewer will know what settings have been made for Filter dimensions: if the OLAP grid is limited to just one product, one gender, and one store, how will this be known? The answer is *OLAP labels*.

When you create an OLAP grid object with either the OLAP Report Expert or by inserting an OLAP grid manually, OLAP labels are added to the OLAP grid by default, as shown here.

These are OLAP labels.

All Customers	All Education Lev	All Marital Status	Profit	All Media
All Promotions	All Stores	All	All	1997
All Yearly Income				

		All Gender		
		F	M	
All Products	Drink	14,706.27	14,652.70	29,358.98
	Food	122,100.72	123,664.15	245,764.87
	Non-Consuma	31,641.74	32,845.31	64,487.05
		168,448.73	171,162.17	339,610.90

Notice that any Filter dimensions, such as 1997, are listed. Otherwise, the All designations appear. This indicates to the report viewer what limits have been placed on the OLAP grid. You may choose to limit the set of OLAP labels that appear—perhaps to just the ones that are used as a Filter dimension. Or, you may want to otherwise customize the way the OLAP labels appear. To do this, click the Labels tab, shown in Figure 16-4, in the OLAP Report Expert or the Format OLAP Grid Object dialog box.

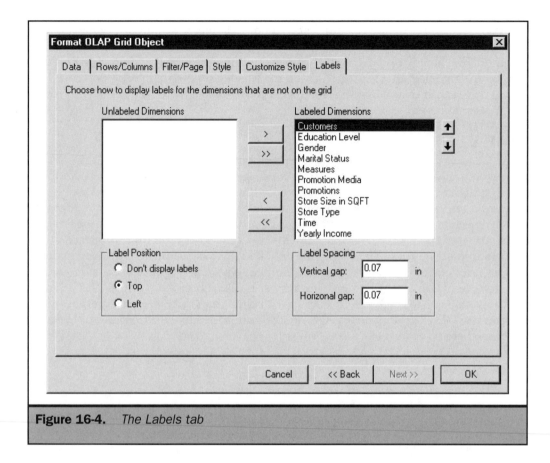

Figure 16-4.   *The Labels tab*

By default, all qualified dimensions (those that are in the cube, but not included as a row or column on the grid) are placed in the right Labeled Dimensions box. You can change the order in which they will appear next to the OLAP grid by selecting a label and using the small arrows above the box to move it up or down in the list. If you don't want a particular label to appear with the grid, select it and click the left arrow to move it to the Unlabeled Dimensions box.

You can also customize the amount of white space Crystal Reports will place between the labels by specifying a new value in the Vertical Gap and Horizontal Gap text boxes. And finally, you can choose to place the entire set of labels on the top or left side of the OLAP grid (or not have the labels show up at all).

After you make your desired choices in the Format OLAP Grid Object dialog box, click OK. An outline of the OLAP grid object will be attached to the mouse cursor. Drop the object in the desired section of the report (if you chose a Page dimension for the OLAP grid object, make sure you place the object in any necessary corresponding report section, such as a group header).

You may make changes or additions to the OLAP grid object by selecting it and then formatting the OLAP grid by using pull-down menu options, the Object Properties button in the Supplementary toolbar, or format options from the right-click pop-up menu.

Changing the OLAP Database Location

An OLAP grid "points" to a specific OLAP cube location on a server. If that location changes, or if you want to report on a different cube without redesigning the entire OLAP grid, you need to change the location of the OLAP database that the grid refers to.

Select the OLAP grid you want to change by clicking its upper-left corner. Right-click and choose Set OLAP Cube Location from the pop-up menu, or choose Database | Set OLAP Cube Location from the pull-down menus. The Set OLAP Database Location dialog box appears.

Set OLAP Database Location	☒
OLAP Database	
Database Type: OLE DB for OLAP	
Database: solo	
Cube: Sales ▾	
Select...	
OK Cancel	

Choose the new OLAP cube or new server location for the associated OLAP database. Then click OK.

Controlling OLAP Grid Appearance

An OLAP grid organizes cube information in a row-and-column format, much as a cross-tab object does. In fact, formatting and changing OLAP grid appearance is essentially identical to formatting a cross-tab object:

- ■ Make choices on the Style or Customize Style tab when formatting the OLAP grid. You can choose from built-in formatting styles on the Style tab, or perform more detailed formatting of individual elements on the Customize Style tab.

- ■ Select individual fields that make up the OLAP grid, and resize or format them individually. When you resize an individual field, the row or column that the field is in will change accordingly. You can change field font face, font size, and color. And, if you're formatting numeric information, such as the OLAP grid value fields, you can choose rounding, decimal places, currency symbols, and other formatting that applies to the type of field you're formatting.

■ Perform conditional formatting on values in the OLAP grid, based on the actual numeric data contained in the cells, or based on the Row or Column field of the cell.

Formatting OLAP grids is virtually identical to formatting cross-tab objects. Refer to Chapter 9 for a thorough discussion.

Interacting with OLAP Grids

Although you don't have quite the "slice and dice" flexibility with Crystal Reports that you may have with your particular OLAP analysis tool, you might be surprised by how easy it is to rearrange the appearance of an OLAP grid object. When you first create the OLAP grid, you choose which dimensions you want to use as rows and which you want to use as columns. If you choose multiple row or column dimensions, the order in which you add them determines the grouping order for the rows or columns.

You may want to change the order of the OLAP grid's row or column grouping, or you may want to swap or *pivot* the rows and columns. This is simple and straightforward, whether you're viewing the OLAP grid in the Preview tab or manipulating the report in the Design tab:

■ To pivot the rows and columns, select the OLAP grid. Then, right-click and choose Pivot OLAP Grid from the pop-up menu. You can also choose Format | Pivot OLAP Grid from the pull-down menus.

■ To reorder dimensions, simply click the row or column heading of the dimension you want to reorder. As you hold down the mouse button, you will notice a little "piece of paper" icon appear on the mouse pointer. This indicates that the dimension can be dragged and dropped below or above another dimension to reorder the dimensions. You can even drag and drop a dimension from a row to a column, or vice versa, provided that at least one dimension will be left in the row or column of the OLAP grid.

The Complete Reference

Chapter 17

Querying SQL Databases with Crystal SQL Designer

Crystal Reports is an excellent tool for organizing and manipulating data coming from corporate databases. However, there are times when a tool for quick and simple database queries is needed. If you just want an easy way to look at your database without having to worry about formatting, fonts, and such, you'll want to look at Crystal SQL Designer. Its easy "expert" user interface makes querying SQL databases very straightforward. And, if you have several Crystal Reports that will be based on the same set of data, you can save the data returned from your SQL Designer query and base several reports on the saved data.

Tip	*In versions of Crystal Reports prior to 7, this tool is known as Crystal Query Designer.*

Defining Crystal SQL Designer

Most popular corporate database systems, such as Microsoft SQL Server, Oracle, Sybase, and Informix, use the common Structured Query Language (SQL) as a means of submitting queries. Once the database server has processed the SQL query, it returns a *result set* (a set of rows and columns of data) that comprises the results of the SQL query.

Although there are trained database professionals who can effectively submit queries to the database by typing in the raw SQL query, the vast majority of database users would prefer not to have to learn "SQL as a Second Language" to get meaningful data from their database. Crystal SQL Designer is Crystal Decisions' original query tool for just such users. By choosing database tables and fields, choosing selection criteria, and supplying sorting requirements with a simple tabbed dialog box approach, users will be able to glean data from their corporate databases without having to learn SQL.

Since Crystal Decisions has also created the Seagate Analysis query tool, you may wonder: "What should I use to query the database—Crystal Reports, Seagate Analysis, or the SQL Designer?" The answer depends largely on how quickly you want to be able to query the database, and whether you need to prepare the results of your query in a fancy formatted presentation.

Caution	*Crystal SQL Designer will only be installed if you specifically choose it when running Crystal Reports 8.5 installation. If you don't choose it when installing, the Crystal Reports Tools submenu (where the SQL Designer is started) won't appear on the Windows Start button. You'll need to re-run Crystal Reports 8.5 installation and choose to install Crystal SQL Designer.*

Crystal SQL Designer Versus Seagate Analysis

The choice of query tools was complicated a bit with the introduction of the Seagate Analysis querying, reporting, and OLAP tool. This free tool is an attempt by Crystal to merge the functions of a direct database query tool, a simplified report designer, and an OLAP analysis worksheet. Although Seagate Analysis doesn't provide the vast array of reporting capabilities of Crystal Reports, it does largely duplicate (and in many cases, improve) the querying capabilities of Crystal SQL Designer. Whether you choose Seagate Analysis or the original Crystal SQL Designer is mostly a matter of personal choice.

 Don't confuse Seagate Analysis, the free query, lightweight reporting, and OLAP cube tool with the recently released Crystal Analysis Professional OLAP reporting tool. They are very different products, and Seagate Analysis is the appropriate tool for relational database queries.

Crystal SQL Designer Versus Crystal Reports

It's often asked, "Why bother using the SQL Designer when I can just create a report in Crystal Reports that gets the same data?" Although this point has some validity, there are definitely times when a simpler query tool without the object-manipulation and formatting capabilities of Crystal Reports is a better choice. The SQL Designer is a good tool for simpler row-and-column data viewing.

Also, you may occasionally have situations where several reports need to access the exact same result set from the database, and you would prefer that each not have to query the database separately. You may create the single query in the SQL Designer, save the result set in the query's .QRY file, and then base the reports on the .QRY file rather than directly on the database.

Creating SQL Queries

Crystal SQL Designer is a separate program on the Crystal Reports Tools program group. Choosing this option will launch the SQL Designer, as shown in Figure 17-1.

Begin creating a new query by choosing File | New from the pull-down menus or clicking the New button in the toolbar. The New Query dialog box appears, giving you three options: use the SQL Expert, enter a SQL statement directly, or start from an existing query.

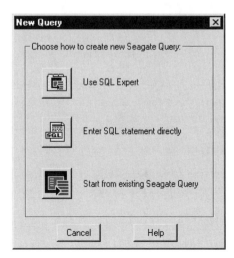

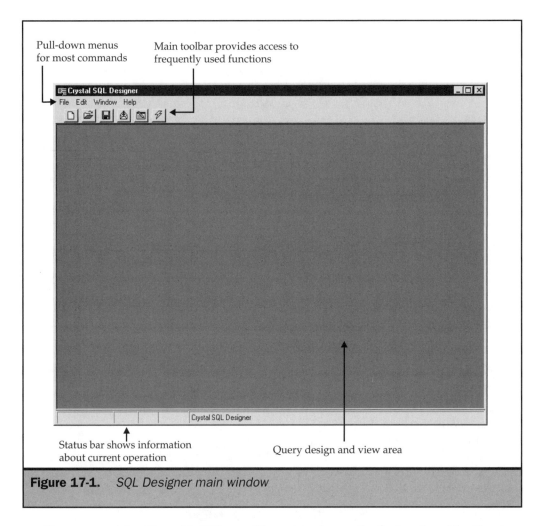

Pull-down menus
for most commands

Main toolbar provides access to
frequently used functions

Status bar shows information
about current operation

Query design and view area

Figure 17-1. *SQL Designer main window*

If you are not familiar with SQL, you'll want to choose the first option. The Create SQL Expert leads you step by step through the query-design process. If you are familiar with SQL and just want to enter a SELECT statement directly, click the second button. Or, if you wish to open an existing .QRY file containing an already created query, click the third button. This simply opens the query in the designer, but does not "save" the filename that was used—when you save the query, it will ask for a new filename.

Entering SQL Directly

If you choose the second option from the New Query dialog box, the Log On Server dialog box appears, allowing you to choose the ODBC data source you wish to use for your query.

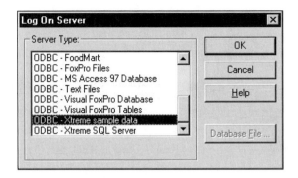

If the database you wish to query is not included in the list of data sources, use the ODBC Administrator application from the Windows Control Panel to add it. If you're unsure of how to set up an ODBC data source, contact your database administrator.

Note *Crystal SQL Designer only operates with databases via Microsoft's open database connectivity (ODBC) communications standard. If you're not sure whether your database is reachable via ODBC, contact your database administrator.*

After you choose the ODBC data source, you are prompted to log in to the database (if the database is secure). Depending on the database you choose, you will be required to supply a user ID, password, and other information such as the name of the database you wish to use. After you make these entries, a message appears indicating that you've successfully logged on to the database. Once you click OK, the Enter SQL Statement dialog box appears, as shown in Figure 17-2.

Tip *If you prefer to log on to one or more databases before beginning to create a new query, you can choose File | Log On Server from the pull-down menus. This will display the Log On Server dialog box, where you can choose a data source and proceed through the logon process. If you are already logged on to a database when you start a query, the Log On Server dialog box will be skipped and you'll proceed directly to the next step.*

You can now type a SQL statement directly into the SQL box. Use the SQL syntax that is particular to the ODBC data source that appears in the drop-down list at the top of the dialog box. To make your statement more readable, you may press ENTER to go to the next line, or CTRL-TAB to add a tab stop in the current line. If you've created a SQL statement in another tool and saved the query as an ASCII text file, you can import it directly into the SQL box by clicking the Import button.

Once you've either imported or typed the SQL query you want to use, click OK to send the query to the server. You'll be asked whether you want to run the query. If you click Yes, the query will be submitted to the server for processing. If there are any errors

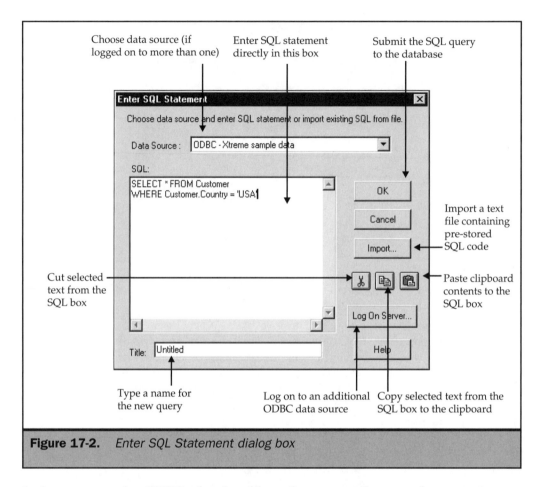

Figure 17-2.   *Enter SQL Statement dialog box*

in the query, or other ODBC-related problems that prevent the query from running to completion, you'll see an ODBC error message.

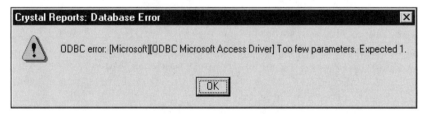

If the query is accepted by the server without any errors, you may have to wait anywhere from a few seconds to many minutes for the server to process the query. While this is happening, you'll simply see an hourglass while you wait. Once the query has completed and the server has returned a result set to the SQL Designer, you'll see the query appear in a simple row-and-column format for online viewing, as shown in Figure 17-3.

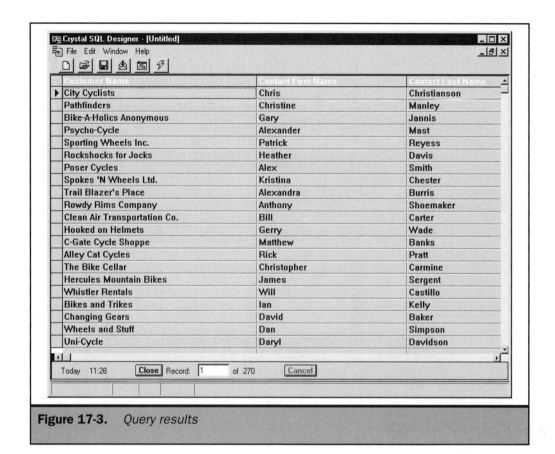

Figure 17-3. *Query results*

Once the query has executed, you may view the results interactively on the screen using the vertical and horizontal scroll bars, or navigate directly to a certain record by typing a record number into the Record text box. If you wish, you can submit the same query to the server again to see if any data has changed. Just click the Refresh button in the toolbar, press the F5 key, or choose Edit | Refresh Data from the pull-down menus. The query will be resubmitted to the server. If any data has been changed, deleted, or added since the last time the query was run, you'll see the changes in the result set.

If you want to modify the SQL statement, click the Edit Query button in the toolbar, or choose Edit | Query from the pull-down menus. The Enter SQL Statement dialog box will reappear, in which you can make changes to the SQL statement and submit it again.

Version 8.5 of SQL Designer includes the capability to export the contents of the query in the exact same manner, and with the same options, as Crystal Reports exporting (discussed in Chapter 13). Click the Export button in the toolbar, or choose File | Export to display the same Export dialog box as in Crystal Reports. You may then choose the type of file format to export the query results in, as well as specify the destination (disk file, e-mail attachment, and so on) for the export.

Using the Expert

Although the SQL Designer may be helpful for SQL-savvy programmers or analysts, its general purpose is to allow casual users who need to query the database to avoid the use of SQL. Crystal SQL Designer features the Create SQL Expert for just such users. Using the Create SQL Expert, a user merely needs to progress through a familiar tabbed interface to create and view a database query.

To use the Create SQL Expert, click the Use SQL Expert button on the New Query dialog box when you first create a new query. The Create SQL Expert dialog box will appear, with the Tables tab showing.

The Tables Tab

Choose the data source for your query on the Tables tab, shown in Figure 17-4. You have two choices: Dictionary and SQL/ODBC. A *dictionary* is a predefined group of database fields that have been set up in advance. Using dictionaries makes it easy for a casual user to work with a database without knowing all the intricate details of table

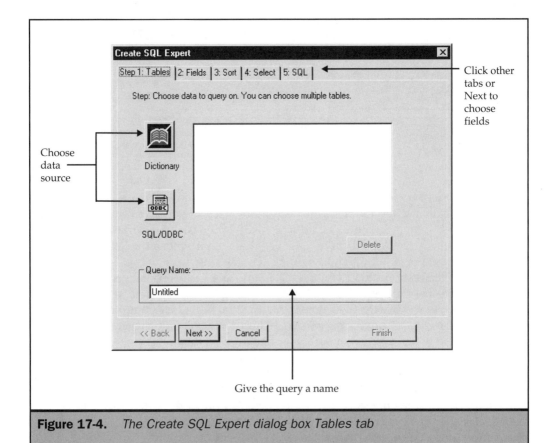

Figure 17-4. *The Create SQL Expert dialog box Tables tab*

and field structure. When you click this button, a File Open dialog box appears, asking you to specify the dictionary file you want to use for your query. Navigate to the correct dictionary file and click OK.

Note   *Since the SQL Designer only works with SQL/ODBC databases, the dictionary must refer to this type of database. You'll receive an error message if you open a dictionary that refers to another style of database. The Crystal Dictionaries tool, used to define dictionaries, is discussed in Chapter 18.*

If a dictionary has not been created, and you need to connect directly to the database, click the SQL/ODBC button. If you aren't already logged on to an ODBC database, the Log On Server dialog box will appear.

Choose the database you wish to use for your query. If the database does not appear, you'll need to use the ODBC Administrator in the Windows Control Panel to add it. Contact your database administrator if you need assistance. If your database is secure, you'll be prompted to log on to the database with a valid user ID and password. Once you've done this, the Choose SQL Table dialog box appears, as shown in Figure 17-5.

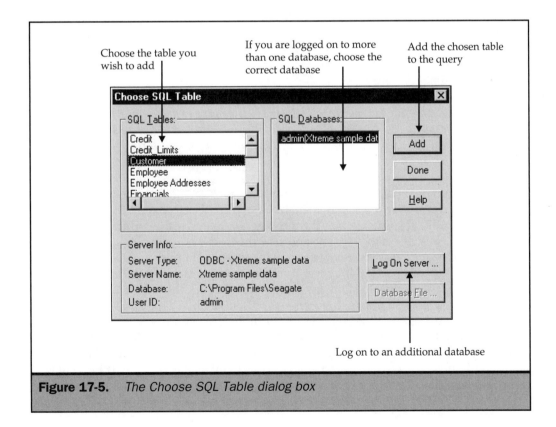

Figure 17-5.   *The Choose SQL Table dialog box*

Choose the tables you wish to use in your query. Since you can only choose one table at a time in the list (CTRL-click and SHIFT-click don't work in this dialog box), you must choose each table individually, by either double-clicking it or selecting it and clicking the Add button. After you finish choosing tables, click Done. If you've chosen more than one table, a new Links tab will appear, as described next.

The Links Tab

If you choose more than one table to include in your query, you must link or join the tables together so they can follow each other properly when returning records. A table *link* must be on a common field. For example, if you want an Employee table to follow a Payroll table properly in your report, you need to link the two tables on a common field or fields.

> **Note** *The Links tab works almost identically to the Visual Linking Expert in Crystal Reports. This Visual Linking Expert is discussed in detail in Chapter 14.*

You'll notice that the tables you chose are displayed at the top of the Links tab, shown in Figure 17-6. You can drag the windows to a new location, or resize them, if that helps. (The Arrange button will move them for you, but not always the way you want them moved.) After you position the table windows, you need to choose the common field or fields to link the tables together. To draw a link, simply drag from the "from" field to the "to" field and release the mouse button. A link line will be drawn connecting the two fields. If you need to link tables on several fields, you can drag and drop as many times as necessary.

> **Caution** *There is a confusing bug in the SQL Designer. If you try to link to the first field in the "to" table, and you drop the link too high on the field, the link will not "stick." If this happens, simply drag and drop again, this time dropping on the very bottom of the first field in the "to" table.*

If you link on fields that may create an unsuccessful link (perhaps they are different data types), you'll receive a warning message. Double-check to ensure that this is in fact the correct link. If so, just ignore the message. If not, draw the correct link. If you need to delete a link, select the link line and click the Delete button or press the DEL key.

The SQL Designer uses an equal join type by default. This may not be the type of join you need for your particular query. To change the join type, select the link you wish to modify. Then, click the Options button or right-click the link and choose Options from the pop-up menu. (Join types are discussed in Chapter 14.)

The default behavior of the SQL Designer is to link tables automatically, using Smart Linking. *Smart Linking* will automatically link fields if their field names and data types are identical. In addition, if the fields are string fields, they both must be the same length. If you deleted links and wish to Smart Link again, or if Smart Linking is turned off, just click the Smart Linking button to automatically link tables in the query.

Drag or resize table
windows to your liking

Drag and drop between tables
to establish a link

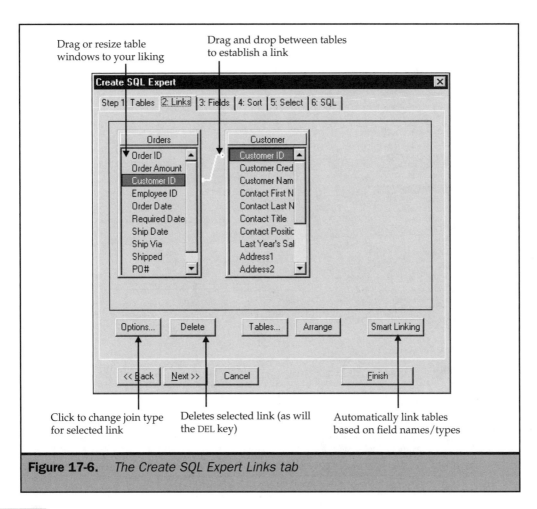

Click to change join type
for selected link

Deletes selected link (as will
the DEL key)

Automatically link tables
based on field names/types

Figure 17-6.   *The Create SQL Expert Links tab*

Tip   *Smart Linking works correctly only in specific cases. In many situations, you'll spend
more time removing incorrect links and adding correct links than you would spend
creating the links on your own. You can turn it off by starting Crystal Reports, selecting
File | Options, and clearing the Auto-SmartLinking check box on the Database tab. This
setting also affects Crystal SQL Designer.*

Once tables have been properly linked, click the Next button or click the Fields tab.
You'll now be able to choose the fields to include in your query.

The Fields Tab

The Fields tab, shown in Figure 17-7, is where you choose the fields you actually want
to appear in the query. You'll see all the fields in the tables you chose in the left
Database Fields box. You can select one or more fields (using SHIFT-click or CTRL-click

Select one or more fields (using CTRL-click or SHIFT-click)

Drag fields from the Database Fields list or double-click to add them

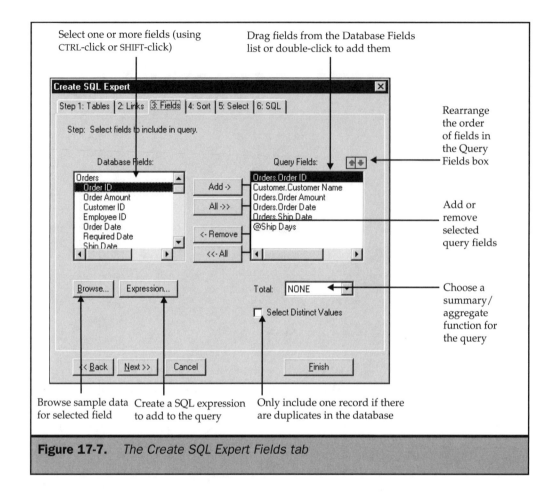

Rearrange the order of fields in the Query Fields box

Add or remove selected query fields

Choose a summary/aggregate function for the query

Browse sample data for selected field

Create a SQL expression to add to the query

Only include one record if there are duplicates in the database

Figure 17-7. *The Create SQL Expert Fields tab*

to select multiple fields) to add to the query. Add fields to the query by double-clicking them, dragging and dropping them to the Query Fields box, or using the Add or All buttons. If you accidentally add too many fields, select any fields you wish to remove from the Query Fields box and click the Remove button.

If you wish to build a SQL expression to add to your query, click the Expression button. A SQL expression is similar to a formula: you specify a calculation using operators or functions built into SQL. You'll be asked to give the expression a name. Once you do so, the SQL Expression dialog box will appear.

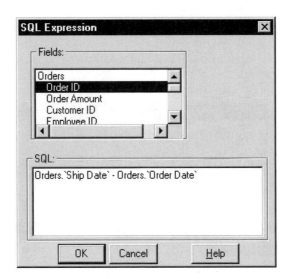

You can double-click fields in the Fields list to add them to the SQL box (and even then, it may not place proper SQL punctuation around the fields). Other than that, you'll need to manually enter the SQL to make the expression work properly for your database. Once you've created the SQL expression, it will appear (preceded by an @ sign) under the SQL Expressions category in the Database Fields list. You can add it to the Query Fields list like any other database field.

 You must have some knowledge of SQL and your database server to effectively create SQL expression fields. Check with your database administrator or a colleague who's knowledgeable about SQL, if you need help.

You may want to perform a summary or aggregate calculation, such as a sum or average. In this situation, the database server will create data "groups" (similar to Crystal Reports groups, discussed in Chapter 3) and return only one database record for each group. The record will contain the summary or aggregate value for all the records in that group.

Choose the field in the Query Fields box that you want to aggregate, and then choose a function in the Total drop-down list. You'll notice the aggregate function is added to the field in the Query Fields list. Then, limit any other fields in the Query Fields list to those that will create the groups that you want to base your aggregate function on.

For example, if you wanted to see a total of all order amounts for each customer, you would choose the Order Amount field and choose Sum in the Total drop-down list. The only other field you would add to the query is Customer Name. Even though there may be many records in the database, the server will group the records by customer, returning just one record per customer. Instead of individual order amounts, the server will total the order amounts for each customer and include the sum in the one-customer group record.

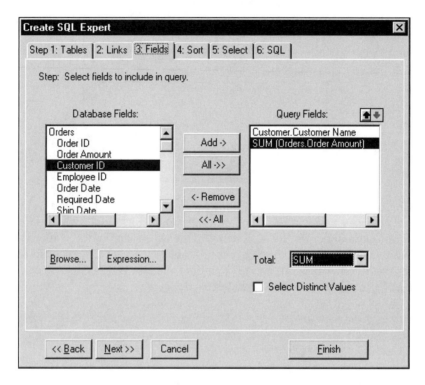

Once you've chosen all the fields, as well as any aggregate functions and SQL expressions you want to include in your query, you needn't specify anymore information in the Create SQL Expert if you don't need to. Click the Finish button to submit the query to the database server and view the results. Figure 17-8 shows the results of a sum aggregate function with Customer Name chosen as the group field.

If, however, you wish to sort the query in a specific order, or restrict the query to certain records, you need to complete either or both the Sort and Select tabs. You can click Next to choose the Sort tab, or click directly on the tab.

The Sort Tab

On the Sort tab, shown in Figure 17-9, you choose the field or fields you want the query sorted by. As with the Fields tab, you can add these selected fields to the Group Fields list by double-clicking, dragging and dropping, or clicking the Add button. Once you've

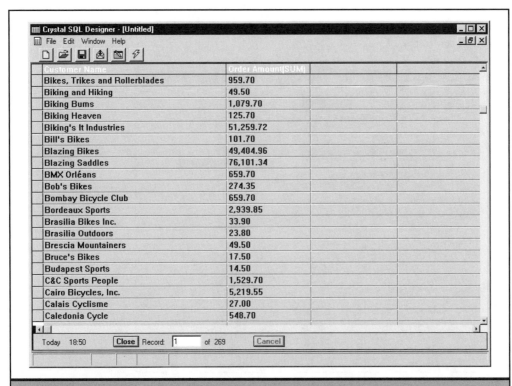

Figure 17-8. *Results of an aggregate query*

chosen the field or fields you want to sort by, you can choose the order you want the query sorted in by selecting a field in the Group Fields list and choosing an option from the Order drop-down list. Ascending order will sort from low to high alphabetically, while descending order will sort from high to low. The Original Order option will simply not sort the records, leaving them in the original database order (if you choose this option, there's actually no reason to even add the field to the Sort tab).

The order in which the fields appear in the Group Fields list is significant. If, for example, you want the query sorted first by country, and then by region, you'll want to make sure the Country field is at the top of the list, followed by the Region field. If you have the fields reversed, the query will be sorted first by region, and then by country if there happens to be more than one country with the same regions. You can reorder the fields with the two small arrow buttons above the list.

After you choose how to sort records in the query, you'll probably want to limit the query to only certain records. Click Next or the Select tab directly.

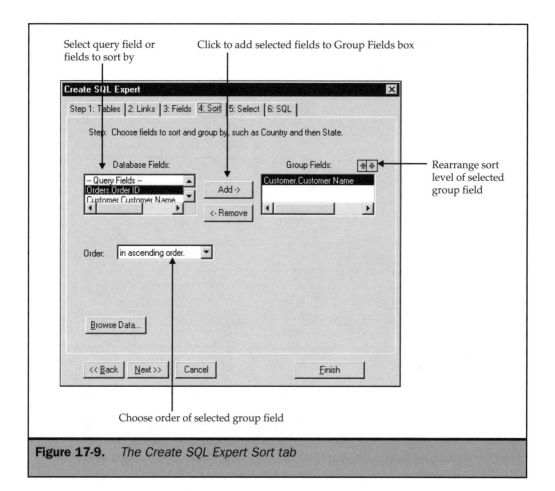

Figure 17-9. The Create SQL Expert Sort tab

The Select Tab

One of the main reasons you'll probably be using the SQL Designer in the first place is to perform some real-time analyses on your database, which means you probably won't want to view every record in the database every time you run the query. To narrow down your query to only a desired set of data, use the Select tab, shown in Figure 17-10.

Select one or more fields in the Database Fields list that you want to use to limit the query results. Add them to the Select Fields list by double-clicking, dragging and dropping, or clicking the Add button. Then, select each field in the Select Fields list. A set of drop-down lists will appear below the lists in the Create SQL Expert. Choose options in these drop-down lists to compare the fields to a fixed value to limit the query.

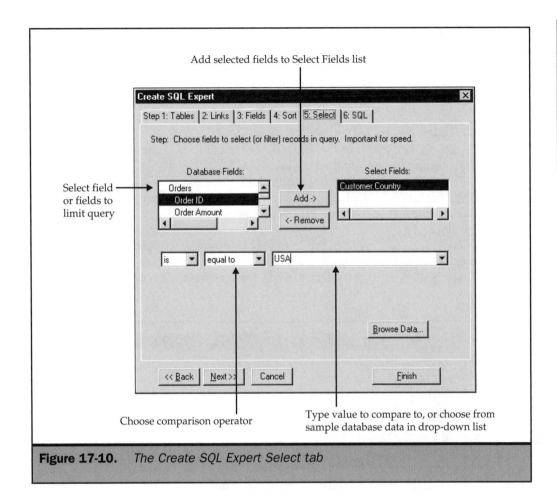

Figure 17-10.   *The Create SQL Expert Select tab*

The first drop-down list simply contains Is, by default. After you choose something other than Any Value in the second drop-down list, you can return to the first list and change the Is to Is Not, if necessary, for your query. The second drop-down list contains a variety of comparison options, such as Equal To, One Of, Less Than, and Greater Than. Depending on which comparison you choose, one or more additional drop-down lists, text boxes, and buttons will appear. Choose the comparison and fixed values to use for your query.

Tip   *The Select tab behaves similarly to the Select Expert in Crystal Reports. For more information, consult Chapter 6.*

Once you've chosen selection criteria, you're ready to submit the query to the server and see the results of your query. However, if you'd like to see what the SQL Designer is actually submitting to the database server, or if you're knowledgeable about SQL and want to make manual modifications to the SQL query, click the SQL tab. The SQL that is automatically generated by the SQL Designer is displayed.

The SQL Tab

On the SQL tab, shown in Figure 17-11, you'll see the actual SQL statement that you've designed by selecting options on the previous tabs. You'll see the fields you chose in the SELECT clause; the tables you chose in the FROM clause; how they're linked together in the FROM or WHERE clauses; any sorting, grouping, and aggregate functions that you chose in the GROUP BY or ORDER BY clauses; and your selection criteria in the WHERE clause.

If you're not familiar with SQL, this is merely informational (perhaps it looks simple enough to you that you might teach it to yourself and consider a career change!). If you are knowledgeable about SQL, you are free to manually change any

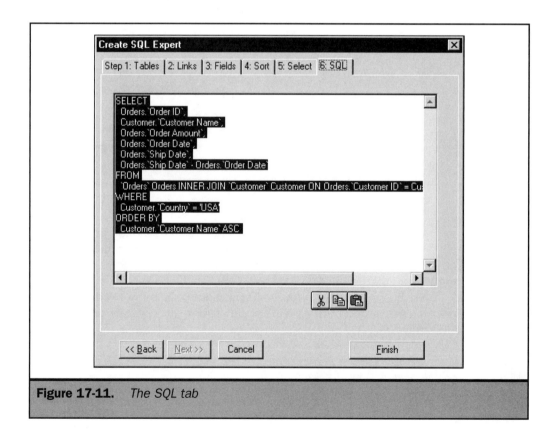

Figure 17-11. *The SQL tab*

aspect of the SQL statement that you wish. You are restricted to the legal syntax of your database server and the ODBC driver that's being used. Also, since the SQL Designer is a *read-only* tool, you won't be able to successfully change the SELECT clause to an UPDATE or DELETE clause—this will result in an ODBC error.

If you make any manual changes to the SQL statement in the SQL tab, you won't be able to return to the other tabs in the SQL Expert to make changes. Make sure you are familiar with SQL before making changes to the query. Once you take the SQL plunge, the other tabs won't even appear when you edit the query.

When you're finished specifying your query, click Finish in the Create SQL Expert to send the query to the server. You'll be asked whether you want to run the query. If you click Yes, the query will be submitted to the server for processing. If there are any errors in the query, or other ODBC-related problems that prevent the query from running to completion, you'll see an ODBC error message.

While the query is processing, you'll see an hourglass cursor pointer. Once the query has completed and the server returns a result set to the SQL Designer, you'll see the query appear in a simple row-and-column format for online viewing. Refer to Figure 17-3, earlier in the chapter, to see an example of the query result set.

Since the SQL Designer is a view-only tool, you will only be able to scroll through the query using the vertical and horizontal scroll bars, or navigate directly to a certain record by typing a record number into the Record text box. You won't be able to change any data. If you wish, you can submit the same query to the server again to see if any data has changed. Just click the Refresh button in the toolbar, press the F5 key, or choose Edit | Refresh Data from the pull-down menus. If you want to modify the query, click the Change Query button in the toolbar, or choose Edit | Query from the pull-down menus. The Create SQL Expert with all tabs will reappear (unless you manually modified the SQL statement—then you'll only see the SQL tab). You can make changes to any tab and resubmit the updated query to the server.

Using Parameter Fields in Queries

If you are performing ad hoc real-time queries on a database, you may find yourself running the same query over and over with only a few changes to the Select tab in the Create SQL Expert, or the WHERE clause if you're entering SQL directly. It may be simpler to create a parameter field to prompt you for a value whenever the query is refreshed, and just supply the results of the parameter field to the query's selection criteria.

You must be viewing the result set from a query before you set up a parameter field. The option is not available when you are working with either the Create SQL Expert or the Enter SQL Statement dialog box. Choose Edit | Parameter Field from the pull-down menus. If this is the first parameter field you are creating, you'll be prompted to give the new parameter field a name. Type in a meaningful name and click OK. The Parameter Field dialog box will appear, as shown in Figure 17-12.

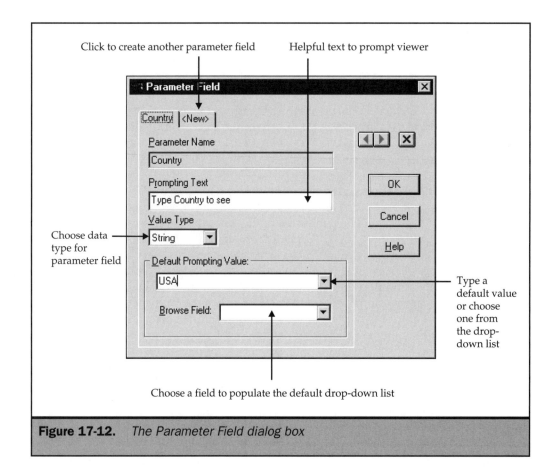

Click to create another parameter field   Helpful text to prompt viewer

Choose data type for parameter field

Type a default value or choose one from the drop-down list

Choose a field to populate the default drop-down list

Figure 17-12.   *The Parameter Field dialog box*

Enter a helpful message in the Prompting Text box to guide the viewer (or yourself) when the parameter field is prompted for. You may want to include entry requirements, such as "all capital letters," "two-character state abbreviations," or other helpful information. Although you can enter a fairly large prompt, only the first 20 characters or so will appear when the prompt is presented.

Choose a data type for the parameter field in the Value Type drop-down list. Make this determination based on the type of field in the query you will be comparing the parameter field to. If you are going to use the parameter field to select a number field, choose a numeric data type, for a string field choose string, and so forth.

The Default Prompting Value section consists of two drop-down lists. You can just type a default value for the parameter field in the first drop-down list. The value you type will appear in the parameter field when you are prompted. If you want some help in choosing the default value, you can choose a database field in the Browse Field drop-down list to populate the Default Prompting Value drop-down list. Then, when you click the down arrow, a list of sample database data from the field you chose will appear. You can pick one of the values as the default.

Caution   *The Browse Field drop-down list may be somewhat misleading. Although it's a good feature request for a future version of the tool, the choice you make in the Browse Field drop-down list won't populate a drop-down list when the parameter field is actually prompted for. It only populates the list so that you can choose an existing value for the default.*

When you've specified all the parameter field items, click OK. This will save the parameter field. It can now be used either in the SQL Expert or directly in the SQL statement that you created earlier. For either situation, click the Edit Query button from the toolbar or choose Edit | Query from the pull-down menus.

If you created the query by entering a SQL statement directly, the SQL statement will reappear. Simply modify the WHERE clause to refer to the parameter field instead of a literal value. For example, if the SQL statement previously read

```
WHERE Customer.Country = 'USA'
```

you would change it to the following for a parameter field named Country:

```
WHERE Customer.Country = '{?Country}'
```

Make sure to leave any necessary punctuation, such as quotation marks or apostrophes, around the parameter field—remember that the parameter field just returns what you type when prompted. There is no automatic punctuation or other necessary SQL syntax. Also, make sure to surround the parameter field name by "curly" or French braces, as well as precede the parameter field name with a question mark.

If you are using the Create SQL Expert, choosing the parameter field in the Select tab is simple. Just display the database browse drop-down list, where you typed the fixed value to compare to. You'll notice that all parameter fields that match the same data type as the database field will now appear in the list. Just choose the parameter field that you want to use. If you don't see the parameter field, you probably used a data type for the parameter field that doesn't match the database field.

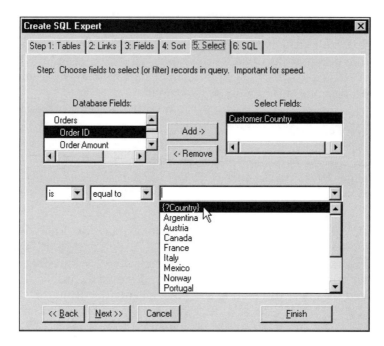

After you make these changes, refresh the query. You now are prompted for the parameter field or fields you added to the query. Type an appropriate literal value and click OK. The SQL Designer will substitute what you typed for the literal value in the query. You can now refresh the query over and over with different values, without having to go back and change the query manually.

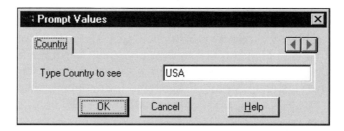

  Query parameter fields are similar to Crystal Reports parameter fields, but they don't have as many features. Crystal Reports parameter fields are discussed in Chapter 12.

Saving the Query

Once you've created and viewed the results of your query, you'll probably want to save the query for future use, either for more direct data analysis in the SQL Designer or for use with Crystal Reports.

First, determine whether you want the result set currently being viewed in the SQL Designer to be saved along with the query definition. If so, make sure Save Data with Query is checked on the File menu. If you don't save the data with the query, the size of the .QRY file will be smaller, but you will have to refresh the query when you later open it in the SQL Designer.

Then, save the query either by using the Save button from the toolbar or by choosing Save or Save As from the File menu; File | Save saves the query with the same filename that currently belongs to the query, overwriting any existing file, whereas File | Save As always asks for a new filename. SQL Designer files are saved with a .QRY extension.

Using Existing SQL Queries

Once you've created and saved queries, you'll want to use them again in the future for additional real-time data analysis. You may also use a .QRY file as the data source for a Crystal Report.

Opening Existing Queries

Opening an existing query in the SQL Designer is as simple as clicking the Open button in the toolbar or choosing File | Open from the pull-down menus. A File Open dialog box will appear, showing all .QRY files in the default folder. Navigate to a different drive or folder and choose the .QRY file that contains the query you want to open. Then, click OK. The query will open with the result set showing (if you saved your query without saved data, the query will be refreshed as soon as it's opened). You can now change the query as described previously in the chapter.

Using Queries with Crystal Reports

One of the main benefits of Crystal SQL Designer is the ability to use its .QRY files as a data source for a Crystal Report. But, you may ask, "Why use a query as a data source for the report, instead of just reporting against the database directly?" There are two main reasons why a query might be preferable:

- A query consists of only the tables (already linked) and fields that you might want a report designer to have access to. The report designer won't need to choose and link tables before being able to choose fields.

- If the query contains saved data, the report will use the saved data. This is helpful if you want to run a query to "hit" the database one time, and then save the data with the .QRY file. You can then create multiple similar reports against the .QRY file with saved data, thereby printing several reports that need to be based on the same data source, without having to hit the database multiple times. An additional benefit of a query with saved data is "point in time" reporting. Queries can be run against the database at various times and saved with data to indicate what the state of the database was at that time.

The steps involved in using a query as a data source for a report vary, depending on whether you use a report expert or the Blank Report option when creating a new report. If you use any of the report experts, Crystal SQL Query will be one of the buttons available on the Data tab. Simply click it to display the Crystal SQL Query Files category of the Data Explorer.

If you use the Blank Report option to create your report, open the Metadata/Query category of the Data Explorer. Then open the Crystal SQL Query Files category. When you click the plus sign next to the Crystal SQL Query Files category, a File Open dialog box will appear, showing only .QRY files. Navigate to the drive and folder where your query files are and choose the desired query.

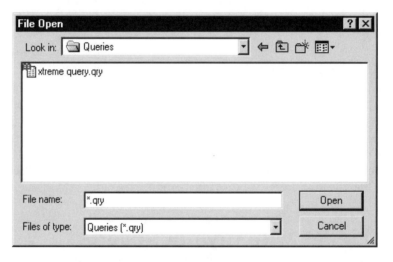

Once you've chosen the desired query, you will proceed directly to the rest of your report design with the query's fields available to you. There will be no need to choose or link tables.

The Complete Reference

Crystal Reports

Chapter 18

Simplifying Databases with Crystal Dictionaries

469

In many cases, once you've learned Crystal Reports, the easy part of your report design process is complete! Often, you'll discover that wading through the intricacies of your corporate database is a much more daunting task than learning the tools to report on it. It's not uncommon for larger databases to contain hundreds of tables, each containing a large number of cryptically named fields. It sometimes seems that some database administrators may be trying to ensure job security by creating a database that only they can understand.

Also, you'll probably run into fairly common situations where some parts of the database are off-limits to certain report viewers and designers. Payroll and accounting applications come immediately to mind. Certain tables in the database may be necessary for some users, while not necessary for others. And, there are often times where even individual fields need to be made available only to certain users.

And, last but not least, databases often don't contain all the data you need for your report, or don't contain it in the form that your company commonly needs it to be presented in. While each individual report designer can conceivably create the same formulas over and over to manipulate data in the necessary fashion, a common predesigned template that already contains these formulas would be immensely helpful.

So, is the only solution to take a week-long course on your database layout, set up elaborate security models to restrict tables and fields to authorized users, and make sure every user adheres to the same formulas? Of course not! Included with Crystal Reports Professional and Developer's Editions is the Crystal Dictionaries tool, which can be used to create a dictionary, or "meta-layer," that insulates a report designer from the actual database layout. By using a dictionary instead of tying a report directly to the database, a report developer can be given a simple set of predefined fields to work with.

Caution *Crystal Dictionaries will only be installed if you specifically choose it when running Crystal Reports 8.5 installation. If you don't choose it when installing, the Crystal Reports Tools submenu (where Crystal Dictionaries is started) won't appear on the Windows Start button. You'll need to rerun Crystal Reports 8.5 installation and choose to install Crystal Dictionaries.*

What Exactly Is a Crystal Dictionary?

The organization of a database, such as the layout of tables and fields and how they all relate to each other (known as the database *schema*), can be very complex. Because of this, there has always been a need for a tool that could present a simplified view of the database to a report or query designer who didn't want to know all the little details of the database. And, there are many situations in which a limited set of fields and predefined formulas, often renamed so they are easier to understand, are in order.

This, in essence, is what a Crystal Dictionary is. Using a dictionary, a user who would normally be intimidated by the complexity of the database can now be given a simplified view of the database, and can use this view to write reports or queries. By using a dictionary, the department responsible for the database can present different views of the database to different users, based on each user's level of database knowledge, "need to know" level, and area of concern. The dictionary can look entirely different from the database it's based on: fields and tables can be renamed, formulas can be predefined and included as if they were just other database fields, and even sample data for browsing and bitmap images can be preloaded inside the dictionary.

Consider the following two illustrations of the Field Explorer box from Crystal Reports. Figure 18-1 appears when the report is based on several actual tables in a database. Figure 18-2 appears when the report is based on a dictionary (a PC-based file with a .DC5 extension). Notice in Figure 18-2 the reduced set of fields, the better organization of field hierarchies, the easy-to-understand field names (some of which are formulas that have been predefined), and the Dictionary Graphics category that contains preloaded company logos and watermark graphics. The second example is much preferable for a report or query designer who isn't familiar with the layout of the huge database, the common fields required to join tables, and the cryptic field names.

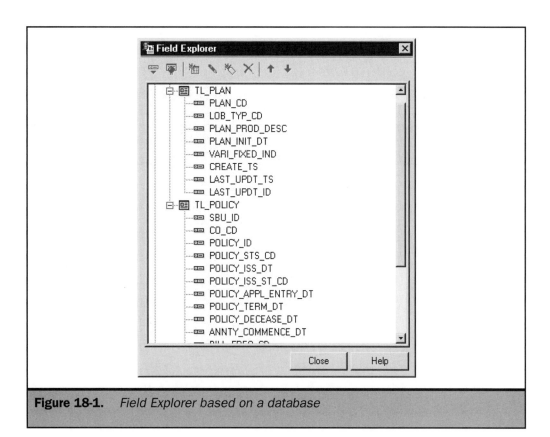

Figure 18-1.   *Field Explorer based on a database*

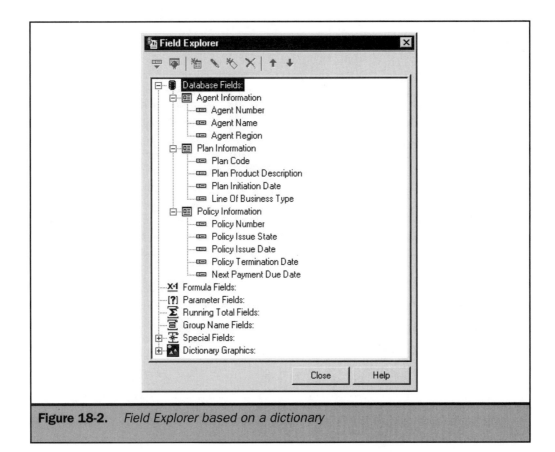

Figure 18-2.   *Field Explorer based on a dictionary*

The Crystal Dictionaries tool is a separate executable program that's run directly from the Crystal Reports Tools program group. Crystal Reports doesn't need to be running to use Crystal Dictionaries. Once it's started, the main Crystal Dictionaries window will appear, as shown in Figure 18-3.

Note   *If you aren't intimately familiar with the table and field structure of your database, you should probably get someone who has this familiarity to create the dictionary, or to help you create it. The whole idea of Crystal Dictionaries is to simplify database access for those who aren't familiar with the actual database layout. The person who creates the dictionary in the first place must obviously have good knowledge of its structure.*

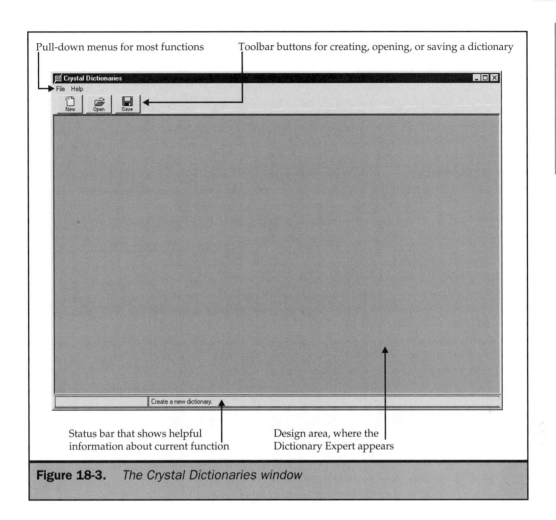

Figure 18-3. *The Crystal Dictionaries window*

Creating a Crystal Dictionary

When you first start Crystal Dictionaries, you have two main choices: open an existing dictionary, or create a new dictionary. To create a new dictionary, click the New button in the toolbar, or choose File | New from the pull-down menus. The Dictionary Expert will appear in the design area of Crystal Dictionaries. This tabbed dialog box is used for the entire dictionary design process.

The Dictionary Expert consists of four main tabs (an additional tab, Links, appears as the second tab if you choose more than one table for the dictionary). Creating a dictionary is somewhat similar to creating a Crystal Report using the report experts (see Chapter 1 for more information on report experts). You supply information on each tab and then click the Next button, or the next tab in the sequence. When the process is complete, the dictionary file is saved. It can then be used in Crystal Reports or the Crystal SQL Designer to create a report or query.

The Tables Tab

The Tables tab is the first tab in the Dictionary Expert, as shown in Figure 18-4. Here, you choose the database and tables you want to use in your dictionary. Your dictionary can contain tables from more than one database, as well as from more than one database type. For example, you might add tables from a Microsoft Access database and a dBASE for Windows database by clicking the Data File button, and include tables from an Oracle database and an Informix database by clicking the SQL/ODBC button.

If you click the Data File button, a File Open dialog box appears, in which you can navigate to the correct drive or folder until you find the PC-style database you want to use. Then, select the database filename. If the database contains multiple tables (such as a Microsoft Access database), you'll be presented with a Choose Tables dialog box, in which you can choose the tables you want to include in the dictionary.

To add tables from ODBC databases, click the SQL/ODBC button. If you are not currently logged in to any ODBC databases, the Log On Server dialog box will appear.

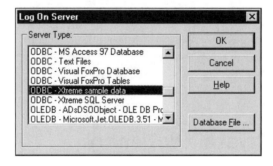

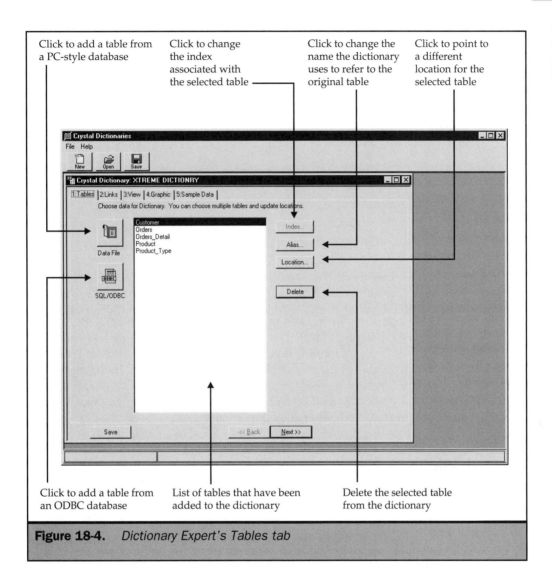

Click to add a table from a PC-style database

Click to change the index associated with the selected table

Click to change the name the dictionary uses to refer to the original table

Click to point to a different location for the selected table

Click to add a table from an ODBC database

List of tables that have been added to the dictionary

Delete the selected table from the dictionary

Figure 18-4.   *Dictionary Expert's Tables tab*

Choose the database you want to use. If the database is secure, you'll need to provide a valid login ID and password to use the database. Once you successfully log on (or if you're already logged on to an ODBC database), the Choose SQL Table dialog box will appear, shown next.

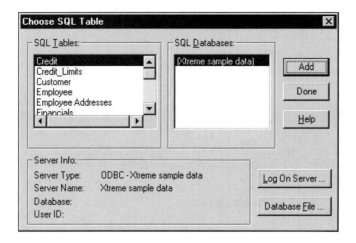

Add tables to the Dictionary Expert's Tables tab by double-clicking each table in the SQL Tables list that you want to add, or by selecting the table and clicking the Add button (selecting multiple tables with SHIFT-click or CTRL-click doesn't work in the Choose SQL Table dialog box). If you need to add tables from a different ODBC database, click the Log On Server button in the Choose SQL Table dialog box and log on to another database. Then, choose the table or tables you want to use from the new database that will be available in the dialog box. Once you've finished choosing tables, click Done.

If you add too many tables to the Dictionary Expert's Tables tab by mistake, select the table you no longer need and either click the Delete button or press the DEL key on your keyboard. You can also choose alternative index files for a particular table (if the table is from a PC-style database that allows index choices) by selecting the table and clicking the Index button. The Alias and Location buttons are helpful if the location of the database or the table or field names in the database change after you save the dictionary. These buttons are described in more detail later in the chapter.

The Links Tab

If you choose more than one table (almost a certainty if you are creating any sort of even moderately sophisticated dictionary), a Links tab will appear after the Tables tab. You use this tab to link the tables together on common fields. You can position and resize the table windows and create links by dragging and dropping fields between tables. If you need to delete incorrect links, just select a link line and click the Delete button or press the DEL key. To change the join type for a particular link, select it and click Options.

Tables added to a dictionary are always smart-linked, regardless of the Auto SmartLinking setting in File | Options in Crystal Reports. Since "real world" smart-linking often creates more incorrect links than correct ones, you'll probably spend a bit of time deleting incorrect links and adding correct ones in the Links tab.

The Links tab works almost identically to the Visual Linking Expert in Crystal Reports. Review Chapter 14 for details on linking issues and join types, and specific details on how to link tables together in the Links tab. Once you've correctly linked tables, click Next or click directly on the View tab to add fields to the dictionary.

The View Tab

The View tab is the heart of Crystal Dictionaries—this is where the real work happens. Figure 18-5 shows the View tab.

The general idea in using the View tab is to move only the fields from the left database list to the right view list that you want the report designer to see—these will be the only fields available when a report or query based on the dictionary is designed.

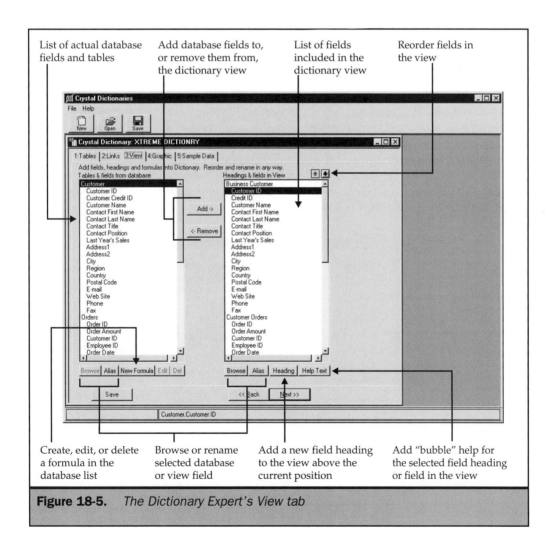

Figure 18-5. *The Dictionary Expert's View tab*

In addition to limiting fields in this fashion, you can create formulas that manipulate database data, and then add these predefined formulas to the right view list as well. And, to make the dictionary more readable and easy to understand, you can rename fields you add to the dictionary, as well as create your own "pseudo table names" using field headings.

Adding Fields

To add a database field to the dictionary view, select one or more fields in the database list. You can select multiple fields by using CTRL-click and SHIFT-click. Then, just drag and drop the selected fields to the view list, or click the Add button to add them. The fields will appear in the dictionary view in the same order as they appear in the view list. If you want to reorder the fields in a more logical order, just select the field you want to move, and drag it to a new location in the view list. Or, you can select the field and click the small up or down arrow above the view list to move the selected field.

Creating and Adding Formulas

One of the many benefits of using Crystal Dictionaries is the ability to create predefined formulas and include them as though they were regular database fields. The person designing the report has no indication that the data from the formula isn't just coming directly from the database. This allows often-used formulas to be created in advance, freeing each individual report designer from having to create them.

To create a new formula, click the New Formula button. Give the formula a meaningful name (though you can still rename it in the view list, if you want to), and click OK. The Edit Formula dialog box will appear, in which you can use the same set of database fields and built-in functions.

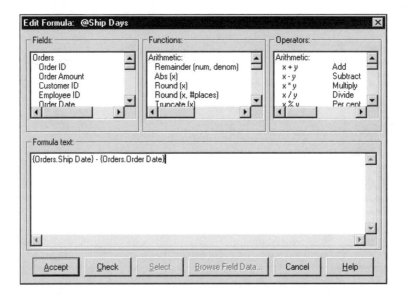

The Edit Formula dialog box used in Crystal Dictionaries has the older layout style of Crystal Reports 6. You'll notice that the newer features, such as toolbars and undockable windows, don't appear in this dialog box. Also, you will not be able to use Basic Syntax for the formula, and newer Crystal Reports formula functions won't be available.

Create the formula as you would in Crystal Reports, and click Accept when you are finished. This will add the formula you created to a separate section labeled Formulas at the bottom of the database list. You can then select the formula in the database list and add it to the view window the same way you would add a database field. If you wish to edit or delete an existing formula, select it in the database list and click the Edit or Del button under the database list.

Adding Field Headings

Another benefit for the report designer when creating a report based on a dictionary is that they won't have to manually choose any specific database or tables. These are already defined in the dictionary. However, the Field Explorer in Crystal Reports can still show fields as though they were contained in individual tables. This *field hierarchy* can be completely controlled by the creator of the dictionary with Field Headings. A field heading will appear in the dictionary as though it is a table name, even though it has no relationship at all to actual tables in the database. You can use as few or as many field headings as you choose (although you have to retain at least the one that's created by default at the top of the list).

To create a field heading, select in the view list the field that you want to place the field heading *above*. Then, click the Heading button. A dialog box will prompt you for the name of the field heading. Type a meaningful heading, such as Customer Information, and click OK. The heading will be added to the view list above the field you had selected. To later delete the heading, select it and press the DEL key.

The Remove button won't work for any field heading—you have to use the DEL key. And, you won't be able to delete the very first field heading that's created by default when you first add a field to the view list. You can, however, rename it to whatever you want.

Renaming Fields and Headings

Another big benefit of using a dictionary is that you can give database fields more meaningful names. Very often, database fields are originally given somewhat cryptic names, often containing strange abbreviations, all uppercase letters, and underscores. By using the Alias button, you can give the fields more meaningful names containing spaces and mixed upper- and lowercase characters.

Select the field or field heading in the view list that you want to rename. Then, click the Alias button. A dialog box will appear with the current field name listed. Just type a new name in the dialog box and click OK. You'll notice that the new name now appears in the view list.

You can actually rename fields or column headings without even using the Alias button. Simply select the field or heading you want to rename and start typing (or start by backspacing). As you type, you'll notice the object name changing.

You may wonder how you can tell what the original field name is, after you've changed the name with the Alias button. Simply select the field in the view list and look in the Crystal Dictionaries status bar. You'll see the original database field name appear.

Adding Help Text

You can add pop-up help (or *bubble* help) to field headings or individual view fields. If you then click the field and wait for a second or two, the help text you entered will pop up, right over the field, as shown in the following illustration. This is helpful if you want to add meaningful information to the field or field heading to assist report designers when they are creating reports with the dictionary.

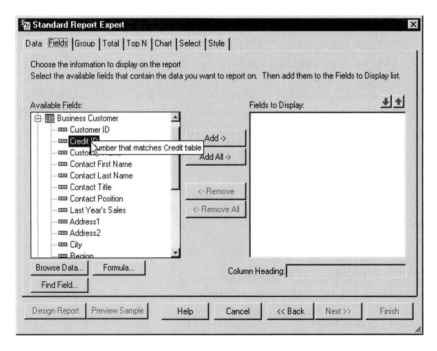

Select the field in the view list that you want to create bubble help for, and click the Help Text button. A dialog box will appear, in which you can type the help text you want to use, and then click OK when you are finished. If you later want to change the bubble help, simply select the field again and click the Help Text button. The existing text will appear, and you can make any necessary changes and click OK.

The bubble help you add with the Help Text button will only appear in a Crystal Reports report expert or the Crystal SQL Designer Create SQL Expert. If you are using the Blank Report option in Crystal Reports, the help text won't be visible in the Field Explorer.

When you're finished with the View tab, you can save the dictionary file by clicking the Save button. Or, you can add bitmap graphics to the dictionary file by clicking either Next or the Graphic tab directly.

The Graphic Tab

If you have a standard company logo or other bitmap graphics files that you want to be easily available to report designers, you can add these to the dictionary in the Graphic tab, shown in Figure 18-6.

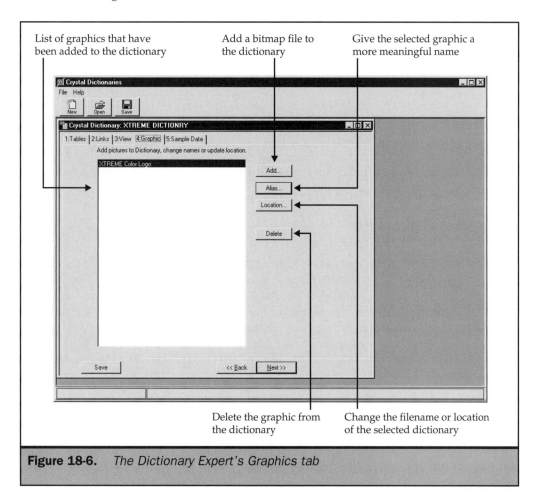

Figure 18-6.   *The Dictionary Expert's Graphics tab*

To add a bitmap image reference to the dictionary, click the Add button. A File Open dialog box will appear, in which you can navigate to the folder that contains the bitmap image. You'll see a list of supported graphics files in the folder. Select the bitmap image you wish to add to the dictionary, and click OK. The filename for the graphic will appear in the dictionary pictures list. You then can use the Alias button to give the graphic a more meaningful name, if you want.

Note *Crystal Dictionaries will read Windows bitmap files (.BMP), PC Paintbrush files (.PCX), JPEG images typically found in Web pages (.JPG), TIFF files (.TIF), and Targa files (.TGA). If you have a graphic in another format, such as vector format or an Adobe Photoshop .PSD file, you'll need to use a graphics program to convert it to a supported format before it can be used in a dictionary or in Crystal Reports.*

If you want to remove the graphic from the dictionary, select it in the list and click the Delete button. This only deletes the reference to the graphic in the dictionary—the original bitmap image remains in its original location.

If you later move or rename an original graphic file, the dictionary will no longer point to the right location—a report designer will get a File Not Found message if they try to use the dictionary graphic. To remedy this situation, click the Location button on the Graphic tab and choose the new location or filename for the bitmap image.

Caution *Since the dictionary merely points to the actual bitmap file, make sure that any PC that might be using the dictionary will have access to the original graphic files that were used when the dictionary was created. You may want to use a UNC (Uniform Naming Convention) name or place the graphic files on a shared network drive that is mapped to the same drive letter on all PCs.*

The Sample Data Tab

When you create a report or query based directly on the database, a Browse function typically is available in dialog boxes and from pop-up menus. If you select a database field and then choose this function, Crystal Reports or the SQL Designer will query the database and return a short list of sample data for that field. The Sample Data tab, shown in Figure 18-7, allows you to control the data that is browsed when a dictionary is being used. This is helpful if the person designing a report or query does not have actual connectivity to the database when the report is being designed, or if the connection is on a slow modem or WAN link, which makes browsing live database data tedious.

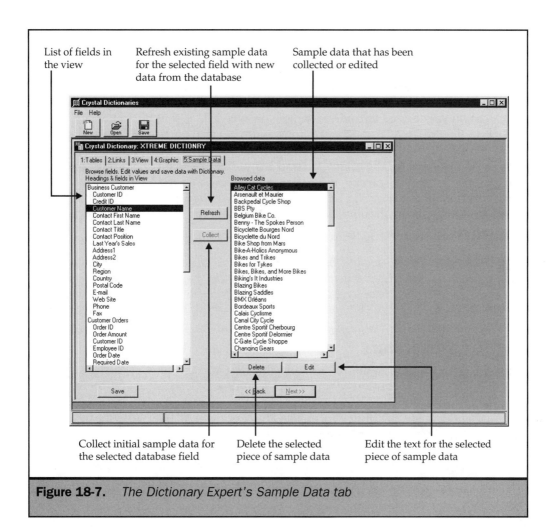

Figure 18-7. *The Dictionary Expert's Sample Data tab*

Sample browse data can be stored right inside the dictionary for selected fields in the view. If you choose not to store sample data for a field, and a user browses it, Crystal Reports or the SQL Designer will go ahead and query the database directly.

To store sample data in the dictionary, you must first collect it from the actual database. Select the field you wish to gather sample data for, and click the Collect button. The database will be queried, and unique sample data will be collected and placed in the Browsed Data list on the right side of the Sample Data tab. You can then scroll through the sample data and delete any pieces you don't wish to keep. You can also select a piece of sample data and click the Edit button. A dialog box will appear, in which you can change the value of the sample data. You cannot add new sample data—just delete or edit existing data.

Once you've collected and edited sample data, you'll see that the same data appears in the Browsed Data list every time you select that particular field in the field list. If you want to reread the database and refresh the sample data, click the Refresh button. The database will be re-queried and any old sample data (including any that you modified) will be discarded and replaced with new data from the database. If you select a field that hasn't had any sample data collected, the Browsed Data list will be empty and the Collect button will be enabled. You can then click Collect to add sample data for that field.

 Remember that the sample data you specify here will only appear when you browse from the Field Explorer. If you create a report based on a dictionary, even though you don't have database connectivity, the sample data will not appear if you try to preview the report.

Saving the Dictionary

After you complete at least the Tables and View tabs, you can save the dictionary to a disk file. Click the Save button either in the Dictionary Expert or from the toolbar, or choose File | Save or File | Save As from the pull-down menus. If you've saved the dictionary previously, the buttons and File | Save option will overwrite the older version of the dictionary with the newer version. If this is the first time you're saving the dictionary, or if you use the File | Save As option, a File Open dialog box will appear asking you to supply a filename. Choose a drive and folder where you want to save the file. The file will be saved with a .DC5 extension, indicating that it's a Crystal Dictionary.

 You may want to set up a shared network directory in which you can save Crystal Dictionaries. That way, many report designers will have ready access to the dictionaries for creating new reports and queries.

Setting Crystal Dictionaries Options

You can choose some default behavior for Crystal Dictionaries by specifying locations for dictionary files that you open or save, as well as choose default locations for PC-style databases and graphic files. You may also set options for logging in to SQL databases. Choose File | Options from the drop-down menus, and the Options dialog box will appear, as shown in Figure 18-8.

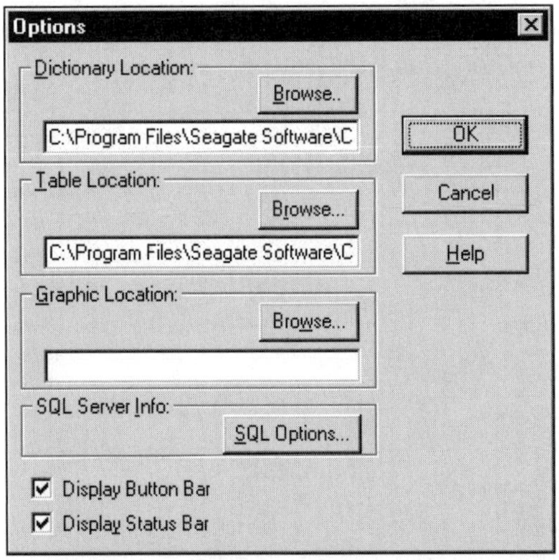

Figure 18-8.   *The Options dialog box*

You can specify default drive and path names for three types of files used by Crystal Dictionaries:

- **Directory Location**   Used when you open or save .DC5 files.
- **Table Location**   Used when you add new tables from a PC-style database.
- **Graphic Location**   Used when you add a bitmap graphic file to the dictionary.

You can type drive and path names in directly, or click the Browse buttons to navigate to the desired locations.

Clicking the SQL Options button displays the SQL Options dialog box, shown in Figure 18-9. Here, you can specify default behavior for SQL and ODBC databases that you add to your dictionary. Specific information about this dialog box can be found in Chapter 14.

Finally, the two check boxes at the bottom of the Options dialog box let you choose whether or not to display the toolbar (referred to as the "Button Bar" here) and the status bar. When you are finished choosing options, click OK. The options will be saved for the next time you start Crystal Dictionaries.

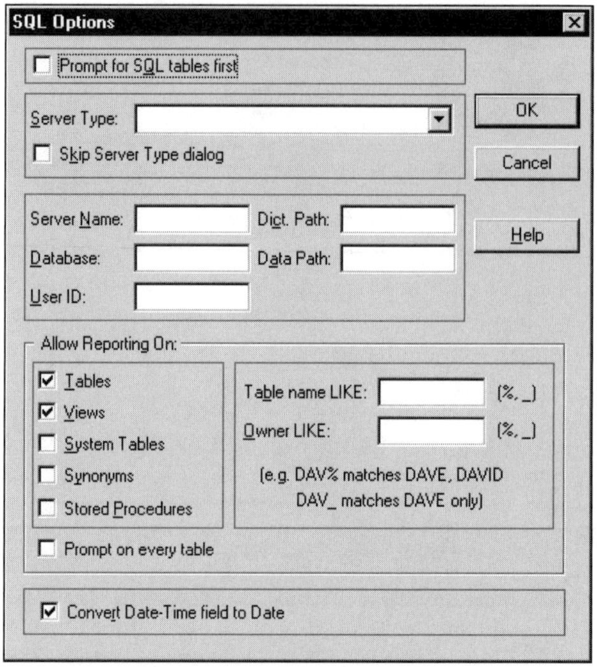

Figure 18-9. *Crystal Dictionaries SQL options*

Opening an Existing Dictionary

Opening an existing dictionary is as simple as clicking the Open button in the toolbar, or choosing File | Open from the pull-down menus. A File Open dialog box will appear, showing any existing dictionary files in the Crystal Reports program folder. Navigate to another drive or folder to locate your existing dictionary. After you locate it, simply select it and click OK. It will be opened in the Dictionary Expert for you to modify as you see fit. After you make any necessary changes, click the Save button in the toolbar, or choose File | Save from the pull-down menus to save your updated dictionary file.

You may notice that Crystal Dictionaries recognizes both .DC5 and .DCT dictionary files. The .DCT extension was used for dictionary files prior to Crystal Reports Version 5. Versions 5 and later (including Version 8.5) use the .DC5 file extension. While Crystal Dictionaries Version 8.5 can read .DCT files, it will only save .DC5 files.

Updating the Database Location

When you create a dictionary, the .DC5 file "points" to a specific database name at a specific database location. The tables the dictionary uses are also referenced by name. Should the location of the database or names of tables or fields in the database change, any dictionaries based on them will need to be modified to point to the new database location or renamed tables.

To simply verify that the database still exists at the location and with the same table and field names it was originally created with, choose File | Verify Dictionary from the pull-down menus. If there have been no changes to the database that affect the dictionary, you'll simply receive a message that the dictionary is up-to-date. If, however, tables can no longer be found at the same location, you'll receive a message indicating that a table can't be found at its original location.

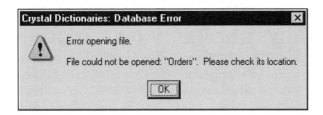

You'll need to then change the location that the table in the Tables tab points to. Click the Location button inside the Tables tab. The previous location of the table will then appear. This location will be displayed in either the Choose SQL Table dialog box, if the dictionary table is from an ODBC database, or a Windows File dialog box, if the table is from a PC-style database. Simply choose the new filename or table name that contains the new table location (use the Log On Server button on the Choose SQL Table dialog box, if necessary) and click OK. Data for the table will now be retrieved from the new location.

If you wish to change the name that the dictionary uses to refer to the original database table, select the table you wish to change. Then click the Alias button. You'll be given the opportunity to change the name, or *alias*, that Crystal Dictionaries uses to refer to the table. Remember that this has no relation to what table names ultimately appear in the dictionary view. Any field headings you create in the View tab will determine the pseudo table names that create a field hierarchy in the actual dictionary view.

If the table location is the same, but fields that were used in the dictionary have been deleted, added, or renamed, you'll receive a message indicating that the table layout has changed. If you click Yes, to "fix up the dictionary," the field names on the left side of the View tab will be updated to reflect the changes to the original database.

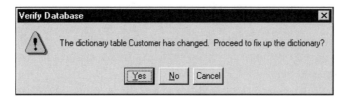

 Crystal Dictionaries has no tool similar to the Remap Fields dialog box in Crystal Reports 8.5. If database field names change, you need to re-add them to your dictionary. You might then give the tables alias names that match the original table names so that any reports based on the dictionary will still work without changes.

Basing a Report or Query on a Dictionary

The true power of Crystal Dictionaries is apparent when it comes time to design a new report in Crystal Reports or a new query in the Crystal SQL Designer. When you create a new report, using either a report expert or the Blank Report option, or when you create a query using the Create SQL Expert, an option allows you to choose a dictionary as the data source for your report. When you choose a dictionary, a File Open dialog box appears in which you can choose an existing dictionary file.

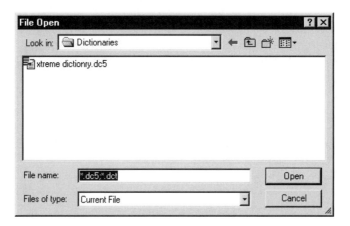

Navigate to the drive and folder where the desired dictionary resides, select it, and click OK. The report or query design process will now proceed as though you had logged on to a database, chosen tables, and properly linked them. You will be able to immediately choose fields.

If the dictionary contains any bitmap graphics and you're using the Field Explorer inside Crystal Reports, you'll see a Dictionary Graphic category as well. Select the category and add any graphics you need directly to the report by dragging and dropping or clicking the Insert To Report button. There's no need to use the Insert Graphic button or menu option to insert dictionary graphics.

Caution	*Make sure you really want to use a dictionary before you spend a lot of time developing a report that's based on one. Once you've created a report using a Crystal Dictionary, you can't convert the report to use an actual database (including a direct connection to the database that the dictionary is based on) with the Set Location or Convert Database Driver command. The Set Location command will only let you choose another dictionary file, and the Add Database To Report and Convert Database Driver commands are not even available from the pull-down menu.*

Here are some tips to keep in mind when setting up Crystal Dictionaries for use within your organization:

- If you are using the Crystal SQL Designer, remember that the dictionary you use must be based only on SQL/ODBC databases. If you choose a dictionary based on a PC-style database, an error message will appear.

- If the dictionary you choose is based on one or more secure databases, you'll be required to provide a valid login ID and password for each database before you can begin to use the dictionary.

- You need to ensure that the same ODBC data source used to create the dictionary is located on the computer that the dictionary is being used on. If the dictionary is based on a PC-style database, the original database must be found in the same path as is contained in the dictionary file. Otherwise, the dictionary won't be able to ultimately resolve dictionary names back to the original database.

- If you created formulas that use any functions from the Additional Functions list in the Formula Editor, ensure that the User Function Library .DLL file that the functions come from is installed on any computers that will be using the formulas. Otherwise, the formula will fail when the report designer tries to use a dictionary field that's based on the formula.

Chapter 19

Reporting from Proprietary Data Types

Crystal Reports is best known as the "reporting tool of choice" for use with any standard corporate database. "Standard" databases might generally be thought to include Microsoft Access or SQL Server, Sybase, Oracle, Informix, IBM DB2, and others that are well known in the mainstream of corporate database technology.

But, what do you do if your data is contained in some other form of database or data file? Well, if the database or data file system is *very* proprietary and out of the mainstream, and the vendor doesn't provide an ODBC (open database connectivity) driver for the database, then you may be, quite simply, out of luck. However, many proprietary databases can be accessed via ODBC, which Crystal Reports will work with. You can also create reports against regular ASCII-delimited text files and against XML files that conform to certain standards, but you'll need to use a supplied ODBC driver to accomplish this. And, Crystal Reports 8.5 supports other data types directly, without even requiring an ODBC driver. You can create reports based on Microsoft Exchange Server and Systems Management Server databases, Symantec's ACT! contact manager, Microsoft Outlook, Windows NT event logs, and Web server activity logs.

The general approach for creating reports against these proprietary types of data sources is similar, regardless of the data source:

1. Ensure that the software you want to report from (such as Microsoft Outlook), or the vendor's "client" application to access a database (such as Enterprise Manager for Microsoft SQL Server), is installed on the same PC as Crystal Reports. Crystal Reports automatically detects these software packages and will list them when you choose a data source.

2. Create a new report using either the report experts or the Blank Report option. If you use an expert, click the Database button and choose the More Data Sources category from the Data Explorer. If you use the Blank Report option, choose the More Data Sources category in the Data Explorer, as shown next, which will reveal the additional "direct" data sources in the list. So, if you want to write reports against a Microsoft Exchange server, choose one of the Exchange data types in the More Data Sources category, such as Exchange Folders/Address Book, Message Tracking Log, or Public Folder Admin.

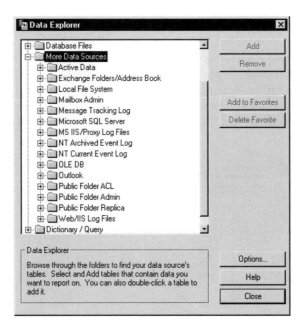

3. Follow any prompts specific to the data source, such as choosing an Exchange server and profile. You'll then see a list of tables and/or fields that are specific to that data type. Use them in your report just as you would use other database tables and fields.

Although Crystal Reports supports many popular data types, most of this chapter will focus on four of the most often used: Microsoft Outlook, the local file system (basically, the disk directory on a PC or network disk drive), the Windows NT event log, and standard Web server activity logs.

The last section of the chapter focuses on reporting from an XML data source, which is handled through an ODBC driver provided with Crystal Reports 8.5.

Reporting from Microsoft Outlook

Microsoft Outlook has become a popular standard on office desktops, because it smoothly integrates e-mail, contact management, and calendar maintenance in one package. Outlook's folder metaphor is handy for organizing your office affairs, and it's also handy for reporting.

The first requirement for creating a Crystal Report based on your Outlook folders is rather obvious—you must have Outlook installed on your PC. More specifically, you must have Outlook installed on the same computer on which you will be running Crystal Reports. Crystal Reports won't report on any other Outlook systems on the network—just your own.

To report on your Outlook data, start a new report just as you would for a standard database. You can use the report experts or the Blank Report option. If you use an expert, click the Database button to display the Data Explorer (which will appear automatically if you choose Blank Report). Click the Outlook folder in the More Data Sources category. If you have not reported from Outlook before, or there is more than one Outlook Profile on your system, you'll be presented with the Choose Profile dialog box, and will need to select your profile (or the default Microsoft Outlook profile) from the drop-down list and click OK. Then you'll be presented with the Choose Folder dialog box, showing the folder hierarchy of your Outlook data. Choose the folder that you want to report on, and click OK.

Note *You cannot report on the Notes folder. You'll receive an error message if you try to select it.*

After you choose the folder and click OK, the Data Explorer appears, and you need to select and add the folder just as you would any database table. When you close the Data Explorer, the list of Outlook fields you can report from will appear in the expert or in the Field Explorer.

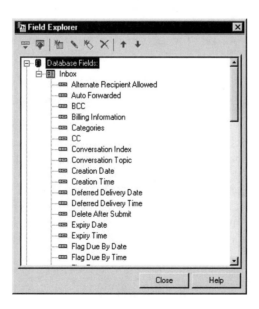

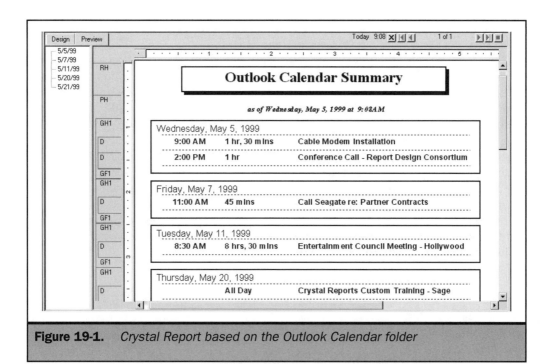

Figure 19-1. *Crystal Report based on the Outlook Calendar folder*

Use the Outlook fields just like other database fields to create your report. You can sort, group, and format the report as you normally would. You can also create formulas, if necessary, to calculate or modify the way Outlook material appears in the report. Figure 19-1 shows a sample report based on the Calendar folder from Outlook.

Note *The field names you see in the Crystal Reports Field Explorer may not always match the field names you see in Outlook. If you don't see the field you expect, look for a reasonable alternative field name. Also, you may need to add other Outlook folders (such as the Contact folder and the Inbox folder) and link the two together to get all the data you expect. Make sure you link on correct fields—Smart Linking typically won't pick the correct fields to perform an Outlook link.*

Reporting from the Local File System

You are probably familiar with Explorer, the Windows application that helps you view the hierarchy and layout of your local and network drives, as well as locate one or more particular files you may be looking for. However, if you want a more powerful reporting-type tool to search or report on drive contents, you need another software solution.

In Crystal Reports 8 and above, the *local file system* is available as a data source, allowing you to write powerful reports against any local or network drive on your PC. By choosing a drive and folder or directory, as well as specifying some detailed criteria (if you choose), you can create reports that select and sort files and folders with the complete power and flexibility of Crystal Reports.

To report on your local file-system data, start a new report just as you would for a standard database. You can use the report experts or the Blank Report option. If you use an expert, click the Database button to display the Data Explorer (which will appear automatically if you choose Blank Report). Click the Local File System folder in the More Data Sources category.

You'll be presented with the Select a Directory dialog box, shown in Figure 19-2. If you simply want to supply a drive or path name, you can either type it or click the Browse button to navigate to the desired drive and directory. If you click the Advanced button, you can add some additional criteria to narrow down the files and directories you want to see.

Make your choices and click OK. A new level in the Data Explorer will appear, with the directory you chose at the top, followed by all directories below it (subject to any limits you may have chosen).

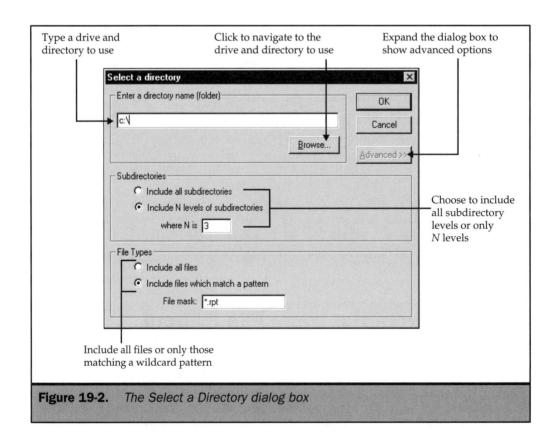

Figure 19-2. *The Select a Directory dialog box*

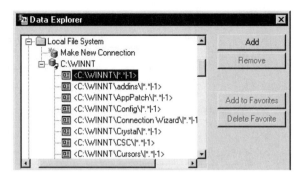

You can choose any directory from the Data Explorer. Files in that directory, as well as directories below, will be included in your report. Once you've made the directory choice and closed the Data Explorer, the list of file-system fields you can report from will appear in the expert or in the Field Explorer.

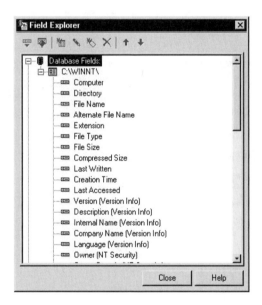

You'll notice many different fields containing information you might not have previously been familiar with. Some fields only apply to certain types of files, such as .EXE or .DLL files. Others only apply to files that belong to certain applications (for example, Number of Words generally only applies to Word or other word processing documents). Use these file-system fields just like other database fields to create your report. You can sort, group, and format the report as you normally would. You can use the fields to create flexible selection criteria to narrow down your report. You can also create formulas, if necessary, to calculate or modify the way file-system material appears in the report. Figure 19-3 shows a sample report based on a local C disk drive.

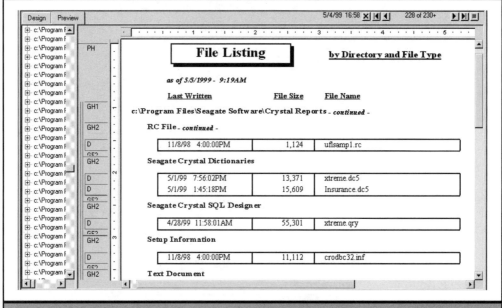

Figure 19-3.   *Crystal Report based on local file system*

Reporting from the Windows NT/2000 Event Log

Windows NT and 2000 have traditionally been the powerful big brothers of desktop operating systems, such as Windows 95 and Windows 98. However, with the advent of more powerful computer hardware available for ever-falling prices, Windows NT and 2000 are finding their way to more and more desktops. And Windows XP builds even further on Windows NT technology.

An integrated part of the Windows NT and 2000 operating systems is the *event log*, a series of files that document events that occur during the general operation of Windows. Several different types of event logs are available, and different types of entries are placed in the event logs as users log on and off, and programs start, stop, and operate. Crystal Reports includes the capability to create flexible reports on the Windows NT event logs.

Note   *Although designing reports against the Windows NT event logs won't harm the computer containing the log, you probably won't find the information returned to be of much use if you're not generally familiar with Windows NT/2000 and its components. This Crystal Reports capability will probably be most useful to system administrators and other technical personnel.*

To report on NT event logs, start a new report just as you would for a standard database. You can use the report experts or the Blank Report option. If you use an expert, click the Database button to display the Data Explorer (which will appear automatically if you choose Blank Report). Click the NT Current Event Log folder in the More Data Sources category to report on current active event logs on Windows NT/2000 computers. Or, you can click the NT Archived Event Log folder to display an Open File dialog box in which to search for archived (.EVT) event log files. If you use this option, upon selecting an event log you will be presented with the Select Archived Event Log dialog box, and you must identify the type of event log you selected (System, Security, or Application).

If you choose the Make New Connection option in the Current Event Log folder, you'll see the Select Current Event Log dialog box, shown in Figure 19-4. This allows you to select an event log on a remote computer—it doesn't have to reside on the computer that you are running Crystal Reports on. You can include event logs from more than one computer in your report, if you choose.

If you know the domain and computer name, you can simply type it in the Computer(s) text box at the top of the dialog box. If you include more than one computer name, separate the names with commas. If you're not sure which computers to include, you can use the Explorer-like hierarchy to select the computers you wish to use. When you see the computer list, you can select one or more computers.

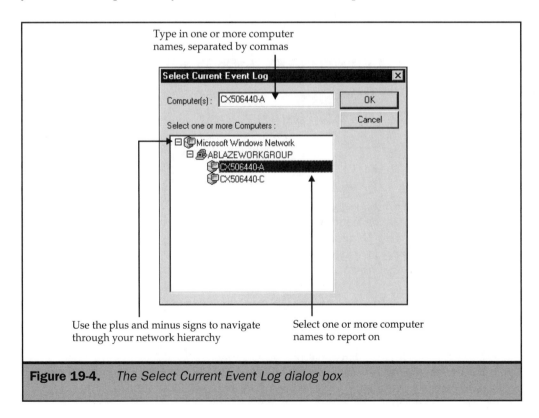

Figure 19-4.   *The Select Current Event Log dialog box*

Make your choices and click OK. A new level in the Data Explorer will appear for the computer you've chosen, showing the three NT event logs that are available: Application, Security, and System.

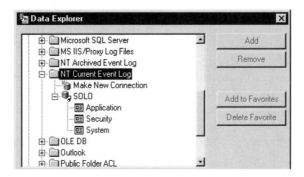

Depending on the types of events you want your report to be based on, choose the appropriate log. If you'd like a better idea of what types of events are contained in each log, use the Event Viewer application from the Administrative Tools program group in Windows NT or the Control Panel in Windows 2000 to view the different event-log entries. Once you've made your log choice, the list of event-log fields you can report on will appear in the expert or in the Field Explorer.

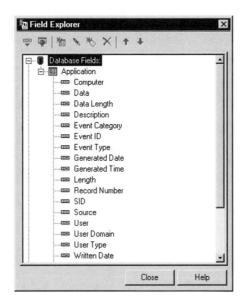

Use these NT Event Log fields just like other database fields to create your report. You can sort, group, and format the report as you normally would. The Event Viewer application can help you identify what some of the available fields contain. You can use the fields to create flexible selection criteria to narrow down your report, and you can also create formulas, if necessary, to calculate or modify the way event-log material appears in the report. Figure 19-5 shows a sample report based on a Windows NT application event log.

Reporting from Web Server Logs

With the ever-increasing proliferation of both the Internet and corporate intranets, there is an equally ever-increasing need to document what pages Web users are pointing their browsers to, as well as when and from where. Most Web servers, such as those from Microsoft, Netscape, and others, keep various amounts and levels of data about Web site visits. What better tool to create Web activity reports than Crystal Reports?

There are several types of Web server logs that you may encounter, depending mostly on the Web server that you are using. All Web server logs are standard delimited ASCII files (a term you don't necessarily need to be familiar with, but it is a common denominator for data-file formats). However, the layout of fields in the files and the information they contain can vary from server to server. There are several "standard" types of log files, including a file type simply known as Standard, and another known as the NCSA Standard, defined by the National Center for Supercomputing Applications for its original Web server. Other Web server developers have adopted both standards. In addition, if you are using Microsoft Internet Information Server (IIS), you'll find additional types of log files available, such as Microsoft's extended log format. When you

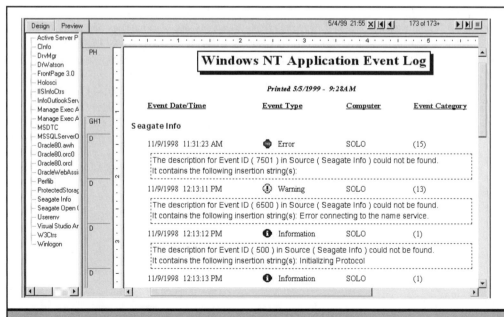

Figure 19-5. *Crystal Report based on Windows NT event log*

configure IIS, you can choose the type of log file that is generated, as well as the fields that are kept in the log file.

As a general rule, Web servers will create a new log file every day, adding statistics to the daily log file as they occur. The filenames consist of variations of the date on which they were created, with a standard file extension. For example, you may see a file named EX990719.LOG, indicating a Microsoft extended-format log for July 19, 1999. These files will be located in a standard directory, such as \WinNT\System32\ LogFiles\W3Csvc1 (this is the default location for Microsoft IIS versions running on Windows NT/2000).

To report on Web server logs, start a new report just as you would for a standard database. You can use the report experts or the Blank Report option. If you use an expert, click the Database button to display the Data Explorer (which will appear automatically if you choose Blank Report). You'll see two categories that may interest you: MS IIS/Proxy Log Files and Web/IIS Log Files. MS IIS/Proxy Log Files will report on "standard" formats, the various Microsoft IIS formats, and Web proxy and Winsock Proxy formats. The Web/IIS Log Files folder will simply report on "standard" and NCSA formatted logs.

Regardless of whether you're using an expert or the Blank Report option, the rest of the prompts will be consistent. If you choose the more generic Web Log option, you'll simply be prompted to choose a drive and directory where the standard or NCSA Web logs are located. You can type or browse to select a local or network drive and directory. If you choose the IIS option, you'll see the Select Log Files and Dates dialog box, as illustrated in Figure 19-6.

Choose the type of log file your Web server uses (look for files in a standard location with the .LOG extension to help determine this). You can also choose the format your Web server uses when writing log files, based on how often it creates a new log file. And, if you prefer to limit Crystal Reports to only using log files within a certain date range, make that selection as well.

When you're finished with your choices, click OK. A new level of the Data Explorer will appear showing the directory name of the log files. Underneath this category, a table-type entry will appear, showing a somewhat cryptic entry for the log files you just chose. Add this table to your report (by double-clicking on the table name or selecting the table name and clicking the Add button) and close the Data Explorer. The list of Web server log fields you can report from will appear in the expert or in the Field Explorer, shown next.

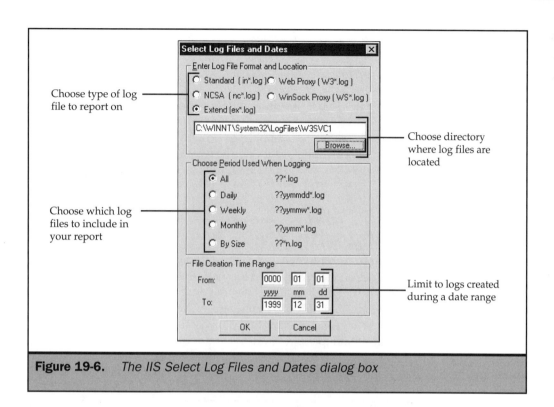

Choose type of log file to report on

Choose directory where log files are located

Choose which log files to include in your report

Limit to logs created during a date range

Figure 19-6.   *The IIS Select Log Files and Dates dialog box*

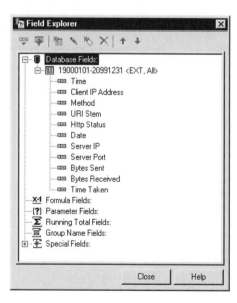

The log fields you see here will vary, depending on the Web server you are using. If you're using Microsoft IIS with NT Server or Windows 2000, you can configure the server to include a variety of helpful statistical fields.

Use these Web server log fields just like other database fields when creating your report. You can sort, group, and format the report as you normally would. You can use the fields to create flexible selection criteria to narrow down your report. You can also create formulas, if necessary, to calculate or modify the way Web server log material appears in the report. Figure 19-7 shows a sample report based on an NT Workstation Personal Web Server log.

Crystal Reporting with XML

The strong expansion of Internet commerce and the proliferation of proprietary data types are combining to produce an increasing need for platform-independent data transfer. A few years ago, a consortium of organizations began collaborating on developing a standard language called eXtensible Markup Language, or *XML*. XML is a format for defining, transmitting, validating, and interpreting data across the Internet, or through electronic file transfers, among independent systems and industries.

While XML has similarities to HTML (HyperText Markup Language, used widely for Internet applications), it has significant differences and advantages. HTML stores

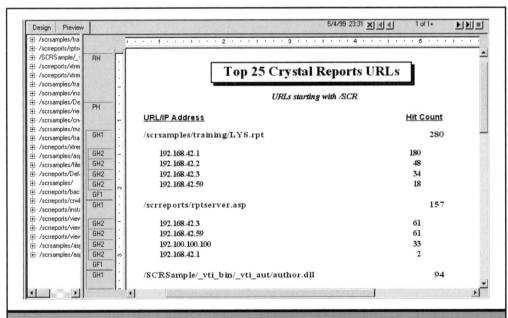

Figure 19-7. *Crystal Report based on IIS Web Server log*

static information and presents it in a static format. XML files can contain a data set, but also can contain or be accompanied by instructions on how to interpret the file content, so that the end user or application can choose how to utilize it. Predictably, several different groups are now working to establish a dominant, widely accepted XML standard, and several standards are emerging. Some standards are focused on certain industries, such as banking or retail, while other standards are intended to be industry independent.

An XML file usually either contains data interpretation instructions (in a "prolog" between the file header and the data content) or is accompanied by an instruction document that defines the XML file content. Generally, these instructions are referred to as *schema*, though some of the types of schema also use "Schema" in their name to confuse the issue. The three most common types of instructions are

- The Document Type Definition (DTD), developed early on primarily for validation of XML file data rather than formatting; DTD instructions can reside within the XML file or as a separate .DTD file, and use a different language syntax than XML.

- The XML Schema, developed by the World Wide Web Consortium (W3C) as an international standard. XML Schema instructions reside in an .XML file, and use XML syntax.

- eXtensible Stylesheet Language (XSL), which has begun to replace DTD due to its broader format-oriented syntax. XSL instructions can reside within the XML file or in a separate .XSL file.

To use an XML file as a source for a report, Crystal Reports 8.5 includes an ODBC driver with a pre-configured ODBC data source name of CRXML V36, allowing you to connect to different types of XML files for reporting.

Note *This driver is a Merant DataDirect ODBC driver, and has some limitations that may preclude connecting to your XML file. Merant supports three standard XML types: XML Data Island files, XML ADO persisted XML files, and raw XML files (with or without schemas). This driver does not support the XML Schema developed by the W3C, and data fields longer than 255 characters are truncated. For more information about these and other restrictions, see "XML" in Crystal Reports online help.*

Figure 19-8 shows an ADO 2.5 persisted format XML file, to which the CRXMLV36 ODBC driver can connect. The file consists of a simple data set of customer names and contact last names, with tags identified in the file header and prolog.

To report on a supported XML file, start a new report just as you would for a standard database. You can use the report experts or the Blank Report option. If you use an expert, click the Database button to display the Data Explorer (which will appear automatically if you choose Blank Report). Expand the ODBC section and select the CRXMLV36 driver. The ODBC XML Driver Connection dialog box appears. You can either type the path to the directory in which the XML file resides, or click the Ellipsis (…) button to browse to the location.

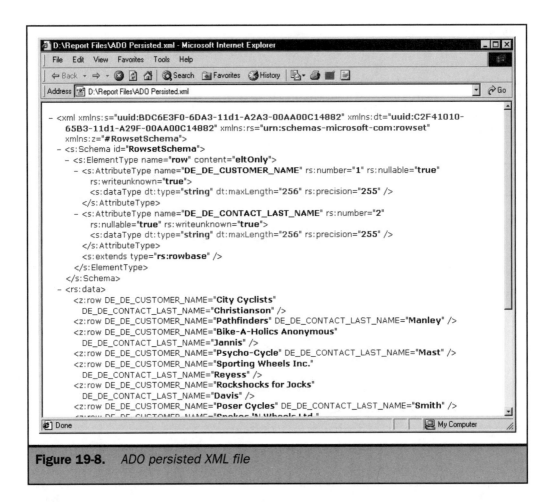

Figure 19-8. *ADO persisted XML file*

Note   *This ODBC connection was created with the default requirement for a user ("user") and password ("password") to be entered. If you set up your own ODBC connection using this driver, you can turn off the user/password requirement on the Advanced tab of the ODBC administration tool.*

When the directory has been selected and user and password entered, click OK. The Data Explorer redisplays, with the CRXMLV36 connection expanded to list all the XML files in the selected directory.

Although all XML files are displayed and can be selected, they will not return valid data to Crystal Reports if they are not organized in a supported XML format.

Select the desired XML file from the list and add it to the report (by double-clicking the table name or selecting the table name and clicking the Add button) and close the Data Explorer. The list of fields you can report from will appear in the expert or in the Field Explorer.

Figure 19-9 shows a Crystal Report generated from the ADO persisted format XML file shown previously in Figure 19-8.

You can also use the ODBC Administrator tool (from your Control Panel) to create your own connections to XML databases using the provided Merant driver. There are specific requirements you'll need to follow to allow Crystal to successfully connect to a supported XML file, and the requirements (for example, the use of table and row hints) differ among the supported types. The Advanced tab of the ODBC XML Driver Setup, shown in Figure 19-10, provides options specific to each XML type.

The Crystal Decisions Web site and the Crystal Reports online help system provide examples and more detailed information on how Crystal Reports connects to and reports from supported XML formats such as IE5 XML Data Islands and ADO 2.5 persisted XML. This information is expected to be augmented as XML standards evolve.

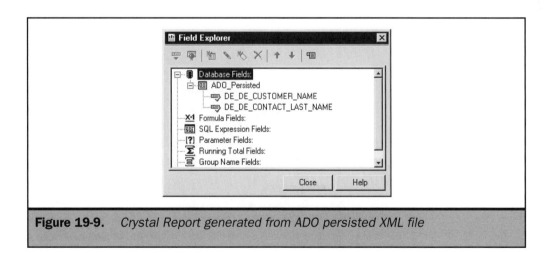

Figure 19-9. *Crystal Report generated from ADO persisted XML file*

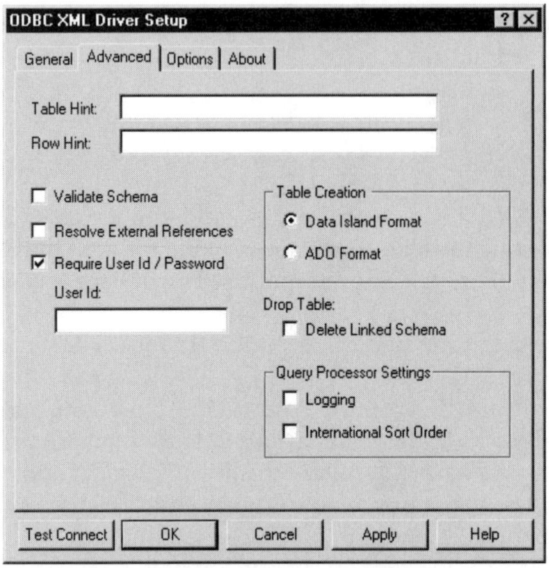

Figure 19-10. ODBC XML Driver Setup Advanced tab

The
Complete
Reference

Crystal
Reports

Part II

Web Reporting with Crystal Reports
and Crystal Enterprise

Chapter 20

Crystal Reports 8.5 Web Alternatives

511

So far, this book has discussed many techniques for creating sophisticated reports with the Crystal Reports 8.5 designer. And, Part III of the book discusses methods for integrating those reports into your custom Windows applications with Visual Basic. However, despite the uncertainty of the "dot-com culture," business organizations, both large and small, continue to turn to Web-based technology for both internal corporate intranets and the Internet. As such, providing a way to display your reports in a Web browser is crucial.

Without argument, the most dramatic change in Crystal Reports 8.5 is the choice of Web reporting alternatives. In particular, the introduction of *Crystal Enterprise* gives you a whole new way to roll your Crystal Reports out to the Web. Whereas previous Crystal Reports Web alternatives were generally limited to supporting a small number of concurrent users, Crystal Enterprise now allows you to implement much larger Web-based reporting environments, potentially serving up to thousands of Web-based report viewers.

Crystal Enterprise has replaced the Crystal Reports 8 Web Component Server. In fact, if you install Crystal Reports 8.5 on a Web server containing an existing Crystal Reports 8 Web Component Server, you'll receive a message indicating that the previous Web Component Server has been removed. The ability of the Crystal Reports 8 Web Component Server to interpret a Crystal Reports .RPT file in a Web server virtual directory and have the .RPT file act as a Web page hyperlink is no longer available with Crystal Reports 8.5 alone. You must install Crystal Enterprise to maintain this capability. However, the ability of Crystal Reports 8.5 to integrate Crystal Reports into Microsoft Active Server Pages remains.

This new architecture provides three general approaches to placing a Crystal Report on the Web—either on your internal corporate intranet or on the entire Internet:

- **Export static reports to HTML format (covered in this chapter)** In this case, you just export your report to one of several different HTML formats, much as you would export a Word or Excel file. Viewers can simply open the HTML file in their browser, or the file can be placed on a Web server for viewing.

- **Use the RDC Runtime Automation Server with Microsoft Active Server Pages (covered in Chapter 21)** This method, which requires installing the Crystal Reports Report Designer Component (RDC) on your Web server, provides a high level of Web integration for reports, virtually identical to the level of flexibility allowed with Visual Basic. This method, however, does not take advantage of the multi-tier, shared processing capability of Crystal Enterprise. As such, it is appropriate for smaller volume Web-based reporting systems.

- **Using Crystal Enterprise (covered in Chapters 22, 23, and 24)** Crystal Enterprise provides a rich, multi-tier/multi-server method of hosting real-time and automatically scheduled Crystal Reports on the Web. You can use the standard "out of the box" user interface provided by Crystal Enterprise, or you may completely customize the user interface using HTML and new Crystal Server Pages.

Crystal Reports Web Alternatives Compared

Each of the Crystal Reports Web approaches listed in the preceding section has advantages and disadvantages, based on your level of Web-development expertise, the sophistication of your reports, how fluid the data you want to present is, the number of users you want to serve, and your budget. It's helpful to examine your reporting requirements, expertise level, and hardware and software environment before you decide on a particular Web reporting direction. Choosing one method won't necessarily preclude you from switching later. For example, it's perfectly acceptable to design a simple report that you initially just export to HTML, and then later decide to give Web viewers real-time access to it via Active Server Pages (ASP) or Crystal Enterprise. However, if you design a very interactive report with drill-down capabilities, you won't achieve the desired level of interactivity with a simple HTML export—you'll need to use ASP or Crystal Enterprise.

Table 20-1 highlights the advantages and disadvantages of each Web reporting method.

If you just want to occasionally allow a simple, noninteractive report to be viewed in a Web browser, you may consider simply exporting to HTML right from Crystal Reports (discussed later in this chapter). This simple approach won't allow interactivity with your report (drill-down, on-demand subreports, or use of the group tree) and won't show data in real time. But, a simple detail or summary report that can be viewed in a few pages can easily be opened directly in a Web browser. A viewer simply uses File | Open (Internet Explorer) or File | Open Page (Netscape Navigator/ Communicator) to view the HTML file directly from a local or network drive without a Web server, or they can click a link or enter the correct URL to view the exported file from a Web server.

Integration Method	Advantages	Disadvantages
Static HTML export	Very simple and fast to implement. No particular HTML or Web development expertise required. Doesn't require a Web server to implement—viewers can just open HTML files from a local or network disk drive in their browser. Can be accomplished with Standard, Professional, or Developer versions of Crystal Reports 8.5.	Reports are static—if the database changes, the exported report won't reflect the change until it's reexported. No interactivity, such as drill-down or group-tree navigation. Only allows limited printing of the report. Full printing and export capabilities require other methods.

Table 20-1. *Comparison of Web Reporting Alternatives*

Integration Method	Advantages	Disadvantages
RDC Automation Server with Active Server Pages	Offers flexible Web integration—capabilities are virtually identical to Visual Basic with the RDC Automation Server. You may modify virtually every aspect of your reports at runtime. Provides complete report interactivity, including drill-down and group-tree navigation. Allows real-time reporting via a Web browser—the report can be refreshed to get the most current data. Low-cost solution—Crystal Reports 8.5 Developer Edition includes five concurrent access licenses at no additional charge.	Requires Crystal Reports 8 Developer Edition—the Standard and Professional Editions don't support this method. Supporting more than five concurrent users requires additional software licenses from Crystal Decisions. Limited performance and capability for large numbers of users—a single-tier solution that can place heavy loads on the Web server. Only compatible with Microsoft Web servers running ASP—Netscape or other Web servers won't work with this method.
Crystal Enterprise Standard	Provides complete interactivity when viewing a report, including drill-down and group-tree navigation. High flexibility for user interface customization with new Crystal Server Page developer interfaces. Allows real-time reporting via a Web browser—the report can be refreshed to get the most current data. Ability to automatically schedule reports to run at regular intervals Ability to place Crystal Enterprise components on a computer separate from the Web server to lighten Web server load. Can operate with any Windows Web server that supports Microsoft, Netscape, or CGI interfaces, as well as certain Unix Web servers.	Requires Crystal Reports 8 Professional or Developer Edition—the Standard Edition doesn't include Crystal Enterprise Standard. No Report Designer. Component-like ability to modify report appearance and behavior at the report object level at runtime. Supporting more than five concurrent users requires upgrade to Crystal Enterprise Professional. No ability to set up multiple user accounts or integrate with NT security. Not capable of scaling components across multiple computers, nor setting up fault-tolerant servers. The exception is the ability to separate the Web server from remaining Crystal Enterprise components.

Table 20-1.   *Comparison of Web Reporting Alternatives* (continued)

Integration Method	Advantages	Disadvantages
Crystal Enterprise Professional	All the same interactivity, scheduling, and developer interface features of Crystal Enterprise Standard. Very scalable, potentially supporting thousands of Web report viewers with multi-server implementation and fault tolerance/load balancing. Complete security model, including multiple users and ability to integrate with Windows NT/2000 security.	Additional administration and knowledge buildup requirements. No Report Designer Component–like ability to modify report appearance and behavior at the report object level at runtime. Can become very expensive, depending on software licensing options chosen and the number of separate computer platforms used for multi-tier processing.

Table 20-1.   *Comparison of Web Reporting Alternatives* (continued)

If you want to provide more interactivity, or your report viewers need access to "live" real-time reporting, you need to choose between the ASP and Crystal Enterprise methods. By using the RDC Runtime Automation Server with a Microsoft Web server running ASP, you can achieve a very high level of report control from a Web page. As with Visual Basic developer interfaces, you can control almost every aspect of the report at runtime, including section formatting, setting formulas, and changing fonts, colors, and other formatting from within your code. However, Crystal Decision's latest product offering, Crystal Enterprise, takes Web reporting to a whole new level. You may still wonder, though, "Which method should I use—Active Server Pages or Crystal Enterprise?"

If your Web reporting requirements are relatively small and can be satisfied with a Web browser connecting directly to the Web server that runs the report against the database (known as a *single-tier* solution), the RDC/Active Server Page scenario may work best for you. It allows you complete control over how reports are customized, formatted, and controlled at runtime, as well as allowing complete interactivity with the displayed report. Just remember: This method is a low-capacity, limited concurrency solution. While you may purchase additional licenses to expand the five concurrent users supported by the Crystal Reports Developer Edition, there are no extensive caching or sharing optimization features in this method. And, your Web server will end up running report queries against the database before returning results to the Web browser—your Web server may become overloaded very quickly in this scenario.

Note *Detailed information on integrating reports on the Web with the Crystal Reports Report Designer Component can be found in Chapter 21.*

The whole concept of Crystal Enterprise is to go beyond the single-tier limitations of the RDC/Active Server Page methodology. By separating the Web server from the rest of the Crystal Enterprise components (Crystal Enterprise Professional can take this separation of components to a possibly absurd level), you are immediately allowing the Web server to do what it is designed to do—serve up Web pages. Other computers on the network can be tasked with formatting reports, running database queries, managing report caches to send already generated report pages to the Web browser, and so forth.

If this "sharing of the reporting load" methodology isn't enough benefit, Crystal Enterprise also allows automatic scheduling of reports. This entirely new concept in Crystal Reporting has been taken from Crystal Decisions' lesser-known product, Seagate Info. This feature allows you to schedule reports to run either on a one-time basis or on some recurring basis, such as once a day, once a week, and so on. When a viewer launches Crystal Enterprise in their browser, they can look at a report's history and view any of the previously scheduled reports without requiring a database query to be run.

And finally, Crystal Enterprise includes a Software Development Kit based on Crystal Server Pages, or CSP. This spin-off of Microsoft's Active Server Page implementation allows you to completely customize the Crystal Enterprise user interface, access Enterprise's scheduling capabilities, and control report customization at runtime. The only piece missing from the Crystal Enterprise Software Development Kit is the flexibility to modify minute report formatting and behavior at runtime, similar to the flexibility provided by the Report Designer Component.

So, there are probably few arguments that should convince you to design a Web-based reporting system around the RDC Automation Server and Microsoft Active Server Pages when a five-user copy of Crystal Enterprise Standard is in the same box as Crystal Reports Developer Edition. If you have an existing RDC-based Web reporting environment that suits you well and you only want to take advantage of a new Crystal Reports 8.5 feature, such as Report Alerts or PDF export capabilities, then you may probably comfortably continue to use this solution. And, if your Web reporting requirements dictate that you be able to completely customize the behavior of a report based on user input, you may want to stick with the RDC. However, if you're looking to create a new Web-based reporting system from the ground up and your reporting customization can be handled comfortably with parameter fields (which are fully supported by Enterprise), you should give most serious consideration to Crystal Enterprise.

When looking to support larger enterprise-wide or Internet-based reporting scenarios that can increase your user count quickly, you'll probably also want to lean toward Crystal Enterprise Professional, the upgraded version of the Crystal Enterprise Standard product included with Crystal Reports Professional and Developer editions. Because of Enterprise's built-in scalability, scheduling, and sharing features, you'll almost certainly realize improved performance over an RDC/Active Server Page–based implementation. Just be prepared—many new customers have raised their eyebrows when presented with Crystal Decisions initial pricing structure for Crystal Enterprise Professional.

Comparisons between Crystal Enterprise Standard and Professional editions, along with much more detailed information on Crystal Enterprise usage, implementation, and customization, can be found in Chapters 22, 23, and 24.

Exporting to Static HTML

More and more, organizations are looking to distribute Crystal Reports to a large audience in a Web format, through a company intranet or the Internet. To provide this capability, you need to convert your report to Hypertext Markup Language (HTML) format—the "markup language" understood by Web browsers. If you've decided to provide only static, noninteractive reports in a Web browser, you simply need to export the report from Crystal Reports, just as you'd export to a Word document or Excel spreadsheet.

Caution *With Crystal Reports 8.5, Crystal Decisions has introduced Crystal Broadcast Licensing. This now affects organizations that generally want to supply online reporting access to more than 50 users. If you are placing your exported reports on a Web server that can reasonably be expected to be available to 50 or more users, consult the Crystal Reports license agreement to ensure you comply with this new requirement.*

Simply start Crystal Reports and open or create the report you want to export to HTML. Remember that whatever is visible on your screen is what will be exported to HTML. If you want to export the main report, make sure the Preview tab is clicked. If you want to export just a drill-down tab, select the correct drill-down tab before exporting. Then, choose File | Print | Export from the pull-down menus, or click the Export button in the Standard toolbar. Figure 20-1 shows a sample report, consisting of a report containing a title surrounded by a border on all four sides and a drop shadow, and an underlain "watermark" graphic.

When you choose the Export command, the resulting dialog box allows you to choose the format and destination of your report. You'll be concerned with the two HTML format options available in the Format drop-down list: HTML 3.2 and HTML 4.0 (DHTML). The different versions refer to the different extensions of the HTML language that Crystal Reports can use. To determine which version of HTML you want to use, experiment with your own exports and the browsers that your report viewers will use. Typically, Version 4 (dynamic HTML) will better represent the actual formatting of the report in the Web browser. However, you'll need newer versions of a Web browser (Internet Explorer or Netscape Navigator/Communicator Version 4 or later) to use DHTML. If you're using an older version of these browsers, you may see better results with HTML 3.2.

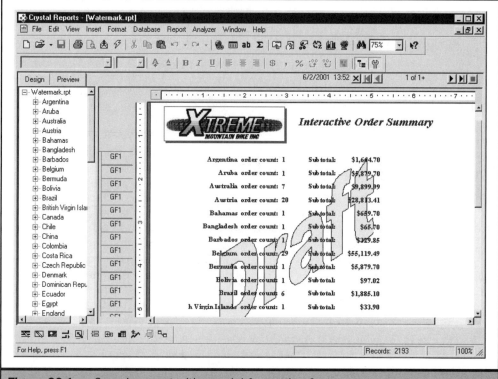

Figure 20-1. *Sample report with special formatting features*

Caution	*Remember that with HTML, particularly HTML 3.2, some "fancy" report formatting (such as drop shadows or special fonts) may not export to HTML properly. You'll want to try some test exports and view the resulting reports in the Web browser that will be used by the majority of your report viewers. That way, you can see what your reports will ultimately look like.*

No matter what destination you ultimately choose from the Destination drop-down list, Crystal Reports must write the HTML code and any associated graphics files (for charts, maps, and bitmaps) to a disk folder. You will be asked to make several choices about how and where you want your report exported, as illustrated in Figure 20-2.

Crystal Reports will create a whole new directory to contain the HTML and graphics files that will make up your report. The drive and folder boxes will let you choose an existing directory *under which* a new directory will be created. Type the name of the new directory in the Directory Name box (Crystal Reports will name the new directory HTML by default). If you wish to place the HTML in a specific folder referred to by a Web "home" page, make sure you export to the predetermined folder on the

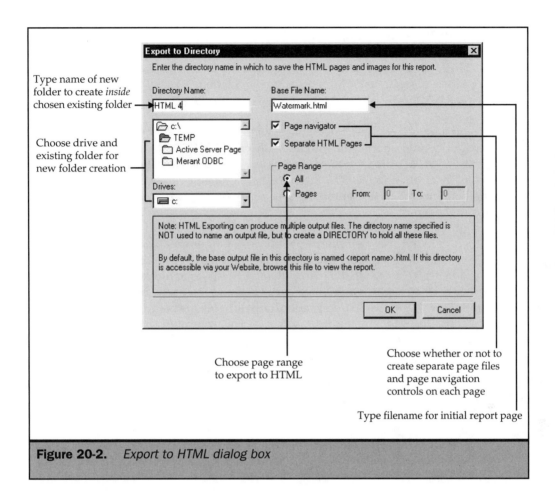

Type name of new
folder to create *inside*
chosen existing folder

Choose drive and
existing folder for
new folder creation

Choose page range
to export to HTML

Choose whether or not to
create separate page files
and page navigation
controls on each page

Type filename for initial report page

Figure 20-2.   *Export to HTML dialog box*

Web server referred to by the page. Crystal Reports will place the name of the report
into the Base File Name box by default. You may want to change this filename to
something your Web server expects (for example, DEFAULT.HTM), if you are
exporting to a Web server folder.

You may also use the Page Navigator and Separate HTML Pages check boxes
(which typically are helpful only with reports that are more than one page in length).
If you check Separate HTML Pages, Crystal Reports will export sequentially numbered
HTML pages, one for each page in the report. For example, if you're exporting a
drill-down tab that consists of four pages, and you chose DEFAULT.HTM as the
base filename, the first page of the report will be exported to DEFAULT.HTM, the
second to DEFAULT1.HTM, the third to DEFAULT2.HTM, and the fourth to
DEFAULTLAST.HTM. If you don't check this box, all three report pages will be
combined into one larger DEFAULT.HTM.

If you check Page Navigator, Crystal Reports will place First, Next, Previous, and Last navigation hyperlinks at the bottom of each page that is exported. If you export to separate HTML pages, these links will navigate to the proper separate HTML page. If you don't export to separate HTML pages, the navigation links will still appear inside the one large HTML page, simply moving the viewer to different locations within the one HTML page.

Once you've specified all export options, click OK. If the folder you specified doesn't exist, Crystal Reports will automatically create it. If the folder already exists and contains an HTML file with the same name as you specified, the old file will be overwritten. In addition to the HTML report file, Crystal Reports will create sequentially numbered .JPG graphics files—one for each bitmap, chart, or map contained in the report.

When you point your browser to the folder and view the HTML file, you'll see the exported report in the browser window, as shown in Figure 20-3.

Notice that not all Crystal Reports formatting options are properly converted to HTML version 3.2. You'll see that the drop shadow on the logo did not export properly. And text was pushed aside by the watermark graphic, rather than be overlain by it. Even with HTML 4.0, the logo drop shadow still didn't export (although drop shadows on textual elements usually will export with 4.0). The watermark appears properly, however. It's a good idea to try sample exports as you're developing your report, to make sure you don't depend on any features that may not export properly.

Note *Don't forget that reports exported to HTML are static. They will simply show database information as it existed when the report was exported. The only way to update the HTML reports is to refresh the report in Crystal Reports and export again. Also, drilling down and using group trees won't work with exported HTML reports. If you want viewers to be able to refresh reports on their own, as well as interact with the report by drilling down and using the group tree, use Crystal Enterprise or Active Server Pages, as described in Part II of this book.*

Hyperlink Capabilities

Crystal Reports 8.5 provides hyperlink capabilities so that you can build in hyperlinks in your reports. Virtually any objects on your report, such as text objects, database fields, charts, maps, or bitmap objects, can be linked to Web pages, e-mail addresses, other Crystal Reports, or other Windows programs. When you point to an object with an attached hyperlink, your mouse cursor turns into the now-familiar pointing finger. Click, and your Web browser will launch the Web site, your e-mail program will launch a new message window, or the Windows program or file that is specified will be launched.

Hyperlinks are created right in the Crystal Reports designer. In either the Design or Preview tab, select the object you want to create the hyperlink for. Then, choose Insert | Hyperlink from the pull-down menus, right-click, and choose Format Field (or a similar format option) from the pop-up menu, or click the Hyperlink toolbar button from the standard toolbar. The Format Editor will appear. If it's not already selected, click the Hyperlink tab, shown in Figure 20-4.

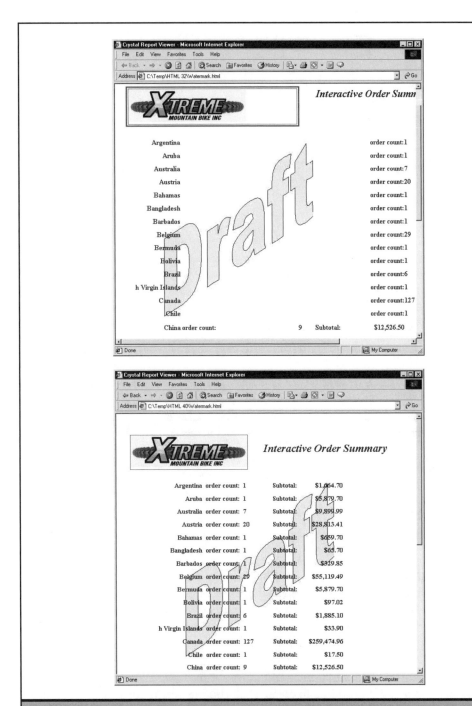

Figure 20-3. *Export comparison between HTML 3.2 and HTML 4.0*

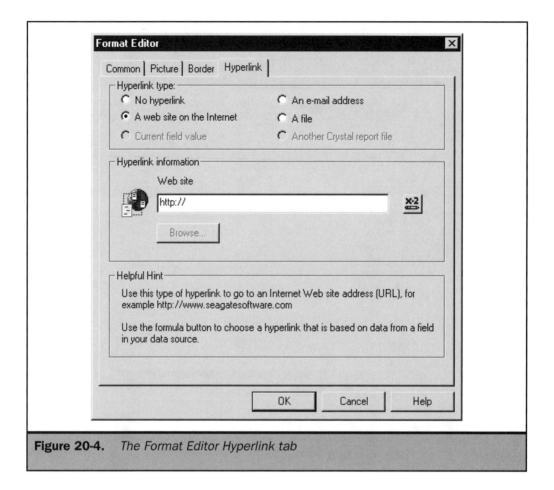

Figure 20-4. *The Format Editor Hyperlink tab*

Choose the type of hyperlink you'd like to create:

- **No Hyperlink** If a hyperlink has already been assigned to this object, clicking this radio button will clear the hyperlink.

- **An E-Mail Address** Click this radio button and add the e-mail address you want the hyperlink to send e-mail to in the Hyperlink Information text box after the mailto: text. If you'd like to create a conditional string formula to customize the hyperlink based on a database field or conditional value, click the conditional formula button next to the text box.

- **A Website on the Internet** Click this radio button and add the Web site URL you want the hyperlink to launch in the Hyperlink Information text box after the http:// text. If you'd like to create a conditional string formula to customize the hyperlink based on a database field or conditional value, click the conditional formula button next to the text box.

- **A File**   Click this radio button and add the path and filename of the file you want the hyperlink to launch in the Hyperlink Information text box after the file:/// text. If you'd like to create a conditional string formula to customize the hyperlink based on a database field or conditional value, click the conditional formula button next to the text box.

- **Current Field Value**   This option is available only if you've chosen a string database field on the report. In this case, the hyperlink will simply be the value of text from the database. To correctly use this option, the database field must return a complete Web site URL (including the http:// prefix), an e-mail address preceded with the mailto: command, or a path and filename preceded with the file:/// command.

- **Another Crystal Report File**   This option is available only if *no objects are selected* on the report. In this case, type the path and filename for another Crystal Report to launch, or click the Browse button to use a file dialog box to look for the .RPT file. The chosen report will be added to this report as an on-demand subreport (discussed in detail in Chapter 11).

To further benefit the report viewer, you may wish to click the Common tab on the Format Editor and add a tool tip indicating what the hyperlink does. Click the conditional formula button labeled Tool Tip text and enter a string formula (perhaps just a string literal between two sets of quotation marks) that will display when the viewer moves his or her mouse over the object.

Caution   *While hyperlinks do export properly to HTML, tool tips aren't retained when you export to HTML. However, if you select the Report Designer Component/ASP option or Crystal Enterprise to display reports, tool tips will appear.*

Once you've specified all necessary information, click OK to close the Format Editor. When you preview the report in Crystal Reports, you'll see the mouse cursor change to a familiar pointing finger hyperlink cursor when you point to the object. If you added a tool tip, it will appear in a small yellow box. When you click your mouse button, the hyperlink will launch the Web page, e-mail Send dialog box, or Windows file.

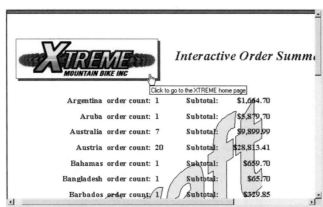

After you create a hyperlink, follow the same steps you used to create it to modify or remove it. If you are modifying your report in the Preview tab, you may find it difficult to select an object that you've defined a hyperlink for. If you point to it with your mouse, your mouse cursor will change to a hyperlink cursor and you'll actually execute the hyperlink if you click. If you need to select an object in the Preview tab that has a hyperlink associated with it, SHIFT-click or right-click on the object to select it.

Hyperlinks aren't applicable only to reports exported viewed on the Web. When you view reports in the Crystal Reports Preview tab, or view a report integrated with a VB program, hyperlinks will work as you expect. Just remember that a viewer who is using Crystal Reports needs a network connection to your corporate intranet or the Internet to successfully use Web or e-mail hyperlinks.

Chapter 21

Crystal Reports and Microsoft Active Server Pages

As discussed in Chapter 20, there are several general ways to integrate real-time Crystal Reports in a Web page. In addition to the Crystal Enterprise (discussed in Chapters 22, 23, and 24), you can integrate Crystal Reports into your Web pages using Microsoft Active Server Pages (ASP) and the Report Designer Component (RDC) Runtime Automation Server. Using this option is quite different from using the Crystal Enterprise. The benefit is that you have complete control and flexibility for your reports, just as you do when using the RDC Automation Server within Visual Basic—Crystal Enterprise doesn't provide this level of individual report customization. The downside is that the process can be much more labor intensive than the "out of the box" Crystal Enterprise user interface. Copious amounts of code are involved. And, you don't gain the scheduling and multi-tier server benefits of Enterprise.

Active Server Pages and VBScript Overview

The original language of the Web, Hypertext Markup Language (HTML), can be used to create attractive, hyperlinked pages with graphics, various font sizes, and (with the advent of newer HTML extensions, such as dynamic HTML) more interactivity and multimedia features. However, being a "markup language" instead of a true procedural or event-driven development language, HTML falls far short of providing all the flexibility you may need to create full Web-based custom applications. To help fill this void, the industry has moved toward *scripting* languages that allow browsers to perform much more sophisticated and intricate procedures. Two scripting languages are established: *JavaScript* is a scripting language based on Java, and *VBScript* is a scripting language based on Microsoft's Visual Basic for Applications (VBA). JavaScript is supported by both major browser vendors, Microsoft and Netscape. VBScript, generally, is limited to versions of Microsoft Internet Explorer (IE).

JavaScript and VBScript are *client-side* scripting languages—both being interpreted by the browser after being downloaded in a Web page. The scripts are not compiled into machine-executable code and generally cannot make database connections to a corporate database. And, because these scripts execute on a browser that can be affected by any number of client-side variables, a developer cannot always expect consistent results.

To provide more flexibility and offer connectivity to corporate databases, Microsoft also implements *server-side* scripting on its Internet Information Server for Windows NT Server and Windows 2000, as well as Personal Web Server for Windows NT Workstation. In this instance, the scripting language is interpreted by the Web server instead of the Web browser client. The results of the server-executed script are then sent to the Web browser as HTML. Because the script is executed on the server, you can create much more robust and flexible applications that are browser-independent—all that is sent to the browser is HTML. Microsoft's implementation of server-side scripting is called *Active Server Pages* (ASP). When a Web server has ASP support installed, pages scripted with ASP are given a file extension of .ASP instead of .HTM. The Web server will then scan the .ASP file for server-side script and execute any it finds, sending the results of the script to the browser.

To enhance ASP even more, Microsoft extends the Component Object Model (COM), which is discussed in more detail in the Visual Basic chapters in Part III of this book, to its Web server platform. Because of this, the RDC Automation Server can be integrated with server-side scripts to create extensive reporting flexibility in Web applications. By using the full VBA power of ASP, combined with the ability of the RDC Automation Server to control almost every aspect of a report at run time, you can create VB-like applications that integrate reports in a Web browser.

Although both VBScript and JScript (Microsoft's version of JavaScript) can be executed in ASP, only VBScript is discussed in this book. Also, Crystal Decision's example ASPs installed with Crystal Reports all utilize VBScript.

Visual InterDev as a Development Tool

Microsoft's Visual InterDev has established itself as the de facto standard for ASP development. It is designed to look very similar to Visual Basic and offers much of the same functionality for developing ASPs as Visual Basic does for Windows applications. In addition to providing a complete HTML page and forms designer, Visual InterDev's code window mimics that of VB, providing automatic code completion and different font coloring to indicate the syntax of VBScript or JScript. Visual InterDev can also debug server- and client-side scripts with integrated debugging tools. Microsoft FrontPage can also edit ASP, but not with the same debugging features and database integration features of Visual InterDev. Since ASPs are straight ASCII files, you can even use a simple text editor, such as Notepad, to edit them.

While you'll derive a good deal of coding and debugging benefit from using Visual InterDev to develop your Web application's user interface, you won't enjoy quite the same level of integration and debugging with the RDC Automation Server that you do with Visual Basic. The RDC Automation Server's object model is implemented in Visual InterDev in such a way that automatic code completion is a little trickier, or not possible. However, this lack of similar interactivity and debugging capability is tempered somewhat by Crystal Reports 8.5 Design-Time Controls for Visual InterDev (discussed later in the chapter). Using a simple "fill in the box" interface, you can add Crystal Reports to your Active Server Pages with a minimum of effort.

Caution   *Because using Active Server Pages requires the RDC Automation Server, you must purchase Crystal Reports 8 Developer Edition. The Standard or Professional Edition doesn't include the RDC. Make sure that the Report Designer Component is specified when you install Crystal Reports on your Web server. If this choice has not been made, you need to reinstall Crystal Reports and specify this option.*

Also, don't forget Crystal Decisions' five-concurrent-user limit with the RDC. If you wish to support more than five concurrent users, you must purchase additional software licenses from the vendor.

Crystal-Supplied Sample ASPs

Probably the best way to begin working with Crystal Reports integration inside Active Server Pages is to view and evaluate the sample ASPs that are installed automatically when you install Crystal Reports 8.5 on a Microsoft Web server. After installing Crystal Reports on a Web server, point your browser to **http://*Web server*/scrsamples**. Choose one of the Active Server Page samples to run ASP examples of different types of report integration. To evaluate the actual ASP code, you need read access to the Crystal Reports directory on your Web server. Use Visual InterDev or Notepad to look in *Crystal Reports program directory*\Samples*language*\Code\Web\Active Server Pages for the different ASP files. They are well documented and give you many good examples of how to implement Automation Server coding inside Active Server Pages.

Or, you can view a sample ASP-based Web site on the companion CD-ROM to this book. Create a virtual directory on your Web server (if necessary, contact your Webmaster for help in creating this directory) and copy files from the Active Server Pages folder of the companion CD-ROM to the folder. When you then point your browser to the new virtual directory, you can interact with a small sample report application. Use Visual InterDev, Notepad, or another editor to view the HTML and ASP code in this application.

What Is RPTSERVER.ASP?

As you look through ASP example files supplied by Crystal Decisions or included on the companion CD-ROM, you'll notice that ASP Web reports are displayed in one of several Crystal Report Viewers. Note that the report viewers are always pointed to another file called RPTSERVER.ASP. This Crystal-supplied ASP is a very important part of Crystal Reports' integration with Active Server Pages.

When you integrate a report with the RDC Automation Server and Visual Basic (as covered in Chapter 26), you use the separate Report Viewer ActiveX control to show the report in a VB window. However, because integrating with the Web means your eventual display target is a Web browser, you need to consider some other viewing alternatives when using ASPs. The available Web report viewers—ActiveX, Java for Browser JVM, Java Plug-In, Netscape Plug-In, HTML Frames, and HTML Page—can all be used with ASPs. In fact, the report viewer for ActiveX is the same CRVIEWER.DLL module used to display reports with the RDC Automation Server in Visual Basic.

Because these viewers use Crystal Reports' page-on-demand architecture, they expect report pages to be fed to them by the RDC Automation Server's PageEngine object. This rather complicated logic and interaction is handled by RPTSERVER.ASP. Although you might be able to write your own ASP code to replace the function of RPTSERVER.ASP, one look at the ASP code in this file will probably convince you that it won't be worth the effort.

The RDC Automation Server Object Model in ASPs

Because Active Server Pages support COM automation servers, you can implement Crystal Reports integration in ASP in much the same way as you do in Visual Basic. The complete RDC Automation Server object model is available for you to use in your

Active Server Pages. You can set properties and execute methods for different Automation Server objects to customize report behavior. Typically, you'll use controls your user has completed on a form, or perhaps values your ASP is retrieving from a database, to control report appearance at run time.

The Application and Report Objects

As with Visual Basic, two base-level objects must be initially declared in your Web project: the Application object and the Report object (the Application object is used in VB only if you are integrating an external .RPT file). The Application object needs to be declared only once, at the beginning of a project. The Application object is then used to open a Report object, and then is generally not used throughout the rest of the project. Because these objects must remain in scope throughout the project and all associated ASP files, they are declared as *session* variables, which retain their values and remain in scope throughout an entire ASP project. Here's sample ASP code to declare them:

```
' CREATE THE APPLICATION OBJECT
If Not IsObject (session("oApp")) Then
    Set session("oApp") = Server.CreateObject("CrystalRuntime.Application")
End If

' CREATE THE REPORT OBJECT
reportname = Path & "Xtreme Orders.rpt"
'Path must be physical path, not virtual path
If IsObject(session("oRpt")) then
    Set session("oRpt") = nothing
End If
Set session("oRpt") = session("oApp").OpenReport(reportname, 1)

' Disable error messages/prompts on the Web server
session("oRpt").MorePrintEngineErrorMessages = False
session("oRpt").EnableParameterPrompting = False
```

A few notes about this sample VBScript code:

■ Variables don't need to be identified with DIM or declared before use. In VB terms, no Option Explicit statement has been executed. While this may seem to ease your coding requirements, you need to remember that this means that all variables used in this fashion are variants. Some RDC Automation Server methods require that variables be passed with a specific data type. In those cases, use VBScript typecasting functions, such as CStr and CInt, to correctly cast variables when passing them.

■ The report file has been preceded with a Path variable, which is assigned in previous VBScript not shown here (look in the sample Crystal ASP or the sample ASP on the book's companion CD-ROM for the routine to generate this variable). The path must be the physical path to the report file (for example, C:\REPORTS) because the RDC Automation Server can't resolve Web server virtual paths. If you know that the .RPT file will be in a fixed, known location, you can skip this entire section of code and simply supply a physical path and filename to the OpenReport method.

■ The Application object is declared only once. If this section of VBScript is executed again, the previous declaration of oApp will remain. However, if there is a previous declaration of the Report object (presumably for a different report that may have been processed in a previous pass through this code), it will be set to Nothing before being set to the new report with the Application object's OpenReport method.

■ The MorePrintEngineErrorMessages property of the Report object is set to false, as is the EnableParameterPrompting property. This reduces the chances of any error messages or prompts appearing on the Web server if unexpected problems occur with a report request. If the RDC Automation Server displays a message or prompt on the Web server screen while a browser is waiting for a report request, the Webmaster likely won't be sitting by, waiting to respond to the Web server message. The browser session will hang, or eventually time out, if this happens.

Note   *For complete information on the RDC Automation Server's object model, methods, and properties, refer to Chapter 26, or look through the CRRDC.HLP file located in Program Files\Seagate Software\Report Designer Component.*

Manipulating the Report Object

Once the Report object has been assigned to an .RPT file, you can use your user interface elements, such as controls on the calling form, to customize the way the report behaves. Use objects, collections, methods, and properties for the Report object to control report behavior.

Here are some examples:

```
session("oRpt").DiscardSavedData
session("oRpt").RecordSelectionFormula = _
   "{Orders.Order Amount} < " & CStr(Request.Form("value"))
```

This code first discards any saved data records that may exist within the .RPT file. It then sets the Report object's RecordSelectionFormula property to limit the report to orders over the amount supplied by the user in a control named "value" on the calling form. Notice that the CStr function is used just to make sure that the entire value being submitted to the RecordSelectionProperty is a string.

The following sample code is used to pass a value to a report parameter field:

```
session("oRpt").ParameterFields(1).AddCurrentValue _
CInt(Request.Form("txtTaxRate")))
```

Again, this code is passing the value from the calling form object "txtTaxRate" to the AddCurrentValue method. This method applies to a member of the ParameterFields collection of the Report object. Again, note that you should use a type declaration function (such as CInt) to ensure that the proper data type is being passed to the RDC Automation Server.

After you set all necessary properties for the report object and are ready to process the report, you may need to execute the Report object's ReadRecords method to actually populate the report with data from the database. If the report is based on a PC-style database or an ODBC connection that the Web server can reach during the report process, this step may not be necessary. However, if you've used the SetPrivateData method to change the data source of the report to an ADO recordset or some other data source that's only in scope in the current VBScript procedure, you need to execute ReadRecords so that the report won't fail. If you don't, and the Report object is used in another VBScript procedure (such as RPTSERVER.ASP) when the recordset is no longer in scope, the report won't be able to read records from the recordset. Here's sample code to execute ReadRecords:

```
On Error Resume Next
session("oRpt").ReadRecords
If Err.Number <> 0 Then Response.Write _
    "A server error occurred when trying to access the data source"
```

The PageEngine Object

The Automation Server exposes a PageEngine object that you normally don't need to worry about in VB applications because of the Report Viewer's ViewReport method. However, since you need to pass the Report object to RPTSERVER.ASP to page out to a Crystal Report Viewer, you need to declare the PageEngine object so that RPTSERVER.ASP can use it to communicate with the report viewers. If you look at RPTSERVER.ASP, you'll be able to get an idea (probably after a significant amount of poking around, though) of how the PageEngine works. Declare it with code similar to the following:

```
If IsObject(session("oPageEngine")) Then
    set session("oPageEngine") = Nothing
End If
Set session("oPageEngine") = session("oRpt").PageEngine
```

Caution   *Because RPTSERVER.ASP is the ultimate ASP that processes the report, you need to think about it when you declare session variables. It expects three session variables to be declared with specific names: session("oApp"), which is the Application object; session("oRpt"), which is the Report object; and session("oPageEngine"), which is the PageEngine object. Don't use alternative variable names for these session variables, or RPTSERVER.ASP will fail.*

Crystal Report Viewers

As discussed in Chapter 20, one of the main benefits of using the RDC instead of just exporting reports to HTML from the Crystal Reports designer is that the RDC can offer full report interaction, such as drill-down and group-tree manipulation. The trick, though, is how to fully implement this interaction in a Web browser. While more flexibility and interactivity is added with each new revision of HTML (DHTML 4 has some, but very few, formatting limitations from a Crystal Reports perspective), it still has inherent limitations that make reproducing every element of a Crystal Report difficult.

To deal with this limitation, Crystal Decisions developed several report viewer applications that can be used with most common Web browsers. The *Report Viewer for ActiveX* is a Microsoft-compatible ActiveX control that can be viewed in Internet Explorer 3.02 or greater. The *Report Viewer for Java with Browser JVM* and the *Report Viewer for Java with the Java Plug-In* are Java-based viewers that can be viewed in 32-bit versions of Netscape Navigator 2.0 or greater, Internet Explorer 3.02 or greater, or other Java-compatible browsers. The Browser JVM version uses your particular browser's Java Virtual Machine, whereas the Java Plug-In version uses the Sun Java 2 Runtime Environment. The *Report Viewer for Netscape Plug-In* views a report inside Netscape Navigator.

These viewers implement almost all the features and functionality of the regular Crystal Reports Preview tab, although there are some visual differences. Both allow you to drill down on group headers and footers, charts, and maps, and offer full interaction with the group tree. Both viewers maintain most font and object formatting, and allow you to print reports in their "native" paginated format on an attached printer.

There are still situations, however, for which an ActiveX control, Java applet, or the Netscape plug-in cannot be used. Perhaps there are security restrictions in your company, performance concerns about network traffic, or noncompatible browsers being used. For these situations, there are two HTML-based alternatives:

- **Report Viewer for Standard HTML with Frames** Requires a browser that can support JavaScript and DHTML 4.0. Frames allow more than one scrollable window to be displayed within the browser at one time, which is used to mimic the group tree as closely as possible in a separate frame on the left side of the browser.

- **Report Viewer for Standard HTML** If your browser doesn't support frames, you can use this alternative, which displays the entire report without a group tree in a single browser window.

Report Viewers Compared

Each of the various report viewers has advantages and disadvantages, based on several factors. The ActiveX, Java, and Netscape Plug-in viewers offer more features, but also place a higher burden on the Web server and network because of their size; they also have higher browser requirements. The HTML viewers have fewer browser requirements, but they may make some formatting compromises and offer less functionality than the ActiveX or Java viewers. Table 22-1 compares the different viewers and their advantages and disadvantages.

Report Viewer	Advantages	Disadvantages
ActiveX Netscape Plug-In	Provides highest mirror-image level of original report and most flexibility, including full group-tree and drill-down interactivity, and accurate printing of reports on your local printer.	Only works with 32-bit versions of Microsoft IE 3.02 or greater, or with newer 32-bit versions of Netscape Navigator. Requires extra time and increases network strain when downloaded to browser.
Java with Browser JVM Java Plug-In	Provides good mirror-image level and high flexibility, such as group-tree and drill-down interactivity, and ability to print report on your local printer. Works with any Java-compatible browser.	Requires extra time and increases network strain when downloaded to browser. Won't work with earlier browsers that don't support Java.
HTML Frames	Will work with browsers that just support frames and JavaScript (such as earlier 16-bit browsers)—ActiveX and full Java capabilities aren't required. Mimics group tree with a browser frame. Faster initial response, and no control or applet download is required.	Makes some formatting compromises because of HTML limitations. Only prints what's in the current browser window—original report pagination and layout are not preserved. Drill-down on charts and maps isn't supported. No Export button on toolbar.

Table 21-1.   *Report Viewer Comparison*

Report Viewer	Advantages	Disadvantages
HTML Pages	Works with even the simplest browsers that don't support frames, while still allowing "pseudo" drill-down by creating links in group headers. Faster initial response, and no control or applet download is required.	Makes some formatting compromises because of HTML limitations. Only prints what's in the current browser window— original report pagination and layout are not preserved. Drill-down on charts and maps isn't supported. No Export button on toolbar.

Table 21-1.   *Report Viewer Comparison* (continued)

Using the ActiveX Viewer with Netscape Navigator

The Report Viewer for ActiveX is the most robust Web viewer that Crystal provides. It maintains the best report-formatting consistency with what was actually developed in the Crystal Reports designer, features the ability to accurately print the report on a locally attached printer, and allows exporting to Excel, Word, Rich Text Format, PDF, and other standard file formats.

Because this viewer uses Microsoft's ActiveX technology, it is only supported "natively" in Microsoft's Internet Explorer browser. Previously, if you wanted similar functionality in Netscape Navigator, you needed to use one of the Java-based viewers. While Crystal has made dramatic improvements to the Java-based viewers as newer versions are released, you now have the option of actually running the Report Viewer for ActiveX in Navigator via an ActiveX plug-in.

To install the plug-in, launch Netscape Navigator and run a Web-based report that "forces" the Netscape Plug-In viewer to be used (specifically choosing it from the SCRSAMPLES Web directly installed with Crystal Reports is one way). If the plug-in has not already been installed, the browser will display a link where you can click to load the plug-in.

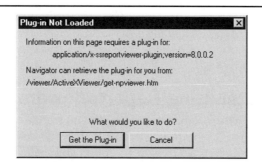

After you follow the prompt to download the plug-in, you are asked to download the file NPVIEWER.EXE. Choose a file location where you want to copy this file. Once it has been downloaded, exit Navigator and use Windows Explorer to find the NPVIEWER.EXE file and run it. This will install the ActiveX plug-in. Once this has completed, restart Navigator and point to the report URL again, and again specify the Report Viewer for Netscape Plug-In. The report will be displayed in the ActiveX viewer within Navigator.

As a general rule, you should use the report viewer that provides the highest level of user functionality for your particular browser and network environment. If your users are all on a 100-megabit intranet with fast PCs and the latest version of Microsoft IE, there can't be too many arguments made against using the Report Viewer for ActiveX. If you have a mix of Netscape and Microsoft browsers, the Report Viewer for Java will work with both. But, if you are providing reports on your extranet that can potentially be accessed by any number of unknown browsers using 28.8Kbps modems, you may want to use either of the Report Viewers for HTML to streamline performance and support the widest variety of browsers.

One thing should always be kept in mind: When you design reports to be distributed over the Web, take your target audience's report viewer choices into serious consideration when you design your reports. If your ultimate goal is that reports look good on a printed page, you need to make serious changes to report formatting and layout if your audience will be using HTML-based viewers instead of the ActiveX or Java viewers. If your reports rely heavily on group-tree and drill-down interactivity (detail sections are hidden, lots of charts are included, and so on), don't realistically expect satisfactory results with the HTML-based viewers. And, don't forget that Crystal Reports includes many formatting options, such as drop shadows, underlaid sections, and object and section background shading, that won't convert properly to HTML when displayed in the HTML viewers. Always test your reports and make sure you're getting the results you expect in your target report viewer.

If you are implementing reporting from a Java application, you may be able to use the Report Viewer Java Bean. Similar to an ActiveX control that can be used in Visual Basic, the Report Viewer Java Bean can be added to a Java application and controlled with properties and methods.

Choosing and Customizing Report Viewers

You'll need to determine which of the report viewers you want to provide to your viewer's Web browser. You can include commonly available VBScript code to query the browser for its type. If you encounter Internet Explorer, you can automatically provide the ActiveX viewer. If you encounter Netscape, you can provide the Netscape Plug-In or a Java viewer. Or, you can create a control on a Web page (perhaps a combo box) that allows the viewer to make the choice.

Crystal Decisions provides some intermediate ASPs that you may include in your ASP code to choose the desired report viewer. You'll find SmartViewerActiveX.ASP, ActiveXPluginViewer.ASP, SmartViewerJava.ASP, JavaPluginViewer.ASP, and HTMStart.ASP in the *Crystal Reports program directory*\Samples*language*\Code\ Web\Active Server Pages folder. You can just copy and paste the code from one of the ASPs into your own file, or use the HTML #*include file* statement to bring in the proper report viewer code. If you've set up a control on your application form that allows the user to choose a report viewer (similar to the viewer variable in the following example), you might use code similar to this to set the chosen report viewer:

```
If cstr(viewer) = "ActiveX" then
%>
<!-- #include file="SmartViewerActiveX.asp" -->
<%
ElseIf cstr(viewer) = "Netscape Plug-in" then
%>
<!-- #include file="ActiveXPluginViewer.asp" -->
<%
ElseIf cstr(viewer) = "Java using Browser JVM" then
%>
<!-- #include file="SmartViewerJava.asp" -->
<%
ElseIf cstr(viewer) = "Java using Java Plug-in" then
%>
<!-- #include file="JavaPluginViewer.asp" -->
<%
ElseIf cstr(viewer) = "HTML Frame" then
        Response.Redirect("htmstart.asp")
Else
        Response.Redirect("rptserver.asp")
End If
```

The Crystal-supplied report viewer ASP for Java and ActiveX set certain viewer parameters to default settings. When you view the ASP code in these files, you'll notice parameters, such as group-tree display, toolbar button display, enabling of drill-down, and so forth, set with PARAM tags. You may modify this report viewer behavior if you so desire. If you want to make permanent changes to these options, simply change the Crystal ASP to use your new desired options (perhaps you don't want to offer a Print or Export button to your users at any time). If you want to hard-code a change only for a particular application, while others still use the Crystal defaults, you need to copy the code from one of the Crystal files into your own ASP file and change the parameter in your own file.

And, finally, if you have set up yet other user options to control report viewer behavior, you can conditionally set the report viewer parameters based on a control on a form. Look at the following sample code:

```
<%' Customize the Report Viewer to turn on/off the group tree
If Request.Form("chkGroupTree") = "ON" Then
    %><param name="DisplayGroupTree" value=1>
<%Else
    %><param name="DisplayGroupTree" value=0>
<%End If%>
```

Tip *The <% and %> characters in the preceding code indicate separation of the server-side ASP script from the actual HTML text to be submitted to the browser. Because the parameters are part of the report viewer Object tag, they need to be returned to the browser, while the If-Then-Else statement will execute on the server. This separation of server-side script from client-side HTML is the basic premise of Active Server Pages.*

Using the Crystal Reports 8.5 Design-Time Controls with Visual InterDev

Crystal Reports 8.5 includes a handy tool for simplifying the inclusion of a report in an Active Server Page. Instead of copying or writing all the detailed code required to add a report to an ASP, you can use a *Design-Time Control (DTC)* to do it for you. DTCs are provided by Microsoft for various other Visual InterDev features. Now, you can use the ones supplied by Crystal Decisions for report integration.

You may use a very simple approach just by creating an Active Server Page in Visual InterDev (VI) that will display a simple report. Or, if you have a more complex, interactive Web page with many controls that interact with the user, you can modify the code the DTC creates to take advantage of your user interface. Either way, the amount of coding is reduced dramatically by the DTC.

To use the Crystal Reports DTC, you must have purchased Crystal Reports 8.5 Developer Edition. Since Visual InterDev uses the RDC Automation Server to integrate with Active Server Pages, only the Developer Edition will suffice—no other edition includes the RDC.

After you install Crystal Reports on the same computer as Visual InterDev, using the DTC is a fairly straightforward process. You will use two Crystal-supplied DTCs to integrate your report. The *Report Source* DTC is used to specify the actual .RPT file you want to integrate, along with logon information for the report, any parameter fields you wish to supply values for, and any modifications you may wish to make to the record-selection formula. The *Report Viewer* DTC is used to actually display the report specified in the Report Source DTC in a report viewer. The Report Viewer DTC allows customization of report viewer features, such as display of toolbar buttons and the group tree.

Perform the following steps to use the two DTCs with your Visual InterDev project:

1. Create a new VI project or open an existing project that you wish to add a report to.

2. Use the Add Item option to actually add the external .RPT file or files to the project. VI will copy the .RPT file or files to the Web server, because they must reside in the virtual directory on the server for the DTC to properly integrate them. Make sure the Web server includes any ODBC data source definitions or native database connectivity options, so that the report will be able to connect to the database. The DTC won't work properly if the report hasn't been added to your project!

3. Ensure the VI Toolbox is displayed. Click the Design-Time Controls button to display a list of available DTCs from the Toolbox. Look for the ReportSource and ReportViewer controls, which may already be placed in the Toolbox. If these two controls don't appear, choose Tools | Customize Toolbox from the pull-down menus, or right-click the Toolbox and choose Customize Toolbox from the pop-up menu. Notice the selection of available DTCs on the Design-Time Controls tab. Look through the list until you find the ReportSource and ReportViewer controls. Check the box next to them to add them to the Toolbox.

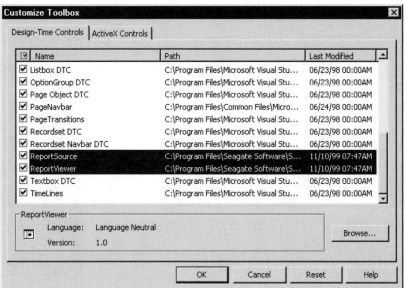

4. Create a new Active Server Page, or open the existing Active Server Page that you want to place the report in. Position the cursor in either VI's Design or Source tab where you wish the report you're going to integrate to appear.

5. Double-click the ReportSource item in the Toolbox to add a ReportSource DTC to the page. VI will automatically number the ReportSource DTC starting with the number 1 (ReportSource1). If you add subsequent ReportSource DTCs to display multiple reports, this numbering will continue sequentially.

6. Ensure that the cursor is *below* the ReportSource DTC that you want to integrate (a ReportViewer DTC must reside below its matching ReportSource DTC in a page). Double-click the ReportViewer item in the Toolbox to add a ReportViewer DTC to the page. You'll now see both DTCs in your Active Server Page.

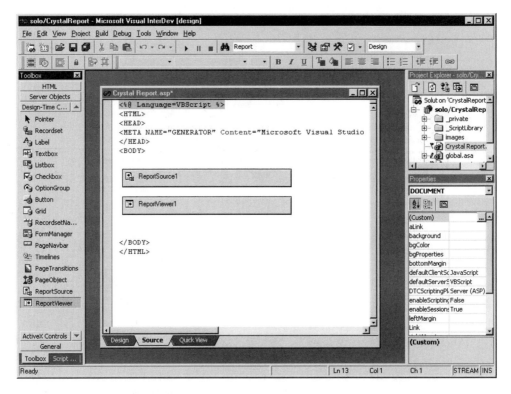

7. Display the Properties dialog box for the controls by selecting the desired control and choosing View | Property Pages from the pull-down menus. You can also right-click the desired control and choose Properties from the pop-up menu. Make selections in the Properties dialog boxes for the report and viewer.

8. Save and view the project in a browser. You'll now see the report appear in the chosen report viewer in the Web page.

Specifying Report Source Properties

When you display the Properties dialog box for the Report Source DTC, you can make several choices for the report that you want to integrate.

Choose an existing report from the VI project from the Name drop-down list on the General tab. If you don't see anything in the drop-down list, you haven't added an .RPT file to your VI project. If you added Report Title and Report Comments text in the Summary Info section of the report, it will appear in the Title and Description sections.

If your report is based on a secure database, supply valid user ID and password information on the Accounts tab. You must either supply this information at design time on this tab, or modify the code created by the DTC to get security information from elsewhere in your project (customizing DTC code is discussed later in the chapter).

If the report you're integrating contains parameter fields, add values for them on the Parameters tab. You'll see a list of each parameter field contained in the report. Select each parameter field and click the Add button to add a value for the parameter field. If the parameter field is defined as a multiple-value or range parameter field, you'll be prompted accordingly, and the value or values you choose will appear in the Current Values box. The Use Defaults check box isn't applicable to a report hosted on an ASP Web server— make sure to leave this unchecked and specify values for the parameter fields. Click the Nullable check box if this is a stored procedure parameter that allows a null value.

If you want to modify the report's record-selection formula, click the Formula tab. If the report already contains a record-selection formula, you'll see it in the Selection Formula box. Click the Modify Formula check box to enable the Selection Formula box, where you may modify the formula. If the report doesn't have a record-selection formula, click the Modify Formula check box to add a new formula. You may click the Check button to perform a syntax check on the formula, or click the Clear button to erase the formula.

The report viewer in an ASP will not prompt for logon information or parameter field values if they are not supplied. If you don't specify this information on either the DTC's Accounts or Parameters tab, or don't supply it by adding code in the DTC-generated VBScript, the report viewer will not display the report. If this happens, close the browser, add the correct values to the DTC, and re-view the report in the browser.

Specifying Report Viewer Properties

After you've specified necessary values for the Report Source DTC, you need to tie the Report Viewer DTC to a Report Source DTC. You can also customize the appearance and behavior of the report viewer by choosing from several options in this DTC.

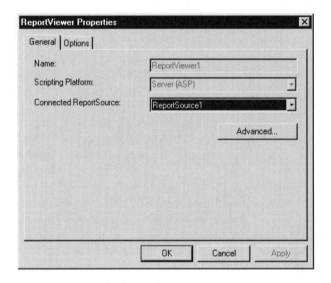

The first choice to make is which Report Source DTC you want the Report Viewer DTC to use. Choose the desired Report Source DTC from the drop-down list. If you don't see the right Report Source DTC (or none at all), it means that the Report Viewer DTC appears *before* the Report Source DTC in the Active Server Page. Move the Report Viewer DTC so that it appears below the Report Source DTC. Then, make the choice from the Connected ReportSource drop-down list.

The Options tab allows you to customize the report viewer. You can choose the viewer to use (you'll find four viewer options in the Report Viewer drop-down list).

You may also choose to customize which controls appear in the Report Viewer toolbar, whether the user can drill down on the report, and other visual and functional options for the report viewer. You may also specify the size of the report viewer.

Modifying the DTC-Generated Code

Unlike an ActiveX control in a Visual Basic program that hides its internal coding from your VB source code, Visual InterDev DTCs actually create VBScript or HTML on-the-fly, based on the values you supply to the Properties dialog box for the particular control. When the page is actually submitted to the Web server for processing, the DTC simply supplies the code as though you typed it yourself.

You may view the code that the DTC creates from within Visual InterDev. To do this, right-click the DTC that you want to evaluate right inside VI (the only Crystal Reports DTC that exposes code is the Report Viewer DTC). Choose Show Run-time Text from the pop-up menu. The VBScript code that the DTC creates at run time will appear below the DTC placeholder in a shaded color.

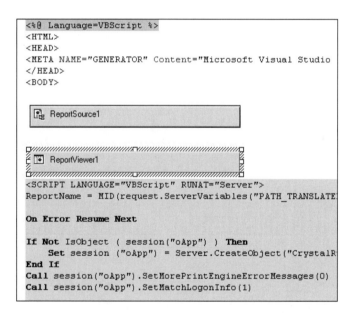

If you choose, you can also convert the DTC to pure code; it will be replaced in Visual InterDev with code reflecting the most recent options you chose before you converted it. Once you convert it, the DTC will no longer exist, and you won't be able to display the Properties dialog box any longer to make changes. If you want to make changes to the behavior of converted code, you can modify the code directly. This will allow you to use the DTC-generated code to interface with other elements of your VI project, such as controls from a form. You may use the RDC Automation Server object model, as described earlier in the chapter, to customize report behavior based on other elements of your project.

To convert the DTC to code, right-click the DTC that you want to convert (typically, you'll convert the Report Viewer DTC—converting the Report Source DTC won't result in anything). Select Convert to Run-time Text from the pop-up menu. The DTC placeholder will disappear and a fragment of VBScript will appear in its place. You may now modify this VBScript as you see fit to further customize the report.

Chapter 22

Introduction to Crystal Enterprise

A good argument can be made that there actually aren't enough new features in Crystal Reports 8.5 to justify an entire new release (not even a "dot-five" release) of the software. So then, the question that may come to mind is, "Why did Crystal Decisions release this software?" The reason that probably comes to mind first is as an avenue for the distribution of Crystal Enterprise, Crystal's new Web-based report distribution system. Crystal Enterprise is, without question, the most far-reaching new "feature" of Crystal Reports 8.5.

Crystal Enterprise Defined

As the World Wide Web has become a more integral part of not only consumer computing, but an important consideration for business computing platforms as well, Crystal Reports has continued to offer more and more Web-based reporting solutions as each new version is released. Version 7 featured the Web Access Server (WAS) for running reports in Web pages. Version 8 introduced a more robust version of the same feature called the Web component server (WCS). And, while Crystal Reports 8.5 has eliminated the Web component server as a Crystal Reports-only Web solution, Active Server Pages and the Report Designer Component (discussed in Chapter 21), as well as basic HTML exports (discussed in more detail in Chapter 20) remain as Crystal Reports–only Web options. All of these options allow end users who wish to view reports to do so from within their Web browsers. A stand-alone copy of Crystal Reports or a custom Windows application integrating Crystal Reports is not required on each of the workstations. And, the workstations don't all have to have connectivity to the corporate database.

However, there has been an increasing demand for more enterprise-oriented, high-capacity Web reporting capabilities. As larger organizations look more and more towards Web-based solutions, Crystal Decisions needed to move beyond the limited-user, Web-server-centric tools it had offered in the past for real-time Web reporting. Companies needed a reporting solution that would scale to potentially support hundreds, or even thousands, of Web-based report viewers.

While Crystal Decisions existing Seagate Info multi-tier reporting tool does include a Web-based interface that can be used, Crystal Decisions has elected to move towards one unified, enterprise-oriented reporting and analysis architecture. Crystal Enterprise is the first example of this new Crystal Decisions direction. Other Crystal tools that fit into this architecture are the recently announced Crystal Enterprise Professional and Report Application Server.

The Two-Tier Web Reporting Method

Crystal Reports 7.0 and 8.0 included a limited Web server-based reporting system that could be described as *two-tier architecture* (and the Version 8.5 ASP/RDC solution described in Chapter 21 still adheres to this architecture). The basic premise of this architecture is to route the report viewing audience through a Web browser and Web server, rather than placing an individual copy of Crystal Reports or a Crystal Reports-based custom application on each user PC. Only the Web server requires connectivity to the corporate database for ad hoc reporting. This architecture is illustrated in Figure 22-1.

| **Note** | *Yes, the argument could be made that the architecture being described here is in fact a three-tier architecture—Web browser to Web server to database. However, by basically moving all of the previous client-based processing to the Web server and transforming clients to simple viewer status, the previous two-tier client/server architecture is just being moved around. It can still be argued that in the typical database/query client/server model, the Web server has become the client and the database remains the server.* |

By centralizing this approach via the Web, much reduced software maintenance on client-side computers is required. Not only do new versions of reports or reporting systems not require any new software to be installed on individual client computers (only the Web pages that comprise the application need to be updated on the Web server), but the application can now support multiple computing platforms, such as Windows-based PCs, Apple Macintosh, and Unix and Linux workstations. As long as a compatible Web browser can be used, Crystal Reports can be viewed on a computer or workstation.

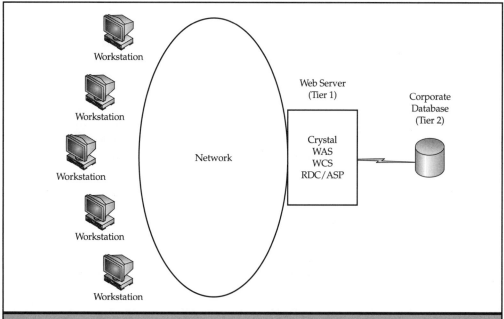

Figure 22-1. *The existing two-tier processing architecture*

Crystal Enterprise Multi-Tier Reporting Method

While the existing architecture just described is an overall improvement beyond the classic client/server computing model of an application on a client with a network connection to a server, there are still bottlenecks and disadvantages that limit this architecture's capacity for large reporting environments. In particular:

■ The Web server suddenly becomes a concentrated reporting and query client instead of the Web page distribution server it's designed for. Every request for an ad hoc report requires the Web server to send a query to the database, wait for a result set, and format the result set before sending the report back to a Web browser.

■ The network connection between the Web server and the database can become overloaded, depending on the types of queries and reports that the Web server submits to the database and the size of the return result sets.

■ There is limited sharing or caching of report requests (particularly for ad hoc real time reports). If 25 users request the same report, the Web server oftentimes will have to submit the report's query to the database 25 times.

■ Earlier Crystal Reports Web systems do not allow reports to be automatically scheduled to run at regular intervals, such as once per day, once per month, and so on.

The answer to these inherent limitations of existing Crystal Web reporting alternatives lies in the new Crystal Enterprise multi-tier report processing architecture, as illustrated in Figure 22-2. Built largely on the existing multi-tier structure of Crystal Decisions Seagate Info reporting product, this multi-tier structure is new to the Crystal Reports user. By creating multiple software functions and creating the ability for them to be rolled out or "scaled" to multiple processors, Crystal Enterprise immediately offers a dramatic improvement in reliability, load capability, and fault tolerance. The Web server can return to its core requirement to serve up Web pages. Additional components now work together to run ad hoc report and query requests, schedule automatically recurring reports, convert completed reports pages to "page-on-demand" viewing files, handle security, and cache recently reviewed report pages for delivery to the next report viewer. The result is a completely scalable multi-tier structure that dramatically improves the capabilities and capacity of Web-based reporting.

Note *Complete discussions of the different server components shown in Figure 22-2 are found in the Crystal Enterprise Architecture section later in this chapter.*

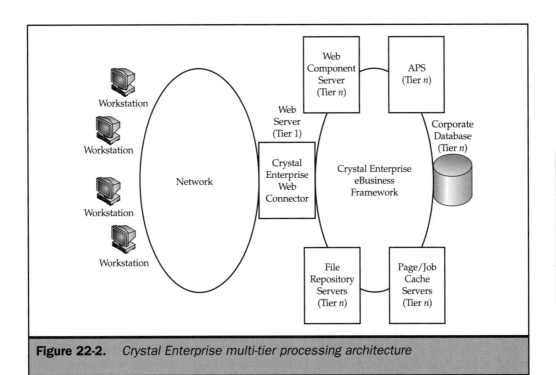

Figure 22-2. *Crystal Enterprise multi-tier processing architecture*

Standard Edition Versus Professional Edition

As discussed earlier in this book, there are three versions of Crystal Reports 8.5 available with differing capabilities: Standard Edition, Professional Edition, and Developer Edition. Crystal Enterprise (actually initially released at Version 8.0) also is available in two versions: Standard Edition and Professional Edition. If you received the Crystal Enterprise CD bundled with your copy of Crystal Reports 8.5, you received Standard Edition. Standard Edition is designed to handle a low-capacity, simple Web-based reporting environment. It might be considered a "light" version of the full Crystal Enterprise product, limited in expandability and capacity. To gain the full benefit of Crystal Enterprise's multi-tier scaled server technology, you'll need to upgrade to Crystal Enterprise Professional. Just bring your checkbook—initial Crystal Enterprise Professional upgrade pricing has raised eyebrows at some of the companies where it has been implemented.

To upgrade to Professional Edition, you'll need to contact Crystal Decisions directly, as they don't offer Crystal Enterprise for sale in the retail channel. Upon purchasing an upgrade, you'll simply receive additional activation key codes that upgrade your current Standard Edition to Professional Edition (Appendix A details procedures for adding the additional key code). There are several significant differences between the features offered in Crystal Enterprise Standard Edition versus Professional Edition. These differences revolve around several core feature areas:

- User capacity
- Security capabilities
- Fault tolerance
- Server scaling

User Capacity

Crystal Enterprise Standard is limited to a five-user concurrent licensing structure. This basically means that any five users can be using the tool at the same time. The sixth user that attempts to log in will receive a message indicating all licenses are in use. Crystal Enterprise Professional, on the other hand, features a wide array of licensing options that you may choose. You may purchase combinations of concurrent licenses, named-user licenses, or processor licenses.

Additional concurrent user licenses allow any user to log in to the system, provided that the total number of users logged in at any one time doesn't exceed the concurrent user limit. Named user licenses allow users with specific user IDs that belong to them to log in at any time, regardless of how many other users are currently logged in. And, processor-based licenses are dependent upon the number of computers or "processors" that are required to implement a Crystal Enterprise system. The proper type and number of licenses will depend entirely on how many users you need to support, what capabilities they need to have, and how often and how long they'll need to use Enterprise. Study and consider these varying options carefully, so you'll have the proper number of licenses for all potential user combinations, without undertaking extra expense that may be incurred for an "overkill" license structure.

Security Capabilities

Crystal Enterprise Standard only supports two user IDs, Administrator and Guest. The Administrator user should be limited to the person in charge of maintaining the system and publishing reports (the Guest user account can't publish reports). The Guest account is for shared use among all the concurrent users (again, of which any five can be connected at the same time). All Guest users will have the same privileges and will be able to see the same folders and reports. And, Crystal Enterprise Standard will not integrate with the Windows NT or Windows 2000 security system—it maintains its own security separate from any existing operating system security.

Crystal Enterprise Professional allows creation of as many user IDs as necessary (based on named-user licenses that are purchased). In fact, the Professional edition even allows users to create *their own* accounts by clicking a link on the ePortfolio (discussed later in the book). In the Professional Edition, users may be assigned to varying *user groups*, each of which is given varying rights and capabilities. Certain groups, for example, can be given the right to publish reports to the ePortfolio or schedule reports on a recurring basis. Other groups, however, may only be able to view reports that have already been published and scheduled by others.

And, Crystal Enterprise Professional allows two choices of user security: Enterprise Authentication or Windows NT/2000 Authentication. With Enterprise Authentication, separate user IDs and passwords are maintained in the Enterprise system database. When a user logs in with Enterprise Authentication, they must specify a separate user ID and password from any existing ID/password combination they may have already used to log in to Windows. However, the Professional Edition allows creation of a specific Windows NT/2000 account group that will interface directly with the Enterprise system database. A user's Windows NT/2000 user ID and password can then be automatically checked against this account group to verify Crystal Enterprise authority. This negates the need for users to specify a separate user ID and password from those they've already used to log in to Windows—they may simply supply their Windows domain name and user ID at the sign-on prompt.

Tip	*Another feature of Crystal Enterprise Professional is Windows NT/2000 Single Sign-On. This allows users to connect directly to the Crystal Enterprise ePortfolio without having to specify any additional user ID or password at all—the user's Windows NT/2000 ID and password are passed on automatically by their Web browser. This feature requires that users connect to Crystal Enterprise through a Microsoft Internet Information Server (IIS) Web server, as well as requiring use of Microsoft Internet Explorer as their Web browser. Get more information on the particular procedures for enabling this feature by viewing the Crystal Enterprise Administrator's Guide (available from the Crystal Enterprise Launchpad). Click the Index tab and search for "NT Single Sign On, setting up".*

Fault Tolerance

Crystal Enterprise Standard does not allow the creation of fault-tolerant server platforms. Only a single set of components can reside on a single computer. Should that computer fail, the entire Crystal Enterprise system will be inaccessible. However, this eliminates one of the major benefits of the Crystal Enterprise architecture—its multi-tier, multi-server technology.

Crystal Enterprise Professional restores this capability, in particular the ability to set up multiple Automated Process Scheduler (APS) machines that back each other up and provide processing scalability (the APS is described in more detail in the Crystal Enterprise Architecture section of this chapter). Should one APS machine fail, the remaining machines will pick up the extra load and continue to process Crystal Enterprise requests. And, when a large processor load is required, multiple APS machines will share that load as necessary, enabling a very large user base to be supported. The *clustering* of APS computers is only provided by Crystal Enterprise Professional.

Server Scaling

As described previously, one of the main benefits of Crystal Enterprise over the previous single-server approach of the Crystal Reports Web component server is the ability to spread the processing load across multiple "tiers." Instead of one computer having to process all report and query processes, report formatting, and HTML page generation, Crystal Enterprise Professional allows these functions to be spread over several computers. Crystal Enterprise Standard, while adhering to this multi-tier software structure, still requires that all these software components reside on a single physical computer. The only exception is that the Web connector (described in more detail in the architecture section of the chapter) can reside on a Web server separately from the remaining Crystal Enterprise components.

Crystal Enterprise Professional Edition, however, allows each software component or "tier," or any combination of components, to reside on separate personal computers on the network. In a very large Enterprise environment, it might be desirable to have each individual software component, such as the APS, the input file repository server, the output file repository server, the cache server, the page server, and the Web component server, each reside on a separate computer on the network. In a high-volume implementation, you might even need to set up multiple computers that share the same responsibility (multiple physical APS machines in a cluster, for example), to satisfy the load requirements of your particular Crystal Enterprise system.

Crystal Enterprise Architecture

Crystal Enterprise is a monumental change from the previous single-server approach of the Crystal Reports Web component server. As discussed previously in this chapter, one of the huge benefits of Crystal Enterprise over earlier tools is its multi-tier, multi-server approach to Web reporting. By spreading the processing load over multiple software and hardware layers, much higher numbers of users and much better sustained performance can be expected.

If you are an end user of Crystal Enterprise, there are several software components that you may encounter as you view reports. Depending on your particular Enterprise implementation, you may also be required to design, publish, and schedule reports as well. You'll want to be familiar with the different components that are required to use Enterprise in these various ways. If you are a Crystal Enterprise administrator who is responsible for installing, maintaining, and supporting Crystal Enterprise, you'll not only want to be familiar with the end-user tools available to your user community, but also the particular server components, communications methods, and administrative tools available for your use.

End-User Components for Reporting

As a Web-based reporting tool, Crystal Enterprise provides interaction almost entirely within a Web browser. If you are using a Windows PC, an Apple Macintosh, or a Unix/Linux workstation, all you need to work with the majority of Crystal Enterprise features is a standard Web browser (a newer browser that supports HTML Version 4 and JavaScript is required). The only exception to the Web browser rule is for designing reports—Crystal Reports 8.5 is used to design reports and must run in a Windows environment. And, there are several ways of publishing reports to Crystal Enterprise. One way, the Crystal-supplied Crystal Publishing Wizard, is also a Windows-only program.

As an end user, you'll normally start using Crystal Enterprise from one of two places: the Launchpad or the ePortfolio. Both are Web pages that can be viewed by pointing your browser to a standard location specified by your Crystal Enterprise administrator. Because Crystal Enterprise is Web-based, it's entirely possible to customize the Web interface to it. Your organization may still use the standard locations for Enterprise pages (but may have customized the pages), or it may have created an entirely customized interface (such as an internal intranet or portal) that interfaces with Crystal Enterprise.

If you wish to add newly designed Crystal Reports to the ePortfolio, you can use either the Crystal Management Console (discussed in the "Server and Maintenance Components for Administrators" section later in the book) or the Windows-based Crystal Publishing Wizard.

Crystal Launchpad and ePortfolio

The Crystal Launchpad is the beginning point for Crystal Enterprise usage. It is simply a home page where you may navigate to other portions of Crystal Enterprise—there are no functional capabilities on the Launchpad itself. From the Launchpad you may click links to online documentation, to the ePortfolio, to the Crystal Management Console, and to Developer Samples that demonstrate customized Crystal Enterprise pages.

You may click the ePortfolio link on the Launchpad, or type in the location (known in Web parlance as a Universal Resource Locator, or URL) of the ePortfolio to display the actual starting point for Crystal Enterprise report viewing.

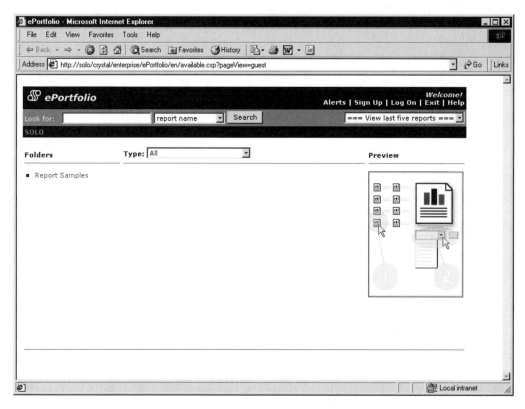

From the ePortfolio, you can create a new user account, log on as a different user, navigate through report folders, view reports and report alerts, and schedule reports to run on a recurring basis. The ePortfolio may appear identical to the previous illustration, or may have been modified to more closely align with your organization's standard Web look and feel.

Customized Web Interface

The ePortfolio is a Crystal Decisions–designed interface to Crystal Enterprise. Based on Crystal Server Pages (discussed in detail in Chapter 24), all ePortfolio source code is provided for perusal and modification. You may modify the existing ePortfolio to more closely match your standard Web interface, or create a completely new set of Web pages to expose Crystal Enterprise features. If a customized intranet page or portal has been created, your administrator may give you a completely different URL to launch your Crystal Enterprise system.

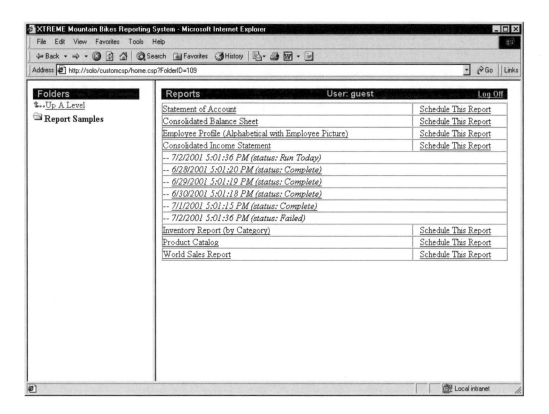

Crystal Publishing Wizard

Depending on how responsibilities for maintaining your Crystal Enterprise system are divided within your organization, you may need the ability to post reports you've designed with Crystal Reports 8.5 to your Crystal Enterprise system. There are two ways to accomplish this: using the Crystal Management Console (discussed in the "Server and Maintenance Components for Administrators" section of this chapter) or the Crystal Publishing Wizard (outlined in Chapter 23, "Using the Crystal Launchpad and ePortfolio").

The Crystal Publishing Wizard provides certain advantages over the Crystal Management Console and is designed to be easier to use overall. This is a Windows program that does require installation on your individual computer from a Windows Setup routine.

Note   *More detailed information on connecting to and using the Crystal Launchpad, ePortfolio, and Crystal Publishing Wizard can be found in Chapter 23, "Using the Crystal Launchpad and ePortfolio."*

Server and Maintenance Components for Administrators

Crystal Enterprise's multi-tier architecture lends itself to a much more flexible, higher-capacity system for Web reporting. It also lends itself to more complexity when it comes to initial setup, operation, and administration. This increased complexity comes, in large part, from the increased number of components that make up the server portion (or "back end") of Crystal Enterprise. While an Enterprise end user simply sees Web pages that allow scheduling and viewing of reports, there are many separate components working together to provide this capability to the user.

Crystal Enterprise has two general types of components that a Crystal Enterprise administrator will be concerned with: back-end servers and administrative tools. The various server components that make up Crystal Enterprise share the overall processing requirements of Enterprise, passing information among themselves as required. The administrative tools (both Web and Windows-based) are used by administrators to control and customize Crystal Enterprise behavior.

Servers

Administrators of Crystal Decisions' other multi-tier reporting system, Seagate Info, will see many similarities between Crystal Enterprise server architecture and Seagate Info server architecture—Crystal Enterprise architecture was borrowed from Seagate Info. However, if you are in charge of administering Enterprise and this is your first experience with a multi-server configuration, there is much to learn about how all these different server components work together and pass information back and forth.

In order for Crystal Enterprise to potentially support up to thousands of Web users, a great deal of processing power must be available for peak processing loads. The idea behind the Enterprise multi-server architecture is to spread that processing load around. Different server components have limited functionality—some are designed to run reports against a corporate database, and with others the sole purpose is to keep track of already viewed report pages, while others keep track of security and report scheduling. Determining how many different computers to use for back-end processing and which components to place on those computers is largely dependent on your individual system and where you think the largest processing loads will be. By studying the remainder of this chapter, by consulting documentation accompanying Crystal Enterprise, and by pure experimentation you'll eventually be able to determine the proper delineation of server resources. And, you may always move components around or "scale out" if you need to—you may initially start with all components running on one physical computer, but later split servers out to multiple processors as your capacity needs increase.

Note	*Don't forget that Crystal Enterprise Standard Edition included with Crystal Reports 8.5 is a low-volume solution designed for small production implementations or for evaluation prior to a Crystal Enterprise Professional upgrade. Crystal Enterprise Standard requires all back-end server components to reside on a single physical computer (the only exception being the ability to place the Web connector on a Web server separate from the remaining server components). To gain full flexibility in loading server components on separate physical computers, you'll need to upgrade to Crystal Enterprise Professional.*

APS The Automated Process Scheduler, or APS, is the heart of Crystal Enterprise. Every other component communicates through the APS (the APS acts as a name server, keeping track of the locations and status of the other server components). The APS also acts as the central security point for Crystal Enterprise login—all user IDs, passwords, and rights lists are maintained on the APS. And, the APS also keeps track of report scheduling. If a report is scheduled to automatically run every day at midnight, the APS sets the report processing cycle in motion at the prescribed time.

Because the APS is so critical to the operation of Crystal Enterprise (the entire system is completely "dead in the water" without it), Enterprise provides for fault tolerance and increased processing capacity with *APS clustering*. With APS clustering, multiple physical computers can run as APS servers. Sharing a common system database hosted on a standard server platform, such as Microsoft SQL Server, Oracle, or Informix, all APS machines appear as one *logical* APS to the entire Crystal Enterprise system. They share processing load, sending processing requests to the least-busy machine in the cluster. If one machine should fail, the remaining APS machines pick up the load and continue to operate—the end user will not even know that one of the APS machines has failed.

Web Component Server/Web Connector The Web component server, or WCS, bears little functional resemblance to the component with the same name in Crystal Reports 8.0. The WCS is the "front line" component of Crystal Enterprise, intercepting all initial requests for Enterprise Web pages and reports from the Web Connector and Web server. The WCS also processes the Crystal Server Page scripting language (covered in detail in Chapter 24) to allow complete customization of the Crystal Enterprise user interface in a Web browser.

The Web Connector is the actual Crystal Enterprise component that resides on the Web server. By moving other Crystal Enterprise components to their own servers and leaving the Web server to its preferred task of communicating with Web browsers, Crystal Enterprise can achieve much higher levels of performance without bogging down the Web server. The Web Connector passes information to and from the WCS, which then communicates among other Enterprise servers to process Web page display, Crystal Server Page script interpretation, report viewing, and other Enterprise functions.

The other benefit Crystal Enterprise derives from placing a very small demand on the Web server is cross-platform Web server support. By minimizing the software footprint on the Web server, Crystal Decisions has been able to support many popular Web servers running on both Windows NT and Unix platforms. While the other back-end servers require Windows NT/2000 to run, there are several Web Connectors that expand Web server support to other platforms.

The following Web Connectors are included with Crystal Enterprise:

- Microsoft Internet Information Server (IIS) running on Windows NT/2000
- Netscape Enterprise or Fast Track Server running on Windows NT/2000
- Lotus Domino running on Windows NT/2000
- Apache, Linux, Solaris (and other servers compliant with Apache Dynamic Shared Objects) running on Unix
- Any Common Gateway Interface (CGI) Web server running on Windows NT/2000 or Unix

Tip   *Complete descriptions and installation steps for all Web Connectors can be found in the online or printed Crystal Enterprise Installation Guide.*

File Repository Servers   As Crystal Enterprise reporting is based on Crystal Reports, procedures for handling the Crystal .RPT files that are published, scheduled, and viewed must be established. This is where the file repository servers come in. These servers store .RPT files that can be viewed on demand and .RPT files that are to be scheduled on a regular basis (perhaps every night, every week, and so on), as well as the finished copies of scheduled reports—the .RPT files with saved data that can be viewed after they've successfully run.

There are actually two different file repository servers (and there can be only one of each in Crystal Enterprise—you can't have multiple copies of these servers running in one Enterprise system). The *input* file repository server is where Crystal Report .RPT files are stored after they've been published with Crystal Reports 8.5, the Crystal Publishing Wizard, the Crystal Management Console, or the Crystal Import Wizard. When a request is received to view a published report on demand, or when the APS runs a scheduled report on a regular basis, the input file repository server is queried for a copy of the .RPT file to run.

The *output* file repository server keeps all the finished .RPT files with saved data (known as report *instances*) that result from reports that are scheduled by the APS on a regular basis. When an end user wishes to view a report instance, the other Crystal Enterprise components query the APS, which keeps track of report instances in the output file repository server. The .RPT file with saved data is transferred from this server to other components for caching and HTML formatting, eventually appearing in the end user's Web browser.

Job Server and Page Server   Of all the servers that comprise a Crystal Enterprise system, only two actually require connectivity to the corporate database: the job server and the page server. Both of these servers need to connect to the database to actually run Crystal Reports that have been published. The difference between the job server and the page server is the group of .RPT files each is dedicated to running.

The job server is dedicated to running reports that are scheduled by the APS. Only reports that run on a regular basis (every day, every week, the first day of the month, and so forth) are submitted to the job server. When the APS needs to schedule a report to run, it passes the request on to the job server. The job server obtains the .RPT file to run from the input file repository server, actually connects to the database to run the report, and sends the completed report instance (an .RPT file with saved data) to the output file repository server.

The page server is dedicated to two tasks: creating EPF files and running on-demand .RPT files. This first task comes into play whenever an end user requests to view a completed report. The page server communicates with the cache server and may be asked to create individual page image files (known as encapsulated page files, or EPF files) that are stored by the cache server and delivered to the end user one page at a time. This "page-on-demand" architecture has been a cornerstone of Crystal Reports performance for several versions. This way, if a report actually encompasses several hundred pages, only the page requested by the viewer will be sent across to the Web browser.

The other task given to the page server is the processing of *on-demand* reports. On-demand reports differ from reports scheduled by the APS on a regular basis, which are handled by the job server. While the automatic scheduling of reports is a very powerful feature of Crystal Enterprise, certain reporting environments require near-instantaneous access to a current set of data. In these situations, the page server is used to run reports against the database whenever a user requests them. By utilizing both on-demand and scheduled reports (and by dedicating servers to each), Crystal Enterprise can satisfy a broad mix of regular production reporting needs versus on-demand ad hoc reporting needs.

| **Tip** | *Depending on how your Crystal Enterprise system will be used, you may find processing bottlenecks occur on the job server or page server. If you schedule a great number of large reports to run on a regular basis, and many of these scheduled reports run at the same time, you may find the need to add additional job servers to your Enterprise system. However, if your primary crunch is on-demand reports, or viewing a large number of reports (which requires a large amount of EPF generation), you'll want to consider adding additional page servers to your Enterprise system.* |

CRYSTAL REPORTS 8.5
ON THE WEB

Cache Server As discussed earlier in the chapter, one of the benefits of Crystal Enterprise (and of several versions of Crystal Reports before it) is page-on-demand architecture. This approach to delivering report pages to the end user's Web browser significantly improves performance, especially with larger reports that comprise many pages. The page-on-demand process will only deliver the page of a report that a viewer currently needs to see. When a report is first viewed, only page 1 is delivered to the viewer. If, for example, the viewer then clicks an entry in the group tree that requires page 210 of the report to be delivered, only page 210 is sent to the browser—pages 2–209 are ignored.

As discussed previously, part of this page-on-demand process is the creation of EPFs, which is handled by the page server. The other very important part of this process, however, is storing already viewed EPFs for later reuse (known as "caching"). This process is handled by the cache server. The cache server and the Web component server communicate very closely with each other. When the Web component server requests that a particular report page be sent to the browser, the cache server keeps track of pages that may have already been viewed (and that are already cached). If the cache server can find an already generated EPF, it simply sends it for viewing. If the cache server needs the EPF to be generated (a user, for example, has asked for a report page that hasn't been viewed previously), it asks the page server to generate the EPF, which it then caches and sends to the Web component server.

All Crystal Enterprise server components, with the exception of the Web Connector (which can run on certain Unix Web servers as well as Windows NT/2000 Web servers), run only on Windows NT or 2000 platforms as "NT services." While you can view reports from within any Web browser on any Windows platform (or other platforms that supply Web browsers), you cannot use Windows 9x or ME to run any of the Crystal Enterprise server components.

Crystal Management Console

The Crystal Management Console is the first of several administrative software interfaces to Crystal Enterprise. Because the Crystal Management Console is Web-based, you can run it on any computer on the network that has a Web browser. You don't need to run it on any of the physical components that make up Crystal Enterprise. You can even run it in a remote location from the Internet, provided your internal network security allows an outside browser to navigate to the proper location.

The Crystal Management Console can be chosen as a link from the Crystal Enterprise Launchpad, or navigated to directly with the following URL:

```
http://<web server>/crystal/enterprise/admin
```

What Is the Crystal eBusiness Framework?

As you peruse marketing materials and documentation for Crystal Enterprise, you'll see frequent referrals to the *Crystal eBusiness Framework*. While you may have reached your limit of technological terms that starts with the letter "e", Crystal Decisions has elected to bestow this name upon its new communications infrastructure first introduced with Crystal Enterprise.

In general terms, the Crystal eBusiness Framework is the common communications structure that ties all the Crystal Enterprise components together. All the back-end servers described in this chapter communicate with each other through the eBusiness Framework. Custom Crystal Server Pages script used to create custom Web pages that expose Crystal Enterprise features includes software "hooks" to allow connection to the eBusiness Framework (Crystal Server Pages are covered in detail in Chapter 24). And, related software products that work in tandem with Crystal Enterprise, such as Crystal Reports 8.5, Crystal Analysis Professional, and the recently announced Report Application Server, all connect to the eBusiness Framework to publish reports, analyze data, or provide extra services and functions to existing Crystal products.

In technical terms, the Crystal eBusiness Framework is a communications layer based on the Transport Control Protocol/Internet Protocol, or TCP/IP (the network protocol that originated with the Internet and that has become the de facto networking standard for most corporate networks). Furthermore, the way servers are named and communicate within Enterprise revolves around the Common Object Request Broker Architecture, or CORBA.

This open standard for network communication is useful from several perspectives, the least of which is cross-platform support. The ability for Crystal Enterprise Windows-based components to work with Web Connectors on Unix is part of the CORBA benefit. The other benefit is ease of communications throughout the corporate network. Crystal Decisions' other multi-tier product, Seagate Info, doesn't use a CORBA communications framework. As such, difficulty often arises when one Seagate Info server needs to communicate with another inside a Windows network. If network security is not set up to support all the possible server communications paths, the system fails. The CORBA-based Crystal eBusiness Framework has eliminated many of these Windows-based security problems.

The first step to take after starting the Crystal Management Console is to log in to the APS. Although most users will be able to successfully log in to the Crystal Management Console, only those with administrative privileges will be able to perform many of the functions offered by the tool. If they choose to perform a function that they're not authorized to complete, an error message will result.

After successfully logging in, you'll be presented with the main Crystal Management Console screen.

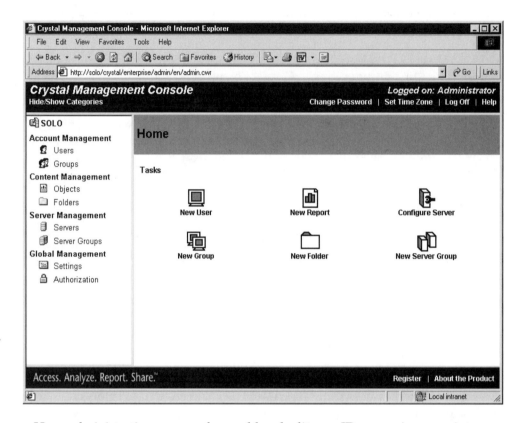

Here, administrative personnel can add and edit user IDs; organize users into user groups; change passwords and grant and deny rights to users; manage back-end servers; add, remove and modify folders to logically organize reports; and add and remove reports in existing folders.

Upgrading to Crystal Enterprise Professional Edition

As described earlier in this chapter, many features of Crystal Enterprise are eliminated or "crippled" in the Crystal Enterprise Standard Edition that's included with Crystal Reports 8.5. To expand Crystal Enterprise beyond its initial five-user limit, to place back-end servers on multiple machines, and so forth requires an upgrade to Crystal Enterprise Professional Edition.

One of the places you'll probably discover the Standard Edition's limitations fairly quickly is when working with the Crystal Management Console. For example, because Crystal Enterprise Standard only allows the two default user IDs already included (Administrator and Guest), you'll immediately run into a limitation if you attempt to add or modify an additional user by clicking the Users link in the left frame of your browser window.

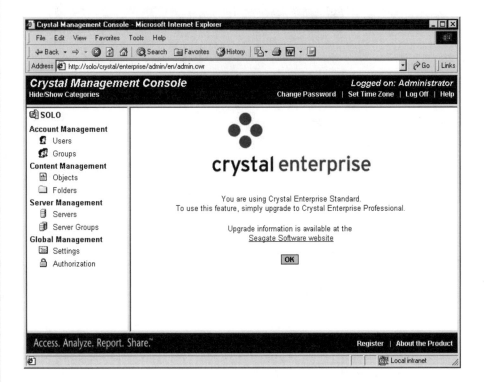

In actuality, there's no physical difference at all between the compact discs that contain Crystal Enterprise Standard and Crystal Enterprise Professional. The only difference is the activation key code that you enter when you initially install the product. The key code that you receive with the CD bundled with Crystal Reports 8.5 will only implement Crystal Enterprise Standard features.

Contact Crystal Decisions for pricing and options for Crystal Enterprise Professional. Once you have purchased the upgrade, you'll probably just receive additional activation key codes—again, the software on the CD contains all features. Once you've received the updated key codes, use the Crystal Management

Console to enter the additional key codes. When you click the Authorization link under the Global Management category, the Authorization screen will appear.

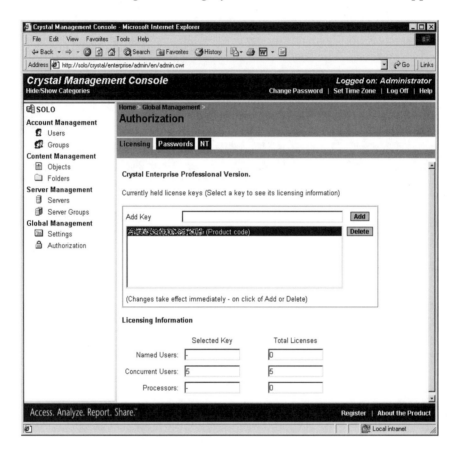

Here, you may add or remove activation key codes to change the version of Crystal Enterprise that you are authorized for. Note that when you select a particular key code in the list of entered codes, you'll immediately be able to see the number of concurrent, named, and processor licenses that the particular key code you've selected provides.

More detailed information about all Crystal Management Console functions and capabilities can be found in the online or printed Crystal Enterprise Administrator's Guide.

Crystal Configuration Manager

Administrative tasks in Crystal Enterprise are split between the Web-based Crystal Management Console (discussed previously), and the Windows-based Crystal Configuration Manager. When you install a Crystal Enterprise component on a back-end server, you'll generally want to install the Crystal Configuration Manager on that machine as well (although you can connect to another server remotely with the Crystal Configuration Manager).

While some administrative tasks or viewing of certain server information can be accomplished from both the Crystal Management Console and Crystal Configuration Manager, more "global" management tasks, such as dealing with user IDs, folders, and reports are accomplished with the Web-based Crystal Management Console. More technical administrative tasks, such as adjusting startup parameters, changing network port numbers, and migrating the APS system database to a SQL server to enable APS clustering are accomplished with the Crystal Configuration Manager.

To start the Crystal Configuration Manager, click the Windows Start button and choose Crystal Configuration Manager from the Crystal Enterprise group. The Crystal Configuration Manager will appear.

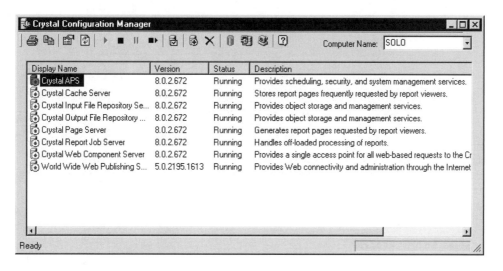

To modify properties of any of the servers listed, highlight the server in the list and click the Properties button in the toolbar. Or, you may right-click on the name of the server and choose Properties from the pop-up menu. When you do so, a tabbed properties page for that server will appear.

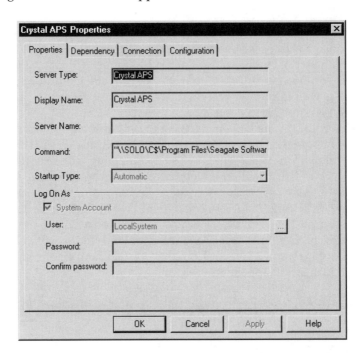

As well as changing server properties, the Crystal Configuration Manager allows you to add additional servers to the Crystal Enterprise system, stop and start servers, disable particular servers, and configure Web Connectors.

Many options for servers shown in the Properties dialog boxes can't be changed while the servers are running. First, stop the desired server using the Stop button in the Crystal Configuration Manager toolbar. Make changes to the server properties, and then restart the server. Of course, you'll want to make sure no critical processes or users are connected to the server before you stop and reconfigure it.

Crystal Web Wizard

As mentioned earlier in this chapter, the Crystal Enterprise ePortfolio is the standard end-user Web interface to Crystal Enterprise. The ePortfolio is designed entirely using standard HTML in conjunction with the Crystal Enterprise scripting language,

Crystal Server Pages (CSP). Your organization may prefer to modify the existing ePortfolio to more closely match the standard look and feel of your company intranet. Or, you may wish to design a completely new user interface separate from the "out of the box" ePortfolio.

While you can write all necessary CSP code from scratch, Crystal Decisions has included the Windows-based Crystal Web Wizard to create a basic set of CSP pages based on responses to a few simple dialog boxes within the wizard. By using the Crystal Web Wizard, you can get a quick jump-start on custom Crystal Enterprise Web pages without tedious amounts of CSP coding. The Crystal Web Wizard is discussed in more detail in Chapter 24, "Customizing the Crystal Enterprise ePortfolio."

Crystal Import Wizard

If you are a user of Crystal Decisions' previously released multi-tier reporting system, Seagate Info, you may be considering a migration to the new Web-based Crystal Enterprise. Or, you may have set up an initial test version of Crystal Enterprise, but wish to copy the existing set of user IDs, the same report and folder structure, and other characteristics to a newer production Enterprise APS.

To prevent an administrator from having to manually re-enter all Seagate Info or Crystal Enterprise information into a new Crystal Enterprise system, Crystal Decisions supplies the Crystal Import Wizard. The Crystal Import Wizard reads the contents of an existing Seagate Info version 6 or 7 APS database, or an existing Crystal Enterprise APS database. It will then allow an administrator to choose which users, user groups, folders, and reports to automatically transfer to a new Crystal Enterprise APS database. When completed, the Crystal Import Wizard will have created a new Crystal Enterprise system that closely mirrors that of the previous Seagate Info or Enterprise system.

The Crystal Import Wizard is a Windows-based program that must be installed from the original program CD. Once installed, you may start the Crystal Import Wizard by clicking the Windows Start button and choosing Crystal Import Wizard from the Crystal Enterprise group. Perform the following basic steps to migrate an existing Seagate Info or Crystal Enterprise system to a new Crystal Enterprise APS:

1. Choose the existing APS that you wish to import from (you'll need to specify an Administrator user ID and password on the existing APS).

2. Then specify an Administrator user ID and password on a new Crystal Enterprise APS that you wish to migrate the existing system into.

3. Choose whether you want to import user IDs and user groups, as well as whether you want to import folders and reports.

4. If you chose to import users and groups, you'll be presented with a user group/user ID "Explorer-like" structure where you may choose the users and groups that you want to migrate.

5. If you chose to import folders and reports, you'll be presented with a folder/report "Explorer-like" structure where you may choose the folders and reports that you want to migrate.

6. Once you've specified all the desired information, click Finish. The migration will occur and a log listing will appear detailing the status of the migration.

Note *For complete information on the Crystal Import Wizard, including descriptions of how users and reports may be affected by a migration, display the Administrator's Guide online help and search the index for "import from Info/Enterprise".*

The Complete Reference

Crystal Reports

Chapter 23

Using the Crystal Launchpad and ePortfolio

T he Crystal Launchpad is the starting point for most end-user interaction with Crystal Enterprise. The primary function of the Launchpad is as a launch point for ePortfolio and the Crystal Management Console; the Launchpad also provides the following links to additional resources for Crystal Enterprise users, administrators, and developers:

- **ePortfolio** is a desktop-style browser environment designed to allow end users to view, schedule, and monitor reports on Crystal Enterprise. As discussed in Chapter 24, your organization might opt to develop a custom Enterprise environment for your users, or modify ePortfolio, rather than use the standard ePortfolio covered in this chapter. However, many of the functions will be similar.

- **The Crystal Management Console**, also run from the Launchpad, is designed to allow administrators to manage the organization, storage, and accessibility of reports through the maintenance of folders, users, and system settings. This chapter discusses only the report publishing function of the Crystal Management Console. Other functions of the Crystal Management Console are discussed in Chapter 22 of this book and in the online Crystal Enterprise Administrator's Guide.

Tip *Like the Crystal Management Console, the ePortfolio (or any substitute Enterprise environment) can be called directly from your Web browser, by typing a URL into the address line. Therefore, you might not end up using the Launchpad at all.*

Several differences between Crystal Enterprise Standard and Crystal Enterprise Professional (discussed in Chapter 22) will directly affect the options available to you in ePortfolio, or your custom environment. The main difference regarding ePortfolio is that Crystal Enterprise Standard only allows two user accounts: Guest and Administrator. Up to five users can log on as Guest at the same time. Furthermore, with Crystal Enterprise Standard, only the Administrator user may publish reports for others to view and schedule.

In contrast, Crystal Enterprise Professional allows the Administrator user (and any other users configured with sufficient security levels) to add and manage users, groups, and folders in accordance with Windows NT security structures; in fact, NT users and groups can be mapped to Crystal Enterprise Professional if desired. Then, users can log on with their own NT identities to use ePortfolio—and all users with sufficient access rights can publish reports to Enterprise Professional.

There are several ways to publish Crystal Reports for use in Crystal Enterprise, whether you are an administrator on Crystal Enterprise Standard or a user on Crystal Enterprise Professional. Publishing methods and options also are discussed in this chapter.

Navigating the Crystal Enterprise Launchpad

To open the Launchpad, select Crystal Launchpad from the Crystal Enterprise program group. If you have not installed any Enterprise components on your computer, you may reach the Launchpad by pointing your browser to http://*<web server>*/crystal/enterprise. The Launchpad will appear in your Web browser, similar to the view in Figure 23-1.

On the Launchpad, you'll find links to many useful pages, including online documentation and tools that reside with Crystal Enterprise, Internet Web sites for support, tools, and samples, and the primary components of Crystal Enterprise: the ePortfolio and the Crystal Management Console. Also available is the Crystal Offline Viewer tool, which, after a one-time setup, allows you to view reports that have been downloaded to your workstation, even when your connection to your Web or network server is unavailable.

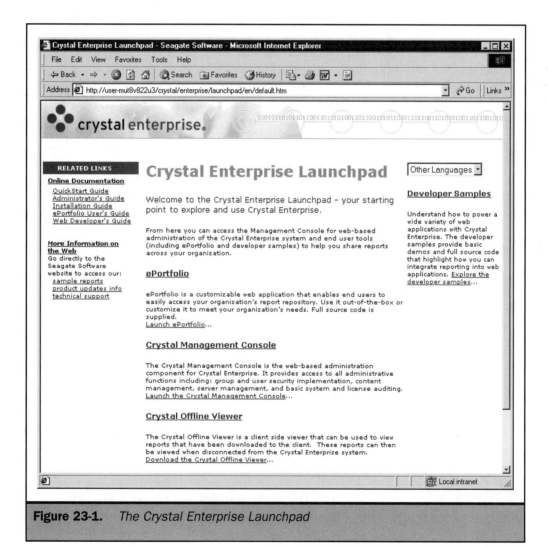

Figure 23-1.   *The Crystal Enterprise Launchpad*

Navigating the Launchpad consists entirely of clicking on the item you want to see. If the link is unavailable, or you don't have security access for it, you'll receive a descriptive message stating this.

If you receive error messages, contact your Crystal Enterprise administrator. You may also search for Crystal Enterprise error messages in online documentation, or search Crystal Decisions knowledge base at http://support.crystaldecisions.com.

Using the Crystal Enterprise ePortfolio

To start the ePortfolio, the end-user interface to Crystal Enterprise, click on the Launchpad link to ePortfolio, or point your browser directly to the URL provided by your administrator. The default page for ePortfolio is loaded as seen in Figure 23-2, with the Guest account automatically logged on. In the example in this figure, the Crystal Enterprise environment has not yet had user or departmental folders and reports published to it for viewing, so there is only one folder showing in the Folders list, called Report Samples.

If the Guest account has been disabled in order to require all users to log on individually, you will see the logon screen prior to the main ePortfolio screen.

To launch ePortfolio (or your custom interface page) directly from a Web browser rather than from the Launchpad, point your browser to http://<web server>/crystal/enterprise/ eportfolio. Your administrator will provide the exact URL applicable to your Web server and interface page.

ePortfolio Elements

The main page of ePortfolio is divided into several basic functional areas that provide other ePortfolio navigation links, search functions, and search result display areas. The page itself can be considered a "view" into the reports, folders, and functions that the logged-on user has access to. The precise appearance of the page, or view, depends on who is logged on, and how the active view has been customized by the user or the administrator. Views are discussed in more detail later in this chapter. Also be aware that the page will appear and behave slightly differently depending on what Web browser you are using. For example, when you roll the cursor over clickable elements on the page, they change color if you are using Microsoft Internet Explorer, but otherwise they may not.

Black Title Bar Functions

The Welcome statement in the black title bar displays the user name, unless the logged-on user is Guest. Also offered in the black title bar are functions and navigation

Use these fields to search for specific reports by name, description, or date, or search for folders by title

Navigation options will vary according to rights of logged on user

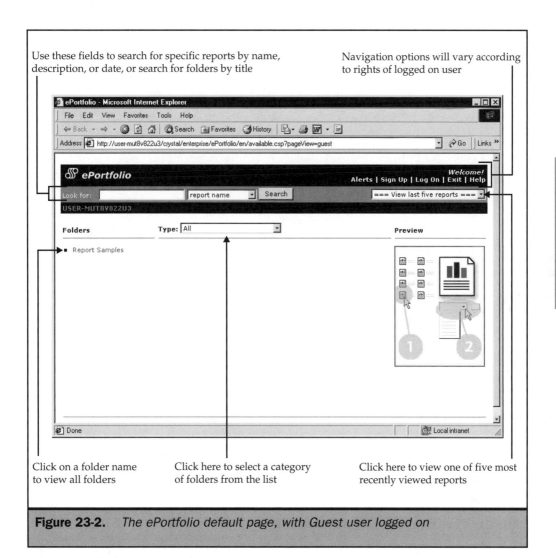

Click on a folder name to view all folders

Click here to select a category of folders from the list

Click here to view one of five most recently viewed reports

Figure 23-2.   *The ePortfolio default page, with Guest user logged on*

CRYSTAL REPORTS 8.5 ON THE WEB

options, which vary depending on whether you are using Crystal Enterprise Standard or Professional, and whether you are logged on as a guest, a named user, or the administrator (who is essentially a named user in either edition of Crystal Enterprise).

Options available to *all* users, and both editions of Crystal Enterprise, include

- **Alerts**   Opens a screen listing any alerts activated by report instances within your viewing rights.

- **Log On**   Allows logged-on user to log on as different user.

- **Help**   Opens online help system.

- **Sign Up**   Allows Guest to create a new, named user account (this option is only available to a *Guest* user with CE Professional, and only if the administrator has set the "Guest users can create their own Enterprise accounts" option).

The following options are available to the administrator with both editions of Crystal Enterprise, and to named users with CE Professional:

- **Favorites / Public**   Toggle between Favorites view or Public view.

- **Organize**   Create and organize folders in Favorites view.

- **Settings**   Customize the appearance of the ePortfolio views, including how much information is displayed about each report, colors scheme, time zone, and other preferences. Also provides access to Account Settings for password changes and so forth.

- **Log Off**   Log off Enterprise, returning to the Guest account or to the logon screen.

The Search Bar

This second section of the ePortfolio allows you to search through your viewable folders for specific reports or folders. Search functions include

- **Text search**   Search for objects by report name, report description (summary info), folder title, or all fields.

- **Date search**   Search for report instances by date.

- **Most recent reports**   Shows the five most recently viewed reports.

Navigation Bar

Below the search bar you will see the folder path and the name of the folder or view you're currently in. Roll your cursor over the path to see that you can navigate directly to any folder in the path.

Folder and Report Display Area

In the main ePortfolio display area, the Folders column on the left lists any folders within the folder or view you're in. The center column shows a report capsule of each report in the open folder, including report title, thumbnail, owner, and the current number of instances. The Preview column, on the right, shows a larger preview of any selected report. Figure 23-3 shows an administrator's view of the Report Samples folder with one of the six reports selected (Also note the different navigation options in the title bar).

Report Action Area

Below the preview is a drop-down box allowing you to take further action with the selected report, such as viewing, scheduling, and so forth.

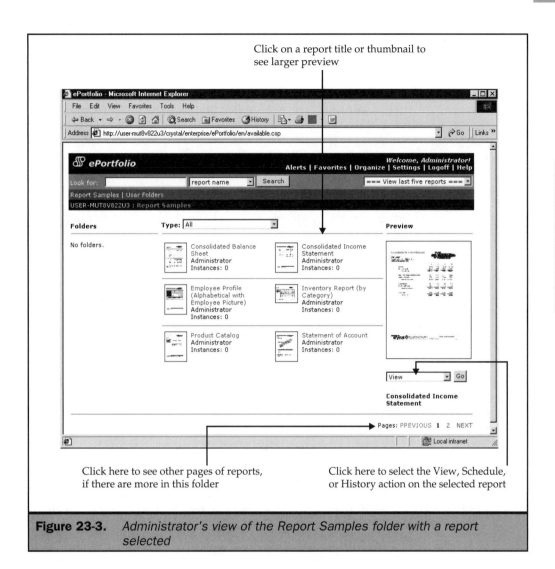

Click on a report title or thumbnail to
see larger preview

Click here to see other pages of reports,
if there are more in this folder

Click here to select the View, Schedule,
or History action on the selected report

Figure 23-3. *Administrator's view of the Report Samples folder with a report selected*

Page Navigation

If there is more than one page of report summaries to display, page navigation elements will appear at the bottom right of the ePortfolio.

Each report that's shown will include certain report elements, to aid in identifying the report. Assuming that your user account settings include displaying all possible elements, you'll see the report title, author, and thumbnail, and if you roll the cursor over the report title or thumbnail, you'll also see the folder path and the report summary info.

The thumbnail will only display if "Save Preview Picture" was activated when the report was saved in Crystal Reports and the administrator has activated the "Generate Thumbnail" feature for the report.

On the main ePortfolio view, the Type drop-down box over the central report summary display column allows you to limit the display to only reports generated by the Crystal Report Designer, or only reports generated by Crystal Analysis Professional. The default setting includes all types of reports.

Searching for Reports

The primary function of the ePortfolio is to search for, view, schedule, and monitor reports. Therefore, navigation and search capabilities are both key to the efficiency of the tool. As outlined above, there are several ways to find the reports you're looking for.

Navigating to Your Report

The basic organization of the ePortfolio page is such that it's easy to navigate through folders to get to the one you need by simply clicking on the folder names in succession until you have drilled down to the correct folder and your report is displayed. You'll find that ePortfolio behaves much the same as Web pages do when viewed in your Web browser. You can even use the browser's Back button to return through previous folders. In addition, you can navigate directly to a particular folder within the path you've followed by clicking on the folder name in the navigation path bar.

Searching for Your Report

If you have specific information about a particular report, you can go directly to it by using one of the searches—if you have a text string that you know is part of a report or folder title, or is even contained within the report description field (created with the Crystal Reports File | Summary Info menu option), you can enter the text in the search box, select the fields you want to search, and click the Search button. If you know the date a report was printed, you can search by date using the search box, selecting the report date field, and clicking the Search button.

As in many Windows applications, including Crystal Reports, you can also always see recently used files. The ePortfolio displays the five most recently run reports in the search bar.

Only public reports that you and other users have viewed, and favorites that you have viewed, will be displayed in the Last Five Reports list. You will not see nonshared recent reports.

Once you have located the report you need, simply click on the desired report title or thumbnail. A larger preview of the report appears in the Preview area. Up to four action options—View, Schedule, History, and View Latest Instance—appear below the preview thumbnail and can be used to process the report.

Viewing and Running Instances and Reports

For most users of ePortfolio, there are four potential actions to take on a report: View, Schedule, History, and View Latest Instance. View and Schedule are both actions that involve actually running the report, either immediately or at a specified time. (When a report is run, it loads the report instructions and accesses the database, then formats and displays the report.) So, your administrator must have granted you "run" rights to a report to perform either the View or the Schedule task in the action list.

The History and View Latest Instance actions require only "view" rights to a report. With view rights, you aren't allowed to run (load and process) the report, but you are allowed to view copies, or instances, of the report saved from when other users did run it. Every time someone with run rights schedules a report to be run, the system saves what the data looked like at run time, and stores it as an *instance* of the report. These instances are saved for a period of time so that users can view them without having to re-access and process data.

> **Tip**   *The terminology is confusing, since you can't view a report with view-level rights. It may help to think of the View action as "run" rather than view.*

No matter which of the actions you take, when a report is finally displayed it will be in a new Web browser window, formatted according to the Format and Viewer options selected by you (or your administrator) in your Settings screen. These settings are discussed later in this chapter.

The View Option

When you ask to "view" a report, it is considered on-demand viewing—you are asking it to run immediately. For an on-demand view request, if a copy of the same report has been run recently, it will be displayed. If you need a fresher view of the database the report is based on, you can refresh the report once it is shown to you in a report viewer. If there is not a recent copy, Enterprise accesses the database, and then creates and displays the report. Several things affect view options and behavior:

- You can only view reports to which you have run rights.
- You can only view and/or refresh a report if you have access to the database. A database logon screen will appear if you view or refresh a report requiring database logon.
- If the report has parameters that must be completed at run time, you will be prompted for this information in your Web browser before the report can display.
- On-demand report copies are retained on the server for a period of time controlled by the administrator—usually 10 to 20 minutes. When the period has expired for an on-demand report, it is cleared from the server and fresh requests will reread the database.

To view a report, locate a report you're authorized to run and select it by clicking on the title or thumbnail. A larger preview image of the report is displayed, and the action box appears below the preview. The default action is View.

Click the Go button. The report is loaded and run, and a new Web browser window appears with a view of the report or a request for any further information required. If additional information is required, such as the database logon ID and password, or a Crystal parameter field, you'll see a request similar to that shown in Figure 23-4.

If you are not familiar with Crystal Reports' parameter behavior, you can click the Help button for additional information. When you have successfully completed any requested further information, using the on-screen prompts, the report is displayed in your Web browser, as seen in Figure 23-5.

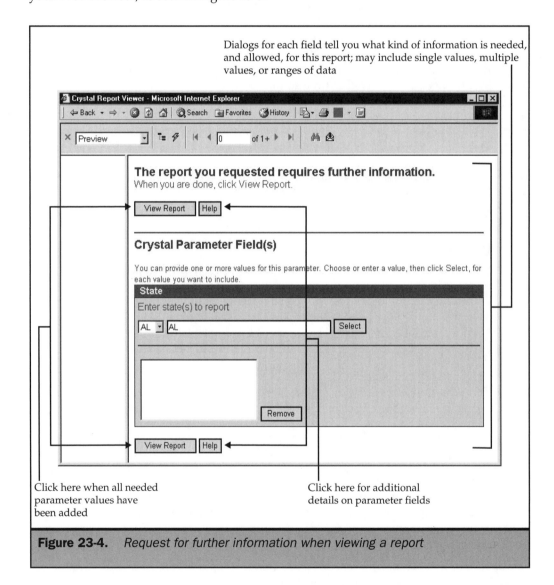

Dialogs for each field tell you what kind of information is needed, and allowed, for this report; may include single values, multiple values, or ranges of data

Click here when all needed parameter values have been added

Click here for additional details on parameter fields

Figure 23-4. *Request for further information when viewing a report*

If drill-down views are open, select among them here

Standard Web browser toolbar

Typical Crystal Reports toolbar buttons

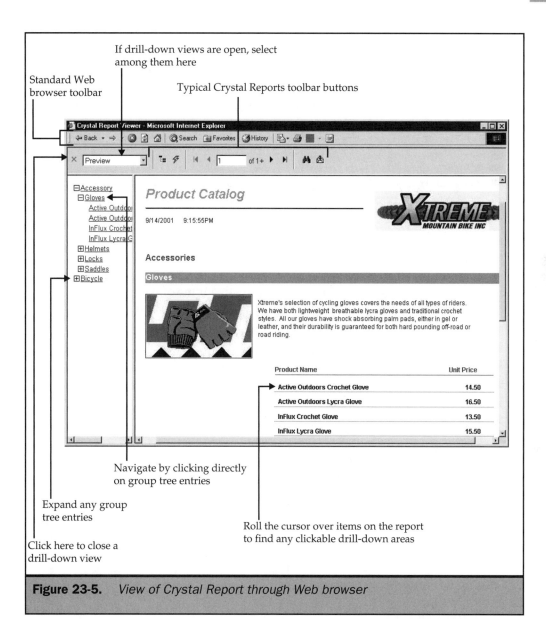

Navigate by clicking directly on group tree entries

Expand any group tree entries

Roll the cursor over items on the report to find any clickable drill-down areas

Click here to close a drill-down view

Figure 23-5. *View of Crystal Report through Web browser*

When you view a report, the toolbars and buttons will vary depending on your Viewer and Format settings. You will always have a Web browser toolbar with whichever tools apply to your viewer (for example, Back, Stop, Refresh, Favorites, and so forth). You will also have an application toolbar for whatever format you've asked to view the report in. If you are viewing a report in Crystal Reports format, you will have a Crystal Reports toolbar limited to those tools available to report management in the chosen Web viewer. When you've requested another application format, like Microsoft Word or Excel, the application toolbar will offer some of the common tools for those applications rather than Crystal Reports tools.

The tools that may be available when viewing in Crystal Reports format are discussed in the following list. If your chosen viewer doesn't support a tool, it won't be offered. For a complete list of the tools supported by each viewer, see "Report Viewers" in Crystal Enterprise Online Help.

- **Page navigation**   All viewers let you click to the first page, previous page, next page, last page, or a specific page number.

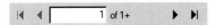

- **Group tree**   If the group tree is enabled and your viewer supports it, this is a powerful navigation tool that shows you an outline of the grouping levels on the report, and allows you to click directly to an item and display that page. The Group Tree button toggles the group tree area on and off.

- **Drill-down and close drill-down**   If the report has further detail supporting some of the data on the report, you may be able to drill down to the detail by clicking on the summary information on the report. The cursor will change when it is rolled over clickable areas, just as it does when rolled over a link on a Web page. When you double-click on a drill-down area, a drill-down page opens in the browser. You can then toggle between the main Preview page and any open drill-down pages by either selecting them in the current view drop-down box (some browsers) or clicking on the drill-down tab. To close a drill-down page, click the red X button when the drill-down page is the current view.

- **Refresh**   Refresh an older instance or a recent view to reflect the latest data. You can only refresh a report if you have run rights to it and have access to the database. If you try to refresh it without those rights, you will receive an error message in the browser.

- **Zoom control**   Some browsers allow you to specify a standard or custom screen magnification value for viewing, in percentages or in relative terms such as page width.

- **Find**   All browsers provide for searching in the report for certain text or data content. Some browsers have the search text box in the toolbar, and others prompt for the text string after you click the Find button.

- **Print** A print request will generate the Print dialog box with such options as printer choice, page range, paper layout, number of copies, and so forth. The options and defaults provided depend on the way the report was saved and the operating system and viewer you're using. Check the default values carefully to see that they are what you want.

- **Export** You have the option to export a report from the viewer to several different file formats, including Crystal Reports 8, Crystal Reports 7, Microsoft Excel, Microsoft Word, Rich Text Format, and Adobe Acrobat. When you click the Export button, you're prompted with a dialog box allowing you to enter a filename, select the file type, and browse to the location you want to store the new file.

Some of the features mentioned here are only available in the ActiveX or Java viewer. If you are using the DHTML viewer (the default when Crystal Enterprise is first installed), you won't see some of these buttons or be able to use some of these features, or some features will behave differently. You may choose a different viewer by clicking the Settings link on the ePortfolio main screen.

When you have finished viewing, printing, and/or exporting the report, you can close the report's browser window, or leave it open. If your user settings dictate that subsequently viewed reports open in the same window, the next report you view will display in place of this one.

Schedule Instances

When you schedule a report, you are setting a time to run the report—either once or on a recurring schedule. You can schedule a report to run immediately, if desired; the difference between doing this and viewing on demand is that Crystal Enterprise saves the "instance" of the report when it is run, and makes it available to other users. Unlike the temporary copy that's available only to you for a little while, after you view a report, the Schedule action puts the report instance in history, and these instances are typically available for a much longer time. As with viewing on demand, you must have run rights to a report in order to schedule it. However, the resulting report instances can be seen by users who only have view-level rights to the report.

Using scheduled reports has several advantages:

- Scheduling instances can optimize server performance by avoiding excess server and database requests.

- The scheduling function provides the ability to enter embedded parameter values, database logon, and/or selection criteria, so that the users don't have to be prompted for these values.

- When you go to view a scheduled instance (from the History list), you can choose the viewing format, such as Crystal Reports, Excel, Word, or Adobe Acrobat. You aren't limited to whatever view the scheduler used.

So, scheduled instances are flexible and informative while still protecting databases from uncontrolled access, and protecting the database servers from unnecessary hits.

To schedule a report, locate a report you're authorized to run, and select it by clicking on the title or thumbnail. A larger preview image of the report is displayed, and the action box appears below the preview.

Select Schedule from the drop-down list and click the Go button. Figure 23-6 shows the resulting Schedule dialog page, with default run-time options.

In order to schedule a report, you must provide information about when to run it, what database logon to use if needed, any parameter values applicable, and any selection criteria you want. Depending on how the report was saved, there may be default values provided and you might not have to go through these options. However, you'll often have to at least provide a database logon or a different run time.

To review and/or change the default options, select each category from the drop-down box titled "Customize your schedule options."

You can click the Schedule link in the title bar to proceed with processing the instance, whenever you've completed the desired options.

Run-Time Options   The Schedule page always opens with the run-time options displayed. These values determine how often and at what time a report instance will

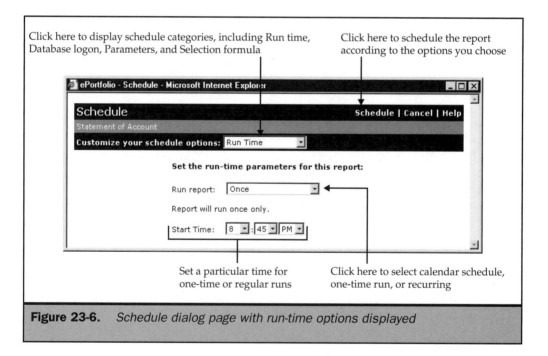

Figure 23-6.   *Schedule dialog page with run-time options displayed*

be created. The default "Once" option means it will run only once—at the time specified and within 24 hours. It defaults to the current time, so accepting the defaults provides an immediate run. The other options run it regularly at the time specified. Options include:

- Run report: Once, Hourly, Daily, Weekly, Monthly, Nth Day of Month, First Day of Month, Last Day of Month
- Start Time: Exact hour, minutes, am/pm

Complete the desired options and click the Schedule link in the title bar, or change the Customize category if you need to change other options.

Database Logon Options   To display the database logon options, select Database Logon from the Customize list.

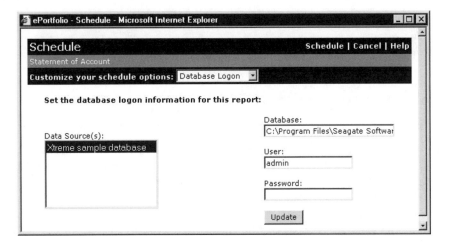

The four fields on the Database Logon page provide a way for the report to access any secure databases when the scheduled instance is being processed. If these fields are not completed, a scheduled instance will fail:

- **Data Source(s)**   Lists all data sources used by the report, with the first one highlighted.
- **Database**   Lists the path to the highlighted database.
- **User**   Requires a valid user name with access to this database.
- **Password**   Requires the password applicable to this user, if any.

If there is more than one database, be sure to click on each and complete the user information for each.

Complete the desired options and click the Schedule link in the title bar, or change the Customize category if you need to change other options.

Parameters Options If this report uses Crystal Reports parameters, which normally prompt the user to make choices about what to include on the report, those parameter values need to be provided in order for an instance to run successfully. Most reports will have default values for parameters, and those defaults may be acceptable to you; if they are, you won't have to change them before scheduling the report. However, if you need different values for this instance, you'll need to complete the Parameters page. To display any parameters active on this report, select Parameters from the Customize list.

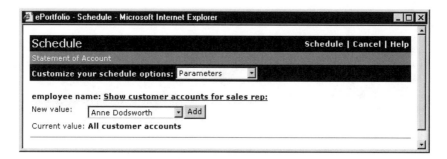

The parameters displayed will vary, depending on what types of parameters exist on the report you're scheduling. Generally, you'll see each parameter listed with its user prompt, and beneath that you'll see an area for adding values for that parameter.

If a pick list has been provided, you can select the value you want from the drop-down list and then click the Add button. If the value you want is not in the drop-down list, you can type the value in the text box and click Add. If multiple values or ranged values are allowed for a parameter, you will be able to add those values.

Complete the desired options and click the Schedule link in the title bar, or change the Customize category if you need to change other options.

Selection Formula You can modify any existing selection formula this instance uses (either record selection or group selection), and you can add any. To display any selection criteria in use, or to enter a new one, choose "Selection formula" from the Customize list.

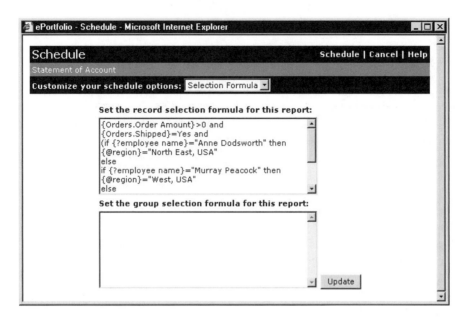

Make any desired changes to either selection formula, and click Update. This is the only options page on which you must update the changes prior to scheduling the report or making other changes.

 You must enter correct Crystal Reports selection formula syntax or the scheduled instance will fail to run. Syntax is not validated during scheduling.

When you have updated any formula changes and all other customization categories, click the Schedule link in the title bar.

The History page is displayed, with the requested instance showing as pending. See the history discussion below for further instructions.

View Instances: History and Latest

When you need to view a report, and you either don't have view rights or you need to view a scheduled instance, one or two options are available to you when you select the report on your public or favorites page. For any report that has a processed instance currently on file, View Latest Instance will be available as an action option. For all reports, the History action is always available to display and select from all scheduled instances.

How long a successfully processed instance remains accessible depends on administrative settings and on server resources—instances that expire and instances that don't get used are automatically deleted if the system needs the space.

History When you select History from the action options for a report, or when you schedule a report to run once right now, the History page opens in your Web browser, similar to Figure 23-7. It displays a list of any scheduled instances on file for this report.

The history display includes the following important elements:

- **Schedule Time** Click on the instance date/time to view an instance of this report if its status is Success.

- **Run By** Name of user who scheduled each instance.

- **Parameters** Any parameter values added during scheduling.

- **Status** Instance status may be Waiting, Recurring, Pending, Running, Stopped, Failed, or Success. "Failed" can be clicked to see reason for failure.

- **View reports as** Drop-down box lists viewing format options, including default Crystal Reports, Microsoft Excel, Microsoft Word, Adobe Acrobat, Rich Text Format, or Text.

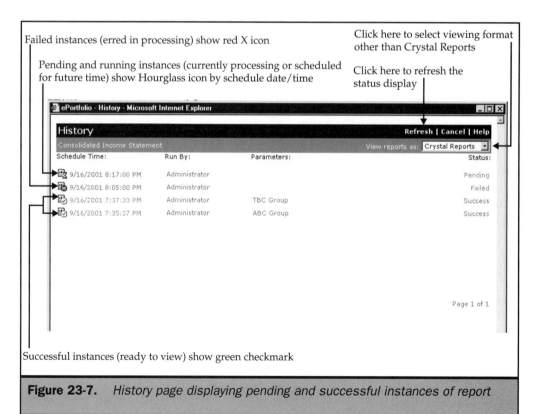

Figure 23-7. *History page displaying pending and successful instances of report*

If the status of the instance you wish to view is Success, you can click on the date/time for that instance and you will be taken to the view of the report. Note that you can first choose a different format to display the report in, if desired, by clicking the "View reports as:" drop-down box in the title bar.

If the status is Pending or Running, you can click the Refresh button periodically to update the status, or you can close the History page and reopen it later to see if the instance has processed successfully. If the status is Failed, you can't view this report instance, but can you view the reason for failure by clicking on the Failed status.

When you click on the date/time of a successful instance, the report opens in a new Web browser according to the format and view settings on your user account. It is the same view you see if you are viewing the report on demand, or viewing the latest instance. The difference is that you had the chance to select a different viewing format first, and could have selected any among the successful instances.

View Latest Instance When you ask to view the latest instance, the most recent successful instance opens in a new Web browser according to the format and viewer settings on your user account, just as if you were viewing a report on demand or from a scheduled instance in the History list.

Only successful scheduled instances will show up as "latest instances." If you have viewed a report on demand, that instance won't be the latest instance (but it will show up in the Last 5 Reports list, in the search bar).

Guest Versus User Account

As discussed earlier, if you are using Crystal Enterprise Professional, you may have the option to have an individual, named user account. Guests and named users can all view reports, report activity history, and report alerts, and can schedule reports for immediate or delayed, one-time, or regular printing. Having a named user account will further allow you to publish reports to the network, and to customize and maintain your ePortfolio folders and views. In order to log on as a named user, you must first have a user account.

Sign Up Page

If users are not allowed to create their own accounts on your system, you will need to contact the administrator to obtain a named user account for yourself so that you can log on as that user in the future. If you are allowed to create the account yourself, open ePortfolio as the default guest user and click Sign Up. Figure 23-8 shows the Sign Up screen.

Note

This is only available if the administrator has activated "Guest users can create their own Enterprise accounts" in the Crystal Management Console.

Complete the fields as desired to create your user identity, and click the Sign Up button. If you are not sure you have completed it correctly, click the Clear Form button and begin again, or click the Cancel link in the title bar.

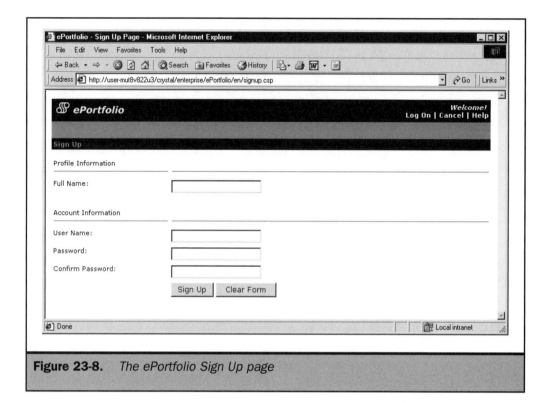

Figure 23-8. *The ePortfolio Sign Up page*

You will automatically be logged on when you complete the sign-up, and the Favorites view for your user account will display with no folders yet organized in it. For more information on the next steps, see " Favorites Versus Public Folder Views " below.

Logon and Logoff Functions

Opening ePortfolio from the Launchpad automatically logs the user on as a guest, and if you are using Crystal Enterprise Standard, there is no need to use either logon or logoff unless you are the administrator. If you are using Crystal Enterprise Professional and are a named user (or the administrator), you will use the logon and logoff functions to access and protect your existing account. Figure 23-9 shows the Logon page, which defaults to the last user logged on at this workstation.

To launch directly to the Logon page from your Web browser without going through the Launchpad or ePortfolio, you may be able to use the complete path to the Logon page—for example, http://<web server>/crystal/enterprise/eportfolio/en/logonform.csp. Your administrator will provide the exact URL applicable to your Web server and interface page.

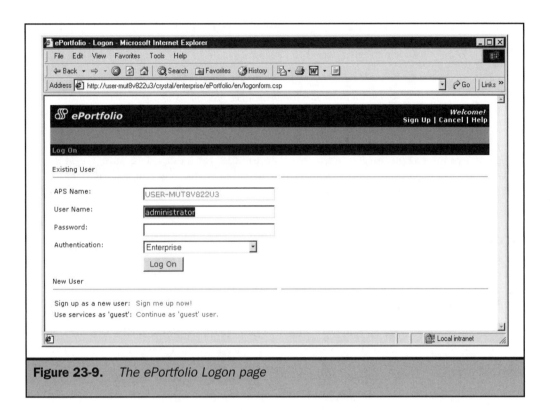

Figure 23-9. *The ePortfolio Logon page*

On the Logon page, fill in the user name and password information for your account. If you are using Crystal Enterprise Professional, make sure that the Authentication drop-down box displays the correct security mode in use on your network—if Enterprise is operating with an independent security structure, leave the default (Enterprise). However, if the administrator has implemented user/group structures that apply to both network security and Enterprise security, the drop-down box should read "NT Authentication."

If you don't have an individual account yet, but believe you're allowed to set one up, use the Sign Up title bar link or the "Sign me up now!" link at the bottom of the screen, and refer to the Sign Up page discussion above.

You can always cancel out of the Logon screen by clicking the Cancel title bar link or the "Continue as 'Guest' user" link at the bottom of the screen.

 The APS field will only be active if you are on Crystal Enterprise Professional in an installation with multiple APS servers. Otherwise, it simply displays the one applicable APS machine name.

When you have finished your session with ePortfolio, be sure to use the Logoff function. It will confirm that you wish to log off, and will automatically return the screen to the Guest view.

 If your network license includes a limited number of guest users as well as named users, be sure to exit ePortfolio after logging off. Leaving the ePortfolio page logged on to Guest will tie up a user license and potentially prevent other guests from logging on.

If you are logged on but leave the workstation idle for a period of time, Crystal Enterprise may log you off. This period of time is controlled by the administrator. If you have been logged off and you request activity, you will receive a logon screen at that time.

Favorites vs. Public Folder Views

The ePortfolio is a view or window into the reports that are available to you on your company's Crystal Enterprise system. There are two basic view types:

- **Public view**   Whether you are a guest user or a named user, you have a view of all the shared (public) reports and folders, and you can also see any other folders your account has the rights to view. You can temporarily narrow your Public view to certain reports by choosing to limit the type of report displayed, or by searching for specific folder or report criteria. If you are a named user (including the administrator), you can also customize the *appearance* of your Public view through the Settings function. But the *contents* of the public view will still be similar to the Public view of other users, because it's a window into the same shared folder structure.

- **Favorites view**   If you are a named user or the administrator, you can toggle back and forth between your Public view and a personal, customizable Favorites view. The Organize function in the title bar is used to customize the *contents* of the Favorites view, adding folders and copying reports and folders into your Favorites view for easy access. Also, most custom settings selected on the Settings page apply to the *appearance* of both your Public and Favorites views.

Organizing the Favorites View   The Organize function allows you to create folders for your own Favorites view in ePortfolio. You can create folders to hold reports, and you can store copies of reports or report shortcuts (links) into those folders, in whatever organizational structure you prefer.

When you are logged on as a named user or the administrator, you can click the Organize link in the title bar to open the Organize Favorites page.

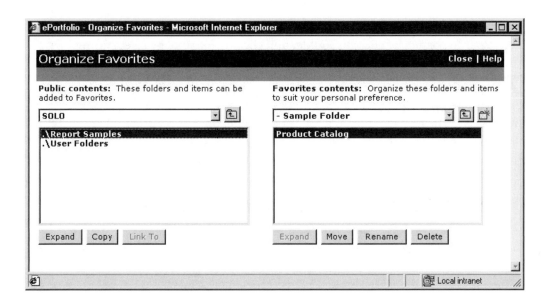

The left side of the screen displays all the reports folders set up by the administrator for shared, public access. The right side shows the current structure of your Favorites folder, including any folders you have created and any folders your administrator might have created for you.

Below each display area there are action buttons:

- **Expand**   Allows you to expand a selected folder in the list.
- **Copy**   Allows you to copy a report from the public folders to a folder in your Favorites view (see further details below).
- **Link To**   Allows you to create a link, or shortcut, in your Favorites view to a report in the public folders (see further details below).
- **Move**   Allows you to move reports and folders around within your Favorites folders.
- **Rename**   Allows you to rename any folder in your Favorites folders.
- **Delete**   Allows you to delete a folder or report from your Favorites folders.

Each of these selections brings a dialog box prompting you for complete information on the action you wish to take. In order to activate the action buttons, you have to select a folder or report first.

You can navigate through the folders on both sides of the screen by double-clicking on a folder to open it, by clicking a folder and clicking Expand, by selecting another folder from the drop-down box, or by clicking the Up-folder button. When you see the report or folder you want, select it and then click the desired action button below it.

Creating Folders   Usually the first thing you'll want to do when organizing favorites is create a few folders to hold different categories of reports for logical access. To create a new folder in the Favorites view, simply click the New Folder button on the upper-right side of the Organize Favorites page. The Add New Folder dialog box is displayed.

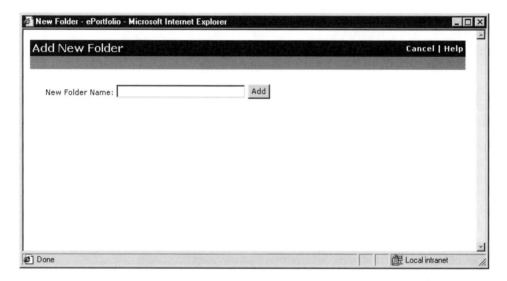

Type the desired folder name in the text box and click the Add button. The folder is added to whichever folder is currently open on the Favorites side. If the resulting location is not at the correct hierarchical level within Favorites, use the Move function to adjust it.

Moving Folders and Reports   If the location of a report or a folder is not in the correct folder, select the item you want to move, and click Move. The Move dialog box is displayed.

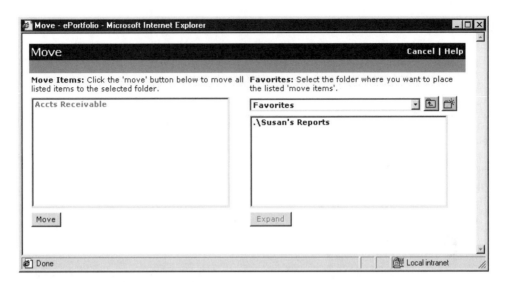

The selected item is displayed on the left side. The Favorites folder structure appears on the right. Clicking the Move button will move the item into whatever folder is currently open on the right. Therefore, before clicking Move, navigate through the folders on the right until the folder name displayed in the drop-down box is the folder into which you wish to move this item. The new folder organization is now displayed on the Organize Favorites page.

Copying and Linking to Reports   The whole purpose of the Favorites view is to organize your reports into efficient locations. Now that you have folders in which to store them, you can add reports. Obviously, one way to do this is to publish reports and save them there (covered later in this chapter under "Publishing Crystal Reports to Crystal Enterprise"), but what if there are already some useful reports in the public folders? You don't have to toggle to the Public view every time you want one if you make them accessible from your Favorites folders.

There are two ways to make public reports accessible from your Favorites view:

- **Copy**   This takes a full copy of the report file and places it in your folder. When you run it, the resulting instances will not be available to other users. If other users run the original report from the Public folders view, those instances will not show up in the History list for your copy of the report.

- **Link To**   This creates a shortcut to a public report, so when you run it, the instances you create are accessible in the History lists in the public folders for other users. And when other users run the report, you will see those instances in the history from your Favorites folder because you are really viewing the public copy.

Though it may be tempting to have your own copy of every report you run, it will overload the servers if you and other users run your own copies of reports that could have been shared. If other instances of a report might suffice for your needs, it is better to use a linked (shared) report to minimize server workload.

To copy or link to a report, first make sure the folder you want it in is open on the Favorites side of the Organize Favorites page. Then select the report(s) on the Public side of the page and click the Copy or Link To button.

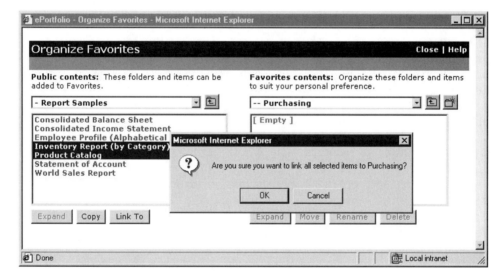 *You can use standard Windows keyboard tools to select multiple items—for example, select a report and hold down the* SHIFT *or* CTRL *key while clicking on additional reports.*

When you click Copy or Link To, a confirmation message appears asking if you want to copy (or link) the selected item(s) to the open folder.

If it's the wrong folder, you can cancel the message, open the correct folder, reselect the items, and try copying or linking them again.

If the folder location is correct on the message, click OK. The Organize Favorites page is redisplayed with the newly copied or linked items in the open folder on the right.

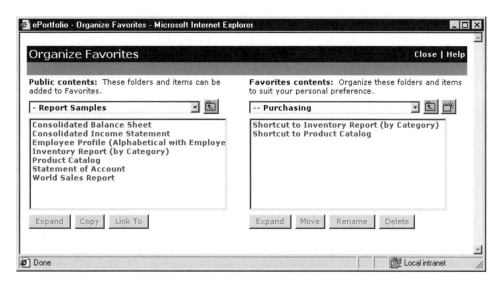

Note that if you chose to link to reports, the item is titled "Shortcut to", followed by the report name. If you copy a report, it will be the report name itself.

Renaming a Report or Folder   If a report name is too long, or you have a more meaningful name for it, you can select the report and use the Rename function to give the report a new name.

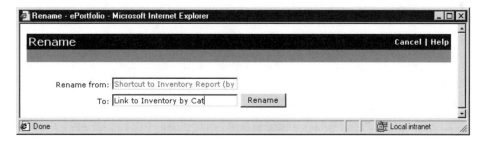

The Rename function can also be used for folders.

Deleting a Report or Folder   If you do not need a particular folder or report, you can select it and click the Delete button. You will receive a message asking you to confirm the action.

If you delete a folder, all of its contents, including instances in the history, will also be deleted; there is no additional warning about this. If the folder contained only links and copies of public reports, it can be re-created (minus the history). But if it contained reports you published directly to an Enterprise Favorites folder, these will be lost.

Customizing Settings for Public and Favorites Views   If you are logged on as a named user or as the administrator, you can use the Settings option on the title bar to customize the desktop/browser appearance and behavior of ePortfolio. Most of the settings, such as color scheme, apply to both your Public view and your Favorites view. Most of the settings are self-explanatory, and you can experiment to see which ones you prefer. These are a few settings of particular note:

- **View reports as...**   This setting allows alternative viewing software as your default application when viewing report objects. The default is Crystal Reports format, but you can select other common office applications such as Microsoft Word, Excel, or Adobe Acrobat, or you can choose Rich Text Format (RTF) or Text only.

- **View my reports using the...**   If you are viewing your reports in Crystal Reports format, this setting dictates which of the many Web-based viewers you need to use. The default is either DHTML, which will work for almost all Web browsers, or a viewer your administrator has deemed more effective for your system. You can choose one of the other viewers if recommended by your administrator. For a complete discussion of the features of each viewer, see "Report Viewers" in Crystal Enterprise Online Help, or check the Crystal Reports viewers section of Chapter 21.

When you finish making changes to your user settings, click the Apply link in the title bar or at the bottom of the page, then click Back to return to your Favorites or Public view.

Changing Your Password   If you are logged on as a named user or the administrator, you can change your password. From the Settings page, click the Account Settings link in the title bar to obtain the Change Password dialog box. You must enter the old password as well as the new password before clicking the Submit button to make the change.

Publishing Crystal Reports to Crystal Enterprise

The main purpose of Crystal Enterprise is to provide a secure, flexible way of distributing reports to people who don't necessarily have or need Crystal Reports, and who may not even have access to the reported databases. But how do you get reports into the Crystal Enterprise environment, where they can be managed and viewed?

There are three basic ways to publish a report so that it is stored in and recognized by Crystal Enterprise:

- **Publish from Crystal Reports 8.5**   If you have the Crystal Reports 8.5 program, you can choose to publish (save) a report to folders in Crystal Enterprise from the Crystal Reports 8.5 application. You can't determine a schedule or modify other run-time criteria, but it gets the report into Crystal Enterprise where it can be viewed and scheduled. The administrator determines whether users are allowed to save reports from Crystal Reports using this method.

- **Crystal Publishing Wizard**   Crystal Enterprise comes with this tool for publishing reports into new or existing Enterprise folders. It can identify and publish multiple reports at a time, and it allows you to establish report properties, scheduling, database logons, and parameters. The administrator determines whether this tool is accessible to users.

- **Publishing with the Crystal Management Console**   The administrator can use the Crystal Management Console to publish an existing report into the Enterprise system of folders. It can be used remotely and has the most comprehensive set of control options, including all of the ones Crystal Publishing Wizard allows plus user rights and selection criteria. However, it can't publish multiple reports at a time.

Each of these methods is discussed below. Keep in mind that the functions offered to you will depend on what rights you've been given by the administrator. Disallowed options will not display, or may display but be disabled (grayed out).

Publishing with Crystal Reports 8.5

To publish or distribute a report from within Crystal Reports to Crystal Enterprise so that you and/or other users can access it from ePortfolio and other Web-based Enterprise tools, you must open the report in Crystal Reports 8.5.

While the report is open, think about how it will be used by Enterprise end users. Will they need any parameter fields for selective viewing? Should you create or modify any selection criteria? Should you activate the Save Preview Picture feature, so that a thumbnail can be activated? Remember that most end users won't have access to the Crystal Report Designer, so you need to provide as much flexibility as you can.

When you are ready to publish the report, select the File | Save As menu function from the toolbar in Crystal Reports.

In the Save As dialog box, your default folder (probably a documents folder) is displayed. Click the Enterprise Folders button in the left column under Save As. You must be logged on to Crystal Enterprise to give you access to the Enterprise folders.

The Connect to APS dialog box appears, with your user name and the APS name filled in, if you are logged on to Enterprise but haven't tried to save a report to Enterprise yet in this Crystal Reports session.

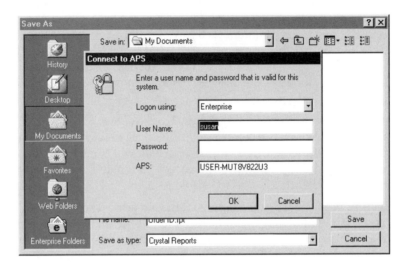

Fill in your password and click OK.

If you try to publish a report to Enterprise before logging on, the Connect to APS dialog box will not have the user or APS fields prefilled. You must provide a valid Enterprise user and password, and the APS machine name. If you don't know the APS name, it may be easier to log on to Enterprise before trying to publish from within Crystal Reports.

If the information you enter is not recognized, the Save As dialog box redisplays with the original defaults.

When your logon information is recognized, the Save As dialog box redisplays with all Enterprise folders available to you (see Figure 23-10).

Browse to the folder you want to place this report in. If you choose a shared public folder, all other Enterprise users will be able to access the report. If you choose your Favorites folder, only you will see the report from within the Enterprise system.

When the correct folder is displayed in the Save in box at the top, verify that the File Name is correct, then click the Save button.

When you browse to subfolders within the Enterprise directory, the filename (which will be the name of the report when saved) may change to match the name of the folder you're browsing to. Be sure to change it to the desired report name.

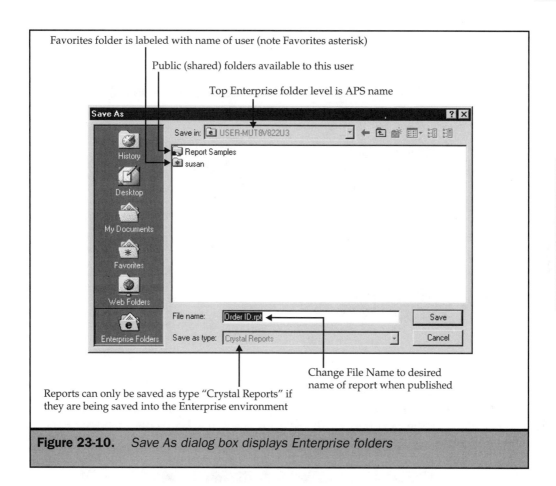

Favorites folder is labeled with name of user (note Favorites asterisk)

Public (shared) folders available to this user

Top Enterprise folder level is APS name

Change File Name to desired name of report when published

Reports can only be saved as type "Crystal Reports" if they are being saved into the Enterprise environment

Figure 23-10.   *Save As dialog box displays Enterprise folders*

When the report is saved, the Crystal Reports screen is redisplayed with the report still open. Continue working, or exit Crystal Reports. When you next view your folders in ePortfolio, or your custom Enterprise end-user environment, you will see the report.

The Crystal Publishing Wizard

The main tool provided for end users to publish Crystal Reports into the Enterprise environment is the Crystal Publishing Wizard. This is a Windows-based program that must be specifically installed from the Crystal Enterprise program CD—it can't be accessed from a Web browser. If it has been properly installed, it will be found in the Crystal Enterprise program group from the Start button.

The Publishing Wizard allows you to identify one or more existing reports and publish them (move copies of them) into existing Enterprise folders on your APS, and allows you to create and organize Enterprise folders if needed. It also prompts you to

CRYSTAL REPORTS 8.5 ON THE WEB

complete any desired scheduling, database logon, and default parameter prompts and values needed, in order for users to view and/or run the reports.

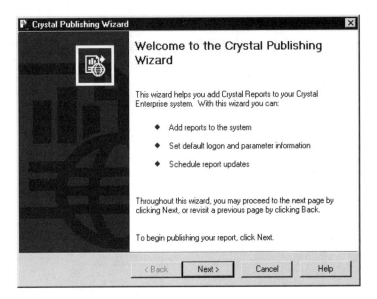

As with all such wizards, the Publishing Wizard walks you through a logical sequence of dialog screens to complete all the information needed, and you can at any time click the Back, Cancel, or Help buttons if you are not ready to go to the Next screen.

To begin, click the Next button. The Select A File dialog box is displayed, with the option to browse to a report file.

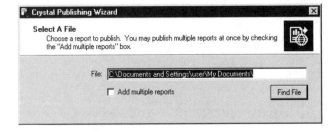

Select a File or Add Multiple Reports

If you are publishing only one report, enter the path to the file in the File field, or click the Find File button to browse to the report location. When the report file path is correctly identified, you can click the Next button.

Otherwise, if you wish to publish more than one report at this time, check the "Add multiple reports" box. Additional prompts appear in the dialog box that allow you to identify a directory containing reports, add those reports to a list of reports to publish, and then modify the list.

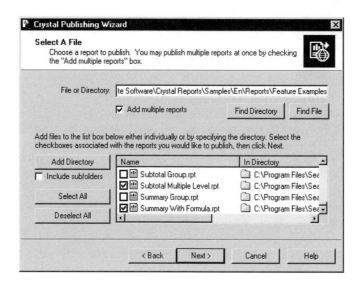

In the File or Directory field, enter the path to the directory (folder) that contains reports you want published, or click the Find Directory button to browse to the folder.

Once you've identified the path to the folder, you can click the Add Directory button to bring all the reports from that directory to the list of potential reports to publish in the center of the dialog box. If the directory has subfolders that also contain reports you might want, check the "Include subfolders" box *before* clicking Add Directory. If you aren't sure whether there are reports you want in any subfolders, check the box, and if there aren't any to add a message will tell you so.

Use the check box beside each report to select the ones you do want. If you want most or all of them, click the Select All button. This checks them all, and you can uncheck the ones you don't need. If necessary, use the Deselect All button to start over with selection.

Click the Next button to continue when you've checked all the reports you want on the list. The Select an APS dialog screen is displayed.

Select an APS

Complete the Authentication, APS, User Name, and Password prompts to ensure that you have the authority to add these reports to the APS. These are usually the same values you use when logging on to your Enterprise environment, discussed in the ePortfolio section of this chapter. The Crystal Publishing Wizard is a separate program, so you have to identify yourself as a valid Enterprise user. This allows the Publishing Wizard to find your folders and access rights for Enterprise.

Click the Next button to begin creating objects for the report(s) you're publishing. If you're only publishing one report, or if your reports all come from one directory, you'll go straight to the APS Folder dialog box to determine where you want your report(s). However, if you're adding multiple reports from more than one folder/subfolder, you will be prompted with the Folder Hierarchy screen.

Folder Hierarchy   If you see this screen, you must decide whether to duplicate existing folder hierarchy on the APS:

- **Yes**   The system will copy the folder names and structure from the local reports directories you've chosen into the existing Enterprise folder system.

■ **No** The system assumes you want to arrange all the reports yourself in the existing Enterprise folder structure, or create different folders there, and the originating folders won't be copied.

Click the Next button to display the APS Folder dialog screen.

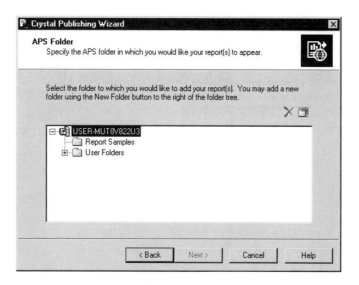

APS Folder (Enterprise Folders)

The APS Folder dialog screen displays the folder structure in your existing Enterprise environment. It only displays folders to which you're authorized full rights. The purpose of this screen is to let you identify or create a destination folder for the report(s) you're publishing. This is just the top-level folder for your reports—you'll still be able to create subfolders for some of the reports in a later step, if desired, as well as move folders and reports around within the structure. If you chose to duplicate an existing outside folder hierarchy, the reports and folders in the original directory will all be copied into the folder you select on this screen.

Find and Select Existing Folder   If the folder you want is showing, click it and then click Next.

   If the folder you want exists but is not showing, expand the top-level folders (click the + beside them) to find the desired destination folder. Select it and click Next.

Create New Folder, or Rename or Delete Folder   If you need to create Enterprise folders, click on the folder in which you want the new folder to reside and then click the New Folder button. Then type a name for the folder. You can also rename folders you've created by clicking in the name field and typing over the old name.

Folders you create are green to show that you can rename and delete them. Folders created by the system can't be deleted or renamed here.

 If needed, you can delete folders you create, by clicking the Delete button when a green folder is selected.

When it's created and named as desired, click on the destination folder for the report(s) you're adding and then click Next. The Location Preview screen appears, with your report(s) listed under the folder you selected.

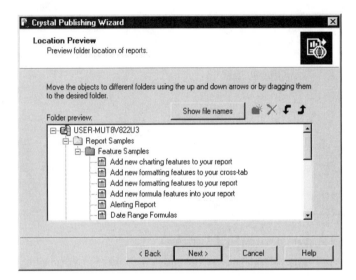

Location Preview

This screen allows you to arrange all the new reports and folders to suit your needs. The reports you added are displayed by title, but you can click the Show Filenames button to display the original file paths and names if it helps you identify them. (You will have an opportunity later to change the titles, if desired.)

Move Report or Folder   To move a report, or a green folder, click on it and click on the Up or Down Arrow button. The report or folder moves through the folder hierarchy. You can also click and drag the report or folder directly to the folder desired.

Create, Rename, or Delete Folder   You can create new folders on this screen, and you can rename and delete your new folders (shown in green) if needed, using the same buttons and methods discussed for the previous screen.

 You have to move all reports out of a folder before you'll be allowed to delete it.

When you've identified the correct location for your new report(s), you're ready to start defining the run-time qualifications and properties that the report(s) will exhibit in the Enterprise environment. Click Next. The Schedule Interval dialog box is displayed.

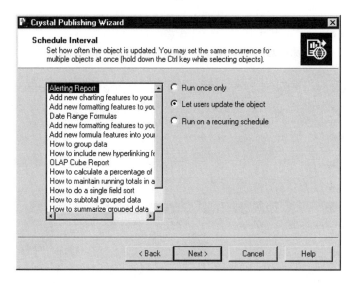

Schedule Interval

The purpose of this screen is to identify how and when each report will be run. The area on the left lists the report(s) you're publishing; on the right are three choices: "Run once only", "Let users update the object", and "Run on a recurring schedule".

The default scheduling option is "Let users update the object". If you do not make any selections on this screen before clicking Next, this option will apply to all the reports in the list.

The first report in the list is highlighted. You can highlight different reports and select a different option for each, or can hold down the SHIFT or CTRL key on your keyboard while you highlight several at once, and have the selected option apply to all.

Depending on the option you select for a report, you may receive additional prompts, as discussed below.

Run Once Only   The "Run once only" option produces an additional prompt asking you to choose whether to run the report as soon as the wizard finishes or at a specified date and time.

Let Users Update the Object   Letting users update the object means the report is not scheduled at all at this time, but will be available for users to view and/or schedule at their convenience.

Run on a Recurring Schedule   If you ask for a recurring schedule, you'll need to click the Set Recurrence button that appears. It provides additional prompts:

- **Occurs**   Choose between Daily, Weekly, or Monthly. The Runs prompt area, below Occurs, changes depending on which option is selected.
- **Starting at**   Set a time that the report will run each recurrence.
- **Daily**   If the report occurs daily, choose between Every *N* days or Every *N* hours and *X* minutes.
- **Run weekly**   If the report occurs weekly, choose the day of the week.
- **Run monthly**   If the report occurs monthly, choose the *N*th calendar day (for example, the 1st of every month), or choose the *N*th weekday (for example, the last Friday of every month).

When you have set any specific scheduling desired for each report, click Next. The Change Default Values dialog box is displayed.

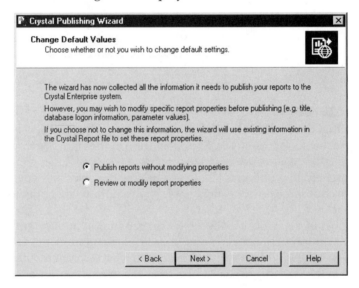

Change Default Values

The question posed on the Change Default Values screen is whether you wish to review and modify report properties before the final publishing step, including parameters, database logons, report titles and descriptions.

If you choose "Publish reports without modifying properties", you'll be advanced directly to the final publishing screens (see the "Final Publishing Dialogs" section later in the chapter); the system does check the reports for complete default information and may issue additional messages, which are discussed in that section.

If you choose "Review or modify report properties", the system displays a progress message as it reads the report file(s) to establish the qualities of each report. Then the Review Report Properties dialog box appears.

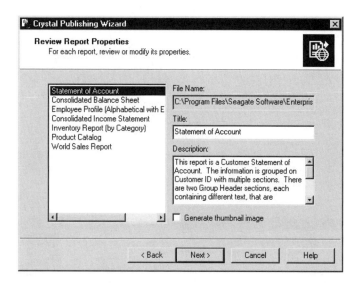

Review Report Properties

Similar to the Scheduling screen, this dialog box lists the report(s) being published on the left, with the first report highlighted. On the right are any existing properties of the highlighted report, including the path to the report filename, text entry areas for the title and description of the report, and a "Generate thumbnail" check box.

- ■ **Title** In the Enterprise environment, reports are listed by their titles, if they have titles (if not, they are displayed by report filename).

- ■ **Description** The description will display in tool-tip text in the Enterprise desktop every time the user points to the report. It helps viewers understand the purpose of the report.

- ■ **Generate thumbnail** If activated, the thumbnail shows a tiny picture of the first page of a report on the Enterprise desktop.

Note *Generate thumbnail is only available for reports that were saved with the Save Preview Picture feature activated. If the thumbnail check box is grayed out, the report doesn't have a preview picture to generate.*

You can set all or several reports to Generate thumbnail by selecting a report, holding down your CTRL key, and selecting other reports. Then check the "Generate thumbnail" check box. Other values are grayed out showing that they will not be affected by this global change.

CRYSTAL REPORTS 8.5
ON THE WEB

When each report is updated as desired, click Next. The Database Logon dialog box should appear.

Caution	*If any of your reports use a file-based data source (for example, MS Access, FoxPro, and so forth) rather than an ODBC or SQL connection to those tables, you will receive a warning indicating that those reports may not be accessible to users in Enterprise. The reports are listed, with the instruction to modify those reports (in Crystal Reports) to use an accepted data source and then republish them through the wizard or another publishing method. This warning will appear at any point that the wizard is verifying data-source choices, which could be here (before the Database Logon dialog box) or could be after choosing to skip report properties altogether.*

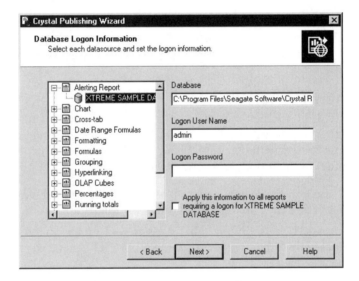

Database Logon Information

The area on the left displays your report(s). Click the + beside a report to see the database(s) it uses, then click on the database. This activates the fields on the right, for entering default database, logon user name, and logon password applicable to that database.

If you want Enterprise users to have to log on to the database any time they run the report, leave the User Name and Password fields blank. Otherwise, if the report will be scheduled rather than run on demand, or if the users who can run it don't have a database use ID and password available to them, complete the screen for the report.

Be sure to highlight each report and its database(s) and complete the information.

To simplify publishing a large number of reports that all use the same database, complete the information and then check the box that allows you to apply this information to all reports requiring a logon for that database.

When all database logons are correct, click Next to review the report parameters.

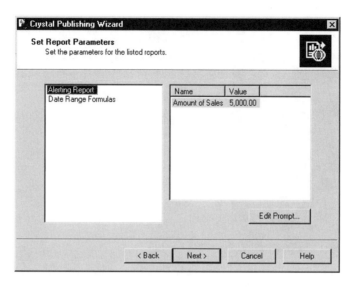

Set Report Parameters

If any reports have parameters, the reports appear on the left, with the parameters that apply to the highlighted report on the right. You may wish to set some default values for parameters, or you may wish to leave them blank.

If each Enterprise user should be allowed to enter different parameters when running this report on demand, do not fill in default values for the report. However, if the report is being scheduled without user intervention, you'll need to provide the parameter values that you want for the scheduled instance(s).

Highlight the report you want, and click the Edit Prompt button.

The Set Parameter Values dialog box appears, and allows you to set up default values for each of the parameters for that report. The options provided will vary according to what type of parameter is being updated. You may be allowed to enter single values, multiple values, or ranged values, for example. When you have established values for all desired parameters on a report, click OK on the Set Parameter Values box to close it.

When you have set parameters on all desired reports, click the Next button on the Set Report Parameters screen. This takes you into the final publishing dialog screens.

Final Publishing Dialogs

When you've been through all the report identification, location, and properties dialogs, or have opted to skip some of them, the Crystal Publishing Wizard lists all the report objects for you, and gives you the opportunity to review your settings and choices before committing to the final publishing steps. At this point, you can use the Back button to check your choices, if desired. This is also your last chance to cancel the publishing process, if needed.

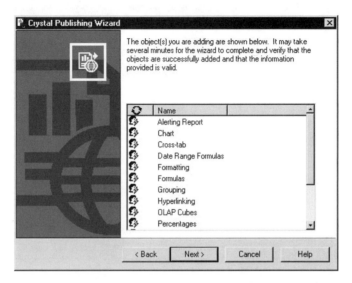

When you click the Next button, the system reviews the report object(s) to ensure all required values and properties are complete. If there are any problems, you will receive a message, such as the file-based data-source issue discussed earlier.

When all properties and values are adequate, the "Committing objects" progress screen will display report names as they are being committed to publishing.

When the commitment process is complete, the final Crystal Publishing Wizard screen appears.

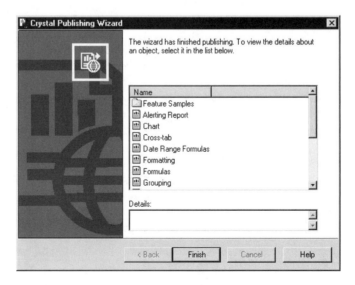

The reports and folders you've added are listed, with a Details area for displaying any comments about that object. Normally the details say, "Object committed to APS successfully." Unusual activity will be marked by a yellow exclamation sign over the object's report or folder icon, and if you click the object you'll see a comment describing the unusual event. For example, if you copied folders that contained duplicate reports, the comment will indicate that the object was committed to the APS with a "(2)" after the filename.

You can't click Back or Cancel at this point, because the reports have actually been published.

Click Finish. The Crystal Publishing Wizard application closes.

Publishing with the Crystal Management Console

This method of publishing is useful for the administrator who is managing several aspects of Enterprise, and has one or two reports to publish as well. It's also useful when your local machine has no access to the Crystal Publishing Wizard or the Crystal Report Designer, because you can use the Console remotely.

Also, you can set or modify selection criteria, which is not available through either of the other publishing methods.

This chapter assumes that you have some familiarity with the Crystal Management Console, and does not explore every option on each page. It is a review solely of the steps needed to publish a report.

When you launch the Crystal Management Console, it displays the home page. Click New Report.

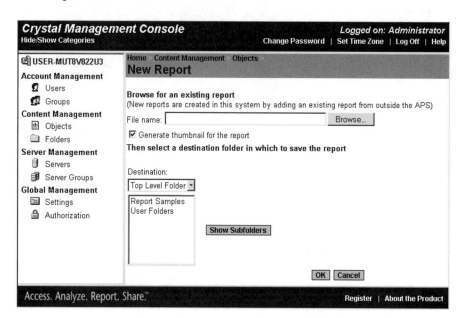

CRYSTAL REPORTS 8.5 ON THE WEB

New Report

The first step is to identify the report you want to publish and choose a folder to put it in.

Enter the path to the desired report, or click the Browse button to browse to it.

Click the "Generate thumbnail" check box, if available. If activated, the thumbnail shows a tiny picture of the first page of a report on the Enterprise desktop.

 Thumbnail is only available for reports that were saved with the Save Preview Picture feature activated.

To identify a destination folder, you must click on a folder in the Destination list, and then click Show Subfolders until the folder you want is in the Destination drop-down box.

Click OK to accept the folder location. A new page is generated for the report, with a tab for reviewing each of the publishing options on the report. Some tabs may be grayed out and inaccessible if those features (for example, parameters) aren't present on or applicable to the report. You do not have to go to every tab. When you do make a change on a tab, be sure to find and click the Update button to save your changes before looking at another tab. Although you can view the tabs in any order, it makes sense to go to the Recurrences tab last, because an update to that tab creates any scheduling requests with all the information updated on other tabs.

Properties Tab

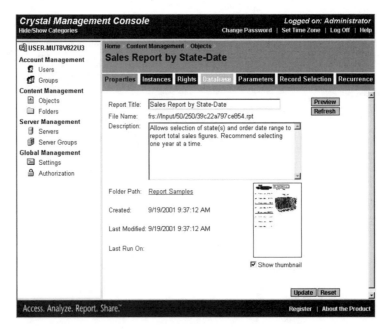

The Properties tab allows you to update the title and description of the report, and request a thumbnail if you didn't do so on the previous page:

- **Title** In the Enterprise environment, reports are listed by their titles—if they have titles (if not, they are displayed by report filename).

- **Description** The description will display in tool-tip text in the Enterprise desktop every time the user points to the report. It helps viewers understand the purpose of the report.

- **Show thumbnail** If activated, the thumbnail shows a tiny picture of the first page of a report on the Enterprise desktop.

Note *Thumbnail is only available for reports that were saved with the Save Preview Picture feature activated.*

When Properties are correct, click the Update button (at the bottom). Go to another tab or click Home (above the report name in the blue title bar) if you're finished publishing the report.

Instances Tab

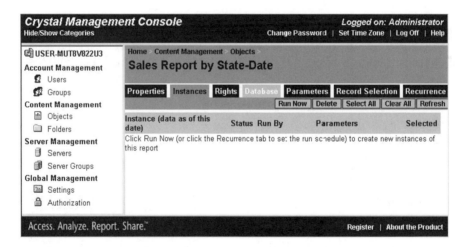

This tab displays all existing (scheduled and historical) instances for a report. For a new report, there are no instances yet, so you normally don't use this tab unless you wish to run the report right now with whatever information has already been provided on the other tabs.

If you do wish to create an instance now, rather than scheduling future or recurring instances, click Run Now (above the instructions, below Parameters tab name). This places an instance in the display area immediately.

From this tab you can go to other tabs, or click Home (above the report name in the blue title bar) if you're finished publishing the report.

Rights Tab

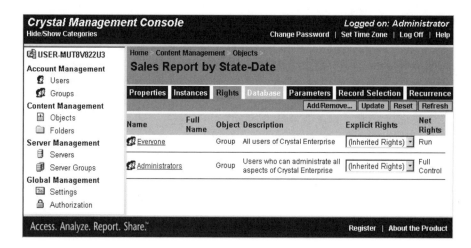

On this tab, you can define what access other users will have to this report. All existing groups and users are displayed, with their net rights to this report (inherited rights based on the folder it's in) listed on the far right. You can change a user or group's explicit rights to this report by selecting a different rights level from the drop-down box.

- **No Access**   User or group cannot see the report at all.

- **View**   User or group is allowed to view scheduled instances, through History and View Latest Instance; cannot run (View or Schedule) the report.

- **Run**   User or group is allowed all viewing and running functions, including View and Schedule.

- **Full Control**   User or group is allowed all viewing and running functions, and can also move, rename, or delete the report.

The report must be in a shared public folder in order for users to find it easily. If the report was published into a single user's Favorites folder, and that folder is not shared, then users with access to the report can find it through the search functions, but will not see the folder it's in.

When you've adjusted the rights to the report, click Update (above the Explicit Rights label) before going to another tab.

Database Tab

In order for instances of the report to be run or viewed by users who don't have database logon information or access, complete information must be provided for any required database logon.

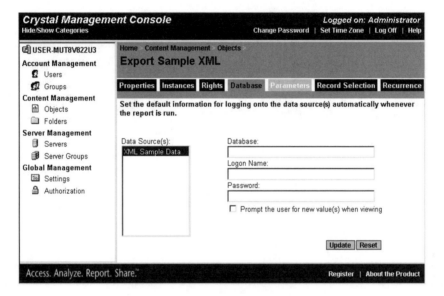

If the Database tab is grayed out, then the information is not needed by the report object (for example, the report was saved with data).

If the Database tab is active, it displays the data source(s) in the report object on the left, and the path to the highlighted database in the Database box to the right. You can change the database a data source points to if there is a different but identical database that should be used; otherwise, leave the database path intact and complete the user Logon Name and Password information if you want it provided for users or for scheduled instances. If you still want users to have to enter valid logon information, check "Prompt the user for new value(s) when viewing".

After you have completed the prompts for each data source in the report, click Update (bottom right) before going to other tabs.

CRYSTAL REPORTS 8.5 ON THE WEB

Parameters Tab

This tab will only be active if there are parameter fields active in the report. If you do not complete any default values for parameters, users trying to run the report on demand will be prompted for parameter values. Users who are scheduling instances are also offered a parameters page. But if there is a standard data set you'd like to generate for users who only have view rights, you should enter the appropriate parameter values here before scheduling instances for those users.

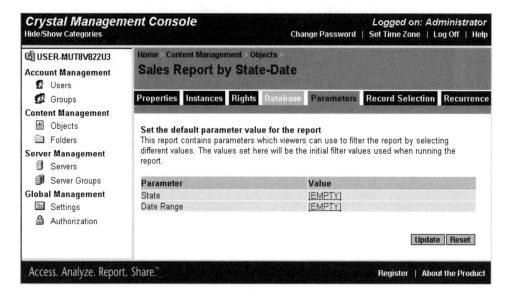

Each parameter in the report is listed, with currently set values displayed. A newly added report normally shows EMPTY in the Values column. Click on the word EMPTY to obtain the dialog box for setting initial values for that parameter.

The Set Initial Values dialog options vary according to the way the parameter was created in the report, allowing for single, multiple, and/or ranged parameter values. When you have set the initial values for a given parameter field, click OK to save these values and return to the main Parameters tab.

When you have established values for each parameter desired, click Update (bottom right) before looking at other tabs.

Record Selection Tab

You can create or modify existing record selection formulas on this tab. If users have the rights to schedule a report, they will be able to modify these, but all other viewing methods will run the record selection exactly as entered here.

 The Crystal Management Console does not check for correct Crystal syntax in the selection formula. If you update an incorrect formula, the resulting report instances will not run successfully.

Add or edit a record selection or group selection formula for this report. Click Update (bottom right) before viewing other tabs.

Recurrence Tab

This tab offers scheduling options similar to, but more extensive than, those in either the Crystal Publishing Wizard or the scheduling page of ePortfolio. You can schedule instances to run on a regular calendar basis, or you can indicate that the report will be available for on-demand viewing. Each calendar option, when selected, provides additional prompts for further defining the schedule.

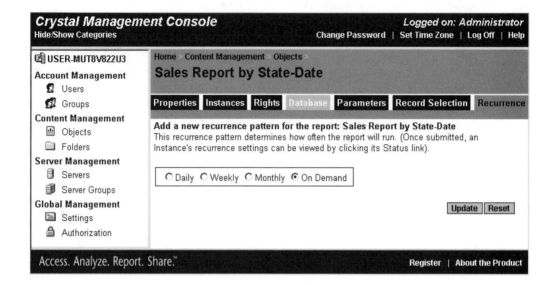

On Demand   Choose On Demand if you do not wish to schedule any recurrent instances at this time. This allows users with run rights to view and schedule the report on demand from their Enterprise environment.

Daily   The Daily option provides additional prompts:

- **Run**   Once each day, Every X days, or Every X hours N minutes.
- **Where X** and **Where N**   Drop-down boxes modify the Run entry.
- **Start Time**   Start time applies to all three Run options.

Weekly   The Weekly option provides additional prompts:

- **Run every week on**   Monday, Tuesday, Wednesday, Thursday, Friday, Saturday, and/ or Sunday; check as many of these as desired.
- **Start Time**   Start time applies to all days selected.

Monthly   The Monthly option provides additional prompts:

- **Run on the Nth day of the month**   Choose this *or* the other Run option.
- **Where N**   Drop-down boxes modify the first Run option, above.
- **Run on the X of the Nth day of the month**   Choose this *or* the other Run option.
- **Where X** and **Where N**   Drop-down boxes modify the lower Run option.
- **Start Time**   Start time applies to both Run options.

When you have established any recurrent or on-demand scheduling, click Update (bottom right).

   If you created a recurrent schedule, you can view the resulting instance on the Instances tab.

When you have reviewed all the desired tabs, and updated any changes on each tab, you can close the report by navigating to another function or page in the Crystal Management Console, or you can close the Console.

Reports and report instances you've published through any of the publishing methods are now visible in ePortfolio and the Enterprise environment.

CRYSTAL REPORTS 8.5
ON THE WEB

The
Complete
Reference

Crystal
Reports

Chapter 24

Customizing the Crystal Enterprise ePortfolio

C rystal Enterprise comes "out of the box" with its own user interface, the ePortfolio. This Web-based application is the default method of interacting with Enterprise when you first install it. While the ePortfolio is fairly complete in the Enterprise feature set that it exposes, it is obviously not designed to mirror your existing corporate intranet or Internet look and feel. As the ePortfolio is entirely Web based, and because Crystal Decisions provides completely open source code for the ePortfolio, you have complete flexibility to customize the ePortfolio to your exacting requirements. In fact, the included Crystal Enterprise Software Development kit, or *SDK*, allows you to completely replace the ePortfolio with your own custom Crystal Enterprise user interface.

> **Note** *If you wish to just use the standard ePortfolio without any customization, you can find detailed information about its features and options in Chapter 23.*

Customization Overview

While the ePortfolio that comes with Crystal Enterprise may be appropriate for many Enterprise installations, you may have a desire to customize its appearance to more closely match your standard corporate web look and feel. Perhaps you already have a corporate intranet or portal in place that you wish to match the ePortfolio to. Or, you may have an Internet site that will benefit from the scheduling or report presentation capabilities of Crystal Enterprise. These are just a few of the many possible instances where you'll find the ability to customize the ePortfolio to be of immense value in your overall Web development direction.

There are several directions you may take to customize the appearance and behavior of ePortfolio, from simple replacement of bitmap images with those more appropriate for your existing Web standards, to a complete redesign of the Crystal Enterprise user interface (in essence, *replacement* of the ePortfolio) utilizing the full capabilities of the Enterprise SDK. The direction you choose will be based on a combination of factors:

- The extent to which you want to change the look and feel of the standard ePortfolio
- The level of Web development and coding expertise in your organization
- The amount of time available for completing the customization

As you might expect, you can generally expect to require less time and less expertise to perform simpler customizations. However, if you prefer to largely redesign the basic look and feel of the ePortfolio, or perhaps even design your own from-the-ground-up user interface using the Enterprise SDK, expect larger time and expertise requirements.

Simple Customization

Relatively simple customization of the ePortfolio can consist of merely replacing some of the included bitmap images with your own, or performing simple customization to the existing HTML and JavaScript code already supplied by Crystal Decisions. This customization can be as simple as replacing the default logo for the ePortfolio with your own custom logo.

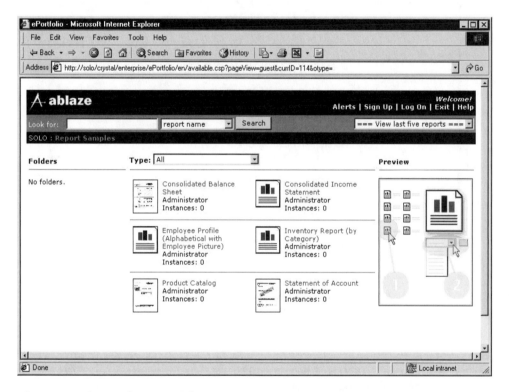

You may also perform modifications to existing JavaScript code (provided you have a basic knowledge of JavaScript), or modify other graphical elements of the ePortfolio by modifying other .GIF files that are shipped with the product.

Complete Customization

Crystal Decisions also includes a complete Software Development Kit (SDK) to allow you to either customize the ePortfolio in larger scale, or completely replace the ePortfolio with your own custom-designed interface to the core Crystal Enterprise components.

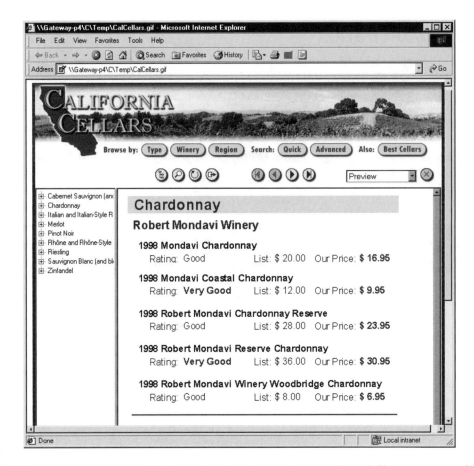

Utilizing your existing HTML and Active Server Page coding skills, you can make use of Crystal Enterprise Crystal Server Pages (CSP) to gain access to the core Crystal Enterprise components, such as Automated Process Scheduler folders, report objects, and report instances. You may then build your own user interface around these elements, displaying reports inside a Web browser utilizing one of the provided report viewers.

Crystal Enterprise even includes the Crystal Web Wizard, an interactive Windows application that generates a basic set of CSP code automatically, based on the parameters you supply to the Web Wizard.

Crystal Decisions provides extensive documentation for different customization options, as well as sample custom applications. After installing Crystal Enterprise, point your Web browser to http://<web server>/crystal/enterprise and click the Web Developer's Guide and Developer Samples links.

Simple Modifications

As discussed earlier in this chapter, if you have minimal customization requirements for your particular Web environment, there are many places you can turn to provide a custom look to the ePortfolio without having to undertake a large customization project. Since the ePortfolio is comprised entirely of HTML, Cascading Style Sheets, JavaScript, and Crystal Server Page code that is completely open and available for your modification, you may make relatively simple changes to the standard ePortfolio offering with limited effort.

By simply replacing some .GIF image files provided by Crystal Decisions, you may replace the older Seagate Software (the previous name for Crystal Decisions) logo with your own company logo. While a specific Crystal Enterprise user can choose between all the available Web-based report viewers, the Guest account is restricted to the DHTML report viewer by default (the differences among report viewers is discussed later in the chapter in "Changing The Default Viewer for the Guest Account"). By performing simple modifications to the supplied Crystal Server Pages, you may change this default to a more desirable report viewer. And, if you do plan on relying largely on the DHTML report viewer, you may easily customize its top toolbar frame by replacing .GIF image files with those more appropriate to your environment.

Tip *Depending on how you've installed Crystal Enterprise, you may need to search on separate computers to find files necessary for customization. If you've installed both the Web Connector and Web Component Server on your Web server, look on this single computer for the pathname \Program Files\Seagate Software\Web Content\Enterprise\ eportfolio\en\. You'll find HTML and Crystal Server Page (CSP) files in this folder, and .GIF files in the Images folder below it. If you have installed the Web Component Server on a computer separate from your Web server, most image files will reside on the Web server, but CSP files will reside on the Web Component Server. You'll need to coordinate modifications on both computers.*

Adding Your Own Company Logo

You can, of course, undertake a more major customization to the ePortfolio look and feel by modifying Cascading Style Sheets or the HTML provided by Crystal Decisions. However, a very simple customization can be undertaken if the general look and feel of the ePortfolio meets your needs, and you merely wish to customize the product with your own company logo. Locate the file eportfolio.gif in the \Program Files\Seagate Software\Web Content\Enterprise\eportfolio\en\Images folder. This image appears in the upper left-hand corner of many ePortfolio pages—by replacing this file with your own company logo, you can easily add your own identity to the ePortfolio.

However, changing this image file alone will not change the Crystal Decisions hyperlink that the image resolves to. You'll most probably want to change the image's hyperlink to your own internal Web site, or perhaps eliminate the hyperlink altogether. In order to accomplish this, you'll need to modify five Crystal Server Page (CSP) files supplied by Crystal Decisions: available.csp, signup.csp, logonform.csp, settings.csp, and settings2.csp. Open each of these files in a Web editor, such as FrontPage, or a standard text editor, such as Notepad. Then, just search for the single occurrence in each file of http://www.seagatesoftware.com (the Web address for Crystal Decisions' predecessor, Seagate Software). Either modify this address to your own desired Web address, or remove the HREF tag entirely to disable the hyperlink for the logo image.

Changing the Default Viewer for the Guest Account

As with the Web Component Server supported by earlier versions of Crystal Reports, as well as with the Crystal Report Designer Component and Active Server Pages, Crystal Enterprise supports multiple browser-based viewers for displaying reports on the Web. The default viewer for all Crystal Enterprise accounts is the DHTML frames viewer, as shown in Figure 24-1. This viewer takes advantage of the latest HTML standard (Dynamic HyperText Markup Language, or HTML 4) to provide very accurate report formatting in a simple HTML frames display.

While this viewer does an admirable job of reproducing most Crystal Reports formatting accurately, there are certain functions (such as printing fully paginated reports to an attached printer) that this viewer does not provide. For this reason, there may be a desire to use one of the available alternate report viewers. For example, the ActiveX viewer (designed for the Microsoft Internet Explorer browser) or one of the Java viewers (designed for Internet Explorer, Netscape Navigator, and other Java-capable browsers) includes a more robust print function, as well as a more seamless export file option. The ActiveX viewer is illustrated in Figure 24-2.

When you log on to Crystal Enterprise as a named user, you will have the ability to choose the report viewer that you'd like to use by clicking the Settings link on the ePortfolio main page (Chapter 23 discusses ePortfolio usage in more detail). However, the default account that the ePortfolio initially presents to a user is the Guest account, which does not have a Settings option and does not allow a customized viewer choice. And, if you are using Crystal Enterprise Standard Edition, the only available user accounts are Guest and Administrator—you won't be able to create additional named accounts for users who can then make their own viewer choice.

The choice of the DHTML viewer as the Guest account default has been hard-coded into various CSP pages by Crystal Decisions. You are free to change this choice, however, should you prefer to present an alternate viewer to the Guest account and to users when they first log in. To make this change, you will be required to edit four CSP files provided by Crystal Decisions.

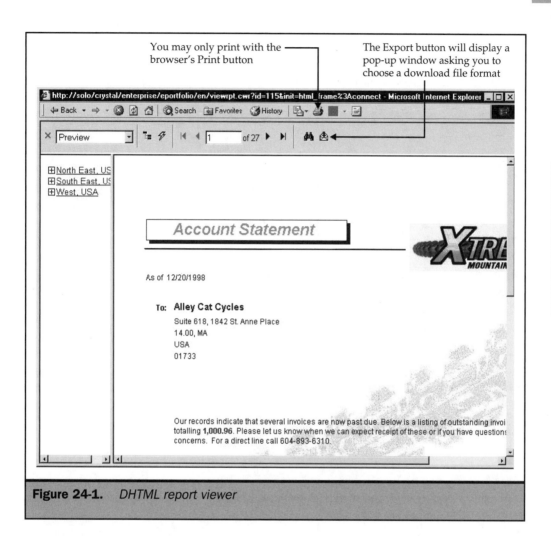

Figure 24-1. *DHTML report viewer*

Make these exact same changes to three of these files—alerts.csp, available.csp, and history.csp:

1. Open each file in a Web editor, such as Front Page, or a standard text editor, such as Notepad.

2. Search for the text "var user_vwr = 1." This is the line of text that sets the default Guest viewer to the DHTML viewer. There will be two occurrences of this text in the file.

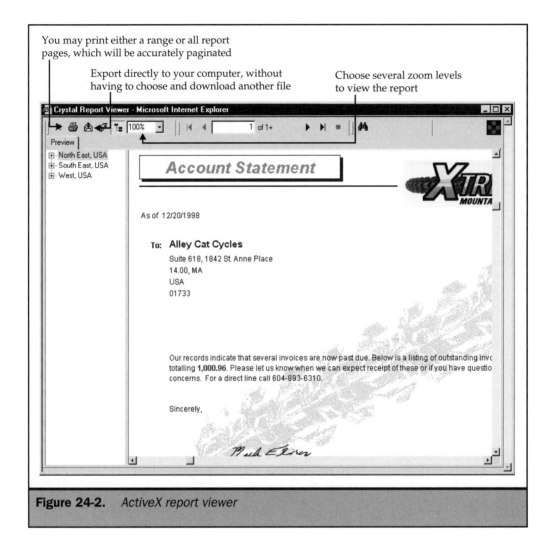

Figure 24-2. *ActiveX report viewer*

3. Replace the number after the equal sign to correspond to the viewer you wish to be the default:

0 ActiveX viewer

2 HTML page viewer

3 Java viewer (using the browser's built-in Java Virtual Machine)

4 Java plug-in viewer

5 Navigator plug-in viewer (provides same functionality as ActiveX viewer, but in Netscape Navigator)

So, default text that originally appeared in the .CSP file as

```
Response.Write "<script> var user_vwr = 1; </script>
```

will now appear as follows, if you choose to have the ActiveX viewer be the new default for the guest user:

```
Response.Write "<script> var user_vwr = 0; </script>
```

In addition to the identical changes you make to the first three files, you must also make a change to reportviewer.csp, which actually displays the report in a browser window when called by the ePortfolio. Perform the following steps to change this file:

1. Open the file in a Web editor, such as Front Page, or a standard text editor, such as Notepad.
2. Search for the following specific line of text in the file:

   &init=" & Server.URLEncode("html_frame:connect") & ExportType

3. After the init parameter, between the initial equal sign and quotation mark, place one of the following specific abbreviations for the viewer that you wish to appear as the default Guest viewer:

actx	ActiveX viewer
html_page	HTML page viewer
java	Java viewer (using the browser's built-in Java Virtual Machine)
java_plugin	Java plug-in viewer
nav_plugin	Navigator plug-in viewer (provides same functionality as ActiveX viewer, but in Netscape Navigator)

4. Place a closing quotation mark after the abbreviation and delete the remainder of the line of code.

So, default text that originally appeared in the .CSP file as

```
url = url & "viewrpt.cwr?id=" & reportNumber & "&init=" & _
Server.URLEncode("html_frame:connect") & ExportType
```

will now appear as follows, if you choose to have the ActiveX viewer be the new default for the Guest account:

```
url = url & "viewrpt.cwr?id=" & reportNumber & "&init=actx"
```

Look in Chapter 21 under "Report Viewers Compared" for a description of available viewers and a comparison of their features.

Customizing the DHTML Viewer Toolbar

While there are certain advantages to using the ActiveX and Java report viewers, you also gain advantage if you use the default DHTML report viewer. Not only do you negate the need to download an ActiveX control or Java applet to the browser, potentially reducing network bandwidth and avoiding any related security issues, but you have more control over how the DHTML viewer appears inside the target Web browser. In particular, you have the ability to customize the appearance and behavior of the toolbar that appears above the DHTML viewer report window.

A simpler approach to this customization is simply reordering the appearance of the elements in the toolbar, (for example, placing page navigation buttons before other elements in the toolbar and so forth) or changing the bitmap images that comprise the toolbar elements. You may edit the existing HTML that creates the toolbar by opening \Program Files\Seagate Software\Viewers\HTML\en\toolbar.html.

You'll notice a large amount of JavaScript code, which implements what Crystal Decisions calls the *HTML Frame API*. While it's arguable that this is really an application programmer interface, or API, in the true sense of the acronym, it does expose a set of JavaScript functions that you can call from your customized toolbar HTML to manipulate the report contained in another browser frame.

Once you've opened toolbar.html, you can make modifications to the order in which elements appear or eliminate elements you may not wish to provide to your end users. Another option is to leave the toolbar basically intact as Crystal Decisions has provided it, but to provide your own image files for such toolbar elements as page navigation buttons, the Refresh button, and other toolbar elements. You can either change references to the provided .GIF files in toolbar.html to refer to your custom images, or you may replace the supplied .GIFs with new files with identical filenames. You'll find toolbar images in the \Program Files\Seagate Software\Viewers\HTML\ en\images folder. Just make sure you provide properly designed replacement graphics. You'll typically notice three images for each toolbar element: an enabled button image, a "gray" disabled button image, and a "mouse over" button image.

Should you wish to completely redesign the toolbar frame to match your own intranet or Internet site, you may engage in a more complex ground-up design. In this scenario, you should perform the following high-level tasks:

- Create a main CSP that creates a frameset for at least two frames: the report frame and the toolbar frame. You may want to consider creation of additional frames for other window elements specific to your desired user interface.

- Create a separate HTML page that includes your custom toolbar code. You'll need to include the Crystal-supplied HTMLviewer.js JavaScript code so that your custom toolbar HTML can call appropriate HTML Frame API functions to move among report pages, refresh the report, export the file, and so on.

You can find a small sample custom toolbar application, and more details on the steps required to create a custom toolbar, by opening the Web Developer's Guide from the Crystal Enterprise Launchpad. Choose the "Tutorial: Developing a Web Application" entry in the table of contents, and then click the "How to create a custom toolbar" link.

 You should make it a practice to always make copies of any Crystal-supplied images, HTML pages, CSP pages, or JavaScript code before you make your own modifications. If you experience technical problems with modified files, you can revert to the Crystal-supplied files to see whether the problems go away.

Complete Customization with Crystal Server Pages

While the procedures discussed previously in this chapter provide you a certain amount of customization capability to the out-of-the-box ePortfolio, you may have a greater need than these techniques satisfy. For example, you may have a radically different intranet or Internet user interface that can't be matched by simple ePortfolio customization. Or, you may have developed a completely customized portal for your employees or customers that only requires limited pieces of Crystal Enterprise to be exposed. Potentially, for as many different Web interfaces that exist, there are options for integrating Crystal Enterprise.

Creating these higher levels of customization and integration will require greater effort on your part, as well as greater knowledge of more base-level Crystal Enterprise interfaces. In particular, you'll need to become familiar with Crystal Server Pages, or *CSP*, the programming interface exposed by the Crystal Enterprise Software Development Kit, or Enterprise *SDK*. As discussed earlier, the ePortfolio is based largely on CSP and is a good place to look when you're first starting to explore this programming interface.

CSP Overview

Crystal Server Pages can be most closely compared to Microsoft Active Server Pages (ASP), Microsoft's server-side scripting language for their Internet Information Server Web server. Like ASP, CSP can support both VBScript and JavaScript code, as well as embedded HTML, Java, and calls to Component Object Model (COM) objects. If you're familiar with ASP, making the transition to CSP should be a fairly straightforward process. Not only does CSP support all the language functions of ASP, but it includes additional calls to the Enterprise SDK to allow you to interact with the Automated Process Scheduler (APS), the central "brain" of Crystal Enterprise.

CRYSTAL REPORTS 8.5 ON THE WEB

Like ASP, CSP operates as a *server-side* development tool—that is, the code is actually processed on a server, not on the Web browser. While you may write fairly extensive CSP code to create your custom interface to Crystal Enterprise, only the resulting HTML or JavaScript will be returned to the end-user Web browser—you may have a 250-line CSP script that ultimately only returns 20 lines of HTML and/or JavaScript to the Web browser.

Examine the following CSP code, which has been saved on a Web server that's set up to run Crystal Enterprise:

```
<HTML>
<BODY>

<%@ Language="VBScript" %>
<%
Dim DayNumber
DayNumber = WeekDay(Date)
If DayNumber = 1 or DayNumber = 7 then
  Response.Write "<B>Have a nice weekend on this " & _
  WeekDayName(DayNumber) & ".</B>"
Else
  Response.Write "Today is " & WeekDayName(DayNumber) & "."
End If
%>
<BR>
</BODY>
</HTML>
```

Notice, in particular, the text between the <% and %> symbols. This text is the server-side script that will be evaluated by the Web Component Server. Only after this script has been evaluated will the actual results of the Response.Write statement be sent back to the Web browser. All text outside of these special symbols will be sent directly to the Web browser as standard HTML. As a result, the following HTML will be returned to the browser, if the system clock on the Web Component Server is set to a Saturday (the WeekDay of the week is 7):

```
<HTML>
<BODY>

<B>Have a nice weekend on this Saturday.</B><BR>
</BODY>
</HTML>
```

The preceding example actually shows standard VBScript that would work just as well when saved as a Web page with an .ASP extension as it would with a .CSP extension. However, there are two immediate stark differences between ASP and CSP code. Unlike ASP, which is evaluated on the Web server (and that Web server *must* be Microsoft Internet Information Server), CSP is evaluated on the Crystal Enterprise Web Component Server. This difference gives you more flexibility with Crystal Enterprise, in that you are not required to use CSP with just a Microsoft Web server. You may use CSP with a variety of Web servers, including Netscape Web servers and "plain" CGI Web servers, as well as certain UNIX Web servers. And, CSP exposes additional software interfaces beyond ASP that can be used to interact with Crystal Enterprise components—in particular, the Crystal Enterprise ASP.

Note   *There are other subtle differences between ASP and CSP. For details, look in the Enterprise Web Developer's Guide, or search the Crystal Decisions support site at http://support.crystaldecisions.com.*

You will typically find there to be much more to a CSP page than the simple example given previously. Here's a small fraction of the code belonging to a relatively small CSP that simply extracts the list of folders from the Crystal Enterprise APS:

```
Folder.csp - Notepad
File  Edit  Format  Help

'Retrieve the parent's ID for the current folder.
Result = RetrieveParentID(IStore,CurrentFolderID,ParentID)

'Check to see if the query was successful.
If Result = TRUE Then

'If this is not the top level of folders display the Up A Level option and just-opened fol
        If Not IsEmpty(ParentID) And (CurrentFolderID<>0) Then
                Result = RetrieveFolderName(CurrentFolderID, CurrentFolderName)
                Response.Write "<tr><td valign=""center""><img src='UpALevel.gif'><A HRef=
                Response.Write "<img src='Folderopen.gif'> "
                Response.Write "<b>" & Server.HTMLEncode(CurrentFolderName) & "</b></td></
        End If

        'If there are sub-folders display a link to them.
        If Not isEmpty(FolderNames) Then
                Dim k
                For k = 1 to UBound(FolderNames)
                        Response.Write "<tr><td valign=""center""><img src=""Folderclosed.
                        Response.Write "<a href='home.csp?FolderID=" & FolderIDs(k) & "' t
                        Response.Write Server.HTMLEncode(FolderNames(k)) & "</a></td></tr>
                Next
        End If
Else
        Response.Write "There was an error trying to retrieve the parent folder."
End If
```

The resulting HTML is very small—simply showing a few .GIF files and the names of the retrieved folders:

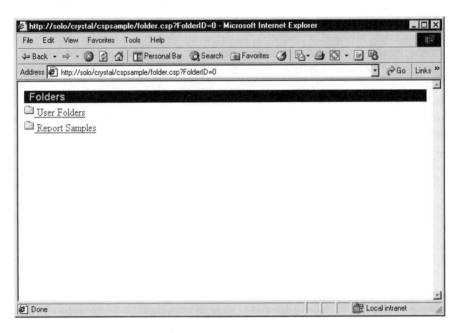

In order for CSP functionality to operate with different diverse Web servers, specific Web page file extensions are "flagged" for special handling on the Web server when a Crystal Enterprise Web Connector is installed on the server. In particular, the following Web page file extensions are automatically routed to the Web Component Server when encountered by the Web server:

CSP   Crystal Server Page

CWR   Crystal Web Request

RPT   Crystal Reports File

As such, any URL containing any of these three extensions will not be processed on the Web server—the file will be routed by the Web server to the Crystal Enterprise Web Component Server, which will process the file according to Enterprise's predetermined processing cycle. The results of that processing cycle (standard HTML or JavaScript from a CSP or a report viewer from a CWR or RPT) will then be sent back to the Web server for return to the Web browser originating the URL.

For more information on Crystal Enterprise Architecture and a discussion of different Enterprise components, such as the APS and Web Component Server, refer to Chapter 22.

Creating Crystal Server Pages

Once you decide to undertake a CSP project (either modification of an existing system or creation of a new ground-up application), you'll have several choices available to you when it comes to code creation. Considering that your custom application will probably make at least minimal use of Crystal Enterprise functionality, be prepared for a fairly code-intensive process. One look at the supplied ePortfolio CSPs will give you an idea of the amount of code required to make even moderate use of Crystal Enterprise features (one of the main ePortfolio files, available.csp, contains some 1,726 lines of code). The choice of your ultimate coding method will depend on a number of factors:

- Your coding skills
- Availability of an existing application that you can modify
- The complexity of the application
- Whether Crystal-supplied tools can create a close enough starting point

You have several choices available, much as you do when creating Active Server Pages. You can use HTML authoring tools, such as Microsoft FrontPage; Web-application development tools, such as Visual InterDev; and even simple text editors, such as Notepad. Crystal Decisions provides some supplementary tools to make CSP creation easier. You'll find the CSP Query Builder to help you create SQL-like queries to retrieve data from the APS. And, the Crystal Web Wizard is an additional choice available to help you create a "starting application" using a simple "expert" interface.

Manual Creation with an HTML Tool or Text Editor

If you are familiar with Active Server Pages, you're aware of various tools used to create them. In general, the development community appears to be evenly divided between a development tool such as Visual InterDev, a "fancy" text editor such as Microsoft FrontPage, and a plain text editor such as Notepad (Microsoft's new development environment, Visual Studio.NET, stands ready to offer a much better alternative to these existing methods). You'll find a similar set of options for Crystal Server Pages. While CSPs are plain ASCII text files, you may want to look for a more robust editing tool—at least one that will highlight different syntax elements inside the VBScript or JavaScript code your CSP is based on. While none of the aforementioned tools will specifically recognize particular Crystal Enterprise CSP syntax elements, you will gain the benefit of at least denoting standard VBScript of JavaScript code included in the CSP.

Note *You may need to set options for Microsoft Visual InterDev or FrontPage to set the tools to properly recognize the .CSP file extension. Look at online documentation for these tools to get more information on adding additional file extensions. Or, you may wish to rename your .CSP files with an .ASP extension for editing, and then rename them back to .CSP before testing.*

You may also be satisfied with the text-editing capabilities of a simple text editor such as Notepad. While you won't see particular VBScript or JavaScript syntax, a simple editor requires no special configuration to recognize file types, and can simply be left open side by side with a Web browser to perform an edit-save-refresh type of development and debugging process.

No matter which method you use to create or modify CSPs, you will need to keep a reference of CSP objects, properties, and syntax close at hand, particularly when you first begin developing your application. While a comprehensive discussion of all Enterprise SDK options is beyond the scope of this Crystal Reports–oriented book, the Enterprise Web Developer's Guide (available from the Crystal Enterprise Launchpad) provides a complete reference to the CSP object models and syntax. You'll also find a complete set of tutorials in this help file, including sample CSP code you can copy to your own editor for use in developing your custom application.

Using the CSP Query Builder Part of the basic requirement for accessing Crystal Enterprise reports, folders, scheduled objects, and instances from within your CSPs is the ability to submit queries to the SDK's "InfoStore" object (an object-oriented interface to the Enterprise APS system database). This process is undertaken using a query language that's very similar to standard Structured Query Language, or SQL.

For example, to retrieve a list of reports in a particular folder to display in a secondary report frame, you might execute CSP code similar to the following:

```
query = "Select SI_NAME, SI_ID From CI_INFOOBJECTS Where "
query = query & "SI_PROGID='CrystalEnterprise.Report' "
query = query & "And SI_INSTANCE=0 AND "
query = query & "SI_PARENT_FOLDER=" & CStr(CurrentFolderID)

'Query the server
Set ObjectResult = IStore.Query(Query)
```

An entire section of the Web Developer's Guide is dedicated to this query syntax, including a reference to all the objects that can be returned and tested. However, Crystal Decisions provides a Web-based tool to allow you to create and execute these queries outside your CSP code. This tool serves several useful purposes—allowing you to see another Web-based example of how to interact with the Enterprise SDK, facilitating a query of the APS database with a stand-alone tool, and giving you an expert-like way of exploring the syntax for InfoStore queries.

To use the Query Builder, choose the CSP Query Builder from the Developer Samples link on the Crystal Enterprise Launchpad, or point your browser to http://*<web server>*/crystal/enterprise/websamples/en/query. The Query Builder will appear in a Web browser, as shown in Figure 24-3.

This Web-based tool allows you to enter an SDK-formatted SQL statement directly into the text box below the login information, or use a simpler step-by-step process of building "rules." Once you've built rules, you may click the Finish button to create a SQL statement at the top of the Query Builder window. When you click the Submit

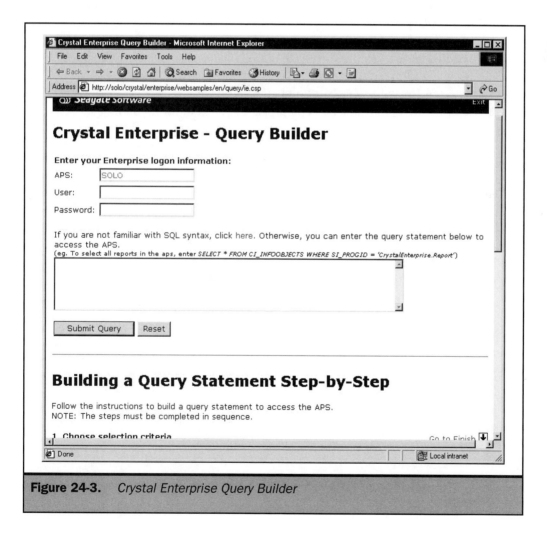

Figure 24-3. *Crystal Enterprise Query Builder*

Query button, your query will be submitted to the APS and a result set of folder, report, or object data will appear in your browser.

To build a SQL statement using the step-by-step process, use the following general guidelines:

1. Supply a valid Enterprise user ID and password to log on to your Enterprise APS.

2. Choose the selection criteria you wish to use in the SQL statement (this will create a WHERE clause). You may do this by either choosing built-in options in the first set of drop-down lists next to the first Add Rule button, or by specifying a free-form WHERE clause in the text box next to the second Add Rule button. For example, to return a list of Crystal Reports in the APS database, choose "Object type" from the first drop-down list, "equals" from the second drop-down list, and "Crystal Report" from the third drop-down list.

3. Once you've chosen from the drop-down lists, or typed in your free-form WHERE clause, click the Add Rule button next to the choices you just made. This will add the rule below the second "Specify the relationship between the rules" portion of the Query Builder.

4. If you've added multiple rules by repeating Steps 1 and 2, you must choose whether to apply an AND or OR logical operator to each of the multiple rules you've chosen. Do this by clicking the check box next to each rule that you want to apply the AND or OR operator to. Then, click the OR or AND button for your desired logical operator.

5. Each of the rules you've selected will then be recombined into one rule with the AND or OR operators included in the rule. If you wish to apply another (probably alternate) AND or OR operator to other rules, check additional boxes next to the rules and click the appropriate button. You *must* have reduced your multiple rules to just one rule containing all the desired AND and OR operators before you may progress to the next Query Builder step.

6. In the list box below the "Choose the attributes that are to be returned" section of the Query Builder, choose the different properties that you'd like the query to return. If you'd like to see more than one property, such as the object name and the object type, you may CTRL-click on the desired attributes. If the property that you wish to see isn't available in the list box on the left side, you may type the attribute name into the text box appearing on the right side of the Query Builder.

7. Click the Finish button. This will build a SQL statement based on the steps you've just performed and place it in the first text box at the top of the Query Builder. You will see a query ready to be submitted to the APS via the query.csp Crystal Server Page.

8. Click the Submit Query button to submit the query to the APS and return the results to your Web browser.

For example, if you build or type the following query,

```
SELECT SI_NAME, SI_PROGID FROM CI_INFOOBJECTS WHERE (SI_PROGID =
'CrystalEnterprise.Report' OR
SI_PROGID = 'CrystalEnterprise.Folder')
```

you'll see the following result showing the name and internal APS "ID" of all Crystal Reports and Folders in the APS system database.

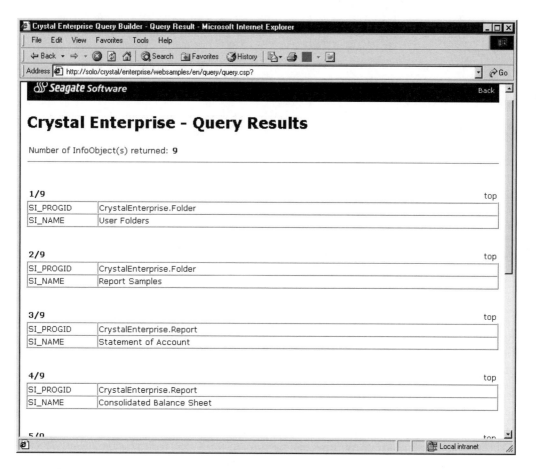

You may choose to now use the query that you built interactively in the Query Builder right inside your CSP code. You may simply copy and paste the query that was displayed from the Query Builder into your text editor, or retype it using the same syntax.

| Tip | *You'll notice that many objects and properties exposed by the Enterprise SDK begin with the letters "SI," while some begin with "CI." This indicates that the Enterprise SDK actually had its beginnings in other Crystal Decisions products—Seagate Info and it's predecessor, Crystal Info. You'll notice a fairly large number of these properties are documented as being unavailable in Crystal Enterprise Standard or Professional Editions. This indicates that these properties are "left over" from Seagate Info and are not supported in this first release of Crystal Enterprise.* |

The Crystal Web Wizard

As discussed earlier in this chapter, even a moderately simple Crystal Enterprise custom application can become very code intensive very quickly. You will want to eventually develop good knowledge of the individual elements of the Enterprise SDK to maximize your coding flexibility. However, you may appreciate a Crystal Decisions–supplied tool that makes initial creation of custom CSP code as simple as using an expert-like interface to specify simple requirements for your initial application. The *Crystal Web Wizard* is available both as a stand-alone Windows program and as an option in the Microsoft FrontPage HTML authoring tool.

The Crystal Web Wizard will present you with a series of screens allowing you to choose particular options for your Crystal Enterprise application. First, you'll have the choice of either creating a new project or installing a sample project. A new project will create a generic user interface, including logon information and a folder/report list. You will then be able to modify the CSP created by the wizard to more closely match your desired look and feel. Choosing a sample project will simply re-create one of the existing five sample applications already available from the Crystal Enterprise Launchpad Developer Samples link: the Report Directory client, the CSP Query Builder, the Report Thumbnail client, the In-Frame client, or the Xtreme Corporate Web site.

In essence, the same things happen when you use either the stand-alone version or the FrontPage version—the FrontPage version simply creates a new Web virtual directory on your Web server and copies the files created by the wizard into it. You'll need to perform the creation of the virtual directory on your own if you use the stand-alone version.

Stand-Alone Version   The stand-alone Crystal Web Wizard is a Windows application that must be specifically chosen when you install Crystal Enterprise. If you click your Windows Start button and don't see a Crystal Enterprise menu option, or don't see the Crystal Web Wizard option within this menu, you'll need to rerun Crystal Enterprise setup from the program CD-ROM and ensure that the Web Wizard is chosen as an option.

To use the stand-alone version of the Crystal Web Wizard, perform the following steps:

1. Start the Crystal Web Wizard from the Windows Crystal Enterprise Start button menu. The Web Wizard initial screen will appear.

2. Choose either the Create a new project or Install a sample project option button. Then, click the Next button. As described previously, the only options available to you if you choose to install a sample project will be one of the samples that are already available from the Developer Samples link on the Crystal Enterprise Launchpad.

3. If you choose to create a new project, you'll next be given the opportunity to determine the logon method you wish to present to your end user when the application first runs. Choose Crystal Enterprise Authentication if you want to only provide Crystal Enterprise–based security (no NT security option will be available). Choose Logon (All Options) if you want to provide a choice of authentication methods (Enterprise or Windows NT) to your end user. Or, choose Windows NT Authentication to only provide Windows NT–integrated security to your end user. Then click the Next button.

4. You'll then be presented with a choice of content templates to control the display of folders, reports, and report instances. Each of the four choices

(Classic Report Listing, Directory Listing, Large Icon View, and Report Listing) will display folders and reports in a different fashion. A thumbnail view of the way the page will appear shows in the preview area when you select each option. Make your desired choice and click the Next button.

5. You'll now be given a choice of a style sheet for the display of your Crystal Enterprise application. As with the content template type, you'll be given choices in a drop-down list, with a matching thumbnail appearing in the preview area when you choose different options. Make your choice of a style sheet and click the Next button.

6. The last screen in the Web Wizard will allow you to select a drive and directory where the CSP, HTML, GIF, and other files should be copied. Either type in a pathname directly or click the Browse button to choose a directory from a directory list.

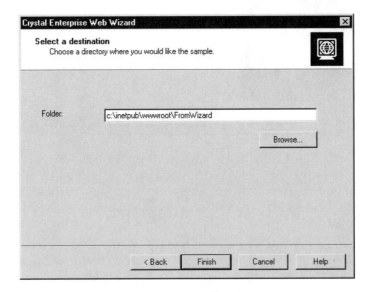

You may choose any pathname you wish (the default being the standard inetpub\wwwroot root directory for Microsoft Web servers). However, you'll probably want to choose a pathname that can be referenced via a Web server virtual directory. If the pathname you choose can't be referenced by a Web server virtual directory, you'll need to map the pathname you specify here to a virtual directory with your Web server administration tools before you can successfully view your completed Enterprise application.

7. After you've specified the location to save the files, click the Finish button. The files comprising your Crystal Enterprise application will be created and placed in the pathname you specified.

You may now modify any of the wizard-created CSPs to more closely match your desired intranet or Internet standards. To view the completed custom application, simply point your Web browser to the virtual directory where you save the application.

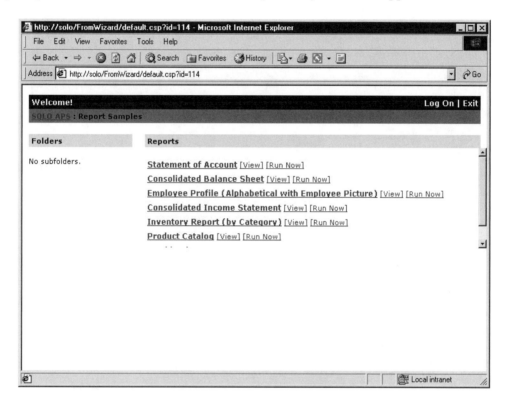

FrontPage Version   Using the Microsoft FrontPage version of the Crystal Web Wizard is almost identical to using the stand-alone Windows version. The only difference is that you can create a FrontPage Web and run the wizard at the same time. When you've completed the various wizard screens, FrontPage will place the files in the FrontPage Web you've chosen and show them in the FrontPage development environment.

To start the Crystal Web Wizard from within FrontPage, perform the following steps:

1. Choose File | New | Web from the FrontPage pull-down menus, or choose the equivalent option from the New toolbar button (steps may be slightly different if you are using FrontPage XP). You'll see a group of icons representing the available wizards provided by FrontPage.

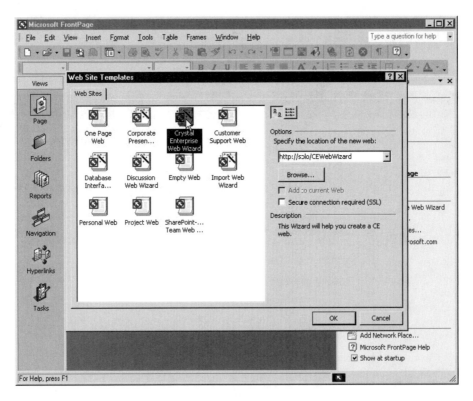

2. Type in a name for the new Web site you wish to create in the "Specify the location of the new Web" drop-down list. Then, select the Crystal Enterprise Web Wizard icon and click OK.

3. FrontPage will create the new site on the chosen Web server and display the introductory Crystal Enterprise Web Wizard where you may choose to create a new project or install a sample project.

4. The remainder of the steps to using the Web Wizard are identical to the steps described previously for the stand-alone version. Refer to the steps listed previously under "Stand-Alone Version" to progress through the Web Wizard.

5. When the wizard has finished creating files, you'll see a folder and file list in the FrontPage window. Because FrontPage doesn't recognize .CSP file types by default, you'll need to change FrontPage options to recognize the .CSP file type if you wish to edit the .CSP files directly in FrontPage. Choose Tools | Options from the FrontPage menus and click the Configure Editors tab. You may modify this tab to recognize .CSP file types.

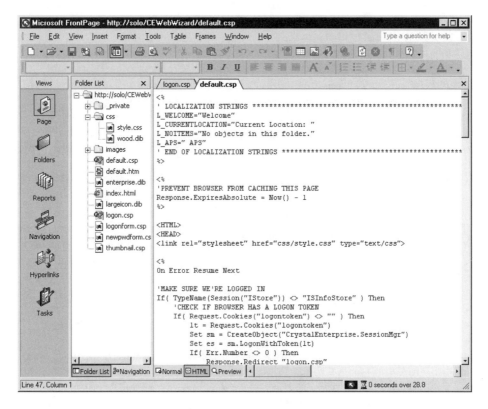

As with the stand-alone Web Wizard, you may view your custom application by pointing your Web browser to the Web page created by FrontPage.

Caution *On some computers, the FrontPage option to run the Crystal Web Wizard is not properly installed by Crystal Enterprise. If this is the case, the Crystal Enterprise Web Wizard icon won't appear in FrontPage. If this happens, just run the stand-alone version from Windows. You may then manually create a Web site using FrontPage or your Web server maintenance tools and copy the files created by the Stand-Alone Web Wizard to the new Web site.*

Introducing the Report Application Server

Shortly before publication of this book, Crystal Decisions released an add-on product for Crystal Enterprise known as the Report Application Server, or *RAS* for short. RAS plugs into the Crystal Enterprise eBusiness Framework (see Chapter 22 for a thorough discussion of the eBusiness Framework and Crystal Enterprise architecture) and allows creation of new reports and very detailed manipulation of existing reports from within a custom Crystal Enterprise application utilizing server-side ASP and CSP coding.

One of the initial limitations of Crystal Enterprise when compared to Crystal Reports Web-based reporting using ASP and the Report Designer Component (covered in Chapter 21) was the inability to control detailed report characteristics at runtime, such as grouping, formula modification, and object and section formatting. In fact, newer Report Designer Component report creation calls allow a developer to create a custom Windows or Web application that creates a complete Crystal Report from the ground up within the application. Crystal Enterprise didn't initially provide this capability, nor the ability to modify report characteristics at runtime.

However, with the introduction of RAS, new flexibility now exists to create a report completely from within a custom ASP/CSP script, as well as do more detailed report modification at runtime from a custom script. The RAS can be considered similar to, although not identical to, the Report Designer Component for Crystal Enterprise. Like the Report Designer Component, the RAS exposes a large COM object model that allows creation and modification of a Crystal Report object entirely within code. While the object model, properties, methods, and collections exposed by the RAS are similar to those exposed by the Report Designer Component, they're not exactly the same. And, unlike the Report Designer Component, the RAS fits into the Crystal Enterprise architecture of the APS, folders, objects, and instances.

The initial aim of the RAS is toward organizations that want to provide the capability for Web-based Crystal Enterprise users to design simple reports right from their Web browser without the need for a copy of Crystal Reports. Crystal Decisions' initial example of the RAS is a Web-based report expert, similar to the tabbed report experts provided by Crystal Reports. Using the RAS, an end user can interact with a series of Web pages that allow choice of database tables, table links, fields to include, sorting, grouping, and totaling options. When the user has finished making these choices, the RAS provides a report object that can then be viewed in any of the Crystal Enteprise viewers, just like a report created in Crystal Reports. While this user interface in no way approaches the drag-and-drop, direct object manipulation capabilities of Windows-based Crystal Reports, it does allow end users to create new reports from scratch right inside a Web browser. A more robust user interface can certainly be designed, only being limited by the knowledge of the developer and any limitations of the Web-based tools at his or her disposal.

The Report Application Server isn't for everybody. First, initial RAS pricing may be of concern to certain organizations—it doesn't come cheap. Also, coding with its object model can be very complex. However, if you have some existing familiarity with the concepts of the object model exposed by the Report Designer Component, you'll be off to a good start. And, if you can also add some CSP knowledge to the mix, you should have little trouble picking up the nuances of the RAS object model fairly quickly.

The Report Application Server requires Crystal Enterprise Professional—you can't use it with the Standard version. The tool is only available directly from Crystal Decisions. Check their Web site at http://www.crystaldecisions.com for more information on the Report Application Server.

Part III

Developing Custom
Window Applications

Chapter 25

Creating Your First Visual Basic/Crystal Reports Application

If you've read even a bit of Part I of this book, you've seen some of the power and flexibility of Crystal Reports. By making the vast array of corporate databases accessible with its simple, straightforward user interface, Crystal Reports has established itself as a valuable tool simply by virtue of its reporting and querying capabilities. And, Part II explored the myriad ways to integrate Crystal Reports with the World Wide Web. But, there's a whole other side of Crystal Reports that has yet to be explored.

Because database reporting and querying is a large part of many standard business applications, you'll often need to include these features in custom applications that you create for your own use. If you develop custom applications for Microsoft Windows in any of the popular Windows development tools, you'll probably soon need some type of database reporting functionality inside the application. While you can develop your own routines to step through the database record by record to generate your own internal reporting mechanism, all the intricacies of formatting, font management, graphics, and other Windows-related printing issues can create a significant, if not impossible, coding challenge.

Crystal Reports has featured developer interfaces for virtually all of its Windows versions. Version 8.5 offers some improved developer integration features that make it an even better choice for inclusion in custom Windows applications. Microsoft Visual Basic 6 (VB) developers, as well as other developers using a development tool compatible with Microsoft's Component Object Model, will appreciate improvements to the Report Designer Component (RDC). In Visual Basic and Microsoft Office 2000 Developers Edition, this interface allows both report design and flexible report integration to occur entirely in the VB integrated development environment (VB IDE). You'll never have to leave Visual Basic to perform any report development or integration tasks!

If you're looking toward Microsoft's significantly updated Visual Studio.NET tool (at Beta 2 status as of this writing) for Windows or Web application creation, you'll find Crystal Reports is an integral part of this new development environment as well. Much like the Report Designer Component with Visual Basic 6, Crystal Reports for Visual Studio.NET is fully integrated with the development environment, allowing complete report development right inside Visual Studio.NET. Finished reports can be made available in both Windows and Web applications, as well as being published as Web services.

Furthermore, Crystal Decisions provides flexibility when it comes to distributing your custom applications. While you are not allowed to redistribute the Crystal Reports design components (such as the Crystal Reports design program itself), your custom programs that merely manipulate and customize existing reports can be distributed without charge. You receive a royalty-free license to distribute the Crystal Reports Print Engine and associated files, such as .OCX and .DLL files. You may purchase a single copy of Crystal Reports, develop your custom application, and distribute the runtime files with as many copies of your application as you like, at no additional charge. If you elect to use newer report creation functions or the embedded Report Designer control that has been added to Version 8.5, you will need to purchase a run-time license from Crystal Decisions.

Don't forget that Crystal Reports 8.5 is available in three different editions. The Developer Edition will be of interest to you if you plan on using any Windows development features. To use any of the developer interfaces discussed in this section of the book, you need to purchase the Developer Edition—the other editions don't provide necessary components for custom Windows integration.

Development-Language Options

Crystal Reports developer interfaces have been designed to work with most popular Windows development tools. The most basic interface is the Crystal Reports Print Engine API. This is simply a Windows dynamic link library (DLL) file that can be called from any Windows language to support calls to external DLLs. This interface can be used with Microsoft Visual Basic and Visual C++, Borland Delphi, and PowerBuilder, among others.

These, as well as other languages and development tools, may also support additional interface options that Crystal Reports supplies. If your development language can use automation servers compatible with Microsoft's Component Object Model (COM), Crystal Reports provides the Report Engine Automation Server and the Report Designer Component Automation Server. And, the Crystal ActiveX control (or OCX control, as it's sometimes known) supplies a simple, object-oriented interface to Visual Basic and other languages that support OCX controls. If you're using Borland Delphi, the Crystal Reports Visual Component Library (VCL) interface makes it easy to create custom Delphi applications. And, if you're using the Informix NewEra development tool, Crystal Reports provides the Crystal NewEra Class Library.

And, finally, Crystal Decisions Software provides a Java-capable interface with Crystal Reports 8.5. The Crystal Reports Java Bean Viewer allows you to integrate a report into your Java applet or application. The Java Bean Viewer exposes a similar set of properties and methods as the Crystal viewer control for non-Java development tools.

Which Development Language Should I Use?

Which development language you should use is a question that cannot be answered simply in this book. It obviously depends largely on your experience level with particular developer tools. Also, your company may standardize on certain development tools that limit your choices. However, if your project will depend heavily on built-in reporting, you may want to consider an alternate tool if the tool you are familiar with doesn't support Crystal Reports' more flexible interfaces.

With Crystal Reports 8.5, Crystal Decisions continues to emphasize its intended direction with developer interfaces. In documentation and the online Developer's Help file, Crystal Decisions strongly urges developers to move toward the Report Designer Component. And, Crystal Decisions backs up its direction by supplying only the newest Version 8.5 functionality in this interface only—the other major interfaces (ActiveX control and the Report Engine Automation Server) have not been updated with new Version 8.5 features. Since most common Windows languages work with

Microsoft's COM, chances are good that you'll be able to program Crystal Reports applications using this method.

Also, the demands of your application will, to a certain degree, determine the language and developer interface that you choose. Almost all of the Crystal Reports functionality can be controlled from within your application. You can customize virtually every part of your report on-the-fly from within your application. You can even trap user events, such as drilling down and mouse clicks. However, not all developer interfaces offer the same level of flexibility for all of these functions. For example, event trapping is supported only by the Report Engine API, the Automation Server (to a limited extent), and the RDC. So, if your application needs to support this level of functionality, you may be somewhat more limited in your development-language choices.

Overall, you need to balance your corporate standards, your knowledge level, the size and speed you want your application to maintain, and the reporting demands of your application when making a development-tool choice. While Crystal Decisions still provides several different interfaces, it makes a strong statement about its direction with the Version 8.5 release. If you plan to integrate Crystal Reports well into the future, you are "on notice!" Strongly consider a development tool that supports Microsoft's COM and use the Report Designer Component.

Why Is This Book Focusing on Visual Basic?

The remainder of this part of the book concentrates on Visual Basic as the development tool for your custom reporting applications, for the following reasons:

- Visual Basic is a wildly popular development environment. Microsoft estimates that there are upward of three million VB developers in the world. Although you might not initially trust these estimates, consider that Microsoft also provides many other popular development tools as well, so inflating VB developer figures would not be particularly beneficial to Microsoft. In any case, it's hard to argue with the popularity of Visual Basic.

- Crystal Decisions estimates that a large number of Crystal Reports developers are using VB. Although other interfaces are provided with the tool, the large corporate and business penetration of Crystal Reports lends itself to VB usage.

Many of the methods and approaches discussed in the following chapters can easily be converted to other languages. For example, if your language compiles with COM, the objects, properties, and methods exposed will be the same in your tool as in VB. As such, very little effort should be required to convert to the syntax of your development tool.

DEVELOPING CUSTOM
WINDOW APPLICATIONS

Tip
The best source of developer-related information from Crystal Decisions is a Windows Help file that ships with Crystal Reports. Use Windows Explorer to navigate to the CrystalDevHelp.CHM file in the Crystal Reports program directory\Developer Files\Help. You'll find information relating to most common development languages, sample code that you can copy from the Help file, and references to sample applications that are installed along with Crystal Reports. More particular to the Report Designer Component is the CRRDC.HLP file located in the Seagate Software\Report Designer Component directory.

You can also find several helpful online documents in Adobe Acrobat PDF format on the product CD-ROM. Look in the Docs folder for DevGuide.PDF, Techref.PDF, and Techrefvol2.PDF. If you prefer to use hard copies of these manuals, they can be purchased from Crystal Decisions. Visit the Crystal Decisions Web site at http://www.CrystalDecisions.com to purchase these materials.

Different VB Reporting Options

One of the big reasons for Crystal Reports' popularity is that it seems to automatically show up whenever you install a great number of other applications. It has been bundled with Visual Basic since VB Version 3, and is also included with other Microsoft development tools, the BackOffice suite of tools, and over 150 other general and specific off-the-shelf applications. This, combined with the introduction of Microsoft's Data Report Designer in VB 6, may beg the question: "Why should I upgrade to the full Developer version of Crystal Reports if I can use the Data Report Designer or already have a bundled version of Crystal Reports with Visual Basic?"

Crystal Reports Versus the Microsoft Data Report Designer

In VB versions prior to 6, the only reporting options you had "out of the box" were excruciatingly painful record-by-record coding options, or the various bundled versions of Crystal Reports. Visual Basic 6 introduced the Microsoft Data Report Designer, as well as continuing to include a bundled version of Crystal Reports. Whereas Crystal Reports was typically installed automatically with VB in versions prior to 6, you have to dig for it with VB 6. Microsoft automatically installs its own Data Report Designer instead.

However, a peek at the Microsoft offering will quickly give you an idea of where you may want to turn for report design. While the Data Report Designer is fairly well integrated with Visual Basic (using the VB Data Environment), it quickly runs out of steam. And Microsoft obviously didn't think that highly of its report designer either—it has been eliminated from Visual Studio.NET to make way for Crystal Reports!

Bundled Crystal Reports Versus the Stand-Alone Version

Even with Microsoft's Data Report Designer included in VB 6, Crystal Reports is *still* bundled in the VB package—you just have to install it separately. And, VB 4 and 5 also included bundled copies of Crystal Reports. The versions that are included with VB differ dramatically from off-the-shelf Crystal Reports 8.5 Developer, however.

In VB 5 and 6, Crystal Decisions bundles a version of Crystal Reports known as Version 4.6. This is interesting, because Crystal Decisions never released an off-the-shelf Version 4.6 of Crystal Reports—stand-alone Crystal Reports versions progressed from 4.5 to 5.0, and then 6.0, 7.0, 8.0, and now 8.5. Why the version of Crystal Reports that's bundled with VB goes so far back is a question for someone who understands software company marketing and upgrade strategies. But for you, the developer, the differences between the 4.6 bundled version and off-the-shelf Crystal Reports 8.5 are vast and significant:

■ Bundled Crystal Reports was brought to market before Microsoft's COM became a standard. It doesn't contain any of the newer programming interfaces, such as the RDC.

■ Crystal Reports 5 and later introduced many new usability enhancements, such as conditional formatting, multiple sections, and subreports. So many capabilities will be severely limited if you choose to use it.

■ The bundled version contains absolutely no Web-reporting capabilities. If your VB apps will ever get *near* the Web, you'll appreciate the stand-alone version's Web-reporting features, such as Crystal Enterprise (discussed in Part II of this book).

These are major reasons to purchase a Crystal Reports 8.5 Developer Edition. Typical upgrade pricing is available if you already have the bundled version with Visual Basic. The greatly enhanced features of Crystal Reports 8.5 should make the outlay well worth the price.

Visual Basic Developer Interfaces

Crystal Decisions provides several methods for you to use Visual Basic to create a custom reporting application. Your choice of a programming interface will depend on several factors, such as your experience level and the particular functions that you need to include in your application. Table 25-1 discusses the different methods and their advantages and disadvantages.

Method	Advantages	Disadvantages
Report Engine API	The API completely exposes most (but not all) Crystal Reports functions that can be changed programmatically. Some newer Crystal Reports 8.5 features, such as Report Alerts, are not exposed by this API.	This interface is the most cryptic and code intensive. If you haven't programmed using Windows DLL interfaces in the past, this is a somewhat challenging place to start. Some of the more advanced functions exposed by the API (such as trapping mouse and drill-down events) require CALLBACK programming, which is difficult to implement in VB. And, some functions, such as report exporting, require the use of a wrapper interface because of some VB limitations in handling data structures.
Report Engine Automation Server	This was Seagate's entry into the standard COM Automation Server arena. It remains in Version 8.5 for backward compatibility with existing applications.	If you're not familiar with object-oriented programming, the Automation Server object model can be somewhat daunting. This interface has not been updated for Version 8.5, so you may not be able to perform some newer functions introduced in the current version.

Table 25-1. *Visual Basic Programming Interfaces Comparison*

Method	Advantages	Disadvantages
Report Designer Component	This interface has been updated completely for Crystal Reports 8.5. It combines both report design and integration functionality completely inside VB. You can accomplish much of your report design work right inside VB, without having to design reports in the Crystal Reports design environment first. In addition, the RDC includes its own automation server (slightly different from the Report Engine Automation Server) that exposes virtually all Crystal Reports' functionality in a property-method-event object model.	There are basically no negatives to using this interface, except for the potential complexity of learning an object-oriented programming model if you haven't used one before.
ActiveX control	This ActiveX control (also known as an OLE control or OCX control) is a very simple interface to Crystal Reports. If you are a relatively new VB programmer who hasn't gotten to automation server or Windows API programming yet, this is a great way to create reporting applications very quickly and easily.	The ActiveX control's simplicity comes at a price—functionality. The ActiveX control doesn't provide the complete Crystal Reports capabilities of the other interfaces. In particular, Crystal Decisions has not updated the ActiveX control since Version 6. This limits your ability to create sophisticated reporting applications with the ActiveX control. Although Crystal still includes the ActiveX control to maintain compatibility with older applications, it strongly urges developers to convert these applications to the RDC when possible.

Table 25-1. *Visual Basic Programming Interfaces Comparison* (continued)

As mentioned previously, the Report Designer component is, without a question, Crystal Decisions' tool of choice for VB integration—and with good reason. The RDC provides a good mix of functionality and ease of use. With its object-oriented interface, you can accomplish any sophisticated report customization that you require without having to get down and dirty with Windows API calls. The RDC also provides report design capabilities right inside VB. And, while the ActiveX control is a great way to integrate a report in simpler applications, you will soon find that it doesn't offer sophisticated features that you will need later on, when your application grows. This is especially true considering that it has not been updated with new features since Crystal Reports Version 6.

One thing to keep in mind when making your choice of a VB interface is that you must choose one option for each individual application. You can't use more than one approach in the same application. For example, if you add the ActiveX control to your application and then try to make direct API calls, errors will result. Evaluate your needs and skills. Then, choose a method and stick with it. Changing an interface in midstream will require you to do significant recoding.

Note   *Due to Crystal Decisions continuing movement toward the Report Designer Component (RDC) as its single developer interface of choice, the remainder of this book section will concentrate on the RDC only. Chapters covering the other integration methods, such as the ActiveX control and Report Engine API, are available for reference on this book's companion Web site at www.CrystalBook.com.*

DEVELOPING CUSTOM
WINDOW APPLICATIONS

Part III Does Not Teach You Visual Basic!

The rest of Part III assumes you have a beginning-to-intermediate working knowledge of Visual Basic. It's not practical to try to teach you VB at the same time you're learning how to integrate reports. You'll need to have a fundamental knowledge of how to create VB forms and how to respond to events. There are many good texts (including several from Osborne/McGraw-Hill), training programs, and interactive tutorials available to teach you these fundamental skills.

Also, this section assumes that you have gleaned report design knowledge from Part I of this book. Crystal Reports features, such as selection criteria, parameter fields, and object and section formatting, will be covered. If necessary, refer to Part I to brush up on these report design topics.

Chapter 26

The Report
Designer Component

Continuing along the direction set with Crystal Reports 8, Crystal Reports 8.5's premier programming integration method is the Report Designer Component, or *RDC*. Although Crystal Reports 8.5 retains all the previously supported methods for integrating reports with Windows programs (Report Engine API, automation server, and ActiveX/OCX control), Crystal Decisions makes no secret of its future direction. Not only do they stress moving to the RDC in most documentation that accompanies the program, but they've stopped adding new features to most other integration methods—to get full use of all new Version 8.5 features, you must use the Report Designer Component.

The following are several reasons why you should give serious consideration to making the RDC your developer integration method of choice:

- The RDC is entirely self-contained. You can create a complete VB-based reporting application from start to finish entirely inside the Visual Basic Integrated Development Environment (IDE).

- The RDC components are all fully compliant with the Microsoft Component Object Model (COM). As such, they'll work with any development environment that supports COM components, including Visual Basic, Visual C++, Borland Delphi, and Microsoft Office.

- Almost all Crystal Reports 8.5 functionality is exposed by various RDC components. If it's a new Crystal Reports 8.5 feature, chances are good that you can control it or customize it from within the RDC.

- Crystal Decisions, more than ever, states publicly and emphatically that its future direction lies with the RDC. Because other integration methods, such as the ActiveX control and Report Engine Automation Server, haven't been updated for several Crystal Reports versions, Crystal Decisions' desire to move developers towards the RDC is clear.

- If you are planning on migrating to Microsoft's new Visual Studio.NET development environment, using the RDC will be the best choice for preparing to migrate to this new environment.

While there aren't major revisions to Version 8.5 of the RDC, there are some notable changes that can make your development activities easier:

- A new combined run-time/design-time library (CRAXDDRT.DLL), in addition to the previously available run-time–only library (CRAXDRT.DLL)

- Full support for new Crystal Reports 8.5 features, such as XML support, PDF export, and Report Alerts

- A new Embeddable Report Designer ActiveX control that allows end users to interactively design reports from within your application programs

The RDC is available only with Crystal Reports 8.5 Developer Edition—it isn't
included with the Standard or Professional Editions. If you're using Visual Basic with
the RDC, you must use Visual Basic 5 or later. The RDC can also be used with other
languages that support standard Microsoft COM automation servers.

RDC Object Model Architecture

The RDC conforms to Microsoft's COM. As such, it can be used in any
COM-compatible development environment that supports a COM automation server
(formerly known as an "OLE server"), such as Visual Basic, Visual C++, Delphi, and
Microsoft Visual InterDev for Web page development. While an in-depth discussion
of COM is better left to Microsoft documentation, you can consider COM to be a set of
standards that allows one software environment to utilize the functions of another
software environment by way of objects, properties, methods, and events.

COM development falls under the category of object-oriented programming (OOP).
An *object hierarchy* is exposed by the COM Automation Server. This hierarchy begins
with high-level objects that contain lower levels of objects. These second-level objects
can contain lower levels of objects, and so on. If it sounds like the levels of objects can
get "deep," they sometimes do. Some objects in the RDC are four or five layers deep in
the object hierarchy.

Objects can contain not only additional single objects below them, but also
collections of objects. A *collection* is a group of related objects contained inside the
parent object. For example, a Report object will contain a collection of Section objects
(an object for the report header, page header, and so on). Each of these Section objects
itself contains its own collection of Report objects, such as fields, text objects, formulas,
lines, boxes, and so on. If the details section of a report has ten database fields, four
formulas, and a line drawing, the Details Section object will contain an object collection
consisting of 15 *members*—one member for each of the Report objects in the section.
And, if a report simply contains the five default sections that are created with a new
report, the report's Sections collection will contain five members—one for each section.

If you aren't using the RDC's internal ActiveX report designer, but instead are
integrating an external .RPT file, the highest level in the object hierarchy is the Application
object—everything eventually "trickles down" from it. Although you do need to
declare the Application object in your VB code, you will rarely (if ever) refer to it again,
or set any properties for it, once it's declared. As a general rule, the highest level of
object you'll regularly be concerned with is the *Report* object, created by executing the
Application object's OpenReport method (or automatically created if you are using
the RDC's internal ActiveX designer). You will then manipulate many of the Report
object's properties (such as the RecordSelectionFormula property), as well as work
with many objects below the Report object (such as report sections, as just discussed).

Because the RDC is a tightly integrated COM component, you will benefit from Visual Basic's *automatic code completion* when you use it. When you begin to enter code into the VB code window for the Report object, the properties, methods, and built-in constant values become available to you from automatically appearing drop-down lists. If you've used Visual Basic 5 or 6, you're probably already familiar with this feature. You'll enjoy the benefit it provides with the RDC, as well.

Whereas the other Crystal Reports integration methods require you to develop the report's .RPT file in the Crystal Reports design tool and *then* integrate it into your VB application, the RDC gives you the choice of actually designing the report right inside VB, as well as integrating existing .RPT files. Not only will you find most of the same design capabilities available from within the RDC that are available in regular Crystal Reports, but virtually all the fields, formulas, text objects, sections, and other parts of the report will be exposed to VB as objects. Like VB forms and controls, Report objects have properties and methods that can be set at both design time and run time. And, if you still choose to use an external .RPT file, the RDC exposes several COM Automation Server interfaces, allowing sophisticated object-oriented report integration with both external .RPT files and the RDC's built-in report designer.

The Xtreme Mountain Bike Sample Reporting Application

The sample application used in this chapter, as well as on the book's companion CD-ROM, is a sample orders report for Xtreme Mountain Bike, Inc., a fictional company used throughout this book. The data for the report comes from the XTREME.MDB Microsoft Access sample database that's included with Crystal Reports 8.5. The application will present a user-friendly, graphical user interface for end users who want to print an Xtreme order report.

This report contains several special features you'll want to enable for your end users in the VB application:

- A user-specified sales-tax rate that is used in the "Order + Tax" formula.

- The ability to group by calendar quarter or customer name, based on user selection.

- A prompt for a highlight value to set orders over a certain amount apart. This value will be passed to a report parameter field.

- An order-date range that will limit the report's record selection.

- A label in the page header of the report indicating the choices the user has made.

- The choice to show detail data, or to just group subtotals and summaries for drill-down. The report contains two different page header sections and two different group header sections, containing column headings that are suppressed and shown according to the summary/detail choice.

- Destination options to preview the report in a window, print the report to a printer, or send the report as a Portable Document Format (.PDF) file, attached to an e-mail message.

If the report is grouped by quarter, given a 5-percent tax rate, restricted to orders from January 1 through December 31, 1997, and the parameter field to highlight orders is given a value of $5,000, the report will appear as illustrated here.

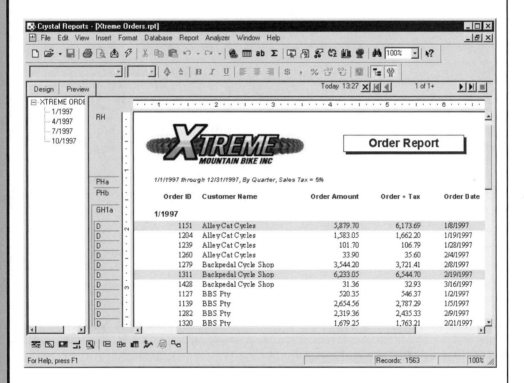

The VB application that will be used to integrate this report is a simple, single-form dialog box that gathers data from the user via text boxes, a combo box, radio buttons, and a check box. When the user clicks OK, the report is previewed, printed, or e-mailed, based on the selections made. The main form from the application is shown next.

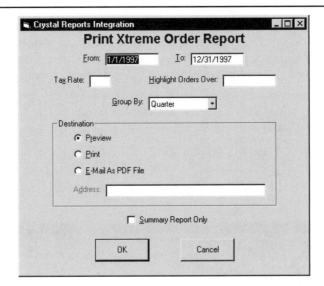

Beginning versions of both the report and VB project (created in VB 6) can be found in the Visual Basic folder on the CD-ROM that comes with this book. You are encouraged to copy these files to your hard disk and practice through the rest of this chapter. The completed RDC application is also included on the CD-ROM in the RDC folder within the Visual Basic folder.

To correctly accomplish the integration, you need to programmatically modify the following report properties from within your VB application:

- Record selection formula
- Report formula
- Parameter field
- Output destination
- Report section formatting (suppress and show)

Different RDC Pieces

The entire RDC actually consists of several parts that work together. In particular, it has four separate pieces:

- **ActiveX designer**   Enables you to actually create and modify reports inside the Visual Basic IDE.
- **Runtime Automation Server**   After you create the report, the RDC Automation Server exposes a set of powerful properties, methods, and events via a COM Automation Server.

- **Report Viewer** Because the RDC doesn't include its own built-in preview window, you use another ActiveX component, the Report Viewer, to view reports on the screen. The Report Viewer also exposes a large set of properties, methods, and events, enabling you to have complete control over how your application users can interact with your report in the viewer window.

- **Embeddable Report Designer** This feature, new to Version 8.5, allows you to place an ActiveX control on your VB form to allow end users to interactively design reports using features almost identical to the report designer available inside the VB IDE. Once users have finished their report design, the Embeddable Report Designer returns a report object that can be further modified and controlled with the Runtime Automation Server.

The ActiveX Designer

The first part of the RDC is an *ActiveX designer,* an interface that works with Visual Basic 5 and 6, and Microsoft Office Developer's Edition (using VBA 6). Whereas other ActiveX controls and automation servers generally extend the capabilities of the Visual Basic language, an ActiveX designer actually extends the capabilities of the Visual Basic IDE. Some common examples are the User Connection Designer and the Data Environment Designer, both of which are ActiveX designers for connecting to remote databases that are available with Visual Basic 6.

The designer portion of the RDC allows you to create a complete report right inside Visual Basic. You no longer need to use the iterative process of creating or editing a Crystal Reports .RPT file, working with it inside your VB code, going back to Crystal Reports to make changes to the .RPT file, and going back to VB to make changes in the code. The RDC looks similar to the Crystal Reports design screen, with multiple report sections, lists of database fields, formulas, parameter fields, and so on. You interact with the RDC via toolbar buttons and pop-up menus.

What the RDC designer features that Crystal Reports doesn't offer is a complete object model for every report section and every object you place in any report section. Every field, text object, formula, parameter field, or any other type of object has its own set of properties that appears in the property sheet, and many of those properties can be set at run time. With the RDC, you can customize formulas, text objects, section formatting, and most other aspects of report behavior and formatting by using VB coding. By creatively using text objects, you can even create report formulas using the Visual Basic language instead of the Crystal formula language, so that the text objects will be under complete VB control at run time. Of course, any Crystal formulas you create will still work, and they can still be modified on-the-fly from within your application, just as with other integration methods.

The Runtime Automation Server

The second part of the RDC is the RDC Runtime Automation Server. This component can accept either a report designed with the RDC ActiveX designer, or an external .RPT file created with Crystal Reports 8.5. The RDC Automation Server then exposes a large number of properties and methods that can be used to completely customize reporting behavior at run time.

The Report Viewer

The RDC Design Time or Runtime components don't include their own built-in preview window for previewing reports on the screen. Therefore, report previewing is provided by yet another ActiveX component that is available with the RDC, the Report Viewer. This ActiveX control is added to a form, where it exposes a large number of properties in the Properties box displayed in the VB IDE that can be set at design time. When your program is run, the viewer is supplied with a Report object from the RDC Automation Server, which it then displays in its window based on the selections you made at design time.

Not only can many of these properties also be set at run time, but the viewer contains its own COM Automation Server, which exposes a large number of other properties, methods, and events that let you completely control report behavior and interaction. You can open drill-down tabs right from within your code, trap a button click in the viewer toolbar, or respond to a drill-down click on a group footer or header. The viewer is versatile enough that conceivably you can design your own container for the Report Viewer window, creating all of your own controls and logic for report interaction.

Note   *The RDC's Runtime Automation Server and Report Viewer also can be used to develop "thin-client" applications that require only a Web browser. Both modules can integrate reports using Microsoft Active Server Pages. Chapter 21 provides complete details of this use of the RDC.*

The Embeddable Report Designer

While Crystal Reports version 8.0 provided the first "design reports at run time" capability, this capability was only available using VB code. Crystal Reports 8.5 goes to the next level by offering a fully interactive report design ActiveX control that can be added directly to a VB form. With this control, end users have full interactive capabilities to design new reports or edit existing reports from within your VB application. By providing an already defined Report object to the Embeddable Report Designer, you can allow users to modify an existing report interactively. Or, simply allow an end user to use the Embeddable Designer to create a complete report from scratch, much as you would using the RDC ActiveX designer inside the VB IDE. In either case, when the end user has completed their report design process, the Embeddable Report Designer simply returns another Report object that can be further manipulated before being printed, exported, or displayed in the Report Viewer.

When Are Royalty Payments Required?

Crystal Reports has always maintained a tradition of a royalty-free run-time license for developers. In the past, you could freely distribute run-time Crystal Reports modules, such as CRPE32.DLL (the Crystal Reports Print Engine API) and CRAXDRT.DLL (the RDC Runtime Automation Server), without having to notify, or pay royalties to, Crystal Decisions. Crystal Reports 8, however, was the first version that potentially required payment of royalties for certain types of application distribution. Crystal Reports 8.5 has expanded these requirements even further.

However, this isn't necessarily cause for concern. All previous run-time functionality, plus most new Crystal Reports 8.5 features, can still be included in your custom applications without requiring any royalty payments to Crystal Decisions. However, previous report-creation-at-runtime functionality from Version 8 that remains in Version 8.5, as well as use of the Embeddable Report Designer, *does* require a separate license and royalty payments to Crystal Decisions.

These new arrangement have a fairly straightforward explanation. In previous versions of Crystal Reports developer interfaces, you had to design a report in advance (either with the Crystal Reports designer or the RDC ActiveX designer) to include with your application—your application could not create and save an external .RPT file. Well, Crystal Reports 8.5's RDC Automation Server allows you to do this entirely from within your application at run time. And, the Embeddable Report Designer allows users of your custom application to create and save their own reports, which your application can save as .RPT files.

Because of this new functionality, Crystal Decisions understandably is concerned about the potential for competing products to its flagship Crystal Reports product (in fact, their license agreement specifically forbids "competitive products"). As such, developers who use the Report Creation RDC calls or Embeddable Report Designer must make licensing arrangements and pay royalties to Crystal Decisions. However, if you *don't* use these report-creation calls, you are still free to distribute the run-time components free of charge and without the need to notify Crystal Decisions.

Crystal Decisions has also introduced the *Broadcast License*, which is a new potential trap you need to watch out for when creating an "automated distribution system" that can distribute reports to 50 or more users. This may potentially involve additional licensing requirements for you if you're developing a system to automatically distribute reports (even if you export them to an alternate file format, such as .PDF, .DOC, or .XLS).

When you are developing applications inside Visual Basic, you'll receive a dialog box notification if you use a property or method that requires special licensing. And, a list of royalty-free and royalty-required application calls, as well as the complete license agreement, can be found in the License.HLP file, located in *Crystal Reports program directory*\Developer Files\Help. You may also search Crystal Decisions Web site at http://www.crystaldecisions.com with the keyword "Royalty."

Adding the RDC to Your Project

The first step in using the RDC is to add it to your project. After installing Crystal Reports 8.5 Developer Edition, the RDC should be properly registered on your system and ready for use.

1. Start Visual Basic and create a new project, or open the existing project with which you wish to use the RDC.

2. Choose Project | Components from the pull-down menus, or press CTRL-T. The Components dialog box will appear.

3. Click the Designers tab. You'll see a list of ActiveX designers registered on your system. Ensure that the Crystal Reports designer is selected and then click OK.

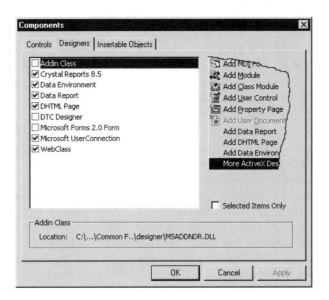

4. Using the Project pull-down menu, choose the Add Crystal Reports 8.5 option (it may appear on the More ActiveX Designers submenu in VB 5). The RDC will be added to Visual Basic and the Report Gallery dialog box will appear, as shown in Figure 26-1.

Crystal Reports 8.5 attempts to add the RDC directly to the Project menu automatically when it's installed. If you need to add it manually with Project | Components, it will "stick" from that point forward. You won't have to add it each time you want to use the RDC with a new VB project.

The RDC begins by displaying its own version of the Report Gallery. The RDC Report Gallery is very similar to the Report Gallery that appears when you create a

The RDC supplies toolbox icons when you click the Crystal Reports button

A new Designers folder will contain ActiveX designers, such as the RDC

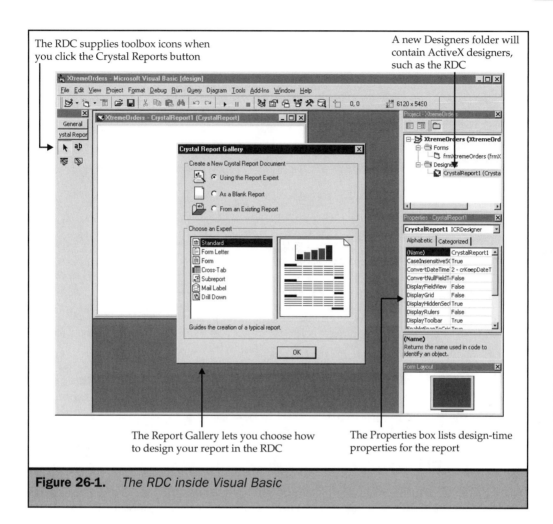

The Report Gallery lets you choose how to design your report in the RDC

The Properties box lists design-time properties for the report

Figure 26-1.   *The RDC inside Visual Basic*

new report in the Crystal Reports program, with a few changes. For example, there isn't an OLAP report option here, and the From an Existing Report option has been added. Your initial choices in the Report Gallery determine how your main report is designed inside the RDC.

Importing an Existing Report

If you've created an .RPT file in Crystal Reports 8.5 or an earlier version, and you want to use that report in the RDC, click the From an Existing Report radio button and click OK. A File Open dialog box will appear, in which you can choose the .RPT file that you wish to import. Once you've chosen the report file, you are prompted to add the Report Viewer to your project.

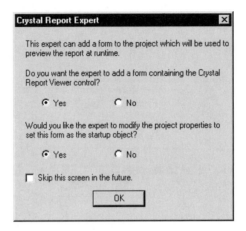

Here, you can determine whether you want the Report Viewer added to a new form in your project and, if you do, decide whether you want the Report Viewer form to be set as the startup form. If you need to preview the report in a window from within your VB application, you need to add the Report Viewer. Although you can do it later if you need to, the RDC will offer to add it automatically, along with some simple code to tie the report to the viewer. If your report will be used strictly for exporting, e-mailing, or printing to a printer, you don't need to add the Report Viewer control because it won't be used.

If you import the Xtreme Orders sample report from the accompanying CD-ROM and add the Report Viewer to a new form, your screen will look something like the one shown in Figure 26-2.

You'll notice that the RDC design window looks quite similar to the regular Crystal Reports design window—many of the features and report design steps apply equally to both environments. There are several ways of carrying out functions in the RDC design window: by using toolbox and toolbar buttons, by choosing items from the Field Explorer at the left of the report, and by right-clicking in the design window and choosing options from the pop-up menus. As with the regular Crystal Reports designer, you can select objects in the RDC design window and then move, resize, format, or delete them. Steps for these functions are basically the same as they are for regular Crystal Reports (with the exception that all RDC functions must be chosen with toolbar buttons and right-clicks—there are no pull-down menus here, as there are in regular Crystal Reports).

Remember that when you import an .RPT file into the RDC, the RDC simply copies the contents of the .RPT file into the design window and then completely disregards any changes that may later be made to the original .RPT file. Also, if you make any changes to the report inside the RDC, there will be no effect on the original .RPT file. You are not creating a real-time link to the .RPT file.

Field Explorer lets you choose
database, formula, parameter, and
other fields to add to the report

The RDC design window

Toolbar buttons for
common report
design functions

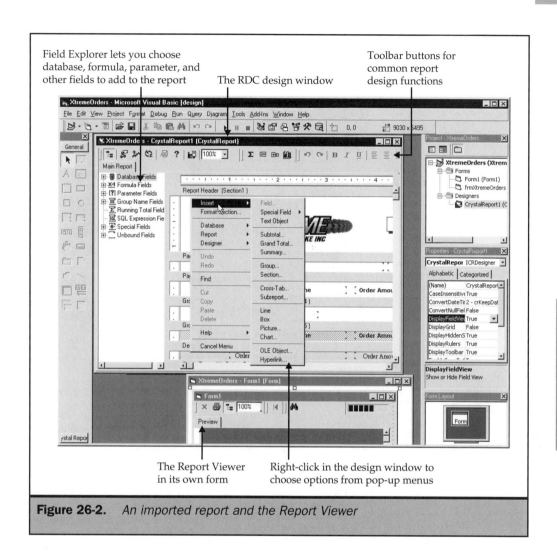

The Report Viewer
in its own form

Right-click in the design window to
choose options from pop-up menus

Figure 26-2.   *An imported report and the Report Viewer*

DEVELOPING CUSTOM
WINDOW APPLICATIONS

Tip   *If you want to save the contents of the RDC designer to an external .RPT file to use for
other purposes, you may do so. Right-click in the design window and choose Report |
Save to Crystal Reports File from the pop-up menu.*

While the RDC design window may not provide any particular functional advantage
over the regular Crystal Reports designer (except that you don't have to exit VB to use
it), the real benefit is the object model that it opens for report contents. When you select
an individual Report object, such as a database field or text object, or a report section,
such as the report header or details section, you'll see design-time properties
in the Properties box. Also, by using the internal report designer, your report design
is saved as a .DSR file along with .FRM, .BAS, and other files that make up your VB

project. When you compile the project, the report design is embedded in the application's .EXE file—there are no external .RPT files that your end users may inadvertently (or purposely) change.

As you can with properties for a combo box, radio button, form, or other regular VB controls, you can set properties at design time for any of these report elements as well. The Properties box and pop-up menu options, such as the Format Editor, interact with each other. For example, you can select a date field, right-click it, and choose Format from the pop-up menu. On the Date tab of the Format Editor, you might choose a spelled-out month and four-digit year, showing no day at all. When you click OK to close the Format Editor and then look in the Properties box, you'll notice that the Day Type property has changed to 2 – crNoDay, the Month Type property has changed to 3 – crLongMonth, and the Year Type property has changed to 1 – crLongYear. The opposite behavior is also true—changes you make in the Properties box will be reflected elsewhere in the RDC dialog boxes.

Tip   *Depending on how you plan to integrate your report and how much customization you want to perform at run time, you may want to rename some of the default names given to objects by the RDC. When you begin looking through report objects in your VB code, recognizing what SubHeading represents is easier than recognizing what Text25 represents.*

After you modify your report as necessary, save the report design the same way you save changes to a form, module, or project file from within VB. Just click the Save button on the toolbar, right-click the Designer object in the Project Explorer window, and choose Save from the pop-up menu, or just close the project or VB. You'll be prompted to choose a filename for the RDC designer, just as you would for a form or module. Choose a path and filename for the designer file—the default file extension for ActiveX designers is .DSR. When you next open the VB project, the .DSR file will load with the rest of the project files, and all properties and characteristics of the report design window will reappear.

Creating a New Report

Although the ability to import an existing .RPT file into the RDC is an excellent way to integrate an existing .RPT file into a Visual Basic application, you may prefer to maximize the power of the RDC and design the report entirely inside the Visual Basic IDE from scratch. The RDC allows you to do this with one of the Report Gallery choices that appear when you first add the RDC to your project.

If you choose one of the report experts, you'll be led through a tabbed dialog box, much as you are when you use the report experts inside regular Crystal Reports (refer to Chapter 1 for more information). If you choose the Empty Report option, you are presented with an empty report design window in which you need to choose database connections, tables, and fields individually to add to the report. Do this by right-clicking in the window and choosing Database | Add Database to Report from the pop-up menu.

Choosing a Report Data Source

When you import an existing .RPT file into the RDC, the report inside your VB application will use the same data source as the imported report did (such as ODBC or a native database driver, perhaps using Btrieve). These data sources are all provided by Crystal Reports functionality, separate from any database-connectivity features within Visual Basic.

However, when you create a new report from scratch using a report expert in the RDC, you have several choices of how your report will "connect" to a database. Because the RDC is so tightly integrated with Visual Basic, you may want to consider using a database connection that can easily be manipulated from within your VB code. In particular, the RDC can connect to data using various Microsoft data-access methods provided by Visual Basic. These include Data Access Objects (DAO), Remote Data Objects (RDO), and ActiveX Data Objects (ADO). In addition, you'll be able to connect directly to an existing data environment that you may have already defined in your VB application (consult the VB documentation for more information on the Data Environment).

When you choose one of the report expert options, the expert's tabbed dialog box will appear. The first tab in the dialog box is the Data tab, as shown in Figure 26-3.

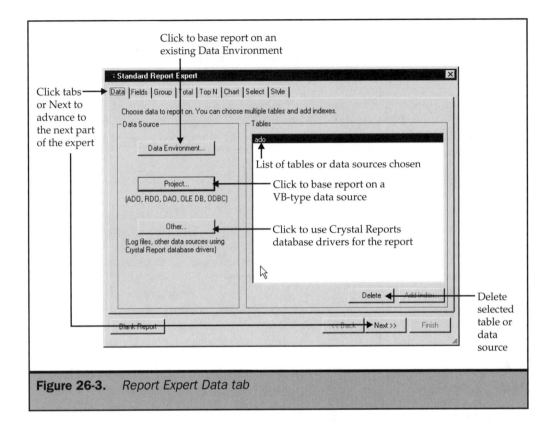

Figure 26-3. Report Expert Data tab

The Data Environment button is available only if you've already added and defined a Visual Basic 6 Data Environment (which is another example of an ActiveX designer) in your project. When you click this button, the set of connections and commands in the Data Environment will be available to be chosen for your report.

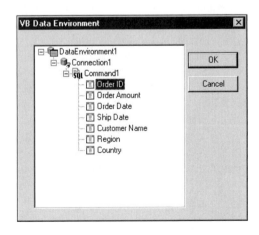

If you want to use Microsoft's "intrinsic" connectivity methods, click the Data tab's Project button to use DAO, RDO, or ADO to connect your report to the database. The Select Data Source dialog box will appear, as shown in Figure 26-4.

Choose the main connection method you wish to use by clicking the appropriate radio button:

- **ODBC** Connects to an ODBC (open database connectivity) data source that has already been set up on your PC. By clicking the Advanced button, you'll be able to choose whether to connect to the data source through the RDO or ADO connection method.

- **ADO and OLE DB** Connects to a data source using the newest Microsoft connection method. This allows you to connect to varied data sources, such as OLAP cubes, Web server logs, and e-mail systems. You need to supply a syntactically correct connection string when prompted (more information about ADO connection strings can be found in VB documentation), or you can click the Build button to create a connection string interactively.

- **DAO** Connects to a local database (typically Microsoft Access, dBASE, and so on). Specify the type of database you want to use, and use the Browse button if you need to search for the proper path and filename for the database.

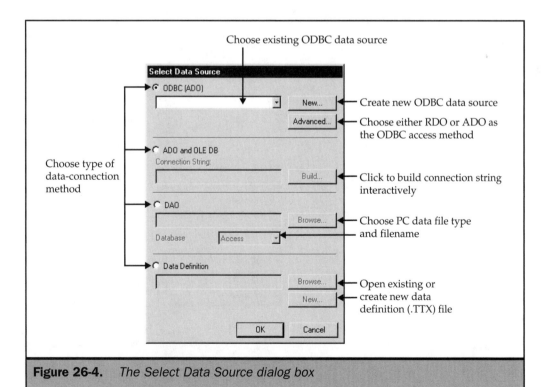

Figure 26-4.   *The Select Data Source dialog box*

■ **Data Definition**   Bases the report on an existing data definition file or allows you to create a new data definition file and base the report on that. A data definition file simply defines a set of field names and data types without actually connecting to any specific database.

Note   *The data definition file options are included here for backward compatibility. The new Unbound Fields feature of the RDC is a much more elegant way to accomplish the same thing: creating a generic report that doesn't connect to a database at design time. This is discussed in detail later in the chapter.*

After you select the data-source type, filename, ODBC data-source name, or other necessary information, click the OK button in the Select Data Source dialog box. If the database you're connecting to is secure, provide the necessary login information when prompted. The Select Recordset dialog box, shown in Figure 26-5, then appears, in which you can choose one or more tables from the data source to use in your report.

You can choose to use just a single table from the database by selecting the Pick From a List of Database Objects radio button and making your desired choices in the Object Type and Object drop-down lists. However, if you want to include and link

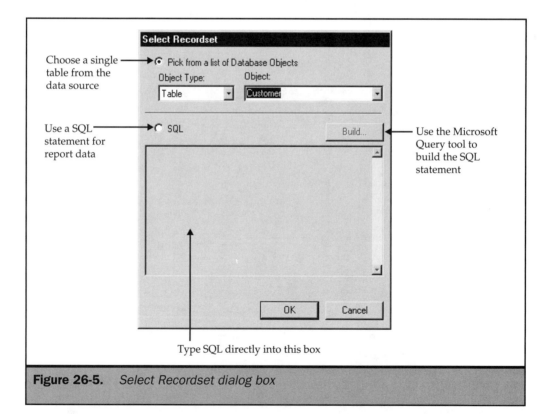

Figure 26-5.   *Select Recordset dialog box*

more than one table, limit the result set to certain records with a WHERE clause, or perform some other SQL function, click the SQL radio button to create a SQL statement to provide report data. If you are familiar with the SQL used by your data source, you can type a SELECT statement into the text box directly. If you'd prefer to be guided interactively through choosing and linking tables, choosing fields, and taking any other steps necessary for creating a SQL statement, click the Build button to launch Microsoft Query. Click OK when you've chosen and linked the necessary tables and fields.

Adding Objects

If you are using one of the report experts, you'll design the report by using the simple tabbed interface. Since this approach is virtually identical to the technique discussed in Chapter 1, you should refer to that chapter if you're unfamiliar with designing a report with an expert.

If you chose the As a Blank Report option (or if you've already closed the report expert but want to add additional objects to the report), use the Field Explorer on the left side of the RDC design window to add objects to the report. For example, to add a field from the database, click the plus sign next to the database fields category to display the data source(s) the report is based on. Click the plus sign next to the data source to see the fields contained in it. Then, just drag and drop the fields you want to the desired section of the report design window.

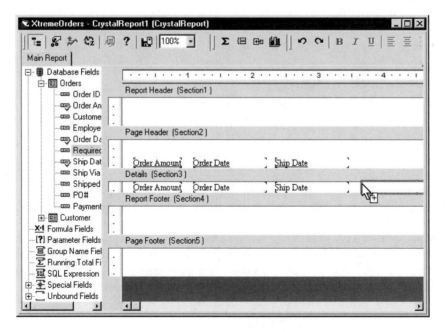

DEVELOPING CUSTOM
WINDOW APPLICATIONS

To create new formulas, parameter fields, running totals, or SQL expression fields, right-click their category in the Field Explorer and choose New from the pop-up menu.

When the new object has been added, you can drag and drop it on the report. Special fields can also be added to the report by dragging and dropping them from their area of the Field Explorer.

After you add objects, you can select them and move or resize them just as you would in regular Crystal Reports. You can format an object that you've selected by right-clicking and choosing the appropriate choice from the pop-up menu. And, don't forget that you also have Visual Basic properties for every object or report section in the report. Select the object or report section and make design-time property choices in the Properties box—that's the power of the VB-integrated RDC.

There are many capabilities and design techniques available that you can apply to the RDC, as you do with regular Crystal Reports. Look at the chapters in Part I of this book for ideas and techniques for designing sophisticated reports.

The RDC Object Model

As discussed at the beginning of the chapter, the RDC actually consists of four different main components that exist in your Visual Basic application: The ActiveX designer, the Runtime Automation Server, the Report Viewer, and the Embeddable Report Designer. When you actually process a report in VB, you design the report within the ActiveX designer window or allow the user to create it with the Embeddable Report Designer and eventually pass a *Report object* to the Report Viewer. The automation server, in essence, appears in the middle to control report customization.

Using the ActiveX Designer

The first step is to assign the design-window report definition to a Visual Basic object variable, as demonstrated in the following sample code:

```
Public Report As New dsrXtreme
```

In this code, from the modXtreme module in the sample application, *dsrXtreme* is the name given to the ActiveX designer object in the Property Pages dialog box. *Report* is the name of the object that will "point" to the report. Because this object is declared to be Public in a module, it will remain in scope and be accessible throughout the entire application. Then, when the report is going to be viewed in the Report Viewer, the Report object is passed to the Report Viewer's ReportSource property. The following code is from the sample application's frmViewer Form_Load event:

```
CRViewer1.ReportSource = Report
```

In this code, CRViewer1 is the default name of the Report Viewer (and it hasn't been changed to another name). The Report object is given to the ReportSource property so that the Report Viewer knows which report to show.

What the RDC Automation Server does between defining the Report object and assigning it to the Report Viewer is the "meat" of RDC integration programming. After you assign the designer to the Report object variable, an entire object model becomes available to you for modifying and customizing the report. By using the RDC Automation Server's object model, consisting of objects, collections, properties, methods, and events, you have extensive control over your report behavior at run time.

When you add the RDC to your report, the CRAXDRT (Crystal Reports ActiveX Designer Run Time) Automation Server is added to your project automatically. This COM interface provides a complete set of properties and methods that you can set at run time. To see the objects, collections, properties, and methods that are exposed by this automation server, use Visual Basic's *Object Browser*. The Object Browser can be viewed in Visual Basic any time your program isn't running. Press F2, or choose View | Object Browser from the pull-down menus. Then, choose CRAXDRT in the first drop-down list to see the object library exposed by the RDC Automation Server.

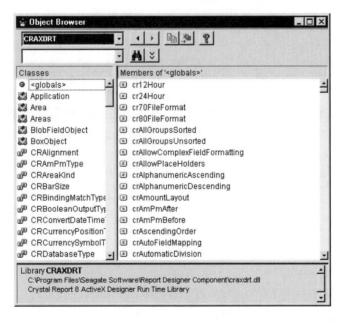

Although an extensive explanation of COM and its general approach to an object model and object hierarchy is better left to Microsoft documentation, navigating the RDC object model will soon become second nature to you. The highest level in the object hierarchy is the Application object—everything eventually falls below it. In general, throughout the RDC, the Application object is assumed by default, so you don't need to explicitly refer to it (unless you use the RDC Automation Server without the RDC ActiveX designer report design window). The highest level of object you'll need to be concerned about is the Report object.

If you are using the Embeddable Report Designer to give your end user interactive report design capability, you'll want to use the new combined design-time/run-time library, CRAXDDRT. Look up this automation server in the Object Browser to explore its objects, collections, properties, and methods. The Embeddable Report Designer is discussed in more detail later in this chapter.

Using an External .RPT File

One of the main benefits of the RDC is the ability to design a report entirely from within the Visual Basic IDE. When you save this internal report design, the designer specifications are saved in a .DSR file along with the rest of your Visual Basic project. When you compile the project, all of the report design specifications are saved in the compiled modules—there are no external report files to be accidentally deleted or modified (either accidentally or otherwise).

However, sometimes you may want to use the flexibility of the RDC Automation Server and Report Viewer with an external .RPT file, similar to the other Crystal Reports integration methods. This is entirely possible, and quite straightforward. In fact, it's virtually identical to the Crystal Reports integration with the Report Engine Automation Server. Examine the following code module from a VB form.

```
Dim Application As CRAXDRT.Application
Dim Report As CRAXDRT.Report

Private Sub Form_Load()
Screen.MousePointer = vbHourglass
Set Application = CreateObject("CrystalRuntime.Application")
Set Report = Application.OpenReport(App.Path & "\Xtreme Orders.rpt")
CRViewer1.ReportSource = Report
CRViewer1.ViewReport
Screen.MousePointer = vbDefault

End Sub

Private Sub Form_Resize()
CRViewer1.Top = 0
CRViewer1.Left = 0
CRViewer1.Height = ScaleHeight
CRViewer1.Width = ScaleWidth

End Sub
```

Notice the code that's very similar to the standard code the RDC automatically adds to your project. Notice a couple of differences, however. Rather than declaring and creating one Report object, consisting of an instance of the ActiveX designer (CrystalReport1), this code declares and assigns two objects: the Application object and the Report object.

The Application Object   When you use the built-in RDC ActiveX designer, you needn't worry about the Application object. However, if you choose to use an external report instead of the built-in designer, you'll need to declare and assign a single instance of the Application object, the highest-level object in the RDC Automation Server's object hierarchy. Don't forget to fully qualify the Application object by preceding the object type with CRAXDRT.

Assign the Application object by using the CreateObject method. The ProgID for the RDC CRAXDRT Automation Server is CrystalRuntime.Application.

The Report Object   The Report object is crucial. You'll use it to perform almost all run-time customization to your reports. You need to declare and assign a Report object for each report you want to have "open" at the same time within your application. For example, if you want to have three separate reports all appearing in their own preview windows simultaneously, you need to declare and assign three different Report object variables. However, if you'll have only one report in use at a time, you can merely declare and assign a single Report object variable, setting it to Nothing and reassigning it as necessary inside your code. Don't forget to fully qualify the Report object when declaring it with the Dim statement by preceding the object type with CRAXDRT or CRAXDDRT, depending on which automation server you're using.

Assign the Report object by using the Application object's OpenReport method. Supply the external report's filename, including the full path name, as the argument.

> **Caution**   *If you decide to use the RDC with an external .RPT file, and don't use the Add Crystal Reports 8.5 option from the Project menu, you need to ensure that the RDC Automation Server and, optionally, the Report Viewer are added to the project. In order for the RDC Automation Server to be available, choose Project | References and ensure that the Crystal Report 8.5 ActiveX Designer Run Time Library option is selected. To use the Report Viewer, choose Project | Components and ensure that the Crystal Report Viewer Control option is selected (setting this option in Project | References won't be sufficient for the Report Viewer).*

An Introduction to the RDC Object Model

While the Report object has many properties of its own (such as the RecordSelectionFormula property), it contains many objects and collections of objects that fall below it. One available Report object collection is FormulaFields, which contains a set of FormulaFieldDefinition objects, one for each formula defined in the report. Each of these objects contains all the properties for that particular formula, such as the formula name, the text of the formula, the data type that it returns, and other properties.

When you're dealing with a collection of objects, you need to identify which member of the collection you wish to manipulate, by using an index pointer to the appropriate member. In the RDC, indexes are "one-based." That is, the first member is numbered 1, the second is numbered 2, and so on. This is in contrast to the ActiveX control and other VB object models, which often expose "zero-based" indexes. The RDC typically numbers the collection members in the order in which they were added to the report.

For example, to print the formula text from the first formula in the Xtreme Orders sample application, you can type the following code into the Immediate window while the program is in break mode:

```
? Report.FormulaFields(1).Text
```

Here, the object hierarchy is being "navigated" to reveal the Text property of the first member of the FormulaFieldDefinitions collection (referred to simply as FormulaFields) of the Report object. Since the Text property is a read/write property, you not only can retrieve what the formula already contains, but also replace it by setting the Text property to a string value, as in the following:

```
Report.FormulaFields(1).Text = "{Orders.Order Amount} * 1.1"
```

Because the RDC and its automation server are tightly integrated COM components, you will benefit from *automatic code completion* (Microsoft refers to it as *IntelliSense*) when you use them. When you begin to enter code into the VB code window for the Report object, the properties, methods, and built-in constant values will become available to you from automatically appearing drop-down lists. If you've used Visual Basic 5 or 6, you're probably familiar with this feature. You'll enjoy the benefit it provides with the RDC.

Manipulating Collection Indexes by Name Instead of Number

Unlike the Report Engine Automation Server, which preceded the RDC as Crystal's initial COM-based integration method, the RDC Automation Server will allow you to use string indexes to refer to members of only certain collections, but not all of them.

For example, the RDC Automation Server requires you to set the contents of a formula with

```
Report.FormulaFields(1).Text = "{Orders.Order Amount} * 1.1"
```

while the Report Engine Automation Server allows you to use

```
Report.Formulas("Order + Tax").Text = "{Orders.Order Amount} * 1.1"
```

You sometimes need to do some experimenting to find the actual member of a collection that you wish to manipulate.

Wouldn't it be nice if, instead of using the numeric index to set the value of a formula, you could use code like this:

```
If SetFormula("Order + Tax","{Orders.Order Amount} * 1.1") Then
   MsgBox "Formula Changed"
Else
   MsgBox "Incorrect Formula Name Supplied"
End If
```

Examine the following function code:

```
Public Function SetFormula(FormulaName As String, _
                           FormulaText As String) As Boolean
Dim intCounter As Integer
For intCounter = 1 To Report.FormulaFields.Count
  If Report.FormulaFields(intCounter).FormulaFieldName = FormulaName Then
    Report.FormulaFields(intCounter).Text = FormulaText
      SetFormula = True
      Exit Function
  End If  'Report.FormulaFields(intCounter).Name = FormulaName
Next intCounter
SetFormula = False
End Function
```

If you examine this code closely, you'll see that the FormulaFields collection can be cycled through using a For loop, looking for the formula that has the same name as the passed FormulaName argument. Once it's found, the value of the passed FormulaText argument is used to set the value of the formula. If a formula with the same name isn't found, the subroutine returns a false value that can be tested for.

If you have a large number of formulas, parameter fields, SQL expressions, or other objects that may be easier to manipulate by name rather than by index number, use this type of logic to make your coding life easier!

In addition to the Object Browser and automatic code completion, there is comprehensive online Help for the RDC and its object model. You can use either the standard Developer's Help file, CrystalDevHelp.chm, located in *Crystal Reports program directory*\Developer Files\Help, or the specific RDC Help file, CRRDC.HLP, found in Program Files\Seagate Software\Report Designer Component.

Note *More information on automation server concepts and COM is available from Visual Basic documentation.*

Controlling Record Selection

One of the main benefits of Visual Basic's integration with Crystal Reports is the ability to control report record selection on-the-fly, based on your user's interactions with the VB application. You can design the exact user interface you need for your application, and build the report record-selection formula based on how your user interacts with it. Because VB has such powerful user-interface features (such as the VB date picker and other custom controls), you have much more flexibility using VB controls than you do using Crystal Reports parameter fields.

Because the record-selection formula you pass to the RDC must still conform to Crystal Reports syntax, you need to be familiar with how to create a Crystal Reports formula. If you are used to using the Crystal Reports Select Expert for record selection, you need to familiarize yourself with the actual Crystal Reports formula that it creates, before you create a selection formula in your VB application. A Crystal Reports record-selection formula is a Boolean formula that narrows down the database records that will be included in the report. For example, the following record-selection formula will limit a report to orders placed in the first quarter of 1997 from customers in Texas:

```
{Orders.Order Date} In Date(1997,1,1) To Date(1997,3,31)
And {Customer.Region} = "TX"
```

> **Tip**   *For complete discussions of Crystal Reports record selection and how to create Boolean formulas, consult Chapters 5 and 6.*

Use the RecordSelectionFormula property of the Report object to set the record-selection formula for the report. You can set the property to either a string expression or a variable. Here's the code from the sample application to set record selection, based on the contents of the user-supplied From Date and To Date text boxes:

```
'Supply record selection formula based on dates
strSelectionFormula = "{Orders.Order Date} in #" & _
    txtFromDate & "# to #" & txtToDate & "#"
Report.RecordSelectionFormula = strSelectionFormula
```

Record-Selection Formula Tips

You need to consider several important points when building a Crystal record-selection formula within your application. Specifically, some tricks are available that you can use to make sure that your string values are formatted properly, and that as much of the SQL selection work as possible is done on the server rather than on the PC.

The string value you pass must adhere *exactly* to the Crystal Reports formula syntax. This includes using correct Crystal reserved words and punctuation. The previous example shows the necessity of including the pound sign (#) around date values in the selection formula.

Also, it's easy to forget the required quotation marks or apostrophes around literals that are used in comparisons. For example, you may want to pass the following selection formula:

```
{Customer.Region} = 'TX' And {Orders.Ship Via} = 'UPS'
```

If the characters TX and UPS are coming from controls, such as a text box or combo box, you might consider using the following VB code to place the selection formula in a string variable:

```
strSelectionFormula = "{Customer.Region} = " & txtRegion & _
" And {Orders.Ship Via} = " & cboShipper
```

At first glance, this appears to create a correctly formatted Crystal Reports record-selection formula. However, if you supply this string to the RecordSelectionFormula property, the report will fail when it runs. Why? The best way to troubleshoot this issue is to look at the contents of strSelectionFormula in the VB Immediate window, by setting a breakpoint or by using other VB debugging features. This will show that the contents of the string variable after the preceding code executes as follows:

```
{Customer.Region} = TX And {Orders.Ship Via} = UPS
```

Notice that no quotation marks or apostrophes appear around the literals that are being compared in the record-selection formula, a basic requirement of the Crystal Reports formula language. The following VB code will create a syntactically correct selection formula:

```
strSelectionFormula = "{Customer.Region} = '" & txtRegion & _
"' And {Orders.Ship Via} = '" & cboShipper & "'"
```

If your report will be using a SQL database, remember also that RDC will attempt to convert as much of your record-selection formula as possible to SQL when it runs the report. The same caveats apply to the record-selection formula you pass from your VB application as apply to a record-selection formula you create directly in Crystal Reports. In particular, using built-in Crystal Reports formula functions, such as UpperCase or ToText, typically causes record selection to be moved to the client (the PC) instead of to the database server. The result is very slow report performance. To avoid this situation, take the same care in creating record-selection formulas that you pass from your application as you would in Crystal Reports. Look for detailed discussions on record-selection performance in both Chapters 6 and 14.

You may also choose to create the SQL statement that the report will use right in your VB application, and then submit it to the report by setting the Report object's SQLQueryString property.

Setting Formulas

The RDC gives you an extra level of flexibility by allowing you to control the contents of Report objects as each record is processed by the report (see "Changing Text Objects at Run Time" and "Conditional Formatting and Formatting Sections," later in the chapter). Using these techniques, you can actually have objects on your report show the results of Visual Basic calculations and procedures. However, it still may be more straightforward to simply modify the contents of Crystal Reports formulas dynamically at run time. This will be useful for changing formulas related to groups that can also be changed from within your code, for changing a formula that shows text on the report, or for changing a formula that relates to math calculations or conditional formatting on the report.

Setting formulas at run time is similar to setting the record-selection formula at run time (described in the previous section). You need a good understanding of the Crystal Reports formula language to adequately modify formulas inside your VB code. If you need a refresher on Crystal Reports formulas, review Chapter 5.

The RDC provides a FormulaFields collection in the Report object that can be read or written to at run time. This collection returns multiple FormulaFieldDefinition objects, one for each formula defined in the report. Although a great deal of information may be gleaned from the FormulaFieldDefinition object, the simplest way to change the contents of a formula is simply to set the Text property for the particular member of the collection that you want to change. The collection is one based, with each member corresponding to its position in the list of formula fields.

In the Xtreme Orders sample application, the Order + Tax formula is modified based on the user's completion of the Tax Rate text box. The formula is changed using the following code:

```
'Set @Order + Tax formula
If txtTaxRate = "" Then
    Report.FormulaFields(1).Text = "{Orders.Order Amount}"
Else
    Report.FormulaFields(1).Text = "{Orders.Order Amount} * " &_
    Str(txtTaxRate / 100 + 1)
End If  'txtTaxRate = ""
```

You needn't change the property for all formulas in the report—just the ones you want to modify at run time. Remember that you can't specify the formula name directly as the collection index argument—you must use a one-based index number. This is determined by where the formula is in the formula list in the RDC design window—the first formula will have an index of 1, the fifth, 5, and so on. Review the sample code earlier in the chapter if you wish to refer to formulas by name instead of index number.

The Text property requires a string expression or variable, correctly conforming to Crystal Reports formula syntax, that contains the new text you want the formula to contain. Take care when assigning a value to the formula. The Order + Tax formula is defined in Crystal Reports as a numeric formula. Therefore, you should pass it a formula that will evaluate to a number. If the user leaves the text box on the form empty, the VB code assumes no additional sales tax and simply places the Order Amount database field in the formula—the formula will show the same amount as the database field.

If, however, the user has specified a tax rate, the VB code manipulates the value by dividing it by 100, and then adding 1. This creates the proper type of number to multiply against the Order Amount field to correctly calculate tax. For example, if the user specifies a tax rate of 5 (for 5-percent tax), the VB code will change the value to 1.05 before combining it with the multiply operator and the Order Amount field in the formula.

If you've used other integration methods from earlier Crystal Reports versions, such as the ActiveX control or the Report Engine API, you've probably used a formula modified at run time to show some form of text on the report, such as the report criteria that has been supplied by the user. Although this can also be accomplished with a formula here, the RDC's capability of manipulating text objects at run time gives you the opportunity to approach this from another angle. Therefore, a formula is not used to accomplish this in the Xtreme Orders sample application with the RDC. The following section explains how this is accomplished by using a text object.

> **Note** *Crystal Reports 8.5 features two formula syntaxes: Crystal syntax, which is compatible with Crystal Reports 7 and earlier, and Basic syntax, which was introduced in Crystal Reports 8. If you need to know which syntax an existing formula is based on, execute some code to access the formula, such as retrieving the Text property. Then, retrieve the Report object's LastGetFormulaSyntax property to determine the syntax of the formula you retrieved before. If you want to assign a specific syntax to a certain formula, set the Report object's FormulaSyntax property first. Then, set the formula's contents by passing formula text in the correct syntax to the Text property.*

Changing Text Objects at Run Time

With other integration approaches, changing textual information on the report, such as a company name or a description of the report's selection criteria, must be done with a formula. Typically, the formula simply contains a text literal (a text string surrounded by quotation marks or apostrophes) that is then changed at run time. While this will still work with the RDC, the RDC permits a new approach that can potentially give you much more flexibility.

Remember that when you add any object to the report (a field, formula, text object, or other object), the object can be manipulated by VB. It has properties that can be set on the Property Pages dialog box at design time, as well as being modified at run time. If you add a text object to the report, a TextObject object becomes available from within the overall Report object. The TextObject object exposes many properties (you can see most of them in the Properties dialog box) that can be set at run time.

You can access the actual contents of the text object with a property and method. The Text property can be read during code execution to see what the text object contains. To change the contents of a text object, you need to use the TextObject SetText method at run time.

In the Xtreme Orders sample application, the Sub Heading formula that was originally created in the .RPT file has been removed in the RDC design window. In its place, a text object has been added and given the name SubHeading. The following code indicates how to set the contents of the text object to indicate what choices the user has made on the Print Xtreme Orders form. This code assumes the strSubHeading string variable has been declared elsewhere in the application. You'll also notice references to the text object and combo box controls on the form.

```
'Set SubHeading text object
strSubHeading = txtFromDate & " through " & txtToDate
strSubHeading = strSubHeading & ", By " & cboGroupBy
If txtTaxRate = "" Then
    strSubHeading = strSubHeading & ", No Tax"
Else
    strSubHeading = strSubHeading & ", Sales Tax = " & txtTaxRate & "%"
End If   'txtTaxRate = ""
Report.SubHeading.SetText (strSubHeading)
'Note: parentheses around argument to SetText method are optional
```

If you have used other integration methods in the past, you may want to change the general approach that you have used for custom formulas. Because you can change the contents of a text object from your VB code, you can essentially create "VB formulas" in your report by using the RDC. Each section of the report will fire a Format event when it is processed at report run time. You can use the SetText method inside this Format event to change the contents of text objects for each report record (in the details section Format event) or for group or report headers or footers (in their respective Format events). More information on the Format event and conditional section formatting is provided later in this chapter.

The RDC limits some of this ease of individual object control to only reports created with the RDC's internal ActiveX designer. If you use an external .RPT file with the RDC Automation Server, you must sometimes navigate much deeper down the object hierarchy to perform this type of customization. For example, if you have just set up Application and Report objects that point to an external .RPT file (there is no ActiveX designer in your project), and you wish to set the contents of a text object, you'll need to execute code similar to this:

```
Report.Sections("PHb").ReportObjects(1).SetText "Order #"
```

This code will set the contents of the first text object in Report Header b to "Order #". This is accomplished by navigating into the Sections collection (one of the RDC collections that allows string indexes to be used, in addition to numbers). Within the Page Header b section, the first member of the ReportObjects collection (the text object) is being changed by executing the SetText method.

Passing Parameter-Field Values

If you are importing an existing .RPT file into the RDC or using an external .RPT file, the report may contain parameter fields that are designed to prompt the user for information whenever the report is refreshed. If you simply leave the parameter fields as they are, the application will automatically prompt the user for them when the report runs. Obviously, one of the main reasons to integrate the report into a VB application is to more closely control the user interface of the report. You'll probably want to alter the mechanism for gathering this data from the user, and then have the application supply the appropriate values to the parameter fields from within the application code.

Because you can control both report record selection and report formulas at run time from within your VB application, there may not be as much necessity to use parameter fields with an integrated report as there might be for a stand-alone report running with regular Crystal Reports. However, if you are using RDC to "share" an external .RPT file with other Crystal Reports users who are not using your custom application, you may need to set the values of parameter fields from within your code.

In this situation, use the Report object's ParameterFieldDefinitions collection to manipulate the parameters. As with formulas, there is one ParameterFieldDefinition object in the collection for each parameter field defined in the report. And, like formulas, the proper member of the collection is retrieved with a one-based index determined by the order in which the parameter fields were added to the report. You can't retrieve a parameter field by using its name as the index (unless you use the looping technique discussed earlier in the chapter for use with formula fields).

The RDC approach for setting the value of a parameter field being passed to a report is to use the ParameterFieldDefinition object's AddCurrentValue method. This passes a single value to the report parameter field. Crystal Reports 8.5 allows multiple-value parameter fields, so you can execute the AddCurrentValue method as many times as necessary (for example, in a loop that looks through a list box for selected items) to populate a parameter field with several values.

The XTREME ORDERS.RPT file in the \VB folder on the book's companion CD-ROM has a parameter field used to conditionally format the details section when the order amount exceeds a value supplied by the viewer. In this RDC example, this logic has been replaced by a direct format of the details section during its Format event (discussed later in the chapter). However, if the original method of supplying the parameter field a value based on the VB user interface had been used, the following code would correctly pass the value to the parameter field:

```
'Set parameter value
'Alternative method is to format Details section within VB
If txtHighlight = "" Then
    Report.ParameterFields(1).AddCurrentValue (0)
Else
    Report.ParameterFields(1).AddCurrentValue (Val(txtHighlight))
End If    'txtHighlight = ""
```

Here, the value is set to 0 if the text box is empty. This is important to note, because the actual parameter field in the report is numeric. Passing it an empty string might cause a run-time error when the report runs. Also, because the AddCurrentValue method is executed at least once, and a value has been passed to the parameter field, the user will no longer be prompted for it when the report is run.

Note *The RDC object model exposes all the features of Crystal Reports 8.5 parameter fields, such as range values, multiple values, and edit masks. Navigate the Online Help table of contents to find the "ParameterFieldDefinition Object" entry. There, you'll find a complete description of the object, as well as all the methods available for manipulating parameter fields.*

Manipulating Report Groups

One of the requirements for the Xtreme Orders report is that the user be able to specify how the report is grouped. A combo box exists on the Print Report form that lets the user choose between Quarter and Customer grouping. In the RDC design window, this is normally accomplished by using the Change Group option from a pop-up menu to change the field a group is based on, as well as the sequence (ascending or descending) that you want the groups to appear in. If the group is based on a date field, such as Order Date, you may also specify the range of dates (week, month, quarter, and so on) that make up the group. To familiarize yourself with various grouping options, refer to Chapter 3.

By being able to change these options from within an application at run time, you can provide great reporting flexibility to your end users. In many cases, you can make it appear that several different reports are available, based on user input. In fact, the application will be using the same Report object, but grouping will be changed at run time based on user input.

Manipulating groups in the RDC object model requires a bit of navigation "down the object hierarchy." Ultimately, the database or formula field a group is based on is specified by the GroupConditionField property of the Area object. A report contains an Areas collection consisting of an Area object for each area in a report. Consider an "area" of the report to be each individual main section of the report, such as the page header, details section, group footer, and so on. If there are multiple sections on the report, such as Details a and Details b sections, they are still part of the overall details *area*, and there is only one member of the Areas collection for them. The Areas collection has one advantage not shared by most other collections exposed by the RDC—the index used to refer to an individual member of the collection can be a string value or a numeric value. This allows you to specify RH, PH, GHn, D, GFn, PF, or RF as index values, or use the one-based index number. Using the string values makes your code much easier to understand when working with the Areas collection, and you don't have to write extra looping code, like that shown earlier for formula manipulation.

Tip *The Areas and Sections collections are similar, but not identical. As shown in an example earlier in this chapter in the section "Changing Text Objects at Run Time," the Sections collection can also accept a string index; but this collection exposes individual sections, with indexes such as PHa for Page Header a and PHb for Page Header b. The Areas collection contains only one member for the Page Header area (referenced with a string index of PH), even if there are multiple page header sections, such as Page Header a and Page Header b.*

However, once you navigate to the specific Area object to specify the GroupConditionField property, you are faced with another peculiarity of the RDC object model. With other integration methods (the ActiveX control, in particular), you may supply a string value containing the actual field name (such as {Orders.Order Date} or {Customer.Customer Name}) to indicate which field you wish to base a group on. The RDC doesn't make life this simple. You must specify a DatabaseFieldDefinition object to the GroupConditionField property—you can't just pass a string containing the field name.

The DatabaseFieldDefinition object is found quite "deep" in the object hierarchy—there is one of these objects for each field contained in the DatabaseFieldDefinitions collection in a DatabaseTable object. And, multiple DatabaseTable objects are contained in the DatabaseTables collection of the Database object, contained inside the overall Report object. To make things even more complex, none of the collections just mentioned will accept a string index value—you must specify a one-based index value.

Although this sounds confusing and hard to navigate, you'll eventually be able to travel through the object hierarchy fairly quickly to find the database table and field you want to provide to the GroupConditionField property. Look at the following code from the Xtreme Orders sample application:

```
'Set grouping
If cboGroupBy = "Quarter" Then
   Report.Areas("GH").GroupConditionField = _
      Report.Database.Tables(1).Fields(5) 'Orders.Order Date
   Report.Areas("GH").GroupCondition = crGCQuarterly
Else
   Report.Areas("GH").GroupConditionField = _
      Report.Database.Tables(2).Fields(3) 'Customer.Customer Name
   Report.Areas("GH").GroupCondition = crGCAnyValue
End If   'cboGroupBy = "Quarter"
```

In this example, notice that the grouping is based on the user choice for the cboGroupBy combo box. In either case, the GroupConditionField property of the GH member of the Areas collection (the group header) is being set. If the user chooses to group by Order Date, the property is set to the fifth member of the Fields collection in the first member of the Tables collection. This indicates that the fifth field (Order Date) in the first table (Orders) will be used for grouping. If the user chooses to group by Customer, the third field (Customer Name) in the second table (Customer) will be used for grouping. As with other collections that don't allow string indexes, you can use quick Print statements in the Immediate window to search through different members of the collection. You can also look at the Database section of the Field Tree view in the RDC design window to determine which index numbers to use to point to the correct tables and fields. Or, you can write a function that uses looping logic, described earlier, to search through the collections until you find a matching name value.

In addition to choosing the database field you want to use for the group, you may have to choose how the grouping occurs, particularly if you use a date or Boolean field as the group field. This is accomplished by setting the Area object's GroupCondition property, which can be set to an integer value or an RDC-supplied constant (see the explanation for the Area object in the online Help for specific constants and integer values). In the sample code shown previously, the group is set to break for every calendar quarter if Order Date grouping is set (hence, the crGCQuarterly constant that is provided). If Customer Name grouping is chosen, the crGCAnyValue constant is supplied, indicating that a new group will be created whenever the value of the group field changes.

Conditional Formatting and Formatting Sections

You'll often want to present your RDC reports in the Report Viewer to allow report interaction in an online environment, instead of having them printed on paper. The Report Viewer provides complete interactive reporting features, such as drill-down, that are invaluable to the application designer. Having control over these capabilities at run time provides for great flexibility.

The Xtreme Orders sample application gives the user the opportunity to specify whether or not to see the report as a summary report only. When this check box is selected, the VB application needs to hide the report details section so that only group subtotals appear on the report. In addition, you need to control the appearance of the report's two page header sections (Page Header a and Page Header b), as well as the two Group Header #1 sections (Group Header #1a and Group Header #1b). This is done to accommodate two different sections of field titles that you wish to appear differently if the report is presented as a summary report instead of a detail report. If the report is being displayed as a detail report, the field titles should appear at the top of every page of the report, along with the subheading and smaller report title. If the report is displayed as a summary report, you only want the field titles to appear in the group header section of a drill-down tab when the user double-clicks a group. Since no detail information will be visible in the main report window, field titles there won't be meaningful.

And, finally, you'll want to show Group Header #1a, which contains the group name field, if the report is showing detail data. This will indicate which group the following set of orders applies to. However, if the report is only showing summary data, showing both the group header and group footer would be repetitive—the group footer already contains the group name, so showing the group header as well will look odd. However, you will want the group header with the group name to appear in a drill-down tab. Therefore, you need to control the appearance of four sections when a user chooses the Summary Report option. Look at Table 26-1 to get a better idea of how you'll want to conditionally set these sections at run time.

You'll notice that, in some cases, sections need to be completely suppressed (so they don't show up, even in a drill-down tab) as opposed to hidden (they show up in a drill-down tab, but not in the main Preview tab). There is a somewhat obscure relationship among areas and sections that make this determination. Specifically, only complete areas (such as the entire Group Header #1) can be hidden, not individual sections (for example, Group Header #1a). However, both areas and sections can be suppressed. To further explain this concept, if you look in the Properties dialog box after you've selected a section in the design window, you'll see a Suppress property but no Hide property.

This presents a bit of a coding challenge for the Xtreme Orders sample application. First, you need to determine the correct combination of area hiding and section suppressing that sets what appears in the Preview window and in a drill-down tab. If an area is set to Hide, none of the sections in it will appear in the main Preview window. And, when the user drills down into that section, you will also want to control which sections inside the drilled-down area appear in the drill-down tab. Then, you must find where to set the Hide property for a particular area. You must also find where to set the Suppress property for sections inside the hidden area, or other sections that aren't hidden.

Section	Detail Report	Summary Report
Page Header b (field titles)	Shown	Suppressed (no drill-down)
Group Header #1a (group name field)	Shown	Hidden (drill-down okay)
Group Header #1b (field titles)	Suppressed (no drill-down)	Hidden (drill-down okay)
Details (detail order data)	Shown	Hidden (drill-down okay)

Table 26-1. *Section Formatting for Different Report Types*

Since the Hide property is only available for an entire area, you need to set the HideForDrillDown property for the appropriate member of the Areas collection. Since the Suppress property needs to be set for individual sections, you can just refer to the individual sections in the RDC design window by name, setting the Suppress property for them as needed. Consider that the Page Header b section has been given the name PHb in the Properties dialog box (it was named Section 3 when the report was imported). Other sections have been given more descriptive names in the RDC design window, as well. Group Header #1a is named GH1A, and Group Header #1b is named GH1B.

Keeping in mind the previous discussion and the hide and suppress requirements outlined in Table 26-1, look at this code from the sample application:

```
'Hide/show sections
With Report
   If chkSummary Then
      .Areas("D").HideForDrillDown = True
      .PHb.Suppress = True
      .Areas("GH1").HideForDrillDown = True
      .GH1A.Suppress = False
      .GH1B.Suppress = False
   Else
      .Areas("D").HideForDrillDown = False
      .PHb.Suppress = False
      .Areas("GH1").HideForDrillDown = False
      .GH1A.Suppress = False
      .GH1B.Suppress = True
   End If   'chkSummary
End With   'Report
```

Notice that both Area objects for the details and Group Header #1 areas are being formatted, as well as individual sections. The areas must be formatted from their collection, whereas sections can be manipulated directly below the Report object by name.

Note   *You can navigate deeper into the object hierarchy and actually set the Suppress property for members of the Sections collection inside the Area object. Although this is a little more code intensive, it is required if you are using an external .RPT file, which doesn't expose individual section names as does the RDC ActiveX designer.*

The Format Event

Another benefit that only the RDC provides to developers (only with reports supplied by the ActiveX designer) is the Format event. This event is "fired" every time the processing of an individual report section begins. Consider the way the first page of a report might be processed. First, the overall report is "prepared"; then the page header prints, followed, in order, by the report header (since this is the first page of the report), the first group header, all the details sections in that group, the first group footer, and so on. Each time any of these sections begins to print (including when the report is "prepared"), its respective Format event fires.

You can intercept these formatting events and change the behavior of the section, or of objects within the section. This gives you complete Visual Basic functionality when it comes to conditional formatting or section formatting. In other integration methods that use .RPT files (including using an external .RPT file with the RDC), you must use Crystal Reports conditional formulas or the Highlighting Expert to set background colors for sections, highlight fields over a certain value, and perform other formatting based on certain conditions. While the RDC continues to support that flexibility, you can now base individual section and object formatting on VB code.

To add code for any Format event, simply double-click a section in the RDC design window. This displays the Format event in the code window for the particular section you double-clicked. You can also right-click the designer in the Visual Basic Project Explorer and choose View Code from the pop-up menu. In either case, each report section appears in the object drop-down list in the upper-left corner of the code window. The only available procedure for each report section is Format, which will appear in the procedure drop-down list in the upper-right corner.

You have all the power of VB at your disposal to control the appearance and formatting of sections and objects, or the content of text objects, while the report is being formatted. This allows you to write VB code to determine how to format a field in the current section being formatted (perhaps to set the background or font color of an object based on some VB code). You can also change the formatting of the entire section, as demonstrated in the following code from the Xtreme Orders sample application:

```
Private Sub Details_Format (ByVal pFormattingInfo As Object)
    If Val(frmXtremeOrders.txtHighlight) > 0 And _
```

```
    Report.fldOrderAmount.Value > Val(frmXtremeOrders.txtHighlight) Then
        Report.Details.BackColor = &HFFFF00
    End If  'Report.fldOrderAmount > Val(txtHighlight)...
End Sub
```

Tip   *The pFormattingInfo argument that is passed into the module is an object that exposes three read-only properties that return true or false: IsEndOfGroup, IsStartOfGroup, and IsRepeatedGroupHeader. You can read the contents of these properties to help determine how to handle logic in the Format event.*

This code is contained in the Format event for the details section (notice that the report section has been renamed Details from its default name of Section 6). Every time the details section begins to format, this event fires. At that time, the contents of the Highlight text box on the Print Xtreme Orders form are checked for a value. If the user has supplied a value, and the fldOrderAmount database field from the report is greater than the value the user supplied, the background color of the details section is set. This logic replaces the parameter field and conditional formatting used in the original Xtreme Orders .RPT file.

Obviously, many other flexible and complex types of formatting and manipulation can occur during the Format event. A common use of this manipulation is to replace formula fields on the report with text objects, and use the SetText method to change the contents of the text objects from within the Format event. Essentially, this extends the complete power of the Visual Basic language to objects you place on your report.

Crystal Reports Version 8.5 exposes some additional events to the report-processing cycle. Not only can you trap the Format event for every report section, but the Report object itself fires several events as it processes. An event of particular interest is NoData. Look at this code fragment:

```
Private Sub Report_NoData(pCancel As Boolean)
    MsgBox "There is no data in this report. " & _
    "Supply different selection criteria"
    pCancel = True
End Sub
```

If the report contains no data when it processes, the NoData event will fire. You may trap this event and perform special handling. In particular, by setting the pCancel value to true, you can cancel the remainder of report processing. Be aware, though, that canceling report processing won't stop the Report Viewer from appearing—you need to add a global variable or some other flag to indicate that the Report Viewer should not be displayed in this event.

As you search through RDC documentation, you may see references to "Formatting Idle" or other processing time references. Certain object properties can be set only

DEVELOPING CUSTOM WINDOW APPLICATIONS

during certain times when the report is processing. This is mostly significant when writing code in the Format event. If you attempt to set a property that can't be set during that particular report-processing time, you'll receive either error messages or unexpected results. Look for a discussion of formatting modes by searching the online Help for "Format event."

Tip	*Formatting events may fire more often than you might expect because of the multiple passes Crystal Reports must make as it processes the report. This may happen, for example, when the RDC encounters a Keep Together section option at the end of a page. If you place code to accumulate values in the Format event without accounting for these multiple passes, your accumulations will be inaccurate. Version 8.5 of the RDC includes a feature called Report Variables that can keep track of these reporting passes. By using Report Variables instead of your own variables, values will accumulate only when an actual "logical" change occurs to a report section. Search the online Help file for "Report Variables" to get complete details.*

Choosing Output Destinations

If your users will have a choice of output destinations (as the user does in the Xtreme Orders sample application), you need to create appropriate code to handle the user's choice. In the Xtreme Orders sample application, radio buttons and a text box allow the user to choose to view the report in the preview window, print the report to a printer, or attach the report as a .PDF file (now supported by Crystal Reports 8.5) to an e-mail message. If the user chooses e-mail as the output destination, an e-mail address can be entered in a text box. Based on the user's selection, you need to set the output destination in your VB code.

If the user chooses to view the report on the screen, you need to activate the Report Viewer. In the sample application, this simply entails displaying the form that contains the Report Viewer control, by executing the form's Show method. The Form_Load event of this form will pass the Report object to the Report Viewer and execute the Report Viewer's ViewReport method.

As mentioned earlier, use of the Report Viewer is completely optional—you are free to answer No when you are prompted about whether or not to add it when first adding the RDC to your project. However, if one of the output options will be to the screen (as in the Xtreme Orders sample application), make sure that the Report Viewer is eventually added to your project.

If you respond Yes to the RDC's "Do you want to add the Report Viewer" prompt, the RDC automatically adds the Report Viewer for you. It will create a new form, place the Report Viewer in the form, and automatically add rudimentary code to supply the Report object to the Report Viewer and resize the Report Viewer to be the same size as the form. If the RDC adds the Report Viewer automatically, you can leave this default behavior as is, move the Report Viewer object to another form, or build additional elements into the form that the RDC created automatically. You can also manually add the Report Viewer to your project later and supply code to pass the Report object to the Report Viewer.

If you wish to print the Report object to a printer, execute the Report object's PrintOut method. The syntax is as follows:

```
object.PrintOut Prompt, Copies, Collated, StartPage, StopPage
```

In this statement, *Prompt* is a Boolean value indicating whether or not to prompt the user for printer options, *Copies* is a numeric value indicating how many copies of the report to print, *Collated* is a Boolean value indicating whether or not to collate the pages, and *StartPage* and *StopPage* are numeric values indicating which page numbers to start and stop printing on. The parameters are optional—if you want to skip any in the middle, just add commas in the correct positions—but don't include the parameter.

If you wish to export the report to a disk file or attach the report to an e-mail message as a file, use the Report object's Export method. The syntax is as follows:

```
object.Export PromptUser
```

In this statement, *PromptUser* is a Boolean value indicating whether you want to prompt the user for export options. If you choose not to prompt the user for export options, you need to set properties of the report's ExportOptions object. The ExportOptions object contains many properties that determine the output destination (file or e-mail), file format (Word, Excel, PDF, XML and so on), filename, e-mail address, and more. Many of these properties accept integer values or RDC-supplied descriptive constants. If you choose MAPI as the destination, the user's PC needs to have a MAPI-compliant e-mail client installed, such as Microsoft Outlook or Eudora Pro. Look for all the available ExportOptions properties by searching the online Help for "ExportOptions object."

In the Xtreme Orders sample application, the following code is used to choose an output destination, as well as to specify a file type and e-mail information, based on user selection:

```
'Set output destination
If optPreview Then frmViewer.Show
If OptPrint Then Report.PrintOut (True)
If OptEmail Then
    With Report
        .ExportOptions.DestinationType = crEDTEMailMAPI
        .ExportOptions.MailToList = txtAddress
        .ExportOptions.MailSubject = "Here's the Xtreme Orders Report"
```

```
            .ExportOptions.MailMessage = _
"Attached is a PDF file showing the latest Xtreme Orders Report."
            .ExportOptions.FormatType = crEFTPortableDocFormat
            .Export (False)
        End With   'Report
End If   'optEmail
```

Caution *If you use the Report object's Export method to export or send the report attached to an e-mail message, make sure you specify all the necessary ExportOptions object properties. If you fail to specify necessary properties, or specify them incorrectly, an error may be thrown. Or, the user may be prompted to specify export options, even though you specifically add a false argument to the Export method. If the export takes place at an unattended machine, your application has to wait for a response, even though no user is available to respond.*

Changing the Data Source at Run Time

Obviously, one of the main benefits of integrating a Crystal Report in a Visual Basic program is the ability to tie the report contents to a data set or result set that the program is manipulating. This allows a user to interact with your application and then run a report that contains the same set of data that the user has selected.

One way to accomplish this is to create a Crystal Reports record-selection formula or a SQL statement based on your user interface. The formula or SQL statement can then be passed to the report, as discussed elsewhere in this chapter. This allows the user to interact with a data grid, form, or other visual interface in the application and create a report based on its contents.

However, you may encounter situations in which you prefer to have the contents of an actual Visual Basic record set from one of Visual Basic's intrinsic data models act as the data source for a report. The RDC provides for this with the SetDataSource method. Using SetDataSource, you can initially design the report using a particular database or data source, or using a field-definition file (discussed in the online Help). Then, you can pass a Visual Basic DAO, RDO, or ADO record set, snapshot, or result set to the report at run time. The RDC will use the current contents of the VB data set to populate the report.

The syntax for SetDataSource is as follows:

```
[form]Object.SetDataSource data, DataTag, tableIndex
```

In this statement, *Object* is the RDC Database object (residing below the Report object) that you want to supply data to; *data* is the DAO, ADO, or RDO data set that you want to supply data to the report; and *DataTag* and *tableIndex* are parameters indicating, respectively, the type of data and the index of the table that you want to change the data source for. The *DataTag* parameter should always be specified as 3, with *tableIndex* being set based on the table you wish to "point" to the new data source.

Thus, if you have created an RDC report and named the Report object "Report," and you have identified an ADO Resultset object elsewhere in your VB application with the name "ADOrs," the following code will pass the contents of the result set to the report. When the report is printed, exported, or passed to the Report Viewer, the contents of the result set will be used by the report's Database object to populate the report.

```
Report.Database.SetDataSource ADOrs,3,1
```

Notice that the last two parameters to the SetDataSource method are 3 and 1, indicating the only allowable data tag (3), and the first table in the database (1).

There are actually two forms of the SetDataSource method available with the RDC. The method described previously applies to the entire Database object, requiring the third argument indicating a table index. There is also a SetDataSource method available for the DatabaseTable object. The syntax is almost the same—the only difference is that a table-index parameter is not required, because the method applies only to a single Table object.

If you use SetDataSource to change the data source for a database table, make sure the data source you pass to the report remains in scope whenever the report runs. For example, you may define a Report object that's global to your application (by declaring it at the module level). But if you pass it a data source that was declared at the form level, and then try to run the report in another form, the data source will be out of scope and the report will fail. The ReadRecords method is available for reading the contents of the data source into the Report object, if maintaining scope for the data source isn't practical. Search the Developer's Help for information on "ReadRecords."

Tip *Version 8.5 provides two other methods available from the Database object (underneath the Report object) that are similar to SetDataSource. AddOLEDBSource will add an ADO data source to the report and make its fields available to the report. AddADOCommand will add a database table to the report through an ADO connection and command.*

Unbound Fields

Depending on the reporting application you are designing, you may choose to create a very basic generic report layout that doesn't connect to any particular database at the time you design it. This might be appropriate, for example, for an application that allows a user to choose from a list of database fields and drag and drop them to a pseudoreport outline in your application. When the report is actually printed, your code would need to match the chosen fields to actual field locations on a Crystal

Report. Or, you may design one report that a user can choose to connect to either a test database or a production database. Although the SetDataSource method, described previously, may be a good alternative for this example, you may also want to manually assign database values to fields on the report.

Version 8.5 of the RDC provides new capabilities to make this type of customized reporting much easier. *Unbound Fields* can be added to your report in the ActiveX designer just like database fields, formula fields, and so forth. The only difference is that the fields don't actually connect to any particular database table or field. This assignment is made at run time, using automatic or manual binding (discussed later in the chapter).

Adding Unbound Fields to a Report

The first step in using Unbound Fields is to add them to the report in the RDC designer. You'll notice the additional Unbound Fields category in the Field Explorer that you don't see in the regular Crystal Reports designer. When you click the plus sign next to this category, you'll see a list of Unbound Field data types. Drag and drop the desired data types to the report just as you would other Field Explorer objects. Figure 26-6 shows Unbound Fields being placed on a report.

The RDC will apply default object names to the Unbound Fields you drag and drop. Depending on how you're planning ultimately to bind the fields to your data source, you may leave the default names if you so choose. But, it probably makes sense to at least give the Unbound Fields meaningful names, to help you remember what you're binding when you begin to write the binding code. And, if you plan to use the RDC's automatic binding method (discussed in the next section), you need to give them names identical to the field names in the data source that you will be binding to them.

Binding Fields to the Data Source

Once you've created the report with your complement of Unbound Fields, it's time to bind them at run time. First, declare and assign any necessary objects. In the following sample code, a Report object is defined to contain the ActiveX designer report, and an ADO record set is created. Fields from this record set will be bound to the Unbound Fields created in the report.

```
Dim Report As New CrystalReport1
Dim rs As New ADOR.Recordset
rs.Open "select * from orders", "xtreme sample database"
Report.Database.SetDataSource rs, 3, 1
```

Remember that even though the Unbound Fields you added to the report aren't "connected" to any particular database fields, the Report object itself must be connected to your desired data source before you can bind any fields to it. This is accomplished with SetDataSource, AddOLEDBSource, or some similar method.

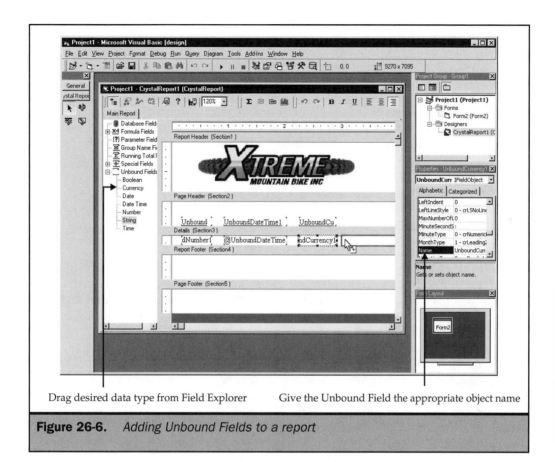

Drag desired data type from Field Explorer   Give the Unbound Field the appropriate object name

Figure 26-6. *Adding Unbound Fields to a report*

After you make the data connection, there are two ways of actually binding the Unbound Fields to a database field: automatic binding and manual binding.

Automatic Binding   Automatic binding uses the Unbound Field's data type and, optionally, object name to bind to actual data fields in the data source. To use automatic binding, execute a single line of code similar to this:

```
Report.AutoSetUnboundFieldSource crBMTNameAndValue
```

By supplying the crBMTNameAndValue constant to the AutoSetUnboundFieldSource method, the RDC will use both the name and data type of the Unbound Field to try to match to a data source field. If you want to base this object-to-field matching on name only, supply the constant crBMTName. The RDC will then attempt to match Unbound Fields to data source fields based solely on name, regardless of data type.

Manual Binding If you have disparate data sources that won't always match field names with the names you've given your Unbound Fields, you can assign data source fields to the Unbound Fields one by one. Examine the following code fragment:

```
Report.OrderID.SetUnboundFieldSource "{ado.Order ID}"
Report.OrderDate.SetUnboundFieldSource "{ado.Order Date}"
Report.OrderAmount.SetUnboundFieldSource "{ado.Order Amount}"
Report.ShipVia.SetUnboundFieldSource "{ado.Ship Via}"
```

In this example, individual Unbound Fields are matched to data source fields using the field object's SetUnboundFieldSource method.

Customizing the Report Viewer

If you've added the Report Viewer ActiveX component to your project, you have a great deal of flexibility in customizing the way the Report Viewer appears and behaves. By default, the RDC will add the Report Viewer to its own form and add a small amount of code to supply the Report object to the Report Viewer and resize the Report Viewer whenever the form is resized.

This default behavior just uses a fraction of the Report Viewer's capabilities. The viewer has many options, exposed by its own automation server, which will meld it more tightly into your application. You can customize how the Report Viewer looks, what controls and toolbar buttons are available, and the Report Viewer's size. You may even perform all the functions from within code that the built-in toolbar buttons would accomplish. This allows you to make the Report Viewer show virtually no controls but the report itself, if you prefer. You can design a completely separate user interface for page control, zoom levels, printing, exporting, and more.

In addition, the Report Viewer contains a flexible event model that will "fire" events as the Report Viewer performs various functions, or as a user interacts with it. You can trap button clicks, drill-down selections, changes in the zoom level, and other events. You can execute extra code when any of these events occurs, or intercept the events and cancel them if you wish to not have the Report Viewer complete them.

When you add the Report Viewer to a form (or when it's added automatically by the RDC), you'll see the outline of the Report Viewer appear as an object inside the form. When you select the Report Viewer object, you'll see a large number of design-time properties appear in the Properties box in VB. This is illustrated in Figure 26-7.

If you want the Report Viewer to exhibit consistent behavior during the entire application, you can change properties for the Report Viewer at design time, such as which toolbar buttons are shown, whether a report group tree is displayed, whether a user can drill down, and so on.

Most of these properties can also be set at run time by supplying the appropriate values to the Report Viewer object's properties. Because the Report Viewer object actually adds its own COM Automation Server to your project, you can get an idea of the object model, properties, methods, and events that are available by looking at the

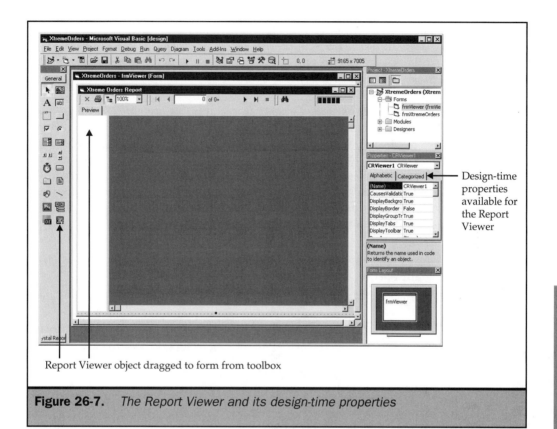

Report Viewer object dragged to form from toolbox

Design-time
properties
available for
the Report
Viewer

Figure 26-7.   *The Report Viewer and its design-time properties*

Object Browser. Press F2, or choose View | Object Browser from the Visual Basic
pull-down menus. Then, choose CRVIEWERLibCtl in the library drop-down list
to see the object model exposed by the Report Viewer's Automation Server.

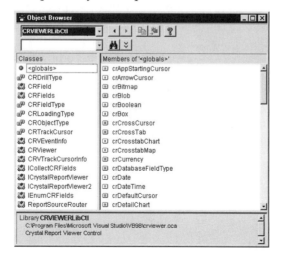

In addition to the Object Browser, the online Help contains thorough information about the Report Viewer object model. Consult either Developer's Help or the stand-alone CRRDC.HLP file and search for "Report Viewer." Then, look for "Report Viewer Object Model" within the Report Viewer Help category.

Here's some code from the Xtreme Orders sample application that customizes several Report Viewer behaviors. The Print button is turned off on the Report Viewer by setting the EnablePrintButton property to false. The Help button is displayed on the Report Viewer by setting the EnableHelpButton property to true. The Crystal Decisions logo animation control is turned on by setting the EnableAnimationCtrl property to true. And, the EnableDrillDown property determines whether or not a user can double-click a group in the Report Viewer to drill down (if the user chooses to show a detail report, drill-down isn't of benefit).

```
CRViewer1.EnablePrintButton = False
CRViewer1.EnableHelpButton = True
CRViewer1.EnableAnimationCtrl = True

If frmXtremeOrders.chkSummary Then
    CRViewer1.EnableDrillDown = True
Else
    CRViewer1.EnableDrillDown = False
End If   'frmXtremeOrders.chkSummary
```

Trapping Report Viewer Events

The Report Viewer's automation server, in addition to offering a good selection of properties and methods, exposes a large number of events that allow you to trap button clicks, report-processing cycles, and drill-down attempts. These events can be used to modify the behavior of the Report Viewer, to execute some additional supplementary code when a certain event occurs, or potentially to modify report contents while it is being viewed.

You can see which events are available for custom coding by searching the online Help for "CRViewer Object," and then clicking the Handling Report Viewer events link. You may also look at the Object Browser. Or, just open the code window for the Report Viewer object and look at the procedure drop-down list in the upper-right corner of the code window.

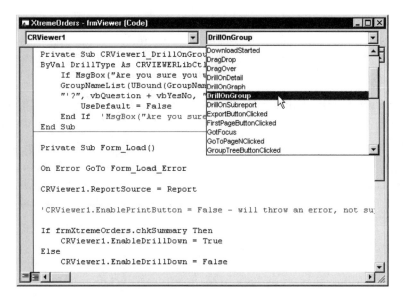

Because you can trap many events that occur during report processing and user interaction with the Report Viewer, you have tremendous power to customize your reporting application. The Xtreme Orders sample application has only three simple examples of these capabilities. If the user clicks the Help button in the Report Viewer (a new event trap added to RDC Version 8.5), a message box appears indicating Custom Help Goes Here. When the user drills down on a group, a confirmation message box appears, asking them to confirm the drill-down. If they answer Yes, the drill-down will occur. If they answer No, the drill-down will be canceled. And, after a user drills down and clicks the Close View button (the red X) in the Report Viewer, another confirmation message box appears, asking them to confirm the closure. As with the original drill-down, the drill-down tab will be closed only if the user answers Yes. Otherwise, the event will be canceled.

One of the more complex parts of these examples is actually determining which group will be affected when the drill-down or drill-down tab closure occurs. Understanding this is crucial for fully exploiting the power of the event model—trapping these events is probably of little use if you can't determine which group is actually being manipulated. The Report Viewer DrillOnGroup event makes this task easier by passing the GroupNameList parameter into the event function. This zero-based array contains an element for each group that has been drilled into previously, with the current group that is now being drilled into being the last element of the array.

If your report contains only one level of grouping (as does the Xtreme Orders sample report), the GroupNameList will always contain just element 0—the group that was drilled down to. However, if your report contains multiple levels of grouping, you'll have the extra benefit of determining how deep and which groups are included in the group that is currently being drilled down to. For example, if your report is grouped on three levels—Country, State, and City—a user may first drill down on Canada. This will fire the DrillOnGroup event, and the GroupNameList array will contain only element 0, Canada. Then, in the Canada drill-down tab, the user might double-click BC. This will again fire the DrillOnGroup event, and the GroupNameList array will now contain two elements, Canada in element 0 and BC in element 1. Then, if the user double-clicks Vancouver in the BC drill-down tab, yet another DrillOnGroup event will fire. Inside this event, the GroupNameList array will contain elements 0, 1, and 2—Canada, BC, and Vancouver.

If you are only concerned about the lowest level of grouping, just query the last element of the GroupNameList array by using the VB UBound function. Even though the Xtreme Orders report contains only one level of grouping (thereby always allowing GroupNameList(0) to be used to determine the group), the UBound function has been used for upward compatibility.

The other argument passed to the DrillOnGroup event is UseDefault. This Boolean value can be set to true or false inside the event to determine whether the drill-down actually occurs. If UseDefault is set to true (or left as is), the drill-down will occur. If it is set to false inside the DrillOnGroup event, the drill-down will be canceled and no drill-down tab will appear for the group in the Report Viewer.

Here's the sample code from the Xtreme Orders application. Note that the actual group being drilled on is included in the message box and that the results of the message box determine whether or not the drill-down occurs.

```
Private Sub CRViewer1_DrillOnGroup(GroupNameList As Variant, _
ByVal DrillType As CRVIEWERLibCtl.CRDrillType, UseDefault As Boolean)
   If MsgBox("Are you sure you want to drill down on '" & _
   GroupNameList(UBound(GroupNameList)) & _
   "'?", vbQuestion + vbYesNo, "Xtreme Orders Report") = vbNo Then
      UseDefault = False
   End If  'MsgBox("Are you sure you want to drill down...
End Sub
```

The other Report Viewer event that is used in the Xtreme Orders sample application is CloseButtonClicked. This event fires whenever a user clicks the red X in the Report Viewer to close the current drill-down tab (known in the Report Viewer object model as the *current view*). Again, the sample application simply displays a confirming message box asking whether or not the user really wants to close the drill-down tab.

By setting the UseDefault parameter inside the event code, the drill-down tab is closed or not closed, based on the user's choice.

As when drilling down, the actual drill-down tab that's being closed needs to be known inside the event (it's just being included in the message box in this example). Because the CloseButtonClicked event doesn't pass a GroupNameList or similar parameter into the event, a little more sleuthing has to be done to determine what the current view is. This is where both the Report Viewer's GetViewPath method and ActiveViewIndex property come into play.

The ActiveViewIndex property simply returns an integer (one based) indicating which drill-down tab is the currently selected tab. While this is helpful, it doesn't return the actual string containing the group name of the tab being viewed. This must be accomplished by using the GetViewPath method of the Report Viewer object. This method accepts one argument, a numeric index indicating the tab in the Report Viewer window for which you want to see the view path. The method returns a one-based string array that includes the actual views (or group names) that are included in the drill-down tab whose index is provided as the argument to GetViewPath. As with GroupNameList, you can then determine the actual name of the current tab being closed by accessing the last element (using the UBound function) of the array.

Examine the following code closely:

```
Private Sub CRViewer1_CloseButtonClicked(UseDefault As Boolean)
    If MsgBox("Close '" & _
CRViewer1.GetViewPath(CRViewer1.ActiveViewIndex)
(UBound(CRViewer1.GetViewPath(CRViewer1.ActiveViewIndex))) _
    & "' Drill-Down tab?", vbQuestion + vbYesNo, _
        "Xtreme Order Report") = vbNo Then
        UseDefault = False
    End If   'MsgBox("Close...
End Sub
```

Caution *Due to width restrictions in the book, the line of sample code in the previous example that demonstrates the CRViewer1.GetViewPath command is broken after the first right parenthesis. If you look at the sample application, you'll notice that this is a continuous line, which is required for proper VB interpretation of the line.*

Notice that GetViewPath is supplied with the ActiveViewIndex property. This will return a string array containing all the groups that are included in the current drill-down tab. Even though the Xtreme Orders report contains only one level of grouping, the UBound function is still used to retrieve the last element of the array returned by GetViewPath. This provides upward compatibility if you ever choose to add multiple groups to the report.

DEVELOPING CUSTOM WINDOW APPLICATIONS

Version 8.5 of the RDC provides additional Report Viewer support for the familiar Crystal Reports Select Expert and Search Expert, as well as a Text Search feature. Buttons for these tools can be enabled or disabled at design time or run time. And, you programmatically perform both formula-based and text-based searches with the Report Viewer's SearchByFormula and SearchForText methods.

Error Handling

You need to set up error-handling code for all aspects of RDC programming. As you manipulate the Report object itself (setting properties and executing methods), you need to plan for the possibility that errors may occur. And, if you use the Report Viewer in your application, it can also throw errors for any number of reasons. Add error-handling logic accordingly.

All Report object and Report Viewer errors will appear as regular Visual Basic run-time errors. These need to be trapped with an On Error Goto routine. The hard part is trying to figure out what error codes to trap. Unlike other integration methods, such as the ActiveX control and Report Engine Automation Server, the RDC is not a wraparound tool for the Crystal Report Print Engine. Therefore, the errors it throws are not the same three-digit codes as those returned by the Print Engine (preceded with 20, to return 20XXX in the ActiveX control and Report Engine Automation Server).

To complicate things further, Crystal Decisions has yet to provide comprehensive documentation for the errors that either the Report or Report Viewer objects might throw. In many situations, you'll see typical VB-type error codes for report-related errors. For example, supplying a string index argument to a Report object collection that only accepts integer arguments won't generate an RDC-specific error; instead, Subscript Out of Range will be returned. However, certain error messages that are Report- or Report Viewer–specific generally throw errors that start with –2147, and are followed by six other numbers.

You'll simply have to test your application thoroughly and create error-handling code appropriately. Try intentionally creating any Report- or Report Viewer–related errors that have even a remote chance of occurring. You can then determine what corresponding error codes the Report or Report Viewer objects throw, and add code to trap those specific errors. Here's sample code from the Xtreme Orders application that traps potential errors when setting Report properties at run time:

```
cmdOK_Click_Error:
Screen.MousePointer = vbDefault
Select Case Err.Number
    Case -2147190889
        MsgBox "Report Cancelled", vbInformation, "Xtreme Order Report"
    Case -2147190908
        MsgBox "Invalid E-Mail address or other e-mail problem", _
            vbCritical, "Xtreme Order Report"
```

```
            txtAddress.SetFocus
        Case Else
            MsgBox "Error " & Err.Number & " - " & Err.Description, _
                   vbCritical, "Xtreme Order Report"
    End Select   'Case Err.Number
```

Other RDC Properties and Methods

This chapter has covered many RDC procedures for handling most common report-customization requirements, but several other areas of RDC functionality deserve some discussion. In particular, RDC functions that pertain to handling SQL database reporting, as well as dealing with subreports, should be addressed. In addition, the RDC DiscardSavedData method for "resetting" or clearing the contents of properties that may have been set in previous VB code should be explored.

The DiscardSavedData Method

If you find yourself displaying a Report object in a viewer, or performing some other output mechanism with the same Report object over and over, you will want to take steps to ensure that any "left over" settings from a previous report process are reset when you run the next report. While you can set the Report object to Nothing and instantiate it again, you may instead want to use the Report object's DiscardSavedData method if you will be running a report multiple times without the Nothing setting.

The Xtreme Orders sample application provides a good example of where this is helpful. The Report object is declared in a global module, and the Print Xtreme Orders form stays loaded during the entire scope of the application. Every time the OK button is clicked, the application sets Report properties based on the controls on the form, and then either prints or exports the report, or displays the form containing the Report Viewer.

The issue of clearing previous settings comes into play when a user runs the report more than once without ending and restarting the application. Because the Report object is never released and reinstantiated, all of its property settings remain intact when the user clicks OK subsequent times. If the Visual Basic code doesn't explicitly set some of these previously set properties, the report may exhibit behavior from the previous time it was run that you don't expect. Executing the Report object's DiscardSavedData method clears many properties of settings from any previous activity, returning them to the state they were in when designed.

Simply execute the DiscardSavedData method for any Report objects that you want to "clean up," as shown in the following sample from the Xtreme Orders sample application:

```
Report.DiscardSavedData 'required for consistent results
```

You may wonder about the significance of DiscardSavedData with the RDC, particularly when you're integrating a report that you designed in the ActiveX designer that does not have a Save Data with Report option. If you are using an external .RPT file that has been saved with File | Save Data with Report turned on, you'll probably want Visual Basic to discard the saved data at run time and refresh the report with new data from the database. Because the RDC is integrating a report that is contained entirely within the VB IDE (even if an .RPT file was imported, its saved data is not imported with it), you may be confused as to how DiscardSavedData applies. The RDC, in essence, "saves" data in the Report object when it is viewed in the Report Viewer, printed, or exported (or when the ReadRecords method is executed). That saved data remains a part of the Report object until it's discarded or the object reference is destroyed.

SQL Database Control

Many corporate databases are kept on client/server SQL database systems, such as Microsoft SQL Server, Oracle, and Informix. Many Visual Basic applications provide front-end interfaces to these database systems and need to handle SQL reporting as well. The RDC contains several properties and methods that help when integrating reports based on SQL databases.

Logging On to SQL Databases

Your VB application probably already handles SQL database security, requiring the user to provide a valid logon ID and password at the beginning of the application. The user will be frustrated if the RDC asks for yet another logon when it comes time to open the report. By using RDC methods and properties to pass logon information to the report, you can pass the valid ID and password the user has already provided, thereby allowing the report to print without prompting again.

One approach to passing logon information to a report is the LogOnServer method, available for both the Application and Database objects. This method logs on to a secure database and remains logged on until LogOffServer is executed, or until the Report object reference is destroyed. Search the online Help for "LogOnServer method."

The other way to provide logon information from within your application is by executing the SetLogOnInfo method for the Report object's DatabaseTable object. If you have tables in your report that originate from different databases, this approach allows individual logon information to be provided for each table in the report. Search the online Help for "SetLogOnInfo method."

Retrieving or Setting the SQL Query

When you submit a record-selection formula, as discussed earlier in the chapter, the RDC automatically generates a SQL statement to submit to the database server. However, if the record-selection formula contains a Crystal Reports formula or other characteristics that prevent the RDC from generating a WHERE clause in the SQL statement, report performance can be dramatically and negatively affected. You may, therefore, want to create directly in your VB application the SQL statement the report uses. As part of this process, you may find it helpful to retrieve the SQL statement that the RDC is generating automatically.

The Report object provides a read/write SQLQueryString property that can be read or written to at run time. By examining the contents of this property, you can see what the SQL query is that the RDC is generating. You can then make necessary modifications to the query, depending on the state of your application and the database on which the report is based. Then, pass the modified query to the SQLQueryString property to be submitted to the server when the report runs.

Note *As with the Crystal Reports designer, you cannot modify the SELECT clause in the SQL query. Only FROM, WHERE, ORDER BY, and GROUP BY can be modified. Don't forget that you must still include the SELECT clause, however, and that it must not be changed from the original clause the RDC created. Also, if you create ORDER BY or GROUP BY clauses, you must separate them from the end of the WHERE clause with a carriage return/line feed character sequence. Use the vbCRLF constant to add the CR/LF sequence inside the SQL query.*

Reading or Setting Stored Procedure Parameters

If your report is based on a parameterized SQL stored procedure, you will probably want to supply parameter values to the stored procedure from within your code, much as you will want to respond to any RDC parameter fields that may have been created.

With the RDC, SQL stored procedure parameters are treated identically to Report parameter fields. The Report object contains the ParameterFieldDefinitions collection, containing one ParameterFieldDefinition object for each Report parameter field *or* stored procedure parameter contained in the report. The ParameterFieldDefinition object's ParameterType property will indicate whether the parameter is a Report parameter or a stored procedure parameter.

By executing the ParameterFieldDefinition object's AddCurrentValue method, you can pass a value to a stored procedure parameter from within your code. More detailed information on interacting with parameter fields can be found earlier in this chapter.

RDC Subreports

The RDC brings all the flexibility of Crystal Reports subreports to Visual Basic. If you import an .RPT file that contains subreports into the RDC, the subreports will be imported along with the main report. And, you can add your own subreports to the RDC design window at any time by right-clicking a blank area of the report and choosing Insert | Subreport from the pop-up menu (see Chapter 11 for more information on creating subreports).

The unique part of the RDC is the way a subreport fits into the object model. When you are displaying the main report in the RDC design window, a subreport will appear as an object outline, just as it does in regular Crystal Reports. However, if you click the subreport object, it has a set of properties that appears in the Properties box, just like other objects on the report. Figure 26-8 illustrates this.

You can set several design-time properties for the Subreport object, the same way you can for other objects on the report. One of the properties you may want to set as a matter of habit is the subreport name. By giving it a descriptive name, you'll be able to more easily identify and work with it as you write code for your application.

After you add the Subreport object to the main report, it's treated just like a text object, field, line, box, or other object that appears on the main report in the main Report object model. But because the subreport contains its own set of fields and objects that are separate from the main report, the object model can expose them in a number of ways. Subreport objects (fields, formulas, sections, lines, and others) actually appear as part of the main Report object. The RDC precedes the object names with the name of the subreport and an underscore.

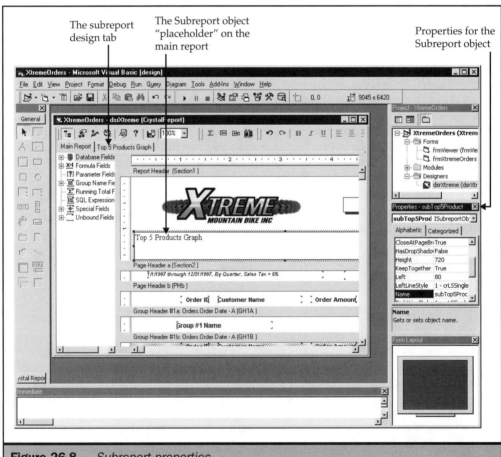

Figure 26-8. *Subreport properties*

Consider a main report that contains several database fields that haven't been renamed since the report was created (Field1, Field2, and so on). The main report also contains a subreport that you've named subTop5Products. The Subreport objects actually become part of the main report. You can now set properties for the Report object named Field1, which will refer to the first field on the main report. If you then set Report properties for an object named subTop5Products_Field1, you are setting properties for the first field on the subreport.

Also, the main report exposes a SubreportObject object for every subreport "placeholder" contained on the main report. This object exposes a variety of properties that can be read and written to at run time to control the appearance and behavior of the placeholder (although not the actual subreport itself). Consider the following code:

```
'Set subreport object borders to blank
Report.subTop5Products.TopLineStyle = 0
Report.subTop5Products.LeftLineStyle = 0
Report.subTop5Products.BottomLineStyle = 0
Report.subTop5Products.RightLineStyle = 0
```

Here, the SubreportObject object is being manipulated from the Report object (referred to with the subreport name subTop5Products). The four line-style properties are all being set to 0, indicating that the border around the Subreport object will be invisible at run time.

Despite this tricky way of sharing objects and setting properties for the subreport placeholder, not all subreport properties, methods, and events are available from the main Report object. And, if you're using an external .RPT file, these options won't be available either. Because the subreport is, in essence, an additional report that appears only on the main report, you need a way to control the behavior of the subreport using the same object model as the main report.

To accomplish this, you must declare an object of type Report from the CRAXDRT or CRAXDDRT Automation Servers (the automation servers the RDC exposes). You then use the main report's OpenSubreport method to create another Report object variable to contain the subreport. You can then set properties, execute methods, and trap events for the main report using its original object variable, and for the subreport using its own object variable. The following code fragment demonstrates this approach:

```
Dim Subreport as CRAXDRT.Report
. . .
. . .
'Put subreport in its own object
Set Subreport = Report.subTop5Products.OpenSubreport

'Set record selection formula for subreport
Subreport.RecordSelectionFormula = "{ado.Unit Price} > 1000"
```

Creating New Reports at Run Time

One of the main improvements first introduced in Version 8 and further improved in Version 8.5 of the RDC is the capability to actually create a new .RPT file from scratch. The *Report Creation API*, as Crystal Decisions refers to this feature, allows your VB code to create a new report entirely from scratch, including tables and fields, report sections, and Report objects. After you create the base report structure, you can further manipulate report sections or format Report objects using code. With Version 8.5 of the RDC, you can even add the Embeddable Report Designer to your application to allow end users to interactively modify the report, virtually identically to the report design capabilities you have with the RDC's internal ActiveX report designer.

And, once all the code-based design and user manipulation is completed, not only can you view the report in the Report Viewer, or print or export the report, but you can save the completed report as an .RPT file, ready to be opened in Crystal Reports or another custom application. Because of the RDC's ability to create a report from scratch, Crystal Decisions considers this a potential threat to its flagship Crystal Reports designer. As such, you must enter into a license agreement and pay royalties to Crystal Decisions if you wish to distribute an application that uses these calls (as discussed in more detail earlier in the chapter). Also, note that Crystal Decisions license agreement specifically forbids you from using these report design techniques to create "competitive products."

There are general approaches to creating a report at run time:

- Creating all report elements entirely within code
- Using the new Embeddable Report Designer within your VB application to allow an end user to create the report interactively.

Creating a New Report with Code

Creating a report with code requires the same basic steps that creating a report interactively in the RDC ActiveX designer or in stand-alone Crystal Reports requires:

1. Create a new report.
2. Choose database tables and link them, if necessary.
3. Add fields, text objects, bitmap images, and other objects to various report sections.
4. Add any desired groups.
5. Add subtotals and grand totals.
6. Format objects for desired appearance.
7. View the report in the Report Viewer, print it, or save it as an external .RPT file.

The RDC object model exposes methods and properties to accomplish each of these steps. Initially, you must add the RDC Automation Server library to your application, using Project | References. Check the Crystal Reports 8.5 ActiveX Designer Run Time Library. And, if you will be viewing the completed report in the Report Viewer, add it with Project | Components.

Tip *Look on the CD-ROM accompanying this book for a sample Visual Basic application that demonstrates these steps. The sample code in the remainder of this chapter is taken from the sample application.*

Declare Application and Report objects as you do with applications that use existing reports. Consider this sample code:

```
Public Application As New CRAXDDRT.Application
Public Report As CRAXDDRT.Report
```

Note references to the new combined design-time/run-time library (CRAXDDRT). This is in preparation for using the Embeddable Report Designer (described later in the chapter). If you will not be using this designer, but just creating a report entirely within code, use the run-time–only library, CRAXDRT.

The first new step involves assigning an object to the Report object variable. Previously, you've either assigned an existing ActiveX designer object to this variable or used the Application object's OpenReport method to assign an external .RPT file. Now, however, you will be creating a new report from scratch. The Application object exposes the new NewReport method to accomplish this:

```
' Create a new empty report
Set Report = Application.NewReport
```

As when creating a new report from scratch in the ActiveX designer or Crystal Reports, you must choose a data connection method and database tables for the report. The Report Creation API requires the same steps. The following sample code illustrates how to assign an ADO connection to the Report object, using the Orders table from the Xtreme Sample Database ODBC data source. The ADO connection string makes this connection (assume that the Microsoft ActiveX Data Objects library has been added to the project, and theADOConnection and ADOCommand objects have been declared earlier in the Declarations section):

```
' Open the data connection
Set ADOConnection = New ADODB.Connection
ADOConnection.Open "Provider=MSDASQL;Persist Security Info=False;
Data Source=Xtreme Sample Database;Mode=Read"
```

```
' Create a new instance of an ADO command object
Set ADOCommand = New ADODB.Command
Set ADOCommand.ActiveConnection = ADOConnection
ADOCommand.CommandText = "Orders"
ADOCommand.CommandType = adCmdTable

' Add the data source (the XTREME Orders Table) to the report
Report.Database.AddADOCommand ADOConnection, ADOCommand
```

Width limits of this book require that the argument to the ADOConnection.Open method be broken in the middle of the line. Note that the actual sample application maintains the string argument for the Open method all on one line.

You now have the beginnings of a report, including an assigned Report object with a data connection. Were you to open this report in the Crystal Report designer or supply the Report object to the Embeddable Report Designer at this point, you'd find an empty report, but the Field Explorer would be populated by fields from the Xtreme Sample Database Orders table. You would then drag and drop desired fields into various sections of the report. The next requirement of your Report Creation application is to add objects to different report sections. Examine the following code fragments from the RDC Report Creation sample application:

```
Report.Sections(1).AddPictureObject "Xtreme.bmp", 1000, 75
Report.Sections(1).AddTextObject "FedEx Order Detail", 6000, 400
```

The first line of code adds a bitmap picture to the report header (Section 1) of the report, placing it 1,000 twips from the left side of the section and 75 twips down from the top of the section. The next line adds a text object containing the text "FedEx Order Detail" to the report header, at position 6,000/400. Both of these lines of code use methods several levels deep in the RDC object hierarchy. The AddPictureObject and AddTextObject methods are available below an individual Section object within the Sections collection (in this case, the first member in the Sections collection) below the Report object.

If you look at the sample application on the accompanying CD-ROM, you'll actually find more involved logic than just demonstrated to add the text object and format it. For simplicity, this code is not demonstrated in the book text.

The sample application proceeds to add four database fields to the details section of the report:

```
' Add fields to details section
' Note that the Sections collection can be accessed via
' number or string index
Report.Sections("D").AddFieldObject "{ado.Order ID}", 750, 5
Report.Sections("D").AddFieldObject "{ado.Order Date}", 3150, 5
Report.Sections("D").AddFieldObject "{ado.Order Amount}", 5500, 5
Report.Sections("D").AddFieldObject "{ado.Ship Via}", 8850, 5
```

RDC object-hierarchy navigation in the details section is similar to that used to add objects to the report header. The AddFieldObject method used adds a database field, requiring the database field, left position, and top position as arguments. Note that the Sections collection can be accessed via either a numeric or a string index.

If you wish to create groups, there are methods exposed in the object hierarchy to allow complete flexibility with group creation. There are also options to create both group summary fields and report grand totals. The RDC Report Creation sample application creates a grand total of Order Amount in the report footer (Section 4) with the following code:

```
' Create and format Order Amount Grand Total in report footer
Dim AmountTotal As CRAXDDRT.FieldObject
' Creating a separate object variable avoids deep navigation
' down the hierarchy when formatting
Set AmountTotal = Report.Sections(4).AddSummaryFieldObject _
Report.Sections(3).ReportObjects(3).Field.Name, crSTSum, 6000, 750)
With AmountTotal
    .Width = 1500
    .Font.Bold = True
End With      'AmountTotal
```

Note several important points about the preceding code fragment:

- A separate object to hold the grand total field was declared and assigned. Note that this wasn't done previously for the bitmap graphic, text object, and field objects. While it is possible to create lots of objects, as shown in the preceding example, this requires extra coding and keeping track of all the additional objects. The purpose in this example is to make formatting easier by eliminating navigation into the object hierarchy to set the Width and Font.Bold properties.

- You can apply every conceivable kind of formatting to objects once they have been added to the report. Note that the grand total has been widened from its default size and given a bold formatting attribute. A glance through the sample application reveals the UseOneSymbolPerPage formatting attribute being applied to the Order Amount field, so only one dollar sign will appear at the top of each page:

```
' Format the Order Amount to have one dollar sign per page
Report.Sections(3).ReportObjects(3).UseOneSymbolPerPage = True
```

At this point, a basic report design has been created and is contained in the Report object. Additional RDC methods and properties that you are probably more familiar with can be applied to the Report object as well. For example, the sample application limits the report to orders shipped via FedEx with the following, now-familiar approach:

```
Report.RecordSelectionFormula = "{ado.Ship Via} = 'FedEx'"
```

Now, you're ready to proceed to view, print, export, or perform other familiar functions with the Report object. You can also now supply the partially designed Report object to the Embeddable Report Designer to allow the end user to interactively modify the report you've already started to design in code.

Assuming you've added the Report Viewer to a form, the following code will now display your report in the viewer:

```
CRViewer1.ReportSource = Report
CRViewer1.ViewReport
```

When you first run this application, you may notice something else you probably haven't seen before (at least, if you're using the run-time–only library, CRAXDRT—the combined design-time/run-time library, CRAXDDRT, doesn't initially appear to create these messages).

Any time your program encounters any of the Report Creation API calls, the RDC displays this message, warning you that you need a license from Crystal Decisions Software to distribute this report. This message will reappear as your code encounters each method that requires a license. You'll probably want to check the Disable This Message check box. This will prevent the message from appearing for the rest of this particular "run" of the application, although the message will reappear the next time you start the application even if you checked the Disable check box before. Regardless, this message *won't* appear when your application is compiled and distributed to your end user.

Saving the Report

As discussed earlier in the chapter, the ultimate result of your application can be a saved .RPT file that can be opened in stand-alone Crystal Reports or other applications or custom programs that utilize .RPT files. The RDC exposes a new Report object method to accomplish this:

```
Report.SaveAs "Sample.RPT", cr80FileFormat
```

Executing the SaveAs method will save the contents of the Report object to the filename supplied as the first argument. The second argument uses an RDC-provided constant to determine whether the report is saved in Crystal Reports 8 or Crystal Reports 7 format (the file format between Version 8 and 8.5 has not changed—Versions 8 and 7 are the only choices).

If the file already exists when SaveAs is executed, it will be overwritten without a warning or any Visual Basic error being thrown. If this is of concern to you, execute additional code prior to SaveAs to check for the existence of the file.

The Report Creation Wizard

In addition to the RDC Report Creation API, Crystal Decisions has provided an additional COM Automation Server to Crystal Reports 8.5 to assist you in developing custom report creation applications. The *Report Creation Wizard* is available to lead your application user step by step through a report creation process. In fact, the Report Creation Wizard object library is the same library used by Crystal Reports 8.5's Microsoft Access and Microsoft Excel add-ins.

This tool allows an end user to create a report with an expert-type interface, complete with Next and Back buttons. If you're comparing the Report Creation Wizard to the Embeddable Report Designer (described later in the chapter) from a Crystal Reports perspective, you might consider the Report Creation Wizard to be a "Report Expert" and the Embeddable Report Designer to be the "Blank Report" option.

Since the Report Creation Wizard is a separate automation server, you must add the library to your VB project. Choose Project | References and check the Crystal Report 8.5 Standard Wizard Library option. And, as with other COM components, you must declare an object variable to hold the wizard object:

```
Dim CRWizard As New CrystalReportWizard.CRStandardWizard
```

If you view the CrystalReportWizard library in the Object Browser, you'll notice that it only exposes the single CRStandardWizard object with one property and one method. The CrystalReport property is used to assign the wizard a partially defined Report object for the wizard to use as a starting point:

```
Set CRWizard.CrystalReport = Report
```

For the wizard to be of any use, the Report object you supply must already have a data source and tables defined, because the wizard doesn't include any capabilities for the user to choose a data source or choose and link tables. This must be done prior to running the Report Creation Wizard. Also, the wizard does not contain any record-selection capabilities. You need to provide your own user interface for record selection, and set the RecordSelectionFormula property prior to or after running the wizard. If the Report object already has fields and groups created, the wizard will recognize them and place them in their appropriate locations in the wizard dialog boxes.

Once you've supplied the Report object, display the Report Creation Wizard to the user by executing the DisplayReportWizard method:

```
CRWizard.DisplayReportWizard
```

The Report Creation Wizard appears as an application-model dialog box on top of any existing forms your application may be displaying.

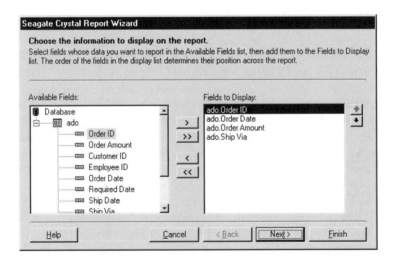

Your user may now progress step by step through the report creation process, clicking the Next button to move to each successive step. These steps can include choosing fields to include on the report; adding groups; creating subtotals, summaries, and grand totals; choosing TopN grouping; and choosing from the usual predefined report styles. When the user clicks the Next button in the Style box, they will be given a choice of what to do next.

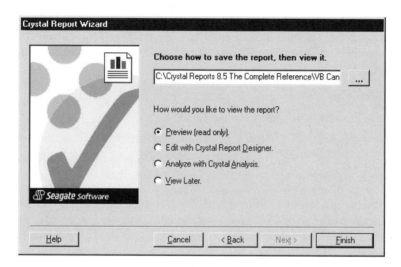

Because the Report Creation Wizard is a completely self-contained object, it will launch Crystal Reports or Seagate Analysis (denoted as Crystal Analysis in this screen) with no further coding required on your part. It will also view the resulting report in the Report Viewer, even if you haven't added it to your project. And, it will save an external .RPT file with no further coding required. Although you might prefer that the wizard merely return the modified Report object to your code to allow you to control what happens next, you have no choice—the options to edit and save are built into the wizard and can't be disabled.

But, once the wizard *does* finish what it's doing, it will return the modified Report object to your application, where you may print, save, or export the report, or supply the Report object to the Report Viewer to be viewed.

A separate online Help file exists for the Report Creation Wizard. Open \Program Files\Seagate Software\Report Designer Component\Wizards_en.hlp (for the English language) to view a small Help file for the wizard.

Using the Embeddable Report Designer

One of the more usable additions to Version 8.5 of the RDC is the *Embeddable Report Designer*. This ActiveX control, when added to a VB form, allows an end user complete interactive report design and modification capabilities, virtually identical to the capabilities provided by the ActiveX report designer that appears in the Visual Basic IDE when the RDC is first added to a VB project. The end result from the Embeddable

Report Designer is a Report object, identical to the Report object that's been discussed earlier in the chapter. It can be further manipulated from within your VB code, supplied to the Report Viewer, exported with the Export method, printed with the PrintOut method, or saved to an RPT file with the SaveAs method.

For all the interactive power it gives to your end users, the Embeddable Report Designer is surprisingly simple to implement inside your VB application. To enable the Embeddable Report Designer in your VB application, there are several general steps required:

1. Add proper references and components from the Project menu.

2. Add the Embeddable Designer to a form.

3. Supply a Report object to the Embeddable Designer.

4. Do any necessary further manipulation to the Report object, such as printing, exporting, saving, or showing in the Report Viewer.

Begin by choosing Project | Components from the VB pull-down menus. You'll see the list of all registered ActiveX controls on your computer. In particular, you'll want to check the Embeddable Crystal Reports 8.5 Designer Control. This will place a Crystal Reports icon on the VB toolbar. You may optionally want to choose the Crystal Report Viewer control as well, if you will be providing an online viewer for your reports within your application.

Selecting the Embeddable Crystal Reports 8.5 Designer Control in Project | Components will add the Crystal Report icon to the toolbox. ⟶

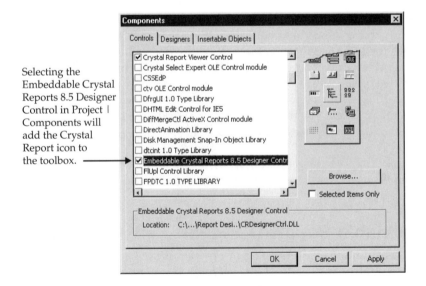

You must also add a reference to the new Crystal Reports 8.5 combined design-time/run-time library. Choose Project | References from the VB pull-down menus and check the Crystal Reports 8.5 ActiveX Designer Design and Runtime Library.

Note *This combined design- and run-time library (CRAXDDRT.DLL) is new to Crystal Reports 8.5. It replaces the previous design-time-only library (CRAXDDT.DLL) that was included with Crystal Reports 8.0. However, the run-time–only RDC library (CRAXDRT.DLL) is still used in Crystal Reports 8.5 as well. When you distribute applications, you'll want to include the combined library if and only if you will be including the Embeddable Report Designer in your application. If you will not require this designer, distribute the run-time–only library (CRAXDRT.DLL).*

Once you've added the proper components and references from the Project menu, you'll notice a new Crystal Reports icon for the Embeddable Report Designer in the VB toolbox. Simply add this control to a form as you would any other VB control. When you do so, you'll see the outline of the designer in your form, along with the designer's design-time properties in the VB Properties box.

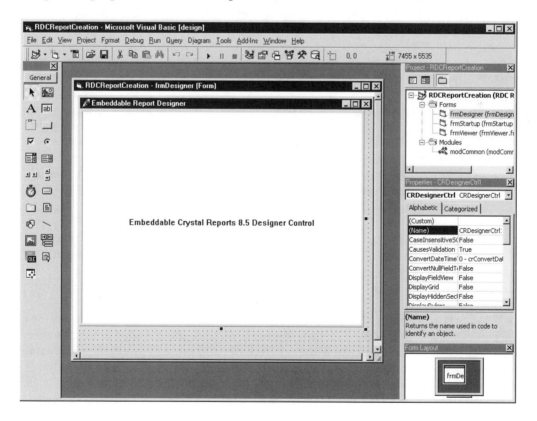

DEVELOPING CUSTOM
WINDOW APPLICATIONS

Enabling the designer is as simple as supplying an existing Report object to the designer's ReportObject property, as in the following:

```
CRDesignerCtrl1.ReportObject = Report
CRDesignerCtrl1.EnableHelp = False
```

This code assumes that the Embeddable Designer object has been left with its default name of CRDesignerCtrl1 and that an already declared Report object named Report is in scope within the current procedure. If you wish the end user to modify an existing report, you will have obtained this Report object by using the OpenReport method of an application object, or perhaps used the application object's NewReport method and programmatically added a database connection, fields, text objects, and other items (as in the sample application included on the CD-ROM accompanying this book).

You'll also notice that the designer's EnableHelp property has been set to false. This property setting will hide the Help button from the designer's toolbar, as well as from pop-up menus. In fact, the Embeddable Report Designer exposes an entire set of properties, a single method, and a few Windows-standard events as part of its own automation server. Most of the report-specific customization of the designer is accomplished by setting properties at design time in the Properties box or at run time in code. A complete description of these properties can be found in either developer's Help file by opening the "Embeddable Crystal Reports Designer Control Object Model" category from the table of contents.

Caution *If you don't disable the online Help button in the Embeddable Designer by setting EnableHelp to false (either in the Properties box or at run time), users will receive a "Help File not found" error message if they attempt to get online help. Information for creating a Windows .HLP file and using it with the Embeddable Designer is available in the CRRDC.HLP file or CrystalDevHelp.chm. Look in the Help file contents and open the "Embeddable Crystal Reports Designer Control Object Model" category. Then, choose "Distributing the Embeddable Designer."*

Once this code has been executed and the form is displayed, you'll note a report designer identical to the designer that appears in the VB IDE when you first begin using the RDC. Users may use the Field Explorer on the left to add fields, create formulas, and so on. They may select objects and format them with right-click pop-up menus or toolbar buttons. The main differences between the Embeddable Report Designer and actual Crystal Reports is that all interaction must be with toolbar buttons, the Field Explorer, and pop-up menus—there are no pull-down menus in the designer. Figure 26-9 shows the Embeddable Report Designer and some of its interface elements.

Once the user has finished interacting with the report, they may simply close the window containing the designer, or use some other user interface element you've built into the form, such as a command button or tab control. However, the designer itself

Use the Field Explorer to add fields, create formulas, and use other elements of the regular Crystal Reports Field Explorer

Use toolbar buttons to perform commonly required report design functions

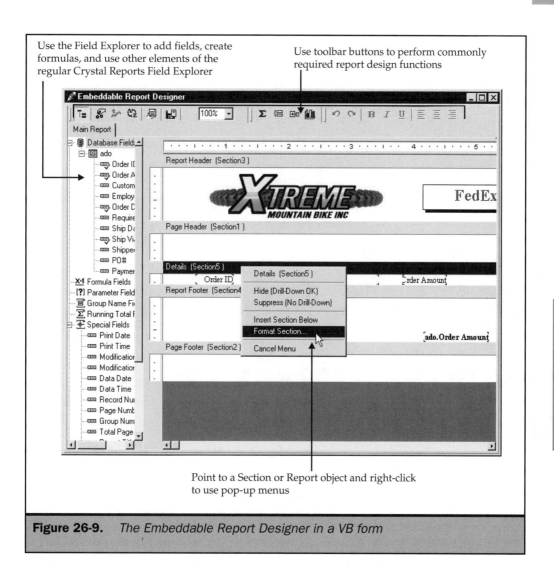

Point to a Section or Report object and right-click to use pop-up menus

Figure 26-9. *The Embeddable Report Designer in a VB form*

doesn't contain the Preview tab familiar to Crystal Reports users—you'll have to facilitate viewing of the modified report in your own code.

The designer simply returns the same Report object to your VB code that you initially supplied with any changes the end user made. You may now pass the modified Report object to a Report Viewer control, export it to a file, e-mail it, or execute the Report object's PrintOut method to print it to a printer. These capabilities are discussed earlier in this chapter.

Distributing RDC Applications

After you create an RDC application that integrates Crystal Reports, you'll want to compile and test the application. This process is unchanged with Crystal Reports 8.5. Unless you're using the application only for yourself, you also need to set up a distribution mechanism to pass your application to your intended audience: the application users.

Because you are distributing Crystal Reports features and components with your VB application, some distribution issues come into play. This section of the chapter discusses both the general points you want to keep in mind when creating your distribution package and specific areas that concern certain reporting features you may want to include or exclude from your application.

Distribution Overview

The days of creating a single .EXE executable file that can be easily copied to a single floppy disk are long gone. Standard Visual Basic projects already consist of the main program executable file, run-time files, and a host of support files. Introducing Crystal Reports into the mix adds a fairly large burden to this process. Because Crystal Reports is designed in a very modular fashion, it's easy to add functionality and upgraded features to the tool. However, this modularity also complicates the distribution process because so many different files are involved in the overall Crystal Reports product.

If you prefer to integrate external .RPT files with your RDC application, rather than using the ActiveX designer within the VB IDE, you must include those .RPT files in your distribution package. A variety of support files also are required, depending on several issues such as the database connections the report uses and the export capabilities that the project entails. The best part is that this is all handled pretty much automatically if you use Visual Basic distribution tools to create your distribution package.

In addition to available third-party distribution products, such as InstallShield and Wise, Visual Basic 6 includes the Package and Deployment Wizard, and Visual Basic 5 includes the Application Setup Wizard. All of these tools are designed to gather all the necessary executable and support files required for a project, compress them into a smaller space, and add them to a setup program. When the setup program is run from floppies or a CD-ROM, run from a network share, or downloaded from a Web server, all the necessary files are decompressed and installed in the proper locations.

> **Note** *Specific instructions for using these distribution tools can be found in the documentation accompanying them—this chapter will not teach you how to distribute VB applications. Examples in the chapter are based on the Visual Basic 6 Package and Deployment Wizard.*

Distribution tools, such as the Package and Deployment Wizard, look through your VB project file and attempt to determine all the necessary files that must be distributed with the project. Depending on the different RDC libraries and modules you have chosen for your application, a different set of files needs to be included in the distribution process. Having a fundamental understanding of this process will help you tailor your project's distribution, based on its individual needs.

Most tools use *dependency files* to determine what files to include in your distribution package. These files consist of the same base filename as the file used to provide Crystal Reports integration, but contain a .DEP extension. For example, the dependency file for the new combined design-time/run-time RDC library (CRAXDDRT.DLL) is CRAXDDRT.DEP. The dependency file is a straight ASCII text file that you can open with Notepad, containing a list of all related DLLs or other files that the "base" file is dependent upon. The distribution package uses the dependency file to include all necessary files (and, in most cases, several that are unnecessary) when the VB application is packaged. If you create VB projects on a regular basis, you may want to customize the appropriate .DEP files to include additional files or exclude files that your applications don't need.

If you let your distribution tool work with default options, you most probably will include necessary files for your application. Simply taking the default options has two potential disadvantages, though:

- More files than you actually need may be included, which likely is a minor inconvenience, eating up a bit more disk space than you really need to use.

- Necessary files may not be automatically detected, which means the application won't work correctly.

By reading on, you'll learn how to selectively remove unnecessary files that are included automatically. However, only by carefully considering your individual application, and the files that it ultimately requires, will you avoid the second problem. In all cases, the rule of thumb is to test and then test again—always try installations on a "clean" machine (similar to what your end users will have in place) to ensure that all files are being installed correctly. Simply installing the package on your development PC (which already has a complete copy of Crystal Reports Developer Edition on it) won't be a sufficient test—you won't detect any missing elements that may be required on a user machine without Crystal Reports already installed.

The RDC is unique among integration methods in that it doesn't use external .RPT files, unless you specifically choose to use them over the internal ActiveX report designer. Report definitions are actually contained in the ActiveX designer (.DSR) files that are added to the project. Because these are an integral part of your application, VB will compile the .DSR files and include them automatically in the project's executable. In addition, the other COM components that make up the RDC will be included in the project.

In particular, the CRAXDRT.DEP or CRAXDDRT.DEP dependency files will include all necessary COM components for the RDC's Automation Server interface. If you are using the ActiveX Report Viewer to view your reports in a form, CRVIEWER.DEP will be used to include its necessary components. While you probably won't have to worry about including external .RPT files, make sure any required database files are included in your package. You may also want to remove some unnecessary database or export-support files to save disk space.

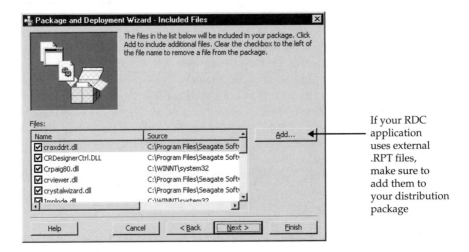

If your RDC application uses external .RPT files, make sure to add them to your distribution package

 Crystal Decisions includes an online Help file that contains a complete discussion of run-time file requirements. Open the RUNTIME.HLP file from the Crystal Reports program directory\Developer Files\Help directory.

Database Considerations

The databases that your reports use must be considered when you are deploying your VB application to end users. Obviously, you need to ensure that each end user is able to connect to the database that the reports require. This may be a PC-style database distributed along with the application, a database shared on a common LAN drive, or a client/server database accessed through either a native Crystal Reports database driver or ODBC. You also need to include only the .DLL files specific to the database and access method being used by your reports. Although it won't necessarily hurt to include database driver DLLs for Microsoft Access in your project, even if your reports all connect to an Informix database via ODBC, you can save disk space by eliminating any unnecessary database drivers.

Direct Access Databases

If your reports use a PC-style database, such as a Microsoft Access .MDB file or a dBASE for Windows .DBF file, you'll want to make sure that the reports will be able to locate the database when the application is installed. If these files were installed on the C drive when you designed the report, but will reside on a network F drive when the end user runs the application, you need to make sure the reports can still find the file.

You can either execute calls inside your VB application to change the data-source location of the reports, or use the Crystal Reports Database | Set Location command in either Crystal Reports or the RDC ActiveX report designer to point to a different database before distributing the application. You may prefer using the Same As Report option in the Set Location dialog box to have the report look in the same drive and directory as the report for the database. In this scenario, you need only ensure that the database and reports reside in the same place, regardless of drive or directory, for the reports to be able to locate the database.

You may be able to save disk space by including only the necessary database drivers for your particular Direct Access database. If, for example, you are using only reports that connect directly to a Microsoft Access database, you don't need to include all the other database drivers in your distribution package. Look in the RUNTIME.HLP file to determine the core set of database drivers required for the particular method your reports use to connect to the database. If you exclude other database drivers, make sure you test your installation on a machine similar to those found in your end-user environment, to make sure all necessary drivers are being included.

ODBC Data Sources

As a general rule, ODBC is used to connect to centralized client/server databases (although some desktop databases you distribute with your application still may use ODBC as the connection method). Therefore, you probably won't have to worry about distributing the actual database with your application. However, you need to make sure that an ODBC data source is set up so that the report will be able to connect to the database from your end user's machine. Your VB application may take care of this automatically if the application itself will be accessing the same ODBC data source. Also, if your report will be using the Active Data driver to connect to a Data Access Objects (DAO) or ActiveX Data Objects (ADO) record set in the application, special provisions probably won't need to be made.

If your report is the only part of the application that will be using a particular ODBC data source, make sure that the setup application creates the correct ODBC data source. You may even need to install ODBC as part of your setup program, if there's a possibility it won't already be installed on the end-user's machine.

You also save disk space if you eliminate other Crystal Reports database drivers that won't be used in your application. Look in the RUNTIME.HLP file to determine which ODBC drivers will be required for the particular ODBC data source and database your reports use. Once you exclude other database drivers, make sure you test your installation on a machine similar to those found in your end-user environment, to make sure all necessary drivers are included.

File Export Considerations

The Xtreme Orders sample application that is used in this chapter allows three output destinations to be used: the preview window, the printer, and a .PDF file attached to an e-mail message. Both exporting the report to a .PDF file and selecting e-mail as the output destination create additional file requirements when you distribute the application. Because Crystal Reports is designed with a modular framework, both the file type (PDF, Word, Excel, HTML, and so on) and output destination (disk file, MAPI e-mail, Exchange public folder, and so on) functions are provided in separate .DLL files. If you are using these export formats and methods, make sure the correct files are included in your application.

Conversely, if you are using only a few output types and destinations, or perhaps none at all, you'll save disk space by eliminating these DLLs from your distribution package. Crystal Reports output destinations are provided by U2D*.DLL files. Output formats are provided by U2F*.DLL files. There are a few additional requirements for certain picture types when exporting to HTML. Look at RUNTIME.HLP for specifics. You need to include only the formats that you specifically call in your application or wish to have available to your end users if they click the Export button in the preview window.

User Function Libraries

If you use formulas in your report that call external User Function Libraries (UFLs), don't forget to include the external UFL .DLL files when you distribute your application. An external .DLL file is called any time a formula uses any functions in the Additional Functions list in the Formula Editor. If you fail to include the .DLL file with your application, the formula will fail when the report runs on the end-user's machine.

By default, Crystal Reports installs several UFLs with the rest of the Crystal Reports package. These are all included in the dependency files that Crystal Reports supplies, so you generally don't have to worry about manually including the UFL files in your distribution package. However, if you've created your own UFLs (Chapter 27 discusses how to create UFLs with Visual Basic), you'll want to either manually add them to your distribution package or modify the .DEP files to include them in all future distributions. You'll also be able to save disk space by removing UFL files that aren't used in any of your formulas.

UFL files generally adhere to the file format U2*.DLL. RUNTIME.HLP contains a description of individual UFL .DLL files and the functions that they provide. If none of the formulas in your report use functions from the Additional Functions list, you can safely remove these UFL files from your distribution package. Again, you should test your installation on a target machine to ensure that your formulas will work properly without the extra UFL files.

Chapter 27

Creating User
Function Libraries
with Visual Basic

The more sophisticated your reports get, the more sophisticated your use of Crystal Reports formulas will become. Although the formula language's built-in functions will satisfy much of your sophisticated reporting requirements, you may eventually encounter situations in which you need extra features that aren't available in Crystal Reports 8.5. This often occurs when a large number of report designers in your company need a business-specific function, such as a way in which to determine the number of days a problem ticket has been open, excluding weekends and company holidays. In some cases, you may be able to create these specialized formulas with a great deal of formula coding. In other cases, the capabilities of the built-in formula language just won't provide the necessary flexibility (perhaps your custom function will need to look up dates in a database of company holidays).

You have several approaches for solving this potential problem. If you're using the Report Designer Component (RDC) to integrate your report with a Visual Basic program (covered in Chapter 26), you can use all the power of Visual Basic to create a value and place it in a text object in the report. But, what if you want to be able to provide a company-specific calculation, such as the problem-ticket example mentioned previously, to anybody using the regular Crystal Report Designer, without having to integrate the report with a VB program? With a User Function Library (UFL), you can extend the capabilities of the Crystal Reports formula language with a Windows development language, such as Visual Basic.

Note   *Chapter 5 discusses the finer points of using the Crystal Reports formula language.*

User Function Library Overview

In the Crystal Reports Formula Editor, the Function Tree box divides functions into logical groups. Arithmetic functions are combined in their own group, date/time functions are located together, and so forth. But, if you look at the bottom of the Function Tree box, you'll see listed in an Additional Functions category an extra collection of functions that run the gamut from Year 2000 date conversions to financial functions, to a sound-alike function (Soundex).

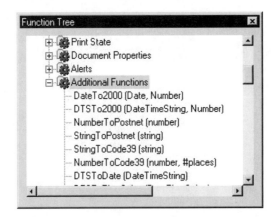

All functions in this Additional Functions category are considered UFLs and are provided to Crystal Reports by way of external dynamic link library (.DLL) files. By creating a Windows .DLL file using a Windows development language, you can extend the power of the Crystal Reports formula language by adding your own functions to the Additional Functions category. Each of these DLLs can expose one or more functions to the Crystal Reports formula language.

Crystal Reports installs several UFL DLLs by default. As with previous versions, when you initially install Crystal Reports 8.5, all the functions in the Additional Functions list are supplied by these .DLL files installed in the \CRYSTAL directory beneath the standard Windows installation directory (typically, \WINDOWS or \WINNT). If you look in this directory, you'll recognize UFL filenames by the first few characters. All UFL filenames begin with the letters *U2*. In many (but not all) cases, the third character is the letter *L*, with the remaining characters describing the function of the UFL. All UFLs are DLLs that have a file extension of .DLL.

| **Note** | *Crystal Reports 8.5 uses 32-bit UFLs only. In previous versions of 16-bit Crystal Reports, you could also have 16-bit UFLs. The filenames for these 16-bit UFLs contained the letter L instead of the character 2 in the second character position.* |

If you wish to create your own UFLs, you have several Windows language choices. The original Crystal Reports language requirement for UFL design was the C language. However, starting with Crystal Reports 6, you have also been able to create UFLs with any language that can create automation servers that conform to Microsoft's Component Object Model (COM). These languages include Visual Basic and Delphi, among others.

UFLs in C and Delphi

If you choose to use C to develop UFLs, the approach is dramatically different from the COM Automation Server approach with Visual Basic. There is plenty of helpful information in Developer's Help (CrystalDevHelp.chm). Look in the table of contents for "Creating User-Defined Function in C." You can also find sample UFL source code in C. Look in *Crystal Reports program directory*\Developer Files\include for UFLSAMP1.C and UFLSAMP2.C.

For information on creating UFLs with Delphi, look in the Developer's Help table of contents for "Creating User Defined Functions in Delphi 3.0."

UFLs in Visual Basic

A UFL that is installed by default with the 32-bit version of Crystal Reports is U2LCOM.DLL. This UFL doesn't actually expose any functions in the Formula Editor by itself. Instead, it acts as a gateway to COM Automation Servers that expose additional functions. By creating these automation servers in a COM-compatible language, you can expose external functions to the Crystal Reports formula language. Using Visual Basic 5 or 6, or the 32-bit version of Visual Basic 4, you can create automation servers that expose additional functions to Crystal Reports through U2LCOM.DLL.

DEVELOPING CUSTOM
WINDOW APPLICATIONS

Although you can use C to develop 16-bit UFLs for use with previous versions of Crystal Reports, Visual Basic UFLs are only recognized by the 32-bit version of Crystal Reports. As such, you must use a 32-bit Visual Basic environment to create them.

Creating a VB UFL requires a specific set of steps. You must start with an ActiveX DLL project to create the automation server. Project names must start with a certain set of characters for U2LCOM.DLL to recognize them. And, functions inside the project's class modules must be declared and created a certain way. When you compile the project into a .DLL file, Visual Basic will automatically register the automation server on your PC. Then, when you start Crystal Reports, U2LCOM.DLL will recognize the new automation server and expose its functions in the Additional Functions list inside the Formula Editor. After you create and test the UFL, you need to use the Visual Basic 6 Package and Deployment Wizard, or another similar distribution mechanism, to install and register the automation server on the end user's computer.

The remainder of this chapter concentrates on developing UFLs with Visual Basic 5 and 6. The steps to create UFLs with 32-bit VB 4 are slightly different. Navigate in the Developer's Help table of contents to "Creating User-Function Libraries in Visual Basic," and then follow lower-level categories to "Using Visual Basic 4.0."

Creating the ActiveX DLL

Visual Basic refers to a COM-based automation server as an *ActiveX DLL*. When you create a new project in VB, choose this project type. A new project will be opened and a Class Module code window will immediately be displayed. Creating the functions to be exposed in the Formula Editor's Additional Functions section is now as simple as declaring public functions here in the class module.

Adding Functions to the Class Module

The CD-ROM accompanying this book includes a very simple sample UFL project that accepts a date value as its only argument and returns the next weekday after the date that is supplied. This might be used to determine when a product could next be shipped, or when a customer could next expect a return call from a sales representative. By adding a database lookup in the routine, you might also be able to include company holidays in the routine, so that Memorial Day or New Year's Day won't be returned as the next weekday.

This function is simply added to the class module as it would be to a form or a .BAS module in a regular Visual Basic .EXE project. Examine the following sample code:

```
Public Function NextWeekDay(DateArg As Date) As Date
    Do
```

```
        DateArg = DateArg + 1
    Loop Until Weekday(DateArg) <> 1 And Weekday(DateArg) <> 7
    ' Could add logic here to look up date in database to
    ' see if it falls on a company holiday, etc.
    NextWeekDay = DateArg
End Function
```

> **Note**   *Because the Crystal Reports 8.5 formula language includes Do Loop functionality, as well as improved date functions, you may be able to do this type of formula just as easily directly in the report, rather than using an external UFL. This formula is included here to show an example of how a UFL is created.*

Notice that the function is declared Public. This is a requirement for the function to be exposed to Crystal Reports. You'll also notice that the arguments to the function aren't specifically designated as ByRef or ByVal. It doesn't matter which method you use to pass arguments; either type of argument, or no type at all, is fine. This function simply uses a Do loop to add one day to the date until the day doesn't fall on a Saturday or Sunday. That date is then set as the function's return value.

You can create as many functions as you need inside the same class module. Just make sure that the functions are named with unique names that won't conflict with other Crystal Reports built-in functions. For example, if you create a UFL function named ToText, it will conflict with the existing Crystal Reports function of that name. Also, there are several reserved words and function names that you cannot use for your function names. In particular, U2LCOM.DLL makes special use of these function names:

UFInitialize

UFTerminate

UFStartJob

UFEndJob

And, COM itself uses the following reserved words, so you can't use any of these for your own function names:

QueryInterface

AddRef

Release

GetTypeInfoCount

GetTypeInfo

GetIDsOfNames

Invoke

DEVELOPING CUSTOM WINDOW APPLICATIONS

Function-name prefixing determines exactly how your UFL function names will appear in the Formula Editor. This is discussed in detail later in the chapter in "Function Name Prefixing."

Your functions can accept as many arguments as necessary, and the arguments can be of any standard Crystal Reports data type. The actual names you give the arguments inside your VB function will be displayed in the Formula Editor as arguments for the Crystal Reports function. This requires you to think carefully about what argument names you want to use in your function. Although you'll notice straightforward argument names like *str* and *date* inside built-in Crystal Reports functions, you're limited to argument names that don't conflict with VB reserved words. With the sample application, an argument named *date* would be consistent with other Crystal Reports functions, but this conflicts with a VB reserved word and thus can't be used as a function argument. You'll notice that *DateArg* is used instead, and it will appear in the Formula Editor as the argument for this function.

When you return the function's value, Crystal Reports automatically converts several VB data types into correct types for Crystal Reports formulas. In particular, functions that return VB's various numeric data types, regardless of precision (integer, long, and so on), will be converted to simple numbers in Crystal Reports. Date, string, and Boolean VB data types will be converted to the corresponding data types in Crystal Reports. You can also pass an array *to* Visual Basic from Crystal Reports. Visual Basic will recognize the array data type and allow you to manipulate the various array elements inside your function. However, the function *cannot* return an array to Crystal Reports—you can only return a single value.

Testing your ActiveX DLL functions is made somewhat more complicated by the ActiveX DLL integrated development environment (IDE). Microsoft recommends creating a project group and actually calling the automation server functions from another project that's loaded in the VB IDE at the same time. You can also choose to create a regular .EXE project and a simple form to test your UFL functions. You can then create the ActiveX DLL project and just copy your already-tested functions from the old project to the new one. Another method of debugging involves "running" your ActiveX project, and then starting a second instance of Visual Basic. You'll find that the functions exposed by the ActiveX project in the first VB instance will appear in the second instance's References list. It's even possible to run the ActiveX project and then start Crystal Reports. You'll see the function exposed in the Formula Editor Additional Functions category.

Special-Purpose Functions

As mentioned previously, several reserved words can't be used for your function names. Four of those names are reserved for special functions that your UFL can use for special UFL processing during your report, as discussed in the following sections.

UFInitialize   This function is called just after the DLL is loaded into memory, before any functions are actually performed:

```
Public Function UFInitialize () As Long
```

One-time initialization of variables, opening of files, or other initialization code can be placed here. Return a value of zero (0) to indicate that the function completed properly. If any errors or problems occur, return any nonzero value to indicate to Crystal Reports that initialization failed.

UFTerminate   This function is called just before the DLL is unloaded from memory, after any other functions are already completed:

```
Public Function UFTerminate () As Long
```

Use this function to deallocate any variables or execute any other cleanup code that you'd like to perform. Return a value of zero to indicate that the function completed properly. If any errors or problems occur, return any nonzero value to indicate to Crystal Reports that UFTerminate failed.

UFStartJob   This is similar to UFInitialize, except that it occurs once for every different report that may be processing:

```
Public Sub UFStartJob (job As Long)
```

You can determine the report that is being started by looking at the job argument that is passed to the function. Use this function for any per-job initialization. Notice that this is actually a subroutine, not a function. You cannot set any return code if errors occur in the routine.

UFEndJob   This function is called when the current job finishes (when all report pages have finished processing, but before a new UFStartJob and before UFTerminate):

```
Public Sub UFEndJob (job As Long)
```

The actual job that is ending is passed with the job argument. Place any per-job cleanup code here. Notice that this is actually a subroutine, not a function. You cannot set any return code if errors occur in the routine.

Naming and Saving the DLL

The combination of your function names, class module name, and ActiveX DLL project name all determine how (and if) your functions appear in the Formula Editor. In particular, you *must* start your project name with the characters "CRUFL." The choice of the remaining characters is up to you, allowing you to give the project a meaningful name. The CRUFL prefix indicates to U2LCOM.DLL that functions in this automation server will be exposed to Crystal Reports. If you don't prefix your project name with these characters, the functions won't appear in the Formula Editor. Name your project as you would any other VB project. Select the project in the Project Explorer window and give the project a name in the Properties window.

After you properly name the project, you need to actually create the automation server .DLL file. Choose File | Make CRUFL*xxx*.DLL from the VB pull-down menus. You'll be prompted to choose a location for the actual .DLL file. To be consistent with other UFL files, you can choose to save it in the \CRYSTAL directory below your regular Windows directory. This is not absolutely required, however, because the actual file location is not significant to U2LCOM.DLL. Instead, the DLL is *registered* by VB when the .DLL file is created. The Registry setting contains the actual location of the .DLL file, so it can be located in any drive or directory you choose.

After you create and register the DLL, start Crystal Reports. Open an existing report or create a new report. Open the Formula Editor and look at the functions that appear in the Additional Functions category. You'll see that your functions and their arguments now appear in the Formula Editor.

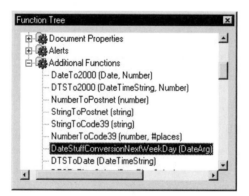

Error Handling

Crystal Reports automatically handles certain error conditions that may occur. For example, if you declare a function argument as numeric in your VB UFL, but pass a string in the Formula Editor, Crystal Reports automatically catches the error. You don't have to provide any special code to trap these kinds of errors.

Even though you design error-handling logic into your UFL functions, you may want to return function-specific error text to Crystal Reports from within your function. Declare and set the UFErrorText public string variable to accomplish this. Examine the following sample code:

```
Public UFErrorText As String
...
On Error GoTo NextWeekDay_Error
...
NextWeekDay_Error:
UFErrorText = Err.Description
```

Here, UFErrorText is declared in the general declarations section of the class module and is set if any error occurs inside the code. Whenever you set the value of this variable inside a function, Crystal Reports will stop the report, display the formula calling the function in the Formula Editor, and display the contents of UFErrorText in a dialog box. Because setting the value of this variable is what triggers the Crystal Reports error, use this only for error handling. Attempting to use UFErrorText to store other values or attempting to read its contents may cause your report formulas to stop prematurely. Also, U2LCOM.DLL resets the value of the variable during report operations, so you can't reliably read its contents inside your code.

Function-Name Prefixing

If you look back at the preceding illustration of the Function Tree, you'll notice that the function name added to Crystal Reports is quite long, and it differs from the actual name you gave the function in your VB code. By default, U2LCOM.DLL uses *function-name prefixing* to actually combine the project name (without the CRUFL characters), class module name, and the function name to create the function that appears in the Formula Editor. For example, the sample UFL application on the companion CD-ROM is named as follows:

- Project name: CRUFLDateStuff
- Class module name: Conversion
- Function name: NextWeekDay (with the DateArg argument)

The resulting function appears as DateStuffConversionNextWeekDay(DateArg) in the Formula Editor.

Function-name prefixing is designed to minimize the chance of duplicate function names appearing in the Formula Editor. If you inadvertently give a UFL function the same name as a preexisting Crystal Reports function (or another function created by a different UFL), errors or unpredictable formula behavior can result. By automatically adding the project and class module names to your function names, the chances of duplicate function names is reduced. However, as you can see, report designers are also presented with rather lengthy function names.

If you wish, you can turn off function-name prefixing, so only the function names themselves will be shown in the Formula Editor, without the project or class module names appended to them. Just be extra careful to make sure you don't use function names that already exist in the Formula Editor. To turn off function-name prefixing, declare the public Boolean variable UFPrefixFunctions in the general declaration section of the class module. Then, set the variable to false in the class's Initialize function. Here's some sample code:

```
Public UFPrefixFunctions As Boolean
...
Private Sub Class_Initialize()
    UFPrefixFunctions = False
End Sub
```

By setting the UFPrefixFunctions variable to false and then creating (or re-creating) the DLL and restarting Crystal Reports, function names will appear in the Formula Editor without prefixing.

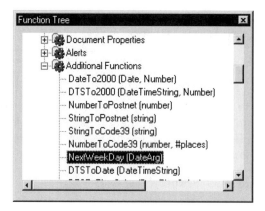

 Don't confuse the class's Initialize event with the UFInitialize function that's reserved for use by Crystal Reports. The class's Initialize event is accessed by choosing Class in the object drop-down list in the Code window and then choosing Initialize in the procedure drop-down list.

Distributing the UFL

Although Visual Basic automatically registers your automation server DLL when you choose File | Make CRUFL*xxx*.DLL from the pull-down menus, you need to distribute the DLL to any other report designer who will want to use the functions of the UFL. You also may want to distribute the UFL as part of a larger VB project that integrates reports, using one of the integration methods discussed earlier.

To simply distribute the UFL to other report designers who will be using the Crystal Reports designer, it's probably best to use the Package and Deployment Wizard with VB 6, the Application Setup Wizard with VB 5, or another distribution tool. This creates a setup program that will install your UFL on the target system and register the automation server on the designer's computer. If you simply wish to pass the .DLL file to a designer, they need to manually register the .DLL file so that U2LCOM.DLL will recognize it. VB provides the REGSVR32.EXE program to register an automation server from the command line.

Although U2LCOM is typically installed automatically with 32-bit Crystal Reports, make sure that the target system has it installed in the \CRYSTAL directory below the Windows program directory. Without this UFL file, no functions exposed by the automation server will appear in the Formula Editor.

If you want to include your UFL in reports that are integrated with a VB program, you'll want to make sure the .DLL file is distributed and registered when the whole VB application is installed by your end users. This can be accomplished simply by adding the UFL Automation Server you created earlier to your new project by using Project | References from the VB pull-down menus. The name of your UFL will appear in the list of available references. Check the box next to the automation server name to add it to the project. When you later distribute the Visual Basic project, the distribution tool will automatically include the .DLL file and register it on the target computer.

The Complete Reference

Crystal Reports

Part IV

Appendixes

Crystal
Reports

Appendix A

Crystal Reports with Visual Studio.NET

It is a sheltered Windows or Web developer who has not at least heard in passing of Microsoft's new Visual Studio.Net (VS.NET) development environment. This new development environment (in Beta 2 release as of this printing) presents not only a whole new way to develop custom Windows- and Web-based applications, but even introduces a new language—C#—to develop with.

One of the more interesting changes noted in VS.NET is the prominence played by Crystal Reports. Whereas Microsoft had moved Crystal Reports "out of the way" for its own embedded report developer in Visual Studio 6, you'll notice that Microsoft's offering is gone from Visual Studio.Net, and Crystal Reports has returned as the report designer of choice for Microsoft Windows and Web development.

> **Note** *This appendix is based on the Beta 2 release of Microsoft Visual Studio.Net, which was available at the time of this printing. The final release of this tool will no doubt have changes to both Visual Studio.Net core functionality and certain Crystal Reports features. Consult documentation with the final release of Visual Studio.Net for current information.*

Crystal Reports for Visual Studio.Net Overview

Crystal Decisions has completely retooled its report offering in VS.NET. Where the reporting tool bundled with Visual Studio 6 was a slight modification of Crystal Reports 4.5, Crystal Decisions is offering a modified version of Crystal Reports 8 inside VS.NET. And, unlike with Visual Studio 6, VS.NET's Crystal Reporting component is an integral part of the VS.NET Integrated Development Environment (IDE), much as is the Report Designer Component when added to Visual Basic 6.

Similarity to RDC

The Report Designer Component, or *RDC*, has emerged as the preferred direction for integrating Crystal Reports, both with Visual Basic 6 applications (covered in Chapter 26) and Web pages with Microsoft Active Server Pages (covered in Chapter 21). Crystal Reports for Visual Studio.Net picks up largely on the same concept as the RDC:

- Integration of a report designer right inside the VS.NET IDE
- A rich object model that exposes virtually all report properties at run time, allowing complete control over report customization from within the application
- Small-footprint Windows Forms Viewer and DHTML Web Forms Viewer for viewing reports in Windows applications and Web pages

Of course, one of the biggest changes between Visual Basic 6 and VS.NET is the more integrated development environment for creating both Windows and Web applications, as well as the common language run time and common features among different development languages. Crystal Reports fits seamlessly into the entire VS.NET environment, being equally functional in Windows and Web applications, as well as being completely accessible by Visual Basic, Managed C++, and C#.

Crystal Reports in Windows Applications

For current Visual Basic developers, the existing Report Designer Component provides many features that go far above and beyond the Crystal Reports product bundled with Visual Basic 6. However, to fully enjoy these benefits (especially for the RDC available in Crystal Reports 8 and 8.5), you need to purchase a copy of Crystal Reports separate from Visual Basic and install the RDC.

Crystal Reports inside Visual Studio.Net is built largely on this same model. If you will be creating custom Windows applications with VS.NET, you'll be able to design a report entirely inside the VS.NET IDE without having to purchase a separate copy of Crystal Reports. In fact, the embedded report designer in Visual Studio.Net, shown here,

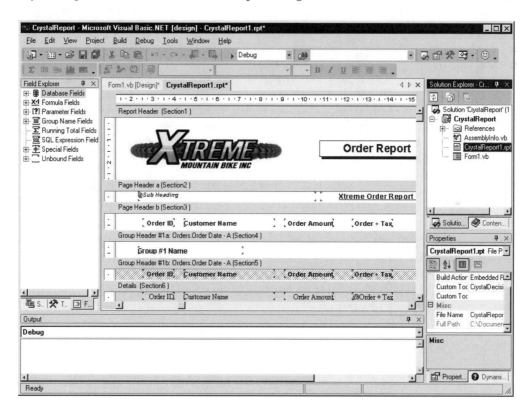

looks very similar to that supplied by the RDC in Visual Basic 6, shown next.

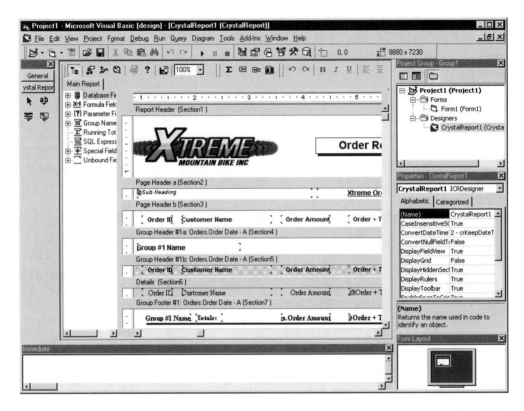

Once you've either created a new report from scratch or imported an existing .RPT file inside the VS.NET IDE, you present the report in your Windows application using a Crystal Report Windows Forms Viewer placed in a Windows form, similar to the ActiveX Viewer provided by the RDC in Visual Basic 6.

As you might expect, the Windows Forms Viewer provided in Visual Studio.Net, shown in the following illustration,

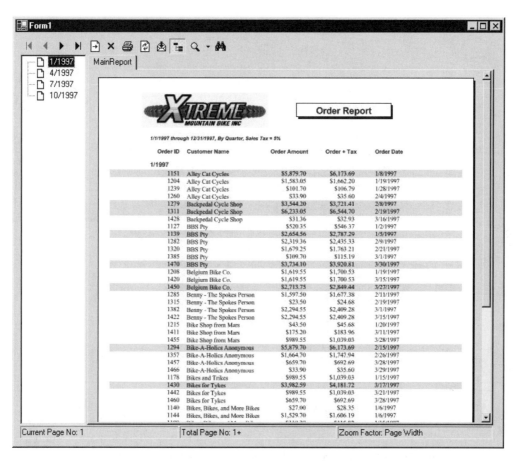

looks similar to the Crystal Reports Viewer supplied by the RDC in Visual Basic 6, shown next.

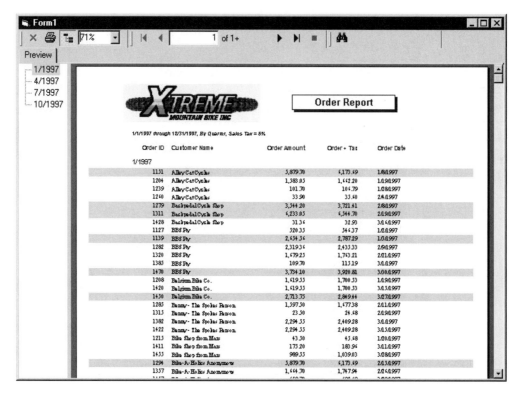

And, as with the RDC and Visual Basic 6, Crystal Reports in VS.NET exposes an extensive object model that not only allows complete report customization at run time from within VS.NET code, but also can trap Windows Forms Viewer events, such as drill-downs, button clicks, and so on. And, you can develop your own user interface elements to replace the standard toolbar in the Windows Forms Viewer, controlling report navigation entirely from within your code.

More information on creating VS.NET Windows applications with Crystal Reports can be found later in this appendix under "Creating Crystal Reports Windows Applications."

While previous versions of Crystal Reports that were bundled with Visual Studio 6.0 and Visual Basic allowed free run-time distribution with Windows-based applications, Crystal Decisions has changed their licensing agreement for Visual Studio.Net. Certain server-based applications require payment of license fees if you will be providing reporting to more than five concurrent users. Visit the Crystal Decisions Web site at http://www.crystaldecisions.com for contact information regarding procedures and costs for acquiring additional licenses.

Crystal Reports in Web Applications

While the RDC with Microsoft Active Server Pages is a very flexible and effective Web reporting method, developing these Web-based applications can be very tedious.

In many cases, you gain very little benefit from using previous Microsoft development tools, such as FrontPage or Visual InterDEV, due to limited support for COM objects and the Crystal Reports Viewers. In many cases, it was often just as effective to use a plain text editor, such as Notepad, to create Crystal Reports Web applications.

The Crystal Reports developer community probably the happiest with VS.NET is Web developers. As VS.NET creates Web applications with virtually the same ease and speed as it creates Windows applications, and because Crystal Reports works just as seamlessly with Web applications, Crystal Reports' Web applications are now infinitely easier to create.

And, if the ease of development isn't enough, you gain a whole new level of flexibility with VS.NET Web applications and Crystal Reports. The same type of rich object model available with the RDC and Active Server Pages is fully exposed to VS.NET Web applications for report customization. But, VS.NET raises the bar for the DHTML-based Crystal Reports Web Forms Viewer. This viewer, as do VS.NET Web-based forms in general, actually exposes its own object model that can be controlled from within code, including the ability to trap viewer events such as page navigation button clicks and drill-downs. This new interactivity in a "plain" DHTML Web browser page is one of the major new features provided by Visual Studio.Net.

More information on using Crystal Reports in Web applications can be found later in this chapter under "Creating Crystal Reports Web Applications."

Crystal Reports as VS.NET Web Services

One of the new features of Visual Studio.Net is the *Web Service*: a server-based "application" that exposes a set of data to other applications using standard Web-based data layouts through standard Web-based communications protocols. The benefit is that any other application, anywhere on the Web (even behind a firewall), can access a Web service. A VS.NET Web service can be written in any of the VS.NET languages, or built using many of the VS.NET-bundled tools such as Crystal Reports.

When you create a Crystal-based Report Web Service, the layout and appearance provided by the report are available to any Web Service client on the Web. A Web Service client can be another Crystal Windows Forms Viewer or Crystal Web Forms Viewer away from your own network—reports can be viewed remotely in Windows or Web applications without any additional effort on your part.

More information on creating Crystal Reports Web Services is found later in this chapter under "Crystal Reports and Web Services."

Creating Crystal Reports Windows Applications

If you've already made significant use of the Report Designer Component with Crystal Reports 8 or 8.5 with Visual Basic 6, you should be familiar with most steps in creating a Windows application using Crystal Reports in VS.NET. Because the VS.NET implementation of a Crystal Report is similar to the embedded designer/object model/

viewer component structure of the RDC, the steps to creating a Crystal-based Windows application basically remain the same:

- Create a new application or open an existing application.
- Either create a new report with the IDE report designer, import an existing report into the IDE report designer, or define a report object in code referencing an external .RPT file.
- Manipulate the report object within code, if necessary.
- Supply the report object to the Windows Forms Viewer for display in a Windows form.
- Design any event-trapping code in the Windows Forms Viewer to handle page navigation button clicks, drill-downs, and so on. Or, design customized code to control behavior of the Windows Forms Viewer from within your own code.

Creating or Modifying Reports in the VS.NET Crystal Report Designer

Once you've created a new VS.NET project, or opened an existing VS.NET project, you have several choices of how you may add a report reference to the project. If you haven't purchased a copy of Crystal Reports or don't have a predesigned .RPT file that you just want to reference directly in your code, you'll need to add the Crystal Report Designer to your project. From this designer, you can create a new report entirely from scratch or import an existing .RPT file to modify.

To add a report to your project, right-click in the VS Solution Explorer and choose Add | Add New Item from the pop-up menu. You may also use File | Add New Item from the VS.NET pull-down menus. The Add New Item dialog box will appear.

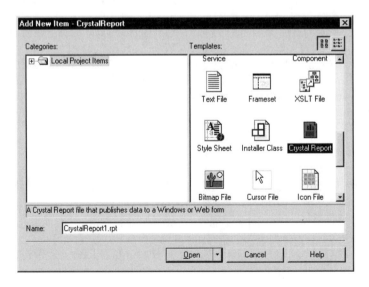

Choose the Crystal Report icon. Then, either accept the default filename given at the bottom of the Add Item dialog box or type a different filename for the report. When you click OK, the familiar Report Gallery will appear, much as it does when initially creating a new report inside Visual Basic 6 with the RDC. You may choose to create a new report using a Report Expert or a new Blank Report, or import an existing .RPT file.

You may also simply add an existing .RPT file you've already created with Crystal Reports to VS.NET. Perform the same initial steps as described above with the pop-up menu or File pull-down menu options—except, choose Add Existing Item instead of Add New Item. A file open dialog box will appear (you may need to change the file type to All Files to see .RPT files in the folder you navigate to). Choose an existing .RPT file to add to your project.

Once you've made your choices (and in the case of using a Report Expert, chosen all necessary items in the various tabs), the Crystal Report Designer will show your report inside the VS.NET IDE, as shown in Figure A-1.

You may work with the Report Designer inside VS.NET much as you work with the regular Crystal Reports program, as discussed in Part I of this book. You may add report objects, format them, create formulas, add parameter fields, and perform virtually all report manipulation techniques that you would with Crystal Reports. As with other elements of your VS.NET project, such as forms, you can save the results of your report design with the VS.NET toolbar buttons or File menu options.

Note   *Importing an existing .RPT file using either of these methods will make a copy of the report into the folder with the remainder of your VS.NET project files. This copy (along with another .RPT file that will be given a unique filename—not the same filename as the report your imported) will be modified as you work in the Report Designer. Your original .RPT file will be unchanged by modifications you make in your VS.NET project.*
Also, the .RPT file format in Visual Studio.Net has changed. If you save an external .RPT file from this environment, it may not be fully compatible with earlier Crystal Reports versions, such as version 8.5

You may also add what's known as an *untyped report* to your project. This type of report object doesn't refer to an actual report that uses the Report Designer inside the project. Instead, an untyped report refers to an external .RPT file somewhere on your network. Untyped reports are added via code. Look in the VS.NET online help index for "untyped report components" for information on how to reference an external .RPT file.

Manipulating Reports Inside Code

Once you've added a report to your project, either via the Report Designer in the VS.NET IDE or as an untyped report, you may create a reference to the report object for the purpose of run-time customization. Once this occurs, you have the complete Crystal Reports for VS.NET object model at your disposal. All report objects (such as fields, formulas, parameter fields, and so forth), as well as report sections (such as the Details section, Page Header, and so forth) are available for run-time manipulation via your custom code.

Use the Field Explorer to add fields, create formulas, create parameter fields, and so forth

Use the Crystal Reports toolbars, much as you would in regular Crystal Reports

Make design-time changes to individual report objects in the Properties window

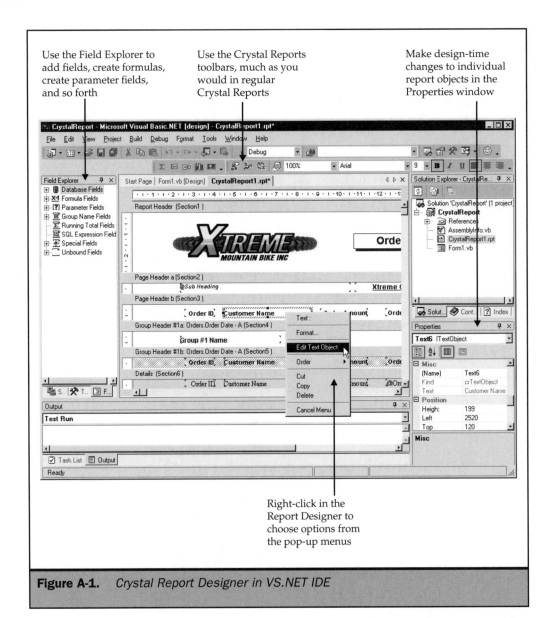

Right-click in the Report Designer to choose options from the pop-up menus

Figure A-1. *Crystal Report Designer in VS.NET IDE*

The report object will expose its object model when manipulated in code.

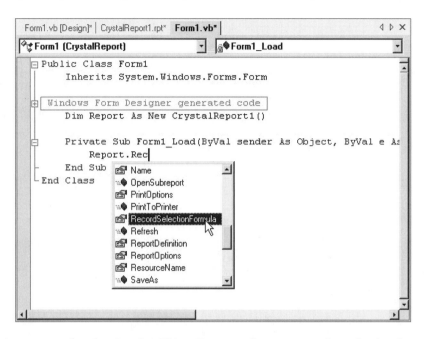

And, you can also display the Object Browser (by pressing the F2 key), where you'll find Crystal Reports objects, properties, and methods.

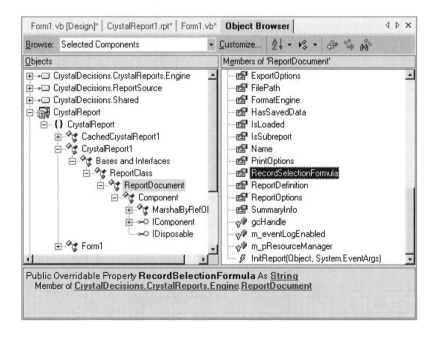

Although the examples shown here are utilizing Visual Basic code, all VS.NET Crystal Reports functionality is also available when using Managed C++ or C# code.

Using the Windows Forms Viewer

Once you've added a report to your project, you need to facilitate some way to show the report in a Windows Form. As with Visual Basic 6 using the RDC, a Crystal Reports viewer control is available from the toolbox to add to a form. Find the Crystal Report Viewer choice in the toolbox and add it to a Windows Form, as you would any other control. Figure A-2 shows a VS.NET Windows Form with the Windows Form Viewer added to it.

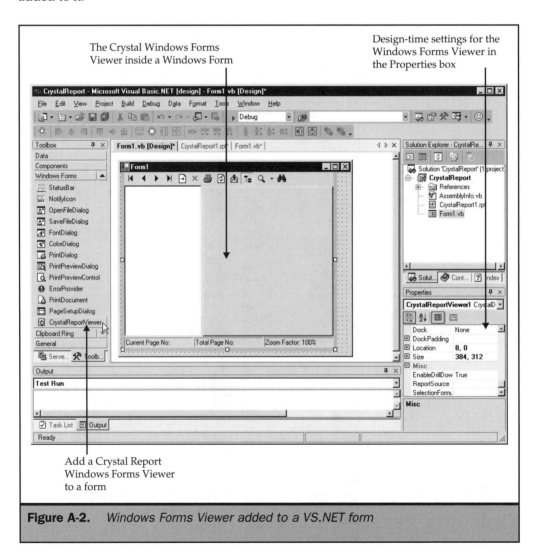

Figure A-2. *Windows Forms Viewer added to a VS.NET form*

One of the first steps required after adding the Windows Forms Viewer is connecting it with the desired report object. You may perform this connection at design time utilizing the ReportSource property or the DataBindings properties. Or, you may dynamically assign a report to the viewer from within code. For example, if you've declared an object named Report and set it to a "New" instance of the Report Designer earlier in your code, you can assign it to the Windows Forms Viewer at run time using the viewer's ReportSource property within code like this:

```
CrystalReportViewer1.ReportSource = Report
```

 There are several different methods for connecting the desired report object to the Windows Forms Viewer in a process called binding. *For a thorough description and examples of these different binding methods, search the VS.NET online help index for "Binding Reports."*

You may control many aspects of the Windows Form Viewer at design time from within the VS.NET Properties box. One of the new properties that saves you some coding is the Windows Forms Viewer Anchor property. This allows you to "attach" the viewer to one or more sides of the Windows Form, allowing the report to automatically resize as the form is resized (using the RDC Report Viewer the same way in Visual Basic 6 required code to be placed in the form's Resize event).

The Anchor property, like most for the Windows Forms Viewer, can be set at design time in the Properties window. However, you may also control viewer behavior at run time, as the viewer exposes its own object model. For example, if you wish to control other aspects of the Windows Forms Viewer, such as the end-user's ability to drill-down on reports, you may wish to execute code similar to the following at run time:

```
CrystalReportViewer1.EnableDrillDown = False
```

Once you've bound a report to the viewer and added any customization code, running the VS.NET project will render the report in a Windows form.

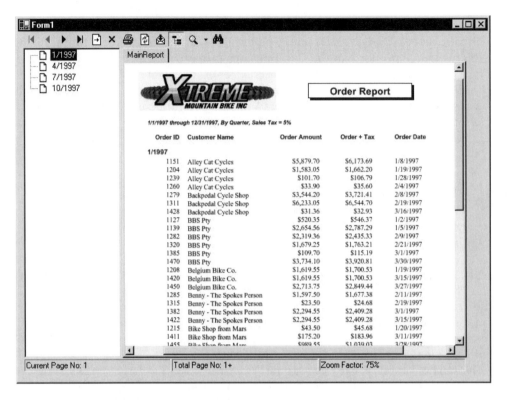

Responding to Windows Forms Viewer Events

Not only can you control behavior of the Windows Forms Viewer at run time, but you can respond to events that may happen due to user interaction with the viewer. For example, you can trap page navigation button clicks, drill-downs on group headers/footers, drill-downs on charts, and so on.

Just open the code view of the Windows form containing the Crystal Report Windows Forms Viewer. Choose the viewer in the object drop-down list at the upper right of the code window. Then, look for available events in the right drop-down list. Choose an event to trap and add code to the desired event.

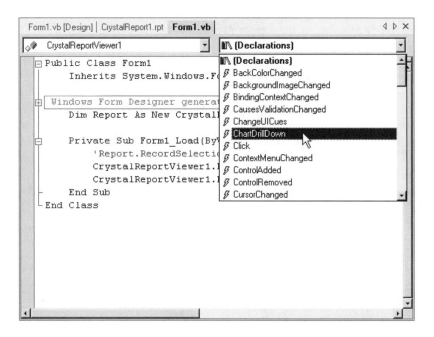

Tip
More detailed information on creating reports, manipulating them in code, and working with the Windows Forms Viewer, including complete documentation for Crystal Reports Object Models, can be found in Visual Studio.Net online help. Also, some simple application examples can be found in Program Files\Microsoft Visual Studio.Net\Crystal Reports\Samples\Code.

Creating Crystal Reports Web Applications

Of course, one of the biggest improvements of Visual Studio.Net over previous Microsoft developer environments is the very fuzzy line between Windows applications and Web applications. The development environment, languages, and associated SDKs and tools are all as Web aware as they are Windows aware. Crystal Reports within VS.NET is no exception.

The steps for adding a report to your Web application are virtually identical to those for a Windows application (see "Creating Crystal Reports Windows Applications," earlier in the appendix). And, steps for customizing the report object with the Crystal Reports Object Model are also identical to those used in Windows applications.

Using the Crystal Web Forms Viewer

The primary difference between Crystal Reports Windows applications and Web applications is the way reports are viewed. While the "internal" coding is similar (and Crystal Reports Web applications use server-side code in VS.NET as they do with the

RDC and Active Server Pages), the report must ultimately be displayed in a Web browser as opposed to in a Windows application. As with the Report Designer Component, this requires some creative approaches to render the report in a Web browser with formatting as close as possible to the original report.

The Crystal Web Forms Viewer is provided to show reports in a Web browser. Based on HTML 3.2 or DHTML 4.0, the Web Forms Viewer can be passed a report object, just like the Windows Forms Viewer. When VS.NET builds the Web application, it includes code to show the report as HTML Frames inside the Web page where the viewer has been added.

Add the Web Forms Viewer to a Web form the same way you might add the Windows Forms Viewer to a Windows form—it will be available in the toolbox. Figure A-3 shows a Web Forms Viewer in a Web form.

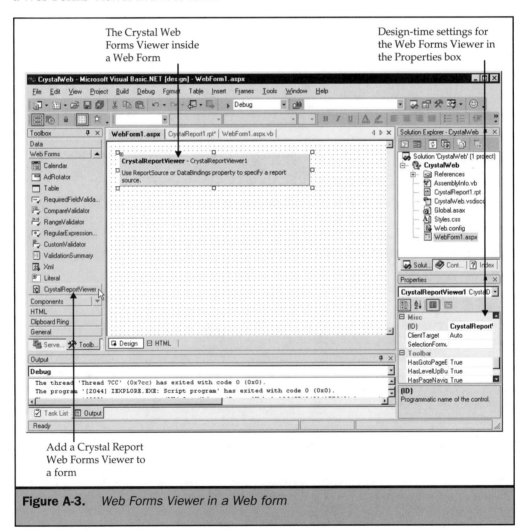

Figure A-3. *Web Forms Viewer in a Web form*

As with the Windows Forms Viewer, you must connect the Web Forms Viewer to the desired report object. You may perform this connection at design time utilizing the ReportSource property or the DataBindings properties. Or, you may dynamically assign a report to the viewer from within code. For example, if you've declared an object named Report and set it to a "New" instance of a ReportDocument object earlier in your code, you can assign it to the Web Forms Viewer at run time using the viewer's ReportSource property within code like this:

```
CrystalReportViewer1.ReportSource = Report
```

  There are several different methods for connecting the desired report object to the Web Forms Viewer in a process called binding. *For a thorough description and examples of these different binding methods, search the VS.NET online help index for "Binding Reports."*

And, as with the Windows Forms Viewer, the Web Forms Viewer exposes an object model that allows you to control viewer behavior at design time from the Properties Window (which isn't possible with the RDC and development tools prior to VS.NET). And, you may also set these properties at run time from within code.

Note that one difference between the VS.NET implementation of the Web Forms Viewer and viewers available in Active Server Pages with the RDC is available choices of viewers. While the RDC provides not only the HTML 3.2 and DHTML 4.0 viewers, additional viewers residing in a browser-based ActiveX control or Java applet may be used. In VS.NET, the Web Forms Viewer is strictly an HTML-based viewer—you cannot provide any browser-based ActiveX control or Java applet to view reports.

Once you've bound a report to the viewer and added any customization code, running the VS.NET project will render the report in a Web browser.

APPENDIXES

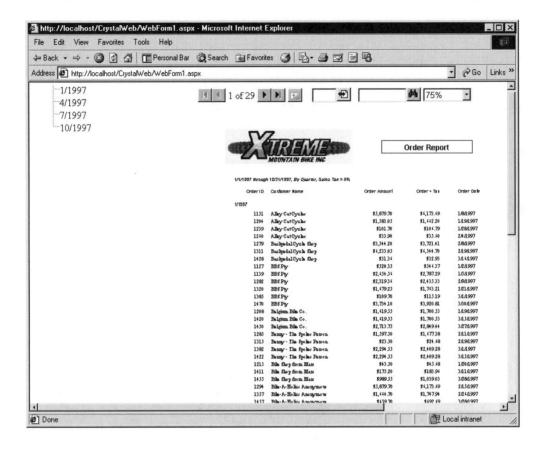

Responding to Web Forms Viewer Events

One of the major new features of Visual Studio.Net is the ability to develop an event-based object model for Web-based applications similar to that for Windows applications. Previously, Windows developers were the only developers generally able to trap user actions, such as resizing windows and so forth. For Crystal Reports developers, the Windows viewer provided by the RDC exposed a large event model. However, Crystal Reports Web developers weren't able to trap report events, such as drill-downs.

With Visual Studio.Net, creative use of client-side script, as well as Web-server interfaces, allow this type of interaction with Crystal Reports viewed in the Web Forms Viewer. As with the Windows Forms Viewer, the Web Forms Viewer exposes a list of events that can be trapped. Just open the code view of the Web form containing the Crystal Report Web Forms Viewer. Choose the viewer in the object drop-down list at the upper right of the code window. Then, look for available events in the right drop-down list. Choose an event to trap and add code to the desired event.

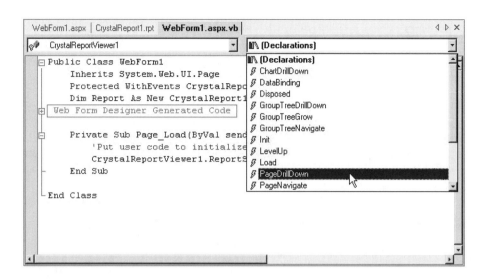

Tip   *More detailed information on using Crystal Reports in Web applications and working with the Web Forms Viewer, including complete documentation for Crystal Reports Object Models, can be found in Visual Studio.Net online help. Also, some simple Web application examples can be found in Program Files\Microsoft Visual Studio.Net\Crystal Reports\Samples\Code.*

Crystal Reports and Web Services

One of the new features of Visual Studio.Net is the *Web Service*: a server-based "application" that exposes a set of data based on Extensible Markup Language, or XML. The Web Service exposes its actual data, as well as its data layout (or *schema*), through HyperText Transport Protocol, or HTTP. Because the XML data layout is simply an extension of HTML and because HTTP is such a ubiquitous communications protocol, virtually all networks, intranet systems, and Internet connection methods (dial-up, firewalls, and so forth) all work with these standards already.

Crystal Reports for Visual Studio.Net fully supports Web Services—being able to both create and "consume" Web Services. Creating a Web Service based on a Crystal Report exposes a report via HTTP to anyone who can consume a Web Service anywhere on the Internet. VS.NET also allows you to create projects that use or "consume" published Crystal Report Web Services. In this scenario, you create a Windows or Web application, including a Windows Forms Viewer or Web Forms Viewer, which is then bound to the report exposed by the Web Service.

APPENDIXES

Creating a Web Service

Creating a Web Service based on a Crystal Report is a very straightforward process—almost identical to creating a Windows or Web application using a Crystal Report. Once you've opened or created your Web Service or Web Application project, add a Crystal Report the same way you would for another application. You may make any design changes and customization to the report in the Report Designer inside the VS.NET IDE the same as you would for any other report.

When you're ready to post the report on a Web server as a Web Service, simply right-click on the report object in the Solution Explorer that you want to publish. Choose Publish as Web Service from the pop-up menu.

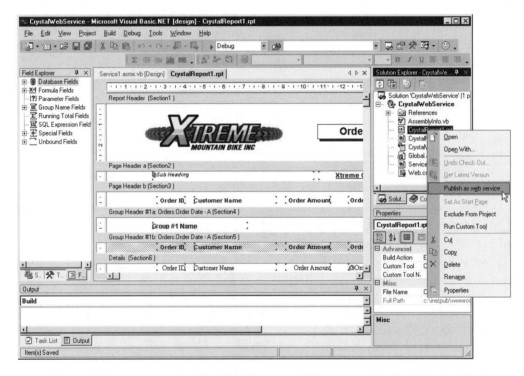

Additional files representing the Web Service will be created in the Solution Explorer. To actually post the Crystal Report Web Service on the Web server that the Web Service project was created on, choose Build | Build from the VS.NET pull-down menus.

Consuming a Web Service

Once a Crystal Reports Web Service has been created, you may access the Web Service using regular HTTP protocols, similar to a standard Web page. You may create either a

Windows or Web application, using the respective Windows Forms Viewer or Web Forms Viewer, to show the contents of the Web Service in your application.

Create a standard Windows or Web application with VS.NET. Add a Crystal Report viewer to the application as described in earlier sections of this chapter. Once you're ready to connect the report viewer to the Web Service, perform the following steps:

1. Add a reference to the Web Service by clicking on the References category of the Solution Explorer. Right-click on the References category and choose Add Web Reference from the pop-up menu. The Add Web Reference dialog box will appear.

2. In the Address line of the Add Web Reference dialog box, type the following URL: **http://<web server>/default.vsdisco**. If you are looking for Web Services on a Web server on the same computer where you are running VS.NET, you may click the Web References on Local Web Server link. A list of references on the Web server will appear in the right frame of the Add Web Reference dialog box.

3. Click the link in the right frame of the reference you wish to add (look carefully at the URLs listed, ensuring you're choosing the right Web Service). You'll see the URL appear in the right frame of the Add Web Reference dialog box by itself, including View Contract and View Documentation links.

4. Once the URL has been narrowed down, you may click the View Contract link to see the XML that is exposed by the Web Service. Once you are ready to add the Web Service to your project, click the Add Reference button. A Web Reference section of the Solution Explorer will appear, followed by the name of the Web server containing the Web Service. Within the Web Services category, you'll find a reference to the Web Service.

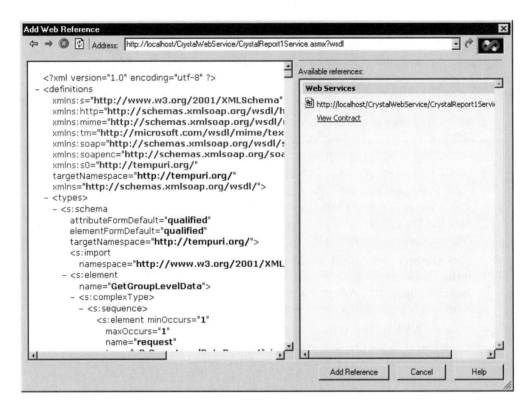

To reference the Web Service in the Windows Forms Viewer or Web Forms Viewer, you may execute code similar to the following in the Load event of the form containing the viewer:

```
CrystalReportViewer1.ReportSource = _
New localhost.CrystalReport1Service()
```

When you run the application, the report exposed by the Web Service will appear in the form containing the viewer.

Appendix B

Installing and Configuring Crystal Reports Components

Installing Crystal Reports is a fairly straightforward process, especially if you are simply installing with a standard set of options on an end-user PC. And, if you've previously installed Crystal Reports 8, you'll see very little difference in the Version 8.5 setup process. The large difference between Version 8 and Version 8.5 falls in the Web reporting arena—the previous Web Component Server from Version 8 is gone, although Active Server Page support with the Report Designer Component remains. Crystal Enterprise Standard (discussed in Part II of the book) has replaced the previous Web Component Server as the typical method for posting reports to the Web. Enterprise is included on a separate CD-ROM in the box with Crystal Reports 8.5 Professional and Developer Editions.

Note *Crystal Reports 8.5 is only available in a 32-bit platform. You must be using Windows 95, Windows 98, Windows NT 4, Windows 2000, or Windows XP to use the software. The minimum memory requirement for Windows 95 or Windows 98 is 32MB, while 64MB is required if using Windows NT, 2000, or XP. You'll see better performance if you use at least 64MB of memory with all platforms. You'll also need at least 60MB of hard disk space for a minimal installation, and up to 235MB for a full installation.*

Installing the Crystal Reports Designer

When you put the Crystal Reports program CD-ROM into a CD-ROM drive, the Setup program starts automatically. If Setup doesn't start automatically (perhaps your CD-ROM drive has Auto-Insert notification turned off), you can choose two different places to start. To see the initial multimedia presentation, as well as to be given a choice to install Crystal Reports 8.5 or view a demonstration, navigate to the root directory of the CD-ROM and double-click START.EXE. To proceed directly to Crystal Reports Setup, navigate to the root directory of the CD-ROM and double-click SETUP.EXE.

Crystal Reports Setup will check to make sure current versions of required base Windows components are installed on your computer. If they're not, Setup will indicate that they need to be installed. Once this is done, Setup will continue. Typical Setup prompts, including a display of the Crystal Decisions license agreement and a prompt for the installation key on the back of the CD-ROM , will appear. Click the Next button after responding to a prompt to continue. Of particular note is the prompt giving you the option to choose a Typical, Complete, or Custom setup. Typical setup includes most common Crystal Reports components. This choice, however, *will not* install some database drivers, Crystal Dictionaries, or the Crystal SQL Designer. If you want to install everything, choose the Complete option. If you want to pick and choose which options to install, choose the Custom option. If you choose the Custom option, a Custom Installation Options dialog box will appear, as shown in Figure B-1.

You'll see a Windows Explorer–like interface, showing the main Crystal Reports elements that can be customized. A plus sign next to an item indicates that there are subfeatures below it that can be selected or deselected. Click the plus sign to see the

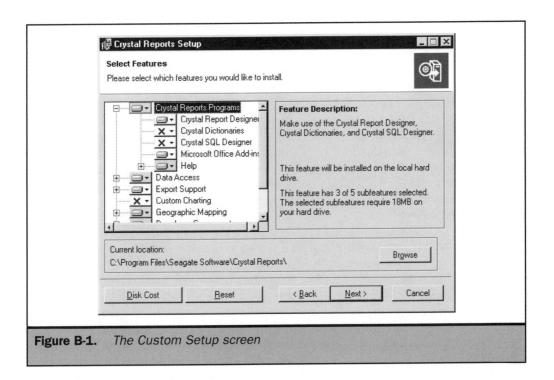

Figure B-1.   *The Custom Setup screen*

subfeature list. If an option is displayed in white, that means that it (and all of its subfeatures, if it has any) will be installed. If the option is displayed in a gray color, it means that *some* of its subfeatures are selected and some aren't. If the object has a red X across it, that means that the item will not be installed.

To change the option, click the down arrow next to it. A menu will appear giving you several choices, such as installing the feature on your hard disk, or possibly running it from the CD-ROM (depending on the chosen feature). If the feature you've selected has subfeatures underneath it, you'll have an option to install the feature and all of its subfeatures. You'll also have the option not to install the feature. Choose the desired option and notice that the color of the feature changes to indicate the choice you've made.

For example, if you're running Setup on your Web server to install the Report Designer Component, you may choose not to install the Crystal Reports Programs (although it's a good idea to install them, in case you need to physically troubleshoot reports on the Web server machine itself). Also, you may want to install the Crystal Dictionaries and Crystal SQL Designer tools, which are not chosen for installation by default. And, you should also double-check the Data Access subfeature list to make sure the proper data drivers will be installed for the types of databases you'll be reporting on.

Installing the Report Designer Component on Your Web Server

If you wish to set up the RDC Automation Server for use with Active Server Pages (discussed in Chapter 21), run Setup on the Web Server computer. While you may be tempted to install a minimal set of components (perhaps just the Report Designer Component from the Developer Components category), don't forget that many of the other options in the Setup list may be required. You'll certainly need to install Data Access components for databases that your Web reports may require. And, you'll probably want to also include other components that may be of use, such as Exporting options, Custom Charting, and Geographic Mapping.

You should seriously consider installing the complete Crystal Reports package on your Web server. Although it's doubtful (and probably unwise) that you'll want to use a production Web server as a report design computer, installing the complete product will allow you to troubleshoot reporting problems that may occur on the Web. If you encounter a report that won't properly run on the Web server, you can launch Crystal Reports directly on the Web server, open the report, and see whether the report will run within Crystal Reports directly. If not, you can more easily troubleshoot the problem, perhaps tracing it to a security or data connectivity problem.

Note that because the Report Designer Component adheres to Microsoft's Component Object Model (COM), you may only use it with Microsoft Internet Information Server with Active Server Pages—Unix and Linux Web servers can't use the Crystal Reports Web components. And, only Windows NT, 2000, or XP Web servers are supported—you can't use Windows 95 or 98 Personal Web Server.

Crystal Reports automatically creates a virtual directory and installs sample reports on the Web server. A quick way to determine whether the Web components have been installed properly on your Web server is to point your browser to http://<Web server>/scrsamples. This should display a Web page in which you can choose to view Crystal Reports samples using Active Server Pages. You'll also have the opportunity with this sample site to view reports using all the available report viewers.

The Crystal License Manager

As the combination of available Crystal Reports Web-based and server-based licensing possibilities grows, so does the complexity of trying to keep track of purchased licenses and the rights they grant. To help with this complexity, Crystal Reports 8.5 now includes the *License Manager*. This stand-alone Windows application (with an associated Web page), allows you to view current usage of your Crystal Reports licenses. You may also add license keys (for multi-user additions, Report Creation API licenses, and so forth), using this application.

To start the License Manager, choose Crystal Reports Licenses from the Crystal Reports Tools group on the Windows Start button. The License Manager will appear, as shown in Figure B-2.

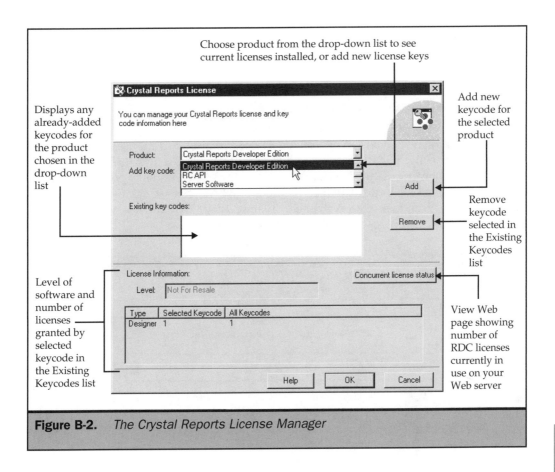

Choose product from the drop-down list to see current licenses installed, or add new license keys

Displays any already-added keycodes for the product chosen in the drop-down list

Add new keycode for the selected product

Remove keycode selected in the Existing Keycodes list

Level of software and number of licenses granted by selected keycode in the Existing Keycodes list

View Web page showing number of RDC licenses currently in use on your Web server

Figure B-2.   *The Crystal Reports License Manager*

In the first drop-down list, choose the product you wish to examine existing licenses for or add new licenses to. If any existing keycodes for the chosen product have already been added, you'll see them appear in the Existing Keycodes list. If you wish to see the specific number of licenses and level of software (such as Standard, Professional, or Developer) provided by a particular keycode, click it in the Available Keycodes list. The bottom of the License Manager will denote the license granted by that keycode.

In many cases, when you purchase additional licenses, such as more concurrent RDC licenses for your Web server or the Enterprise Broadcast License, you won't receive any additional software CD-ROMs from Crystal Decisions—you'll merely receive a piece of paper containing additional red stickers containing additional keycodes. To activate your additional licenses, use the drop-down list to choose the product that you wish to upgrade with additional licenses. Then, type the new keycode in the Add Keycode text box and click the Add button. The new keycode will be added to the Available Keycodes list, where you may select it to confirm the additional licenses it has granted you. To remove a keycode (perhaps to transfer the license to another computer), select the desired keycode in the Available Keycodes list and click the Remove button.

Viewing Web-Based RDC Licenses

If you install the Report Designer Component (RDC) included in the Crystal Reports Developer Edition on a Web server, you are granted five concurrent user licenses for Web-based reporting. The RDC object model actually exposes a function that allows you to query its license status. An example of how the object model exposes this can be found in a sample Web page displayed by the License Manager. Click the Concurrent License Status button to see the Web page, or launch your Web browser and navigate to http://<web server>/crystal_license/license_info.asp.

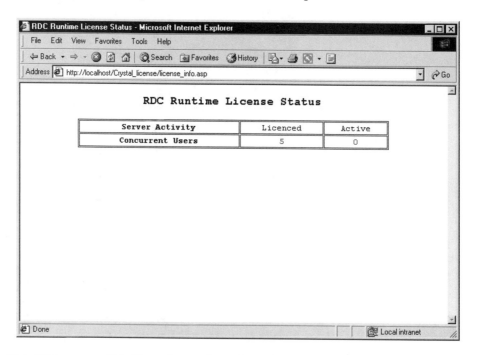

This Web page will indicate the total number of available concurrent licenses (you may see more than five if you've purchased additional RDC licenses), and those that are currently in use. If you see an excessive number of active licenses that you believe are not actually in use, you may wait for a period of time for these Web sessions to "time out," or you may stop and restart the Web server, which will reset the active user count.

There are finer points to some functions of the License Manager and its associated Web page. For details on these issues, view the help file available when you click the Help button on the License Manager.

Index

E

X

INTERNATIONAL CONTACT INFORMATION

AUSTRALIA
McGraw-Hill Book Company Australia Pty. Ltd.
TEL +61-2-9417-9899
FAX +61-2-9417-5687
http://www.mcgraw-hill.com.au
books-it_sydney@mcgraw-hill.com

CANADA
McGraw-Hill Ryerson Ltd.
TEL +905-430-5000
FAX +905-430-5020
http://www.mcgrawhill.ca

**GREECE, MIDDLE EAST,
NORTHERN AFRICA**
McGraw-Hill Hellas
TEL +30-1-656-0990-3-4
FAX +30-1-654-5525

MEXICO (Also serving Latin America)
McGraw-Hill Interamericana Editores S.A. de C.V.
TEL +525-117-1583
FAX +525-117-1589
http://www.mcgraw-hill.com.mx
fernando_castellanos@mcgraw-hill.com

SINGAPORE (Serving Asia)
McGraw-Hill Book Company
TEL +65-863-1580
FAX +65-862-3354
http://www.mcgraw-hill.com.sg
mghasia@mcgraw-hill.com

SOUTH AFRICA
McGraw-Hill South Africa
TEL +27-11-622-7512
FAX +27-11-622-9045
robyn_swanepoel@mcgraw-hill.com

**UNITED KINGDOM & EUROPE
(Excluding Southern Europe)**
McGraw-Hill Education Europe
TEL +44-1-628-502500
FAX +44-1-628-770224
http://www.mcgraw-hill.co.uk
computing_neurope@mcgraw-hill.com

ALL OTHER INQUIRIES Contact:
Osborne/McGraw-Hill
TEL +1-510-549-6600
FAX +1-510-883-7600
http://www.osborne.com
omg_international@mcgraw-hill.com